KU-033-607

HISTORY OF THE UNITED STATES

# FIGHTING FORCES

40

HISTORY OF THE UNITED STATES

# FIGHTING FORCES

cp

# ARMY

WRITTEN BY
MARK LLOYD

# MARINE CORPS

WRITTEN BY
ROBIN CROSS

First published by Chevprime Limited
27 Swinton Street, London WC1



Printed in Yugoslavia

ISBN 1 85361 107 7

# NAVY

WRITTEN BY
RICHARD HUMBLE

# AIR FORCE

WRITTEN BY
BERNARD FITZSIMONS

HISTORY OF THE UNITED STATES
ARMY

Victorious American troops from the 28th Infantry Division join in the Victory Parade down the Champs Elysées on 25 August 1944, four days after the liberation of Paris.

# 1: THE BIRTH OF AN ARMY

## THE EARLY MILITIAS

From the outset the early British colonies were left virtually defenseless by the mother country, having to rely entirely upon their own resources for survival. Settlements would occasionally band together in the face of a large-scale Indian attack, but support from distant neighbors, perhaps under threat themselves, could not be relied upon. Most colonies depended for their salvation on the time-honored European concept of the trained-band or militia, by which all fit men between the ages of 16 and 60 were conscripted.

Militiamen, who supplied their own muskets, ammunition and provisions, would, meet regularly at the county seat to practise marching and musketry under the watchful eye of locally elected officers. However, with few exceptions, none of the men, including the commanding officers who were themselves appointed by the governor, had any military experience, with the inevitable result that gatherings often disintegrated into social festivities.

Fortunately when trouble did occur it was invariably localized and short-lived, with the result that the militia's chronic lack of logistical support was rarely, if ever, put to the test.

Unencumbered by the conventions of European warfare, the militias learned their irregular tactics from their Indian adversaries whom they soon began to conquer as much by their stealth and skill as their superior firepower.

As the Indian threat receded, the militias began to win the respect and loyalty of the colonists who now regarded them as a viable local defense force. Although this had its disadvantages, (trained bands became excessively parochial with many refusing to serve far from home), it did succeed in forging a link between the military and the independence-minded colonies.

## THE COLONIAL WARS

During the early eighteenth century, as the Indian threat lessened, new and potentially more dangerous enemies in the form of France and Spain rose to take its place. Whilst Britain had been colonizing the eastern seaboard from Maine to Georgia, France had been consolidating her hold on the St. Lawrence seaway, steadily extending her colonies to the Great Lakes and eventually down the Mississippi to the Gulf of Mexico itself. Simultaneously, Spain had been securing her position in Florida.

The British colonies thus found themselves surrounded by potentially hostile enemies at the

Indians attack a New England stockade in a typical skirmish of the early eighteenth century. There was no standing army and settlers had to rely on themselves for their defence.

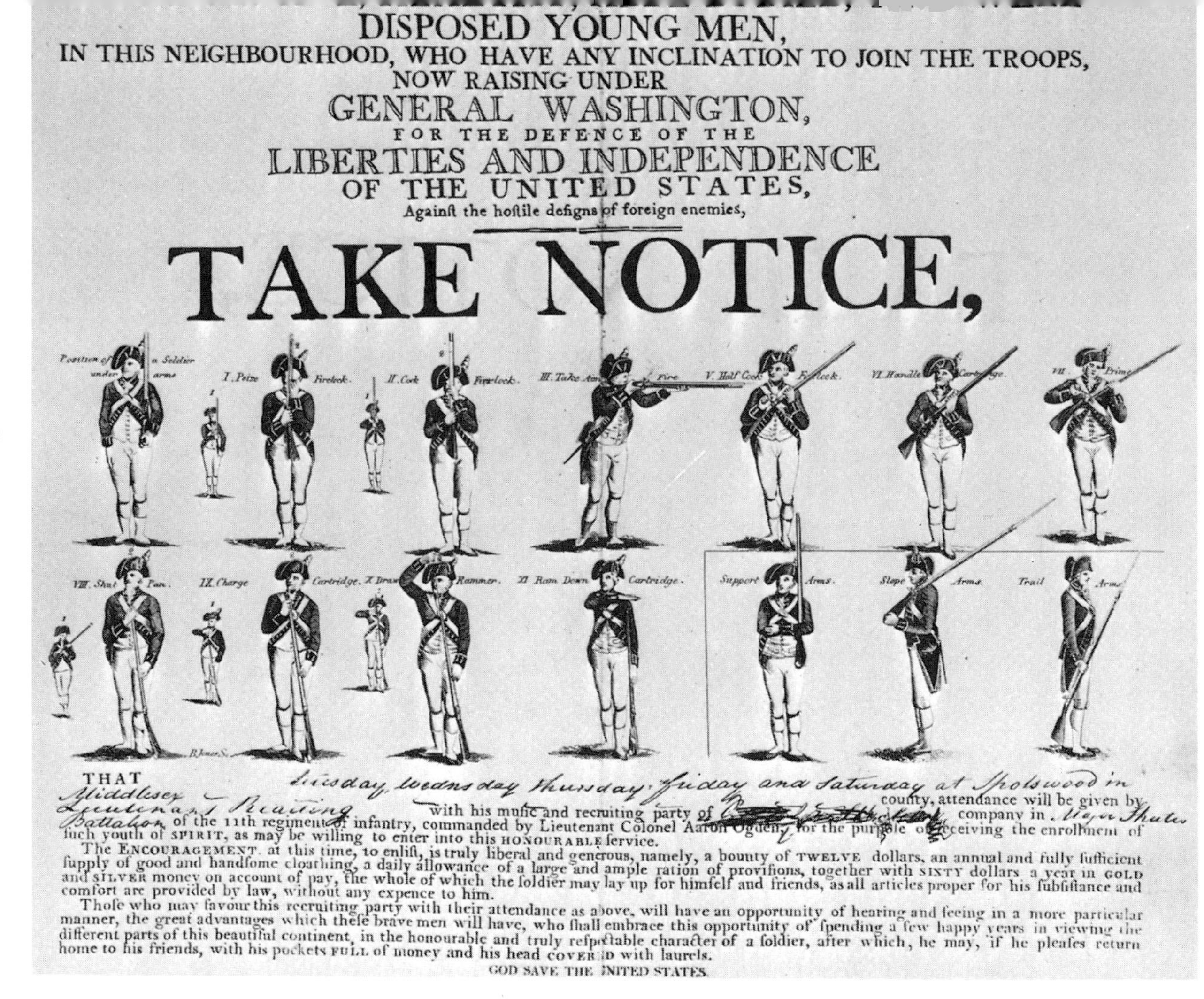
DISPOSED YOUNG MEN,
IN THIS NEIGHBOURHOOD, WHO HAVE ANY INCLINATION TO JOIN THE TROOPS,
NOW RAISING UNDER
GENERAL WASHINGTON,
FOR THE DEFENCE OF THE
LIBERTIES AND INDEPENDENCE
OF THE UNITED STATES,
Againſt the hoſtile deſigns of foreign enemies,

TAKE NOTICE,

THAT Tuesday, Wednesday Thursday Friday and Saturday at Spotswood in Middlesex county, attendance will be given by Lieutenant Recruiting with his muſic and recruiting party of company in Major Shute's Battalion of the 11th regiment of infantry, commanded by Lieutenant Colonel Aaron Ogden, for the purpoſe of receiving the enrollment of ſuch youth of SPIRIT, as may be willing to enter into this HONOURABLE ſervice.

The ENCOURAGEMENT at this time, to enliſt, is truly liberal and generous, namely, a bounty of TWELVE dollars, an annual and fully ſufficient ſupply of good and handſome cloathing, a daily allowance of a large and ample ration of proviſions, together with SIXTY dollars a year in GOLD and SILVER money on account of pay, the whole of which the ſoldier may lay up for himſelf and friends, as all articles proper for his ſubſiſtance and comfort are provided by law, without any expence to him.

Thoſe who may favour this recruiting party with their attendance as above, will have an opportunity of hearing and ſeeing in a more particular manner, the great advantages which theſe brave men will have, who ſhall embrace this opportunity of ſpending a few happy years in viewing the different parts of this beautiful continent, in the honourable and truly reſpectable character of a ſoldier, after which, he may, if he pleaſes return home to his friends, with his pockets FULL of money and his head COVERED with laurels.

GOD SAVE THE UNITED STATES.

Young men flocked to the militia where they learned basic skill at arms and tactics which would stand them in good stead against the more orthodox British regulars: This recruiting poster demonstrates the 12 stages in priming a musket.

very time that their settlers were feeling strong enough to push their boundaries to the west. Although the French in particular were heavily outnumbered they had taken the precaution of establishing trading contacts with the Indians whom they were able to recruit as allies in the border disputes that followed.

When, inevitably, the Franco-British War being fought in mainland Europe spilled west into the colonies, these local disputes soon developed into full scale hostilities.

During the four wars which followed in close succession between 1689 and 1763, the British colonial militias gave sterling support to the more orthodox regular troops sent to "protect" them. In 1690 a group of 700 volunteers raised from the trained bands of Massachusetts captured Port Royal, Nova Scotia, only to be forced to surrender it through lack of numbers, and later that year a force of 2,000 laid siege to Quebec. In 1710 Port Royal was attacked again, (this time by a joint militia-regular force of 8,500), recaptured and held permanently as a British possession.

Early settlers had to rely upon their own resources to defeat any hostile Indians.

During the War of Austrian Succession (1744-48) known locally as King George's War, the New England colonists demonstrated their growing military prowess and independence by successfully mounting a full-scale expedition against Louisburg, the so-called "Gibraltar of the New World," on Cape Breton Island.

Regardless of the precarious peace which followed the cessation of hostilities in mainland Europe, the British colonists, particularly those of New England who had borne the brunt of the fighting to date, now felt themselves strong enough to challenge French expansion to their west. They made a series of unsupported attacks against the chain of forts such as those at Frontenac, Niagara and Duquesne then being built at strategic points along the crucial north-south waterways. A force of militia from Virginia which had so far played little part in the anti-French fighting was sent under the command of Colonel George Washington to attack the French at Fort Duquesne, constructed on the confluence of the Allegheny and Monongahela Rivers, thereby freeing Pennsylvania of foreign influence. Overwhelmed by superior numbers and forced to surrender, the Virginians were released and sent back home.

During the fourth and final stage of the lengthy Franco-British conflict, the Seven Years War (1756-63), Britain sent strong naval forces and 25,000 regular troops to fight alongside the American colonial regiments placed in regular service and the volunteer militia units. After an initial setback in which a combined force of 16,000 regulars and militia failed to take Fort Ticonderoga, victory followed upon victory until French influence in the Americas was all but destroyed.

In 1758 Louisburg was captured by regular forces after a text-book siege and Fort Frontenac fell in more irregular fashion to a force of 3,000 militia. Quebec fell to British regulars in 1759, a victory made Pyrrhic by the death of their commander Major General James Wolfe in the battle, whilst the river forts of Niagara and Ticonderoga surrendered to a mixed regular-militia force under the command of General Amherst.

When seventy years of intermittent fighting was finally brought to a close by the Treaty of Paris in 1763, Britain and her colonies were left in total mastery of the American continent.

However problems soon arose from this very fact. The colonial volunteer-militia which had borne the brunt of the fighting in the first three wars and had made sizeable contributions in the fourth, had developed their own style of fighting far more suited to the wilderness than that adopted by the more conventional British regulars. They had learned to fight away from home in wars which did not directly affect their own or their families' well-being. They had in fact become in every respect an army which no longer felt it necessary to rely on the British for help or protection.

Both Britain and France had Indian allies in their conflicts, and eventually learned that the rigid formations of European warfare were unsuited to American conditions. On 9 July 1755, the British commander-in-chief in America, Edward Braddock, was ambushed and defeated at the battle of the Monongahela near Fort Duquesne by a smaller mixed force of French and Indians. He and half his force were killed, but George Washington who was a volunteer with the expedition, helped lead the remainder back to Virginia.

# 2: THE AMERICAN REVOLUTION

With the Treaty of Paris of 1763 and the end of the French Wars, both Britain and her colonists looked forward to a period of stability but, as so often happens, peace brought with it new-found tensions. Nearly bankrupted by the War, Britain found herself having to station 10,000 extra troops in the colonies which were now expanding fast to fill the void left by the French.

New taxes would have to be raised as a matter of priority and it was to her colonies, whom she felt had gained most directly from the victory, that Britain turned. Steps were taken to increase taxation on imports and exports through the Navigation Acts, existing legislation was enforced more rigorously and plans were made to bring the increasingly independence-minded colonists more firmly under direct governmental control.

The colonists on the other hand resented the presence of the redcoats whom they saw more as a restraint on territorial growth than a protection against the frontier Indians whom they had earlier proved inept in fighting. More fundamentally they were adamant that in providing excellent militia throughout the Wars, the costs of which had been borne locally, they had contributed more than adequately to the campaign and should not now have to suffer higher taxation.

Initial half-hearted Parliamentary attempts to raise taxation through the Sugar and Stamp Acts were abandoned in the face of peaceful resistance and local boycotts. Britain realized that if she were to stem the rising tide of independence sweeping the colonies she would have to act with a newly-found sense of firmness and resolution. Her fateful opportunity came when in 1773, in response to the recently passed Tea Act, a group of Bostonians thinly disguised as Indians boarded ships in the harbor, broke into the holds and unceremoniously dumped their valuable cargoes of tea overboard. Parliament over-reacted unwisely and in haste. Punitive legislation, known locally as the "Intolerable Acts," was passed, closing the port of Boston and placing Massachusetts under military rule. The stage was set for armed resistance.

The British victory at Quebec on 13 September 1759 broke French resistance in Canada, but was marred by the death of General James Wolfe who was one of the finest military leaders of the eighteenth century. This famous painting is by the Pennsylvanian-born artist Benjamin West (1738-1820).

## LEXINGTON GREEN

Determined to resist military rule, the Massachusetts Provincial Congress at once prepared for action by stockpiling ammunition and supplies in Concord, a small settlement some 20 miles from Boston. General Gage, the commander of the British garrison, upon learning of this

from his network of spies, immediately sent a force of 700 men to seize the illegal stores. However, the minutemen, an elite among the militia, were forewarned of the coming military and formed on the village green at Lexington to block their advance. A short sharp battle ensued on the morning of 19 April after which the militia retired having sustained 8 dead. The redcoats proceeded to Concord where they destroyed the remaining stores before beginning the long return march to Boston. Their route was harried throughout by militiamen sniping at them from vantage points along the way to the extent that they were only saved by a relief force sent from Boston.

By the end of the day the British regulars had sustained nearly 275 casualties and the militiamen 95, a demonstration of the latter's excellent use of guerrilla tactics.

Initially the British swept aside the Minutemen in their advance to Concord. Subsequently, however, they were to lose a quarter of their force. This cartoon was engraved by the American patriot Paul Revere (1735-1810).

The fuze of insurrection was now lit. Within days the British garrison was under siege from the New England militia, and forces from Connecticut under Benedict Arnold and from Vermont under Ethan Allen had seized the key forts of Ticonderoga and Crown Point.

After a short period of stalemate during which both sides steadily received reinforcements, the British began to fortify Dorchester Heights to the south of Boston, and the colonists Bunker Hill at the neck of the Charleston peninsula to the north. Inexplicably the work party sent to Bunker Hill began to fortify Breed's Hill instead, thus presenting the British with an irresistible target. On the afternoon of 17 June 1775 General Howe was dispatched with 2,200 men to dislodge the militiamen then occupying Breed's Hill in fairly equal numbers. Although they succeeded in their third attempt the British sustained over 1,000 killed and injured in what became known erroneously as the Battle of Bunker Hill. The colonists became convinced, however over-optimistically under the circumstances, that their irregulars were more than a match for the British redcoats.

## THE BIRTH OF AN ARMY

Britain determined to fight the War by the implementation of the tried and tested tactics of large-scale set-piece battlefield engagements supported by a naval blockade. However, this necessitated a period of intransigence during which the garrison was steadily increased for the anticipated conflict ahead.

Foreseeing the need for a regular, disciplined force to protect the colonies against the inevitable onslaught, the Second Continental Congress adopted the irregular New England Army assembled around Boston as the Continental Army on 14 June 1775, and the next day appointed George Washington of Virginia as its Commander-in-Chief. The American Army had been born.

Although Washington was appointed primarily for political reasons in an attempt to unite the southern colonies behind a conflict which many still saw as a northern irrelevancy, the choice proved to be fortuitous. Washington was an inspired and dedicated leader who despite his limited battlefield experience in the Indian and French Wars nevertheless enjoyed a tremendous degree of military perception and foresight.

Steps were taken immediately to form an army of 20,000 men under the command of four major-generals and eight brigadiers, all of whom had seen service in New England or in the British Army itself.

Washington led his men across the River Delaware in a fierce snowstorm on Christmas night, 1776 and defeated the Hessians at Trenton.

Early enlistment was disappointing as many colonists were unwilling to sacrifice even a year away from their farms and families.

Despite the perilous lack of supplies (he was relying heavily upon booty taken from a few captured supply ships to provision his forces), Washington decided to launch a major expedition into the north in the hopes of adding Canada to the coalition of rebellious states whilst securing a potential invasion route from the St. Lawrence through Lake Champlain to the vital Hudson Valley.

The expedition consisting of 2,000 men under the command of Major General Schuyler of New York met with limited success. Montreal fell on 13 November but Quebec held firm. Decimated by illness and desertions, the American forces made a last disastrous attempt to storm the city under the cover of a snowstorm on the night of 13 November 1775. Brigadier Montgomery was killed, Colonel Arnold wounded and the attackers thrown into disarray. When the British received reinforcements and counter-attacked in June 1776 the colonists retreated without a fight, leaving Canada and the St. Lawrence firmly in British hands.

This defeat was mitigated in part by the British withdrawal from Boston on 17 March 1776. Although General Howe, who had succeeded General Gage, made the decision to abandon Boston on sound military grounds, the militia had placed artillery on the recently captured Dorchester Heights and Nook's Hill to harrass the garrison. Although Halifax, to which the British redeployed, was strategically far safer, the colonists saw the evacuation as their first concrete victory.

## THE DECLARATION OF INDEPENDENCE

On 4 July 1776 the Declaration of Independence was proclaimed and a struggle for home rule became at once a war for total independence. However, the colonists were far from united and many were actively against the continuation of hostilities. Supplies for the Continental Army were kept to a minimum, enlistments remained short term and the incidence of desertions high. Although in theory the Continental Army consisted of 110 battalions or 80,000 men, in reality it rarely numbered more than 30,000 of whom no

Left: The Continental Congress drew up the Declaration of Independence in Philadelphia in 1776 by which time the war was already a year old.

Overleaf: The Battle of Valcour Island, Lake Champlain took place on 28 October 1776. The makeshift American fleet under the command of Benedict Arnold was defeated by a stronger British force. Most of the American ships were captured or sunk, but the battle had delayed the British advance on Fort Ticonderoga and instead caused them to withdraw to winter quarters in Canada.

Some Continental Army Uniforms from the early years of the war. The man in the foreground is one of 'Morgan's Rifles' (see page 27).

more than half were battle-ready at any one time. Consequently Washington was forced to supplement his forces with locally raised militia whose standards varied greatly and who remained solidly under the influence of the domestic legislatures, with the result that rarely, if ever, did he enjoy the military independence for which he yearned.

## THE CONTINENTAL ARMY

At the outset, the Continental Army consisted almost entirely of infantry supplemented by cavalry and artillery supplied by the militia. This was far from satisfactory and in the summer of 1776 Colonel Henry Knox was tasked with the formation of four battalions of artillery each consisting of 10 companies equipped with between 6 to 10 guns per company. A cavalry formation of four regular regiments each of 360 light dragoons organized into six troops was created in the following year.

The infantry carried a hotch-potch of weapons varying from the British "Brown Bess" 0.753 caliber musket to the Pennsylvania long rifle, so lethal in the hands of a marksman. As the War progressed, an increasing number of French 0.69 caliber Charleville muskets reached the American forces but, even so, weapons were never standardized.

Generally speaking, the artillery fared no better, although by the end of the War domestic armories were producing standard 4-, 12- and 18-pounder cannon along standard French lines to supplement the ordnance captured earlier from the British.

Despite early attempts at centralized dress-regulations, uniforms remained a sea of divergent color throughout the War. Many units refused to adopt the brown coats recommended by Congress in 1775 and those that did found that the dyes supplied were so unreliable that "regulation" coats varied in hue from light sand to dark umber.

Although the standard infantry blue coat of 1779 with its distinctive lapel facings (white for New England, buff for New York and New Jersey, red for Pennsylvania, Delaware, Maryland and Virginia, and blue with white for the southern states) proved more popular, by the time of its introduction many states simply had neither the finances nor the resources to introduce it.

Despite the introduction of nearly 30,000 uniforms supplied by France between 1776 and 1778, the Continental Army finished the War as it began it, dressed in a mixture of uniforms and colors cobbled together by any means possible. Prior to 1778, military training was piecemeal and often ineffectual. Veterans of the militia who had relied traditionally on enthusiasm and woodsmanship rather than iron discipline for success, now felt unwilling to adopt what many saw as discredited British regular tactics, and as a consequence were of little value in open battle.

Matters improved considerably in 1778 when Washington appointed Frederick Wilhelm, Baron von Steuben, a former staff officer in the Prussian Army of Frederick the Great, to be his Inspector-General.

Von Steuben at once set up at Valley Forge a training program which was highly professional, comprehensive and adapted specifically for American conditions. Cadres taught personally by Von Steuben returned to their units to inaugurate local training programs, thus ensuring that the new tactics were disseminated throughout the Army with the minimum of delay. In 1779, at the Baron's instigation, the

Continental Army Infantry in regulation dress.

"Regulations for the Order and Discipline of the Troops of the United States", destined to be the Army's "bible" for the next 33 years, were published.

The Army itself was restructured into battalions each consisting of eight companies of about 60 men. The standard tactical unit was reduced to two companies, the largest force cap-

The British retreated from Boston on 17 March 1776.

An artilleryman in the Rhode Island militia.

able of command by a single man in the heat of battle.

By 1776 the British were at last able to move but, ominously for them by the end of that year had made few of the gains anticipated.

While it was recognized that the majority of fighting would necessarily take place in the north, Parliament was aware that large elements of the south remained loyal to the Crown. Accordingly, plans were made to send an expedition transported by a fleet commanded by Admiral Sir Peter Parker to their assistance.

The fleet was delayed and did not reach American waters until May, by which time the majority of loyalist pockets of resistance had been neutralized by the local militia. Nevertheless, Parker decided to attack Charleston, the largest and most secure American base in the south. Inevitably his troops were beaten back until eventually Parker was forced to sail north to join Howe in Halifax. Thereafter the south was left virtually untouched by the War.

## THE BATTLE FOR NEW YORK

Howe himself had intended to attack New York before moving along the Hudson into Canada, thus cutting off New England, the center of the

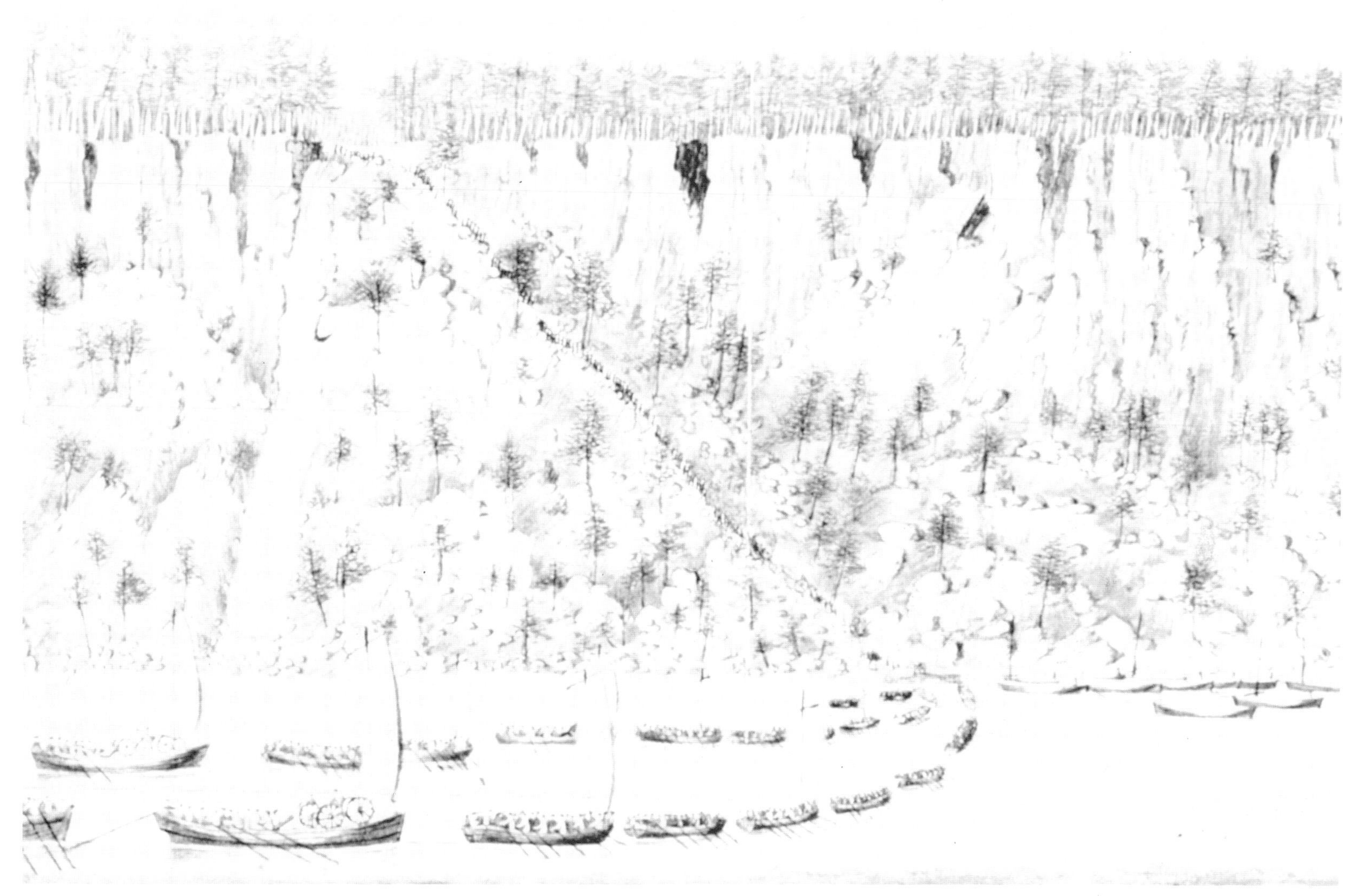

Lord Cornwallis's troops scaled the Hudson Pallisades in November 1776 forcing the Americans to evacuate Fort Lee.

resistance, from the other states. However, reinforcements were delayed, with the result that the expedition could not be mounted until August. The delay meant the British could hope to do no more than capture New York, securing it as a staging area for a campaign in the following year.

Howe, with an army of 32,000 supported by a powerful naval contingent under the command of his brother Admiral Richard Howe, confronted Washington, who had a force of no more than 19,000 men. The latter compounded his problems by making the fundamental mistake of fortifying Brooklyn Heights in an attempt to defend Manhattan Island, leaving himself open to infiltration from the flanks and rear. Landing on 22 August 1776, Howe attacked the Americans from the unguarded Jamaica-Bedford road, forcing the defenders back onto the Brooklyn Heights positions. Fortunately for Washington, Howe was an extremely cautious man who delayed his attack long enough to allow the Americans to escape across the East River on the night of 29 August.

Two weeks later, Howe secured a beachhead on Manhattan, but again his lack of tenacity allowed the Americans to dig in on the Harlem Heights from which they were able to hold off the British for a further month. When in mid-October Howe landed at Pell's Point behind the American lines, Washington ordered the evacuation of Manhattan and moved north to White Plains, leaving some 6,000 men to guard the Hudson River from the key points of Forts Washington and Lee. Howe seized both forts, taking some 3,000 prisoners in the process, whilst simultaneously pursuing Washington out of New York, south into New Jersey, and into Pennsylvania. When Washington finally halted, his force of 19,000 had disintegrated into a shattered rump of no more than 2,000 men.

Whilst Washington was retiring in disorder before the might of Howe's Army in New York, Benedict Arnold was securing a small but significant victory for the Americans in the north. General Guy Carlton, in an attempt to capture

General Burgoyne surrenders his sword and his army at Saratoga in October 1777. This American victory was one of the turning points of the war, and helped gain France's alliance.

Fort Ticonderoga, constructed a small flotilla of boats with which to cross Lake Champlain. Arnold and his men built their own flotilla with which to join battle and, although they lost the subsequent naval engagement at Valcour Island, so delayed Carlton that he was forced to return to Canada.

As the winter of 1776-77 set in, the British Army seemed in total control. It had established itself in winter quarters in Newport, Rhode Island, and in New York, in Brunswick, Preston, Trenton and Bordentown, New Jersey. Victory seemed no more than a matter of time.

## THE WINTER CAMPAIGN

Washington realized that the desperate situation called for equally desperate measures, and hastily assembled a mixed force of 7,000 Continentals and Pennsylvania militia to hit the British in their winter quarters. To compound his difficulties, any offensive would have to be completed by the end of December, at which time many of the American soldiers would complete their enlistment and return home. Washington's forces crossed the Delaware River at McConkey's Ferry, a few miles from Trenton, on Christmas night, split into two columns and entered the town at both ends on the morning of 26 December. Taken completely by surprise, the Hessian mercenaries surrendered after only 90 minutes, conceding 40 dead and 900 prisoners. Although a similar attack planned against the garrison at Bordentown failed, Washington felt secure enough to lead an incursion with 5,000 men across the Delaware River on the night of 30 December. Blocked by Major General Cornwallis at Trenton, the Americans left their camp during the night, leaving their camp fires burning to deceive the enemy, and appearing next morning at Princeton, where they inflicted severe casualties on the two incumbent British regiments.

Washington thereafter withdrew into winter quarters at Morristown, New Jersey, his prowess as a military leader now beyond dispute.

The year 1777 saw none of the victories so eagerly anticipated by the British. Washington's Army was now supplemented by a nucleus of foreigners such as Thaddeus Kosciuszko, the Polish engineer; Von Steuben, the German tactician; and Lafayette, the French field commander. Washington placed the majority of the 8,000 men then under his command between Philadelphia and New York to bar Howe's path to the capital, but found himself outflanked by the British who sailed up Chesapeake Bay to Head of Elk, southwest of Philadelphia, where they landed unopposed.

Washington attempted to redeploy his forces but was outflanked by Cornwallis, and forced to retire to Chester leaving the capital undefended. Philadelphia fell virtually without a fight on 26 September, and was immediately adopted by Howe as his winter headquarters. For his part, Washington retired to his winter quarters at Valley Forge, some 20 miles away, to resettle and rebuild his army for the battles to come.

## SARATOGA

Ironically, Howe's single-mindedness in capturing Philadelphia and putting Washington to flight may well have cost Britain the war. In order to carry out the complex Chesapeake Bay landings, Howe had been forced to reduce the New York garrison to a minimum, leaving it with no opportunity to support the advance then being made from the north by Major General John Burgoyne.

Burgoyne had been tasked with leading a mixed force of 8,000 British regulars, Hessians, Loyalists and Indians from Canada via Lake Champlain and Lake George to Albany. A second force of 1,700 regulars and friendly Indians under Colonel St Leger was to sail to Lake Ontario, move down the Mohawk River, capture Fort Stanwix and attack Albany from the west.

After initial successes, including the capture of Fort Ticonderoga on 27 June 1777, Burgoyne's advance began to slow down under the weight of its own baggage. Incensed by the British use of Indians, the New England militia did all in its power to frustrate the British, destroying over 10 per cent of their numbers in a single skirmish at Bennington, Vermont.

More seriously, St Leger, deserted by his Indians, was forced to abandon the siege of Fort Stanwix and return to Canada, leaving Burgoyne's left flank perilously exposed.

Foolishly, the British continued towards Vermont, regardless of the fact that the Americans were becoming stronger by the day, and their own forces weaker. In a series of battles fought between 19 September and 17 October 1777, the British were halted, forced to withdraw, and finally encircled.

Denied aid of any kind by the depleted New York garrison, Burgoyne and 6,000 of his men were forced to surrender at Saratoga.

Spurred on by this victory, France threw in her lot with the Americans, and by February 1778 an alliance had been made between the two countries. What had once been a localized war was rapidly turning into an international conflict.

In the spring of 1778 General Clinton, who had succeeded Howe in overall command, was ordered to abandon Philadelphia, to retire to New York and to dispatch part of his forces to the West Indies to counter a possible French offensive.

Attempts by the Americans to hinder the withdrawal ended in near disaster when a force under General Lee, who was subsequently court-martialled for incompetence, was heavily mauled at Monmouth Court House, New Jersey.

An abortive attempt by Washington to capture Newport, Rhode Island, was followed by a stalemate in the north.

Britain, who still harbored ideas of rallying southern loyalists to her cause, laid siege to Charleston in May 1779. Although Charleston itself did not fall, the British fleet gained a major victory at Savannah, enabling Clinton to move a large force south with impunity.

Brigadier General Daniel Morgan (1736-1802) was an American commander who fought with distinction in the Saratoga campaign and later won a brilliant victory at Cowpens, South Carolina on 17 January 1781.

Above: American cavalry attack Tarleton's right flank in the American victory at Cowpens.

Opposite: A contemporary map of the siege of Yorktown.

Below: General Cornwallis (center) surrenders at Yorktown. This effectively ended the war.

Charleston was attacked again, this time by 14,000 men, and fell to the British in February 1780. Clinton returned to New York with one-third of his men, leaving the residue under Cornwallis to pacify the southern states. Loyalists were less eager than had been anticipated to show their true allegiances in the face of threats from guerrilla bands led by Sumpter, Pickens and Marion, with the result that Cornwallis found his task virtually impossible.

Dangerously over-committed, Cornwallis sent a number of expeditions into the interior, but all met with failure and often disaster. A force of Tory militia under Ferguson was destroyed by Carolina mounted militia at King's Mountain, whilst Tarleston was annihilated by Brigadier Morgan and his mixed force of militia and Continentals at Cowpens, North Carolina.

Virtually abandoning the Carolinas hinterland to its fate, Cornwallis moved the residue of his troops north to Virginia in pursuit of the elusive enemy. After a few insignificant victories against the vastly outnumbered Continentals, Cornwallis was ordered by Clinton to establish a sea base from which to evacuate the majority of his remaining troops to New York.

Cornwallis chose Yorktown, a small deep water harbor on the Chesapeake Bay. Before the British fleet could arrive the Army was blockaded by a French fleet under the command of Admiral de Grasse. Yorktown was besieged by a strong force of 9,000 Americans and 6,000 French regulars, and on 19 October 1791 Cornwallis was forced to surrender.

The surrender ended the formal fighting of the War of Independence. Parliament and the British people were heartily sickened by a war they could not win, and in which they had little interest. British power was being challenged by France, Spain and Holland on two continents and on half the oceans of the world.

With the Treaty of Paris in 1783, Britain formally recognized America as a fully independent country. The United States Army had been comprehensively blooded and had won its first victory.

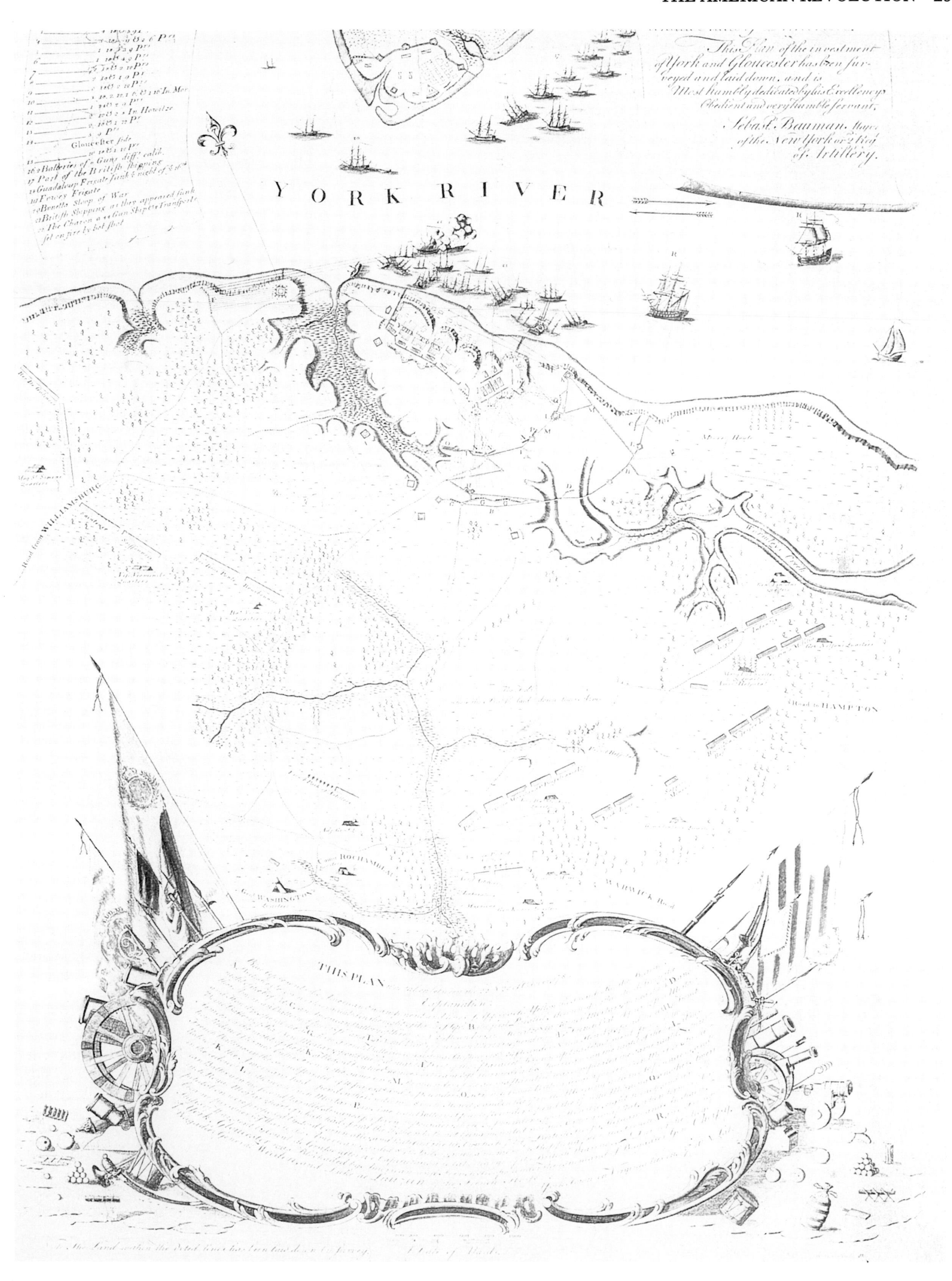
This Plan of the investment of York and Gloucester has been surveyed and laid down, and is Most humbly dedicated by his Excellency's Obedient and very humble servant,
Sebast. Bauman. Major of the New York or 2 Reg. of Artillery.
YORK RIVER
Gloucester side
THIS PLAN
WASHINGTON
ROCHAMBEAU
HAMPTON
WARWICK Road

# 3: THE YEARS OF GROWTH AND CONSOLIDATION

The need for a large standing army ceased with the signing of the Treaty of Paris in 1783, and immediate steps were taken by Congress to reduce the size of a force which was rapidly becoming a burden on the economy. Although America had no external enemies, the ever present danger of attack by hostile Indians remained, and with it the necessity for retaining a standing army under federal control.

Original plans formulated by George Washington to create a full time force of 2,630 officers and men, supported by reserves drawn from state volunteer militia were rejected out of hand by Congress on the grounds of cost. Eventually in June 1784 Congress compromised and allowed the creation of a regular army of 700 men drawn from volunteers from Pennsylvania, New Jersey, New York and Connecticut. America had its first, if inadequate, peacetime standing army.

So small a force could only be a stopgap, and indeed within two years a reformed army protected by the new Constitution had been created. Independent of the states, control of the army was vested both in the legislative and executive branches of the government. Congress was given the power to declare war and to raise a navy, but the Commander in Chief, both in peacetime and in war, was the President. A single Department of War for the Army and Navy was created, to continue in existence until after World War II. Major General Henry Knox was created the first Secretary of State for War, and Brigadier General Harman confirmed as field commander.

Under the terms of the Militia Law of 1792, states were encouraged, but not forced, to create local forces drawn from able-bodied white men between the ages of 18 and 45 to assist in local defense. However, central financial assistance was not offered, to the detriment of discipline and training, until inevitably the militias became militarily non-effective.

Far from receding, the Indian menace had, if anything, increased with the expulsion of the French and victory over the British. Britain, which refused to relinquish control of the forts in the western territories until monies owed in reparations to the loyalist Tories who had fled post-Independence America were paid, con-

American soldiers respond to an attack by Maumee Indians in the frontier forests of Ohio. General 'Mad Anthony' Wayne completely defeated the Maumees in the Battle of Fallen Timbers on 20 August 1794, and there was peace on the frontier for nearly two decades.

The Battle of Tippecanoe Creek was hard-fought but inconclusive although the Indians were forced to withdraw.

tinued to supply and even arm the Appalachian Indians. Settlers demanded protection from the fledgling government, threatening to turn to England for assistance if help was not forthcoming.

Congress responded by authorizing an increase in the size of the Army to 2,283, whilst ordering Knox to mount a major offensive in the "Ohio Country." An initial expedition against the Miami Indians in 1790, led by Arthur St Clair, the Governor of the Northwest Territory, failed completely.

Attempts at expansion were almost abandoned completely when, in the November of the following year, a punitive expedition of 600 regulars and 1,400 militiamen was attacked by 1,000 Indians whilst encamped on the Wabash River and virtually annihilated.

A third expedition, this time led by the impetuous if competent Revolutionary War veteran "Mad Anthony" Wayne, consisting of 5,000 men specially trained for warfare in the wilderness, was dispatched from Fort Washington in 1793 and in the following year moved north. Battle was joined with the Indians near the British-held Fort Miami, on the site of modern-day Toledo, where the Indians were forced into open ground at the point of the bayonet and decimated by mounted militiamen.

Subdued by this show of force, the Western Ohio tribes sued for peace and, in the Treaty of Greenville signed in August 1795, ceded their lands. Pioneers, until then held in rein by the threat of massacre, now flooded west in unprecedented numbers.

Inevitably, settlers began spilling over into lands not ceded by treaty. Tecumseh, the far-sighted chief of the Shawnee Indians, began to organize a defensive federation, until spurred on by local pressure William Henry Harrison, the Governor of Indiana, led a pre-emptive expedition against Tecumseh, destroying his principal village at Tippecanoe Creek. Once again the Indian threat was momentarily abated.

In 1793, revolutionary France declared war against a coalition of European states, including Britain, determined to restore the Bourbon monarchy. France and Britain at once set about cutting off each other's lines of supplies by interdicting trade and seizing vessels on the high seas.

As an emerging neutral, the United States found herself deeply involved in a war in which she had no obvious interest. Determined to avoid actual combat, Congress negotiated Jay's Treaty of 1794 with Britain under the terms of which the latter withdrew her remaining troops from her outposts in the American west. Seeing this, however erroneously, as a flagrantly pro-British act, France immediately accelerated her seizure of American shipping. Congress countered by authorizing the mobilization, although only for three months, of 80,000 militia and the formation of a Provisional Army for the protection of domestic harbors and borders. The anticipated invasion never came, the French threat abated, and in 1800 Congress felt secure enough to disband the Army.

President Thomas Jefferson took the bold step in 1803 of purchasing the State of Louisiana, including the vital port of St Louis, from an impecunious France for only $15 million, thus securing once and for all a secure trade route to the south.

## WAR WITH BRITAIN

When Thomas Jefferson assumed the Presidency in 1801 he brought with him an avowed policy of prosperity through peace. The army was reduced to 3,000 men and the navy virtually scrapped.

The resumption of hostilities between Britain and France however led to an intolerable increase in the harrassment of American merchant shipping, exacerbated by the new British policy of pressing American seamen into service in the Royal Navy. Early American attempts at a trade embargo failed, causing far more suffering to the domestic producers than the European merchants. Demands for war against Britain, particularly from southern and western traders most hit by the British blockade, grew to fever-pitch until Congress was forced by the pressure of public opinion to declare war on Great Britain on 18 June 1812.

On the face of it Britain was vastly superior in manpower and resources. Her regular army numbered 300,000 supported by a large militia, her fleet of 700 ships included 125 ships of the line and her treasury was full. To counter this the United States had an army of only 11,000 including 5,000 raw recruits, a militia not contracted to serve abroad and, to fight a war in which control of the seas would be crucial, a fleet of less than 20 ships including no more than six frigates.

Britain, however, was currently fighting Napoleon in Europe and could only afford to regard this latest confrontation as a minor irritant to be contained until Napoleon was crushed, after which forces for its prosecution would become available. She could not afford to reinforce the Canadian garrison of 6,000 regulars and 2,000 militia for long, nor could she hope to release more than the 80 ships then engaged on blockade duty.

The United States Army itself was suffering from years of neglect. Supplies were short, training and morale were low, and experienced officers rare. With the exception of the Corps of Engineers, who had established a small academy at West Point (later to become the United States Military Academy), in 1802 support units were sadly ill-equipped to wage an all-out war.

The United States Army could at least now

William Henry Harrison (1773-1841) became a national hero after the Battle of Tippecanoe Creek. His reputation for ruthlessness in battle stood him in good stead when he ran for the Presidency. He died of pneumonia just one month after his inauguration as President.

British infantry advance during the Battle of Lundy's Lane, Ontario (25 July 1814). This was the bloodiest battle of the war, but was also indecisive.

boast a plentiful supply of domestically produced weapons, notably the 0.69 caliber flintlock musket and the 0.59 caliber flintlock cavalry pistol manufactured at the government arsenals at Springfield and Harper's Ferry respectively, and uniforms had now taken on a degree of regimentation.

United States Army soldiers now at least looked like soldiers; whether or not they would act as such when faced by a well-trained and disciplined enemy remained to be seen.

The war began badly for the American land forces when three independent offensives against Canada were repulsed with heavy losses. By the end of 1812, Fort Dearborn (now Chicago) had been destroyed by pro-British Indians and its inhabitants massacred; Fort Mackinac and Detroit had fallen to a small British force commanded by General Brock, placing the entire Northwest territory under British control; a force of 900 militia under the inexperienced Major General van Rensselaer had been forced to surrender; and an attack on Montreal had ended in a costly fiasco.

The next year was only a little better for the Americans. An early attempt by Brigadier Henry Harrison, the hero of Tippecanoe, to recapture Detroit ended in failure made even more

The death of General Zebulon M. Pike, after whom Pike's Peak is named. He was killed in the successful taking of York (now Toronto), Canada on 24 April 1813.

unpalatable by the subsequent massacre of 500 prisoners by their Indian captors. A small force under General Pike successfully stormed York (now Toronto), a victory lessened when Pike himself was killed in an accidental powder magazine explosion. An amphibious assault under the command of Colonel Winfield Scott and Commander Oliver Hazard Perry of the navy took Forts George and Queenston on the western shore of the Niagara River.

Subsequently, Commander Perry secured Lake Erie, destroying a six-ship Royal Navy flotilla in the process, enabling American forces to continue unimpeded into upper Canada.

Similar attempts to bring lower Canada under American influence in late 1813 ended in unmitigated disaster when forces totalling 10,000 men led by General Wilkinson and Brigadier Hampton fell back in disorder when confronted by vastly inferior British forces.

One of the bloodiest engagements of the year was fought in the south between Andrew Jackson, an avowed Indian hater, and the Creek Indians. In the summer of 1813 the Creeks attacked Fort Mims, in the southern Mississippi Territory, massacring over 500 men, women and children. In retaliation, Jackson, with a band of 600 regulars, 2,000 militia and hundreds of friendly Indians, pursued the 900 Creeks to Horseshoe Bend, destroyed them in battle and thereafter set about a systematic massacre of the survivors every bit as bloody as that perpetrated at the Fort.

Throughout 1813 the Royal Navy continued its blockade of American ports, denying the tiny American Navy access to the seas.

American attempts to seize lower Canada in 1814 met with failure. The British were now being reinforced by veterans of the Napoleonic Wars and decided to take the initiative. In August a force under the command of Major General Ross captured Washington, burning the Capitol and White House before withdrawing in good order. Subsequent attempts to take Baltimore were less successful in the face of a spirited defense engineered by Samuel Smith and his force of 10,000 Maryland militiamen.

The last great battle of the War, the disastrous British attack on New Orleans in which over 2,000 regulars were killed or injured, took place on 8 January 1815, some two weeks after peace had been negotiated.

For the second time in America's short history, her regular forces and militia had come together to defend the nation. It was becoming increasingly apparent, however, that despite the militia's occasional bravery (they had comprised the majority of troops at New Orleans and in the defense of Baltimore), America's future security would inevitably depend almost exclusively on the proficiency of the regular armed forces.

# 4: THE INDIAN AND MEXICAN WARS

Popular support for the Armed Forces soon diminished with the coming of peace and cutbacks inevitably followed to the extent that by 1823 there were no more than 6,000 men serving the colors.

A number of major changes were, however, taking place within the Army. The Military Academy at West Point, which had been pioneered by the Corps of Engineers, was expanded in 1816 and the cadets given ceremonial gray uniforms reminiscent of those worn by their forebears at Chippewa and Lundy's Lane.

Brevet Major Sylvanus Thayer, appointed superintendent in the following year, immediately set about a number of administrative and educational reforms within the Academy, expanding its curriculum to incorporate infantry, artillery and cavalry tactics. During the 30 years that followed, over 1,000 cadets graduated from the Academy, of whom nearly one half remained as career officers to give the US Army its first real professional continuity.

Under the auspices of Secretary for War John Calhoun, an artillery school was established at Fortress Monroe at the mouth of Chesapeake Bay and an infantry school at Jefferson Barracks, St Louis, in which whole units rather than individuals attended training courses of up to a year's duration.

Although the United States met with no foreign enemies during this period, the Indian problem remained to the extent that the Army found itself involved in three wars before the lands east of the Mississippi were finally pacified.

During the First Seminole War of 1817, Andrew Jackson, the inveterate Indian fighter and now commander of the Southern Department, led 800 regulars and 1,000 Georgian militia, (later supplemented by 1,000 Tennesseans), into Spanish Florida in pursuit of bands of Seminole and Creek Indians recently incited by rogue British adventurers to raid across the border. Hanging two British traders for allegedly aiding the Indians, Jackson soon gained total control of central and western Florida. When Spain issued half-hearted political protests, a solution was speedily reached and the entire area ceded to the United States in exchange for a small cash sum.

The second of the Indian Wars, or Black Hawk

American soldiers capture Monterrey, Mexico on 24 September 1846 while under the command of General Zachary Taylor (1784-1850).

War, took place on the Illinois and Wisconsin frontiers in 1832, after Chief Black Hawk recrossed the Mississippi with 500 warriors and 1,000 women and children to reclaim his lost ancestral lands. Alarmed by this unilateral act of aggression, the Illinois government dispatched 1,000 militia supported by 500 regulars under the command of Colonel Henry Atkinson to the troubled area. Realising that his position was hopeless, Black Hawk attempted to escape north into Wisconsin Territory before recrossing the river but was brought to battle first at Wisconsin Heights and subsequently on the Bad Axe River where his forces were annihilated.

The final and largest Indian War, the Second Seminole War, began in 1835. Essentially a guerrilla campaign, the Seminole chief Osceola shunned from meeting the US Army in open combat, preferring to harry small detachments and lightly defended outposts from the relative safety of his strongholds in the swamps. The campaign which was marked by savagery on both sides was only brought to a successful conclusion when Osceola and several of his chiefs were tricked into attending a peace conference under a flag of truce and subsequently arrested.

Sac and Fox Indians were forcibly resettled in Western Iowa after being decisively beaten at the Battle of the Bad Axe River, Wisconsin on 2 August 1832.

THE MEXICAN WARS

Between the years 1820 and 1835 some 35,000 Americans poured into the Mexican territory of Texas. Initially welcomed by the Mexicans, the Americans became increasingly independent and their relations with the government strained. When Mexico froze immigration in 1836, American anger expressed itself in armed insurrection. Within the year General Sam Houston had defeated the Mexican forces sent to bring him to his knees and independence had been declared. Overtures sent to the United States requesting admission to the Union were fraught with danger, for whereas the vast majority of Americans welcomed integration, Mexico steadfastly refused to recognize the *de facto* independence.

After nearly ten years of prevarication in Congress, President John Tyler agreed to admit Texas into the Union on 1 March 1845. Mexico immediately suspended diplomatic relations and war became inevitable. Anticipating hostilities, Brigadier Zachary Taylor was ordered to move his forces from Louisiana into Texas to a point "on or near" the Rio Grande. Taylor marched to the mouth of the Nueces River where he camped for six months until ordered to move his force of 4,000 regulars, volunteers and Texas Rangers to the Rio Grande, 100 miles down the coast in land claimed originally neither by Texas nor the United States. On 25 April 1846 a Mexican army crossed the river and attacked a squadron of dragoons, killing 11 men. War inevitably followed.

Leaving a small detachment at his base in Fort Texas, Taylor withdrew to Point Isabel and the supply ships awaiting him. On his return to Fort Texas he met and with the aid of his superior artillery defeated a Mexican army of 4,000 men at Palo Alto. Having sustained 500 casualties, the Mexicans withdrew across the Rio Grande in disorder. Taylor pursued them over to the river but was unable to cross until 18 May due to the lack of pontoon bridging, by which time the Mexicans had extricated themselves to safety.

When War was declared on 13 May, Congress authorized an increase in the Army from 734 officers and 7,885 men to 15,540 regulars and 50,000 volunteers.

The American Army of 1846 was better equipped than any before it to fight a war. Despite its small size - it consisted of only eight regiments of infantry, two of dragoons and four of artillery - it was well trained, professionally officered and had learned valuable lessons from the Indian Wars.

Weapons and tactics had also improved immeasurably. The percussion lock rifle first introduced in 1841 and accepted immediately by the cavalry albeit if less readily by the infantry, offered considerable enhancements in range accuracy and rate of fire to the well trained soldier.

For the first time in the military history of the United States, the militia were not to play a major role in the War, their place being taken by one-year volunteers. Although the new system had its obvious disadvantages, the volunteers were easier to control, discipline and train and above

The reformed American Army had effectively won the Second Seminole War with the victorious Battle of Lake Okeechobee on 25 December 1837, although guerilla attacks persisted for several more years.

Opposite above: Santa Anna tried unsuccessfully to block Scott's advance on Mexico City.

Opposite below: The Kentucky Dragoons twice broke up Mexican infantry charges at the Battle of Buena Vista.

all were not precluded from fighting abroad.

At the beginning of the war it was decided to mount a three-pronged offensive into Northern Mexico. One prong under General "Old Zack" Taylor was to advance westward from Montamoros to Monterrey; another under Brigadier Wool to move from San Antonio west to Chihuahua and then south; and a third under Colonel Kierney to march from Fort Leavenworth to Santa Fe and thence onward to San Diego. Only subsequently was it decided to send a further larger force under Major General Winfield Scott, commanding general of the army, to invade Vera Cruz before proceeding inland to strike at the very jugular of Mexico City itself.

Early successes on the battlefield were soon marred by political in-fighting. Taylor took Monterrey on 24 September but only after conceding an eight-week armistice, which so angered President Polk that the latter ordered its unilateral termination. Forced to continue his advance against his better judgement, Taylor took Saltillo on the main road to Mexico City and joined forces with Brigadier Wool, only to be ordered to hand over command of his remaining 4,000 regular troops to Scott, then pushing towards Vera Cruz.

Enraged by this decision, Taylor chose to regard Scott's further order to pull back to Monterrey as mere "advice" to be ignored. Far from consolidating as ordered, Taylor pushed his remaining 4,650 troops deeper south, halting at Agua Nueva some 300 miles north of Mexico's General Santa Anna, then assembling a powerful army. Assuming incorrectly that Santa Anna would not be able to move his 15,000 men through the barren desert which divided them, Taylor was outmanoeuvered and forced by the Mexicans to join battle at Buena Vista.

After two days of often bitter fighting, victory was pulled from the jaws of defeat when the Mississippi Rifles under Colonel Jefferson Davis broke the murderous Mexican cavalry charges which had earlier thrown the American infantry into disarray, giving the latter the opportunity to reform and thereafter to gradually assert its superiority. By the end of the second night Santa Anna was forced to retreat, leaving 1,500 casualties to America's 800.

The fighting spirit of the volunteers, the outstanding bravery of Zachary Taylor who had positioned himself on his horse in the center of the line throughout, the marked superiority of the 6-pounder cannon and the sheer *elan* of her cavalry, had compounded to bring America one of her greatest victories.

Having secured Northern Mexico, Scott assembled a force of over 13,000 men at Lobos Island, 50 miles south of Tampico, for the long-awaited attack on Vera Cruz. On 5 March, three miles south of Vera Cruz, the United States Forces made their first amphibious landing in history. Within four hours 10,000 men, plus their artillery and stores, were rowed ashore to be joined later by six naval guns which were subsequently successfully employed to breach the walls of Vera Cruz and its fortress San Juan de Ulua. The now defenseless city fell on 27 March leaving the road to the capital open.

Despite the unexpected loss of 4,000 volunteers, who refused to renew their enlistments, Scott met and yet again defeated Santa Anna at Cerro Gordo. Mexico City was then besieged, falling to numerically inferior forces on 14 September 1847.

The war with Mexico ended on 2 February 1848 with the signing of the Treaty of Guadalupe Hidalgo. The United States now had clear title to Texas, with the Rio Grande as its recognized southern border, and to over one million square miles of new territory, including all of present day Arizona, New Mexico, Utah, Nevada and California. Over 13,000 American lives had been lost in the War, 11,000 from disease and accident, but the United States now had firm borders to the North and South and could hope to expand steadily to the west. However, the overriding feelings of optimism now pervading the country were soon to be sorely shattered.

Below: Scott executed a text-book landing at Vera Cruz. It was the first important amphibious landing in the history of the American military.

# 5: THE CIVIL WAR

THE BUILD UP TO WAR

Attempts to reconcile the many deep-seated differences between the North and South came to nothing in the years immediately following the Mexican War.The admission of California into the Union in 1850 left many Southerners embittered, whilst others saw the passage of the Kansas-Nebraska Act of 1854, delegating the question of future slavery to the individual states, as an unacceptable sign of things to come.

With Abraham Lincoln's accession to the Presidency in 1860 the die was cast. Southern states took immediate steps to draft ordinances of succession and even before Lincoln's inauguration on 4 March 1861, seven states, led by South Carolina, had seceded from the Union to form the Confederate States of America. Two days later on 6 March, Jefferson Davis, the President of the Confederacy and one-time hero of the Mexican War, called for 100,000 volunteers to defend the new Confederacy.

As open war approached, it seemed that the North had all the advantages. Her 23 loyal states had a population of 21 million people against less than 9 million, including 3 million slaves, in the South. She controlled 80 per cent of the nation's factories, including all of those involved in heavy industry, and 67 per cent of the agriculture. Furthermore, the North enjoyed a developed and integrated transportation system, especially in railroads, which would enable her to move men and equipment quickly and cheaply about the countryside.

The North likewise enjoyed a preponderance of naval and maritime power. The 90 strong US-Navy, not in itself strong enough to fight an all-out war, was nevertheless capable of speedy expansion and indeed grew to 670 ships and 50,000 men within three years of hostilities. To counter this the South was never able to muster more than 130 vessels and 4,000 men; far too small a force to defeat the forthcoming blockade.

Lulled into a false sense of security by its preponderance in numbers and material, the Union Army, still led by the ageing and now uninspiring Winfield Scott, settled upon a simple three-pronged strategy to bring about the Southern downfall.

The Confederate capital of Richmond was to be captured, the Mississippi was to be secured along its entire length, effectively bisecting the enemy landmass, and an economic blockade, codenamed the "Anaconda Policy," was to be implemented to starve the Confederacy into submission.

For its part, the South hoped only to wage an "offensive-defensive" war of attrition on the basis that Northern resolve would break first and

The Battle of Shiloh, 6-7 April 1862, was the bloodiest in American history up until then. The Union had 13,000 killed or wounded while the Confederacy had 11,000 casualties.

Above: The new (1855) percussion lock muskets were much deadlier than their predecessors.

Above right: Jefferson Davis (1808-89): the President of the Confederacy.

Opposite above left: Abraham Lincoln (1809-69): 16th President of the USA.

Opposite above right: 100,000 Confederate volunteers enlisted in the first year of the war.

Opposite below: Zouaves (special infantry) often wore unusual uniforms such as these.

a compromise be agreed. It had however reckoned without the iron resolve of Abraham Lincoln, who from the outset would countenance nothing short of total re-integration.

The seccession of the seven states placed Lincoln on the horns of a dilemma. Fort Pickens and Fort Sumter, the only remaining Union strongholds in the South, were under threat. If he were to send reinforcements this would be interpreted by the eight remaining neutral slave states as unacceptable provocation, which would almost certainly drive them into the Confederacy; but if he were to abandon the forts this would be regarded as intolerable weakness. Eventually, on 8 April, a small supply column was dispatched to Fort Sumter. Brigadier Beauregard, the Charleston military commander, immediately demanded the surrender of the Fort. Having sustained a bombardment for 34 hours, Fort Sumter surrendered on 14 April. Lincoln immediately signed a proclamation declaring the seven states in rebellion. The remaining eight states began the process of seccession and both sides mobilized for all-out war.

## THE CONTENDING ARMIES

Neither combatant was remotely geared for the terrible carnage to follow during the next four years. Davis's original 100,000 volunteers had enlisted for one year only, and by the end of 1861 it had been deemed necessary to extend the terms of enlistment for up to three years. Conscription for up to three years, which proved both complex and unpopular, was introduced into the South in 1862. Militia were exempt as were the larger slave owners, whilst the wealthier conscripts could hire proxies to fight in their place.

In all over 900,000 men fought for the Southern cause. However at the height of the War there were no more than 450,000 on the roll, of whom only half were ever on duty simultaneously. In 1864 when manpower was at its most critical, the Army had shrunk to 200,000 with perhaps 100,000 effective.

The position for the North was if anything more perilous in the early stages. The vast majority of the regular forces were based west of the Mississippi, leaving only 15 companies to guard the Atlantic seaboard, the Canadian and southern borders. Within a year, however, 600,000 volunteers had come forward, with the result that training rather than manpower became the predominant problem. Although the North was forced to resort to conscription, it did so fairly and only on a small scale.

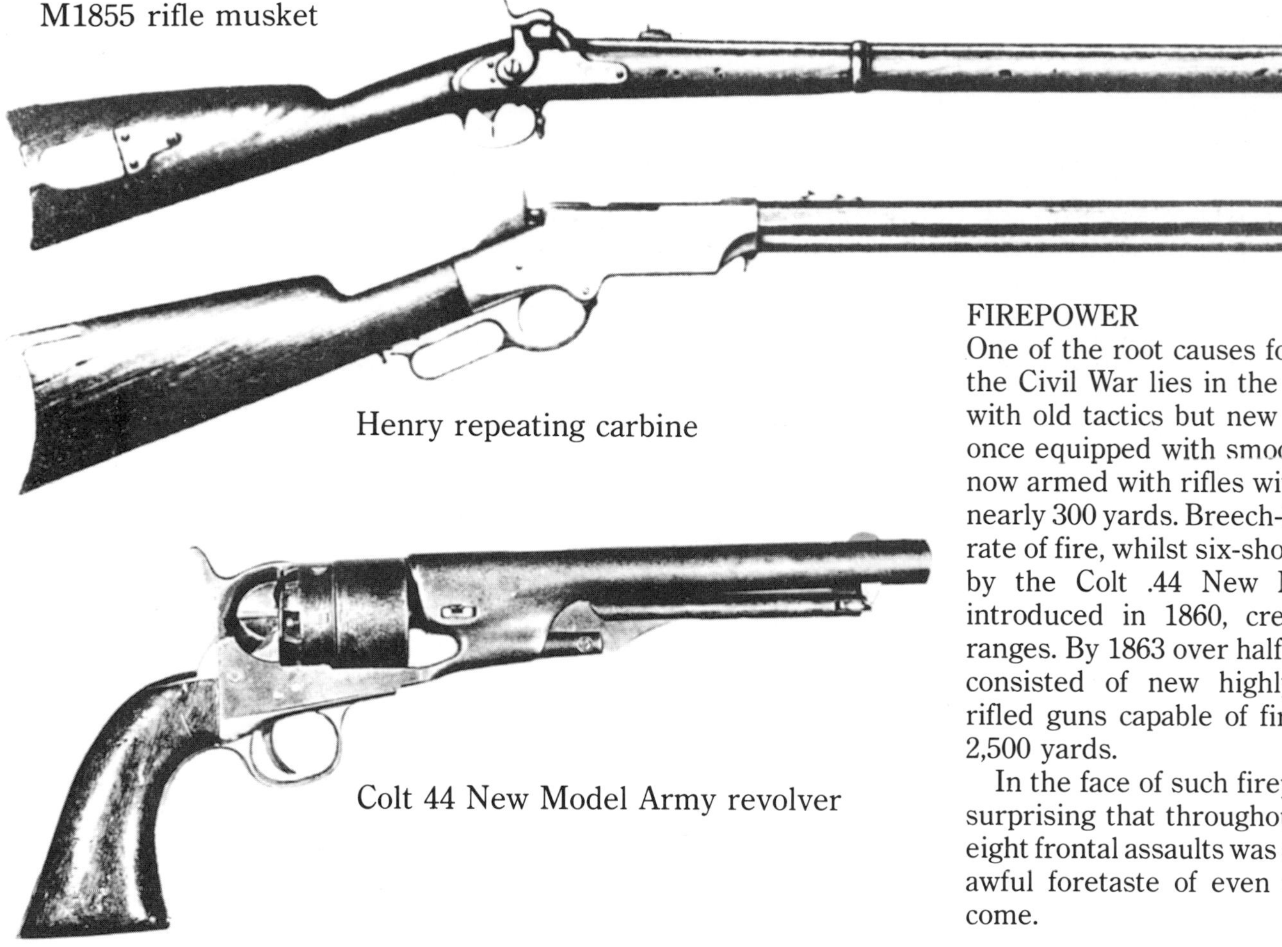


Above: Firearms improved greatly during the war.

## FIREPOWER

One of the root causes for the sheer carnage of the Civil War lies in the fact that it was fought with old tactics but new weapons. Infantrymen once equipped with smooth bore muskets were now armed with rifles with an effective range of nearly 300 yards. Breech-loading quadrupled the rate of fire, whilst six-shot revolvers, epitomized by the Colt .44 New Model Army revolver introduced in 1860, created bedlam at close ranges. By 1863 over half of the North's artillery consisted of new highly accurate three-inch rifled guns capable of firing an explosive shell 2,500 yards.

In the face of such firepower it is not perhaps surprising that throughout the War only one in eight frontal assaults was destined to succeed; an awful foretaste of even more terrible wars to come.

The Gatling Gun was an early machine gun with a revolving cluster of barrels. Each barrel was automatically loaded and fired during each revolution. Suprisingly, it was little used during the war.

Confederate soldiers fire a piece of heavy artillery.

A 15 inch Rodney Siege gun.

Ulysses Simpson Grant (1822-85) was the 'fighting general' Lincoln had been seeking, but his victories were won at the cost of many lives.

EARLY CONFLICT

The War commenced with a peroid of inactivity during which both protagonists concentrated on the training of their raw recruits. However, in June 1861, pressured by public opinion, Lincoln ordered Brigadier McDowell, then stationed south of Washington with 30,000 men, to advance into Virginia.

General Beauregard, in command of 22,000 Confederates at Manassas Junction a few miles to the south, moved his forces behind Bull Run to await McDowell's slowly advancing Federals.

The two virtually equal armies met on the morning of 21 July, at which time each immediately attempted to turn the other's right flank. Although initially successful, McDowell's forces were halted by an unexpected counter-attack and turned. Defeat disintegrated into a rout until, unable to regain control, McDowell was forced to order a withdrawal to the outskirts of Washington.

For the rest of the year both armies faced each other uneasily, neither wishing to make a move until its numbers and strength had been increased.

THE WESTERN CAMPAIGN

The western campaign of 1862 began well for the Union, whose forces in that area outnumbered the Confederates by nearly five to one. Fort Henry on the Tennessee River fell to Grant on 6 February, followed by Fort Donelson some twelve miles to the east on the Cumberland River a week later. By early March over 15,000 Confederate prisoners had fallen into Union hands and the road south into Tennessee lay wide open and undefended.

Halleck, in overall command of the Western Theatre, ordered Grant to proceed to Shiloh to await the arrival of Buell's Ohio Army before proceeding deeper into enemy territory. Fully apprised of the Union plans, General Johnston, in command of the local defenders, elected to attack Grant at Shiloh before Buell could join him.

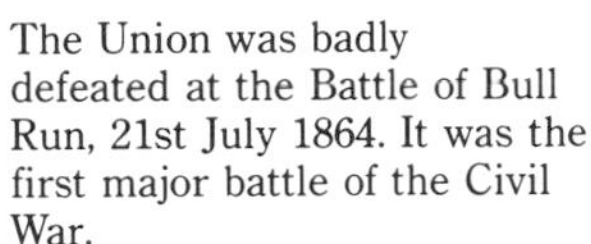

The Union was badly defeated at the Battle of Bull Run, 21st July 1864. It was the first major battle of the Civil War.

After a hard march Johnston fell upon Grant on the morning of 6 April, taking the latter completely by surprise. However at his very moment of victory Johnston was wounded, command passed to Beauregard and the Confederate attack was halted. During the course of the following night Grant received 17,000 reinforcements from Buell and in the morning was able to regain the initiative. During the course of the battle the North sustained 13,000 casualties, over 20 per cent of their entire force, but the South itself had lost 11,000 men from the 40,000 committed and had been forced to retire. The road into Tennessee remained open.

When Memphis fell on 6 June the central Mississippi fell firmly into federal hands. Later that month a force of 18,000 men under General Butler, supported by a flotilla of 46 ships under Captain Farragut, sailed into the lower Mississippi, fought their way past the coastal forts

Robert E. Lee (1807-79) was one of history's great generals. He led the Confederate forces throughout the war.

On 15 February 1862, Grant led the Union forces that captured Fort Donelson on the Cumberland River, Tennessee.

and captured the vital sea port of New Orleans.

By early August, Baton Rouge and Natchez had fallen, leaving the lower river securely under Union control. Lincoln had only to take the small stretch between Port Hudson and Vicksberg to fulfil his aim of bisecting the Confederacy.

Far from down-hearted, the Confederates immediately planned a massive counter-offensive in the West. General Bragg, who had replaced Beauregard after the latter's surrender of Corinth, moved north against Buell in the hopes of inducing neutral Kentucky into the Confederacy. However despite severe losses inflicted on the Union at the battles of Perryville and Stones River in October and December 1862, Buell's forces proved too powerful, Kentucky remained undecided and Bragg was forced to fall back upon Chattanooga.

In the East, 1862 began in stalemate with General McClellan assiduously refusing to move his 150,000 Union troops south against the far smaller numbers of General Johnston, without adequate preparation. Eventually, having retained McDowell and his 30,000 men for the protection of Washington, Lincoln grudgingly consented to McClellan moving the residue of his troops by sea to Fort Monroe, to the south-east of Richmond, to put pressure on the enemy capital.

Despite his having more than enough troops to complete the mission, McClellan moved with such caution that the Confederates were able to gather 70,000 troops to meet him. Panic-stricken, McClellan requested and was granted McDowell's 30,000 troops as reinforcements, but this contingency was foreseen by Davis who immediately dispatched Jackson with 17,000 men to threaten Washington.

Although never more than a diversion, Jackson succeeded in drawing off all available troops in the Washington area, including McDowell's much needed reinforcements, before retiring in good order down the Shenandoah Valley.

Simultaneously, Johnston attacked the heartily demoralized McClellan on 31 May at Fair Oaks and Seven Pines but could not dent his lines. The badly wounded Johnston was replaced by Robert E. Lee, who immediately mounted a spirited offensive culminating in the Seven Days' Battle (25 June-1 July), after which the Union forces pulled back south-east to the protective mantle of their naval base on the James River.

Lee followed, constantly harrassing the still numerically superior enemy, suffering 11,000 casualties in the process.

McClellan was ordered back to Washington to support General Pope, recently brought from the West to rejuvenate sagging Union spirits. As

Lee's invasion of Maryland was stopped at Sharpsburg (Antietam) in September 1862.

Andrew 'Stonewall' Jackson (1824-63) was an outstanding leader of the Confederate cavalry. His death deprived Lee of his most valuable supporter.

ever, he moved too slowly and too late.

When Lee, who had moved his forces north with all the dash and determination which was later to make him legendary, attacked Pope in what was later to become known as the Second Battle of Bull Run on 29 August, the latter had yet to be joined by more than a few of McClellan's promised reserves. Half-hearted Union probes were halted and turned, and not for the first time Northern indecisiveness was exploited by the far more dynamic Confederacy to turn disorder into a rout. The Army fled to the protection of Washington where, perhaps strangely, Pope who had at least fought, was replaced in overall command by McClellan whose failure to do so had played so large a part in the defeat.

Unwilling to surrender the initiative, Lee ordered Jackson to capture the Union stronghold of Harper's Ferry before rejoining his main forces which he himself would lead across the Potomac into Maryland. Attempts by McClellan to destroy the two Confederate forces before they were able to reunite failed, as ever due to tardiness and indecision, with the result that by the time McClellan was able to join the enemy in battle behind Antietam Creek, Lee had been reinforced by the majority of Jackson's veterans.

On the morning of 17 September 1862 90,000 Union soldiers were committed against 50,000 Confederates. Although casualties on both sides were horrific (within the day over 12,000 Unionists and 10,000 Confederates were to be killed or wounded), the outcome was indecisive. Lee was allowed to retire south into Virginia in good order, whilst McClellan was at last removed although his replacement, General Burnside, was hardly more assertive.

An early plan by Burnside to cross the Rappahannock at Fredericksburg before proceeding to Richmond met with disaster on 13 December, when 15,000 of his troops were killed or injured attempting to cross the river in the teeth of strong Confederate defences.

By the end of 1862 the Confederacy was as strong as ever in the East. It was however losing ground in the West, the blockade was beginning to bite and Union resolve was far from crumbling. To the astute few, the outcome of the war was already a foregone conclusion.

Below: The Union advance into the South was halted by General Brixton Bragg at Chickomauga Creek on 19-20 September 1863.

## 1863: THE CRUCIAL YEAR

The badly shaken Burnside was replaced early in 1863 by General "Fighting Joe" Hooker, an inveterate boaster but a tenacious fighter and good tactician. Hooker had no intention of repeating his predecessor's folly at Fredericksburg. Instead, late in April, he transferred three of his corps 30 miles up river, to execute an easier crossing, whilst leaving two corps conspicuously facing Lee on the far side of the Rappahannock. Initially all went well until, realizing the nature of the ruse, Lee moved quickly and savagely against the complacent Hooker to his rear. Completely unnerved and contrary to all the tenets of war, Hooker halted his offensive, taking up a defensive position outside Chancellorville. Seizing his opportunity, Lee moved all but a covering force west against the Federals, employing Jackson's cavalry in a flanking attack.

Completely outmanoeuvred, the Union lines nevertheless held for two days of bloody fighting. When, tragically for the South, Jackson was mortally wounded - ironically by his own troops - on 5 May the attack lost momentum. The Union forces were allowed to withdraw, leaving behind them 13,000 casualties, and Virginia was once again secured for the Confederacy.

Ignoring strong pressure to send help to Johnston's hard-pressed forces in the West, Davis authorized Lee to make a limited offensive into Pennsylvania in the hopes of pressurizing the Union into agreeing peace terms.

Early in June 1863, Lee with 75,000 men moved north across the Potomac. Almost immediately his plan began to falter. General James Stuart and his cavalry, tasked with the mundane duties of

General George G. Meade was methodical rather than brilliant as a general yet his victory over Lee at Gettysburg put the Confederacy on the defensive from then on.

reconnaissance and flank protection, misinterpreted their orders and began to move parallel to the main force. Denied his "eyes", Lee was unable to know that Hooker had been replaced by General Meade, whose substantial forces were now rapidly closing with him.

On 30 June the two armies met at Gettysburg. During four days of bitter fighting during which the pendulum swung first in favor of and then against the Confederacy, Lee gradually lost the initiative until on 4 July he was forced to retire southwards towards Virginia.

During his second offensive culminating in Gettysburg, Lee sustained 25,000 irreplaceable casualties. Although Union losses reached 20,000, recruitment was at its peak and the vacancies soon filled. The South was now forced firmly on the defensive. Defeat was inevitable.

## VICTORY IN THE WEST

Whilst the Union Army was securing its position at Gettysburg, no less vital a campaign was being waged in the West. Late in December 1862, Grant moved his forces south from Memphis towards Jackson, Alabama, with a view to moving west as a prelude to taking Vicksburg, the last great Confederate stronghold on the Mississippi. The attack was repulsed with inevitable heavy losses.

Undeterred, in January 1863 Grant gathered his forces at Memphis and with the aid of naval support moved down the Mississippi to lay siege to the fortress. Although his 75,000 troops outnumbered the entire Confederate forces in Mississippi, Grant appreciated the magnitude of the task ahead of him. Vicksburg was a natural fortress surrounded by marshes on three sides with

'Stonewall' Jackson was accidentally shot by one of his own sentries during the Battle of Chancellorsville, 2 May 1863.

only the eastern approaches, then firmly in enemy hands, susceptible to assault.

Initial plans to build a canal to bypass the city failed, as did subsequent attempts to negotiate the shallow and winding bayous to the north of the citadel.

Eventually Grant decided to throw caution to the wind. Commodore Porter, the naval commander, was ordered to run the gauntlet of the batteries at night, taking such casualties as were necessary. The infantry were instructed to march south through the Louisiana swamps for 50 miles, after which they would be transferred to firm ground across the river by the waiting ships. At the same time Colonel Grierson was to move his cavalry rapidly south towards Jackson and on to Baton Rouge, causing as much pandemonium as possible.

Audacity won the day and the plan succeeded. On 14 April Porter's ships ran the gauntlet of the fortress guns with minimal losses and within two weeks had ferried Grant's army safely into the very heart of enemy territory. Grierson, his cavalry covering 600 miles in 16 days, took Jackson on 14 May, forcing Johnston and his battered forces north-east away from the battle zone.

After a siege of six weeks, during the final stages of which the civilian occupants had been

The Confederate infantry and cavalry charge on Seminary Ridge, Gettysburg was repulsed with heavy losses.

Union soldiers successfully storm Lookout Mountain on the first day of the Battle of Chattanooga (24 November 1863). This became known as 'the battle above the clouds'.

reduced to eating mules and rats to keep alive, General Pemberton, the city commander, surrendered unconditionally. The surrender was accepted on 4 July, within hours of Lee's defeat at Gettysburg.

While Grant was laying siege to Vicksburg, General Banks with 15,000 men from the New Orleans garrison had been besieging Port Hudson to the south. With the news of the surrender of Vicksburg, Port Hudson capitulated, leaving the Mississippi firmly in the hands of the Union.

The Confederacy was now effectively severed.

## THE CHATTANOOGA CAMPAIGN

The Union was aware that it could not hope to exploit its victories on the Mississippi until it captured the vital communications center of Chattanooga, nestling on the Tennessee-Georgia border. The retiring and nervous General Rosecrans was dispatched with an Army to take the city, but delayed so much that the more experienced General Bragg was able to withdraw his troops into superb defensive high ground to the south.

Exhilarated by his bloodless capturing of Chattanooga, Rosecrans rushed headlong into the mountains in search of his foe, only to find himself confronted by superior forces. After two days of bloody fighting at Chickamauga Creek, in which the Confederates lost 18,000 men (an astounding 25 percent of their numbers!), the Union center broke, as a result of which the entire Army was forced to retire in considerable disarray to the protection of the city's defenses.

The superiority in numbers now enjoyed by the Union was clearly demonstrated by Grant when, his forces supplemented by Hooker and 20,000 men transferred by train from the East, he relieved the city with little difficulty.

Once established, Grant began slowly but purposefully to clear the enemy from the high ground to the south. When Bragg was forced to release a large part of his forces required urgently in the east, Grant seized his opportunity, attacked the center of the Confederate stronghold of Missionary Ridge, and drove the enemy from the battlefield.

Disheartened, the Southerners withdrew to Dalton, Georgia, where Bragg, little more than a scapegoat, was relieved of his command and replaced by Johnston.

The road to Atlanta, the very nucleus of Southern resistance, lay open.

Above: General Joseph Eggleston Johnston (1807-91) was one of the Confederacy's best generals. He distinguished himself at the first Battle of Bull Run, July 1861, and later commanded the Confederate Armies in Tennessee and Mississippi.

Opposite: 'Grant in the Wilderness'. Grant's drive on Richmond, Virginia was a prelude to the ultimate Union victory and the end of the war.

## UNION VICTORY

Lincoln recognized in Ulysses S. Grant a general who would fight without fear and in March 1864 promoted him to Lieutenant-General and soon thereafter to General-in-Chief in the place of Halleck, whom he retained in Washington as a senior administrator.

Grant's plan for the final destruction of the Confederacy relied upon three offensive movements. General Meade's Army, resting near Fredericksburg after its victory at Gettysburg, would move south towards Richmond whilst General Sherman would drive south east from Chattanooga, sieze Atlanta and drive south. Simultaneously, General Banks would move up the Red River, take Shreveport and enter Texas as a counter to Napoleon III of France whose forces had recently quelled the unrest in Mexico. Thereafter he would strike east, take Mobile and move north to threaten Montgomery.

Placing himself at the head of Meade's Army, Grant began his move south on 4 May 1864 and at once began a lateral movement to the left in order to stay close to his rail links with Washington and to the various tributaries of the Chesapeake along the Virginia coast. Seeking to thwart this vulnerable manoeuvre, Lee launched an attack on 5 May and for two days fought a bloody engagement in the wilderness west of Chancellorville.

Unlike his predecessors Grant was impervious to losses and minor set-backs. His advance continued until Lee, seeing no virtue in a Pyrrhic victory, disengaged to reform to the south astride the vital crossroads at Spotsylvania. Anticipating a counter-attack, Grant at once ordered Sheridan, and his cavalry toward Richmond to meet and destroy Stuart's cavalry. In a 16-day series of running skirmishes culminating in the Battle of Yellow Tavern, Stuart destroyed his enemy at once, denying Lee what most tacticians agreed had been the cream of his Army.

Grant then assaulted Lee's stronghold of Spotsylvania, but after four days of bloody fighting broke off the engagement and on the 20 May simply continued his march to the south. The remnants of Lee's forces were left stranded and impotent to the rear. Lee raced south to cut off Grant, digging-in along the North Anna River. Grant simply ignored the challenge completely, continuing his relentless march to the south.

Lee followed until finally the armies faced each other at Cold Harbour on the outskirts of Richmond itself. Grant attacked on 3 June but as ever was unable to crack the determined Confederate resistance.

Despite his losses, then in excess of 55,000 against the South's 32,000, Grant continued on relentlessly, crossing the James River by way of a, brilliantly engineered 2,100-foot pontoon bridge. A supply base was established at City point and on 18 June the City of Petersburg placed under siege.

To break the pressure and relieve the siege, Lee ordered General Early and his cavalry north along the Shenandoah Valley to threaten Washington. Lincoln, refusing to be panicked by what he regarded as a forlorn gesture, strengthened the city's defenses but resisted the temptation to withdraw badly needed troops from Grant's Army.

Lacking manpower and chronically short of supplies, Early was unable to penetrate the outer perimeter of the city's defenses before he himself was forced to withdraw. Pursued back down the

Shenandoah Valley by Sheridan, Early's exhausted cavalrymen were defeated at Winchester, Fisher's Hill and Cedar Valley. So as to deny the Confederacy the use of the Shenandoah Valley again, the entire area was systematically destroyed in the first of a series of scorched earth actions which were to play so brutal a part in the final stages of the War.

Whilst this was occurring General Sherman, based at Chattanooga and Nashville, prepared to move his 100,000 troops south-east into Georgia. Jackson, who had only 65,000 men to guard the entire state, employed complex manoeuvering tactics to slow Sherman, successfully reducing his advance to less than 100 miles after 74 days. However this was not enough for the impatient Davis, who replaced Johnston with the more aggressive Hood. Despite his willingness to meet the Northern juggernaut head-on, Hood was quite unable to halt Sherman's massive Army which began its triumphant entry into Atlanta on 1 September 1864.

Pausing only to consolidate, Sherman detached 30,000 troops to join General Thomas in the defense of Nashville, and with his remaining

Right: General William Tecumseh Sherman (1820-91), an outstanding Union general. He became supreme commander in the west in 1864 and made his famous 'march through Georgia' in that year.

Far right: Grant's victory at Petersburg made the capture of Richmond, the Confederate capital, inevitable and was effectively the end of the war.

62,000 men began the famous "march to the sea". Determined to destroy the Southern will to fight before quitting Atlanta, Sherman ordered the destruction of its railroad system together with its provincial municipal buildings and infrastructure. Between then and his arrival at Savannah, which he took on 21 December 1864, Sherman ensured that his troops wrought maximum havoc wherever they went, regardless of whether the towns and villages en route surrendered or put up a token resistance. Southern morale, both civilian and military, was shattered.

## THE FINAL MONTHS

Hood's problems were compounded when, in an attempt to circle north and capture Nashville, he lost 11 general officers and 6,000 veterans, one-third of his total, at the Battle of Franklin. Too weak to advance and unable to retire, Hood was forced to bivouac a few miles to the south of Nashville, his fate now entirely in Federal hands. Realizing the full extent of his enemy's weakness Thomas launched a devastating three-pronged cavalry and infantry attack against Hood on 15 December. Within two days of fighting, the Confederate Army was a defeated shambling ghost of its former self. Destroyed as a fighting unit, it would never again be able to take the field.

The ports of Wilmington and Charleston fell early in the new year, leaving Richmond the only major city remaining in Confederate hands. Lee made a desperate attempt to escape encirclement with the remnants of his troops but was intercepted by Sheridan at Appomattox, Virginia. Realizing that escape was impossible, Lee began surrender talks, and on 9 April 1865 the bloodiest war in American history came to its inevitable end.

The defense of Richmond was the last great Confederate act of defiance.

Union ecstasy was however soon to turn to grief. Within five days President Abraham Lincoln, the undoubted author of the Northern victory, lay dead, the victim of an assassin's bullet.

## THE ROAD AHEAD

The Union's infatuation with its Armed Forces was so short-lived that by 1876 the regular army had been reduced to 27,000 officers and men. However, initial attempts to restore the Southern states to normality by peaceful means met with little success due to the complete refusal of most of their citizens to accept the new place of the black ex-slave in society. Accordingly, the Army was often called upon to restore order and ensure the implementation of unpopular measures, a task which most of its members found highly distasteful. Inevitably military rule became increasingly tainted by civilian opportunists, or "carpetbaggers," exploiting the situation for their own ends. Organizations such as the Ku Klux Klan and the Knights of the White Camellia mushroomed in response, and in some rural areas actually began to challenge the power of the over-stretched Army.

The situation improved somewhat for the Army if not for the country as a whole when in 1877, in return for supporting Rutherford Hayes' candidature for the Presidency, the South was granted virtual autonomy, the blacks were returned to a position of subjugation, and the majority of the military was withdrawn to the North or West.

Although the immediate post-war Army consisted almost exclusively of veterans, by the 1870s most of these had retired to be replaced in the main by immigrants and those unable to find alternative employment.

Morale, discipline and self-esteem sank to an all time low with desertion at one time reaching a staggering thirty per cent of all enlisted men.

Inertia and inefficiency were rife at all levels and initiative discouraged. Equipment suffered badly to the extent that the single-shot .45 caliber "trap-door" Springfield Rifle, so named because its breech snapped upwards like a trap door, was not adopted until 1872 and then was itself only replaced by a magazine-rifle, the five-shot .30 caliber Danish Krag-Jorgensen, in 1893.

Despite its devastating potential, the Gatling Gun was never fully exploited, being regarded more as an artillery asset than an aid to the infantry,and the full implication of rifled artillery, then being introduced into Europe, was not fully grasped until the end of the century.

Surprisingly, despite its obvious lack of

After the Civil War, Congress reduced its expenditure on the army. However, the Krag bolt-action breech-loading rifle was introduced in 1893 and is shown in this illustration of an American infantryman by Frederic Remington.

Right: After the war, the army became increasingly involved in the suppression of industrial unrest - a duty detested by the ordinary soldier.

Below: Troops protect a train during the Pullman railroad strike of 1894.

Indian leaders were dealt with mercilessly by post-war governments. This public hanging of the leaders of a Sioux uprising in 1862 was not an especially uncommon occurrence.

leadership the post-war Army enjoyed some of the finest training establishments in the world. The Corps of Engineers relinquished control of West Point Military Academy in 1866, after which its curriculum was broadened considerably. Several post-graduate professional schools were set up and the Artillery School at Fort Monroe was reopened in 1868 after a gap of eight years. Most important of all, the School of Application for Infantry and Cavalry, later to become the General Service and Staff College, was opened at Fort Leavenworth.

## INTERNAL STRIFE

Morale within the Army hit its lowest ebb during the 1870s and 1880s when troops were called out to curb the increasingly violent spate of strikes then occurring throughout the industrial North-East. Throughout, the Army exercised tremendous restraint, often in the face of extensive provocation, and in only one instance, during the Pullman Strike of 1894, was a rioter killed by military action. Even so the role of the military in domestic matters was questioned, and in several instances individual states and the federal government were deeply divided as to whether or not to employ troops.

As a direct result many governors and local legislatures began to see the reformation of the volunteer militia as the only way of ensuring the preservation of their powers against encroachment from Washington. By 1892 every State had its own local force, or "National Guard" as they began to be known, free of Federal control. By the turn of the century over 100,000 men, mainly middle-class conservatives, had enrolled in the Guard which was by then considerably larger and in many respects more influential than the regular army it was intended to support.

Above: The Wagon Box Fight between the Army and Sioux in 1867. The Indian Wars were bloody and uncompromising with quarter neither asked for nor given.

Above right: Sitting Bull (1834?-90) was the most famous of all the Sioux.

Opposite top left: George Armstrong Custer (1839-76).

Opposite top right: *Custer's Last Stand* by Otto Becker.

Opposite center right: Geronimo (1834-1909) with three fellow Apaches photographed after his surrender in 1886.

Opposite bottom right: A mass grave for the dead of Wounded Knee, 1890.

## THE INDIAN WARS

West of the Mississippi some 270,000 Indians, over 100,000 of whom were potential combatants, co-habited uneasily with two million white settlers. Up to 9,000 soldiers, many but not all of whom were cavalry, were allotted the thankless task of policing this huge, hostile area. Caught between a humanitarian faction which regarded all Indian deaths as murder and the frontiersmen who wanted the Indian lands at any cost, the role of the Army as mediator was all but impossible.

The Plains Indians themselves constituted arguably the finest light cavalry of their era. Brave and tenacious in the extreme, they were at the same time cruel, suspicious and argumentative.

The Indian Wars, which lasted from 1866 to 1890 and which resulted in the deaths of 2,000 soldiers and 6,000 Indians, invariably relied on the use of converging columns to force the Indians to stand and fight, on the wholesale destruction of their camps, livestock and shelter and on the employment of friendly Indians both as scouts and combatants.

The initial campaign, fought in the South against the Cheyenne, Arapahoes and Kiowas, ended in the year-long Red River War of 1874 when 3,000 soldiers herded the unhappy Indians into reservations in present-day Oklahoma.

The Sioux federation in the North with its 30,000 members proved a more difficult adversary. Enraged by what they considered a flagrant breach of earlier treaties, the Sioux under the leadership of Red Cloud left their reservation, joined the "hunting bands" of Sitting Bull and migrated en masse to their ancestral homes in the Black Hills of Montana.

General Sheridan, commanding a division in Missouri, was ordered to return the recalcitrant Sioux to their reservations. One column of 1,000 men supported by 250 Crow and Shoshone allies under the command of Brigadier Crook, marched north from Fort Fetterman in Wyoming. A second column of 450 soldiers and 25 Crow under Colonel Gibbon was dispatched against the Sioux encampments in south-east Montana and a third force of 950 soldiers and 40 Indian scouts, including the 7th Cavalry, under the overall command of Brigadier Terry, moved westward from Fort Abraham Lincoln.

Crook's column was attacked by 1,500 Sioux and Cheyenne warriors along the Rosebud Creek just north of the Montana border, and in the ensuing six-hour battle was so badly mauled that it was forced to retire. Unaware of this setback or of the enemy's vastly under-estimated numbers, the remaining columns continued. Custer and the 7th Cavalry were detached to the Little Big-Horn to drive the Sioux into the arms of the waiting infantry. Inexplicably Custer split his already stretched command into three independent columns. Two of the columns under Benteen and Reno were able to reunite before being brought to battle by an overwhelming number of Sioux and managed to hold out for two days before the survivors were relieved by Terry. Custer

however was less fortunate. His column was suddenly surrounded by thousands of Sioux under Crazy Horse and in a two-hour battle were wiped out to the last man. After the "massacre" the Sioux dispersed to their homelands. The nation however, its centenial celebrations in ruins, clamored for vengeance. A large army under the command of General Crook was dispatched to Montana and in a savage winter campaign broke the Indians completely. The final period of large-scale tribal resistance ended when Sitting Bull and Crazy Horse surrendered in the spring of 1877.

Geronimo with his renegade Apaches continued to resist in the south-east, but even he was forced to accept the inevitable and surrender in 1886.

A small group of Sioux, intoxicated by a new brand of ultra-nationalistic religious fervor, left their reservation in 1890. Intercepted at Wounded Knee, the Sioux surrendered, but a misunderstanding occurred and fighting broke out. In the ensuing massacre over 200 Indians, many of them women and children, were killed. Indian resistance was finally broken forever and the Army was able to return to its barracks and depots. It would not however be left in peace for long.

# 6: THE SPANISH-AMERICAN WAR

As if by fate, the return of the Army to its barracks coincided almost exactly with a newfound national confidence and desire for self-assertion. Relations with Canada were good, whilst Mexico, if still far from stable, presented no challenge. Only the dying embers of the Spanish Empire, personified by its iron-fisted control of Cuba and Puerto Rico, remained to affront United States' sensibilities.

Cuba, which had been attempting to gain her freedom since the 1860s, rose again in 1895. Realising that success would be impossible without United States aid, the rebels established an office in New York and began at once to lobby for support. Although Congress was quick to recognize the new Government, neither President Cleveland nor his successor William McKinley wanted war and both prevaricated. The President, however, was powerless to stem the ground swell of public opinion when the battleship "Maine" blew up in Havana Harbor on 15 February 1898. Despite expert evidence to the contrary, the population as a whole was sure that the "Maine" had fallen victim to Spanish sabotage and demanded revenge.

On 20 April, Congress declared Cuba free and authorized the use of the Army to defend its latest ally. As anticipated, Spain felt that she had no option but to declare war.

Although the United States Navy was strong, recently modernized and quite capable of fighting the war, the Army was not. Reduced to 26,000 officers and men, the Army had little, if any, jungle warfare experience, nor did it have the resources to train and equip the thousands of willing volunteers now flocking to the colors.

Friction between Major General Miles, Commanding General of the Army, and Alger, Secretary of War, was apparent from the outset. Whereas Miles wished to assemble a force of 80,000 men at Chickamauga Park, Georgia, with a view to training them for a landing in Cuba in October immediately after the rainy season, Alger, with an eye to public opinion, demanded immediate action.

Accordingly the bulk of the regulars, now increased to 59,000 officers and men, and the 210,000 volunteers, were sent piecemeal to southern ports to await embarkation even though at that stage no battle plan or overall strategy existed.

Meanwhile the Navy, freed from such confusion, won the first decisive victory in the Philip-

Theodore 'Teddy' Roosevelt (in center with glasses) poses with his famous volunteer 'Rough Riders'.

Above: Although the sinking of the "Maine" was almost certainly accidental, it led to a demand for war against Spain.

Opposite above: More than 200,000 men volunteered for service against the Spanish.

Opposite below: Having expelled Spain from her colonies in the Philippines the United States found itself supressing Filipino insurgents demanding independence.

Below: The naval victory at Santiago Bay on 1 May 1890 destroyed the Spanish Pacific fleet.

pines. Immediately after the declaration of war, Admiral Dewey had steamed with his Asiatic Squadron from Hong Kong to Manila Bay where he encountered a large but totally unprepared Spanish fleet. The fleets engaged and by the end of 1 May Spanish naval power in the Pacific had ceased to exist. The 15,000 strong VIII Corps under General Merritt was dispatched at once to the Philippines in the optimistic hope that the local population would welcome the United States as its new imperial master.

Unlike the Spanish garrison, which was more than willing to surrender if honor could be upheld, the Philippino guerillas who had been fighting for independence for decades were not willing to exchange one foreign overlord for another, and would tolerate nothing short of total sovereignty.

Despite this setback the attack on Manila went ahead, and after a contrived "battle" in which the American attackers and Spanish defenders agreed to miss their targets, honor was deemed to have been settled and the city passed to United States control on 13 August 1898.

At the subsequent Treaty of Paris, to which the guerillas were not invited, the entire Philippine archipelago was ceded to the United States, which thus unexpectedly found itself, albeit somewhat unwillingly, a major Pacific power.

The mainstream war in Cuba was progressing less satisfactorily. Despite Army protestations that it could not hope to move its forces to Cuba until the Navy had secured total sovereignty of the sea lanes, V Corps under Major General Shafter was dispatched from its temporary base at Tampa on 14 June and arrived off Santiago six days later. Unopposed amphibious landings were made at Siboney and Daiquiri, east of Santiago, and the city placed under siege. The subsequent attack on 1st July was marred by American confusion and an almost total lack of cohesion. Units failed to support each other, artillery support was lacking and the naval bombardment virtually non-existent. Nevertheless Colonel Theodore Roosevelt's volunteer Rough Riders, supported gallantly by the black troopers of the 10th and 19th Cavalry Regiments, stormed and took nearby Kettle Hill.

Two days later, contrary to all sound military reason, the Spanish flotilla, anchored safely in

the protected waters of Santiago Bay, made a dash for the open sea where it met and was destroyed by the superior American fleet. Disheartened, surrounded and totally alone, the Spanish military leaders surrendered Santiago with its garrison of 23,000 on 16 July.

While Shafter was gaining victory at Santiago General Miles, with 3,000 troops, was securing Puerto Rico which finally surrendered on 13 August 1898.

Reeling from defeat after defeat, Spain sued for peace in the hopes of mitigating her losses at the conference table. The United States, however, proved to be uncompromising. The Philippines and Puerto Rico were ceded to her whilst Cuba, now nominally independent, was placed under her protection.

Peace in the Philippines was not fully restored for a further year. 40,000 guerillas under the experienced Emilio Aquinaldo made a final desperate bid for freedom. It was not until the summer of 1899, by which time 35,000 troops had been deployed to the islands, that the insurgents' power was finally broken.

# 7: EXPANSION INTO EMPIRE

## THE BOXER REBELLION

By September 1899 Secretary of State John Hay felt secure enough to declare a unilateral "Open Door" policy guaranteeing equal trading rights in China for the Occidental powers and Japan. Despite subsequent public protestations that it was not the intention of the great powers to dismember the tottering Chinese Empire, and although it was certainly in the United States' best interest for China to retain its national identity, his policy was soon to disintegrate in shreds.

Resentful of Western incursions upon their way of life, nationalistic Chinese, calling themselves The Fists of Righteous Harmony, with the tacit approval of the Manchu Dowager Empress, began to attack foreigners on sight. Missionaries, traders and religious converts were slaughtered out of hand and the foreign legations in Peking placed under siege. Defending the 500 foreign civilians and 3,000 Chinese Christians from the 140,000 rioters, now known as Boxers, was a small mixed force of 450 soldiers assigned to the various legations.

Despite her policy of non-dismemberment, the United States at once joined with her European allies in putting together an expeditionary force to relieve her nationals. When the original force of 2,000 proved inadequate for the task, President McKinley at once dispatched the 9th and 14th Infantry together with supporting artillery from the Philippines. Although this force represented no more than ten per cent of the 25,000 strong "International Relief Force" which eventually stormed Peking, its members played a significant part in its capture and the bringing to an end of the 55-day siege.

The American Forces played no part in the subsequent occupation, although a small armed contingent did remain in China, ostensibly to guard the legation, until 1938.

## INTERNAL REFORMS

The United States had by now proved her willingness to play a full part in international affairs. Her Armed Forces had deported themselves bravely against the Boxers but their equipment had often been found wanting. It was realized that if America were to challenge the established European powers in the world arena, her Army would have to undergo a drastic and expensive modernization program.

In 1903 the old Krag rifle was replaced by the Springfield M1903 rifle, a .30-caliber five-round

The Boxer Rebellion represented the United State's first foreign incursion into foreign policy in the Far East.

weapon capable of high-velocity sustained fire, and in 1911 the .38-caliber revolver was retired in favour of the lethal .45-caliber seven-round Colt automatic pistol. The artillery received the M1902 3-inch gun as its standard field piece and coastal fortifications were rendered virtually impregnable by the introduction of the new 16-inch rifled gun.

Ominously, Congress showed itself blind to the needs for a new heavy machine-gun to replace the Gatling and it was not until 1917, three years after the weapon had shown itself king of the battlefield on the Western Front, that the United States adopted the Browning.

Although the commanders in the Spanish-American War had proved themselves perfectly able, they had often been let down by their logistics. Conceding the necessity for fundamental change, Secretary of War Root commissioned Grenville Dodge to investigate all areas of administrative weakness, and in 1903 began to implement the findings. Over the next few years the so-called "Root Reforms" would drag the military hierarchy however unwillingly into the twentieth century.

The office of Chief of Staff was created and that of Commanding General scrapped. The new Chief of Staff, supported by a General Staff, would be responsible for administration as well as for tactics, and as such would be able to plan every aspect of a future campaign. The Army War College and General Staff College were set up, as were new schools for the artillery, cavalry and the support units. In 1903 steps were taken to rationalize the militia. Under the terms of the Dick Act two separate groups, an organized militia or National Guard and a reserve, were set up. Initially the Guard could be mobilized for up to nine months only and could not serve abroad. However, legislation in 1908 and 1914 extended the President's powers, enabling him to appoint Guard officers personally when the force was acting under federal jurisdiction and authorizing their deployment abroad.

Casualties in the Spanish-American War were caused as much by an atrocious lack of sanitation as by enemy action.

The Wright Brothers' first flight at Kitty Hawk in 1903. In 1909 the US Army's Signal Corps purchased Aeroplane Number 1 thereby establishing its aero division.

LATIN AMERICAN INTERVENTIONS

By the turn of the century the United States felt strong enough to exert total sovereignty over Latin America as a whole. It sent a 5,000-strong "Army of Pacification" to Cuba between 1906 and 1909 to re-establish law and order on the island, and subsequently sent smaller forces in 1912 and 1917.

In 1907, after an earlier expensive French failure, Colonel W. Goethals, one of the finest military engineers in the world, master-minded the construction of the Panama Canal, at once allowing the United States Navy free passage between the Atlantic and Pacific Oceans.

Less successful were the Army's several interventions into Mexico between 1911 and 1916. In 1914 as the result of an incident largely inspired by President Woodrow Wilson, the United States Navy imposed a blockade of part of the Mexican coast and subsequently siezed the port of Vera Cruz. After mediation from Argentina, Chile and Brazil, the military were withdrawn but the situation remained tense. Two years later President Wilson again ordered his troops into Mexico in

Fransico 'Pancho' Villa (1877-1923). His revolutionary activities led to President Wilson sending troops into Mexico in pursuit of him.

this instance in pursuit of Francisco ("Pancho") Villa, a rebel opposing the regime of President Carranza. Despite the inspired leadership of Brigadier Pershing the invading forces failed to corner the elusive Villa. They did however become embroiled in a series of escalating clashes with the regular Mexican Army until, fearing all-out war with Carranza, Wilson was forced to order a withdrawal.

Although the expedition had been far from successful, it had nevertheless highlighted a number of weaknesses remaining in the Army. As history would demonstrate, the lessons learned would soon prove invaluable.

Above: General John J. Pershing (1860-1948) (center) with General Leonard Wood (right) - his chief of staff.

# 8: THE GREAT WAR

## THE PATH TO CONFLICT

Prior to the United States entry into the War, the major European combatants had fought themselves into a bloody stalemate. Neither superpower alliance was strong enough to destroy the other, yet neither would countenance defeat. Millions had died, the victims of massed artillery, the machine-gun and suicidal frontal assaults across no-man's land, yet the tactics of attrition remained unaltered.

Desperate to break the deadlock, the Allies set about tightening their blockade of the Central Powers. Determined to break the blockade and in turn cut Britain off from her Empire, Germany accelerated her use of the U-boat. In so doing she realized that she would have to renege on her agreement with the United States not to sink neutral shipping, but nevertheless felt that the danger of forcing America into the War was outweighed by the necessity for early victory.

In February 1917 Germany made its declaration of unrestricted submarine warfare, contemporaneously entering into secret negotiations with Mexico to invade the United States in the hope that this would keep the latter too occupied to bother with a war over 3,000 miles away. Domestic public opinion in America turned sharply in favour of the Allies, and when the terms of the Zimmerman Telegramme, offering Mexico military assistance for its intended invasion, were leaked to Washington by British Intelligence, the United States declared War on Germany on 6 April.

## MOBILIZATION

As if anticipating eventual involvement in the European conflict, Congress had been moving slowly but surely towards a war footing since the outbreak of hostilities. The National Defense Act of 1916 allowed for a massive growth in the regular forces over five years to 175,000 men supported by a federally organized National Guard of 400,000 under joint State-Pentagon control but subject to Presidential conscription. Additionally it provided for an officer reserve corps, for a volunteer army in case of war and for the formation of a Reserve Officers' Training Corps (ROTC) program. The United States thus had the organization and structure, if not the trained manpower, to fight a major war several months before its actual declaration. For the first time in her history she could call upon an Army incorporating regulars, Guardsmen, reservists, volunteers and conscripts to fulfil her inter-

American 'doughboys' advance through the Argonne Forest, France in 1918. The battle lasted 47 days and involved one and a quarter million US troops (more than were in any previous single American Army). Despite its huge scale, the battle often resolved itself into fierce hand-to-hand combat.

President Woodrow Wilson (1856-1945) addresses Congress. The German adoption of unrestricted submarine warfare forced the President to declare war on 6 April 1917 despite his repeated promise to keep America out of the war.

national obligations without the passage of time-consuming and often contentious legislation.

The Army of April 1917 was nevertheless hardly ready for instant action. Including those Guardsmen in federal service on the Mexican border, the entire force numbered no more than 200,000 officers and men with a further 100,000 Guardsmen in state service. A small ill-equipped American Expeditionary Force under the command of General Pershing, consisting almost totally of the 1st Infantry Division was dispatched at once to France as a token of American involvement whilst the residue of the Army took desperate steps to expand and bring itself up to battlefield standards.

The Guard, reserves and volunteers were augmented by draftees conscripted under the Selective Service Act of May 1917. Administration of the draft was vested in local citizens boards and originally limited to men between the ages of 18 and 30 although this was later extended to those between 18 and 45. Substitutions and bounties, so shamelessly abused in the Civil War draft, were specifically outlawed.

The initial Act increased the regular Army strength to 286,000, the Guards to 400,000 and allowed for one million volunteers but these numbers were steadily increased as the War progressed until, by the Armistice of November 1918, over 3.6 million men were serving in 62 divisions.

Training and supply remained a nightmare. Still on a peacetime footing, the home market was totally incapable of supplying so large a force without assistance, so much so that it became necessary to supplement Springfield rifles with the arguably better British Lee Enfields and to accept Allied, particularly French, machine-guns and artillery.

INTO ACTION

As Pershing led his small force to France he was ever-mindful of its deficiencies in training and of his orders to retain it as a "separate and distinct component" free of French or British control. Accordingly he refused to commit his men to action without a further period of training in all aspects of trench warfare, demanding instead that they be placed in a quiet sector of the line until able to acclimatize.

Recognizing the degree of exhaustion of all the major Armies, yet failing totally to realize the lack of preparedness of the Americans, the German High Command determined to launch a final major offensive before United States involvement could swing the balance in favor of the Allies.

Without warning, a 3.5 million-man offensive was launched against the British and French positions. The initial attack launched on 21 March 1918 against 50 miles of the British front met initially with limited success but failed in its overall task of breaching the British lines. A second attack one month later, also launched against the British, was supported by a feint against the French in the region of the Chemin des Dames to the north-east of Paris. Unknown to the Germans, that sector had recently been taken over by exhausted troops brought from the north for rest and recuperation. The feint was a total success and within three days the Germans were on the Marne within 50 miles of Paris, their deepest penetration since August 1914.

George S. Patton (1885-1945) who was an unofficial aide to Pershing in 1915.

Two divisions of American soldiers and Marines were rushed to the aid of the French, taking up defensive positions around Chateau-Thierry. Despite their total lack of battle experience the green "doughboys" played a major part in halting the advance, before themselves going on to the offensive in Belleau Wood.

When Ludendorff's exhausted and dispirited Germans made their final desperate assault in June they were halted by, among others, 10 American divisions. United States troops were by now arriving at the rate of 250,000 per month and were eager to play a full part in the coming push to Berlin.

FORWARD TO VICTORY

The Allied offensive when it came had two basic objectives: the elimination of the three salients encroaching into positions held by the British in the North, the French in the center and the Americans in the South, and the disintegration of the enemy front line, followed by a rapid advance

into the industrial heartland of Germany.

Eight American divisions supported the French in the initial, and highly successful, Aisne-Marne Offensive, whilst a single division aided the British in their subsequent equally successful attack on the Amiens salient. The third and final offensive was carried out almost exclusively by United States Forces. On 12 September some 550,000 troops aided by 260 tanks under the command of Lieutenant Colonel George Patton attacked the St. Mihiel salient, driving the enemy back after four days of bitter fighting. Thereafter the Americans moved north, keeping the Meuse to their right and the Argonne Forest to their left in an attempt to secure the rail junction at Mézières and cut off the German retreat.

In the space of one week General Pershing's staff, inspired by the brilliant Colonel George Marshall, contrived to move 600,000 men, their supplies and equipment from St Mihiel to Verdun to enable the northern thrust to jump off on time, a feat which would have been considered impossible less than ten years earlier.

During the subsequent battle for the Argonne Forest, which lasted for 47 days of often savage hand to hand fighting, the American Army deployed over 1,250,000 men, a force far larger than ever deployed by the United States before.

By 5 November the Americans had crossed the Meuse and were striking west. By now Germany, exhausted, its monarchy in disarray and the Government threatened by revolution,was suing for peace and at 1100 hours on 11 November 1918 the Armistice came into effect.

Although United States losses were minimal compared with those of the European powers (Britain had lost 947,000 men, France 1,400,000, Russia 1,700,000 and Germany 1,800,000 compared with America's 50,280 dead and 200,000 wounded), her contribution to the final victory had been considerable.

The United States had now fought a major war abroad and on equal terms with the great European powers. Her position in the center stage of world policy making was now assured.

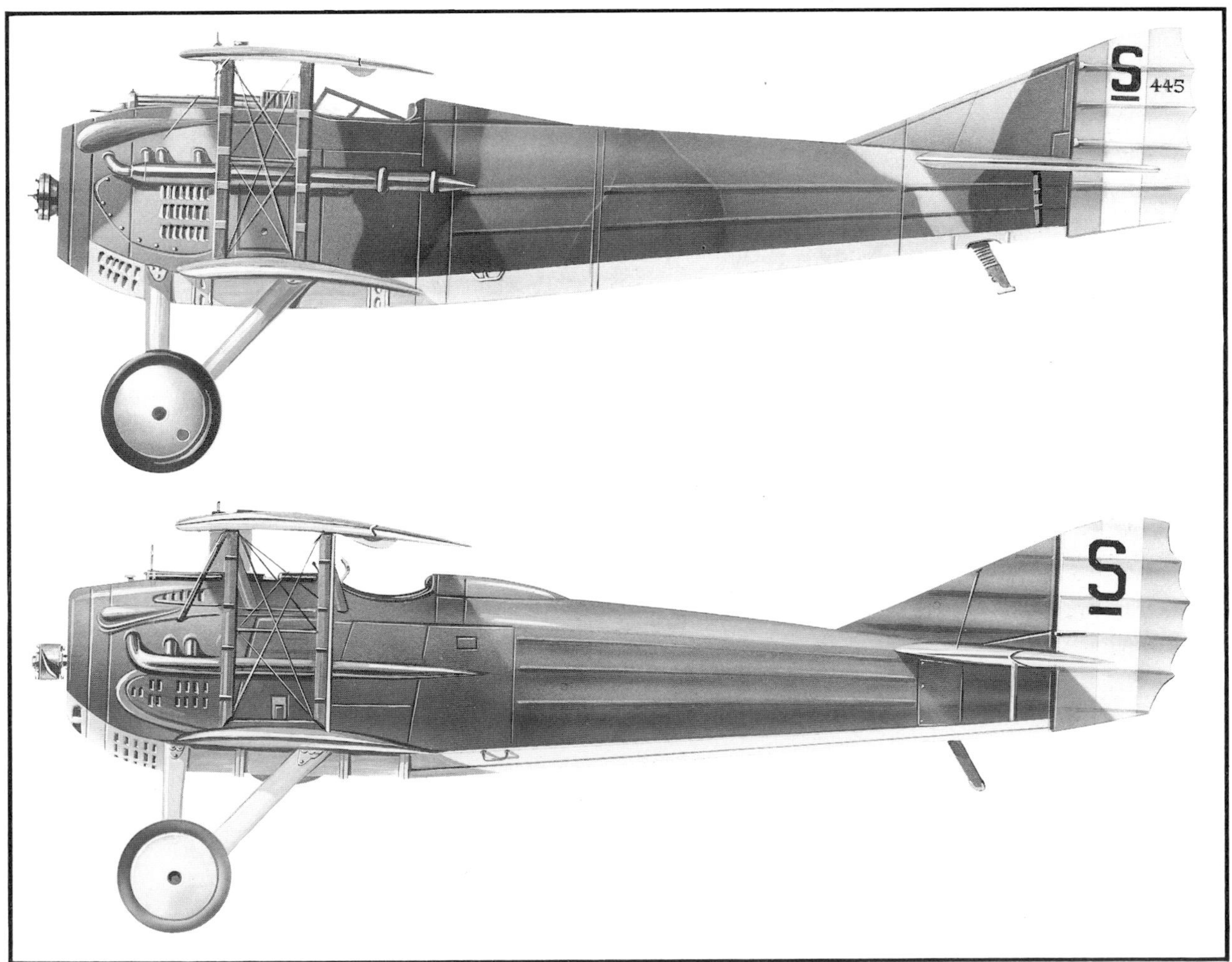


Above: American machine-gunners on duty in a French cemetery. The weapon is a French Hotchkiss 8mm machine-gun.

Opposite above: An American infantryman involved in bitter street fighting at Chateau Thierry in May 1918. The Americans were totally inexperienced, but fought well and halted the German advance before themselves going onto the offensive.

Opposite below: Black American troops of the 369th Infantry, 93rd Division. The Army was still segregated with the exception that white officers were mainly in command.

Left: American pilots mainly flew European combat aircraft during the war, and especially French Spads. The Spad VII (above) was a strong, stable fighter: it was replaced in 1917 by the Spad XIII (below) which had a maximum speed of 134 mph.

## THE YEARS OF PEACE

Despite fervent pleas from the regular army to retain a standing force of 600,000 men, such was the post-war desire to return to normality that within a year of the Armistice over 3 million men had been demobilized, conscription had been abandoned and the Army reduced to a peacetime strength of only 19,000 officers and 205,000 men.

## RUSSIAN INCURSION

Anti-communist sentiments did however overcome the mounting desire for isolationism in the short term. Revolution had broken out in Russia and threatened to envelop the Western democracies. Determined to destroy this menace in its infancy, the United States ordered 5,000 troops to Murmansk to join a British-led expedition against the Northern Red Armies. A further force

Right: The *Ostfriesland* is sunk by Brigadier Billy Mitchell in the first effective demonstration of air power.

of 5,000 was subsequently ordered to the Far East where it remained until April 1920. The Red Armies, under Trotsky's brilliant leadership, proved more of a challenge than expected, whilst service in Russia became increasingly unpopular particularly among Great War veterans awaiting demobilization. Eventually both forces were withdrawn having gained nothing save the distrust and hatred of the new Soviet regime.

## THE PERIOD OF REORGANIZATION

After careful study, the National Defense Act of 1920 was passed by Congress in an attempt to create a balanced land force capable of rapid growth in the event of hostilities. A regular army of 17,000 officers and 280,000 men was to be supported by a National Guard of 436,000 and an unquantified officer and enlisted reserve force.

Fact however was not as accommodating as theory. Due to financial restraints the regular army rarely rose above 12,000 officers and 125,000 men until the danger of conflict in the 1930s forced its growth. The Guard averaged no more than 180,000, whilst the non-commissioned reserve proved highly unpopular. Only among the officer reserves, drawn mainly from the ROTC, were allocations actually fulfilled.

Staff reorganization was however more positive. When in 1921 Pershing was promoted to Chief of Staff, an appointment which he had greatly distrusted when serving in the trenches, he began at once to strengthen his position. Three new major branches, the Air Service, the Chemical Warfare Service and the Finance Department, were created to serve alongside the Infantry and Artillery. The General Staff was reorganized into five divisions; personnel, intelligence, training and operations, supply and war plans. Training continued in the 31 special branch schools whilst the General Staff and Service College at Fort Leavenworth was streamlined and renamed the General Staff School, a

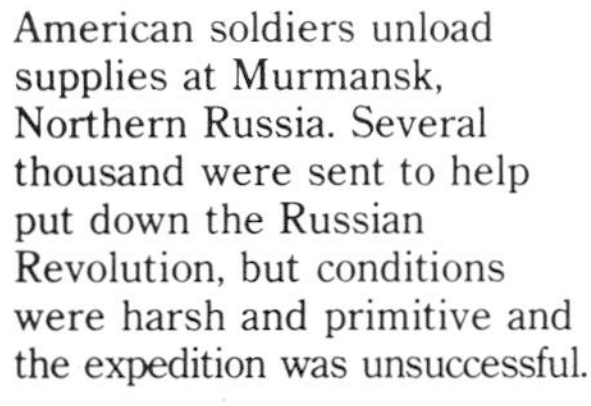

American soldiers unload supplies at Murmansk, Northern Russia. Several thousand were sent to help put down the Russian Revolution, but conditions were harsh and primitive and the expedition was unsuccessful.

title more appropriate to its duties.

Strangely the Tank Corps, which had done such sterling work in the last few weeks of the War, was largely ignored, remaining a part of the Infantry.

The creation of the Air Corps was particularly significant, although not without its problems and petty intrigues. Brigadier Mitchell, who along with General Trenchard of the Royal Air Force was an unyielding exponent of an independent air wing, willingly risked the unpopularity of his superiors to establish his point. In 1921 he forced an unwilling Navy to allow his bombers to prove their prowess by sinking the old German battleship "Ostfriesland" in Virginia Bay. The ship was sunk and Mitchell claimed an unqualified success, although others were not slow in pointing out that the ship had been unmanned and at anchor at the time of the "attack."

Unwilling to suffer the troublesome Mitchell further, Pershing appointed the more diplomatic Major General Patrick head of the Air Service. Patrick shared Mitchell's faith in the Air Force, but unlike his uncompromising colleague was willing to see it subordinated to overall ground command. Mitchell objected publicly, was court-martialled for insubordination and resigned his commission.

Even without Mitchell's aid the Air Force made steady technical progress. The Martin B-10 twin-engine monoplane introduced in 1934 was one of the most advanced light bombers in the world whilst the prototype Boeing B-17, or "Flying Fortress," which entered service two years later, was arguably the finest heavy bomber of the decade.

By the time that it went to war the Air Force would boast such aircraft as the Curtiss P-40 Tomahawk and Lockheed P-38 Lightning.

The Army's development of armored fighting vehicles during the same years was, however, less successful. By 1920 the Tank Corps of 5,000 vehicles and 20,000 men had all but disappeared. Although steps were taken to mechanize the ground forces in the 1930s, the necessity for the tank as an independent strike force was simply not appreciated. America lagged far behind Europe in the production and exploitation of the tank and would continue to produce models far inferior to the German Panthers and Tigers throughout the War.

The Infantry, however, fared better. The Springfield was replaced in 1936 by the vastly superior .30-caliber gas-operated semi-automatic Garand M1, whilst the Browning Automatic Rifle, the heavy and unwieldy section support weapon, was supplemented by the .45-caliber Thompson sub-machine-gun, made famous by the Chicago mobsters of the 1920s.

At about the same time the Army introduced the 81mm M1 and 60mm M2 mortars into the infantry, and the 57mm anti-tank gun, the 105mm M3 howitzer and the massive 155mm Long Tom into the artillery, weapons destined to remain in the American arsenal for the next twenty years.

Brigadier Billy Mitchell (center) strongly advocated airpower and was finally court martialled for insubordination.

35
231

# 9: WORLD WAR TWO

## THE ROAD TO WAR

Despite all portents to the contrary, the American people stalwartly refused to countenance the possibility of a second global war until the inevitable was virtually upon them. By the outbreak of war in Europe in September 1939, Italy had seized Abyssinia and was firmly embroiled in Albania. Nazi Germany had engulfed Austria, the Sudetenland and ultimately the rest of Czechoslovakia without serious hindrance from the Allies, and Japan, greedy to expand her empire in the East, had invaded China.

However strong her desire to isolate herself from Europe's war, the United States was inexorably drawn in by the emergence of modern technology. British air bases in the Caribbean, had they been allowed to fall into Nazi hands, would have been able to threaten the Eastern seaboard whilst submarines would have had little difficulty in blockading the Panama Canal.

Although President Roosevelt was careful to declare American neutrality, at the same time he raised the Army to 227,000 and the Guard to 235,000 to ensure that such neutrality would not be threatened. Nevertheless, as Nazi Germany grew in stature many Americans found it increasingly difficult to hide their true feelings. Weapons and supplies were sold and later "lease-lent" to the British, whilst 50 elderly destroyers, vital to the Royal Navy's anti-submarine program, were traded in exchange for long leases on eight bases in Newfoundland and the Caribbean. Secretly, but crucially for Britain, Roosevelt extended United States naval patrols further into the Atlantic, rendering Prime Minister Churchill every assistance short of a formal alliance.

As America moved closer to war she found herself mobilizing in order to meet the challenges ahead. The draft was reinstated on a limited scale in 1940, and the National Guard and reserves called up to federal service in 1941. An armored force was belatedly created and the existing teeth arms brought up to strength. By the summer of 1941 the United States Army boasted 27 infantry, five armored and two cavalry divisions comprising 1,500,000 officers and men.

Meanwhile the war in Europe grew in intensity. Germany overran Norway, Denmark and the Low Countries, and in less than six weeks of fighting destroyed the "unbeatable" French Army. All attempts to defeat Britain however were frustrated by the gallantry of the Royal Air

American forces disembark at Nisida, Italy after the Anzio operation.

Opposite above: Troops disembark near Casablanca, North Africa, during Operation Torch in 1942. This was the first combined American-British offensive.

Opposite below: General Erwin Rommel (1891-1944) on the left, was arguably the finest field commander of the entire war.

Below: The Japanese attack on Pearl Harbor was completely unforeseen, and much of the fleet was destroyed.

Force. When Hitler invaded the Soviet Union, in total disregard of the Molotov-Ribbentrop mutual defense pact, it seemed as if it were only a matter of time before he dominated the entire continent of Europe.

Without warning on 7 December 1941 a large Japanese naval armada launched an air attack on the American naval base at Pearl Harbor. Simultaneously other forces attacked installations in the Philippines, Guam and Wake Island. Incensed, the United States vowed to destroy the Japanese Empire completely.

Hitler, sensing that the United States would now be fully involved in the East, declared war against America in the hopes that in so doing he would be able to starve Britain of American material aid.

Once an exclusively European conflict, the war had now spread to every continent and ocean. Before its conclusion in 1945, 16,300,000 Americans would have served in the Armed Forces, 11,200,000 in the Army, 4,100,000 in the Navy and 669,000 in the Marines. Those who did not serve in uniform would rally to the factories and farms in unprecedented numbers. The United States would truly become the "Arsenal of Democracy."

## FROM AFRICA TO ITALY

### OPERATION TORCH

Operation Torch, the American landings in North Africa, were the climax of a lengthy British-American compromise. Whereas domestic public

opinion demanded the defeat of Japan with all possible haste, the United States military planners accepted that victory in Europe would have to take priority. Although it was realized that an invasion of the continental mainland would eventually be necessary, it was felt in 1941 that the Allies were nowhere near strong enough for such a venture at that time. It would first be necessary to secure the Mediterranean to deny Hitler the oil fields of the Persian Gulf.

Despite Soviet demands for a Second Front and a strong American desire to take the war to the enemy, Britain resisted any suggestion of a full scale invasion until her lifeline with the Empire through the Suez Canal was firmly secured.

Thus the United States, against her better judgement, accepted as a compromise the invasion of North Africa in November 1942. The German situation in North Africa was tenuous. General Erwin Rommel, arguably the finest field commander of the entire war, had pushed the British VIII Army back to El Alamein, 60 miles west of Alexandria, and had taken the crucial port of Tobruk. His troops however were exhausted, a problem made more difficult by the existence of a 1,400-mile supply line. General Montgomery, his troops refreshed and revitalized, had just defeated the Afrika Korps at El Alamein and the latter were pulling back. An invasion in the west would effectively leave them entrapped.

Above: Generals de Gaulle (right) and Giraud shake hands at the Casablanca Conference in January 1943. These were the leaders of the Free French forces but mistrusted each other. Roosevelt and Churchill are also present.

Right: American M-3 tanks move into action during the Battle of the Kasserine Pass.

Below: A destroyer 'makes smoke' to protect itself from enemy aircraft during the Salerno landing on 9 September 1943.

The invasion force, to be known collectively as the British First Army despite its preponderance of Americans, was to be divided into three task forces; the Western Force under General Patton consisting of 35,000 men was to sail from Hampton Roads, Virginia, and land in the vicinity of Casablanca and Rabat; the Centre Force containing 39,000 American and British soldiers under General Fredenhall was to sail from Scotland and land in the area of Oran, whilst the Eastern Force of 33,000 men under General Ryder was to take Algiers.

Prior to the landings it was hoped that the French troops guarding the coast would do nothing to hamper the invasion. General Giraud and Admiral Darlan commanding the French forces were contacted but with limited success resulting in spirited French defence in Algiers and Morocco before Darlan, with 200,000 troops, eventually switched his alligience to the Allies.

The initial landing went well with Algiers falling on 8 November, Oran two days later and Casablanca on 11 November. The move east into Tunisia however soon slowed down under the combined weight of vastly superior enemy armor and impossible logistics, so much so that by the time the winter rains and mud set in in mid-December, the Allies were still far short of their objectives.

Field-Marshal Kesselring, commanding the southern Wehrmacht from Italy, poured all available reserves into the area and in February 1943, taking advantage of poor American troop displacements in the area of Tunis and Bizerta, launched a counter-attack with General Von Armin's V Army through the center of the Allied position.

The German counter-attack very nearly succeeded, and indeed had it not been for Von Armin's lack of resolve borne of his Army's chronic lack of reserves, the First Army might well have been destroyed. As it was, the US 2nd Corps sustained 6,500 men killed, wounded or captured and the British a further 4,000 in the Battle of the Kasserine Pass alone.

In the aftermath, Rommel was removed and Patton took over control of the 2nd Corps. Under the experienced control of General Alexander the Allies went on the offensive again, linked up with the VIII Army advancing from the east and slowly but surely forced the remaining Axis soldiers north towards Tunis. On 7 May the British took Tunis and the Americans Bizerta. The entire North African land mass was now firmly in Allied hands and the invasion of the Continent could proceed. Germany and Italy between them had sustained 40,000 casualties and lost 275,000 prisoners of war. The Allies had sustained 60,000 dead, wounded and missing. More fundamentally the Americans had realized that the German soldiers facing them were battle-hardened and dedicated. More training would be required before the next battle if unacceptable losses were not to be sustained again.

SICILY AND ITALY

Whilst the fighting raged in North Africa Roosevelt and Churchill met in Casablanca to discuss the future. Again the American desire to invade France met with British objections and again a compromise was reached.

An invasion of Italy to take place in the late summer of 1943 was agreed upon on the basis that this would draw German reserves from the Russian Front, strengthen Allied supply lines in the Mediterranean and put pressure on the Italian Government, already reeling from the losses in Africa, to sue for peace.

Above: US Paratroopers in 1943.

Above: An American tank enters a Sicilian village with the infantry advancing in its shelter.

Operation Husky, the invasion of Sicily, was to be the largest amphibious operation in history. Some 80,000 troops with 7,000 vehicles, 600 tanks and 900 artillery pieces were to be landed on the beaches within 48 hours, supported by 4,600 paratroops and glider troops who would drop behind enemy lines within hours of the invasion.

The airborne landings were a tragic fiasco. Due to poor navigation, American paratroops were scattered over south-east Sicily, over half of the British gliders due to land near Syracuse fell short (although a crucial bridge was taken and held by a small party), and a group of American gliders flying over the invasion fleet was shot at by its own forces and 23 aircraft brought down.

Despite early catastrophes and the total inability of Montgomery and Patton to work in harmony, Allied preponderance in numbers forced a slow Axis withdrawal. When Messina fell to Patton on 17 August the Allies at last had a firm foothold on the mainland. 45,000 Germans and 70,000 Italians had however escaped across the Straits of Messina to fight another day.

In July 1943 Mussolini was deposed by the war-weary Italians and replaced by Field-Marshal Badoglio, who pledged to continue the war but with little conviction. Enraged, Hitler ordered the rescue of Mussolini, setting him up as a puppet ruler in Northern Italy. It was obvious however that the Italian Army could no longer be relied upon and plans were laid to take over the administration of the country as and when necessary. When Italy surrendered on 3 September 1943, Hitler immediately moved eight divisions into Central and Southern Italy and disarmed the Italians.

That day the British VIII Army crossed the Straits of Messina, and six days later the British 19th Corps and US 6th Corps, constituting the American 5th Army under the command of General Mark Clark, landed at Salerno some 25 miles south of Naples. After four days of bitter fighting Kesselring withdrew his forces behind

Above: A reconnaissance unit moves through the war-torn streets of Messina, Sicily in August 1943.

Right: Soldiers of the Fifth Army in action in Italy, May 1944.

the prepared defensive positions along the Gustav Line, where they frustrated every Allied attempt at incursion for the rest of the winter.

Attempts to outflank the German defenses failed when the landing at Anzio met with near disaster. 40,000 troops of the British 1st Division and US 3rd Division were landed at Anzio, to the south of Rome, on 22 January 1944. The initial successful landing was not exploited, with the result that Kesselring was given time to cobble together a makeshift defensive force and push the Allies back to the bridgehead. Before they eventually broke out on 23 May, the Allies were to suffer 59,000 casualties, a third from disease, exhaustion and neurosis, in one of the most futile operations of the war.

Although Kesselring was forced to withdraw to the Gothic Line north of Florence, he was able to hold this position until September 1944, by which time the Allies were faced with yet another winter. Only in the spring of 1945 were the Allies able to continue their advance North, by which time Germany itself was under threat.

The campaign, which ended on 2 May 1945, proved one of the harshest and bloodiest of the war

## FROM NORMANDY TO VICTORY

Even before the Allies had landed in Sicily, steps were being taken to plan for a much larger invasion of Northern France by American, British and Canadian troops. Roosevelt and Churchill agreed that the invasion would take place in the summer of 1944, and by the summer of that year over 1,500,000 US soldiers and airmen supported by 500 million tons of supplies and equipment had been landed in the United Kingdom to supplement the 1,750,000 British and Commonwealth troops already assembled.

For political reasons supreme command was vested in the American General Eisenhower and command of the land forces in the British General Montgomery a decision which although considered strange at the time would later be proved by history to have been inspired.

After extensive research it was decided to land on the coast of Normandy directly south of England rather than on the more proximate Pas-de-Calais. Strenuous steps would however be taken up to the very moment of the invasion to convince the German High Command that the landings would be elsewhere. So successful was this subterfuge that, when eventually the Allies did land, Hitler refused to commit his reserves convinced that the landings were a feint and that the main force had still to be put ashore in the Calais area.

Although the German defenses along the "Atlantic Wall" were formidable, they were in parts unfinished. The 300,000 troops who controlled the 15,000 strong points along the coast were too sedentary, and control and communications were weak. Hermann Goering, in total control of the Luftwaffe, remained in Germany, whilst four of the seven armored divisions comprising the backbone of the defenses were directly assigned to Wehrmacht headquarters under the command of Hitler. Rommel, in nominal command of Army Group B responsible for driving the invaders into the sea as and when they landed, was thus denied the very troops whom he needed the most. Not only did Hitler frustrate his most competent leaders but he slowed the chain of command so drastically that the Allies were given a valuable breathing space once ashore before the panzers were permitted to counter-attack. Without this the invasion might well have failed.

## THE NORMANDY BEACHES

After several days of frustrating delay due to unexpectedly bad weather, D-Day was eventually set for 6 June 1944. Throughout the pre-

Overleaf: Landing craft in action.
Page 94 inset: Assault troops wade ashore during the D-Day landings.
Page 95 inset: Infantry take shelter behind the protective front of a landing craft as it nears a beachhead during D-Day.

From 1942 onwards, the German rushed to improve their defenses on the 'Atlantic Wall'.

A1377

vious night airborne troops, taking part in Operation Neptune, landed to secure key areas behind the beaches. The British 6th Airborne Division landing in the East secured the Caen Canal and Orne River bridges, the American 82nd Division under General Ridgeway landed near Sainte-Mère-Eglise at the base of the Cotentin Peninsula whilst the 101st Airborne Division under General Maxwell Taylor landed in support to secure the western flank of the invasion area. After extensive air and naval bombardment at 0630 hours, 176,000 soldiers began to come ashore in 4,000 landing craft. Forced by Hitler to keep two armored divisions in reserve, von Rundstedt, in command of the defenses, was unable to react quickly.

Conditions on the five beachheads varied greatly. The US VII Corps under General Lawton landed with comparative ease on Utah Beach in the extreme west due in no small part to the stalwart efforts of the paratroopers dropped in the rear area the night before. In contrast Omaha Beach was a bloodbath. The US V Corps under General Gerow encountered well dug-in artillery and machine-gun posts with the result that they suffered over 3,000 casualties compared with VII Corps' 197 before securing the beachhead.

The British and Canadians, landing at Gold,

Juno and Sword, initially met light resistance although they were later to attract heavy counter-attacks from the German panzers once it was accepted that the main invasion had taken place and they were released from the reserve.

In the weeks of bloody, occasionally hand to hand fighting that followed, the Allies gradually consolidated until it became obvious that their position ashore was secure. Hitler however refused to countenance retreat to better defensive ground.

By the end of June the British had encircled Caen, the US 7th Corps had captured the majority of the Cotentin Peninsula and the US 7th and 8th Corps had fought their way south through the hedgerows of the "bocage." By August the US First Army had moved into Brittany whilst the newly constituted Third Army, under Patton, who, to his great annoyance, had played no part in the landings, was preparing to advance East.

Attempts at a counter-attack in the "Falaise Gap" slowed the Allies for a time, but ultimately failed at a cost of 60,000 German casualties. By 20 August Patton was on the Seine at Fontainebleau and on 25 August Paris was liberated by Free French forces. By the end of July over 1,000,000 Allied soldiers supported by 150,000 vehicles

Above: Troops wade ashore in the landings on the Gilbert Islands in the Pacific.

Left: George Patton was a 3-star general by the time of the invasion of Europe as shown by the insignia on his helmet.

Opposite above: Omaha Beach, Normandy shortly after the D-Day landings.

Opposite below: GI's fight their way through the woods and hedgerows of Normandy.

Right: GIs take a break during the invasion of Saipan Island in the Marianas.

were in France eager to push on into Germany itself.

In the meantime Operation Anvil, the invasion of Southern France between Cannes and Toulon by General Patch's US Seventh Army, took place against little resistance. Once established, the Free French 2nd Corps passed through the American lines, subsequently leading the advance into Marseilles and up the Rhône to Lyons and Dijon before turning eastwards into Germany. France was liberated and the drive to Berlin was on.

## THE INVASION OF GERMANY

Perhaps inevitably, taking into account their characters, once securely ashore the Allied field commanders began to squabble about tactics. Montgomery, supported by Bradley, wished to operate on a narrow front on the left, advancing through Belgium and Holland into the Ruhr basin and onwards towards Berlin. Patton, supported by the other American generals, preferred an advance across the entire front. Eisenhower acceeded to Patton's wishes. The British moved into Belgium seizing the giant ports of Brussels and Antwerp whilst the Americans proceeded east into the Verdun area, the scene of much heavy fighting in 1918.

Montgomery's advance against the Germans in the north met with stiff resistance and he failed to clear the 60-mile wide Scheldt Estuary. Until the Allies could command the Scheldt they could not gain access to the port facilities of Antwerp and were unable to shorten their supply lines. Consequently the Americans in the south began to run out of supplies and were forced to slow their advance.

In order to break the deadlock in the North

Below: Paratroopers land near Arnhem during Operation Market Garden.

Montgomery devised Operation Market Garden, a combined airborne operation to punch a gap through the enemy defenses to allow the British 30th Corps to advance and turn the northern limits of the Siegfried Line. The key to success was the speedy capture of the bridges at Veghel, Zon, Grave, Nijmegen and Arnhem by British and American airborne troops.

On 17 September the 101st Division captured the bridges at Veghel and Zon and the 82nd took Grave. That day the British 30th Corps under Horrocks advanced to Zon and within two days had reached Grave. However the operation which had begun so well was about to disintegrate into chaos. A joint US-British force had been landed at Nijmegen and the British 1st Airborne at Arnhem. Unknown to the Allies and quite coincidentally two German panzer divisions were refitting at Arnhem before pro-

Patton's Third Army captured Coblenz only after fierce street-fighting.

ceeding westward to the battle front. Although the British secured the bridge and through tenacious fighting held it for seven days, they were eventually forced to withdraw in the face of overwhelming and unexpected opposition. About 2,200 men managed to escape across the Rhine leaving over 7,000 of their comrades killed or taken prisoner.

In the meantime von Rundstedt had rushed 85,000 men of the XV Army to the Scheldt Estuary which remained firmly in German hands.

Denied the use of Antwerp, the Allies in the form of the Canadian First Army continued the capture of the Channel ports, driving the Germans from Dieppe, Le Havre, Bologne and Calais. On 8 November the Scheldt was eventually taken but remained unusable until cleared of mines later that month, by which time winter had set in. The invasion of Germany would have to wait until the following spring.

Desperate for a victory, Hitler ordered a winter counter-offensive into the forests of the Ardennes with a view to striking for Antwerp 100 miles away and splitting the Allied forces in two. Ignoring his generals' protestations that there were simply not enough supplies for such a venture, Hitler began to gather together reserves from all over the Reich and on 16 December began what has come to be known as the "Battle of the Bulge."

Over 250,000 men, 1,900 artillery pieces and

970 tanks, supported by 1,500 aircraft, went onto the offensive. The VI SS Panzer Army under Dietrich and the V SS Panzer Army under Manteuffel spearheaded the attack directly through the American lines, whilst the VII and XV Armies protected their flanks. Simultaneously 20,000 men under the command of the brilliant Skorzeny, and dressed as US soldiers, spread confusion behind the American lines.

Plagued by faulty intelligence and exhausted by the recent assault on the Hurtgen Forest the American 8th Corps, destined to sustain the initial attack, was dangerously overstretched and totally unprepared for the task ahead of it. Furthermore, low clouds and bad weather were grounding the Allied air forces.

The initial attack on 16 December was a complete success with confused and vastly outnumbered American forces falling back everywhere. However, as soon as Eisenhower realized the extent and implications of the offensive all available reserves were rushed to the area. The

Above: An American 105mm howitzer in action during the Battle of the Bulge.

Sherman tanks ready for action during the Battle of the Bulge.

A paratrooper with a bazooka climbs aboard a C-47 prior to Operation Market Garden in September 1944.

George Patton (left) led the 3rd Army during the Battle of the Bulge. Omar Bradley (right) commanded the 12th Army Group.

82nd Airborne, recovering from Market Garden, linked with the 7th Division and managed to halt the advance in the Saint-Vith area throwing the tight German timetable into confusion.

At the same time even greater dramas were occurring at Bastogne, some 30 miles to the southwest. On 18 December 3,000 men of the 101st Airborne, the "Screaming Eagles," under the command of Brigadier McAuliffe, advanced to relieve the defenders. By 20 December the entire 11,000-man division was under threat. Secure in the knowledge that Patton's 4th Armored Division would soon relieve them the paratroopers held out tenaciously. When offered terms of surrender by the Germans, McAuliffe simply replied "Nuts!" - and in so doing earned himself a place in the annals of American military history.

The siege of Bastogne was lifted on 26 December but not until the 101st had sustained 2,000 casualties and the 4th Armored Division a further 1,000 men killed and wounded. Yet the

Snow-covered Sherman tanks prepare to counterattack near St Vith during the Battle of the Bulge.

Germans had been stopped, their fuel tanks empty, some 30 miles short of their objective. As the skies cleared and the Allies were able to re-establish complete mastery of the air, counter-attacks were made by the First Army from the north and the Third Army from the south. On 16 January the giant pincers met at Houffalize north of Bastogne and on 28 January the "Battle of the Bulge", the last great German offensive of the War, was over.

In February and March the Allies began to cross the Rhine. The British 21st Army Group drove for the Ruhr whilst the 6th and 12th US Army Groups headed for Cologne. The US First Army crossed over the still intact Remagen Bridge on 7 March, and Patton's Third Army forded the river at Nierstein on 22 March.

Much to British consternation, Eisenhower refused to join the Soviets in a race for Berlin, halting his advance on the Elbe. On 25 April American and Soviet troops met for the first time at Torgau on the Elbe east of Leipzig, and on 30 April Hitler committed suicide. On 4 May Montgomery accepted unconditional surrender from representatives of Admiral Dönitz as Hitler's successor; on 8 May the War officially ended and by 11 May all German troops had laid down their arms.

5,400,000 Allied troops, including 3,000,000 Americans had taken part in the invasion and subsequent battles, of whom 135,000 were killed and 435,000 wounded.

Above: A convoy of supplies moves through the streets of Bastogne.

Right: A 57mm gun crew of the 3rd Army drives towards Bastogne on 22 December 1944.

## THE PACIFIC WAR

Japan did not declare war on the might of the United States lightly. For two decades prior to 1941 she had been steadily expanding her empire. She had taken Manchuria, Korea, Formosa and the Ryukya Islands and was now heavily embroiled in war with China. She had occupied French Indochina with the tacit approval of the Vichy government, and was now looking for further conquests. With Britain heavily committed in Europe and her fleet employed elsewhere she regarded the dismemberment of the British Empire in the East as a formality, yet realised that her own imperial aspirations could not be met in toto without the domination of the American-owned Philippines, Guam and Wake Island.

Japan could only succeed if she were able to drive the United States from the Pacific forcing the latter to wage war from its own western seaboard. Under such circumstances she believed that the United States would sue for peace.

Control of the Pacific would be impossible whilst the United States maintained so large a fleet at Pearl Harbor. The destruction of the fleet, by subterfuge if possible, became of paramount importance.

At 0755 on the morning of 7 December 1941, without formal warning, the Japanese launched a superbly executed attack on Pearl Harbor. Within two hours most of the fleet battleships were sunk or damaged and the port installations totally destroyed. In addition 177 planes were destroyed, 159 damaged and 2,000 servicemen killed.

General Short and Admiral Kimmel, in command of the base, were roundly blamed for having failed totally to evaluate the intelligence build-up which should have given them ample indication of the attack and were replaced.

Despite the chaos and recriminations, the United States could count herself lucky that her aircraft carriers, the prime target of the raid, were at sea at the time and had thus been preserved to fight another day.

## EARLY DEFEATS

Five hours after the attack on Pearl Harbor, 108 Japanese bombers protected by 84 fighters attacked Clark Field near Manila. Unbelievably, despite ample knowledge of the morning attack nothing had been done to disperse the aircraft on the Field, with the result that 18 bombers, 50 fighters and 30 support vehicles, virtually the total of McArthur's air force, were destroyed on the ground.

Simultaneously Guam and Wake Island were attacked. Guam fell two days later but Wake held out, frustrating two enemy attacks, destroying one enemy ship and damaging five others, until 23 December.

Japan now turned her attention to the Philippines, currently being defended by General

Below: The Pacific Fleet suffered major losses at Pearl Harbor. This pall of smoke almost completely covers the hulks of the *Maryland* and *Tennessee* (both badly damaged) and the *Oklahoma* and *West Virginia* (both sunk).

The American flag is raised again over Corregidor in the Philippines on 27 February 1945 less than three years after its conquest by the Japanese.

McArthur with a mixed force of the Philippino Division; some 12,000 Philippino Scouts, a division of Philippino regulars and a few Marines. When 43,000 men of the Japanese XIV Army landed in Lingayen Gulf north of Manila on 22 December, General Wainwright's forces in that area were soon forced to retreat towards Manila. When a second army landed at Lamon Bay, 70 miles southeast of the capital, McArthur ordered a general retreat to the Bataan Peninsula at the northern end of Manila Bay and to Corregidor, the fortress island in the Bay itself. Manila, now unprotected, fell on 2 January. Despite shortages of food, equipment and medicine the 15,000 American troops with their Philippino allies dug in and awaited the onslaught. The Japanese when they attacked on 11 January fought ferociously but were unable to dislodge the stalwart defenders, so much so that by mid-February the Japanese commander had lost 7,000 men and was forced to call a two-month halt to the attack pending the arrival of reinforcements.

When Roosevelt revealed in mid-February that reinforcements would not be sent, and subsequently ordered the evacuation of McArthur to Australia, morale among the defenders plummeted. Nevertheless the defence continued. Bataan held out for six days after the offensive was renewed on 3 April, and Corregidor for a further month. On 5 May the Japanese eventually gained a foothold on the fortress and two days later Corregidor, and with it the Philippines, surrendered.

Japan had extended her Empire to the limit of her expectations but would not be left in peace to enjoy her gains. She and her people would soon bitterly regret their greed.

THE SOLOMONS

The United States launched her first offensive on 18 April 1942 when 16 land-based Army B-25 bombers, under the command of Colonel Doolittle, launched a bombing raid on Tokyo from the decks of the carrier "Hornet" steaming some 700 miles out to sea. Despite the morale-raising effect of the raid, it otherwise caused little damage. The American forces remaining in the Pacific were able to do little to halt the steady Japanese expansion into the South-East Pacific. Malaya, Singapore and Hong Kong, the latter with their vast harbor facilities, fell to the seemingly unstoppable Japanese until at one time it seemed that Australia itself must fall.

Only at sea could the United States retaliate on equal terms. In the first Battle of the Coral Sea, fought between 4-8 May 1942, a task force turned back a Japanese invasion fleet steaming for New Guinea and a month later two carrier task forces (with only three carriers between them) sank four enemy carriers in the Battle of Midway. Unknown to both sides, Japanese expansion had now been halted and the die of American victory cast.

The Allies' first step to victory came in the Solomon Islands, north-east of Australia. In March 1942 the Japanese had taken Guadalcanal and Tulagi in the southern Solomons with a view to interdicting traffic to and from Australia. On 7 August 1942 the 1st Marine Division began to assault both islands. Japan responded by rushing reserves to the area, especially to Guadalcanal with its vital airstrip, but to no avail. In early December the 1st Marine Division was replaced by the 2nd Marine Division supported by the 25th

Japanese flamethrowers attack an American strong point during their conquest of Corregidor in 1942.

and Americal Divisions under General Patch. After a bloody but fruitless attempt to take Mount Austen, commanding the air base at Henderman Field, Patch by-passed the high ground concentrating instead on the annihilation of the remaining ground troops. Although 13,000 Japanese, out of an original invasion force of 36,000, escaped by sea, the Solomon Islands were returned to Allied control. Australia was safe and for the first time the Japanese infantryman had suffered a comprehensive defeat. Given America's vast preponderence in manpower and materials, victory could only be a matter of time.

## THE BATTLE FOR NEW GUINEA

Frustrated in their attempts to take Port Moresby, the capital of Papua, by sea, the Japanese now attempted to take it by land. In June 1942 an invasion force was landed at Gona on the north coast of the island. The troops at once began their perilous trek across the Kokoda Track south towards the capital. For three months the Japanese pressed on against the often ferocious resistance of the Australians, until on 17 September they reached Ioribaiwa some 30 miles north of their objective. At this point destitute of stores and reinforcements, the Japanese began their slow retreat hampered the entire way by the 7th Australian Division.

After a bloody rear-guard action, the Australians in conjunction with the US 32nd Infantry Division finally drove the Japanese into the sea. By 19 November 1942 the island was once again free of enemy activity and the Allies were at last in a position to plan the ultimate downfall of Japan.

After the recapture of Guadalcanal, it was decided to execute a two-pronged attack toward Japan with the pincers converging on the Phillipines.

For the Army this now meant clearing New Guinea prior to attacking the great Japanese base at Rabaul, on New Britain. MacArthur's forces would clear the Huon Peninsula in northeast New Guinea, prior to moving across the Vitiaz and Dampier Straits and landing in New Britain, whilst Halsey's troops would move through the Solomons directly to Rabaul.

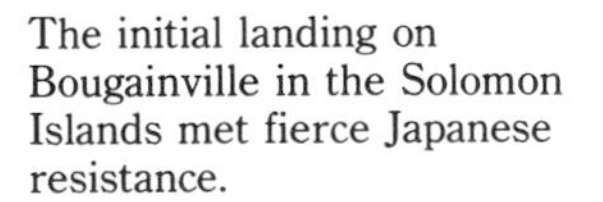

The initial landing on Bougainville in the Solomon Islands met fierce Japanese resistance.

On 30 June 1943, elements of the 41st Infantry Division landed in New Guinea to link up with the Australians moving across the mountains. Simultaneously, Krueger's Sixth Army took the islands of Kiriwana and Woodlark, and began the immediate construction of improvised airstrips. Even with the aid of an airdrop by the US 503rd Airborne Regiment, in which 1,700 paratroopers were dropped in the space of one minute, Japanese resistance proved difficult to overcome, with the result that the Huon Peninsula, initially considered a soft target, was not cleared of the enemy until December.

On 15 December 1943, soldiers from the 112th Cavalry Regiment finally crossed the Vitiaz and Dampier Straits to land in New Britain. On 25 December, the 1st Marine Division attacked and after three weeks captured Cape Gloucester, opening the Straits securely to Allied shipping.

Halsey's advance up the Solomons towards Rabaul met with equally fierce resistance, compounded by the atrocious climate and conditions. After five weeks of bitter fighting, first by the 43rd and subsequently by the 25th and 37th Divisions, the islands of New Georgia and Rendova fell, but only after appalling casualties had been sustained by both sides. Fearful that an attack on Kolombangara, the next island to the north, would result in similar carnage, the island was bypassed. Thus was born almost by accident the policy of island-hopping, which was to play so vital a role in the subsequent campaign.

Bougainville, some 250 miles by air from Rabaul could however not be bypassed. The 125-mile long island, guarded by 40,000 China War veterans, contained six airfields, and as such could not be left in the rear of the main advance to threaten the ever-increasing supply lines. Initial landings by the 3rd Marine Division and the Army's 37th Division met with such resistance that a beachhead was only secured after 17 days of close quarter fighting. By the time the island fell in April 1944, 7,000 Japanese and 1,000 Americans lay dead, victims of some of the heaviest localized fighting of the War to date.

Well before the fighting ended, three airfields had been built on the island leaving Rabaul well

Top: Seabees (CB's or Construction Brigade workers) construct a pre-fabricated landing strip on Bougainville in the Solomon Islands in 1943.

Above: A platoon of the 43rd Infantry moves inland on Rendova Island, New Georgia in June 1943.

within US Air Force range. With the base effectively neutralized from the air, it was decided once again to bypass Rabaul and to continue the advance northwest into the Pacific.

THE SOUTH PACIFIC

The prime objective of the Navy's Central Pacific offensive was the capture of the Gilbert Islands, some 1,500 miles southwest of Hawaii. Makin and Tarawa Atolls, the two principle objectives, were to be taken by the Army and Marines respectively. Although Makin was defended by no more than 300 soldiers, the 27th Infantry Division took four days to secure it completely. Likewise, the battle for Tarawa was a bloodbath. Less than half a square mile in area, the island was interlaced with fire trenches and pill boxes in which the Japanese fought to the death. In three days of ferocious hand to hand combat the Japanese were to lose 4,700 dead, the Marines 1,000 dead and 2,200 wounded.

It was clear that future attacks would require far greater co-ordination between the Navy, Air Force, artillery and assaulting infantry, if they were not to end in catastrophe. Prior to the next assault, artillery shells would be enlarged to facilitate the destruction of enemy reinforced emplacements, and armored amphibious tractors would be introduced to afford the infantry a modicum of protection.

On 1 February 1944, Kwajalein Atoll was taken after which the huge naval base at Truk, 1,100 miles west, was neutralized from the air. When Einwetok and Engebi fell to elements of the 106th Infantry, 27th Division and the Marines, the Marshall Islands were effectively bypassed or secured, and the route to the Marianas and the Philippines lay open.

Over 600 ships of the US Fifth Fleet, the Marines of the 2nd, 3rd and 4th Divisions and the Army's 27th Division, 127,000 men in all, were assembled to take the Marianas. On 15 June the 2nd and 4th Marine Divisions launched their attack on Saipan nestling in the center of the island group.

Desperate to save the defenders, the remnants of the Imperial Japanese Navy in the guise of the First Mobile Fleet and Southern Fleet sailed to meet the US Fifth Fleet and in the two-day Battle of the Philippine Sea (19-20 June), they were destroyed. The Japanese Navy, and with it her long range air wing, had ceased to exist.

In the meantime, the attack on Saipan was progressing slowly, amid largely unjustified Marine-Army recriminations. On 7 July, the 27th Division faced and defeated a suicide attack by 3,000 Japanese intoxicated on sake and intent on death. Two days later the island was secured at a cost of 16,000 American dead and wounded, and 29,000 Japanese dead. Nearby Tinian fell by the end of July, and Guam soon thereafter.

NEW GUINEA

Whilst the right arm of the pincer was moving across the Central Pacific, MacArthur to the south was taking Papua New Guinea. Although New Britain Island was in Allied hands, the remainder of New Guinea remained under Japanese sovereignty and would have to be taken if the Americans were to gain a springboard for the Philippines. Accordingly, the Australians moved inland through New Guinea paralleled by MacArthur moving along the North Coast. Having failed to cut off a large enemy force near Saidor in February 1944, MacArthur surprisingly attacked the Admiralty Islands to the north to gain air bases from which to attack Madang.

Madang was subsequently captured by the 1st Cavalry Division (Armored) after strenuous fighting, although the majority of the Japanese succeeded in escaping west to new defensive positions. Ignoring the new enemy defensive emplacements entirely, MacArthur now moved north to attack Hollandia some 500 miles up the

coast. Once Hollandia had been secured by elements of the 163rd Regimental Combat Team, together with the 1st and 24th Divisions, ignoring the 55,000 Japanese of the XVIII Army between himself and the Australians to the south, MacArthur at once struck west towards the Vogelkop Peninsula in the far west of New Guinea.

The Peninsula secured, and despite Naval objections that such an assault would be futile, MacArthur now obtained Roosevelt's permission to press forward to Mindanao and thence onwards to the Philippines. He had promised the islanders that he would return and now intended to keep his word whatever the tactical consequences.

On 10 July, the XVIII Army stranded between MacArthur and the Australians counter-attacked in the hope of diverting troops from the attack on the Philippines. Within a month the Japanese Army had been destroyed. 10,000 enemy were killed, against 400 American dead and 25,000 wounded, leaving the remainder to melt into the mountains where they remained undisturbed until the end of the War.

Above: General MacArthur inspects a captured Japanese supply dump in Hollandia, New Guinea.

Left: The Pacific forces became experts at island invasions through 1944 and 1945.

Opposite above: Marine flamethrower teams in action on Iwo Jima in February 1945.

Opposite below: Soldiers of the 163rd Infantry Regiment, 41st division wade ashore from Higgins boats during the invasion of Wake Island.

In July MacArthur was cleared to bypass the Japanese stronghold of Mindanao and proceed direct to Leyte in the Central Philippines. United States tactics had now undergone a fundamental change. Iwo Jimo and Okinawa, less than 400 miles from the mainland, would be attacked, and when taken would provide air bases from which the Superfortresses would be able to attack the majority of Japan's principal cities.

## THE PHILIPPINES

Four Army divisions under General Krueger, supported by the Fifth Air Force under General Kennedy, and a naval task force under Admiral Halsey hit the beaches on Leyte on 20 October 1944. Stalemate ensued until December, when the 77th Division executed a surprise landing on the west coast. The stalemate was broken and although several elite Japanese units continued to hold out for several months, MacArthur was now able to proceed onto the main island of Luzon. Supported by five divisions landed at Lingayen Gulf and by aircraft operating from a captured airbase on the island, MacArthur then began his move down the Central Plains to Manila. Although many Japanese melted into the hills, over 20,000 remained to fight for the city. By the time Manila was liberated after a month of street fighting it was all but destroyed, and 100,000 of its citizens lay dead, many of them butchered by the retreating Japanese.

Meanwhile, the 503rd Parachute Infantry retook Corregidor, the 38th Division landed at Subic Bay, and the 11th Airborne hit southern Luzon. Pressured by overwhelming odds, the Japanese defenders retired slowly towards the mountains. They were not however fully neutralized until June 1945, and an outstanding 50,000 combatants remained to harass the Americans until the very end of the War.

## IWO JIMA

Iwo Jima, in the Bonin Islands some 600 miles southeast of Tokyo, was attacked by 70,000 Marines on 19 February 1945. The Japanese defended the eight square mile island with such fanaticism that after a month of hard fighting 6,800 Americans and virtually the entire

Below: GIs cautiously move forward through the jungles of Leyte in the central Phillipines which was successfully taken in October 1944.

Japanese garrison of 22,000 lay dead.

A landing by the 77th Division was made on the Kerama Islands off Okinawa on 26 March, and on Easter Sunday, 1 April 1945, Okinawa itself was attacked. In 83 days of bitter and bloody fighting the soldiers and Marines lost 7,600 killed and 31,807 wounded. The fanatical Japanese who contested virtually every square inch of the island, and who ultimately committed suicide in large numbers, lost 110,000 men dead.

The United States now had its staging post for the all-out air assaults, which were designed to bring the Japanese civilian population to its knees.

## THE FINAL VICTORY

During the summer of 1945, the 1,000 Boeing B-29 Superfortresses of XXI Bomber Command conducted incessant raids against the major Japanese cities. Simultaneously, surface ships and submarines blockaded the outer islands. The War in Europe was over and the full Allied might could now be dedicated to the total destruction of Japan. Rumours of horrific treatment metered

out to prisoners of war by their Japanese captors were proving to be horribly accurate, and an enraged public was demanding vengeance.

All expectations were that the Japanese would defend their homeland fanatically, and that up to 1,500,000 Allied casualties might be anticipated. Plans were made for the invasion of Kyushu, the southernmost mainland island, in November 1945, and for the invasion of the main island of Honshu during the spring of 1946.

All plans for the invasion were however cut short when on 6 August 1945 a XX Air Force B-29 bomber dropped an atomic bomb on Hiroshima. Two days later the Soviet Union declared war on Japan and on 9 August a second bomb was dropped on Nagasaki. Although Japan still had two million men under arms and 10,500 aircraft operational, (of which half were assigned to kamikaze attacks), the Government had no way of knowing how many more atomic bombs remained at the Allies' disposal.

Japan formally surrendered on 14 August 1945. The bloodiest war in the history of the world, which had claimed some 50 million lives, including those of 235,000 American servicemen, was over.

Opposite top right: General MacArthur ratifies the Japanese surrender aboard the USS *Missouri* on 2 September 1945.

Opposite top left: The second atomic bomb to be used fell on Nagasaki on 9 August 1945.

Opposite bottom left: General Yoshio Tachibana signs the surrender of Iwo Jima aboard the USS *Dunlap* on 3 September 1945.

Left: This scene of devastation is Hiroshima after the dropping of a single atomic bomb.

# 10: KOREA

## THE FALL OF THE IRON CURTAIN

Despite the usual protestations from the Army that its ranks should not be completely denuded with the coming of peace, such was the desire for the return to normality that President Truman realised that it would be political suicide not to release the draftees as soon as possible. By the end of 1945, half of the eight million men under arms had been demobilized. By mid-1946 its numbers had been reduced to two million and within a year of that to 680,000 ground troops and 300,000 airmen. The draft was phased out and the military returned to its traditional all-volunteer status.

Yet the world to which the G.I.s returned was far from that which they had left less than five years earlier. Most of America's allies had been reduced to poverty by the war, made worse in many cases by a period of vicious occupation. The Soviet Union had, however, grown in influence and stature within Eastern Europe. Totally uncaring of his soldiers' feelings and of the financial hardship caused them by keeping them in uniform, Stalin refused to demobilize. America had only her fleet and the threat of the atomic bomb to protect her way of life against her one-time ally and now ideological enemy. Within a few years, a series of spies headed by Klaus Fuchs would ensure that the Soviets, too, enjoyed the secret of atomic power.

While the size of the military was being reduced, its planning and operational ability were being enhanced. Under the terms of the National Security Act of 1947, the Air Force was promoted to equal status with the Army and Navy, and a National Security Council to co-ordinate national security was set up. The position of Secretary of Defense, a post enjoying cabinet rank, was introduced, and area commands established throughout the world. In 1949 the Department of Defense, with the Secretary of Defense at its head, was set up, and has changed little since.

## THE COLD WAR

Disputes soon arose between the wartime allies over the fate of Germany and Korea. After Russia's failure to remove the Western powers from Berlin by a blockade of the City in 1948-49, an independent Soviet satellite was set up in East Germany. Slowly but surely one sovereign state after another in Eastern Europe succumbed to Stalin, until eventually the "Iron Curtain" prophesied by Winston Churchill in 1946 became a reality.

A mortar is fired in one of the many skirmishes of the Korean War.

Berlin children watch as an aircraft flies in supplies to beat the Soviet blockade of the city in 1948.

The United States responded with a policy of "containment" under the terms of which friendly countries were offered assistance to combat the threat of Communism. In 1947, Congress voted for $400 million to aid Greece and Turkey, and a year later implemented the Marshall Plan, whereby $16 billion was funneled into Western Europe to facilitate its reconstruction.

In 1948, despite earlier specific agreements to facilitate the country's reunity, Korea was divided permanently along the 38th parallel. In response, the United Nations held free elections in the South and later that year established the Republic of Korea in the South. In 1949 both Russia and the United States withdrew their armies of occupation, and the stage for the first great post-war ideological battle was set.

In 1947 the United States signed the American Treaty of Reciprocal Assistance with 21 of her continental neighbours, and in 1949 became one of the first signatories to the North Atlantic Treaty Alliance.

## THE KOREAN WAR

While the Western powers had continued to disarm, the Soviet Union and her massive new ally the Chinese People's Republic, maintained and extended their military strength. In 1950 the Soviet Union had two million men under arms, compared with the United States' 640,000.

The inevitable confrontation between the two superpowers came on 25 June 1950, when thousands of soldiers of the North Korean People's Army swept south across the 38th parallel. The 90,000 lightly armed soldiers comprising the South Korean Army proved no match for the 250,000 Communist invaders supported by Soviet-supplied T34/85 tanks. Within three days Seoul had fallen, and the Northern armies were proceeding steadily south on all fronts.

In the absence of the Soviet Union, the United States condemned the aggression unequivocably, authorizing the use of force to resist it. President Truman ordered General MacArthur, based in Japan with the VIII Army, to use all available means to halt the Communists. However, the single armored division and three infantry divisions comprising the VIII Army were all under-strength and ill-equipped to fight a sustained campaign. Unable to wait for reinforcements, MacArthur committed his troops piecemeal, but was unable to do more than slow the enemy advance. By early August the Americans had sustained 6,000 casualties, and their Korean allies a further 70,000. They had been forced back behind the "Pusan Peninsula" in the extreme

The North Koreans used Soviet-supplied T-34/85's. This formidable medium tank was arguably the leading tank design of World War Two, and remained in production for many years afterwards.

The South Korean Army worked closely with the American forces and were mainly equipped by them.

Right: Infantry of the 38th Infantry Regiment, 2nd Infantry Division dig trenches and bunker positions on 'Old Baldy' in September 1952. This hill had no strategic significance but was the scene of intensive Chinese attacks in 1952 and 1953, and was eventually captured by them.

Opposite above: General Douglas MacArthur (1880-1964) (seated) was Commander-in-Chief of American forces during most of the Korean War.

Opposite below: UN soldiers fire a 57mm recoilless rifle at a North Korean target.

south-east of the country, and were in imminent danger of being driven into the sea.

The 140 mile-long perimeter did, however, hold long enough for American and British forces to be rushed to the area until, with the aid of the Air Force which had rapidly mastered the art of close air support, the area became impregnable.

MacArthur, realising the vulnerability of the North's long supply lines, now decided upon the most audacious plan of his distinguished military career. X Corps, consisting of the 7th Division, the 1st Marine Division and 9,000 Korean soldiers under the overall command of General Almond, was to make an amphibious landing at Inchon some 25 miles from Seoul, thus cutting the Northern Army off from its supply bases and forcing its withdrawal through the mountainous east.

MacArthur's plan was as audacious as it was unconventional. Inchon could be approached only through mile-wide mud flats at high tide. The troops would have to negotiate a high sea wall before landing, and would have no time to consolidate before committing themselves to battle in the built-up areas abutting the harbor. Furthermore, X Corps comprised the Americans' total reserves. Failure would mean total defeat for the Korean people.

Despite the strenuous opposition of more conservative minds, the landings took place on 15 September 1950. The astonished defenders offered only minimum resistance, a beachhead was quickly established, and elements of the 7th Infantry and 1st Marine Divisions began to move inland toward the Kimpo Airfield, and toward Seoul itself. After two weeks of often desperate

fighting, on 29 September MacArthur was able to return Seoul to the Government of South Korea.

General Walker with the VIII Army now broke out of the Pusan Perimeter driving the dispirited North Koreans before him. 30,000 soldiers escaped north beyond the 38th parallel, but 135,000 were killed or taken prisoner. For the time being, South Korea was once again secure.

On 27 September, President Truman ordered MacArthur north in pursuit of the remaining enemy troops. By late October the Americans and South Koreans, now supplemented by troops from numerous United Nations countries, had driven the enemy to within 50 miles of the Chinese border.

Consumed by the scent of victory, MacArthur refused to accept intelligence reports suggesting that Chinese soldiers were now being found in increasing numbers in the war zone, and pressed on relentlessly for the Yalu River, the northern border of the country.

By early November it was clear that thousands of Chinese "volunteers" had now been committed to the war. By the end of that month over 300,000 Chinese had crossed the border, and it was now MacArthur's turn to order a retreat in the face of overwhelming odds.

This photograph conveys an impression of the massive scale of the Inchon beach head in Korea. Four LST's can be seen unloading men and equipment in the background.

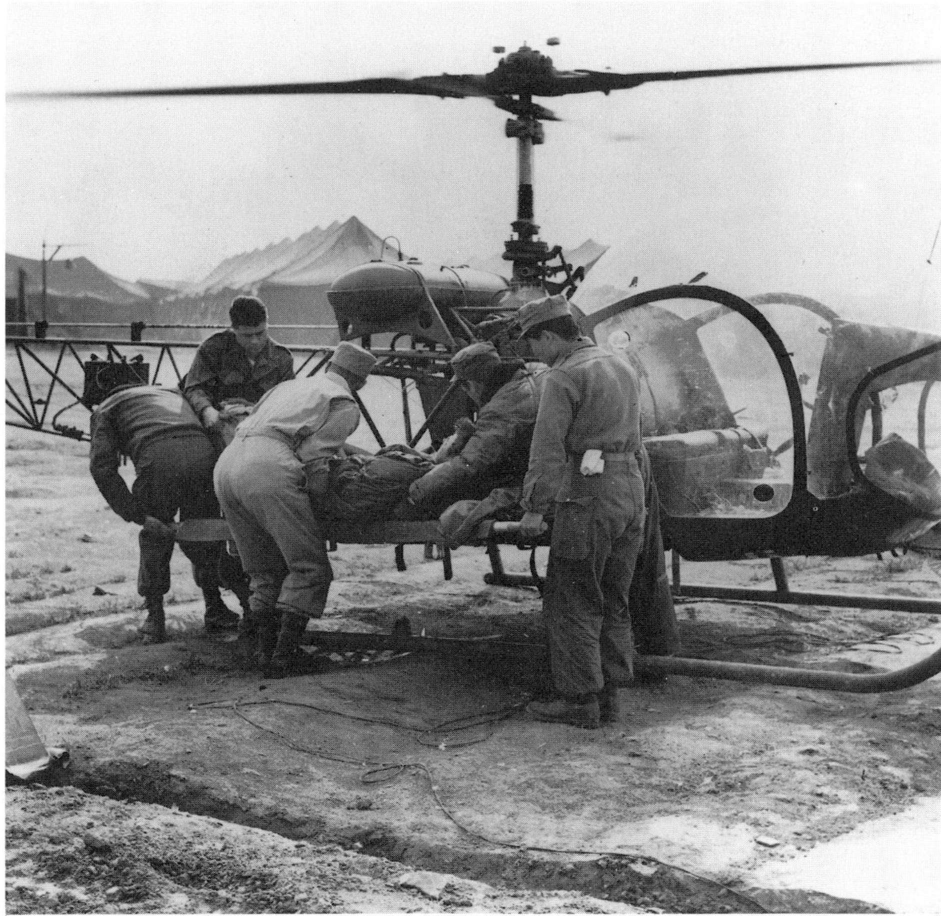

Above: US Army medics lift a wounded soldier off a helicopter to carry him to a MASH (Mobile Army Surgical Hospital) tent for emergency treatment.

Left: A mule helps the Korean war effort. Pack animals proved to be invaluable in the rugged terrain and carried on working when machinery broke down.

Above: US infantry in Korea.

Right: A mortar crew in action.

Left: By the end of the war, the front had stabilized enabling permanent signs such as these to be erected.

A signals crew on Hill 602, Korea in December 1951.

Right: A Soviet-built Korean T34/85 tank lies wrecked amid the ruins of a bridge in South Korea in October 1950 after an air strike by the USAF.

Despite the intensity of the Korean winter, and the unrelenting pressure of the Chinese, the United Nations forces were able to withdraw in good order to the 38th parallel.

When General Walker was killed in a motor accident on Christmas Eve, his place was taken by General Ridgeway who at once took steps to consolidate his weak and over-stretched front line. However, the United Nations troops were forced to withdraw in the face of massed Chinese attacks launched on New Year's Eve, and by 4 January 1951 Seoul was once again in Communist hands.

Despite this setback, Ridgeway succeeded in holding a line roughly along the old 38th parallel and, in March 1951, actually managed to recapture Seoul. President Truman now contented himself with holding the line pending a negotiated settlement. MacArthur however demanded victory whatever the cost, and by whatever means. The General, never renowned for his diplomacy, began to advocate his policies to whomever would listen, despite direct orders to clear all public statements before their release. On 11 April 1951, Truman relieved MacArthur of command, appointing the more compliant Ridgeway in his place.

During the next few months the United Nations forces advanced a few miles north to the so-called "Kansas-Wyoming line", but were unable to advance further in the face of dogged Chinese resistance.

Below: House to house fighting near Seoul.

President Eisenhower visited Korea in January 1953 shortly before his inauguration.

After months of negotiations the Chinese agreed to an armistice on 27 November, but before it could be augmented, reneged on its terms. The talks continued throughout most of the following year, frustrated invariably by the question of prisoners of war. North Korea demanded the return of all prisoners as a basis for settlement, but the United Nations refused as over half had expressed a strong desire to remain in the South. Eventually, in September 1952 the talks were suspended.

Negotiations were resumed in 1953 when, true to his election pledge, the newly-elected President Eisenhower visited Korea in an attempt to resolve matters directly. Unlike General Clark, his Far East Commander, Eisenhower had no wish to resume the war, preferring to negotiate by coercion if need be. China, the Soviet Union and North Korea were warned through diplomatic circles that if an armistice were not forthcoming the United States would be forced to escalate the war by any means at its disposal: a thinly veiled threat to use atomic weapons.

The talks were resumed in March 1953 and although battles flared to the very moment of peace, an armistice was finally signed on 27 July 1953.

When the War ended after 37 months of fighting, 142,000 Americans had been killed, wounded or captured. China and North Korea had lost 1,500,000 casualties. Neither side gained territorially, yet neither side lost face. The world was now a far more dangerous place.

## THE YEARS OF CHANGE

The years from Korea to Vietnam represented a period of fundamental reappraisal for the Armed Forces. Korea was fought largely along World War II lines, but any future conflict would without doubt be subject to entirely different tactics. The power of the atomic, and later, hydrogen bomb, would dictate every decision, often subordinating military strategy to political contingency.

Inter-continental ballistic missiles, the most powerful in the nuclear arsenal, could be delivered by land-based missile, by submarine or by long-range bomber. Intermediate missiles could be launched by the air force or from land-based sites in Europe, but only with the agreement of America's allies, particularly the United Kingdom and West Germany.

The sheer cost of the new nuclear program necessitated a reduction in conventional arms spending, to the extent that during the 1950s the Army was forced to scrap six divisions. Greater emphasis was placed on intelligence gathering, whether by high-flying U2 aircraft, radio interception or espionage, in an attempt to keep abreast of the Soviets' intentions.

In an attempt to maintain a viable army whilst cutting costs, Eisenhower introduced legislation permitting citizens to undertake a part of their commitment in the reserves or National Guard.

In the interim, the reduced regular army enhanced its firepower by introducing new generations of tanks, by mechanizing the infantry, and by exploiting the lifting power of the new generation of helicopters then coming into service.

When John F. Kennedy came to power in 1961 he abandoned the policy of massive retaliation with its dangers of over-reaction, in favour of "flexible response", requiring large-scale conventional forces as well as powerful nuclear warheads.

Conscious that his new policy would prove expensive, yet determined to keep waste to a minimum, Kennedy appointed experienced financiers headed by Robert McNamara to oversee the Department of Defense budget. Inevitably, standards were sacrificed at the altar of cost-cutting expediency, and for the first time in decades the Army found itself receiving equipment chosen as much for its cheapness as for its effectiveness.

Ominously, many of America's allies began to

The Cuban missile crisis reached its most dangerous point when the USSR sent missiles to Cuba on the *Kasimov* and other ships.

question whether or not flexible response would offer adequate defense to Europe, or whether it would be used as an excuse not to escalate a conflict if only European interests were under threat. Refusing to subjugate his country's future to an American whim, the xenophobic de Gaulle removed France from NATO.

Whatever the shortcomings of "flexible response", the policy did result in a degree of improvement in the equipment and tactics of the regular army. Mechanized and armored divisions were up-gunned, the role of the two airborne divisions was streamlined, and "air cavalry" units, utilizing a combination of armored helicopters and ground troops, were introduced.

Despite the total failure of the Bay of Pigs operation, organized and funded almost exclusively by the CIA, Kennedy remained committed to counter-insurgency operations, championing the cause of the new elite special forces groups specially trained in sabotage and counter-revolutionary activities.

Kennedy won his greatest victory when he forced a brow-beaten and ill-advised Kruschev to back down over the Cuba crisis. During October and November 1962, the Soviet Union attempted to position a number of intermediate missiles in Cuba. Kennedy immediately responded by blockading Cuba and putting his own nuclear facilities on stand-by. In exchange for a promise by the United States not to invade Cuba, (something she had no intention of doing), the Soviets agreed to withdraw the missiles.

Kennedy and his policy of flexible response had won a remarkable victory. Other aspects of his foreign policy were less inspired.

A reconnaissance photograph of a nearly completed missile site in Cuba, October 1962.

# 11: FROM VIETNAM TO THE PRESENT DAY

American involvement in Vietnam began in 1950 when limited funds and a few advisers were made available to the French, then trying to re-establish post-war control over Indochina. At the time, Ho Chi Minh, the leader of the Communist Viet Minh with its power base in the North was vying with Bao Dai, the French puppet, for control. Weakened by lack of domestic support, and defeated at Dien Bien Phu, France agreed to talks in 1954. The result was that the country was divided along the 17th parallel. 100,000 communist sympathisers moved north leaving an unknown number of Viet Minh behind to act as power bases for later guerilla units, and 800,000 North Vietnamese moved south.

It was clear from the outset that a lasting peace formula had not been found. Both adversaries built up their armies, aided by 400 American advisers in the case of the South, and awaited events.

Having consolidated his position in the North by a policy of ruthless suppression, Ho Chi Minh activated his supporters (now designated the Viet Cong) in the South, and within a short time was dangerously destabilizing the Southern Government. In response to the thinly veiled presence of North Vietnamese regular troops with the Viet Cong, the United States increased the number and scope of its advisers until by 1960 its troops were actually taking the field with front line South Vietnamese units.

Reacting to the support given freely to Ho Chi Minh by China and the Soviet Union, President Kennedy increased American support dramatically, until by 1962 11,000 military personnel, many of them Green Beret specialists, were operational. Still they were unable to prevent the infiltration of the Viet Cong and NVA (North Vietnamese Army) along the Ho Chi Minh Trail.

After the assassination of the unpopular and corrupt President Diem, a period of near anarchy prevailed in the South, during which the Communists grew considerably in power and influence. President Johnson, Kennedy's successor, found himself on the horns of a dilemma. If he were to send more troops the fighting would inevitably escalate, but if he were to hesitate history, and the electorate, would certainly regard

Vietnam was fought in conditions alien to the GI. No amount of training at home could prepare him for the swamps and jungles in which he would be expected to fight.

Opposite: A section of GIs protect the outer perimeter of a fire base against NVA nsurgents in 1966.

him as the man who lost the war. Eventually, using an attack on United States warships in the Gulf of Tonkin as an excuse, Johnson sought and was granted "carte-blanche" to pursue the war more vigorously.

In February 1965, Army and Marine combat troops went into direct action against the enemy in the Central Highlands, and for the first time targets in the North were bombed. Still enemy pressure grew unabated. The United States responded with more troops, until by the end of 1965 over 180,000 were operational.

Despite a few notable victories, such as that in the Ia Drang Valley, and the popularity of General Westmoreland's search-and-destroy policy, the enemy was not contained, nor was his will to fight weakened. By February 1968 the United States had 490,000 men committed in support of 640,000 Vietnamese. Between them they had killed 180,000 enemy and captured a further 70,000, but still they could not subdue the remaining 240,000 Communist combatants in the field.

Seemingly willing to accept losses often ten times greater than the Americans, the Communist will to win seemed to grow at the very time that American domestic opinion was turning sharply against the War. Ill-equipped, inadequately trained for a jungle war, and some would say badly led, the young American soldier, with an average age of only 19, never fully came to grips with his environment.

## THE TET OFFENSIVE

Reconciled to the fact that the forces under his command had neither the manpower nor the resources to defeat the United States in open battle, yet believing that the vast majority of the population in the South hated the Saigon Government sufficiently to countenance its overthrow, General Giap and his Staff planned a complex series of attacks on a series of key cities and provincial capitals.

Strategic points and municiple buildings were to be stormed and held to prove irrefutably that Saigon did not exercise control beyond its own immediate geographical environment. ARVN soldiers who layed down their arms were to be offered an amnesty, whilst the local civilian population was ,to be encouraged to rise in support. Politically it was felt that the Viet Cong would be more welcome than the NVA, who were therefore limited operationally to their strongholds along the border.

Towards the end of 1967. despite ample evidence to the contrary, US Intelligence officers on the ground did not acccept that a large-scale offensive was imminent. Increased infiltration by the Viet Cong into the major population centers, the growth in the size and number of their training camps outside of such towns, the virtual cessation of defections and the new-found optimism manifested by the majority of recently captured prisoners were all indicative of an offensive but not of its scale. Ironically the US

Members of the 151st (Ranger) Infantry Long Range Patrol open fire against the enemy. The Ranger in the foreground is armed with an M-16 rifle.

Command in Saigon captured, translated but discounted a prophetically accurate plan of the intended campaign only a short while before the city itself was attacked.

The scale of the Communist redeployment was hidden in part by the advent of the Tet holiday, a time of general relaxation and merriment during which the Viet Cong had been known to return home for a few days' respite from the jungle. As if to emphasise the temporary de-escalation of hostilities, Hanoi had announced a unilateral Tet truce of seven days, a gesture reduced to a period of 36 hours between 29 and 31 January by the wary South Vietnamese.

Fortunately for the Central Government, General Fred Weynard, commanding the Saigon sector, unwilling to accept the assurances of well-being generated by his Staff, had persuaded General Westmorland to released to him 15 battalions then deployed on the Cambodian border. Thus when the attack came he was able to call upon the resources of 27 battalions of US infantry, a luxury denied his fellow commanders.

Due to excessive secrecy within the surprisingly unwieldy Viet Cong command structure, a fundamental and potentially lethal confusion arose as to the exact start date designated for the overall attack, with the result that only Kontum, Pleiku, Binh Binh, Darlac, Khanh Hoa and Quang Nam were hit on the first day. However, although alerted to the likelihood of a new general offensive by such premature attacks, neither the US nor the ARVN forces realized its immensity until the following night, by which time the possibility of mounting preemptive counter-attacks had been lost.

The bulk of the attacks on the second night fell on Saigon and within the provinces of Quang Tri, Thua Thien, Quang Tin, Quang Ngai, Binh Thuan, Vinh Long and Phong Dinh. During the following night a further eight provinces were attacked. In all the Viet Cong involved 36 provincial capitals, five autonomous cities, 64 district capitals and 50 hamlets in the bitter fighting which was to last for over a week in Saigon and for nearly a month in Hue.

Inevitably the battle for Saigon attracted the majority of press footage, not always accurate, and from the American point of view highly selective and often counter-productive. Photographs of the summary execution by Nguyen Ngoc Loan, the highly volatile police chief, of a captured Viet Cong officer were flashed around the world, yet equally gruesome accounts of Viet Cong massacres of local government officials, paticularly in Hue, were largely ignored.

The attack on the United States Embassy by a squad of aproximately 20 volunteers from the C-

A convoy moves down the streets of Pleiku, Vietnam in 1972.

Above: Base camp operations. Members of the 82nd Airborne Division fill and stack sandbags around personnel bunkers.

Right: An infantryman climbs aboard an AVC to be driven to his patrol area.

Waiting for action.

10 Sapper Battalion provided the greatest drama. At 2.45 am a small group of Viet Cong who had earlier stolen a taxi and secreted it in a garage close to the main complex rushed the gateway. Fortunately the Military Police on guard were alert and managed to secure the entrance before radioing for assistance. During the suicidal distraction at the gate, other guerrillas blew a hole in the wall to gain entrance to the compound. However at that moment their commander was killed and the others, now lacking direction, made no attempt to enter the main complex. Within six hours Marine and heliborne reinforcements had arrived and the fighting was over. In reality very little damage was sustained by the Embassy. The Ambassador, Ellsworth Bunker, was quite safe (at the outset of the operation he had been escorted to a place of safety, the wine cellar, by his marine guards) and only five US soldiers were killed. However the first newsflash mistakenly reported that the Embassy had been seized and later reports clearly depicted the bodies of the dead Sappers, their blood-soaked brown uniforms a clear testament to the previous night's fighting. United States public opinion would never again fully accept the credibility of the Saigon Government's claim to be the total master of its own country.

During the course of the night the Viet Cong, supported on occassions by NVA soldiers, continued to attack positions in the Saigon area. Two aircraft were destroyed and 20 damaged in an attack by two reinforced battalions on the airbase at Bien Hoa. The French colonial cemetery, its massive headstones offering ideal if ghoulish protection for the defenders, was taken over by the enemy in battalion strength whilst the main military airfield at Tan Son Nhut was brought under attack, by a full regiment with Sapper support. Twenty-three US personnel were killed and another 85 wounded in the attack for the loss of a staggering 962 enemy killed!

During the next few days troops drawn from five US battalions, supported by those ARVN who were not on leave or who had not deserted, were tasked with clearing the city, in some instances block by block. Not trained in street fighting, a mode of warfare more reminiscent of the Phillipines than Vietnam, and faced with an enemy committed to a fight to the death, many commanders relied expressly on air power to suppress enemy strong-holds to the detriment of the local civilian population; a matter which did not go un-noticed by the press. Nearby guerrilla-occupied towns such as Can Tho and My Tho were devastated by air strikes, as a result of which tens of thousands of civillians were injured or rendered homeless, whilst the town of Ben Tre was levelled to the ground. American protestations that 'we had to destroy to save it" met with little support from a confused and increasingly cynical population at home.

## THE BATTLE FOR HUE

Hue, the ancient capital of Vietnam nestling on the banks of the Perfume River, was destined to be attacked by no less than six Viet Cong and four NVA battalions, nearly 75,000 men in all!

The focal point of Hue was the Citadel, a massive defensive bastion some two miles in circumference. Once the residence of the Annamese emperors, its brick walls were sixteen feet high and in places between 60 and 100 feet thick. The initial attack on the Citadel, made by the 4th and 6th NVA regiments, was fragmented and only partially successful, leaving the all-important heli-pad, crucial for the introduction of reinforcements, still under US Army control.

The Communist forces tasked with the capture of the rest of the town were however more successful and by day-break all but a few suburbs had been, in the parlance of the North, "liberated."

There followed an orgy of violence in which an estimated 3,000 "class-enemies" were executed. Professional men including doctors, lawyers, teachers and government officials were summarily shot, bayoneted, clubbed to death or simply buried alive until, sickened by the butchery, the North Vietnamese commander ordered the blood-thirsty Viet Cong to cease.

Initially there was marked reluctance among the authorities to use heavy armament to destroy the city in order to save it. However on February, long after the Tet Offensive had been crushed elsewhere, the Government granted permission for aircraft to attack targets outside the Citadel walls. A week later the order was extended to the Citadel itself.

Eventually 18 battalions, four drawn from the US Army, three from the marines and 11 from the ARVN, recaptured the Citadel and with it the city. Attempts by the Communists to withdraw to the east proved disastrous when the retreating forces were ambushed by elements of the US 1st Cavalry Division positioned specifically to counter such a contingency.

Early on the morning of 24th February peace returned to the shattered streets of Hue. By then the US forces, both Army and Marines, had lost 119 killed and 961 wounded. The ARVN, who had demonstrated a high degree of valor throughout the engagement, had lost 363 killed and 1,242 wounded. An estimated 5,000 Communists had died in the City and a further 3,000 in the adjoining countryside, many of them the victims of the 1st Cavalry Division.

Opposite: A Viet Cong sapper lies dead in the garden of the US Embassy in Saigon. Very little damage was actually sustained at the Embassy, but the credibility of the Saigon Government's claim to total mastery of the country was irreparably damaged.

Below: Soldiers of Company A, 30th Ranger Battalion of the ARVN keep in radio contact as they move against the Viet Cong during the Tet offensive.

### THE AFTERMATH

During the Offensive as a whole, the Communists lost 32,00 dead and a further 6,000 captured at the expense of only 4,000 defenders. Justifiably the US Army and the ARVN regarded theirs a victory. However public opinion at home, fed a diet of biased and often uninformed television, interpreted Tet as a defeat. The loss and suffering amongst the innocent civilians, always a problem in war, was highlighted and found to be unacceptable. General Westmoreland, due anyway for replacement, was promoted to Chief of Staff and his place taken by General Creighton Abrams. More fundamentally, President Johnson felt it

Opposite: ARVN Rangers guard some Viet Cong infiltrators who were captured during street fighting in Cholon.

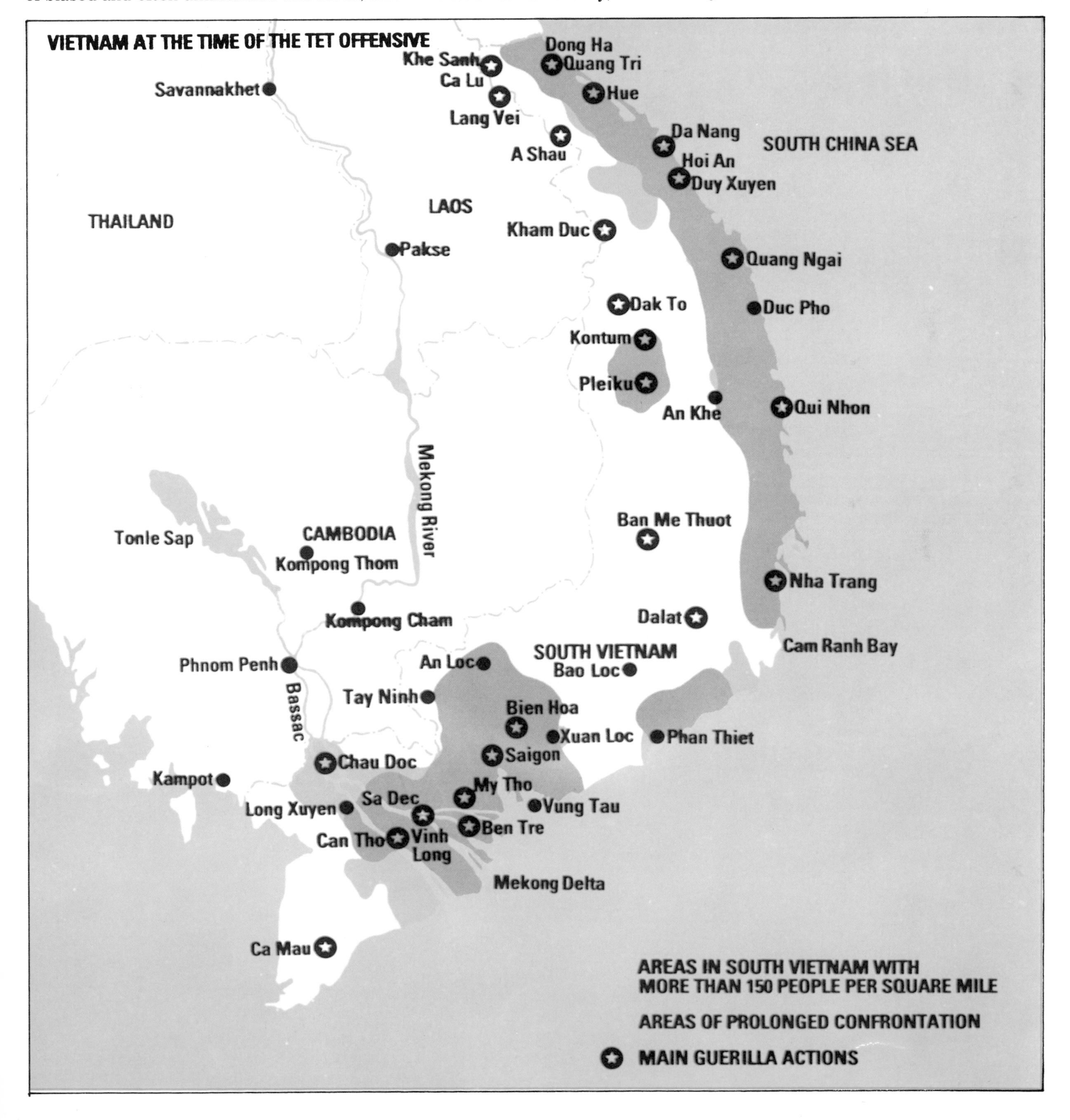

Main picture: Air Cavalry Regiments were trained to deploy quickly and in force behind enemy lines. Here troop ships land to pick up soldiers after a search and destroy mission near Chu Lai. Support helicopters such as this Chinook (inset left) often acted as 'packhorses'. This one is lifting an M198 155mm howitzer. Helicopters of the Delta force (right inset) wait on the USS *Nimitz* for the beginning of the ill-fated attempt to rescue the hostages from Iran.

politically expedient to halt the bombing of the North and to seek negotiation.

When Nixon replaced Johnson as President a policy of withdrawal in favour of the Vietnamization of the War was actively pursued.

Troop withdrawals in 1969 were accompanied by the first incursions by the Air Force into neutral Cambodia. By now however the War had been lost in the minds of the American civilian public and total evacuation could only be a matter of time. Although the Communist "Easter Offensive" of 1972 was bloodily rebuffed by the South Vietnamese the United States was by now doing all in its power to distance itself from the fighting. By October 1972 spurred on by a particularly savage spate of bombing of its major cities the North Vietnamese agreed to end the fighting in exchange for an American commitment to withdraw leaving the Vietnamese to settle their differences internally.

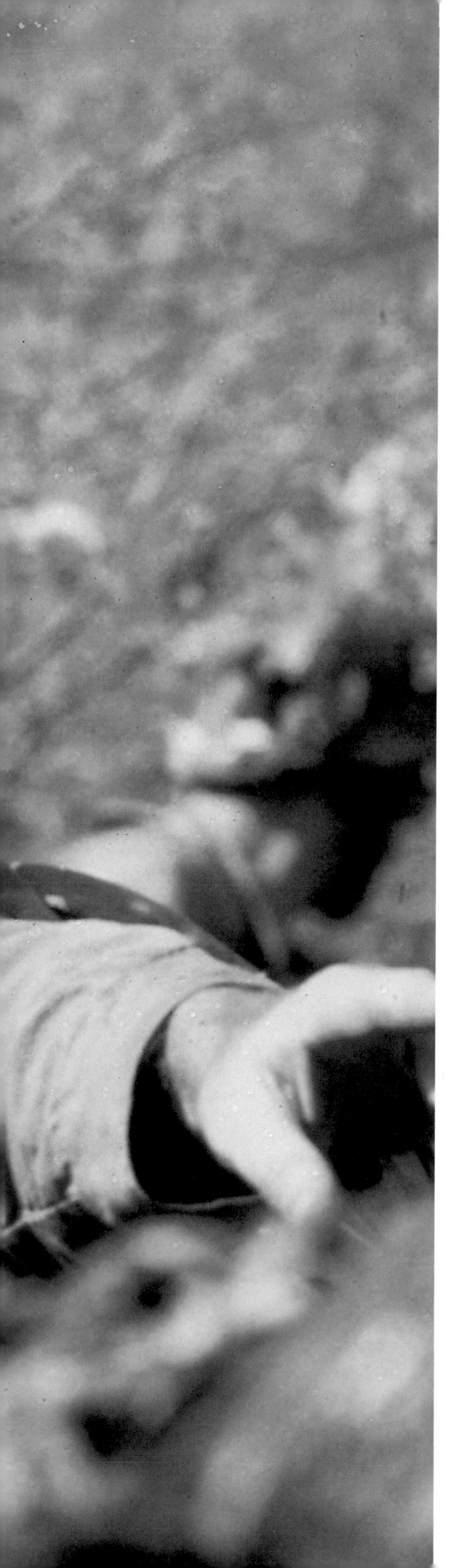

# 12: THE ARMY TODAY

Immediately upon his assumption of the Presidency in January 1977, President Carter set about the fundamental alteration of the United States' foreign policy. The B-1 bomber program was cancelled, only to be reintroduced at a later date, and naval expenditure was heavily restricted.

Carter's optimistic hope for a more peaceful and secure future was, however, shattered by events. The equanimity of the Middle East was thrown into turmoil in 1979 when the Shah of Iran was deposed by the Ayatollah Khomeini. When subsequently the staff of the embassy in Tehran were seized and held captive by Moslim fundamentalists for 444 days, America was impotent to act, her only attempt at a rescue ending in tragic fiasco. Carter responded by emphasizing the American presence abroad. Suggestions that the army division in South Korea might be withdrawn were quashed, and troops were sent to the Sinai in response to the Camp David Accord, to ensure peace between Israel and Egypt.

Ronald Reagan came to power in 1980 with a promise to "rearm America", and at once set about keeping his word. The Navy was increased, although not to the strength of 600 ships demanded by John Lehman, who subsequently resigned, and a series of inter-continental and medium range missiles were introduced or modernized. Marines were sent to the Lebanon, in many cases tragically to their deaths at the hands of bombers, and in 1982 a multi-service force was despatched to Grenada to thwart Cuban expansionism.

As the Army grew in size and strength so it regained public support. Educational standards increased and the ROTCs were revitalized. The world at present stands poised to see if the two great super-powers can agree to further reductions in their nuclear arsenals. Whether or not they are successful, it is certain that the 781,000 officers, men and women who comprise the regular army, supported by the 700,000 personnel of the National Guard, can be relied upon to support American policy, whether domestic or foreign, wherever and whenever called upon to do so.

A modern combat soldier.

The modern American Army is better equipped than ever before including heavy artillery (main picture) and mobile firepower. The M-1/M Abrams (center left) is now replacing the M-60 (top) as the main battletank while the M-2 Bradley (bottom left and right) and the M-113 APC (center right) now provide the infantry with excellent firepower as well as mobility.

The modern US Army is better armed and equipped than ever before. Figures published by the International insitute of Strategic Studies state that $282.90 bn was voted for defence in 1987 and that over $300.00 bn will be spent throughout 1988. Over 13,300 front line tanks are now operational including 4,500 of the latest M-1/M Abrams.

Today's infantry are transported in over 3,600 Bradely MICVs (Mechanised Infantry Combat Vehicles) and 23,200 APCs including the ubiquitous M-113 many of which are fitted with TOW (Tube Optical Wired) anti-tank weapons.

Increasingly the infantryman himself is being re-equipped with the much improved Colt M-16 A2 rifle. For his personal defence his uniform now includes several life-saving characteristics including the Kevlar "Fritz-hat" helmet so named because of its marked outward similarity to the World War II German headgear.

Since 1987 Special Operations Forces, the cream of the army, have been under the control of the grandiosely named Assistant Secretary of Special Operations and Low Intensity Conflict, a new position within the department of defence. A new special Operations Command, based at MacDill AFB Florida has been set up to incorporate the Rangers, Army Special Forces and special warfare schools into a single integrated fighting concept thus ensuring unanimity of action and purpose in any future emergency.

The US Army in all its facets is stronger, more efficient and better prepared than ever to wage war. It is to be hoped that war will not come again. If however it does, the US Army will certainly give an excellent account of itself.

VMA-231
MARINES
158390
MARINES
VMA-231

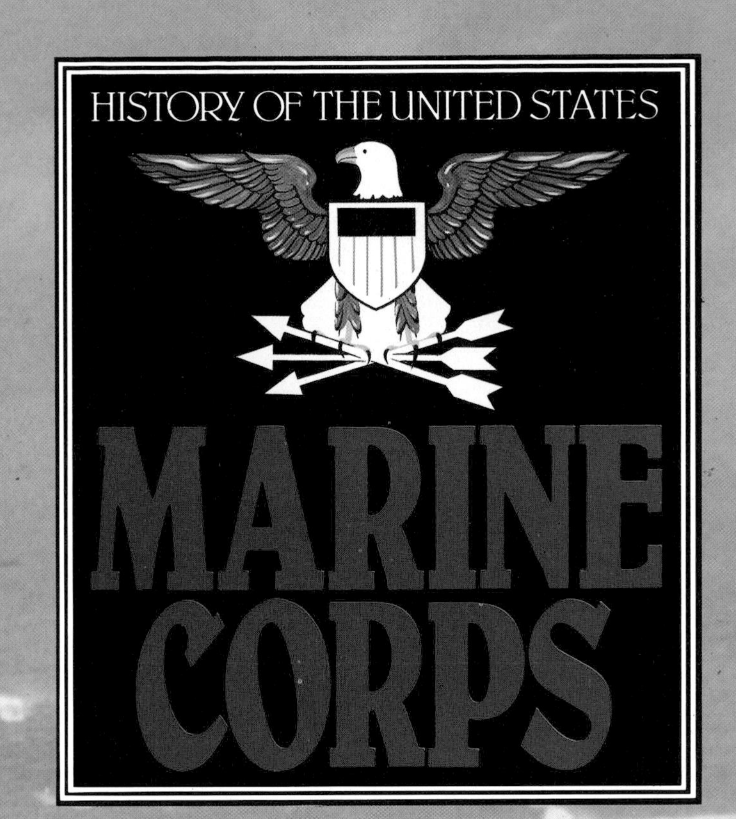
HISTORY OF THE UNITED STATES
MARINE
CORPS

*Right:* Jungle warfare is one of the Marines' special skills.

# 1: FIRST TO FIGHT
## 1775-1914

### THE AMERICAN WAR OF INDEPENDENCE

The origins of the Marine Corps can be traced back to the colonial battalions of Marines raised in America before the Revolution and modeled on their British counterparts.

In 1740 four battalions of Marines — some 3,000 men — were raised for service in Britain's war with Spain, the so-called "War of Jenkins' Ear", allegedly triggered off by the arrest and mutilation of a British captain. Designated 43rd Regiment of Foot, they became known as "Gooch's Marines", after their commander, Colonel William Gooch. Serving under the British Admiral Vernon, Colonel Gooch led his Marines into battle at Cartagena, Colombia, in April 1741. In July of the same year, Marines landed unopposed at Guantanamo Bay, in Cuba, to secure it as a base for a British fleet.

The War of Jenkins' Ear soon expanded into a Franco-British confrontation coinciding with, and merging into, the War of the Spanish Succession. In this new struggle, the Colonial Marines found employment in the British Navy, serving as marksmen aboard its ships and providing the cutting edge of boarding parties. Their duties also included shipboard security and maintaining discipline among the seamen, the latter a task calculated to encourage the sometimes prickly relationship between Marines and sailors, a phenomenon which persists today.

### The Continental Marines

The British soldier has lost many battles, but the only important war he has lost is the American War of Independence, which began with shots on the village green at Lexington on 19 April 1775. The unity of opposition felt by the American colonies to British rule had already been demonstrated at the First Continental Congress, which met in Philadelphia in September 1774. In May 1775, the Second Continental Congress prepared for war, appointing George Washington on 14 June as commander-in-chief of the army to defend the 13 colonies.

Initially, this predominantly militia force did not fare very well against British regulars. An invasion of Canada (June 1775–July 1776) proved beyond their resources and

*Left:* George Washington at Valley Forge.

came to grief at the end of December 1775 when an attempt to storm Quebec was repulsed and the colonists' commander, General Montgomery, was killed.

Two months earlier, the Congress had approved a resolution calling for the creation of a new military force, the Continental Marines. The resolution had been drafted by a committee of Congress in the Tun Tavern, Philadelphia, whose owner, Robert Mullan, was appointed a Marine Captain under the command of another inn-keeper, Samuel Nicholas, proprietor of The Conestoga Wagon.

However, Marines had already made their mark on the war. In May 1775, the Continental Congress reacted to news of the enfeebled state of the American forces holding Fort Ticonderoga and Crown Point by requesting the governor of Connecticut to reinforce the garrisons with his colony's forces. A body of troops set out from Hartford, and with them was "money escorted by eight Marines [from the Connecticut Navy] well spirited and equipped". The Marines — later dubbed "The Original Eight" — and the soldiers evaded hostile Indians and British forces to relieve the hard-pressed garrison.

In October 1775, American merchantmen were requisitioned and armed in a successful bid to capture two unescorted British ships carrying quantities of ammunition, of which Washington's forces were in acutely short supply. The vessels were placed on "Continental risque and pay", an arrangement whereby Congress paid the crews and assumed responsibility for insuring the ships against loss or capture. Congress also instructed Washington to "give proper encouragement to the Marines and seamen" — the first written reference by Congress to "Marines".

The Continental Marines went into action in March 1776 when an American squadron raided the Bahamas with the principal aim of seizing gunpowder for Washington's army. On 3 March, 220 Marines, under the command of Captain Samuel Nicholas, landed on New Providence Island. In two weeks the raiding party captured two forts, a quantity of guns, occupied Nassau and took the British Governor prisoner. But the gunpowder had been spirited away by the canny Governor Browne. Nicholas reported, "We found in this fort [Nassau] a great quantity of shot and shells, with 15 brass mortars, but the grand article, gunpowder, the Governor had sent off before, viz 150 casks." The Marines re-embarked on 17 March for Rhode Island. On the homeward journey the squadron was engaged by the lone 20-gun British corvette *Glasgow*. In a night action with the American *Cabot* and the squadron's flagship, the 24-gun *Alfred*, the British inflicted the first combat losses suffered by the Marines — Second Lieutenant John Fitzpatrick and six enlisted men.

The expedition earned Nicholas promotion to the rank of Major, and in December 1776 he and 300 of his men joined Washington's army in Pennsylvania. The Marines did not participate in Washington's morale-boosting victory at Trenton on 26 January, remaining on the Pennsylvania side of the River Delaware as a reserve force. Nevertheless, this was the first occasion on which Marines served as part of the Army.

*Right:* The capture of the British Ship *Sandwich*, during the "undeclared" naval war with France, by Captain Daniel Carmick of the Marine detachment of the USS *Constitution*, 11 May 1800.

The Marines fought in the second battle of Trenton (2 January 1777), using the ruse of false campfires to slip through General Charles Cornwallis' lines, and took part in the action at Princeton on the following day.

In the spring of 1777, Washington reorganized his army, incorporating some of the Marines in his artillery and returning the remainder to their naval duties. In October–November 1777, the Marine artillerymen played a prominent part in the defense of Fort Mifflin, on the River Delaware, against a squadron of British warships and Hessian shore batteries.

In January 1778, a small force of Marines, commanded by Captain James Willing, sailed down the Mississippi aboard a venerable vessel which Willing had renamed *Rattletrap*. During the next 12 months Willing's force operated in the region of New Orleans, harassing British traders, before returning north to fight against hostile Indians.

In July 1798, a force of 300 Marines, under Captain John Welsh, distinguished themselves in an unsuccessful combined operation against a British fort at Penobscot Bay, Maine, making "a forcible charge against the enemy". In May 1780, 200 Marines fought a gallant holding action against a vastly superior British force at Charleston, South Carolina.

Continental Marines serving with John Paul Jones aboard *Ranger* took the war to the enemy, making two raids on the British

mainland in April 1778. In the winter of 1780–81, Marines from the frigate *South Carolina* made an amphibious attack on the island of Jersey in the English Channel, the last such operation of the war. On 8 May 1782, 300 Marines on the *South Carolina* assisted in the capture of the Bahama Islands for Spain. In January 1783 the Continental Marines ended their part in the naval war when a detachment aboard the warship *Hague* boarded and seized the British ship *Baille* in the West Indies.

The military outcome of the War of Independence had been effectively settled two years earlier, when General Burgoyne surrendered at Yorktown on 19 October 1781. Britain finally acknowledged the loss of her colonies at the Treaty of Versailles on 30 November 1783. With peace came the disbandment of the American Navy and the Continental Marines, whose peak strength during the war had been 124 officers and 3,000 men. Major Samuel Nicholas is held by the Marines to have been their first Commandant.

## Birth of the Marine Corps

When the first Congress assembled in 1789 in New York, the United States had no Navy. A number of states maintained small warships, but the Republic had not a single armed vessel. It was not until March 1794 that Congress took steps to reactivate the Navy, authorizing the construction of six frigates, each of which was to have a detachment of Marines.

However, two years passed before the funds were found for the construction of three ships, *United States*, *Constellation* and *Constitution*, all three of which were launched in 1797. A Congressional Act of 1 July 1797 laid down the number of Marines to serve on the ships: five lieutenants, eight sergeants, eight corporals, three drummers, three fifers and 140 privates. At this point the Marines were considered to be part of the Navy.

An early supporter of the idea of a Marine Corps with its own separate identity and command structure was the Secretary of War, James McHenry, who in a letter of 9 April 1798 to the House Naval Committee Chairman, Samuel Sewell, recommended that an organization of Marines be formed. In Congress, wheels were grinding. The House of Representatives passed a Bill calling for the creation of "a battalion to be called the Marine Corps". The Senate increased the size of the proposed Corps to a regiment and on 11 July 1798, with House agreement, sent "An Act for Establishing and Organizing a Marine Corps" to President John Adams for his signature.

The Corps was initially placed under the direct orders of the President, to be attached either to the Army or the Navy, "according to the nature of the service in which they shall be employed" and subject either to the Articles of War or the Naval Regulations. The ambiguity inherent in this agreement — particularly when the Marines were serving ashore — was removed in June 1834 with the passing of an Act "For the Better Organization of the Marine Corps", which

attached the Marine Corps to the Navy unless the President ordered part of it to come temporarily under the control of the Army.

The table of organization for the new body of Marines prescribed a total of 33 officers and 848 "non-commissioned officers, musicians and privates". They were provided with striking uniforms: blue shortcoats and trousers, edged in brilliant red; their hats, with one side turned up, sported a yellow band and a cockade. Sergeants bore yellow epaulettes on their shoulders; officers wore long blue coats with red cuffs and golden epaulettes. All the uniforms had stiff leather collars, which quickly earned the Marines their famous nickname, the "Leathernecks".

On 12 July 1798, President Adams appointed William Ward Burrows as the first commandant of the Marine Corps. Burrows set up his first headquarters in Philadelphia, but in July 1800 moved the Marines HQ to Washington DC, selecting a location "near the Navy Yard and within easy marching distance of the Capitol". By 1806, Marine Barracks, Washington, was completed, and it is here that the Commandant of the Corps makes his home to this day.

### War at Sea

One of the most pressing problems facing President Adams was the protection of American commerce against the depradations of French privateers, who were harassing the shipping trade between the United States and Britain, with whom France was at war. Persistent French disregard of American neutrality led to the "undeclared" naval war with France which began in May 1798.

Marines serving aboard Federal vessels played a prominent part in all the sea engagements of the war. They also participated in land action on foreign soil and were given the responsibility of guarding French prisoners of war held in Philadelphia.

In 1799, Marines serving on *Constellation*, under the command of Lieutenant Bartholomew Clinch, were involved in the capture of the French frigate *Insurgente*. In 1800 *Constellation* bested the French ship *Vengeance* in a four-hour night engagement. Between October 1799 and March 1800, the Marines aboard Navy ships saw action against the armed barges of Haitian pirates ("picaroons").

On 11 May 1800, sailors from *Constitution*,

Replica of the Tun Tavern, birthplace of the Marines.

*Right:* The engagement between the American ship *Planter* and a French privateer during the "undeclared" war with France, 10 July 1799.

and its Marine detachment, seized the captured British ship *Sandwich*, held by the French in the supposedly neutral port of Puerto Plata on the northern coast of Santo Domingo. Employing a *ruse de guerre* reminiscent of the wooden horse of Troy, a party of sailors and 90 Marines sailed into the harbor hidden below-decks on the American ship *Sally*, took over *Sandwich*, captured the local fort, spiked its cannon and then made good their escape with their prize, the ship *Sandwich*. This was the first combat landing made by the Marine Corps on foreign soil. In September, Marines from *Patapsco* and *Merrimack* went into action against French units besieging the Dutch garrison at Willemstad on the island of Curacao. The arrival of the Marines forced the French to lift the siege.

One of the most successful of the US Navy's ships was the *Enterprise*. In 1800 she defeated or captured 10 enemy vessels and recaptured 11 American ships. Her 16 Marines, delivering a hail of fire from the fighting tops, played an important part in all these victories.

The "undeclared" naval war came to an end in February 1801, by which time the US Navy had captured 85 French vessels. In 1802, however, President Thomas Jefferson instituted a policy of economic retrenchment aimed at reducing the national debt. He ordered the selling of naval vessels and halted all warship construction. The majority of the frigates which remained were dismantled to save expense. The Marines did not escape the financial axe, and the Corps' strength was reduced to 26 officers and 453 men.

### Barbary Pirates

These economies were shortsighted measures at a time when the United States was about to enter into a war in the Mediterranean against the Barbary states. For many years the Muslim states of Morocco, Tunis, Algiers and Tripoli had been extorting money from the United States and the European powers, either as ransom for prisoners or as the price of allowing merchant ships to navigate the Mediterranean unmolested by the Barbary pirates. By the spring of 1801, the United States had parted with two million dollars, one-fifth of its national revenue.

Matters came to a head when the Pasha of Tripoli, Yusuf Caramanli, demanded even greater tribute. When this was refused, he declared war on the United States in May 1801. A month later, four vessels of the United States' exiguous Navy — *President*, *Philadelphia*, *Essex* and *Enterprise* — were formed into the Mediterranean Squadron and despatched from Hampton Roads to Tripoli. There were about 180 Marines in the Squadron.

The Mediterranean Squadron was far too small to protect American merchant ships or threaten the supremacy of the Barbary

*Above:* Lieutenant O'Bannon and his men raise the Stars and Stripes over Yusuf Caramanli's citadel at Derna in April 1805.

*Right:* Lieutenant Stephen Decatur, USN, who led a daring action against the Barbary Pirates in February 1804.
*Below:* Decatur and his raiding party board the captured frigate *Philadelphia* in Tripoli harbor prior to burning her.

pirates. On 31 October 1803 the frigate *Philadelphia* ran aground on a reef off Tripoli, was captured by pirate ships, floated free and towed into port, where its crew (including 44 Marines) were imprisoned by the Pasha.

*Philadelphia* was saved from the ignominy of becoming a pirate ship by the daring of Lieutenant Stephen Decatur, USN. On the night of 16 February 1804, Decatur slipped into the harbor aboard the captured ketch *Intrepid*. With his raiding party were eight Marines under the command of Sergeant Solomon Wren. Decatur's party boarded *Philadelphia*, overpowered the pirate crew, burned the ship to the waterline, and in the subsequent confusion in the harbor escaped without suffering a single casualty. However, *Philadephia*'s crew remained in Yusuf's hands, and their freedom was purchased with another massive ransom.

One of the most remarkable episodes in the Tripoli war was the expedition undertaken by William Eaton, American Consul in Tunis, to replace the troublesome Yusuf with his elder brother, Hamet Bey. In Alexandria, Eaton assembled a force comprising a small number of US Navy and Marine Corps personnel, 40 Greeks, a squadron of Arab cavalry, 100 Turks and other mercenaries and a caravan of camels. In February 1805, he set out across the Libyan desert on a 600-mile trek to Derna, Yusuf's capital. Accompanying him was Marine Lieutenant Presley N. O'Bannon with a sergeant and six privates from the *Argus*.

During their seven-week march, Eaton and O'Bannon had to deal with mutiny, extremes of hunger and thirst and constant brawling between the diverse elements of their motley expeditionary force. Arriving at Derna in late April 1805, they immediately demanded Yusuf's surrender. When the tyrant declined to hand himself over, they drew up an assault plan to capture his stronghold.

Under cover of three American warships in the harbor, Hamet Bey and his Arabs were to attack Yusuf's castle while the Marines, Greeks and Turks seized the harbor fort. Things did not go according to plan. The naval gunfire made no impression on Yusuf's garrison, and Hamet and his Arabs held back, waiting to see how the situation developed.

Under heavy fire, and with an enemy force approaching, O'Bannon led a charge in which Eaton and three Marines fell wounded. Yusuf's men were driven from the walls of the harbor, the Stars and Stripes was raised and the unspiked guns turned on the castle. Hamet Bay rallied his Arabs and swept away the last remnants of resistance. Within two hours of the first shots being fired, Derna was in the hands of Eaton's polyglot army. A peace treaty with Tripoli was concluded in June 1805.

Hamet Bey reputedly rewarded O'Bannon with his sword, a weapon of Mameluke design, decorated with an ivory hilt topped with a golden eagle's head. The "Mameluke sword" served as the pattern for the swords still carried by Marine officers on ceremonial occasions.

### The War of 1812

In military terms, 1812 was dominated by Napoleon Bonaparte's invasion of Russia. But far from the great European war fronts, a small, bitter struggle was being waged across the Atlantic. The American War of 1812 was ostensibly caused by British violation of American neutrality during British naval operations against the French and their allies. The United States declared war against Britain on 18 July 1812, to "defend the freedom of the seas", but also with an eye on the acquisition of British territory in Canada. On the outbreak of war, the total of US military personnel stood at 12,631, with the Marine Corps comprising 10 officers and 483 enlisted men. There were only three first-class warships in the Navy, *Constitution*, *President* and *United States*. Their task was to harass the British by chasing down commerce and whenever possible to engage single British warships.

In this they were conspicuously successful. *Constitution* destroyed the British *Guerrière* on 19 August off Nova Scotia; on 25 October *United States* seized *Macedonian* off Madeira; and, on 29 December, *Constitution* sank *Java* off Brazil, earning the nickname "Old

*Below:* British forces, under Major-General Robert Ross, advance on Washington in August 1814.

Ironsides". Marines were involved in all these actions, leading boarding parties and delivering musket fire from the fighting tops. In 1813, Marines participated in the actions which gave Commodore Perry a superiority over the British naval forces on Lake Erie, which he retained until the autumn of 1814 when reverses in other sectors forced the US Navy to relinquish control of the lake.

Once again the war threw up a Marine Corps hero, in the youthful form of a 23-year-old Lieutenant, John Marshall Gamble. On 22 October 1812, Gamble and 31 Marines sailed from the Delaware Cape on board *Essex*, under the command of Captain David Porter. In April 1814, off the Galapagos Islands, Porter intercepted and captured three British whaling ships. One of the captured vessels was then commissioned as the USS *Greenwich* and put under the command of Gamble with a crew of 14 men. Thus Gamble became the only Marine ever to captain a ship of the US Navy.

In July 1813, Gamble displayed great coolness and seamanship when *Greenwich* outmaneuvered and captured the *Seringapatam*, an armed British whaler. In October, Porter left him in charge of three British prize ships at Nukuhiva in the Marquesas Islands, hastily fortified and garrisoned by 22 men. Within an ace of being overwhelmed by mutiny, hostile natives and his British prisoners, Gamble fled for his life aboard one of the prize ships, *Sir Andrew Hammond*, with a crew of seven wounded men.

After a 15-day voyage, Gamble landed in the Sandwich (Hawaiian) Islands, where his ship was given a refit by friendly traders and natives. In return, Gamble undertook a mission to ferry tribute to the chieftain of a nearby island. En route he encountered the British warship *Cherub* and was forced to surrender. Gamble and his men remained prisoners for the rest of the war. The young Lieutenant returned to New York in August 1815 and resumed a distinguished career with the Marine Corps, from which he retired in 1834 with the rank of Lieutenant-Colonel.

Napoleon's abdication in April 1814 released large numbers of British Peninsular War veterans for service in the American theatre. The British mounted three geographically separate operations against the United States. In the north, 14,000 troops, transferred from Europe and led by General Prevost, marched on New York from Montreal at the end of August. Prevost was forced to withdraw after an attempt to secure the strategically vital Lake Champlain and was defeated in a naval engagement on 11 September.

The British were more successful in the Chesapeake Bay area, where on 19 August 1814 Admiral Cockburn's squadron landed 5,400 veterans of the Peninsular War under General Robert Ross. The British advanced on Washington, scattering 6,000 local militia at Bladensburg, a few miles outside the capital. The militiamen took to their heels at the first rattle of musket fire, but a battalion of 114 Marines, commanded by Captain Samuel Miller, and sailors under the command of Commodore Joshua Barney, stood their ground. They inflicted 250 casualties on the British with their muskets and an 18-pdr cannon, delaying the British advance for two hours.

The British lingered only to burn the Capitol and the White House, although leaving the Marines' barracks untouched, before withdrawing to mount an unsuccessful attack on Baltimore.

*Above:* The death of General Pakenham during the Battle of New Orleans, 8 January 1815.
*Left:* The Battle of Lundy's Lane, 25 July 1814.

The Marines gained sweet revenge for the burning of Washington in January 1814. On 13 December 1814, a British expeditionary force of 7,600 Peninsular veterans, under the command of Major-General Sir Edward Pakenham, landed on the Gulf Coast. Their objective was New Orleans. Already well-placed to counter this threat were the militiamen commanded by Andrew Jackson, who had originally been despatched to Alabama in March 1814 to put down an Indian rising. Jackson's force was an extraordinary mixture of fighting men, among them Jean Lafitte's pirates and 300 Marines under the command of Major Daniel Carmick, who was mortally wounded in action against the British on 28 December.

Pakenham's main thrust against Jackson's base at New Orleans began on 8 January 1815, the British advancing in close order to be mown down by the well-dug-in defenders. Over 2,000 British troops were killed or wounded, with Pakenham among the dead. American casualties were fewer than 100. The war, and British violations of American neutrality, was brought to an end by the Treaty of Ghent, signed on 24 December 1814, ironically a month before Pakenham lost his life before the defenses of New Orleans.

Congress expressed its thanks "for the valor and good conduct of Major Daniel Carmick, of the officers, non-commissioned officers, and Marines under his command". The same, alas, cannot be said for Marine Commandant Franklin Wharton, who had fled Washington after the Battle of Bladensburg. Charges of neglect of duty and conduct unbecoming an officer and a gentleman were brought against Wharton by Marine Captain Archibald Henderson, an exemplary fighting man who had commanded the Marine detachment aboard *Constitution.* At a trial in September 1817, Wharton was acquitted, but he died under a cloud.

Wharton's successor, Major Anthony Gale, was another bad lot, lasting only two years before he was court-martialled and dismissed the service. Fortunately for the Marine Corps, he was succeeded by one of its outstanding Commandants, the 38-year-old Archibald Henderson.

## At Home and Abroad

Under Henderson's vigorous command, training, discipline and the Marines' personal appearance underwent dramatic improvements. Although the complement of the

Seminole Indians observe a waterborne Marine patrol in the Florida Everglades during the Seminole War. Marine Commandant Henderson was rewarded for his role in the suppression of the Seminoles by promotion to Brigadier-General. He was the first Marine officer to hold general officer rank. For the enlisted Marines of the 1830s and '40s, life was tough. Drunks were forced to drink several quarts of salt water, an extremely unpleasant way of sobering up. Falling asleep on watch was punished by several months of walking guard duty wearing an iron collar and ball-and-chain. Disobeying the commands of a sentry earned 12 lashes with the cat o' nine tails. As late as 1843 a private's pay was only $6 a month, plus $30 a year uniform allowance.

Corps was small, it found employment in a wide range of duties: suppressing piracy in the Caribbean; landing on the Falkland Islands in 1832 to protect American interests in the South Atlantic; and in the same year participating in a punitive expedition in Sumatra after the harassment of American shipping by Malay pirates.

At home the Marines saw service as emergency firefighters — notably during the Boston fire of 1824 — and guardians of public order. They successfully combined both roles when arsonists set fire to the US Treasury in Washington DC. Marines from "Eighth and Eye" — Corps headquarters located at Eighth and I Streets, SE — helped to put out the fire and then stood guard over the nation's treasures.

A milestone in Marine history was reached in 1834 with the passing by Congress of an "Act For the better Organization of the Marine Corps", which frustrated attempts to merge the Corps with the Army and preserved it as a semi-autonomous body within the Naval establishment, ashore and afloat, except when detached for service within the Army by order of the President. It also set the Corps' peacetime strength at 63 officers and 1,224 enlisted men.

Almost immediately, President Jackson detached all able-bodied Marines for service with the Army in the war against the Creek Indians of Georgia and the Seminoles of the Florida Everglades. Commandant Henderson quickly assembled a two-battalion regiment consisting of 38 officers and 424 enlisted men. The story goes that before leaving Marine headquarters, Henderson pinned the following note to his door: "Gone to fight the Indians. Will be back when the war is over. A. Henderson. Col. Comdt." The Marines played an important role in bringing the Creek war to an end in the summer of 1836. The Seminoles proved more intractable, and the campaign against them was brought to an end in 1842 without a treaty having been signed. During these operations against the Indians, the Marine Corps gained field experience which was to prove of immense value in the Mexican War.

### The Mexican War

The war of 1846–47 with Mexico sprang from the hectic period of American expansion which followed the Louisiana purchase of 1803. As its frontiers pushed westwards and southwards, the United States came into conflict with Mexico over the latter's territory in California and Texas, which was annexed by the United States in 1845.

Contention over the lands north of the Rio Grande River flared into hostilities on 18 May 1846, when Marine detachments from vessels under the command of Captain John H. Aulick, USN, clashed with Mexican troops at Burrita, 15 miles upstream from the mouth of the Rio Grande.

This skirmish was quickly overshadowed as Marines from the Gulf Coast Squadron began operations to establish a blockade in support of General Zachary Taylor's march south from the Rio Grande. The squadron's senior Marine officer, Captain Alvin Edson, combined all the ships' detachments to form a 200-strong Marine battalion. In October 1846, the battalion, reinforced by sailors and supported by the guns of the squadron, made a series of successful raids against the ports of Frontera and San Juan Bautista.

On 16 November, General Taylor occupied Saltillo. Thereafter he was obliged to assume a defensive posture while General Winfield Scott mounted an invasion of Mexico from Tampico, which on 14 November had been seized by a landing party including Edson's Marines. Vera Cruz was Scott's first important objective.

Following General Taylor's defeat of Santa Anna at Buena Vista on 22/23 February 1847, the focus of the war shifted to central Mexico, where Scott's offensive was about to begin. On 9 March his force made an unopposed landing at Vera Cruz, which surrendered after an 18-day siege. Pushing westwards, Scott routed a Mexican army under Santa Anna at Cerro Gordo on 18 April. However, early in May his advance came to a halt at Puebla. He now had barely 6,000 men under his command, as 4,000 of his original force had returned to the United States on the completion of their agreed period of service.

Commandant Henderson — taking advantage of a 1,000-man increase in the Corps' strength authorized by Congress on 3 March 1847 — immediately began a recruiting drive, and obtained Scott's permission to make good some of his losses with Marines. A battalion of Marines, some 350 strong, joined Scott's forces at Puebla on 6 August and was attached to General John A. Quitman's 4th division under the command of Major Levi Twiggs, a hard-fighting veteran of the campaign against the Seminole Indians. In Scott's rear, Marines of the Gulf Coast Squadron had played an important part in the operations which closed the last remaining ports of entry on Mexico's western coast.

On 7 August, General Scott's reinforced army of 11,000 men began its advance on Mexico City, defeating Santa Anna at Molino del Rey on 8 September. Still outnumbered by at least 2:1, Scott pressed on to clear the last major defensive obstacle before Mexico City. This was Chapultepec, a 200ft-high outcrop topped by a fort. He launched his attack on Chapultepec at 0800 hrs on 13 September. Major Twiggs, armed with a double-barreled shotgun, was killed in the advance to the base of the Mexican fortifications. Under heavy fire, the American troops scaled the walls and seized the fort. The Marines suffered 24 casualties in the attack, and among the wounded was Second Lieutenant C.A. Henderson, the son of the Commandant.

Thrusting on to Mexico City with elements of 4th Division and Marines, General Quitman was held up by fierce enemy resistance. Marine Captain George H. Terrett — a veteran of the 1832 campaign against the Malay pirates — moved his company forward without orders to attack a line of Mexican batteries. He pursued the fleeing gunners and then broke up a counter-attack by Mexican lancers. Mexico City was taken on 14 September. With the city secured, Marine Lieutenant Augustus S. Nicholson cut down the Mexican colors and

*Top and centre:* Two views of the fighting at Churubusco during the final stages of the advance on Mexico City in the summer of 1847.
*Left:* The ill-fated Mexican General Santa Anna, who was unequal to the task of halting the American advance on Mexico City.

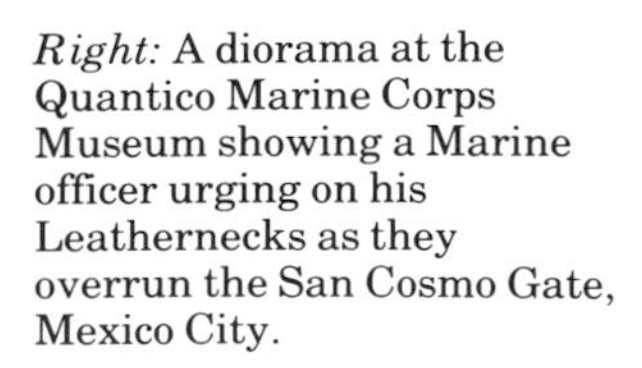

*Right:* A diorama at the Quantico Marine Corps Museum showing a Marine officer urging on his Leathernecks as they overrun the San Cosmo Gate, Mexico City.

ran up the Stars and Stripes. In the Treaty of Guadulupe Hidalgo, signed on 2 February 1848, the United States acquired 500,000 square miles of territory up to the Rio Grande, including California, Nevada, Utah and large tracts of Arizona, New Mexico, Colorado and Wyoming.

In honour of the Marines' contribution to victory, the citizens of Washington DC presented Commandant Henderson with a blue and gold standard bearing the motto: "From Tripoli to the Halls of Montezuma". Later, Marine service in the war was immortalized in the opening line of the Marines' hymn, "From the Halls of Montezuma to the shores of Tripoli".

**Prelude to the Civil War**

After the Mexican War, the Corps' establishment was cut back to its authorized peacetime strength of 1,224 enlisted men. This did not prevent the Marines from continuing to fulfil a worldwide role. During this period the Corps' expanding range of duties was linked to the United States' growth as a maritime power. Widening American commercial interests overseas frequently required a strong Navy presence to protect the lives and property of its citizens in troublespots torn by revolution or civil strife.

Marines were active in the suppression of

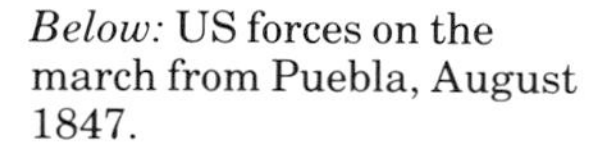

*Below:* US forces on the march from Puebla, August 1847.

the slave trade; the safeguarding of American interests in Nicaragua, Uruguay, Panama, Argentina, Fiji, Hong Kong and Shanghai; the establishment of diplomatic relations with Japan; and military action in China.

From the mid-nineteenth century, China was torn apart by the Taiping religious war, a conflict which claimed 20 million lives before it ran its 15-year course. Warring factions exploited the crisis to make regular raids on foreign property, and the Marines were frequently called upon to protect American citizens from the mob.

In September 1856 the situation near Canton boiled over when the four "Barrier Forts" on the Pearl River — bristling with 176 cannon and garrisoned by 4,000 troops — opened fire on American ships. A force of Marines, placed under the command of Captain John D. Simms, was conveyed up the Pearl by the Navy steam frigate *Jacinto* and two sloops-of-war, *Portsmouth* and *Levant.*

Simms' attack on the "Barrier Forts" began on 20 November. In three days' hard fighting the 287 Marines and sailors under his command captured the four Chinese strongholds, killed an estimated 500 of their defenders and routed an army of thousands. American losses were seven killed and 20 wounded.

Marines were also required to keep the peace at home. On 1 June 1857, elections in Washington DC were disrupted by an armed gang, the self-styled "Plug-Uglies", from Baltimore. The city police were overwhelmed and Mayor Magruder called for assistance from Marine Headquarters. The Marines and the "Plug-Uglies", now deploying a cannon, came face to face near Fifth and K streets. At that moment, a ramrod-straight, white-haired figure in civilian clothes and carrying a gold-headed cane stepped from the crowd and advanced on the gang from Baltimore. It was the 74-year-old Commandant Henderson, who placed himself squarely in front of the cannon's muzzle and calmly told the mob: "Men, you had better think twice before you fire this piece at the Marines."

One of the bolder "Plug-Uglies" thrust a pistol in Henderson's face, whereupon the Commandant seized the man in a vise-like grip and hauled him away to be placed under arrest. Then a ragged volley of shots was aimed at the Marines, who "poured in an answering fire". The rioters fled.

Two years later, on 6 January 1859, Henderson died while still in office. He had served as Commandant for 39 years, under ten Presidents and during the United States' turbulent early years of nationhood. There can be no better description for him than "The Grand Old Man of the Corps".

### The Civil War

In the autumn of 1859, the Marines were faced with a civil disturbance which dramatically reflected the tensions between the Northern and Southern states which were inexorably tearing the Union apart.

On the night of 16 October, the fanatical abolitionist John Brown seized the government arsenal at Harper's Ferry, Virginia, in a bid to raise the slaves in revolt in the Shenandoah Valley. The Navy Department ordered all available Marines in Washington to proceed at once to Harper's Ferry.

The new Commandant, Lieutenant-Colonel John Harris, despatched 86 men by rail from Corps HQ, led by Lieutenant Israel Greene. On the following day they reported to the overall commander of the operation at Harper's Ferry, Colonel Robert E. Lee, USA.

Brown had barricaded himself in the engine house of the arsenal, and on the morning of the 18th Greene was ordered to prepare a storming party. Following Brown's rejection of an ultimatum, delivered by Lieutenant J.E.B. Stuart, USA, Greene's men forced their way into the engine house. As Greene burst through the shattered doorway, Brown fired a shot, killing Marine

*Below:* Marines parade outside the barracks in Washington in 1861, on the eve of the Civil War.

Union Zouave units engage Confederate cavalry during First Bull Run, a battle noted for the general incompetence displayed by both sides. It was here that a Marine unit broke and ran.
*Below right:* Union forces cross the Potomac during the Civil War.

Private Luke Quinn. Before Brown could reload his carbine, Greene had cut him down with a sabre slash, which brought an end to all resistance. When Brown had recovered sufficiently from his wounds, Greene and his detachment escorted him to Charles Town. Subsequently he was tried for treason by the State of Virginia and hanged.

Following the election of Abraham Lincoln as President in November 1860, the battle lines were drawn up between the North and the seccessionist Southern States. On 18 February, Jefferson Davis was elected president of the Confederacy. Hostilities began on 12 April when shore batteries from Charleston, South Carolina, fired on Fort Sumter.

During the months preceding the outbreak of war, the divided loyalties felt by many officers had a debilitating effect on the United States' armed forces. As the prospect of secession by the South loomed, many officers from the South, or whose sympathies were strongly in favor of the South, resigned their commissions and offered their services to the Confederacy. The Army lost one-third of its officers (among them Robert E. Lee and J.E.B. Stuart) and the Navy one-sixth. In the Marine Corps, approximately half of its captains resigned, including officers of the caliber of George H. Terrett. Nearly two-thirds of the Corps' lieutenants, and half the second lieutenants, left the service, among them John D. Simms, the hero of the "Barrier Forts", and Israel Greene. With the exception of Major Henry B. Tyler, the field officers of the Corps remained loyal to the Union.

The Corps quickly appointed 38 new officers, but few of them had any previous military experience. In July 1861, Congress authorized an increase of 28 officers and 750 enlisted men for the Marines, raising the strength of the Corps to 3,000. Later in 1861, President Lincoln authorized two increases of 500 men, but at no time during the Civil War did the strength of the Corps exceed 3,900 men. (The Confederate Marine Corps reached a peak strength of 600 men.)

During the course of the war, the Marines' principal function was to serve as detachments on board ships of the Navy. The chances for action ashore were limited and confined to small bodies of men. Marines who served ashore did so either as part of a ship's landing force or directly assigned to the Union Army. Although the Civil War saw many gallant acts by Marines, it was not the Corps' finest hour.

An ominous note was struck at the First Battle of Bull Run on 21 July 1861, when an inexperienced Marine unit under the command of Major John G. Reynolds broke and ran after a series of attacks by Confederate riflemen and cavalry commanded by Colonel J.E.B. Stuart. Any criticism of these raw troops must be tempered by the general incompetence displayed by both sides at Bull Run, a battle cuttingly described by the German commander Helmuth von Moltke as little more than "two armed mobs pursuing each other".

Clearly the Marines were better suited to the amphibious operations conducted along the Southern coast as part of the Union's strategy of blockading the Confederacy's ports. In August 1861 Marines attached to the ships *Minnesota*, *Cumberland*, *Susquehanna* and *Wabash* took part in the

capture of Fort Clark and Fort Hatteras in North Carolina, closing the Hatteras Inlet to British blockade runners and Confederate privateers, who were using it as a base from which to harry Union shipping. In October–November 1861, a 300-man Marine battalion, under the command of Major John G. Reynolds, was earmarked for an amphibious operation against Port Royal, South Carolina, planned by Naval Flag Officer Samuel F. DuPont, commander of the South Atlantic Blockade Squadron. However, the Marines took no part in the action as their unseaworthy transport, the sidewheeler *Governor*, foundered in rough weather on the way to Port Royal. After two more equally abortive missions, the amphibious battalion was disbanded and the men assigned to their ships' detachments.

On 11 May 1862 the scuttling of the Confederate warship *Virginia* (the refitted

*Above:* Petersburg, Virginia, an important supply base for General Robert E. Lee's Confederate Army of North Virginia. At the end of the Civil War it endured a 10-month siege. Lee's defence was a tactical masterpiece, and he was forced to abandon Petersburg only a week before the surrender of the Army of North Virginia at Appomattox on 9 April 1865.

*Merrimack*) during the evacuation of Norfolk opened up the James River. Four days later Union warships approached Drewry's Bluff on the James, about eight miles from Richmond. Here they came under fire from Confederate shore batteries stationed on the bluff. The *Galena* was returning fire when a direct hit caused a violent explosion. Marine Corporal John Mackie rallied the survivors, carried off the dead and wounded and got three of the ship's guns back in action. These acts of heroism made him the first Marine to win the Medal of Honor. By the end of the war he had been emulated by 17 of his fellow Marines.

Nevertheless, frustration rather than derring-do was the keynote of the Marines' war. In August 1863, Marines under the command of Major Zeilin were tasked with assisting Union forces in the attack on Fort Wagner, South Carolina. Fired with enthusiasm, Zeilin attempted (unsuccessfully) to expand his 300-strong battalion into a regiment and instil in his men a set of basic amphibious tactics. The results were not encouraging, and Zeilin's Marines were left to kick their heels. Zeilin was replaced by Lieutenant-Colonel John Reynolds, who reduced the regiment to a battalion and turned it over to Captain Charles G. McCawley. In September, Marines were attached to the expeditionary force assembled by Rear-Admiral John A. Dahlgren for an attack on Fort Sumter. The assault was a dismal failure; 44 of the Marine party of 150 men were killed, captured or wounded. The battalion was taken out of combat for rest and recuperation, but suffered further losses from disease and was broken up in 1864.

The demoralized Commandant, John Harris, died on 12 May and was succeeded by Major Zeilin. On the previous day, Secretary of State Gideon Welles had retired all Marine officers who ranked senior to the new Commandant.

By the end of 1864 the only Southern port which continued to defy the Union was Wilmington, North Carolina. Entrance to the port was by the appropriately named Cape Fear River, guarded by the 44 large-caliber cannon of Fort Fisher and over 1,000 troops.

The first attempt to take Fort Fisher was a fiasco engineered by a bumbling amateur soldier, Major-General Benjamin F. Butler, a politician from Massachusetts. The Union's General-in-Chief, Ulysses S. Grant, replaced Butler with a professional, General A.H. Terry, leading a force of 8,500 men under the overall command of Rear-Admiral David D. Porter.

Porter devised a plan of attack which bordered on the reckless. Following a "softening-up" bombardment from his

*Left:* Major-General Benjamin F. Butler, the incompetent amateur soldier who bungled the first attempt to take Fort Fisher.

warships, 1,600 of Porter's seamen and 400 Marines would make a frontal attack on Fort Fisher while Terry's troops launched the main thrust from the rear. Throwing seamen armed with cutlasses and pistols — and covered only by Marine riflemen — against the walls of a heavily defended fort displayed an optimism which one of Porter's subordinates characterised as "sheer murderous madness".

Amid scenes of great confusion, the seamen and the Marines were landed before Fort Fisher on the afternoon of 15 January 1865. The Marines arrived too late to support the bluejackets, who were mown down by the fort's defenders. Ordered into the attack themselves, they suffered a similar fate. Combined casualties were 309 dead and wounded. Nevertheless, the diversion served its purpose and Terry's troops stormed Fort Fisher from the rear. But the bloody price of victory triggered off a furious controversy over Porter's tactics, in which the Admiral defended himself with the improbable assertion that, "Had the covering party of Marines performed their duty, every one of the enemy would have been killed".

The furore over the attack on Fort Fisher did little to promote the cause of the Marines as an independent force specifically trained and equipped to undertake amphibious operations. The Civil War came to an end on 9 April 1865 without the Corps having found a basic role which would dispel the clouds still hanging over its future. Moreover, its marginal influence on the course of the war can be gauged from its casualty figures of 148 killed in combat and 312 dead from other causes. The combined losses of North and South from all causes are estimated at approximately 520,000 men.

*Below:* The bombardment and assault on Fort Fisher, 15 January 1865. The high casualties suffered by the Marines and bluejackets in the action led to a political furore which did little to enhance the reputation of the Corps.

## From Korea to the Philippines

The Marine Corps emerged from the Civil War with its morale and reputation at a low ebb. In the summer of 1866, the House of Representatives considered a resolution for the abolition of the Corps and its transfer to the Army. Marine Commandant Zeilin mounted a fierce political counter-offensive, enlisting support from the Navy. In February 1867 the resolution was thrown out by the House Naval Affairs Committee, which recommended that the Marines' "organisation as a separate corps should be preserved and strengthened . . . [and] that its commanding officer shall hold the rank of brigadier-general".

Service at sea continued to be the primary role of the Marines, although the advent of steam ships meant that they were no longer stationed as sharpshooters on the fighting tops. The Marines serving on foreign sea duty after the Civil War were soon re-acquainting themselves with far-flung parts of the world in the role of peacekeepers and protectors of American lives and property: in the 1860s, small-scale landings were made in Formosa, Japan and Uruguay; in the 1870s Marines went ashore in Mexico, Colombia and the Hawaiian islands; in the 1880s it was the turn of Egypt, Korea, Haiti, Samoa and the Hawaiian islands; followed in the 1890s by

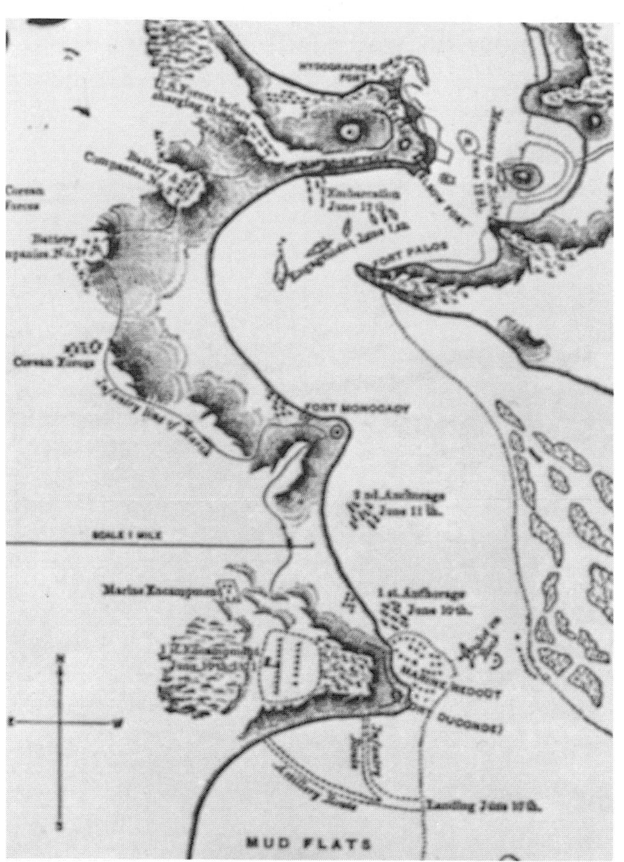


*Right:* A contemporary sketch map of the American operations in Korea in 1871, including the positions taken by the Marines and bluejackets.
*Opposite, top:* Marine headgear of the late 1870s. Clockwise from top left: field officer, full dress; company officer, fatigues; all officers, undress pattern; full dress, enlisted men; fatigue, enlisted men; undress, bandsmen; full dress, company officer.
*Opposite, bottom:* A Marine racing crew pose proudly for the camera aboard USS *Olympia*.

Argentina, Chile, Korea, North China, the isthmus of Panama and Nicaragua.

In most cases, the mere presence of the Marines was sufficient to counter a threat to American interests. But there were exceptions. In the summer of 1871, the American Minister in China, Frederick Low, was despatched on a peace mission to Korea, whose people had already displayed their xenophobia by massacring the crew of an American ship, *General Sherman*, which had gone aground in the Han River.

Low arrived on the west coast of Korea in the latter part of May on board the *Colorado*, flagship of the Asiatic Fleet, accompanied by four other ships under the overall command of Rear-Admiral John Rodgers. Arriving off the mouth of the Han River, Rodgers sent a small scouting party upstream to find an approach to the Korean capital, Seoul. As it worked its way up the channel, the party came under fire from one of five forts which guarded the lower reaches of the Han River.

The Koreans showed no inclination to apologize for this incident, and ten days later Rodgers and Low set about mounting a punitive expedition. A force of bluejackets and a Marine brigade of four officers and 105 enlisted men, led by Marine Captain McLane Tilton, were ordered to capture the Korean forts. This was made no easier by the Marines' armament of obsolescent breech-loading muskets. In contrast, the garrisons of the Han River forts were armed with modern repeaters.

The operation began on 10 June with an assault across a mud flat against the smallest of the forts. Cowed by a naval bombardment, the defenders offered little resistance. A second fort was captured with equal ease on the following day. Tilton then turned his attention to the heavily fortified "Citadel", which had to be approached over mountainous terrain which concealed Korean riflemen. The final assault was pressed home under heavy fire up a 150-ft hillside. After a fierce hand-to-hand fight, the enemy flag was torn down by Marine Corporal Charles Brown and Private Hugh Purvis, both of whom were subsequently awarded the Medal of Honor. Four more Medals of Honor were awarded for this action, in which the Marines accounted for over 200 Koreans at a cost of only two casualties. Their opponents must have been very poor marksmen. Thereafter the Koreans prudently refrained from hostile acts against Americans.

On 11 July 1882, the British fleet bombarded the Egyptian city of Alexandria after a serious outbreak of rioting by *fellah* mobs against foreign influence in the region. With large sections of Alexandria ablaze, 60 blue jackets and 73 Marines from the European Squadron, under the Command of Captain H.C. Cochrane, were landed to assist in restoring order, prevent the spread of fires and protect the American Consulate, which had thus far escaped serious damage. Cochrane, a brilliant officer and legendary martinet, quickly swept through the streets around the Consulate, establishing a riot-free zone and earning these words of praise from the British commander Lord Charles Beresford, whose arrival with a force of 4,000 men had brought the uprising to an end: "To your smart, faithful force great credit is due . . . I have represented these facts to my government."

Much nearer home, the Marines were called in to restore order in the strategically sentitive region of Panama when in 1885 its population rebelled against its Colombian rulers. In April of that year two battalions of Marines were sent to Panama City and formed into a brigade under Colonel Charles Heywood, the first time in its history that the Marines had operated as a brigade. By the last week in April the Marines had secured and maintained military control over

Panama City, handing over to Colombian regulars on 30 April. The Marines had now gained a well-earned reputation for the efficient execution of such operations. When the captain of a British warship at anchor in Panama City's harbor was informed of the arrival of the Marines, he said, "Tranquillity is then assured".

The enforced tranquillity of Stateside garrison duty was often relieved by such law-and-order assignments as assisting the authorities in the destruction of illegal distilleries and the enforcing of the revenue laws. In the spring of 1877, two battalions of Marines assisted the Army in suppressing labor riots in Baltimore and Philiadelphia which flared up during a major railroad strike.

Throughout this period, the eighth Commandant of the Corps, Charles G. McCawley, worked hard to improve its status. McCawley supervized the drawing-up of the first standardized table of organization for the Corps; introduced the first mass-produced uniforms; reorganized and reinvigorated the Headquarters Marine Corps cadre; and improved career prospects for non-commissioned and enlisted men. He also succeeded in drawing Marine Corps officers from the ranks of Naval Academy graduates; between 1881 and 1897 all 50 officers who entered the Corps were Academy graduates.

One of McCawley's less popular measures was his ban on the sale of beer in Marine canteens, and his somewhat quixotic encouragement of a group calling itself the Marine Temperance Union. McCawley also provided an imprtant footnote to musical history when in 1880 he appointed 26-year-old John Philip Sousa as leader of the Marine Band. Under Sousa's inspiring leadership, the Band became one of the world's finest musical groups.

McCawley's reforming work was continued by Colonel Charles Heywood, who succeeded him as Commandant in 1891. Heywood took an important step in the further professionalization of the Corps, creating the School of Application in Washington, forerunner of the Marines Basic Schools system. Under his leadership, the number of Marine bases increased from 12 to 21; one of them, located at Port Royal, South Carolina, was to become Parris Island, the most important training area for Marines on the eastern seaboard. In training, Heywood placed great emphasis on target practice and

*Top:* Marines and seamen drawn up for inspection aboard USS *Essex* in 1888. *Above:* Marines at bayonet drill, c. 1890. In the background is the receiving ship USS *New Hampshire*.

marksmanship. In the wider political sphere, he skilfully preserved the integrity of the Corps against renewed pressure to combine the Marines with the Army's regiments of artillery.

## War with Spain

The Spanish—American War of 1898 was once described as a "glorious national picnic", which nevertheless signalled the emergence of the United States as an imperial power. The immediate *casus belli* was an incident in which the US battleship *Maine* exploded and sank in Havana Harbor, Cuba, on 15 February 1898, with the loss of 238 sailors and 28 Marines. (In all probability, the explosion was caused by unstable ammunition.)

American public opinion — cynically manipulated by the newspaper baron William Randolph Hearst — was already incensed by the brutal manner in which the Spanish had put down the Cuban insurrection of 1895–8, and war was declared on 25 April on a floodtide of emotion.

There were two theaters of war: the Spanish possessions in the Caribbean (Cuba and Puerto Rico) and the Philippines. On 1 May, Commodore George Dewey's Asiatic Squadron annihilated Admiral Montojo's fleet in Manila Bay. On 3 May, Dewey landed a contingent of Marines from the USS *Baltimore*, under the command of Lieutenant Dion Williams, to occupy the Spanish naval station at Cavite. The Marines were the first to land on Spanish territory and raise the American flag. Manila capitulated after the arrival of American Army troops at the end of June. Nine days earlier, Marines from Charleston had landed unopposed on the Spanish island of Guam. The Pacific phase of the war was over.

At home the Marines were preparing for a landing on Cuba. On 16 April, Commandant Heywood had been instructed to organize a Marine battalion to serve in Cuba. With great drive and efficiency, the Marines assembled 647 men, organized into four infantry companies and an artillery battery, under the command of Lieutenant-Colonel Robert W. Huntington. Heywood personally oversaw the equipping of the force: "... [the battalion] was supplied with all the equipment and necessities for field service under conditions prevailing in Cuba, including mosquito netting, woolen and linen clothing, heavy and light weight underwear, three months' supply of provisions, wheelbarrows, pushcarts, pick-axes, shovels, and a full supply of medical stores".

Within a few weeks the Marine battalion had been transported by the *Panther*, commanded by Commodore G.C. Reiter, to Key West in Florida, there to await orders.

It soon became clear that Commander Schley's Flying Squadron needed a shore base to support the blockade of the Spanish fleet in Santiago. Huntington's Marines were ordered to seize Guantanamo Bay, about 40 miles east of Santiago, as a coaling station. Intelligence reports indicated that there were about 8,000 Spanish troops in the area. On the afternoon of 10 June, Huntington's battalion was landed from *Panther*, becoming the first American troops to establish a beach-head on Cuban soil.

The landing was unopposed, which was just as well as the prickly Commodore Reiter initially refused to send ashore the Marines' small-arms ammunition, on the grounds that he needed it as ballast for his ship. He was quickly brought into line by the senior Naval officer in the area, Commander Bowman McCalla, captain of the cruiser *Marblehead*, who ordered the immediate landing of 50,000 rounds of small-arms ammunition. The grateful Marines named their beach-head

*Above:* The wreck of the USS *Maine* in Havana habor, Cuba. Twenty-eight Marines died in the explosion, which is now thought to have been caused by the spontaneous detonation of unstable ammunition. But the Spanish took the blame, and in the ensuing war the United States took the Philippines, the Pacific Island of Guam and Peurto Rico.

*Left:* Commodore George Dewey, whose Asiatic Squadron annihilated the Spanish fleet in Manila Bay.

*Above:* The Battle of Manila Bay.

bivouac Camp McCalla.

On the afternoon of 11 June, the Spanish roused themselves from their torpor, attacking a Marine outpost and killing two men. After three days of desultory fighting, Huntington decided to cut off the Spanish water-supply, which was located at a fortified well in the village of Cuzco, six miles southwest of Camp McCalla. On the morning of 15 June, two rifle companies, under the command of Captain George F. Elliott (later the 10th Commandant of the Marine Corps) and 50 Cubans marched on Cuzco. Supporting fire for the attack was provided by the warship *Dolphin*. However, its salvoes began to creep dangerously close to the Marines. Disaster was averted by the initiative and coolness of Marine Sergeant John H. Quick, who improvised a semaphore flag and, with enemy fire whistling about his ears, redirected the *Dolphin*'s fire on to the enemy position. The author Stephen Crane was at Cuzco as a war correspondent and left this memorable thumbnail sketch of the gallant Quick: "I saw Quick betray only one sign of emotion. As he swung his clumsy flag to and fro, an end of it once caught on a cactus plant. He looked annoyed."

Victory in the action at Cuzco dealt a severe blow to the already fragile Spanish morale. On 22 June, 17,000 US Army troops under General Shafter landed at Santiago, defeating General Linares' 35,000-strong army at San Juan on 1 July. Two days later, Admiral Cervera's attempt to break out of Santiago harbor was thwarted, and the city surrendered on 17 July. Fighting continued in Puerto Rico, where General Miles had landed at the head of an expeditionary force on 4 August. On 10 December, hostilities were brought to an end by the Treaty of Paris. Spain relinquished sovereignty over Cuba and ceded Puerto Rico and the Pacific island of Guam to the United States, which also acquired the Philippines at the knock-down price of $20 million.

The war was a turning point for the Marine Corps. The United States had gained a quick victory, but most "picnics" are rather better organized than the American campaign in 1898, which was notable for its chaotic staff work. Army troops sweltered in the tropical

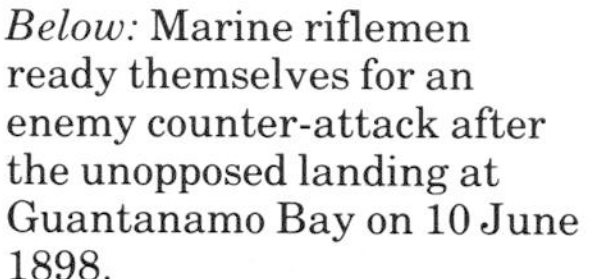

*Below:* Marine riflemen ready themselves for an enemy counter-attack after the unopposed landing at Guantanamo Bay on 10 June 1898.

*Above:* The first picture taken of Marines — and feline mascot — on the island of Guam.

heat in woolen uniforms; at least half of them contracted yellow fever and enteric disease. The Marines, however, were a shining exception — well-organized, well-prepared, quick to respond when the call came, and considerably fitter than their Army colleagues. Only two percent of the Marines personnel suffered from enteric fever, and none of them contracted yellow fever.

On 3 March 1899, Congress approved a bill calling for a permanent Marine Corps consisting of 201 officers and 6,062 men, a 100 percent increase over its strength in 1896. In the longer term, the success of the operation at Guantanamo encouraged the development of amphibious tactics and a detailed consideration of the Corps' role in seizing and holding advanced bases.

As the newly-formed Navy Board acknowledged in 1900, the Marine Corps was "best adapted and most available for immediate and sudden call" in such operations. It directed the Corps to select the personnel and develop the techniques for this task, and by 1902 an Advanced Base battalion was in training.

In July 1910 an Advanced Base school was established at New London, Connecticut (it was moved to Philadelphia a year later). Although principally aimed at the training of officers in the Advanced Base concept, its first class consisted of 40 enlisted men. By 1914 the Marines' combat-ready element was centered on the Advanced Base Force, a brigade-sized combined-arms formation whose prime function was to assault and defend bases for the US Navy.

Before the creation of the Advanced Base Force, each Marine barracks had its own "rookie squad" which gave rudimentary training to new recruits. However, the Advanced Base Force needed men with a standard level of training, and the solution was provided by the setting-up of small Marine recruit depots at the larger Naval stations. The search for greater economy and efficiency soon led the Corps to consolidate all its recruit training at two bases, one on each coast. The Marine Barracks, Parris Island, South Carolina, established its attached

*Above:* A Marine firing line in action against insurgents in the Philippines in 1901.

recruit depot in 1915. A similar depot was set up at Mare Island, California; the latter moved to San Diego in 1923.

In 1914 the Advanced Base concept was tested when trouble flared with Mexico after Washington learned that Germany was about to supply arms to the insurgent General Huerta. On 21 April, President Wilson ordered naval forces to land and seize the customs house at Vera Cruz. Sailors and Marines went ashore that day, and by 24 April Vera Cruz had been pacified. On the 28th, Army troops occupied the area. They were supported by a Marine brigade of 3,000 officers and men, which remained in Vera Cruz, under Army command, until November 1914.

*Below:* Marines patrol the tropical jungle near Olongapo, Luzon, during operations against Filipino guerrillas in 1900.

### "He Served on Samar"

The Marine Corps' involvement with the Philippines did not end with the war of 1898. By 1900, Filipino agitation for independence led to the stationing in the Philippines of four Marine battalions, comprising two rifle regiments and two artillery companies, a total of 58 officers and 1,547 enlisted men.

The Marines' service in the Philippines was characterized by long periods of boredom, familiar to everyone who has endured garrison duty, and short spells of savage fighting. Among the Corps' fiercest adversaries were the Moros of Samar Island. In September 1901 450 Moros had surprised and wiped out US 9th Infantry's C Company as it sat down to breakfast, making off with all their rifles and 28,000 rounds of ammunition.

On 24 October 1901, a battalion of Marines landed on Samar, under the command of a brilliant, peppery officer, Major Littleton W.T. Waller. In a month of hard fighting — during which no quarter was given by Waller's men — the Moros were driven deep

into the jungle and then overwhelmed in their stronghold in the cliffs of the Basey River.

With peace restored on Samar, General Jacob M. Smith, USA, ordered Major Waller to reconnoiter a telegraph route from Basey to Lanang. Waller's 52-mile march through the jungle began on 28 December, and quickly turned into a nightmare. Boats and provisions were lost in treacherous rivers; bearers mutinied; ten of the 50 Marines died of to fever and exhaustion, and one of them went mad. After emerging from the bush on 15 January 1902, Waller set up a drum-head court-martial, which tried and then executed 11 of the Filipino bearers, a drastic disciplinary measure which resulted in Waller being hauled before an Army court-martial on 11 counts of murder. Waller was eventually acquitted, but a shadow was cast over his subsequent career and probably prevented him from becoming Commandant of the Corps. Nevertheless, his jungle march became a Marine Corps legend. Whenever one of Waller's men was present at a brigade mess, the toast would be raised: "Stand, gentlemen. He served on Samar".

### From China to the Caribbean

In the summer of 1900, the Boxer Rebellion burst upon China. Much of its ferocious energy was channeled against foreign influence in China, and the legations of the Western nations, alarmed for their physical safety, requested military protection from their respective governments.

Marines were quickly on the spot. Late on the night of 29 May, a detachment of Marines and sailors from the US warships *Newark* and *Oregon* arrived in Tientsin, some 80 miles south of Peking. Among those who watched them arrive was a young engineer named Herbert Hoover, who later recalled: "I do not remember a more satisfying musical performance than the bugles of the American Marines entering the settlement playing 'There'll be a Hot Time in the Old Town Tonight'."

The Marines were shortly followed by British, Austrian, German, French, Italian, Japanese and Russian landing forces. Two days later a Marine detachment led by Captain John T. ("Handsome Jack") Myers and Captain Newt H. Hall, formed part of the international force which set out by train from Tientsin for Peking, where they marched to the American Legation through dense crowds of silent and hostile Chinese.

On 5 June the rail lines between Tientsin and Peking were torn up by the Boxers. Five days later an international relief force, commanded by Vice-Admiral Sir Edward Seymour, RN, set out to repair the rail line and reach Peking. Harassing attacks by the Boxers brought Seymour's force to a halt 25 miles short of Peking and then forced it back to the outskirts of Tientsin, where it was bottled up in the Hsi-ku arsenal. At the end of June a fresh international force, including 138 Marines commanded by Major Waller, lifted the siege of the arsenal and then joined Seymour in crushing the Boxers in the area,

*Below:* Members of the International Relief Force pose for the camera in Peking. They include Japanese and British infantry, French Chasseurs Alpin, men of the German East Asia Division, Russian Cossacks, men of the British Royal Navy and Marines, Russian sailors and — seated on the right — US Marines.

*Top:* A stylized contemporary rendering of the street fighting in Peking between rampaging Boxers and appropriately jut-jawed Marines.
*Above:* A battalion of Marines parades in Peking's Forbidden City after the defeat of the Boxers.

which was pacified by the end of July.

In Peking, the siege of the legations began on 20 June. At the beginning of August an international force of approximately 18,000 men — including a fresh regiment of Marines under Major William P. Biddle — began its march on Peking, eliminating hostile Chinese forces on the way. They reached the outskirts of Peking on 13 August and raised the siege of the legations on the same day. On the 14th the Allied force made its final assault on the Imperial City, driving the Boxers out. By the end of the month all organized resistance had collapsed. The Marines remained in Peking until the end of September, when they returned to the Philippines.

In the years leading up to World War I, the Marines became increasingly embroiled in the turbulent politics of the Caribbean and Central America, both of which were, and remain, vital to the hemispheric interests of the United States. In the winter of 1903, Marines landed in Panama, whose people were in open revolt against their Colombian rulers. The stakes were high, as the United States was in the middle of negotiating with Colombia for the right to dig a canal across the isthmus of its Panamanian province. The Marines restored order and forestalled intervention by Colombian troops. In the words of President Theodore Roosevelt, who had personally ordered the operation: "I took the Canal zone and let Congress debate, and while the debate goes on, the Canal does also." Things were simpler in the days before Watergate and Irangate. The United States quicky recognized Panamanian independence, the price of which was at treaty with the US government which gave it the sovereign right to a canal zone 10 miles wide and the right to keep order within Panama.

When mob violence erupted in Cuba in

August 1906, following fraudulent elections, two battalions of Marines were despatched to assist President Tomas Estrada Palma in restoring order. Within a few weeks there was an entire brigade of Marines in Cuba, totalling 97 officers and 2,795 enlisted men. Shortly afterwards, President Roosevelt ordered the formation of the Army of Cuban Pacification, in which Marines served under the US Army's jurisdiction, remaining in Cuba until 1909. Renewed outbreaks of unrest in May 1912 resulted in the despatch of 1st Provisional Regiment of Marines to Cuba, reinforced by a second regiment which arrived at Guantanamo at the beginning of June. Under the command of Colonel Lincoln Karmany, a provisional brigade was formed which restored order in 26 towns in the Santiago and Guantanamo region until the situation was stabilized in July. Thereafter they handed over their responsibilities to the civilian authorities, pulled back to Guantanamo and then sailed for the United States.

Similar operations were undertaken in Nicaragua, following the outbreak of revolution in 1909 and civil war in 1912. High on the list of Marine priorities was the protection of the substantial American fruit, lumber and mining interests in Nicaragua. In 1912 a Marine regiment was sent to the Dominican Republic — whose economy was wholly dependent on the United States — when political unrest threatened to topple the government. On this occasion, the Marines' presence in their ships in the harbor was sufficient to restore order, but in 1916 a civil war led to the stationing of a brigade of Marines in the Dominican Republic, where they remained until 1925.

In neighbouring Haiti, what passed for politics was a blood-drenched *danse macabre*, which in July 1915 erupted into a sanguinary paroxysm disgusting even by Haiti's grisly standards. On 28 July, a detachment of Marines and sailors from the USS *Washington* went ashore at the Haitian capital, Port au Prince. The next day they were reinforced by a company of Marines rushed from Cuba. Later the Marine force on Haiti was augmented by 2nd Marine Regiment, 1st Marine Regiment and Headquarters, 1st Marine Brigade, the latter commanded by Colonel Waller. Serving with brigade headquarters was a young Marine Lieutenant, Alexander Archer Vandegrift.

In a three-month campaign, the Marines dealt with the principal troublemakers on Haiti, a group of lawless guerrillas known as the Cacos. Once a relative degree of order had been restored, the Marines on Haiti devoted their energies to training Haitian officials in the business of government and directing such civic works as road-building, communications and education. The gendarmerie was staffed and trained by Marines and was gradually transformed into an all-native Haitian force. The Marines were to remain in Haiti until August 1934.

*Left:* President Theodore Roosevelt, who in 1908 ordered Marine detachments to be removed from ships of the US Navy and threatened to reduce the Corps to little more than a naval station guard. Congress stepped in to preserve the Corps' integrity, much to the fury of the mercurial Roosevelt.

*Above:* Marines comes ashore at Port-au-Prince in the early stages of the Corps' involvement with the chaotic fortunes of Haiti.

# 2: RETREAT, HELL! WE JUST GOT HERE!

## World War One

On 1 June 1916, a small combined force of US Marines and sailors went into action against Dominican insurgents in the town of Puerto Plata. At the same time on the other side of the Atlantic, the British Army was suffering the greatest one-day loss in its entire history — the 60,000 casualties it sustained on the first day of the Battle of the Somme.

The Somme became a symbol of the new kind of war which held Europe in a paralysing grip. On the Western Front, strategy was placed in a straitjacket by the domination of "bullet, spade and barbed wire". Movement had been replaced by mud and the machine-gun. In 1916, an average of 56,000 British soldiers were dying every month.

President Wilson had been elected in 1916 on the slogan "He kept us out of the war". But German unrestricted submarine warfare, and an attempt to push Mexico into action against the United States, forced the President's hand. On 6 April 1917 the United States entered the war as an "associated power", a status which gave her armies a measure of independence from the French and British high commands.

However, in 1917 the US Army was tiny in comparison with the millions locked in combat in Europe. In A.J.P. Taylor's memorable phrase, America's declaration of war was only a "promissory note for the future". It brought handicaps rather than immediate help to the Allies. Tens of thousands of men would have to be conscripted and trained. New munitions factories would have to be built. Tanks, artillery, and even rifles, would have to be provided by the British and French. The Allies would have to hold on until the United States could bring its enormous economic resources to bear and make its presence felt on the battlefields of France.

In April 1917 the Marine Corps strength was 462 officers, 49 warrant officers and 13,213 enlisted men. By December 1918, it had risen to 75,000 officers and men (including the newly-formed Marine Corps Reserve), of whom some 30,000 saw service on the Western Front. Statistically a drop in the ocean, they nevertheless played a part

*Left:* Marines advancing through a wood shredded by shellfire during the Meuse-Argonne offensive in 1918.

out of all proportion to their numbers.

In June 1917 the first US troops were shipped to Europe under General John J. Pershing, commander of the American Expeditionary Force. Among them were 5th Regiment of Marines, composed of 70 officers and 2,689 enlisted men, completely organized and ready for active service. They made up one-fifth of the first American force to land.

Having arrived in France, 5th Marines were forced to champ at the bit behind the lines, broken up to perform labor and guard duties while inferior units were sent up to the front. This enforced inactivity was in part due to Pershing's doubts about the Marines' ability to adapt to conventional infantry operations, a scepticism which was soon to prove unfounded.

By February 1918, 6th Regiment of Marines and 6th Machine-Gun Battalion had arrived in France. They combined with 5th Marines to form 4th Brigade of Marines, part of 2nd Infantry Division, with a strength of 258 officers and 8,211 enlisted men. They were later joined by 5th Brigade of Marines, with a similar strength.

In March 1918 the Marines were introduced to the front line, in a quiet sector south of Verdun on the Meuse River. They were pulled out for further training after 53 days, having suffered 872 casualties. It was not long before they were thrown into the cauldron of war.

*Left:* General Pershing, commander of the American Expeditionary force, is welcomed by enthusiastic French crowds.
*Far left, top:* A vivid recruiting poster with a famous call to arms.
*Far left, bottom:* They answered the call: applicants arriving at the recruit depot, Parris Island, South Carolina, in 1917.

In the winter of 1917, Germany's warlords, Field-Marshal Hindenburg and General Ludendorff, decided that they must clinch victory before American intervention irrevocably tipped the balance against them. In March 1918 Ludendorff launched a series of massive offensives: on the Somme, penetrating to within 75 miles of Paris; in the Lys–Aisne sector in April–May; and in the Noyon–Marne sector in June–July. On 27 May, 14 German divisions broke through on the Aisne, achieving an advance of ten miles in a day, a distance unequalled since the first weeks of the war in August 1914. Thirty-six hours later the Germans had reached the Meuse at Château-Thierry and were within 40 miles of Paris.

French reserves thrown in to stem the German tide were reinforced by the US 2nd and 3rd Divisions. The sector assigned to 4th Brigade of Marines was Belleau Wood, three miles north of Château-Thierry and at the tip of the German advance. Here 1,200 troops of the battle-hardened 461st Imperial German Infantry had established a formidable defensive position in a square mile of rocky woodland.

The fight for Belleau Wood lasted 20 days. The Marines quickly earned the respect of the Germans with the quality of their marksmanship at ranges of up to 800yds. But much of the fighting was at close quarters as the Marines attacked and the Germans counter-attacked through the stony outcrops and shattered tree-stumps of Belleau Wood. The final enemy strongpoints were neutralized by 3rd Battalion, 5th Marines, on 24 June. The casualty lists reflected the fierceness of the fighting. Two attacks by 1st Battalion, 5th Marines, on 6 June resulted in nearly 1,500 Marines dead or wounded, losses in a day's fighting not exceeded by the Marines until the battle for Tarawa in 1943. In honor of the Corps, the French renamed the wood "Bois de la Brigade de Marines".

*Above:* Marine Major-General John A. Lejeune, who assumed comand of US 2nd Division in July 1918, becoming the first Marine officer to command an Army division. After World War One, Lejeune became a distinguished Commandant of the Marine Corps.

*Above:* Marines pause in a French village on their way up to the front at the end of May 1918. They were shortly to face their first major test at Belleau Wood.
*Opposite, top:* Figures in a bleak landscape; Marine machine-gunners on maneuvers in the winter of 1917-18.
*Opposite, bottom:* Marines man 3-in guns abord the battleship *Pennsylvania* in World War One.

More significantly, the action at Belleau Wood, and 2nd Division's counter-attack at Château-Thierry, had halted the German drive on Paris and provided a vital moral tonic for the war-weary British and French. It also marked an important moment in the Marine Corps' history, demonstrating its effectiveness when employed in numbers against seasoned infantry. Above all, it provided the Marines with an arena in which to display the daring and *esprit de corps* of an élite formation. These fighting qualities were succinctly summed-up on 5 June as 4th Brigade moved up to the front through roads clogged with refugees and demoralized French units heading fast in the opposite direction. When a French officer suggested to Marine Captain Lloyd W. Williams that his men should join the retreat, the American replied, "Retreat, hell! We just got here!"

The Germans had exhausted themselves with their triple offensive, and the Allies now possessed the advantage of 300,000 American troops arriving every month. In July—August 1918, the Allied Supreme Commander, Marshal Foch, launched a limited series of counter-attacks — the British in the north, the French in the center and the Americans at the southern end of the line near Verdun — with the aim of squeezing the Germans out of the three huge salients they had driven into the Allied front in the spring and early summer.

On 18 July, Marines spearheaded the counter-offensive against the rail center at Soissons on the northern shoulder of the Marne salient. Casualties were heavy. On the first day of fighting, 2nd Battalion, 6th Marines, lost 50 percent of its men in 30 minutes. Overall casualties in pinching out the salient — a maneuver much favored by World War One commanders and much disliked by their men — were 1,972. Shortly after the Marines established themselves in positions overlooking the Soissons–Château-Thierry road, Marine General John A. Lejeune took command of 2nd Division, becoming the first Marine officer to command an Army division in combat.

In September the focus shifted to the Saint Mihiel salient, jutting across the Meuse between Verdun and Nancy, a thorn in the Allied side and a constant threat to movement in the Champagne area since 1914. The removal of this ugly feature was to be the preliminary to the final offensive against the Hindenburg Line — the immensely strong line of defenses built along an arc running through Lens–Noyon–Rheims — and the first battle of the war to be

fought independently by US 1st Army.

On 12 September seven American divisions — each more than twice the size of their French and German equivalents — attacked the two sides of the salient while the French nibbled away at its nose. Marine 4th Brigade was held back as a reserve. The attack caught the Germans in the middle of a tactical withdrawal, and I Corps, under General Liggett, USA, achieved its second-day objectives within a matter of hours. But the opportunity was not fully exploited and all but 4,000 of the 50,000 Germans threatened with encirclement slipped through the closing jaws of I and IV Corps. The Marines were then given the task of reducing the fortifications which screened the Hindenburg Line, and the salient was finally cleared by 16 September. Marine casualties were light, with 132 killed and 574 wounded. Some of the sharpest fighting was seen in the Bois de la Montagne by 2nd Battalion, 6th

*Above:* An artist's impression of Marines storming German machine-gun posts at the height of the battle for Belleau Wood.
*Opposite:* A wounded Marine is given first aid treatment before being stretchered to the rear.

Marines, who overran positions held by a substantial enemy force and then repelled four counter-attacks supported by artillery and gas.

The Germans had now abandoned the three salients they had carved out since March, but nowhere was their line broken. What had snapped was their morale and their faith in victory. The Allies launched a renewed counter-offensive on 26 September. The vital stroke was to be delivered by the Americans in the Argonne, with the aim of destroying the Germans' lateral line of communications running behind the Hindenburg Line.

After St Mihiel, 2nd Division had joined the French Fourth Army. Initially, considerable pressure had been exerted on General Lejeune to allow the Division to be broken up to provide shock troops for a number of French units. Lejeune succeeded in preserving the Division's integrity, and it was tasked with seizing Blanc Mont Ridge, on the heights of the Meuse, a primary position in the German line against which the French had been vainly battering for several weeks. The assault on Blanc Mont began on 3 October and, in two days of exceptionally hard fighting, 5th and 6th Marines, in a co-ordinated assault with an Army brigade of 2nd Division, overran the enemy positions. This action won the Marines their third citation from the French Army, earning them the right to carry the Croix de Guerre on their colors. The price of this honor was 2,538 casualties; in one company only 23 men remained of the 250 who had begun the battle.

The Marines ended the war serving with US 1st Army in the northern sector of the Argonne forest, punching their way through the Hindenburg Line. On 1 November, 4th Brigade took the last major strongpoint in the Line — "Freya Stellung" — after a lightning advance of more than five miles. By

*Right:* A signpost for the future — a Marine seaplane stationed in postwar Cuba takes off on an aerial survey mission.

9 November the Germans had withdrawn across the Meuse, and 4th Brigade was readying itself to attack across the river at Mouzon and Villemontry. On the 10th they crossed the Meuse under heavy enemy fire. They were preparing to renew their advance on the 11th — the day of the Armistice — when the guns fell silent.

### Marine Aviation

The first Marine airman had been Lieutenant Alfred A. Cunningham, who in August 1912 became Naval Aviator No 5. In 1914, military aviation was still in the embryonic stage, but by April 1917 — when the United States entered the war — tactical air power over the battlefield, and strategic bombing operations against industry and centers of population, had become significant secondary factors in the waging of war.

However, when the United States declared war, the Marines' aviation section had only six officers (designated Naval Aviators), one warrant officer and 34 enlisted men. In September 1917 the first Marine Aeronautic Company was formed, and in January 1918 its 12 officers and 133 enlisted men were transferred to the Azores, from where it flew seaplanes on anti-submarine missions for the rest of the war.

In the spring of 1918 the 1st Marine Aviation Force was organized, with its headquarters at the former Curtiss Flying Field in Florida, Miami. On 30 July 1918 it despatched three landplane squadrons to France, with a fourth following in October. Upon their arrival they became the Day Wing of the Northern Bombing Group, stationed in northern France, flying the British-supplied De Havilland DH4, the best single-engined bomber of the war. From October 1918, Marines flew DH4s in operations in the Dunkirk area against German submarines and their bases at Ostend, Zeebrugge and Bruges. By the Armistice the Marine Aviation Force numbered some 2,500 officers and men and fielded 340 aircraft. They claimed 12 victories over enemy 'planes and delivered 52,000lb of bombs in 57 raids. They also performed the first recorded aerial resupply operation when they dropped food to a beleaguered French regiment, cut off for several days in the front line. It was a modest beginning for Marine aviation, which was to come into its own in World War Two.

# 3: FOUNDATION FOR VICTORY

## The Interwar Years 1919-1941

With the arrival of peace, the Marine Corps suffered the wholesale cutbacks affecting all the armed services which had fought "the war to end all wars". By July 1920, its wartime strength of 75,000 had been reduced to 17,165 officers and men on active duty.

In that month, General John A. Lejeune was appointed Commandant, a post he held until 4 March 1929. It was a difficult time for the Corps which, in common with all the services, had to cope with the drastically reduced funding resulting from the mood of isolationism which gripped the United States in the 1920s. Nevertheless, under Lejeune's shrewd leadership the Corps initiated a number of programs — most notably in the field of amphibious warfare — which laid the foundations of victory in the Pacific in World War Two.

### Nicaragua and New Methods

Initially, however, active service was principally confined to the familiar troublespots of Haiti, Cuba and Nicaragua. In 1925 Nicaragua was once more threatened with civil war, and by May 1927 the Marine presence there had been reinforced to brigade strength.

The need for air support in Nicaragua's difficult terrain was quickly recognized, and in February 1927 VO-1-M, under the command of Marine Major Ross E. "Rusty" Rowell, was despatched to Managua, the Nicaraguan capital. VO-1-M was subsequently joined by VO-4-M and the two units combined to form an Aircraft Squadron, under Rowell's command, flying their DH4s on reconnaissance patrols over the two opposing Nicaraguan factions while the representative of the US government, Henry L. Stimson, was negotiating an armistice. In June a general pacification agreement was reached, the liberal insurgents laid down their arms, and a process of troop withdrawals began.

However, the United States' overriding role in Nicaragua's destiny had produced a strong armed nationalist movement — Ejercito Defensor de la Soberania Nacional (EDSN) — committed to ending all foreign influence in Nicaraguan affairs. Under the charismatic leadership of Augusto Cesar

*Left:* Bringing the boys back home; Red Cross women welcome men of 2nd Marines as they parade in New York on their return from France in 1919.

Marines pick up their rations while on board ship.

Sandino, the EDSN refused to accept the accord and moved into the inaccessible mountains of the north-east to wage a guerrilla campaign against the Marines and the newly-formed Nicaraguan National Guard.

The Marines established a number of garrisons in the jungle in an attempt to contain Sandino in the highlands. They were defeated by the rebels' superior knowledge of the terrain and the hostility of the local population, but the campaign provided a number of young Marine officers — among them Merritt A. Edson, Evans F. Carlson, and Lewis B. "Chesty" Puller — with an introduction to the tactics and techniques of jungle warfare. They were to make their mark in the Pacific in World War Two.

The fighting in Nicaragua also saw the beginnings of modern air–ground co-operation. On the night of 15 July 1927, Sandino launched a surprise attack with 600 men against the small outpost of Ocotal, held by 62 Marines under Captain Hatfield and 48 ill-equipped and poorly trained National Guardsmen, commanded by a Marine NCO. Sandino's attack was beaten off but, when dawn broke, the town was completely cut off. The nearest friendly outpost was 125 miles away, which meant 14 days of hard marching for a small Marine relief force. Sandino settled down to wait for the defenders of Ocotal to run out of ammunition.

Two aircraft of Rowell's unit — now known as VO-7-M — made aerial contact at 1010 hrs on 17 July, strafing Sandino's guerrillas before returning to make a report. Rowell had five DH4s ready for operations and these immediately took off, armed with 17-lb fragmentation bombs.

Rowell was one of the postwar pioneers of dive-bombing and all his pilots were thoroughly trained in this technique.

The time had come to put Rowell's dive-bombing theories to the test. The DH4s reached Ocobal against the dramatic backdrop of a threatening tropical storm, circling the target area once at 1,500ft and then forming their bombing column. Rowell led the attack, pulling out of his dive at 600ft. Sandino's men had never been exposed to serious aerial attack and disdained to take cover, losing as many as 80 men in the first attack. Subsequent dives were made from 1,000ft with the DH4s pulling out at 300ft. Sandino's men broke and fled. Although dive-bombing by individual aircraft had been a feature of the closing months of World War One, this was the first use of co-ordinated dive-bombing techniques in combat.

The value of air–ground support was underlined in January 1928, when Marines besieged at Quilali were sustained from the air by First-Lieutenant (later General) Christian F. Schilt. Using an improvized airstrip cut through the center of the town, Schilt flew in supplies and ammunition and flew out the wounded, his ten missions winning him a Medal of Honor. As the campaign against Sandino wore on, it became standard procedure to use aircraft in support of patrols and garrisons.

Sandino's army fought on for six years, and by 1933 the war had spread to 10 of Nicaragua's 16 provinces. Unable to secure a decisive victory against the rebels, and under considerable domestic pressure to end American involvement, the Marines were withdrawn from Nicaragua in 1933. Sandino was assassinated a year later, but his ghost — in the form of Nicaragua's Sandinista regime — came back to haunt the US government in the 1980s.

**The Orange Plan**

In the interwar years there was a ferment of new ideas about the tactics and technology of future conflicts. In Germany the revolutionary theories of armored warfare advanced by the British military writers Fuller and Liddell Hart were taken up by a brilliant young Army officer, Heinz Guderian, principal architect of Blitzkrieg warfare. The Italian General Douhet and the merican polemicist General William Mitchell argued that air power, in the form of massive fleets of strategic bombers, would become the single, dominant factor in war, rendering all others obsolete. Mitchell's enthusiasm for the long-range bomber was eventually proved correct by the global application of his theories, and confirmed his tireless advocacy of the importance of Alaska as the strategic key to the Pacific.

Another less-famous military visionary obsessed with the perils and potential of American strategy in the Pacific was a Marine Corps staff officer, Major (later Lieutenant-Colonel) Earl H. Ellis. As early as 1913 Ellis had delivered a series of lectures at the Naval War College in which he warned of a future war with Japan, the outcome of which would hinge on the possession of the islands and atolls of the trans-Pacific. To meet this threat, Ellis evolved a wide-ranging and revolutionary approach to the waging of amphibious warfare.

Unlike Mitchell, Ellis was not a voice in the wilderness. Prior to World War One, War plans derived their titles from the codenames of the probable enemy. Japan was codenamed Orange, and the strategic concept and missions to be followed in the event of a war with that country were contained in the Orange Plan. The Orange Plan was constantly revised as the international situation changed.

Before 1914, the broad strategy was for the Army to defend the Philippines until the Fleet could carry reinforcements across the Pacific. Naval strategists were keenly aware that Japan would almost certainly seize Guam before a relief force could be despatched, depriving the US Navy of its only Fleet anchorage between Pearl Harbor and Manila Bay. Thus Guam would have to be retaken or another island occupied as a coaling and repair station.

After World War One, Orange assumed new dimensions when Japan gained control of the former German possessions in the Marshalls, Carolines and Marianas. The Philippines were now more vulnerable, and Guam ringed with Japanese outposts. The Orange Plan came under review.

In 1920 the Office of Naval Intelligence proposed a study of the possibility of a trans-Pacific war against Japan, and various agencies were directed to assist the study with plans of their own. In 1921 Ellis was assigned to the newly-formed Division of Operations and Training at Headquarters, Marine Corps. It was in this year that Ellis' 1913 paper, "Naval Bases: Location, Resources, Denial of Bases, Security of Advanced Bases", was published, along with his "Advanced Base Operations in Micronesia in 1921". The latter became the basis of Operation Plan 712D, the Marine Corps' contribution to the Orange Plan, approved by the Commandant, General John A. Lejeune, in July 1921.

Ellis' plan concentrated on one aspect of a future war against Japan — the seizing of a base which would be urgently needed by the Navy as a coaling or a repair station. Focusing his attention on the islands in the Marshalls Group, Ellis outlined the tactics to be used in such an operation. He wrote: "It will be necessary for us to project our fleet and landing forces across the Pacific and wage war in Japanese waters. To effect this requires that we have sufficient bases to support the Fleet, both during its projection and afterwards. To effect [an amphibious landing] in the face of enemy resistance requires careful training and preparation, to say the least, and this along Marine lines. It is not enough that the troops be skilled infantrymen or artillerymen of high morale; they must be skilled watermen and junglemen who know it can be done — Marines with Marine training."

The practical application of Ellis' theories was limited by the rudimentary nature of the equipment then available to the Corps, but he made a number of significant recommendations, not the least of which was the stress he placed on naval gunfire support for troops fighting ashore. Crucially, Ellis' approach radically altered thinking about the role which the Marines were expected to play. Ellis outlined a scenario in which they would no longer be used primarily to defend advanced bases; now they would seize bases from the enemy.

This shift in the Marines' priorities was underlined in February 1921 when Lejeune suggested that the Corps' primary wartime function was to act as a mobile force accompanying the Fleet for operations in support of the Fleet. Addressing the Naval War College in 1923, Lejeune laid great stress on the importance of the Marine Corps as a force in readiness: "On both flanks of a Fleet crossing the Pacific are numerous islands suitable for utilization by an enemy for radio stations, aviation, submarine or destroyer bases. All should be mopped up as progress is made . . . The presence of an expeditionary force with the Fleet would add greatly to the striking power of the C-in-C of the Fleet . . . The maintenance, equipping and training of its expeditionary force so that it will be in instant readiness to support the Fleet in the event of war, I deem to be the most important Marine Corps duty in time of peace."

Ellis did not live to see his ideas take concrete form. He died in mysterious circumstances in 1923 while making a lone reconnaissance of the Japanese-held islands in the Pacific, having almost certainly confirmed that they were being fortified in contravention of the 1921 Five Powers Naval Treaty. It was left to others to develop his technical and tactical guidelines into a coherent body of doctrine.

In the immediate postwar years, precedent was not encouraging. Waterborne landings in World War One had been uniformly chaotic, with the Gallipoli landings of 1915 providing a bloody reminder of what could happen when a large-scale amphibious operation unravelled in the face of determined opposition. The majority of strategists remained deeply sceptical about the usefulness of amphibious operations. However, after an internal study of the Gallipoli campaign, the Marine Corps concluded that it was sheer incompetence, rather than any inherent flaw in the amphibious idea, which had undermined the operation.

Amphibious exercises conducted in Cuba between 1922 and 1925 confirmed the inadequacy of conventional tactical doctrine and the converted wooden Navy launches which were used as landing craft. But the Corps' expeditionary duties during the rest of the 1920s diverted its attention from

*Above:* A Marine mans a heavy machine-gun aboard a river patrol boat during the postwar occupation of the Rhineland.

amphibious warfare, and it was not until the following decade that the momentum was regained.

As the Marine Corps withdrew from its policing operations in Central America and the Caribbean, more troops became available for training in landing operations. However, before any real progress could be made, a substantial and permanent force of Marines — with its own command staff — would have to be organized for the purpose. The Assistant Commandant, General John H. Russell, proposed that the old "Expeditionary Force" should be replaced with a new formation called either the "Fleet Marine Force" or the "Fleet Base Defense Force". The new force would form an integral part of the US Fleet, under the operational control of the Fleet Commander when embarked on vessels of the Fleet or engaged in Fleet exercises ashore or afloat. These proposals were rapidly approved by the Commandant and the Chief of Naval Operations, and the designation Fleet Marine Force (FMF) chosen. The decision became official with the issuing of Navy Department General Order 241 on 8 December 1933.

The creation of the FMF provided the Marine Corps with the tactical framework within which it could execute the primary war mission of seizing and securing advanced bases. In 1934 the Corps produced a textbook whose purpose was to embody the theory and practice of landing operations, *The Tentative Manual for Landing Operations*. It was approved by the Chief of Naval Operations for "temporary use . . . as a guide for forces of the Navy and the Marine Corps conducting a landing against opposition". In spite of its engagingly modest title, this manual laid the foundations for all modern amphibious thinking in the American armed forces. In 1938 the Navy adopted it as official doctrine with the issuing of Fleet Training Publication 167; and the Army followed suit in 1941 with Field Manual 31-5. The fundamental elements of amphibious warfare covered by *The Tentative Manual for Landing Operations* included: command relationships; naval gunfire support; close air support; ship-to-shore movement; combat unit landing; and the organization of shore party personnel.

### Tools for the Job

Flowing directly from the evolution of a body of amphibious tactics was the development of the technology to put it into practice. The overriding requirement of all amphibious operations is to get the troops on to the beaches with as few casualties as possible. By the early 1930s, pioneering work on amphibious craft was underway in the United States.

In 1933 a retired manufacturer, Donald Roebling, developed a remarkable amphibious vehicle for rescue work in the swamplands of the Florida Everglades. His design comprised an aluminum hull fitted with tracks which, by paddle-wheel action, propelled the amphibian through the water and enabled it to move across country. In 1937 Roebling's "Alligator" came to the attention of the Marine Corps, whose Equipment Board authorized a series of tests. In 1939 the board ordered three "Alligators" and put them through their paces at Quantico Marine base. Encouraged by the results and the basic soundness of the design, the Corps made some minor modifications to the amphibian and then gave Roebling a contract to produce the vehicle in quantity. This marked the birth of the Landing Vehicle, Tracked (LVT).

Subsequently the Navy Bureau of Ships produced an LVT design of its own, passing the blueprints to the Borg-Warner Corporation for manufacture. The principal modifications were the adoption of a sprung suspension and the installation of the engine and drive train from the M3 tank. Designated LVT2, the vehicle went into production in 1942.

At the same time, the executive officer of the Marine Equipment Board, Major Ernest E. Linsert, was developing an armored amphibian, the Landing Vehicle, Tracked (Armored), or LVT(A), based on the original "Alligator" design. Turrets made of steel casings housed the LVT(A)'s main armament: a 37-mm gun and 7.62-mm machine-gun mounted in an M3 turret; one 12.7-mm gun in each of its two side turrets; and two fixed 12.7-mm guns fired by the driver manipulating buttons on the steering levers. The first LVT(A)s came off the production line in the winter of 1940/41.

Although the tracked amphibians were destined to play a vital role in the Pacific War, the rapid build-up of men, machines and materiel could not have been achieved without the development of a new type of landing craft. The pioneer in this field was Andrew J. Higgins, who in the mid-1920s produced the "Eureka" boat for fur trappers

in the Louisiana swamplands. To cope with the region's shallow, weed-infested waters, the boat had shallow draft and a protected propeller.

In 1934 Higgins took his "Eureka" design to the Marine Corps, who were interested but had no money to fund a long-term development project. Undaunted, Higgins continued to liaise with the Corps and by 1939 had produced an improved landing craft which in a series of tests consistently outperformed all comparable vessels. It retained one serious design drawback — the troops had to disembark by jumping over the side. In April 1941 Higgins visited the Marine base at Quantico, where he agreed to redesign the craft with a ramp bow. Working with Brigadier-General Moses, the head of the Marine Equipment Board, Higgins produced a design which met the Corps' specifications. At the beginning of 1942 the Board of Ships authorized full-scale production of the Higgins Boat.

## Marine Aviation in the 1930s

The 1930s also saw significant changes in Marine aviation. Flying aircraft off ships was one such change, and from 1931 to 1934 VS-14M and VS-15M, the first Marine squadrons to become part of the Fleet air organization, saw service aboard the carriers *Saratoga* and *Lexington*.

Marine aviation also adapted to the establishment of the FMF and the emphasis now placed on the seizure of advanced bases in the event of war. In 1935 the aviation section at Headquarters, Marine Corps, was removed from the Division of Operations and Training and established as an independent section under the Commandant. In 1936 it became a Division under a Director of Aviation, who served as an advisor to the Commandant on all aviation matters. The Director also acted as liaison officer between the Marine Corps and the Navy Bureau of Aeronautics.

The Marine Corps remained completely dependent on the Navy for its aircraft and equipment. But it was the Marines who in June 1940 took delivery of the first 57 Douglas SBD-1 Dauntless dive-bombers. The Dauntless was to be one of the most important US combat aircraft of World War Two, sinking more Japanese shipping than any other Allied weapon, stopping the Imperial Fleet at Midway in June 1942 and later playing a major role in the Solomons campaign.

*Above:* The Douglas SBD Dauntless dive-bomber, all of the first batches of which went to the Marine Corps. Although obsolescent by the Battle of Midway (June 1942), the rugged Dauntless was a war-winner, sinking more Japanese shipping during the Pacific war than any other Allied type. The SBD-1 had a maximum speed of 252mph, ceiling of 24,300ft and range (as dive-bomber) of 456 miles and as a scout bomber of 773 miles. Armament comprised two 0.3-in Browning machine-guns fixed above the nose; one (later two) 0.3-in Browning manually aimed from the rear cockpit; and one bomb or other store of up to 1,000lb on a swinging crutch under the belly. Additionally, there were outer-wing racks for two 100-lb bombs or depth charges.

By the summer of 1939 there were 210 officers and 1,142 enlisted men on active duty with the Marine Corps' aviation arm. In June 1940, Congress authorized the Navy's 10,000-'plane program, out of which the Corps was allotted 1,167 aircraft. This led to the preparation of plans for four groups, each comprising 11 squadrons. Landing exercises in 1941 indicated that a single division making an amphibious landing would require air support from a minimum of 12 fighter, eight dive-bomber, two observation and four utility squadrons. However, progress towards achieving this level of support was slow. When the two brigades of Marines were reorganized into divisions in February 1941, their air support groups were redesignated 1st and 2nd Marine Aircraft Wings (MAWs). When war broke out, there was still only one group in each wing and a total of 251 aircraft and 708 pilots in Marine aviation.

On the eve of war, the Marine Corps was spread far and wide across the globe. Some 18,000 of its 65,000 officers and men were deployed overseas. A brigade built up around 6th Marines (reinforced) had been despatched to Iceland to relieve a British garrison and pave the way for the arrival of more US troops. There were Marines on duty in China, the Philippines, Guam, Wake Island, Midway, American Samoa, Panama and a number of British islands in the Caribbean. Another 4,000 Marines were serving aboard Navy ships or at Navy stations, and 20,000 were in training at land bases. And there were some 4,500 Marines on the Hawaiian island of Oahu, on duty at the great US naval base — Pearl Harbor.

Boeing F4B biplanes of VF-10, part of the West Coast Expeditionary Force, c. 1930.

# 4: THEIR FINEST HOUR:

## World War Two

### JAPAN IN THE ASCENDANT: WORLD WAR TWO

Just before dawn on 7 December 1941, the first wave of Japanese aircraft — 43 Mitsubishi A6MZ Zero-Sen fighters, 89 Nakajima B5NA "Kate" level-altitude bombers and 81 Aichi D3A2 "Val" dive-bombers — took off from the carriers of Admiral Nagumo's task force, lying some 250 miles north of the US Pacific Fleet's base at Pearl Harbor. The Japanese aircraft were picked up by radar as they approached Pearl Harbor, but no action was taken. In the calm, clear light of early morning, the naval base remained to all intents and purposes undefended: battleships berthed alongside each other in the harbor; nearly all the anti-aircraft guns unmanned and the ammunition under lock and key. The attack on Oahu began at 0755 a.m. and continued, with a brief lull, for nearly two hours. Using torpedoes and specially-adapted armor-piercing bombs, the Japanese inflicted most damage in the first five minutes of the attack, when resistance was non-existent and the targets were not obscured by smoke. Four battleships were sunk and a fifth, *Nevada*, crippled and beached. Three destroyers and a minelayer were also sunk and 188 aircraft destroyed, including all but one of the 48 'planes of Marine Air Group 21 (MAG-21). There were 2,403 American dead, including 112 Marines. Japanese losses were 29 aircraft and 555 men.

Superficially, the pre-emptive strike on Pearl Harbor had been an overwhelming victory. Hindsight enables us to see that on 7 December the Japanese took their first step on the road to defeat. The greater part of the US Navy escaped unscathed. After Pearl Harbor the US Navy still retained 18 heavy cruisers — 12 of them in the Pacific — 168 destroyers and, crucially, 112 submarines. Above all, the three aircraft carriers of the Pacific Fleet — *Enterprise*, *Saratoga* and *Lexington* — were absent from Pearl Harbor when the Japanese attacked. The urgent need for Marine aircraft to strengthen outpost defenses had sent *Lexington* and *Enterprise* to sea on aircraft-ferrying missions. On 7 December *Lexington* was en route to Midway with aircraft of Marine

*Left:* The face of the Pacific war. Bitter fighting in the Marshall Islands, February 1944.

Scout Bomber Squadron 231 (VMSB-231). She turned back when news of the attack was received. On that fateful day *Enterprise* was steaming back to Pearl Harbor after flying off the fighters of VMF-211 to reinforce the defenses of Wake Island. She should have tied up in Pearl Harbor at about 0730 hrs on 7 December, but she was delayed by refueling problems and was some 200 miles west of Oahu when the attack went in. Warned of the situation by some of her aircraft, which had encountered the first Japanese wave, the carrier sailed westwards and out of danger.

## Guam and Wake

In the Japanese war plans, the small concentration of forces based on Truk was earmarked to secure the islands of the south-west Pacific. The first phase of operations including the seizing of the American islands of Guam and Wake.

As US strategists in the 1920s had anticipated, Guam was virtually indefensible. The most southerly of the major islands in the Marianas, Guam was hemmed in on all sides by Japanese possessions, particularly to the south in the Carolines. To defend Guam's 225 square miles there was a garrison of 153 Marines, armed with nothing heavier than .30-caliber machine-guns and reinforced by about 80 local militiamen. Within hours of the attack on Pearl Harbor, Guam was subjected to an air offensive which lasted two days before the Japanese put 6,000 troops ashore on the morning of 10 December. The tiny garrison was overwhelmed within an hour, the Marines surrendering to prevent the possibility of Japanese reprisals against the local population. Four Marines and 15 Guamanians had died in the defense of the island.

Wake Island was a different proposition. Wake is a small bleak atoll of three islands and a lagoon, 2,000 miles from Hawaii and over 600 miles from the nearest Japanese base. Before the war it had been a Pan-American Airways staging post. Any major or prolonged Japanese attempt to seize Wake would run the risk of a fleet engagement. The likelihood of such a clash depended on timely intelligence and the ability of the Wake garrison to hold out against the Japanese attack for a length of time.

However, Wake was only marginally more heavily defended than Guam. In October 1941, command of the Marine garrison of 178 officers and men was assumed by Colonel James Devereux. On 2 November he was reinforced by 200 Marines led by Major George H. Potter, and at the end of the month Commander Winfield Scott Cunningham of the US Navy arrived at Wake to take overall command of the island.

Devereux remained in command of the

*Left:* The battleship *Pennsylvania* and the destroyers *Cassin* and *Downes* in the aftermath of the attack on Pearl Harbor. *Pennsylvania* was in dry dock at the time of the attack and thus saved from the attentions of Japanese torpedo-bombers. *Cassin* and *Downes* took the brunt of the enemy dive-bombing attacks. *Pennysylvania* lived to fight another day and played an important part in The Battle of Leyte Gulf, in October 1944, which saw the last battleship-against-battleship engagement.

### MARINE DEFENSE BATTALIONS

In the years following the formation of the Fleet Marine Force (FMF), the prevailing mood of isolationism in the United States restricted the funding of the armed services by Congress. With some ingenuity, the Commandant of the Marine Corps, Major-General Thomas Holcomb, argued that an increase in the Corps' manpower would bolster the nation's defensive, rather than offensive, capability. Thus the Defense Battalion Program eventually got underway on 10 October 1939 with the activation of 3rd Defense Battalion. The aim was to provide the Corps with a force capable of seizing and securing bases for the US Fleet. Tables for four different types of Defense Battalion appeared in October 1941. Each had a Headquarters and Service Battery, and a 90-mm or 3-in anti-aircraft artillery (AAA) group. The addition of two of the following components would complete the battalion's organization: a 155-mm artillery group; a special weapons group; a machine-gun group; or a 7-in artillery group. Combat strength of the battalion was approximately 1,000 officers and men, including a naval component of 25 doctors, dentists and hospital corpsmen. When the United States entered the war, a number of understrength Defense Battalions were stationed in the Pacific, notably at Wake and Midway. In the 1944 drive to increase the strength of the six Marine divisions, 17 of the 20 Defense Battalions were redesignated anti-aircraft battalions. Where possible, their men were transferred to AAA units; the remainder were retrained as field artillerymen and transferred to line artillery regiments.

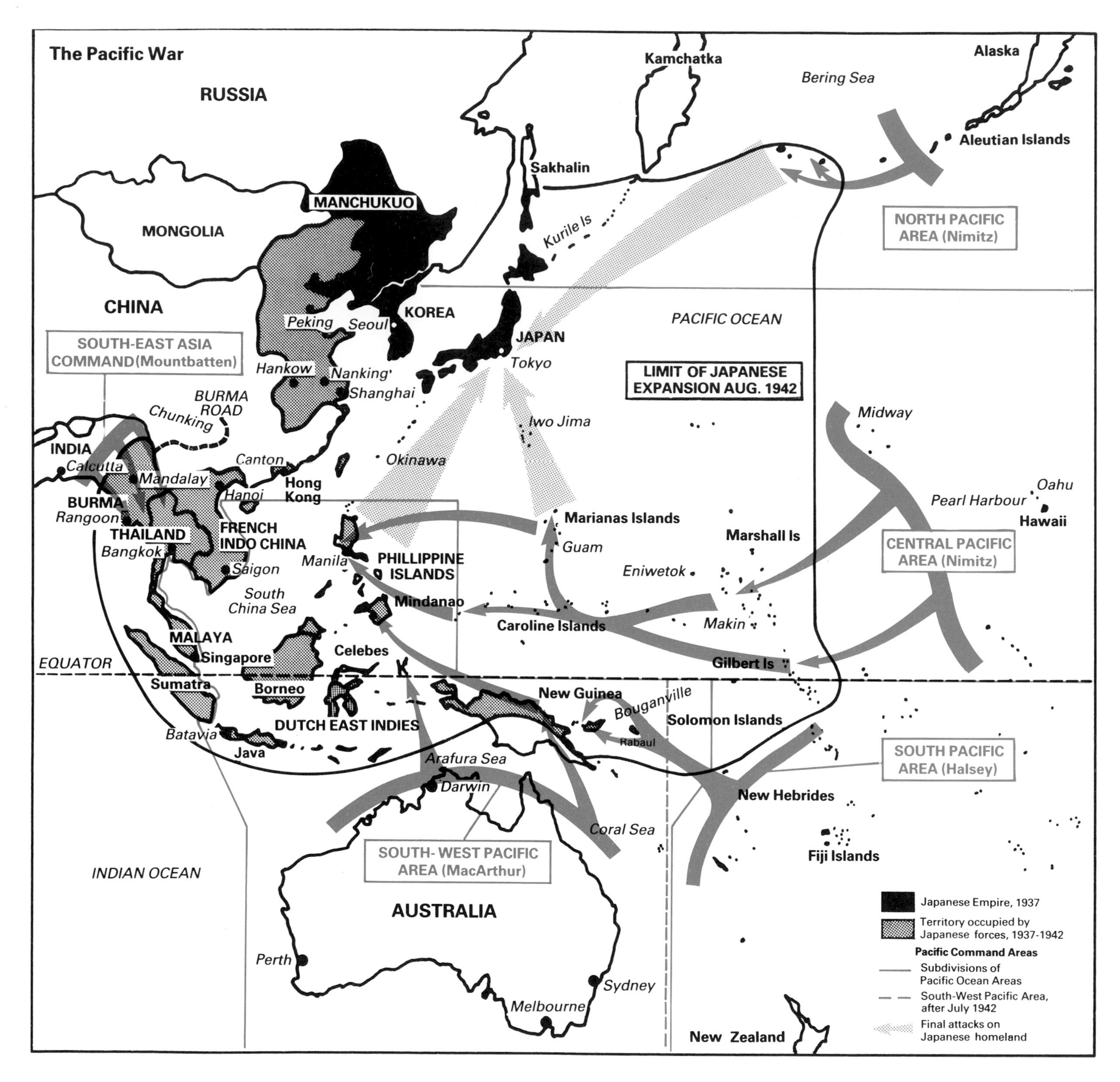


The map shows the strategic situation in the Pacific in February 1944, with the taking of the Gilbert and Marshall Islands, but before the trap closed completely on Rabaul.

Marine detachment, and was responsible for co-ordinating the operations of the Defense Battalion and the Marine Fighter Squadron VMF-211. The latter, led by Major Paul A. Putnam and comprising 12 Grumman F4F Wildcats, had flown in from the flight deck of the carrier *Enterprise* on 4 December.

The Marines' artillery consisted of six 5-in coastal guns and 12 3-in anti-aircraft pieces. But the understrength Defense battalion could not man these guns simultaneously and possessed only half the numbers sufficient to operate the 0.5-in and 0.3-in machine-guns which were to be used for air and ground defense respectively. An SCR-270B search radar had been promised but not delivered. Wake's improvised air-raid warning system was supplied by Marines stationed atop two 50ft water towers.

The air raids were not long in coming. At noon on 8 December, 30 Japanese bombers appeared over Wake, dropping a dense pattern of bombs on the atoll's airfield. Seven Wildcats were destroyed on the ground, and the squadron's 25,000-gallon fuel tank erupted in a ball of flame. Twenty-three Marines died in the attack and 11 were wounded. Crossing the lagoon, the bombers strafed the Pan American facilities, setting fuel tanks ablaze and killing 10 American civilians.

The bombers reappeared at 1145 on the

9th. Twenty-seven aircraft flew in from the south and were met by four patrolling Wildcats, which claimed one kill. Fourteen of the bombers flew away with heavy flak damage. On the 10th, 18 bombers arrived over Wake, two of which were shot down by Captain Henry Elrod.

Meanwhile, a Japanese assault force was closing on the atoll. The preparations for the attack were uncharacteristically slipshod, influenced perhaps by exaggerated reports of the success of the bombing raids and a fatal underestimation of the resolve of the Marine garrison. Very few troops — less than 450 in the assault phase — were embarked for the landings at dawn on the 11th. The Japanese covering force comprised three lightcruisers (the flagship *Yubari*, *Tatsuta* and *Tenryu*) and six destroyers (*Hayate*, *Kisaragi*, *Mochizuki*, *Mutsuki*, *Oite* and *Yayoi*).

Although most of the garrison's Wildcats had been destroyed, the 5-in and 3-in guns remained intact. As the Japanese assault force approached Wake, the Marines held their fire until the range had closed to 4,500yds, at which point Colonel Devereux gave the order to commence firing. The 5-in guns on Wilkes Island and Peacock Point, commanded by Lieutenant Clarence A. Barninger, scored two hits amidships on the port side of the cruiser *Yubari*. These were followed by two more shells which slammed into the ship slightly aft of the first two hits. *Yubari* limped away billowing smoke and steam. One of the escorting destroyers attempted to cover her withdrawal by laying down a smokescreen, but was herself driven off when a 5-in shell exploded on her forecastle.

One of the transports, a converted destroyer, was hit and crippled and another transport damaged. In an effort to draw the Marines' fire from the transports, three of the destroyers immediately closed to engage the shore batteries. Battery L, commanded by Lieutenant John A. McAlister, quickly found the range and blew *Hayate* out of the water. She was the first Japanese warship to be sunk by US forces in World War Two.

*Oite* and *Yayoi* sustained hits during these exchanges, also coming under attack from Wake's four Wildcats. Able to carry only two 100lb bombs, the fighters had to return to the airfield to re-arm after each bombing run. At 0730hrs, during his final sortie, Captain Elrod scored a direct hit on *Kisaragi*, setting off her depth charges. She sank almost immediately with all hands. The Japanese withdrew. Without being able to put a man ashore, they had lost two ships and 700 men. Amidst the tide of victory in the Far East, this had been a uniquely disastrous operation.

Inevitably, the Japanese redoubled their efforts to seize Wake, whose capture was vital to complete their defensive perimeter across the width of the Pacific and to prevent the atoll being used by the Americans as a jumping-off point for future operations in the Western Pacific. Moreover, the possession of Midway would facilitate future Japanese operations against Midway and the western Hawaiian group. The failure of the attack on 11 December had made a second operation against Wake markedly more hazardous, as it gave the Americans a chance to reinforce the garrison and deploy a powerful task force to counter the Japanese assault.

This the Americans failed to do. The ill-fated Admiral Kimmel, C-in-C of the Pacific Fleet at the time of Pearl Harbor, had ordered the reinforcement of Wake, instructing *Saratoga* to support the atoll's garrison and ordering *Lexington* and *Yorktown* to stand by their sister carrier. But *Saratoga* was delayed in Pearl Harbor by refueling problems, and then lost two days topping up her destroyers at a time when speed was of the essence. On 17 December, Kimmel was removed from his command and temporarily succeeded by his deputy, Admiral William S. Pye, pending the arrival of the new C-in-C Pacific Fleet, Admiral Chester W. Nimitz. Unsure of the strength of Japanese forces in the area of Wake, Pye shrank from risking his carriers so soon after the débacle at Pearl Harbor. Ultimately, Wake was expendable, but the carriers were not. Pye decided against the relief of Wake.

Meanwhile, the atoll was being pounded twice a day by Japanese aircraft: at noon by land-based bombers and at dawn by flying boats. On 14 December the tail of one of the two remaining Wildcats was set on fire during a raid. Three men from the squadron's engineering section, Second Lieutenant John Kinney, Technical Sergeant William Hamilton and Aviation Machinist's First Mate James Hesson, left their cover, removed the undamaged engine from the burning aircraft and dragged it clear. By ingeniously cannibalizing the squadron's damaged 'planes, they had within three days provided VMF-211 with four operational Wildcats.

The damaged destroyer *Downes* in the dry dock at Pearl Harbor. She was repaired and saw service in the Pacific.

On 20 December, Wake's battery positions were hit by 29 Japanese Navy bombers escorted by 18 Zero fighters. This was the first time that the atoll had been attacked by carrier-based aircraft and a sure indication that an enemy task force was closing on Wake. The assault force consisted of the survivors of the 11 December defeat, supported by four heavy cruisers from Guam, the carriers *Hiryu* and *Soryu* from Admiral Nagumo's Strike Force and the seaplane tender *Chitose*. It was a powerful group but, with grim irony, inferior to US naval forces in the general area.

By the evening of 22 December, Wake's remaining Wildcats had been destroyed. At 0120 hrs on the 23rd, 1,000 Japanese Special Naval Landing Force troops came ashore at four points on the southern shore of Wake, skilfully seeking the security of dead ground for their landfall. Prudently, the heavy cruisers stayed out of range of the shore batteries. As the Japanese moved up the beach, a 3-in shell from one of the Marine batteries blew up an ammunition magazine on one of the destroyer-transports, turning the night into day.

The Marines put up a ferocious resistance, and there was bitter hand-to-hand fighting on the water's edge. The dawn came up, revealing 17 enemy warships ringing the atoll. Three destroyers steamed in to finish off the gallant shore batteries, and in a final act of defiance the 5-in guns hit and heavily damaged one of them, *Mutsuki*. By 0700 hrs all the Marines' forward positions had been overrun, and Commander Cunningham ordered them to lay down their arms. The order went out: "Cease firing. Destroy all weapons. The island is being surrendered." After performing this melancholy task the Marines sat down in their positions and — perhaps mindful of what lay ahead — began to eat as much as they could.

The garrison had held out for 15 days after the first raid. During the raids, shelling and assault on the island, they had suffered 81 killed and wounded and had inflicted approximately 1,000 casualties on the enemy. Four Japanese ships had been sunk and eight more damaged. Twenty-one enemy aircraft had been shot down by the island's fighters and anti-aircraft guns. On 12 January the Marines were loaded aboard the *Nitta Maru* and sailed off into four long years of captivity. Their heroic example prompted President Roosevelt to declare that millions had "been inspired to render their own full share of service and sacrifice".

### The Fall of the Philippines

The opening weeks of the Pacific war were characterized by the brilliant Japanese concentration and co-ordination of all arms against the enemy's points of maximum weakness. On 8 December, heavy bombing raids crippled US air power in the Philippines. By the end of the afternoon, for the loss of just seven Zero fighters, the Japanese had destroyed 103 US aircraft, most of them on the ground and over half of them fighters. When General Homma's XIV Army landed on the northern tip of the island of Luzon on 10 December, American aircraft had ceased to pose a serious threat. Two days later a Japanese force from Palau captured Legaspi, in the extreme south of Luzon. The main landings went in on 22 December in the Lingayen Gulf. After establishing a strong beach-head, the Japanese advanced south, meeting only limited pockets of stiff resistance.

Without adequate naval and air support, the policy of forward defense against the Japanese adopted by General Douglas MacArthur, commanding US Army forces in the Far East, proved a forlorn hope. On 23 December, MacArthur withdrew from Manila into the Bataan peninsula. The Japanese entered the Philippines capital on 2 January and then confronted MacArthur at the northern end of the Bataan peninsula. MacArthur remained confident, claiming, "The Japanese may have got the bottle but we have the cork."

Marines of the 4th Division, recently arrived from Shanghai, were not placed in the immediate front-line. They were assigned the task of defending the island fortress of Corregidor at the entrance to Manila Bay, and two of its three supporting forts, Hughes and Drum. It was not long before these "impregnable" bastions became the last-ditch defenses of the Philippines.

In the Bataan peninsula, the Japanese threw in their first attack on 9 January. They were beaten back with heavy losses on both sides, but by the end of the month the Americans had been forced back to their reserve line, running across the peninsula from Bagac to Orion. More than once in the last week of January the Japanese attempted amphibious landings against the south-west coast of Bataan, but two Japanese battalions were destroyed on their beach-heads. Two months of stalemate followed, during which both sides began to feel the effects of disease and malnutrition.

On 12 March, MacArthur reluctantly left his headquarters in Corregidor for Australia, handing over command to General Jonathan Wainwright. On 3 April the Japanese launched a new attack, breaking through the American line and turning the flank of 2nd Corps. On 9 April the 80,000 US and Filipino troops on Bataan surrendered. The Japanese Army had not prepared for a capitulation on this scale and adopted the most expedient course, marching the troops 65 miles to a railway line and then shipping them to Camp O'Donnell. En route, the Japanese treated their prisoners with extreme brutality, giving them no food or drink for five days, shooting stragglers and inflicting many other hardships. This was the infamous Bataan Death March, in which about 16,000 US and Filipino troops died and for which General Homma was tried and executed after the war.

After the surrender, about 2,000 troops escaped to Corregidor. Japanese aircraft had made their first raid on the "Gibraltar of the East" on 29 December. Three days later the garrison was placed on half rations. From the end of March, the Japanese began a regular artillery bombardment of the island which increased in intensity after the surrender on Bataan. For the men of 4th Marines, dug in behind Corregidor's beach fortifications in foxholes, it was "like living in the center of a bullseye". The bombardment continued day and night, churning up the defenses faster than they could be rebuilt and transforming the "Rock" into a landscape of rubble. It reached a crescendo on 29 April, when more than 150 heavy guns thundered out a murderous salute to the Emperor's official birthday, setting the remaining undergrowth ablaze, throwing up such a pall of dust that the mainland was completely obscured, and smashing the last vestiges of co-ordinated defensive zones on Corregidor's beaches.

Conditions on Corregidor were intolerable. The only secure refuge from the ceaseless bombardment was the Malinta Tunnel, a

A Marine unit in the Bataan peninsula March 1942.

bomb-proof underground complex located at the base of Corregidor's long tadpole-like tail. But it was now fetid with the stench of hundreds of wounded, jammed into its stifling, dust-choked side chambers. Malnutrition, malaria and dysentery had remorselessly eroded morale. On 3 May General Wainwright radioed MacArthur that, with less than five days of water left, the situation was critical. On 4 May, 16,000 shells fell on Corregidor, and that night Homma despatched assault boats carrying 2,000 men against the fortress. Their landings were preceded by another furious barrage, but the assault craft were caught by a strong current and missed their landing points by more than a mile. When the Japanese came ashore, they were met with fierce enfilading fire from 1st Marine Battalion, which took full advantage of the rising moon to inflict heavy casualties.

The men of 4th Marines — their numbers swollen to nearly 4,000 officers and men by Army, Navy and Filipino troops — fought valiantly, sustaining nearly 700 casualties before their commander, Colonel Samuel L. Howard, ordered them to surrender. Their last pockets of resistance in the Malinta tunnel area were overcome on 6 May. The survivors joined the infamous Death March into captivity.

*Right:* Admiral Yamamoto, the strategic genius who promised, and delivered, to the Emperor Hirohito six months of victory between December 1941 and June 1942. He never fully recovered from the defeat at Midway and was shot down and killed by US fighters on 18 April 1943 while flying from Rabaul to Bougainville.

## The Long Road Back

In a six-month explosion of military energy, the Japanese had overrun Malaya, taken Singapore, bundled the British out of Burma, swallowed up the Dutch empire in the East, isolated China, menaced the borders of India, brushed the north coast of Australia and gained control of nearly half the Pacific. They had acquired vast oil, tin and rubber resources and their safe passage to the Japanese home islands.

There was now an immense buffer zone against an American counter-attack, but its very size posed strategic problems which the Japanese failed to resolve. If the United States, with its immeasurably superior economic and industrial resources, could not be decisively defeated, Japan would be committed to the forward defense of a hugely-extended perimeter, where the enemy would enjoy the luxury of choosing the time and place of attack. Admiral Yamamoto, C-in-C of the Japanese 1st Combined Fleet and architect of Japan's stunning victories, had warned that he could promise only six months of victory. The six months were now up.

In May and June 1942, Japanese expansion was checked at two naval battles, Coral Sea and Midway. At Coral Sea (7/8 May) — the first of the carrier battles of the Pacific war — the Japanese were thwarted in their attempt to outflank New Guinea, seize Port Moresby and isolate Australia. Still wrestling with their self-imposed strategic dilemma, the Japanese then implemented an immensely elaborate plan — involving the movement of eight separate task forces — for the capture of Midway Island, which offered a base within striking distance of Hawaii. It was Yamamoto's aim to draw the US Pacific Fleet into a decisive naval battle, but the tables were about to be turned on the triumphant Japanese.

Yamamoto's plans had been fatally compromised by the Americans' breaking of the Japanese Fleet Code, which gave them ample foreknowledge of the attack on Midway on 4 June. The resulting battle was indeed decisive, but it was Admiral Nagumo's 1st Carrier Strike Force which was destroyed. On 4 June, the US Task Forces 16 and 17 sank three Japanese carriers — *Kaga*, *Akagi* and *Soryu* — for the loss of the carrier *Yorktown*. On the following day the crippled Japanese carrier *Hiryu* was scuttled.

The victory at Midway was won principally by carrier-borne Navy aircraft, but the Marine Corps played its part. Stationed on Midway Island was Marine Air Group 22 (MAG-22), comprising Marine Scout Bomber Squadron 241 (VMSB-241), equipped with obsolescent Vought SB2U Vindicator dive-bombers; and Marine Fighter Squadron 221 (VMF-221), flying equally vulnerable

Brewster F2A-3 Buffaloes and a handful of rugged, agile Grumman F4F-3 Wildcats. The Vindicators had flown direct to Midway from Hickam Field, Oahu, covering 1,137 miles in 9hrs and 20 minutes, at the time the longest massed flight of single-engined land 'planes. The Brewster Buffaloes had arrived at Christmas, flown from the deck of *Saratoga* after her abortive mission to relieve Wake Island. By the end of March, MAG-22 had received further reinforcements in the form of 16 Douglas SBD-2 Dauntless dive-bombers. On the eve of the Japanese attack on Midway there were 107 Marine, Army and Navy aircraft on Midway.

At 0555 hours on 4 June, Midway's radar logged the approach of "many planes" — a Japanese strike force consisting of 36 "Val" dive-bombers, 36 "Kate" torpedo-bombers and 36 escorting Zeros. Within 10 minutes MAG-22 — which already had fighters up to cover a sortie by the island's Consolidated PBY flying boats — had every available aircraft in the air. VMF-221, dividing into two groups, took off to intercept the incoming strike force. VMSB-241 headed for a rendezvous station 20 minutes to the east, where the dive-bombers' pilots were to receive further instructions.

The VMF-221 fighters, under Major Floyd B. Parks, sighted the Zero-escorted "Val" bombers at about 0616hrs, 30 miles from Midway. Captain John F. Carey, leading one of Parks' divisions in a Wildcat, flew into the attack from 17,000ft. His fighters had time for only one pass at the bombers before they were overwhelmed by the Zeros. Outclassed and outmaneuvered, nine of the 12 Marine fighters were shot down in the ensuing *mêlée*.

Like the fighter squadron, VMSB-241 had divided into two striking units, the first composed of 16 SBD-2s led by Major Lofton R. Henderson and the second of 11 SB2U-3s commanded by Major Benjamin W. Norris. Climbing to 9,000ft, Henderson's unit sighted the enemy carriers at 0744hrs, but were almost immediately set upon by Zeros flying cover. Only eight SBD-2s returned to Midway, having scored no hits. Henderson was among those lost.

Major Norris attacked the carriers in the wake of the bombing run made by 15 USAAF B-17s led by Lieutenant-Colonel Walter S. Sweeny. Roughly handled by the ever-present Zeros, Norris selected the nearest targets to hand, the battleships *Haruna* and *Kirishima*. No hits were scored and three of the SB2Us were shot down. One pilot who made it back counted 259 hits on his aircraft.

By 1100hrs all the surviving Marine aircraft had returned to Midway. Of the 25 fighters from VMF-221 involved in the action, there were only 10 left, and only two of these were fit to fly; 13 Buffaloes and two Wildcats were missing. Midway was covered in a pall of smoke from oil fires set off by the Japanese bombing, and ruptured fuel lines left two-thirds of the aviation fuel supply temporarily unavailable.

At 1700hrs a burning enemy carrier was reported 200 miles north-west of Midway. Major Norris prepared VMSB-241's six operational SBD-2s for a night attack. They took off at 1900hrs, but failed to locate the carrier. Norris did not return from the mission.

*Left:* An SB2U-3 Vindicator dive-bomber of VMSB-241 takes off from the airstrip at Midway.

**CACTUS AIR FORCE**

The original units of 1st Marine Aircraft Wing (MAW-1) to fly into Guadalcanal and lay the foundations of Cactus Air Force arrived on 20 August 1942 with Marine Air Group 23 (MAG-23). They were VMF-223, an F4F Wildcat squadron, and VMSB-232, an SBD Dauntless Squadron. On 22 August they were joined by the P-400 (a version of the Bell P-39 Cobra) aircraft of 67th Pursuit Squadron. The first of the Navy carrier detachments arrived from *Enterprise* on 24 August, and on the 30th the rest of MAG-23 landed in the form of VMF-224 and VMSB-231. On 3 September the command echelon of MAW-1 arrived on Guadalcanal, led by Brigadier-General Roy S. Geiger. During the period September–November 1942, many units served with Cactus Air Force for periods varying from three days to over six weeks. These detachments from Navy carrier groups included VS-3, VF-5, VT-8, VMSB-141, MAG-14, VS-71, VMF-121, VB-6, VMF-212, VMSB-132, VMF-112, VMSB-131, VMSB-142, VF-10, VB-10, VS-10 and VT-10. During the period 7 August–15 November, Guadalcanal-based aircraft (mainly SBDs) sank or wrecked 20 ships and damaged 14 more. Marine Wildcat pilots had claimed 407 victories, to which must be added 59 by Guadalcanal-based Navy squadrons and 18 by the Army's P-39s and P-400s, plus over 20 claimed by the bomber crews. Estimated Japanese losses to these units give a probable total of 260 aircraft. Cactus lost 101 aircraft, but of 126 Marine and 34 Navy fighter pilots who served on the island only 38 were killed or seriously wounded and, of these, 17 fell during the first week of combat. Outstanding aces of the 'Canal included Captain Joe Foss of VMF-121, the first American of the war to reach 20 victories, who gained the majority of his 26 kills at Guadalcanal; Major John L. Smith of VMF-223, who accounted for 19 enemy aircraft during the battle; and Lieutenant-Colonel "Indian Joe" Bauer of VMF-212 (11 victories), one of the great all-round fighter pilots of the Pacific war.

## Guadalcanal

The Marine airmen at Midway had not died in vain. The gallant Henderson's name was soon to be immortalized when it was given to the jungle airstrip — Henderson Field — which became the focus of the bitter six-month struggle for Guadalcanal.

Guadalcanal is a jungle-carpeted island some 90 miles long and 25 miles wide in the Solomons group, which lies on the north-eastern approaches to Australia. Early in 1942 it assumed a critical strategic importance. If seized by the Japanese, Guadalcanal could be used to cut the sea supply routes between the United States and Australia. In American hands, it could serve first as a shield to the Allied build-up in Australia and then as a springboard for pushing the Japanese out of the South Pacific.

Before the Battle of Midway, the Imperial General Headquarters had authorized a series of ambitious operations in the islands

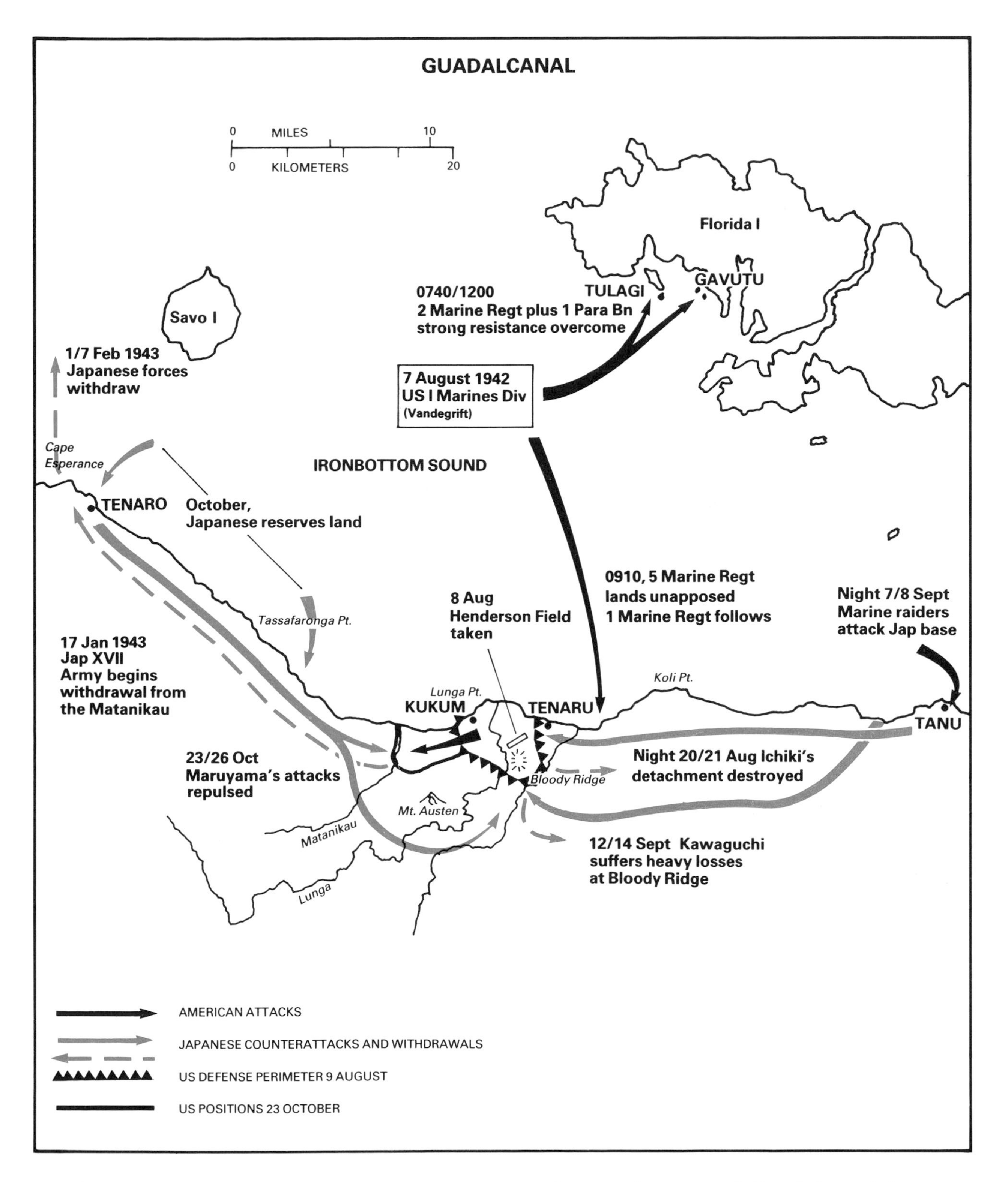


north and north-east of Australia, including the establishment of air and naval bases in the Solomons. After Midway, however, these plans were drastically revised and scaled down.

In May 1942, the Japanese had seized the island of Tulagi, with its magnificent anchorage, 30 miles north of Guadalcanal. At the end of the month they inserted troops on Guadalcanal. By mid-June, Australian coastwatchers were sending back reports that the Japanese were building an airstrip on the north coast of Guadalcanal between Tenaro and Kukum. When completed, it would enable Japanese aircraft to dominate the area. The number of Japanese troops on the island rapidly rose to about 2,400.

In the first six months of 1942 the United States' commitment to the "Europe First" policy had limited the men and materiel available for large-scale operations in the Solomons. Now Admiral Ernest J. King, Chief of Naval Operations and a powerful advocate of the allocation of greater resources

*Opposite, top:* A Marine F4F Wildcat takes off from the airstrip at Henderson Field, focus of the bitter seven-month struggle for Guadalcanal. With a maximum speed of around 330mph, the Wildcat was rather slow, but this was offset by its strength and maneuverability. The Wildcat was virtually the only Navy and Marine fighter facing the massive Japanese onslaught from Pearl Harbor until the arrival of the F6F Hellcat at the end of August 1943.
*Opposite, bottom:* Major-General Alexander A. Vandergrift, architect of victory at Guadalcanal, takes a back seat to Lieutenant-General Thomas Holcomb, the Corps Commandant, in December 1942.

to the Pacific, urged an operation to deny the Japanese the Solomons once and for all. In spite of their reservations, the Joint Chiefs of Staff gave their consent. Eight months after the humiliation of Pearl Harbor, the United States launched its first offensive against the Japanese in the Pacific — Operation Watchtower.

The US 1st Marine Division, reinforced by Marine Raider and parachute units, was tasked with landing in the Tulagi/Guadalcanal area at the beginning of August and establishing a "permanent lodgement". The landing force reserve was to be provided by Marines of 2nd Marine Division. This bold plan belied the difficulties which lay ahead and the preparedness of the Marines for so important an operation.

Operation Watchtower was a stab in the dark. In the summer of 1942 there was not a single accurate map of Guadalcanal. There was no reliable information on the target area's tides and reefs, and no accurate assessment of the strength and dispositions of the enemy. These were, perhaps, the least of the problems facing 1st Marine Division's commander, Major-General Alexander A. Vandegrift.

Rapid expansion following Pearl Harbor had brought the division up to wartime strength, but thousands of its men were raw recruits with no experience beyond basic drill and weapons training. The division had not participated in any large-scale exercises and many of its units had no experience of amphibious maneuvers. When the division had been despatched from its base in North Carolina, General Vandegrift had been assured that his men would be given plenty of time for training and acclimatization as they were not likely to go into action until 1943. The first Vandegrift learned of the Marines' task was when he called on Admiral Ghormley of the US Navy, the commander of the South Pacific area and overall commander of the expedition, in New Zealand on 25 June. Half of Vandegrift's division had not yet arrived and D-Day — eventually fixed for 7 August — was just six weeks away.

The US Navy forces assembled for Watchtower were as inexperienced in amphibious operations as many of Vandegrift's Marines. A dress-rehearsal for the operation was held off Koro in the Fijis on 26 July. The aim was to test the fundamentals of an amphibious assault: air and naval gunfire support, air-ground communications, ship-to-shore communications, ground-controlled aerial bombing and disembarkation procedures. The result was a fiasco. Coral reefs prevented many assault craft from landing on their assigned beaches; many of the landing craft broke down; and the naval gunfire and close-air support was wildly inaccurate. Vandegrift could only hope that everything would be all right on the night.

In the early hours of 7 August, Martin Clemens, an Australian coastwatcher on Guadalcanal , was woken in his mountainside hideout by the sound of heavy guns. As dawn came up he had a grandstand view of the the landings on the island. The grey transport ships of the South Pacific Amphibious Force, commanded by Rear-Admiral Richmond K. Turner, moved deliberately toward their allotted positions off Guadalcanal and the neighboring islands. Simultaneously, the British Rear-Admiral Victor Crutchley deployed three Australian cruisers (*Australia*, *Hobart*, *Canberra*), two US cruisers (*Chicago*, *San Juan*) and nine destroyers north-east and north-west of Savo Island on the most likely Japanese avenue of approach. Over the horizon, Vice-Admiral Frank Fletcher's three carriers (*Saratoga*, *Wasp*, *Enterprise*) maneuvered 100 miles south of Guadalcanal. Screened by six cruisers and 16 destroyers, they provided air cover for the assault force.

The assault force had achieved total tactical surprise. The Japanese on Guadalcanal and the neighboring islands of Florida, Tulagi, Gavutu and Tanambogo did not know the enemy were on them until the first bombs and shells fell on their positions. At 0641hrs, after a 30-minute bombardment, the order was given to land the Marines on Guadalcanal. Thousands of tense, grim-faced Marines clambered down the cargo nets hanging from the decks of the transport ships and into the assault craft below. The landing craft churned through the calm sea to their assembly areas, forming into "boat groups" and closing with Red Beach in regulated waves. At 0910 hrs the first wave (1st and 2nd Battalions, 5th Marines) hit the beach on a 1,600-yard front. The landing crafts' hulls juddered into Guadalcanal's white sand, and the bombardment shifted inland as the Marines waded ashore through the warm, greenish-blue water, their weapons held high.

Pushing into jungle, they hastily established a defensive perimeter 600yds

inland. The Marines found it heavy going. Two weeks in cramped troop transports had sapped their stamina. Heavy packs, insufficient water and salt tablets, and the steamy unfamiliar jungle terrain, reduced many of them to a state of exhaustion. Advanced units had moved about a mile inland when General Vandegrift ordered a halt to re-orientate and establish internal contact. When night fell, the jungle reverberated with the sound of nervous sentries' fire against imaginary targets. General Vandegrift noted the "uniform and lamentable" failure of all units properly to patrol their fronts and flanks.

The Japanese failure to contest the landings on Guadalcanal gave Vandegrift a crucial breathing space. On Red Beach, 500

*Above:* Marines coming ashore at Guadalcanal take advantage of a short rest before moving into position.

men of 1st Pioneer Battalion struggled to prevent the logistical build-up from turning into a shambles. The landing area rapidly became clogged with a jumble of randomly dumped materiel through which the later waves of Marines wandered in search of orders. Off the shore, scores of LVAs sailed to and fro, searching for a clear space to leave their supplies. If enemy aircraft from Rabaul had struck hard at the congested beaches, Operation Watchtower might have failed at the first obstacle.

On the islands neighboring Guadalcanal — Tulagi, Gavutu and Tanambogo — the Japanese offered fierce resistance. Vandegrift had carefully picked his disembarkation point on Guadalcanal where there was no enemy. On Guadalcanal's smaller neighbors there could be no avoiding the Japanese, and the task of securing them had been given to the most seasoned Marine units.

Colonel Merritt "Red Mike" Edson, commander of 1st Marine Raider Battalion, tasked with the capture of Tulagi, ordered his men to strip down to the minimum combat equipment, telling them, "Don't worry about food. The Japs eat it, too. All you have to do is get it."

It took three days to crush the Japanese resistance on Tulagi, Gavutu and Tanambogo. Their defenders, fighting from coral caves, natural redoubts and heavily fortified emplacements, had literally to be blasted into submission. In the final assault on Tanambogo, the destroyer *Buchanan* was called in to pour shells into the last Japanese strongpoints at point-blank range. Resistance collapsed and within minutes the Marines had secured the island. The Marines had lost 144 dead or missing and almost 200 wounded. About 700 Japanese had been killed — about 90 percent of their number — many of them in mass suicide charges. This savage passage of arms gave the Marines a grim foretaste of the fanatical Japanese will to resist to the last man from fortified emplacements, and the extreme difficulty of assaulting heavily defended islands.

The first Marine patrols reached Guadalcanal's airfield late in the afternoon of the 8th. Everywhere were signs of the panic which had gripped the Japanese construction teams and the Naval Landing Force garrison when they had fled into the jungle after the initial American bombardment. Behind them they had left a large number of heavy vehicles, repair facilities, fuel dumps and quantities of food.

Satisfaction at the capture of the airfield was shortlived. From the outset, Admiral Fletcher had promised the land forces only two days' support, and he was now about to withdraw his carriers. At the same time a force of seven Japanese cruisers under Vice-Admiral Mikawa moved in to attack US transports unloading off Guadalcanal. On the night of 8/9 August, Mikawa encountered Crutchley's cruisers, which were patrolling the approaches to Savo Island. The Japanese had superior torpedo and night-fighting techniques, and in the engagement four of Crutchley's cruisers were sunk. The remaining elements of the naval force were now withdrawn, the last of Admiral Turner's ships sailing away on the afternoon of the 9th. The 11,145 Marines on Guadalcanal were on their own, with 50 percent of their equipment and supplies disappearing over the horizon in Turner's transports.

General Vandegrift was now in a perilous position, short of supplies and heavy equipment and holding a small enclave surrounded by dense jungle in which lurked the survivors of the original Japanese occupation force. The Marines had five units of fire and food for 37 days. (The original loadings of 60 days' supplies and 10 units of fire were, respectively, 33 and 50 percent below the 90-day and 20-unit levels considered normal for this kind of operation).

The Japanese enjoyed complete air superiority, and the Marines were subjected to constant air raids as they labored to complete the airfield, now known as Henderson Field. The waters around Guadalcanal were controlled by Japanese warships, which regularly shelled the Lunga Point beach-head. At one point, a Japanese cruiser landed a 200-strong advance echelon and supplies along the coast in broad daylight.

Using the heavy equipment abandoned by the Japanese, work was quickly completed on the airfield and a start made on two subsidiary strips. On 20 August, two squadrons of 1st Marine Aircraft Wing (MAW-1) flew into Henderson Field: VMF-223, an F4F Wildcat squadron under Major John L. Smith; and VMSB-232, an SBD Dauntless squadron commanded by Lieutenant-Colonel Dick Mangrum. These were the first elements in what soon became known as Cactus Air Force, "Cactus" being

*Below:* A detachment of Marines pause in a jungle clearing, December 1942. The Marine in the right foreground has added netting to his helmet for use in camouflaging himself in dense undergrowth. Conditions on Guadalcanal were punishing, with an exceptionally high number of men suffering from dysentery, malnutrition, virulent fungus infection, exposure and battle fatigue.

*Above:* A Marine Raidar unit comes ashore at Guadalcanal in November 1942.

the codename for Guadalcanal.

Within hours of Cactus Force's arrival, the Japanese attacked from the east. Lieutenant-General Hyakutake, commanding XVII Army in the South Pacific, had been ordered to "eliminate" the American force on Guadalcanal, a task he assigned to Major-General Kawaguchi's XXXV Infantry Brigade. However, the brigade was not fully assembled, and the decision was taken to send in two echelons from the only units available, the regiment commanded by Colonel Ichiki and a Special Naval Landing Force.

On the night of 18/19 August, six destroyers under the command of Rear-Admiral Tanaka landed the 815 men of Ichiki's first echelon 20 miles east of Lunga Point. Japanese intelligence was extremely poor — Ichiki had been told that there were no more than 2,000 Marines on Guadalcanal — and their plans fatally compromised by a reckless contempt for the enemy.

At 0700 hrs on 19 August, one of Ichiki's units encountered a patrol from A Company, 1st Marines. A fierce fire fight left 31 Japanese and three Marines dead. Examination of Japanese bodies revealed detailed maps of the Marines' defences.

Disturbed by the Marines' discovery of his landings, Ichiki immediately moved on to the offensive. On the night of 20/21 August, he ordered an attack on the left flank of Vandegrift's defensive perimeter. The initial attack went in at 0310hrs as 200 men waded across the River Ilu with fixed bayonets and hurled themselves on the Marines' lines. Most of them were mowed down by small-arms fire and canister-firing 37-mm anti-tank guns of the 1st Special Weapons Battalion. A second bayonet charge met a similar fate, following which Ichiki withdrew into the jungle.

Although it had been grievously mauled, Ichiki's echelon regrouped. When daylight came, the Marines were subjected to harassing fire from across the Ilu. Vandegrift, anticipating the arrival of Japanese reinforcements, moved swiftly to deliver the *coup de grâce* to the survivors of Ichiki's formation. Led by Lieutenant-Colonel Leonard B. Cresswell, the 1st Battalion, 1st Marines, crossed the Ilu further upstream and swung north to envelop the Japanese.

By early afternoon, Ichiki's men had been encircled and the final bloody phase of "The Battle of the Tenaru" began to unfold. Bombed and strafed by Cactus Air Force and

pounded at short-range by artillery, the Japanese were squeezed back towards the sea. The last pockets of resistance were overcome by Vandegrift's light tanks, which remorselessly crushed the dead, dying and living beneath their tracks. In his report Vandegrift wrote that "the rear of the tanks looked like meatgrinders". The Marines had lost 34 men dead and 75 wounded. Ichiki had lost all but a handful of his élite troops. Escaping with a few men, he marched eastwards to Taivu, where he tore up and burned the regimental colors and then committed *hara-kiri*.

The Battle of the Tenaru was only the opening exchange in the see-saw battle for Guadalcanal. The arrival of Marine aircraft on Henderson Field had conferred an immediate tactical advantage on the Americans. On 25 August, Rear-Admiral Tanaka's transport group, carrying Ichiki's second echelon and screened by a light cruiser and destroyers, was pounced upon by Cactus Air Force's dive-bombers. Tanaka's flagship, *Jintsu*, and the transport *Kenryu Maru*, were both hit and set on fire. Further attacks by USAAF B-17s from Espiritu Santo sent one of his destroyers and the transport to the bottom. Tanaka, frustrated in his aim of reinforcing Guadalcanal, retired to the advanced base in the Shortland Islands, north-west of Guadalcanal.

Japanese movement in the waters around Guadalcanal was now restricted to the hours between dusk and dawn. Accordingly, Tanaka reverted to his original tactic of reinforcing Guadalcanal by using fast destroyers on nocturnal "Rat Runs". By the end of August the resourceful Tanaka's destroyers were operating with a clockwork precision which earned the American nickname of the "Tokyo Express".

To investigate the Japanese build-up outside his enclave, Vandegrift despatched Edson's Marine Raiders by sea on 7/8 September to make a reconnaissance in force of the enemy base at Taivu. The Raiders returned with vital intelligence of Japanese strength and intentions. The news that General Kawaguchi had moved off into the jungle with the bulk of his force was a clear indication that a second Japanese attack was imminent. Vandegrift anticipated correctly that the main Japanese thrust would be launched against the low 1,000yd ridge extending south of Henderson Field and parallel to the Lunga River, an inviting avenue of approach to the Marine airstrips.

He placed 1st Raider Battalion in this sector supported by the 105-mm howitzers of 5th Battalion, 11th Marines and elements of the Special Weapons Battalion. His reserve, 2nd Battalion, 5th Marines, was placed immediately to their rear.

Kawaguchi had planned a three-jawed envelopment of Vandegrift's enclave from the west, south and south-east, co-ordinated with air and naval support. To the normal difficulties associated with such a plan, he added the complication of cutting a trail over the steep jungle-clad ridges and gorges from the Tasimboko area to a point south of Henderson Field. The aim was to avoid observation, but what little Kawaguchi gained in surprise he lost in co-ordination and the stamina of the troops under his command. From the outset he lost control of the battle. His troops were exhausted by the march through the jungle, and communications broke down. Kawaguchi pressed on.

The Japanese showed their hand at mid-day on 12 September when bombers launched a heavy attack on the ridge south of Henderson Field. As darkness fell, a Japanese cruiser and three destroyers began to shell the ridge.

The shelling gave way to a series of probing attacks, but it was not until 2100 hrs on 13 September that the "Battle of Bloody Ridge" reached a crescendo. Without artillery preparation, Kawaguchi drove a two-battalion charge against the center and right of the Raider-Parachute line. Marine mortars, sited in defilade, poured shells into the human waves as fast as their loaders could slide them down the tubes. Behind them the artillery on the ridge laid down a devastating fire, some of it falling within 200yds of the Marines' lines. Japanese mortar fire began to drum the ridge and at 2230hrs, after a violent barrage, they shifted their attack to the thin flank held by the Parachute troops. Screaming in English, "Gas Attack! Gas Attack!", they swarmed from the jungle through a smoke screen, driving the Parachute troops back along the ridge. The Marines' defenses buckled but did not break. The Raiders' communications with the artillery in their rear and Vandegrift's headquarters were severed. But Japanese flares "telegraphed" each successive attack, providing 11th Marines' gunners with reference points for the all-night firing in which they expended 1,992 rounds of 105-mm projectiles, some at ranges as short as

1,600 yards.

At one point the Japanese surged to within 1,000 yards of Henderson Field in some of the most savage fighting of the Guadalcanal campaign. They were thrown back, only to launch two more attacks before daybreak. But their strength was now ebbing away. When cannon-firing fighters from Henderson Field began strafing the jungle at the foot of the ridge, Kawaguchi gave the order to withdraw. He had lost over 1,200 men killed, wounded and missing. Demoralized, disease-ridden and starving, the survivors of XXXV Brigade straggled away westwards to link up with other Japanese units at Port Cruz.

The Marines had also taken heavy losses. Of just over 750 Raiders who had landed on 7 August, 234 had become casualties; of the

The debris of battle. A Japanese landing barge which never reached its destination, wrecked by fire from Marine half-tracks during the Guadalcanal campaign.

377 Parachute troops, 212 had been killed

The response of Imperial General Headquarters was to despatch the veteran XXXVIII Division to the South Pacific to join XVII Army. Lieutenant-General Maruyama's II Division — already in the area — was ordered to Guadalcanal. Japanese operations on New Guinea were suspended in order to facilitate a concentration of all available naval, air and military resources on the recapturing of Guadalcanal. General Hyakutake transferred his headquarters to the island, where he had direct control of 20,000 men, including a regiment of three batteries of heavy artillery, a mortar battalion and a tank company.

The Marines also received much-needed reinforcements: 7th Marines, an artillery battalion, motor transport companies, communications personnel and 164th Infantry Regiment. This brought the number of US troops on Guadalcanal to 23,000, but many of them were suffering from malnutrition, dysentery, virulent fungus infection, exposure and battle fatigue. In other less crucial battle zones, more than one-third of them would have been invalided out.

Cactus Air Force was also stretched to the limit. Japanese attempts to feed in reinforcements led to a naval battle off Cape Esperance at the northern end of Guadalcanal. On the night of 11/12 October, a Japanese convoy sailing down the "Slot" — the narrow channel inside the Solomons chain — clashed with the cruisers commanded by Rear-Admiral Norman Scott. After a confused and ferocious engagement, the Japanese withdrew, although the transports they wei e escorting got through to Guadalcanal, landing heavy artillery and other reinforcements unopposed.

At first light on the 12th, all available SBDs, F4Fs and P-39s took off in search of any cripples from the night engagement. They were led by Colonel Al Cooley, whose MAG-14 had relieved MAG-23, and Lieutenant-Commander John Eldridge, commanding VS-71. The attack group found the survivors north of the Russell Islands, sinking two destroyers and inflicting heavy damage on the remaining enemy ships.

During the night of 13/14 October, the battle ships *Kongo* and *Haruna* sailed close into the Guadalcanal coastline and delivered a 90-minute bombardment of the Marines' positions with their 14-in guns. Over 900 shells were fired into the beach-head, most of them landing on Henderson Field and in the coconut grove at the north-eastern side of the strip, where the pilots and crews were billeted. Forty-one officers and men were killed; of the 38 SBDs operational 24 hours before, only seven remained fit for flying. The Field was pockmarked with huge craters and strewn with blazing wreckage but, miraculously, the fighter strip was virtually unscathed and 29 of Cactus Air Forces' 42 F4Fs were still in flyable shape.

Air raids on the 13th and 14th inflicted further damage, and another bombardment from the battleships in the small hours of the 15th left so few aircraft serviceable, and petrol in such short supply, that a Japanese convoy of six transports — sailing in broad

*Above:* Lieutenant Mitchell Paige of 7th Marines receives the Medal of Honor from General Vandegrift for gallantry during the fighting on Guadalcanal. The US Marines who served on the 'Canal composed a little verse which vividly conveys their feelings about the campaign: "And when he gets to Heaven, To St Peter he will tell: 'One more Marine reporting, Sir — I've served my time in Hell!' "

daylight down the Slot — was able to put 3,500 troops ashore at Tassafaronga.

In a supreme effort, Cactus Air Force put 12 SBDs and eight fighters in the air for an attack on the enemy transports. Flying with them was a Consolidated PBY Catalina flying boat piloted by General Geiger's aide, Major Jack Cram, and rigged with two torpedoes. In one of the most remarkable torpedo attacks in military history, Cram glided in from 6,000ft, releasing the torpedoes at 200ft and scoring a direct hit on one of the transports. The lumbering Catalina flew back to Henderson Field with Japanese fighters swarming all over it, but Cram made it back with the help of a landing F4F, whose pilot shot down the last of his pursuers without bothering to pull up his gear.

On 23 October the Japanese II Division — some 5,600 men — attacked the western perimeter of Henderson Field across the Matanikau River. The Marines were well dug in and ready for them, smashing the attack with concentrated artillery fire. Twenty-four hours later, General Maruyama launched the main thrust from the south with more than 7,000 men. For two days the Japanese force battered itself to destruction on the ridges to the south of Henderson Field. Then, like Kawaguchi's brigade, they fell back into the jungle, having lost 3,500 men.

Poor co-ordination had doomed Maruyama's offensive. His arduous approach march through the jungle had held him up and forced him to abandon much of his artillery. Twice he postponed his attack, but news of the second postponement failed to reach the commander on the Matanikau. The plans for a simultaneous two-pronged assault on Henderson Field were destroyed, and with them the dwindling hopes of victory on Guadalcanal. Operating on interior lines, Vandegrift had defeated each attack in turn. American losses had been fewer than 350, and they now began to expand the perimeter.

Maruyama's attack on Henderson Field was to have been supported by aircraft of the Combined Fleet, stationed north of Guadalcanal. Simultaneously, US Task Forces 16 (with the carrier *Enterprise*) and 17 (with the carrier *Hornet*) were ordered to patrol the area around the Santa Cruz islands to intercept Japanese forces approaching Guadalcanal. The fleets clashed on 26 October. The Japanese carrier *Zuiho* was disabled by dive-bombers from *Enterprise*, which in turn was hit by air strikes. *Hornet* was swamped by dive- and torpedo-bomber attacks and reduced to a blazing hulk which was later sunk by the Japanese. The battle was broken off with the disabled enemy carrier limping away in company with *Zuiho*. Having lost *Hornet*, and with *Enterprise* out of action, there was not a single carrier operational with the Pacific Fleet. But the Japanese had won a Pyrrhic victory, having lost about 100 aircraft and their irreplaceable experienced aircrews.

Refusing to accept defeat, the Japanese continued to pour men and supplies into Guadalcanal. But in mid-November 11 transports carrying the bulk of Lieutenant-General Sano's XXVIII Division to Guadalcanal were intercepted by aircraft flying from Henderson Field. Seven of the transports, and 4,000 men, were lost. Only 2,000 men, most of them without equipment, reached Guadalcanal. Thereafter General Hyakutake was isolated; the supplies and reinforcements reaching him shrank to a trickle.

Preparing to go on the offensive, the Americans brought in fresh units to replace the war-weary 1st Marine Division, which was relieved at the beginning of December by the 25th Infantry Division, 2nd Marine Division and the Americal Division, designated 14th Corps under the command of General Alexander Patch. At the end of the month, Emperor Hirohito authorized the withdrawal of XVII Army from Guadalcanal. In a text-book evacuation during the first nine days of February, the destroyers of the "Tokyo Express" took off the 12,000 exhausted survivors.

Overall Japanese casualties in the fighting on Guadalcanal were 14,800 killed or missing in action, 9,000 dead from disease and 1,000 taken prisoner. Marine and Army casualties

## MARINE RAIDERS AND PARACHUTE UNITS

In the 1930s, the Marine Corps experimented with the idea of using raider teams to operate behind enemy lines. The concept achieved formal recognition in January 1942 when 1st Battalion, 5th Marines, was redesignated 1st Separate Battalion. A month later a Marine officer, Lieutenant-Colonel Evans F. Carlson, was ordered to raise men to form the 2nd Separate Battalion. Lieutenant-Colonel Merritt A. Edson was appointed commander of 1st Battalion. Within weeks the units were redesignated 1st and 2nd Raider Battalions and readied for combat. Each battalion was made up of 850 officers and men, divided into six rifle companies and a small headquarters. In addition to standard infantry equipment, Raiders used shotguns, bangalore torpedoes, chainsaws and rubber dinghies. They had three specific roles: spearheading amphibious landings; launching hit-and-run raids against enemy-held islands; and conducting protracted guerrilla operations behind enemy lines. By mid-1942 both Raider Battalions had been blooded. In August, Carlson's Raiders hit Makin Island in a lightning raid, and Edson's men were tasked with the taking of Tulagi in the initial phase of the battle for Guadacanal. The success of the Raiders led to the formation of more units, which were formed into 1st and 2nd Raider Regiments.

The first Marine parachute unit was raised in 1941, taking part in combined US Army Corps/Marine Corps exercises at Camp Lejeune that year. Subsequently two more companies were raised, and as 1st Parachute Battalion, Fleet Marine Force, the unit fought on Tulagi, Gavutu and Guadalcanal. Three more parachute battalions were then formed. Early in 1943, 2nd and 3rd Battalions joined 1st Battalion as 1st Parachute Regiment; 4th Battalion was never deployed as a unit from the United States. In spite of their name and training, none of the parachute units ever jumped in combat. The Parachute Regiment (minus 2nd Battalion) fought at Bougainville in November 1943. The 2nd Battalion participated in the operation in Vella Lavella under the command of 8th New Zealand Brigade, suffering heavy casualties during the initial landings when the ship carrying the battalion HQ was sunk. In October 1943 2nd Battalion was in action in the diversionary operation against Choiseul. The Parachute Regiment was disbanded in 1944 and its units merged with 5th Marine Division, fighting at Iwo Jima in 1945.

totalled 1,598 officers and men killed and 4,709 wounded. Of these, Marine ground forces dead were 1,152 and 2,799 wounded.

For the Allies, the seizure and successful defense of Henderson Field brought crucial strategic gains. Australia and New Zealand were now safe, and Allied forces stood on the flank of the Palau–Truk–Marshalls line, the outer cordon of the Japanese empire.

The battle for Guadalcanal was also a psychological victory over the previously all-conquering Japanese Army. The Marines had demonstrated that the Japanese could be beaten on their own ground. Not the least of their achievements was the 150-mile trek behind enemy lines undertaken by 2nd Marine Raider Battalion under Colonel Evans F. Carlson. Landing at Aola Bay on 4 November, Carlson's Raiders fought their way through the jungle, in four weeks killing over 500 Japanese in a dozen actions for the loss of only 17 men and driving the enemy deep into the interior of Guadalcanal. No longer could the Japanese claim absolute supremacy in the jungle.

Above all, Guadalcanal was a primer of amphibious and jungle tactics. As the official history of the US Marine Corps observes, "It was everything the United States could do at the moment against everything the Japanese could manage at that place". General Vandegrift summed up the importance of the campaign in characteristically pithy fashion: "We struck at Guadalcanal to halt the advance of the Japanese. We did not know how strong he was, nor did we know his plans. We knew only that he was moving down the island chain and that he had to be stopped. We were all well-trained and as well-armed as time and our peacetime experience allowed us to be. We needed combat to tell us how effective our training, our doctrines, and our weapons had been. We tested them against the enemy, and we found that they worked. From that moment in 1942, the tide turned, and the Japanese never again advanced."

## The Battle for the Solomons

Guadalcanal was a setback for the Japanese. But they had anticipated a shift to a defensive strategy once their perimeter had been anchored, and the defeats at Midway and Guadalcanal had taken place beyond the limits of the perimeter as they had originally envisaged it. They were more concerned with the alarming attrition of trained carrier pilots. They still nursed hopes that a series of defeats on the main line of their perimeter would force the Americans to give up.

On the Allied side, the victory at Guadalcanal marked the beginning of the Pacific drive on Japan. General MacArthur, Supreme Commander South-West Pacific, was to outflank the Japanese base at Rabaul and approach the Philippines from the south. Admiral Halsey, commanding the South Pacific area, was to co-operate with MacArthur in isolating the fortress of Rabaul and driving north-west from Guadalcanal along the Solomon Islands. Admiral Nimitz, commanding the Eastern and North Pacific areas, was to channel resources to the other two commanders while launching a central drive through the Pacific. The axes of the final assault on Japan were to run from the Philippines through Okinawa; from the Marianas through Iwo Jima; and southwards from the Aleutians.

In the South-West Pacific area, units of the US Army would shoulder the burden of the fighting. The Marines would carry the landings in the Central Pacific. To meet this challenge, the Corps was to be expanded to 300,000 officers and men by mid-1943. This rapid expansion led to the abandonment of the Corps' policy of segregation and the admission of blacks into its ranks, a reform

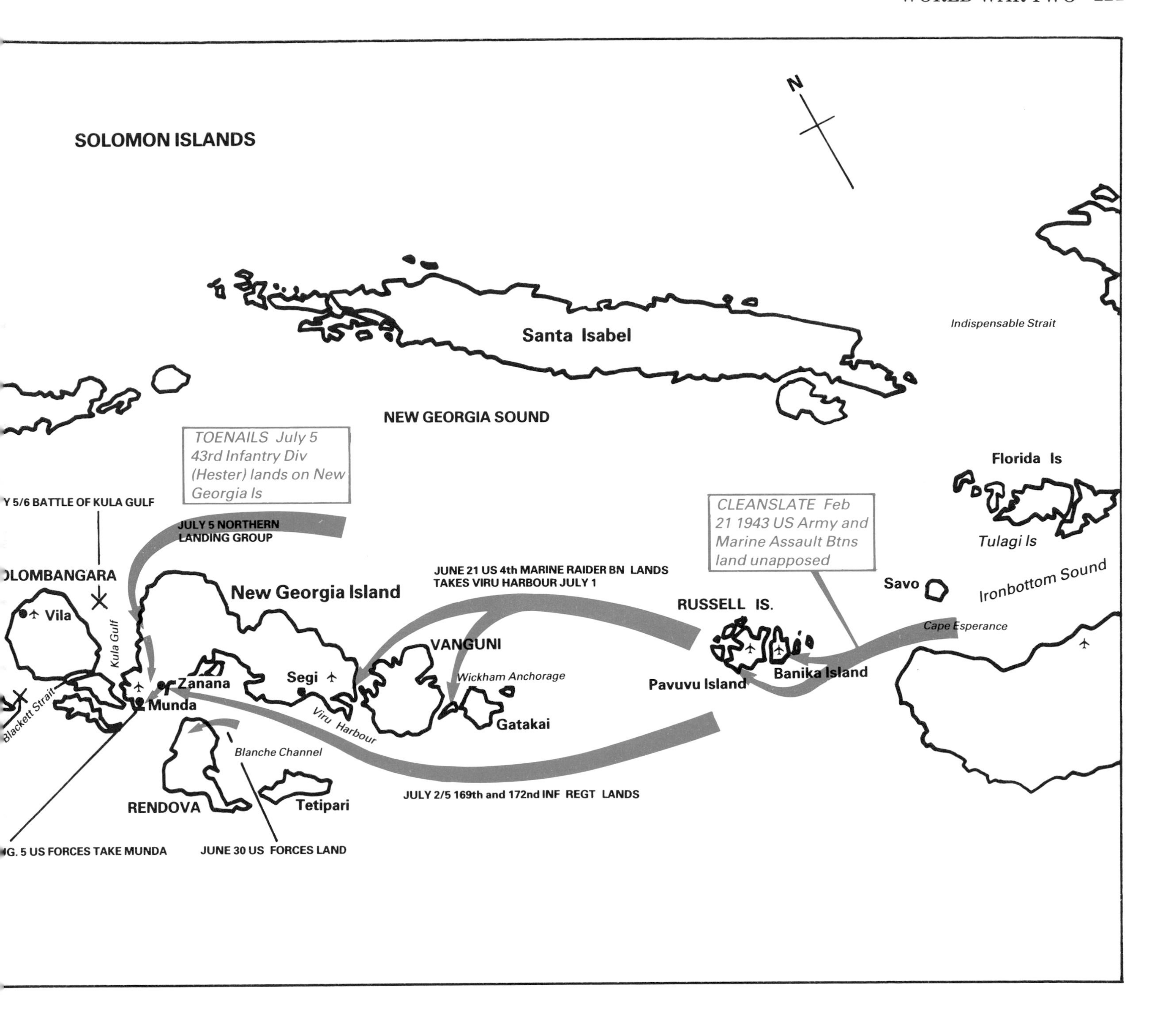


*Following page:* Marine Raiders and their dogs on Bougainville.
*Below:* Marine infantry and light tanks encounter heavy going in the jungle on Bougainville.

initially undertaken with the greatest reluctance. At first blacks were confined to segregated units, under white officers and NCOs, and given only defense and labor duties. Black Marines were eventually introduced to combat, and by the end of the war over 15,000 had passed through.

For the Allies, the Guadalcanal campaign had been only the beginning of the battle for the Solomons. Further advances along the island chain to seal off Rabaul from the south-east set the pattern for subsequent operations in the Pacific. Key air bases were seized by outflanking moves, to provide an overlapping system of controlled air space. Intermediate enemy-held islands were mopped up while preparations were made for the next advance. Principal objectives in the Solomons were the New Georgia group and Bougainville.

Between February and June 1943, there was a breathing space while Admiral Halsey prepared for the assault on New Georgia. On 21 February, in Operation Cleanslate, the Russell Islands — between Guadalcanal and New Georgia — were seized in an unopposed operation. The capture of the Russell Islands provided the Americans with sites for fighter bases to cover movements through the central Solomons. Further support came from new airstrips constructed on Guadalcanal.

On 18 April Admiral Yamamoto, Japan's foremost strategist, was intercepted and shot down by US fighters while flying from Rabaul to Bougainville. At the end of the month, General MacArthur issued his final plan for Operation Cartwheel, a co-ordinated drive in the South and South-West Pacific towards Rabaul.

The campaign in the central Solomons was

opened on 21 June when 4th Marine Raider Battalion landed at Segi on the eastern tip of New Georgia. Principal target on New Georgia was the airfield at Munda.

The Army units tasked with taking Munda — 169th and 172nd Infantry Regiments and 43rd Infantry Division — were reinforced with two Marine Raider and two Defense battalions. The Marines were also assigned a role in the capture of Rendova, the island to the south of Munda, from which artillery support could be provided for the assault on the airfield. Between 2 and 5 July, troops were landed to attack Munda from north and south. As this was the most important airfield in the Solomons, it was heavily defended and was not taken until 5 August. Marines played a vital role in beating off successive Japanese counter-attacks around the airfield and provided artillery support from Rendova with their new 155-mm "Long Toms". They also supplied six of the 32 fighter and bomber squadrons flying out of Guadalcanal and the Russells during Operation Toenails. On the night of 6 August, Japanese reinforcements were destroyed in a naval battle in the Vella Gulf. By 22 August the enemy had evacuated northern New Georgia, and three days later all resistance on the island had ceased.

In mid-August, a US Combat Team had

landed on Vella Lavella, west of New Georgia, and established an airbase which leapfrogged the intermediate island of Kolombangara. New Zealand troops replaced the US forces on Vella Lavella in mid-September and cleared the island of the remnants of the Japanese garrison. This forced the enemy to abandon Kolombangara, and by the end of the first week in October the campaign in the central Solomons had been brought to a successful conclusion.

On 1 October Admiral Halsey ordered an invasion of the island of Bougainville. Its capture would place the Japanese base at Rabaul within range of American fighters and dive-bombers. However, it presented a formidable obstacle. Approximately 125 miles long, Bougainville offered a nightmarish prospect for military operations, carpeted with swamps and jungle from which rose the jagged peaks of a mountainous spine. A line of Japanese airfields stretched from Bonis, on Bougainville's northern tip, to Buin in the south. Defending them were 40,000 troops.

To disguise their intentions, the Allies launched two diversionary operations. In Operation Blissful, on 28 October, 2nd Battalion, 1st Marine Parachute Regiment under Lieutenant-Colonel Victor H. Krulak, made a feint assault on the island of Choiseul, to the north of New Georgia. Simultaneously, in Operation Goodtime, the 8th New Zealand Brigade landed on the Treasury Islands, south-west of Vella Lavella.

These feints successfully distracted Japanese attention. When the attack on Bougainville — Operation Cherryblossom — opened on 1 November, 3rd Marine Division met only light resistance as it went ashore at Cape Torokina on the island's southern coast. By nightfall, 14,000 troops had been put ashore.

*Top:* Marines pinned down on the beach at Bougainville. *Above:* A flamethrower is turned on a Japanese pillbox on Russell Island.

*Above:* Bougainville, November 1943. Casualties disembark from a tank landing craft after being ferried across Empress Augusta Bay to Puruata Island, where another LST waits to evacuate them.

One of the principal lessons of Guadalcanal had been that it was cheaper and easier to build a new airfield than to capture and then improve one the Japanese had already built or were building. This also coincided with one of the fundamentals of amphibious warfare — never hit a defended beach when the objective can be reached over an undefended one.

At first the Japanese commander on Bougainville, the ill-fated General Hayakutake, believed that the 1 November landings were another diversion, holding back his forces while the Americans began to dig in and construct an airfield. A Japanese counter-attack, launched from Rabaul on 7 December, failed to dislodge the American assault force. By the end of the year they had established a defensive perimeter stretching 5,000 yards inland and had turned Empress Augusta Bay into an Allied naval base with three airstrips in operation. Even though much of Bougainville remained in enemy hands, Admiral Halsey was now poised to close the pincers on Rabaul.

By the time the Japanese launched a belated March offensive against the American perimeter, 3rd Marine Division had been replaced by the Americal Division. The Japanese threw themselves on the carefully prepared American positions, and in 17 days of bitter fighting suffered 7,000 casualties; American losses were 1,000. By the end of April, US aircraft from the Torokina strips were joining carrier-based 'planes in regular missions against Rabaul.

The trap was closing on Rabaul. MacArthur's next move was the capture of Cape Gloucester, on the western end of New Britain Island, which controlled the Vitiaz and Dampier Straits between New Britain and New Guinea. With the straits in American hands, the sea lanes to the north-west would be safe for passage. In a three-week operation beginning on 26 December, elements of 1st and 7th Marines overcame 10,000 Japanese troops in and around Cape Gloucester. The capture of the Admiralty Islands and the St Matthias Group northwest of New Britain (February–March 1944) completed the encirclement of Rabaul, whose 135,000-strong garrison was left to "wither on the vine".

### Tarawa

During the summer and autumn of 1943, before the pincers finally closed on Rabaul, Admiral Nimitz assembled an armada of ships, men and aircraft for the atoll-by-atoll drive in the Central Pacific. The offensive was designed to secure MacArthur's right flank and to provide forward bases for a strategic bombing campaign and a jumping-off point for landings on Japan itself. The three stepping stones in Nimitz's Central Pacific drive were the Gilbert Islands, the Marshalls and the Marianas.

The island chains of the Central Pacific presented operational problems markedly different from those which had been encountered at Guadalcanal and on Bougainville. They were made up of small atolls, rings of islets which were the tops of submerged mountains. These specks in the ocean had formidable natural defenses in the razor-sharp reefs which uniformly surrounded them. Their low contours offered little or no cover for amphibious assault forces coming ashore. Secure in fortified emplacements and bunkers, their Japanese defenders could survive the heaviest air and naval bombardments.

On 20 November 1943, the Central Pacific campaign opened with the launching of Operation Galvanic, the taking of the Gilberts, on the outer edge of Japan's Pacific empire. The forces assembled for Galvanic comprised the US 5th Fleet, under Vice-Admiral Raymond Spruance, and V Amphibious Corps, under the overall command of Major-General Holland M. "Howlin' Mad" Smith, a Marine veteran of the Aleutians campaign and one of the founding fathers of modern amphibious warfare.

By 23 November, Makin Island — the

*Below:* On the beach at Tarawa. Heavily-laden Marines climb the sea wall to attack Japanese positions around the atoll's airstrip.

scene of a daring Marine Raiders operation in August 1942 — had been secured by an Army landing force consisting of 165th Regimental Combat Team (reinforced) of 27th Division. But the toughest objective in the campaign lay ahead — Tarawa, a bracelet of tiny coral islands which was of crucial strategic importance. On one of its islets — Betio — there was a heavily defended airstrip suitable for fighters and light bombers. No thrust north-west to the Marshalls and Marianas could be undertaken until Tarawa had been seized.

Betio was only a few feet above the water, containing a scant 300 acres of sand, coral and palm trees. The Japanese had crammed 4,800 troops of the Special Naval Landing Force on Betio and added to the natural barrier of its twin coral reefs with a fearsome network of man-made defenses. The waters offshore were laced with mines, concealed obstacles and barbed wire, aimed at channelling attackers into prepared killing grounds. At the edge of the water a four-foot-high sea wall was defended by machine-gun posts with interlocking fields of fire.

Coastal defences included four 8-in guns, several smaller pieces, and a network of interlinked bunkers reinforced with concrete roofs up to 6½ft thick. Running out to sea were the island's coral reefs. Unknown to the Americans, the inner reef rose sufficiently high to ground their landing craft. It was planned to send only the first three waves of Marines ashore in LVTs, which could negotiate the barrier of the reefs. The remainder would have to carry the assault in LCVPs (Landing Craft Vehicle, Personnel) and LCMs (Landing Craft, Mechanised), both of which were likely to go aground on the edge of the reef, several hundred yards offshore.

The bombardment of Tarawa had begun on 13 November with a series of air strikes. Neither these, nor the 16-in shells of the battleships *Carolina* and *Maryland*, succeeded in suppressing the Japanese defenses. H-Hour was planned for 0830 hrs

on 20 November. The assault force was 2nd Marine Division, under Major-General Julian Smith. The attack was to be spearheaded by Colonel David Shoup's 2nd Marines and the 2nd Battalion, 8th Marine Regiment, with the remaining two battalions of 8th Marines being held back as a divisional reserve. Additionally, a corps reserve of three battalion landing teams of 6th Marines was held to cover the entire operation in the Gilberts, to be released to the division on request. Three landing areas were designated on Betio: Red Beaches 1, 2 and 3 on the island's lagoon side. The blunt western end of the islet, where no landings were planned, was designated Green Beach.

As the first wave of LVTs crossed the reef, the fire support lifted. Gazing at the dense cloud of smoke and coral dust swirling above Betio, the naval gunfire support commander, Admiral Kingman, thought it "impossible for any human being to be alive on Betio Island". But the enemy were ready and waiting.

Only the destroyers in the lagoon were close enough to give accurate suppressive fire during the Marines' first run-in to Betio. Thus the island's defenders had a breathing space in which to reach their posts and open up with a storm of machine-gun fire and 75-mm airburst shells.

The first Marines ashore, at 0855 hrs, were men of the scout and sniper platoon of 2nd Marine Regiment, led by Lieutenant William Hawkins, who took the end of the long pier which ran out from the corner of Red Beach 2. Behind Hawkins, the LVTs were taking heavy punishment. Half of them were destroyed in the water. Many of the remainder landed on the wrong beaches. None of them could surmount the sea wall. The Marines were pinned down on a few square yards of black sand in front of the barricades. There was no way back across the blood-tinged waters of the lagoon, and seemingly no way forward. The landing craft in the following waves were grounded hundreds of yards from the shore by an unexpectedly low tide, forcing the Marines to

LVTs churn towards the shore at Tarawa, 20 November 1943.

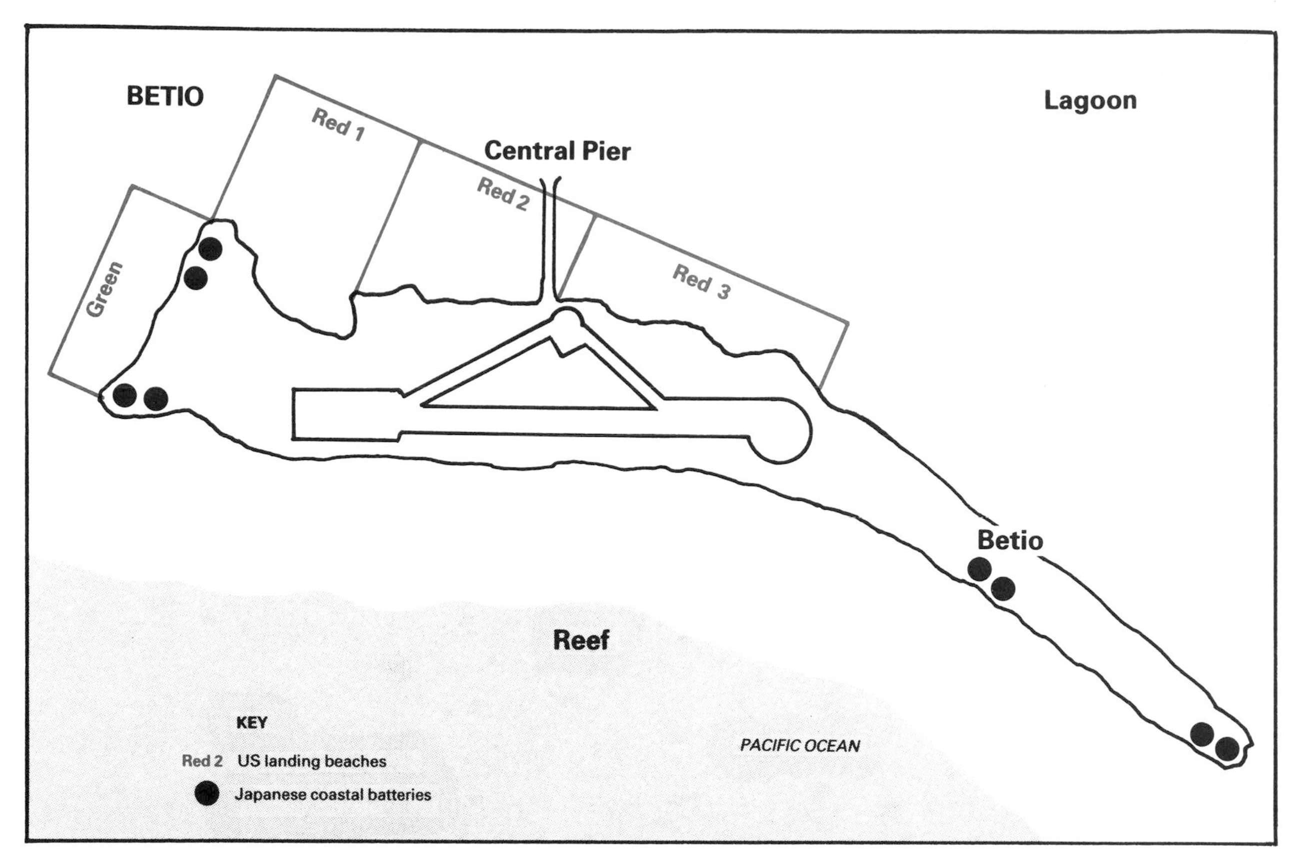


Fire-shredded palms, abandoned equipment and bloated corpses bear testimony to the savage fighting at the water's edge of Red Beach 2 during the landings on Tarawa. This was the objective of 2nd Battalion, 2nd Marines, under Colonel Herbert Amey. He and many of his men were cut down by withering fire from carefully hidden enemy bunkers.

wade in through the fire-lashed lagoon, past the bobbing corpses of their comrades.

The 3rd Battalion, 2nd Marines, tasked with landing on Red Beach 1, was virtually annihilated, its survivors forced to the western edge of Betio by furious Japanese fire from strongpoints dominating the landing area. On Red Beach 2, 2nd Battalion, 2nd Marines, took heavy casualties coming ashore, and at noon was reinforced by 1st Battalion, 100 of whose men were forced off course by enemy fire, joining the remnants of 3rd Battalion clinging to the western tip of Green Beach.

Only on Red Beach 3 was a firm lodgement made, by Major Henry Crowe's 2nd Battalion, 8th Marines. Accurate covering fire from the destroyer *Ringgold* ensured that casualties did not rise to 10 percent until the arrival of the fourth and fifth waves. By mid-day Crowe had a platoon of medium tanks available. Covered by 37-mm guns, his men began to push inland with the tanks and demolition teams in close mutual support. Soon afterwards Crowe's forces made contact with 1st and 2nd Battalions, 2nd Marines, on Red Beach 2, where Colonel David Shoup had placed his command post next to an enemy strongpoint. Shoup later recalled: "I was never off my feet for 50 hours, standing for most of the time by an enemy pillbox with 26 live Japs therein."

Having linked up, Shoup and Crowe's forces mounted an attack, supported by medium tanks, across the airstrip taxiway, establishing a joint perimeter some 300 yards deep.

The approach of darkness brought with it fears of a Japanese counter-attack, and 3rd Battalion, 8th Marines, was now committed to Red Beach 2, taking heavy casualties as they came in on both sides of the pier. On the extreme right flank of Red Beach 1, some scattered elements of 1st, 2nd and 3rd Battalions, 2nd Marines — driven to the western edge of Betio by fire from a chain of enemy strongpoints in the cove that comprised most of Red Beach 1 — launched an attack southwards along Green Beach at 1630 hrs. Supported by two tanks, they advanced about 500 yards before being brought to a halt. The tanks were knocked out and they lacked the flamethrowers and heavy equipment to deal with the network of Japanese bunkers which held them up. They withdrew to a defensive position for the night at the north end of Green Beach.

There was no Japanese counter-attack that night, probably because their communications had been wrecked by the naval bombardment and their strongpoints were unable to co-ordinate their actions or assess the overall situation.

Before dawn on the 21st, General Smith committed the remaining divisional reserve, 1st Battalion, 8th Marines, who had spent an uncomfortable night offshore in their LCVPs. On the long walk ashore they were badly mauled, losing 350 of their 800 men before joining the right flank of Shoup's forces in the centre of the island. An artillery battalion of 10th Marines had also arrived with five 75-mm pack howitzers, but could make no impression on the enemy defenses of Red Beach 1. There seemed little hope of joining hands with the Marines on Green Beach.

But during the morning two medium tanks and the vital flamethrowers arrived on Green Beach. Air strikes were called up to pulverize the Japanese batteries on Betio's western coast. At 1100 hrs the Marines advanced southwards, supported by naval gunfire. Green Beach was secured an hour later,

*Right:* First Lt. Marvin Rankin and Cpl. Southard plot the situation on Roi Island while under enemy fire, February 1944.

opening the way for the landing of reinforcements in battalion strength with minimum casualties and with their organization, command and equipment intact. The corps reserve, 6th Marines, was now on its way, and by late afternoon its 1st Battalion was coming ashore. The 2nd Battalion, 6th Marines, was deployed with artillery from 10th Marines on the neighboring island of Bairiki to add its firepower to the final assault and cut off a Japanese retreat across the narrow stretch of water separating the two islands.

The tide in Tarawa's lagoon shifted, allowing the LCVPs to clear the reefs with vital supplies. By nightfall, elements of Shoup's forces had fought their way across the airstrip and reached the south coast of the island. Shoup reported to General Smith on *Maryland*: "Casualties many; percentage not known; combat efficiency; we are winning."

By the morning of the third day on Tarawa, the Marines had clawed their way out of Red Beach 3 and were closing on the bombproof blockhouse which served as the headquarters of Rear-Admiral Shibasaki, commander of the island's defense forces. This was reduced to a smoke-blackened shambles as Marine assault engineers threw grenades down the blockhouse's air vents, followed by gasoline, to be detonated by TNT charges. That night the Japanese put in the long-expected counter-attack, but it was smashed up by naval gunfire as their troops assembled.

On 23 November, 3rd Battalion, 6th Marines, arrived on Betio, penning the remaining Japanese in the eastern end of the island while the weary survivors of the initial assault force reduced the lingering pockets of enemy resistance along Red Beach 1. The task was completed by the early afternoon, and at about the same time 3rd Battalion, 6th Marines, reached the eastern end of the island. At 1312 hrs General Smith declared Betio secure.

A small enemy force of about 175 men put up a final stand on the northern island of Buariki, but by 28 November the gruelling battle for Tarawa was over. Of the original Japanese garrison, only 146 were taken prisoner. Marine losses were 985 dead and 2,193 wounded, approximately 10 casualties per acre. Losses during the six-month campaign on Guadalcanal were just twice as heavy as those incurred in six days on

Tarawa. Nevertheless, the human cost of the operation was more than justified by the strategic results which flowed from it: the isolation of Rabaul, the move into the Marshalls and a drive through the Central Pacific as far west as the Palau Islands.

The savage struggle for Tarawa forced US planners to review their tactics for the assault of heavily defended islands. In spite of the ferocity of the naval barrage, the Japanese defenders had weathered the worst of the bombardment. In future operations the scale and duration of the "softening up" process would be increased and rockets and high-angle armor-piercing shells used to smash the enemy's heavily fortified bunkers and trench systems. Henceforward, Underwater Demolition Teams (UDTs) would precede landings to clear the way for improved LVTs. During the fighting on Tarawa, the Marines had been hampered by the unreliable radio links between the assault troops and the command ships lying offshore, which increased the difficulty of bringing in reinforcements to bolster a hard-pressed sector or of calling down artillery support on an enemy position. As the Marines fought their way inland, they were held up by a network of defenses which could not be silenced by relatively inaccurate naval gunfire. Short of heavy weapons, they took severe casualties when they closed on their well-dug-in enemy. The answer was provided by the development of "go-anywhere" amphibians, some armed with bunker-busting weapons. The American planners were confident that, with these improvements, an amphibious assault could get ashore, no matter what the obstacles.

### On to the Marshalls

The campaign for the Marshalls — Operation Flintlock — began on 1 February 1944 when the newly-formed 4th Marine Division stormed ashore on the islands of Roi and Namur, the latter the site of a major Japanese air base on the northern tip of Kwajalein atoll. At the same time, 7th Infantry Division attacked Kwajalein Island, at the atoll's southern tip, while Majuro atoll — some 400 miles to the south-west — was secured by Army units for use as a fast carrier base.

In four days the central Solomons had been

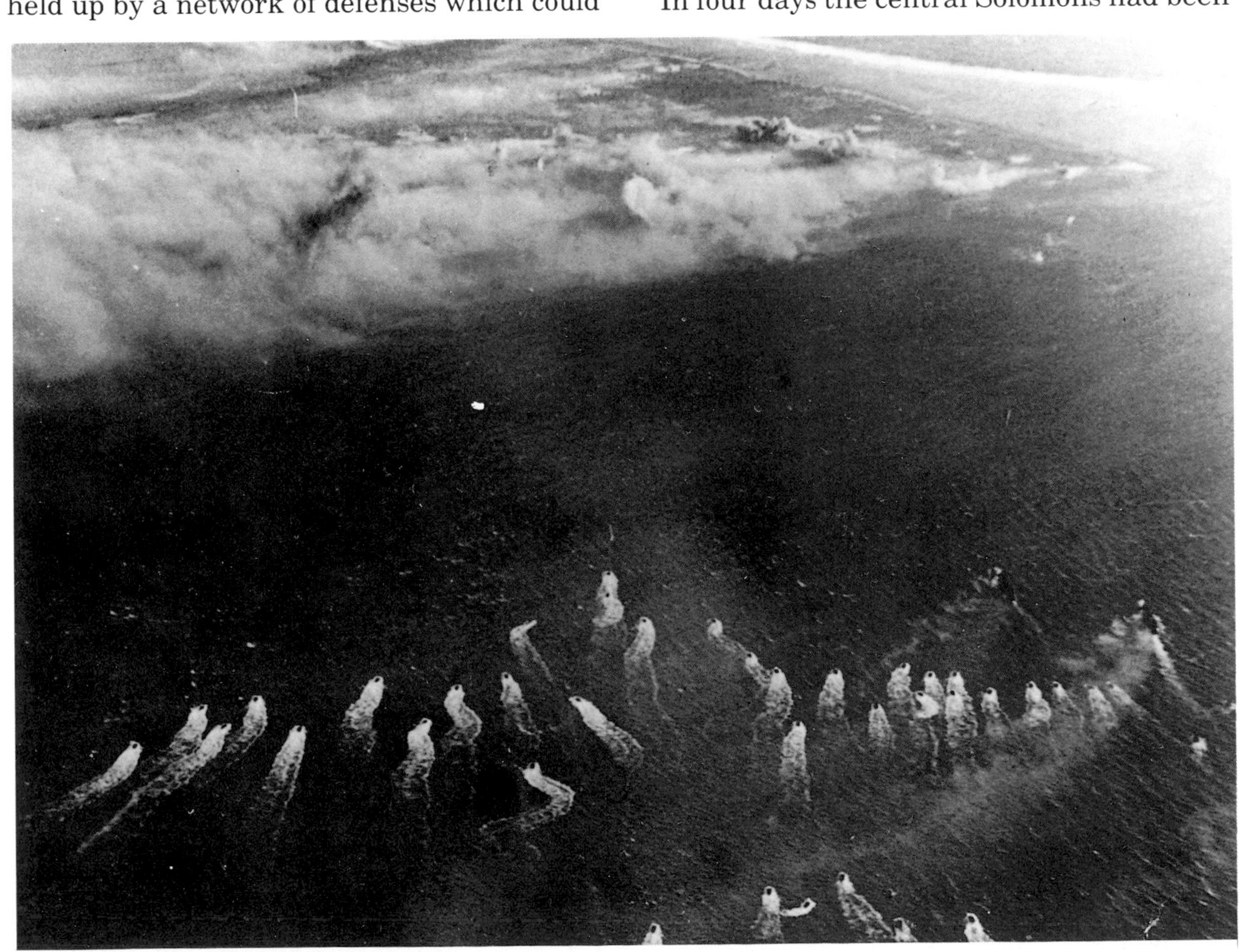

*Below:* Marine LVTS snake towards Engebi Island, in the Marshalls, on 18 February 1944. A dense pall of smoke raised by the naval and air bombardment hangs over the landing area. The LVT was one of the key elements in the Pacific campaign. LVTs were first used at Guadalcanal in August 1942, but only in a logistical role, ferrying ammunition and other supplies to the troops on the beaches. They were first in a tactical role employed at Tarawa in November 1943, clambering over the coral reefs which prevented deep-draughted vessels from reaching the shoreline. Their success at Tarawa resulted in the allocation of 300 amphibious craft to each Marine division. Inevitably, the LVTs suffered heavy losses, as they had to take the full brunt of the enemy's fire during the first phase of the assault. Further losses were caused by design faults. The LVT's bilge pumps were driven by the engine; if it failed, the LVT would quickly sink. Another fault lay in the organization of the amphibious assault units. Mother ships, tasked with delivering LVTs within range of their objective, often refused to repair or assist craft from other ships, condemning them to float off and eventually founder because of some minor defect. These initial shortcomings were ironed out and the LVT — of which 18,000 of various types were built between 1942 and 1945 — went on to play a vital role in the Pacific, enabling the troops to reach the shore relatively unscathed and providng them with their own heavy firepower.

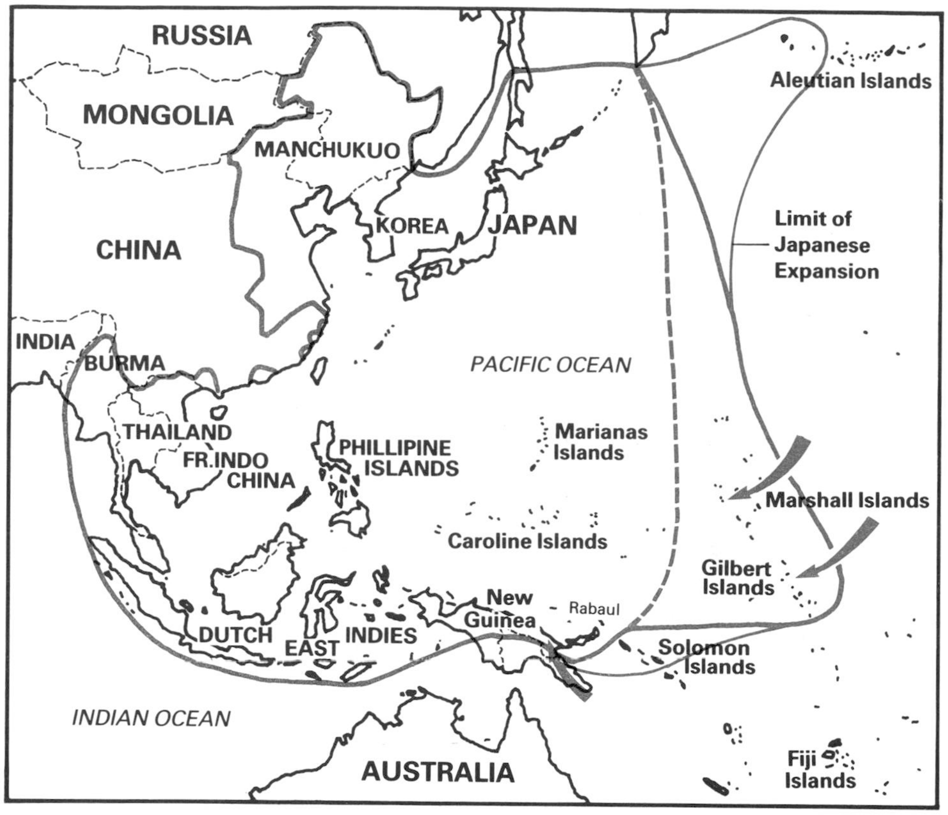

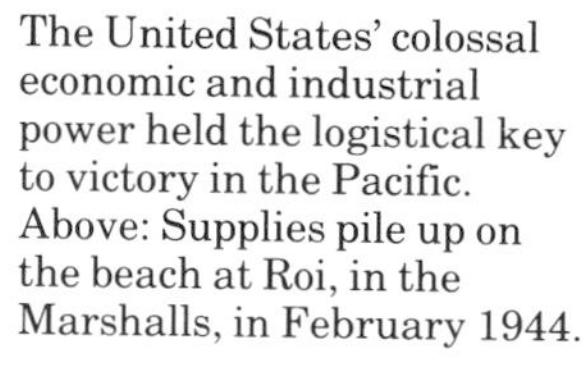

The United States' colossal economic and industrial power held the logistical key to victory in the Pacific. Above: Supplies pile up on the beach at Roi, in the Marshalls, in February 1944.

*Right:* A week after the landings on Green Island (15 February 1944), equipment and men move quickly off LSTs after a rough road has been cleared through the jungle by bulldozers.

*Left:* Seated in the back of a jeep during a tour of inspection in the Marshalls are Marine General Harry Schmidt (left) and Admirals Turner (center) and Connolly.

*Below:* Marines pause to salute the flag during the mopping-up operations on Roi. In the background are the smoldering remains of a three-storey enemy blockhouse knocked out after a furious bombardment.

taken at a cost of little more than 300 lives. The final target in this phase of the Pacific campaign was Eniwetok atoll, an important Japanese naval base 325 miles north-west of Kwajalein.

The threat of enemy naval or air intervention from the stronghold at Truk — 800 miles to the east — was eliminated by two days of bombing which destroyed 41 ships and 200 aircraft, turning Truk lagoon into an underwater graveyard

On Eniwetok, Marines of the 22nd Regiment and troops of 106th Infantry and 27th Division encountered stiff resistance when they went ashore on 17 February. In spite of a heavy air and naval bombardment, the atoll's defenders had to be winkled out yard by yard. The fighting was over by nightfall on 23 February, with not a single survivor from the atoll's garrison of 2,000 men. Overall Marine casualties in the Marshalls had been fewer than 600 killed.

### The Battle for the Marianas

The next stepping stone in the slog across the Pacific was the Marianas chain, 1,000 miles north-west of Eniwetok, whose capture would provide bases from which naval and air forces could cut the lines of communication to the southern half of Japan's Pacific empire, and from which heavy and continuous bombing of the Japanese home islands could be made by the USAAF's new Boeing B-29 Superfortress long-range bombers.

As a preliminary to Operation Forager, Vice-Admiral Marc A. Mitscher's Task Force 58, comprising one battleship and four fast carrier task groups, secured total air supremacy over the Marianas. The islands of Saipan, Tinian and Guam formed the main Japanese defenses in the chain, garrisoned by troops of XXXI Army. For the amphibious operation, Admiral Nimitz assembled an assault force of 600 vessels and 127,000 men. The attack on the first objective, Saipan, inaugurated a new phase in the Pacific war. With the exception of Guadalcanal, all the American offensives in the Pacific had been directed against small islands, atolls or single small places on an extended coastline. The ensuing battles had been savage but short, with the Japanese dying to the last man. But the taking of Saipan, with its 72 miles of murderous terrain defended by 30,000 enemy troops, threatened a long campaign which, additionally, would have to be fought over a sizable civilian population.

At 0843 hrs on 15 June, after a prolonged bombardment, 2nd and 4th Marine Divisions (V Amphibious Corps) went ashore on Saipan's south-west coast. Within 30 minutes, 8,000 troops had been put ashore on a six-mile front. The plan was for 2nd Division to swing north to attack the 1,550ft Mount Tapotchau, the dominating feature on Saipan, while 4th Division thrust across the island to take Aslito airfield, five miles east of the beach-head.

By nightfall on 15 June, 20,000 troops had been landed on Saipan. In addition to both units landed in the first wave, the Americans had disembarked reserve units, seven pack howitzer battalions and elements of two armoured units.

Nevertheless, progress inland was slow. By sunset on 15 June, the assault troops had fought their way off the beaches, but only in the extreme south — the sector held by 25th Marines — had a line been consolidated along the first-day objective. Elsewhere the Marines had established only a shallow

*Left:* Dead Japanese soldiers litter the beach at Eniwetok.
*Opposite, top:* Seabees and Marines aboard an LVT at Roi, waiting for the order to land.
*Opposite, bottom:* Blood plasma is administered to a wounded Marine on Eniwetok.
*Below, left:* Sergeant Charles G. Bowers goes after a Japanese sniper with his Thompson sub-machine-gun on Eniwetok. The Marines had used the Thompson since the 1920s, and were probably the first military force to adopt the weapon, in Nicaragua in 1928. Although utterly reliable, the Thompson was expensive, slow to produce and in great demand by 1942. Its immediate replacement, the Reising 11.43-mm-caliber machine-gun, was not a success, rapidly clogging with dirt in combat, and was withdrawn after Guadalcanal. From 1943 the Marines adopted the M3 sub-machine gun, popularly known as the "Grease Gun", because of its resemblance to a mechanic's greasing tool.

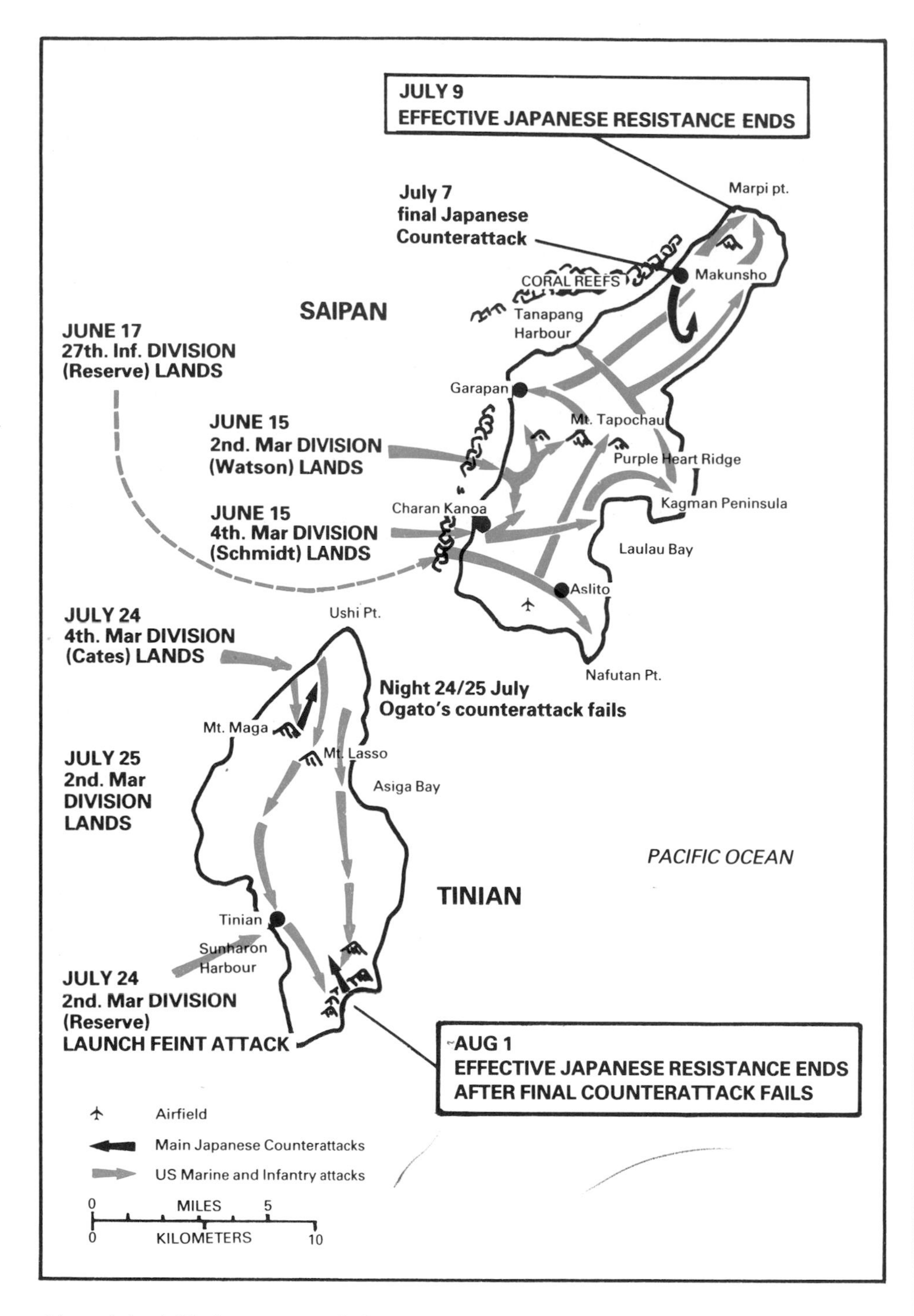

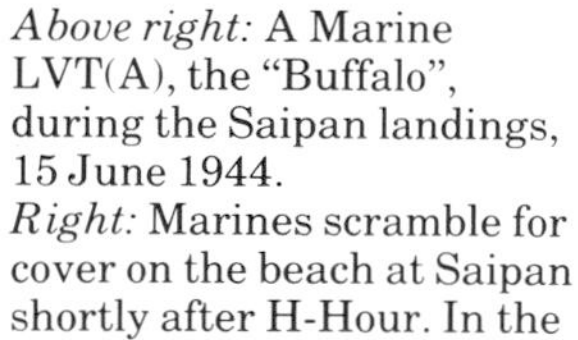

*Above right:* A Marine LVT(A), the "Buffalo", during the Saipan landings, 15 June 1944.
*Right:* Marines scramble for cover on the beach at Saipan shortly after H-Hour. In the background, smoke pours from a crippled "Buffalo".

defensive perimeter, and at the end of the day barely half of the designated beach-head had been secured. Enemy troops still clung to the ridges which overlooked the landing areas.

In gaining a foothold on Saipan, the Marines suffered about 2,000 dead and wounded, a casualty list which grew bigger that night when the enemy launched a counter-attack against 6th Marines, using Marines of their own and a reinforced armored battalion. But they had missed their chance to hit the Americans when they were at their most vulnerable — during the initial landings — and were thrown back by the Marines with the aid of naval gunfire, including that of the battleship *California*.

At this crucial point in the Marianas campaign, the Japanese suffered a crushing naval defeat. The American invasion fleet presented an irresistible target, and for its

*Above:* Which way to the front? Confusion on the beach at Saipan. In the background is a "Buffalo" mounting a 75-mm howitzer for heavy infantry support.

destruction the Japanese assembled a Mobile Fleet under Admiral Ozawa with nine aircraft carriers, five battleships, 13 cruisers, 28 destroyers and 478 aircraft. Opposing them was Admiral Mitscher's Task Force 58, with 15 carriers, seven battleships, 13 cruisers, 69 destroyers and 473 aircraft. Battle was joined on 19 June, when the first wave of Ozawa's carrier-borne aircraft was intercepted by 450 Grumman F6F Hellcat fighters. These powerful, chunky fighters were more than a match for their lightly armed adversaries and, in what became known as "The Marianas Turkey Shoot", over 250 Japanese aircraft were shot down at a cost of only 23 US 'planes. Meanwhile, American submarines had located Ozawa's Main Body, sinking the carriers *Taiho* (Ozawa's flagship) and *Shokaku*. Down to 100 aircraft, Ozawa headed north-west as darkness fell. Under the mistaken impression that he had inflicted heavy damage on the Task Force 58, he planned to renew the attack as soon as he had refueled and rearmed.

The Americans struck first. Late on the afternoon of 20 June, Mitscher found and attacked Ozawa's fleet, sinking the carrier *Hiyo* and two oilers as the Japanese withdrew towards Okinawa. Flying at the

limit of their range, many US aircraft were forced to ditch in the sea. In all, between 300 and 400 Japanese aircraft had been destroyed, with the disastrous attendant loss of aircrews. The carrier force survived, only to be annihilated later at the Battle of Leyte Gulf (24/25 October 1944).

On Saipan, the reserve 27th Infantry Division had been committed on 17 June. By nightfall on 22 June, the whole of southern Saipan had been cleared with the exception of the Nafutan headland. Thereafter, the commander of V Amphibious Corps, General Holland M. "Howlin' Mad" Smith, decided on an advance up the length of the island. Progress was slow, and the Army and Marine commanders fell to squabbling over what were essentially doctrinal differences. The Army believed in a cautious step-by-step approach. The Marines, aware of the vulnerability of the offshore fleet behind them, believed in taking ground at the utmost speed with scant regard for casualties. Holland Smith won the argument, and 27th Division's commander, Major-General Ralph Smith, was dismissed on 24 June.

His removal had little immediate effect in speeding up the breakthrough in "Death Valley", the Japanese defenses in the central part of Saipan. Mount Tapotchau fell to the 2nd Marine Division on 27 June, but it was not until the end of the month that 27th Infantry Division straightened the front by breaking through the center of the main line of Japanese resistance. By 6 July, the Japanese were penned in the northern third of Saipan. With defeat staring him in the face, Admiral Nagumo, Japanese naval commander on Saipan, committed suicide. His example was followed by the commander of the enemy Army forces, Lieutenant-General Sato, who slit open his belly with his sword and was then despatched by an officer with a pistol shot to the head. His final message to his troops was an invitation to follow him to glory against the enemy. They obeyed with a massed suicide charge in the Makunsha sector against two battalions of 27th Infantry, which lost about 1,000 men killed and wounded as they and the Marine gunners behind them were swamped by the banzai charge. The American reply was a concentrated artillery barrage which left some 3–4,000 Japanese corpses littered in heaps before their lines.

Saipan was secured on 9 July amid scenes of horror as the island's remaining troops and

22,000 civilians — driven mad by an irrational fear of being taken prisoner — performed an act of mass self-immolation. At one point, American troops watched helplessly as in the distance Japanese soldiers lined up to await decapitation by one of their officers. Lemming-like, whole families of civilians threw themselves off the 1000ft "suicide cliff" on to the jagged rocks below and from the bluffs at Marpi Point into the sea, deaf to frantic Japanese-language loudspeaker appeals assuring them that they would not be harmed. At Marpi, the dead and dying were clogged so thick that they fouled the propellers of the destroyers trying to pluck them from the sea. Of the Japanese military, the garrison of 32,000 men died almost to the last man. American casualties were almost as sobering — over 16,000 killed and wounded, of whom 12,934 were Marines.

After the fall of Saipan and the Battle of the Philippine Sea, the Japanese high command was forced to recognize that there was no longer any way of avoiding defeat. In the United States these victories laid the basis for President Roosevelt's nomination for an unprecedented fourth term. In Japan they led to the resignation, on 18 July, of the Tojo cabinet.

Tinian, three miles to the south of Saipan, was another tough proposition, its high, rocky coastline bristling with concealed batteries. The only chink in the coastal wall lay in front of the town of Tinian, on the south-west coast, but this had been heavily fortified by the Japanese. Accordingly, a landing was planned on the north-west tip of the island, where two undefended gaps in the jagged cliffs offered access to the interior. On 24 July an invasion fleet, spearheaded by 2nd Marine Division, made a demonstration in front of Tinian while 4th Marine Division landed in the north-west of the island. Achieving complete tactical surprise, they established a perimeter sufficiently firm to beat off a determined Japanese night attack. On 25 July, 2nd Marines went ashore, and within a week the island was in American hands.

The capture of Guam was of both strategic and symbolic importance. Not only did it contain three airstrips and a superb harbor, it had also fallen to the Japanese at the beginning of the Pacific war and would be the first piece of American territory to be liberated. On 21 July a combined assault on Guam was undertaken. 3rd Marine Division

*Above:* A Marine marksman takes aim at a Japanese sniper during the fighting on Saipan.
*Top left:* Marines in action with a captured Japanese mountain gun on Saipan.

*Left:* Waiting for the order to move out. The Marine in the foreground is carrying boxed mortar rounds lashed to his back.

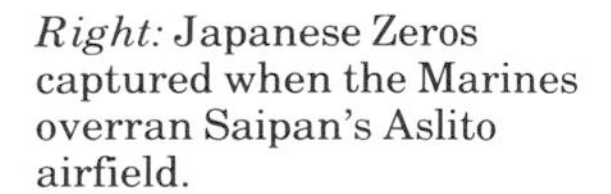

*Right:* Japanese Zeros captured when the Marines overran Saipan's Aslito airfield.

landed on the west coast of the island four miles south of its capital, Agana; and 1st Provisional Marine Brigade and 77th Infantry Division came ashore to the south, at Agar, with the aim of trapping the Japanese forces in the Orote Peninsula, where the principal airfield was located.

The peninsula had been sealed off by 25 July, but that night the Japanese launched two frenzied counter-attacks, the first from the airfield and the second against 3rd Marines' beach-head. Both were driven back with horrific losses. Effective Japanese resistance on Guam had ended by 10 August 1944, after 10,000 of their troops had been killed. Mopping-up continued for a long time. The last Japanese to surrender on Guam did so in 1960.

A view of the beach at Pelelieu on D-Day, 15 September 1944. The landing area is shrouded with the smoke raised by a three-day naval and air bombardment.

## Hell at Peleliu

With the capture of Guam, the Marianas were secured and the Carolines and Truk bypassed. The American high command now had their eyes fixed on the Philippines, and Admiral Nimitz decided that the next move was to be against the western Carolines and the Palau Islands. Lying 500 miles east of Mindanao in the southern Philippines, the Palau Islands stood athwart the left flank of the Central Pacific drive and threatened MacArthur's right flank as he moved up through the South-West Area towards the same goal. Nimitz insisted that the Palau Islands be taken rather than bypassed.

The main target was Peleliu, the principal island in the Palau group. Only two miles wide and six miles long, Peleliu's highest point is a hill named Umurbrogol Mountain, which was soon to earn the name "Bloody Nose Ridge". It was garrisoned by 10,000 Japanese troops dug deep into a honeycomb of interconnecting caves and bunkers — many of them fortified with sliding steel doors — lavishly stocked with food and ammunition. There were to be no mass suicide charges on Peleliu. The garrison's commander, Colonel Nakagawa, had been ordered to contain the Americans on their beach-head. If this failed, his troops were to withdraw to their prepared positions to enfilade the assault force with mortar and artillery fire. When overrun, they were to remain hidden and then strike at the enemy in the rear.

The Japanese defenses were subjected to a three-day air and naval bombardment before 1st Marine Division went ashore on the

*Above:* LVTs ferrying troops ashore at Pelelieu on D-Day.

south-west corner of Peleliu on 15 September. As they hit the beach, the Marines were met with a storm of fire from the island's defenders, who had sat out the barrage secure in their bunkers. Taking heavy casualties, the Marines fought their way across the island's airstrip, at which point Colonel Nakagawa ordered the withdrawal into the caves and strongpoints of Umurbrogol Mountain, by now stripped of all of its vegetation by gunfire and bombing.

On 17 September, the men of 1st Marine Regiment, commanded by Colonel Lewis B. "Chesty" Puller, began the nightmarish task of digging the Japanese out of their last-ditch defenses squad by squad, sometimes one by one. After three bloody days the 1st was replaced by 7th Marine Regiment, having suffered 1,700 casualties since landing on Peleliu.

At the same time, the Army's 81st Division was moved on to Peleliu, enabling 5th Marines to clear the northern sector of the island before turning to attack "Bloody Nose Ridge" from the rear. The ridge was surrounded by 321st Army Combat Team, 5th and 7th Marines, who then inched their way up its slopes, destroying Japanese

*Opposite, top:* Marines move up the beach at Pelelieu. They are wearing standard two-piece herringbone-twill fatigue suits and M1 helmets with "beach" camouflage cover.
*Left:* A Marine 4FU Corsair unleashes a rocket salvo against Japanese positions on Okinawaw, May-June 1945.

strongpoints with flamethrowers, grenades and satchel charges.

It took the Marines seven weeks to secure Peleliu and the surrounding islands in the group. The Japanese, who had succeeded in bringing in 4,000 reinforcements during the fighting, had lost 13,600 killed. Only 400 were taken prisoner. Each dead Japanese soldier had cost the Americans 1,600 rounds of light and heavy ordnance. They had also incurred 7,900 casualties (including 1,750 dead), of which over 6,000 were Marines.

## Marine Aviation

In the New Georgia campaign, Marine air groups had developed highly effective close-support techniques under the direction of Major Wilfred Stiles. The basis of the system was the Air Liaison Party (ALP), operating in a radio-equipped jeep to call down strikes with maximum precision, thereby increasing hitting power and avoiding casualties among friendly troops.

The Marines were also the first to take delivery of the immensely powerful Vought 4FU Corsair carrier-borne fighter-bomber. Teething problems with the Corsair's carrier-landing ability led to all early deliveries going to the Marines, most notably to the flamboyant Major Gregory "Pappy" Boyington's "Black Sheep", VMF-214.

Combat with land-based Marine squadrons began in the Solomons in February 1943, and the Corsair quickly gained supremacy over the previously untroubled Japanese. Boyington was appointed commander of VMF-214 in September 1943 and led the unit until 3 January 1944, when he was shot down and became a prisoner of war. During his service with VMF-214, Boyington claimed 22 personal victories which, when added to his earlier six scores in China with the American Volunteer Group, made him the war's top-scoring Marine pilot, with 28 kills.

VMF-214's combat tour in the Solomons ended on 8 January, five days after Boyington was shot down over Rabaul. After carrier training in the United States, it briefly re-entered combat in March 1945 aboard the USS *Franklin*. The "Black Sheep" ended up as the seventh-highest-scoring Marine squadron of the war, with 127 victories, all but 30 of which were gained during Boyington's period of command.

The Marines achieved another first when, on 18 March 1944, VMF-111 exploited the Corsair's potential as a dive-bomber, attacking enemy anti-aircraft batteries with 1,000-lb bombs. Subsequently it was shown that the Corsair could be employed to devastating effect as a dive-bomber, delivering twice the payload of the specially-designed Dauntless in dives of up to 85 degrees. The fighter's six .5-in guns were used for strafing in the latter stages of the dive.

In the autumn of 1944 a vast amphibious armada carrying 200,000 men of Lieutenant-

*Opposite, bottom:* A Corsair of MAW-2 bombs enemy positions on Five Sisters Peak, Pelelieu, October 1944. Although designated a carrier-based fighter, the Corsair was rejected by the US Navy because its big nose restricted visibility and its undercarriage tended to make the aircraft bounce on touchdown. The Corsair entered service with the Marines in February 1943 in the South Pacific. Powered by a 2,000hp Pratt and Whitney engine, the Corsair had a maximum speed of 415mph at 20,000ft and a normal range of 1,000 miles. Variations of the F4U carried different armaments: for example, the F4U-1 had six 0.5-in Brownings while the F4U-1D fighter-bomber had provision for underwing bombs or rockets. In World War II, 2,140 enemy aircraft fell victim to the Corsair — a kill ratio of 11:1.

General Walter Kreuger's 6th Army sailed towards the eastern shore of Leyte in the Philippines. On 20 October, US 10th Corps and 24th Corps established a beach-head against light opposition from XVI Division of General Suzuki's XXXV Army. Japanese battleships and carriers attempted to draw off the US fleets from their support of the landings, but in a series of engagements between 23 and 25 October — the Battle of Leyte Gulf — the last vestiges of Japanese sea power were shattered.

Once the Americans were firmly established ashore, Marine air groups — many of them still equipped with the faithful Dauntless — were flown in to newly-liberated airfields to provide close support. Using the ground-attack techniques perfected during the Pacific war, these units gave the Army invaluable assistance in the protracted period of land fighting in the Philippines, and in the mopping-up operations which continued until the end of the war.

The Marine SBD squadrons swung into action during the Lingayen landings in January 1945, flying 255 sorties and dropping 104 tons of bombs for the loss of just one aircraft. During the capture of San Jose, north of Manila, 1st Infantry had suffered heavy casualties from strafing "friendly" USAAF fighters. Understandably, this made them extremely sceptical about the value of close support. However, on 18 February they required Marine dive-bomber assistance in a difficult operation. Nine SBDs made pinpoint attacks, placing all of their bombs within 30 yards of the target. Thereafter the SBDs remained on standby at the request of the Army.

*Top:* A Dauntless of VMSB-331 flying over Majuro atoll, in the Marshalls, in June 1944.
*Above:* A Marine Consolidated Vultee PB4Y-2 Privateer maritime patrol bomber in flight over the Pacific in April 1945. Derived from the B-24 Liberator, the Privateer saw postwar service in an electronic intelligence-gathering role.

### Iwo Jima

While US 6th Army was fighting for control of Luzon, the northernmost island in the Philippines, V Amphibious Corps was preparing for the landings on the small volcanic island of Iwo Jima, and the bloodiest fight in the history of the Marine Corps.

Iwo Jima was a Japanese stronghold which could not be bypassed and left to "wither on the vine". Lying some 700 miles south of Tokyo, it formed an integral part of the inner ring of defenses around the Japanese home islands. From its two completed airfields, Japanese fighters could strike at the B-29 bomber streams flying to raid Japan's cities, and launch harassing raids on American forces on Saipan, Tinian and Guam. Less than two hours' flying time from Japan, Iwo Jima also provided an early-warning station from which to monitor US attacks on the home islands. The capture of Iwo Jima would provide the Americans with the bases from which short-range escort fighters could fly top cover for the B-29s and also act as an emergency stopping point for damaged bombers on their return journey.

Iwo Jima was administratively part of the prefecture of Tokyo, and its loss would deal a hammer blow to Japanese civilian morale. Recognizing its importance, and knowing that he could expect no help, the island's

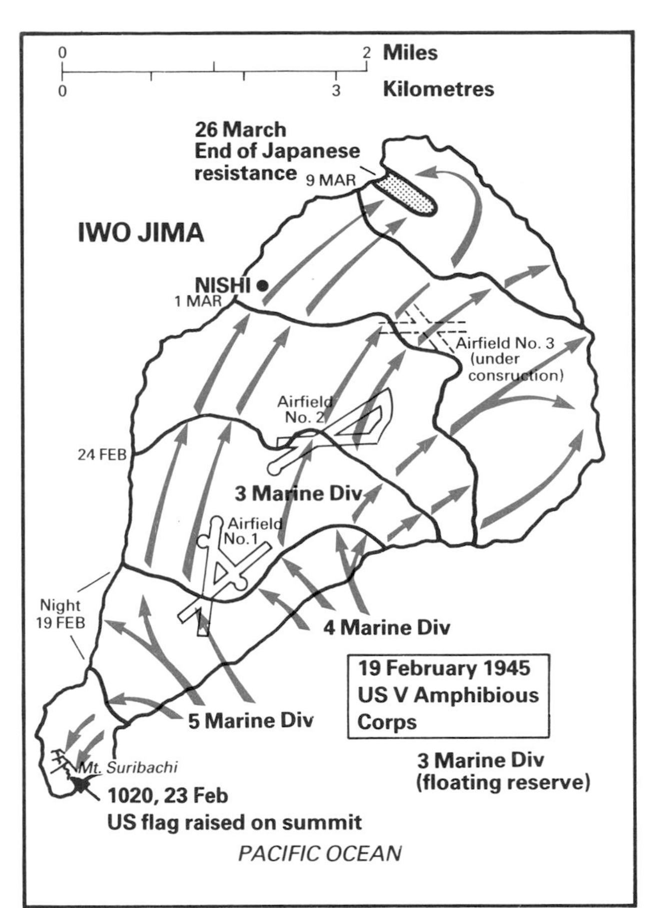


*Below:* Marines of 4th Division hug the black sand of Iwo Jima on D-Day, 19 February 1945. This was the division's fourth amphibious assault in 13 months.

commander, Lieutenant-General Kuribayashi, set about turning it into a death trap. Although only eight miles square, Iwo Jima was garrisoned by 21,000 men, packed with 1,500 pillboxes and blockhouses and criss-crossed with tunnels, trenches and minefields. The island's dominating natural feature, Mount Suribachi, a 600ft volcanic outcrop at the island's southern tip, was honeycombed with defensive positions.

Kuribayashi's artillery comprised 361 guns over 75-mm calibre, 300 anti-aircraft guns, 20,000 light guns, 130 howitzers, 12 heavy mortars, 60 anti-tank guns and 70 rocket launchers. Over 20 tanks were dug in, hull-down.

American preparations had been equally thorough. Preliminary planning for the operation had begun as early as September 1943. After the securing of the Marianas, General Holland M. "Howlin' Mad" Smith was placed in overall command of the assault on Iwo Jima. Spearheading the operation, under Major-General Harry Schmidt, was V Amphibious Corps, veterans of the Guadalcanal, Marshalls and Marianas campaigns.

Schmidt was given three divisions: the battle-hardened 3rd Marine Division, under Major-General G.B. Erskine, to be held offshore as a corps reserve; 4th Marine Division, under Major-General C.B. Cates; and 5th Division, under Major-General K.E. Rockey, untried as a formation in combat but containing a substantial percentage of veteran troops.

Having landed on Iwo Jima's south-eastern shore, under the glowering bulk of Mount Suribachi, the plan was for 4th and 5th Divisions to wheel north to assault the heavily fortified Motoyama Plateau, while 28th Marine Regiment undertook the daunting task of capturing Suribachi, from which the Japanese could observe every American movement.

On 8 December 1944, the Americans began the longest and heaviest aerial bombardment of the Pacific war, a 72-day "softening up" of Iwo Jima by B-24s and B-25s. Naval bombardment had begun in November and continued, with intervals, until 16 February 1945 when a 72-hour pre-assault barrage burst on Iwo Jima. Six battleships and their escorts pounded the Japanese positions, expending some 1,950 rounds of 16-in shell, 1,500 rounds of 14-in, 400 cf 12-in, 1,700 of 8-in, 2,000 of 6-in and 31,000 of 5-in. Flying over the pitted, lunar landscape of Iwo Jima,

*Above:* Iwo Jima, 10 March 1945. Lieutenant-General Holland M. Smith (center) and Major-General Harry Schmidt in V Amphibious Corp's command post.
*Above, left:* Marines push inland on D+21, as the battle for Iwo Jima nears its end.

*Left:* Amid a litter of equipment, Marines entrench beneath the glowering bulk of Mount Suribachi.

US aircraft napalmed and rocketed the Japanese defenses.

On 17 February, LCI gun- and rocket-boats came close inshore to cover the UDT teams clearing the beach approaches and checking the beach and surf conditions. Mistaking them for the first wave of the assault force, the Japanese opened up with their heaviest artillery, revealing their carefully-concealed positions.

D-Day, 19 February, dawned bright and clear, with a blue sky and calm sea. Offshore, 450 vessels of the US 5th Fleet maneuvered for the assault, while around them buzzed the 482 LVT(A)s which would carry the Marine battalions into action. As the Navy's ships laid down a creeping barrage — the first of the Pacific war — 68 LVT(A)s left their start line for the 4,000-yd dash to the shore. If all went according to schedule, the first seven battalions of Marines would be ashore within 45 minutes.

The Marines hit the thick black sand of Iwo Jima's beaches at 0902 hrs, 5th Division on the left, 4th on the right. Initially there was only light resistance, but when the Marines had pushed about 300 yard inlands they were suddenly raked with a hail of fire from concealed positions. Casualties were heavy, but the Japanese had made a fatal miscalculation. They had allowed the Marines to establish themselves ashore with all the equipment they needed to weather the storm. By 1030 hrs, elements of all eight assault battalions were ashore, and the bigger LSMs were bringing in tanks,

*Above:* One of the indelible images of World War II — the Stars and Stripes are raised on Mount Suribachi.

bulldozers and artillery. By nightfall, nearly 30,000 Marines had been fed into the beach-head, securing the neck of the island, sealing off Mount Suribachi and gaining a lodgement at the corner of Airfield No. 1. But they had already sustained 2,400 casualties, including 600 dead.

It took 28th Regiment nearly three days to capture Mount Suribachi, an ominous bare mound resembling an ant-heap crawling with vicious soldier-ants. Fighting was frequently hand-to-hand. Private First Class Leo Jez was advancing towards a pillbox when a Japanese officer rushed him, wielding a sword. Jez deflected the blow, wrenched the sword from the officer's hand and, in a single movement, hacked off his head. The mountain was taken yard by yard, grenades, flamethrowers and satchel charges burning and blasting the Japanese in their dug-outs and bunkers.

The summit, now eerily silent, was reached at 1015 hrs on the 23rd by a platoon from 2nd Battalion led by Lieutenant Harold G. Schrier. They planted a small Stars and Stripes and were photographed by Sergeant Louis R. Lowery, a *Leatherneck* magazine photographer. The proceedings were interrupted by a brief firefight, during which Lowery was forced to roll some way down the mountain to avoid a grenade, smashing his camera in the process but saving the film. Two hours later, a second photographer, Associated Press man Joe Rosenthal, arrived at the summit, where the Marines were preparing to raise a second, bigger flag. It was one of the 18 pictures which Joe Rosenthal took during this flag-raising ceremony which became a symbol of the entire war for the United States.

There was much bitter fighting to come. On 24 February, 4th and 5th Divisions — reinforced by 3rd Division — confronted the main Japanese defensive line along the Motoyama Plateau. Their advance through a surreal landscape of jagged rocks and stinking sulfur pits was measured in tens rather than hundreds of yards; 28th Regiment, once again in the thick of the fighting, suffered 240 casualties daily for three days in a row. Artillery was useless against the Japanese positions and tanks were unable to maneuver in the broken terrain. Brilliantly camouflaged, the Japanese would often allow the Marines to pass through their positions before taking them in the rear with murderous bursts of fire.

On 28 February the assault began on the complex of trenches and bunkers on Hills 382 and 362A. On the following day, these objectives claimed the lives of three of the men who had helped to raise the flag on Mount Suribachi: Sergeant Hanson, Sergeant Strank and Corporal Block. Hill 382 fell on 1 March and Hill 362A was taken on the following day after a night attack.

It was not until D+18 (9 March) that patrols of 3rd Division broke through to the north-eastern shore of Iwo Jima. Another week elapsed before organized resistance collapsed, and mopping-up continued for another 10 days. On 4 March, 12 days before the island was declared secure, the first crippled B-29 flew in to land. On 7 April, 108 North American P-51 (Mustang) fighters took off from Iwo Jima to escort a daylight B-29 attack on Tokyo. Within three months over 850 B-29s had made emergency landings on the island. Without Iwo and its two airstrips, the majority would have been lost.

The price had been high. Of the 21,000 Japanese, only 200 were taken prisoner. Some 6,821 American soldiers and sailors lost their lives, of whom 5,931 were Marines. Over 18,000 were wounded, 17,372 from the Corps. The 28th Marines, in particular, had suffered grievous losses. Of the 3,900 men who had landed on Iwo Jima on 19 February, only 600 remained fit for action when the fighting ceased.

*Left:* D+18 on Iwo Jima: Marines wait warily as one of their comrades throws a hand grenade into an enemy emplacement.

The battle for Iwo Jima had been the only large-scale land action in the Pacific war in which American casualties outnumbered those of the Japanese. Its savagery prompted the pugnacious General Holland M. Smith to observe that it was the "toughest [fight] we've run across in 168 years". Admiral Nimitz declared that for the Marines on Iwo Jima, "uncommon valor was a common virtue", a tribute borne out by the awarding of 22 Congressional Medals of Honor — 12 of them posthumously — for acts of heroism during a single month of fighting. This tally represented more than one-quarter of the total awarded to Marines throughout the whole of World War Two. It was a chilling portent of what lay ahead if Japan itself was to be invaded.

## Okinawa: the Last Battle

The final objective before the invasion of the home islands was Okinawa, the most important of the Ryuku Islands, almost exactly equidistant from Manila and Tokyo.

Okinawa was strategically located across the sea lanes to the south. Its capture would isolate Formosa and enable American medium bombers to strike at Japan. In enemy hands, it remained within range of land-based 'planes from Japan, but was out of range for similar American aircraft flying from the Philippines. Air cover for an invasion would have to be provided by carrier-based aircraft. In turn, the carriers would have to stay on station, making them highly vulnerable to kamikaze attacks.

A vast naval armada of more than 1,200 vessels was readied for the task of transporting 183,000 men of the US 10th Army (24th Army Corps, III Amphibious Corps) for the landings on Okinawa, codenamed Iceberg. The Marine element comprised 1st, 2nd and 6th Marine Divisions, plus a number of Marine air groups assigned to the covering Tactical Air Force.

On 1 April, after a week-long bombardment, the Americans went ashore on the south-west coast of the island, north of the city of Naha. Simultaneously, a feint was made against Okinawa's south-eastern shore by 2nd Marine Division. Initially, all went according to plan. Within three days the island had been split at the Ishikawa isthmus, with 6th Marine Division pushing northwards and the Army units advancing south. The Marines met only light resistance until they reached the Motobu Peninsula, which was secured by 20 April after a hard fight.

In the south, however, the Japanese had planned an unpleasant surprise for the Americans. General Ushijima was under orders to hold on until the kamikaze aircraft had sunk or driven off the American amphibious support ships. When this had been accomplished, he was to counter-attack and drive the invaders into the sea. Accordingly, he had fortified the southern third of Okinawa with a series of defensive lines, of which the most formidable began at Naha on the west coast, ran through the dominating high point of Shuri Castle and was anchored on the eastern shore at Yonabaru. It was Iwo Jima all over again, with the Japanese burrowed into caves and with reinforced emplacements on both forward and reverse slopes of their defensive lines.

While US 5th Fleet was assailed by waves of kamikaze aircraft, American soldiers and Marines battered away at Ushijima's lines. The first, the Machinato Line, held out for six days. Ushijima then fell back on his main line of defence — the Shuri Line — on which the Americans could make little or no impression. In desperation, the commander of 10th Army, General Simon Bolivar Buckner, considered an amphibious end-run, but all possible landing places were covered by heavy concentrations of Japanese artillery. There was nothing for it but to continue slogging away at the Shuri Line. The 6th Marine Division was brought down from the north and 1st Marine Division, until then

held in reserve, was thrown into action. The Marines of 6th Division took heavy casualties securing "Sugar Loaf Hill", and 1st Division was badly mauled in its fight for the Dakeshi Ridge and Wana Ridge. Under intensive bombardment, the Japanese fought every step of the way — during the campaign, American field artillery expended 1.7 million rounds. At sea the final toll of both kamikaze and conventional attacks was 36 US ships (most of them smaller types) sunk, 368 others damaged and 10,000 Navy personnel killed or wounded. But 5th Fleet still stood offshore.

The tide began to turn at the beginning of May. Unwisely, Ushijima yielded to demands from his subordinates for a major offensive, which was beaten back with the loss of 5,000 men, destroying his final reserves. On 21 May, he abandoned the Shuri Line and withdrew into last-ditch positions at the bottom of the island, across the Naha Plain, around the Yaeju Dake Escarpment. By the end of the month, Naha had been secured by the Marines after a savage house-to-house battle.

Not until mid-June did Marines and Army troops break the enemy positions on the escarpment. Okinawa's southern shore was reached on 19 June, and mopping-up operations continued for several more days. Three days before the battle ended, General Buckner was killed by an artillery shell. He was succeeded by Major-General Roy S. Geiger, a Marine aviator, who became the only Marine officer to have commanded a field army. Ushijima committed suicide,

*Left:* With a rifle lined on the entrance to a Japanese-held cave on Okinawa, Marines await the result of an explosive charge and prepare to shoot any enemy who attempt to escape. These bitterly contested cave positions formed the Japanese "Little Siegfried" line, defending the capital city of Naha.

*Right:* Marines are pinned down by enemy sniper fire behind the gravestones of Okinawa's "Cemetery Ridge".
*Opposite, top:* Major-General Lemuel C. Shepherd, commander of 6th Marine Division, studies a map during the battle for Okinawa.
*Opposite, bottom:* A Marine Corps Grumman TBM Avenger drops two 500-lb bombs on enemy positions on Okinawa.

along with thousands of soldiers and civilians. Years after the war, one could still see grisly mounds of bleached bones at the bottom of the cliffs on Okinawa's southern shore.

Overall Japanese casualties in the campaign were 117,000, of whom 110,000 were killed. Marine Corps casualties were 19,000, including 3,000 dead. The complete 10th Army casualty list stood at 65,000 killed and wounded, another terrible reminder of the losses which would inevitably be incurred if the Japanese mounted an equally fanatical defense of the home islands.

President Truman decided to shorten the war, and at the same time send a pointed strategic message to the Soviet Union, by dropping the first offensive atomic bomb on Hiroshima, an important military headquarters and supply depot, on 6 August 1945. The bomb exploded over the center of the city, killing approximately 80,000 of its inhabitants. The Japanese high command still believed that continuing resistance might secure "honorable conditions". Accordingly, a second bomb was dropped on the seaport and industrial centre of Nagasaki on 9 August. Japan immediately surrendered unconditionally. A general cease-fire came into operation on 15 August and the official surrender was signed on 2 September aboard the battleship *Missouri* in Tokyo Bay. General MacArthur, resplendent in victory, declared "These proceedings are closed".

## The Final Count

For the Marines, World War Two had been

overwhelmingly a Pacific War. Nearly 98 percent of all Marine officers served in this theatre, and 89 percent of enlisted men. It had been a unique campaign, fought in the steaming jungles of Guadalcanal, on the fire-swept beaches of Tarawa and the caves of Peleliu. The Corps' six divisions had made 15 landings. Its air arm, which by the war's end numbered 145 squadrons in 31 aircraft groups, scored 2,355 kills (top-scoring unit was VMF-121 with 208 victories). In the fighting from Wake to Okinawa, 19,733 Marines had died and 67,207 had been wounded in action. During the course of the war, 669,000 men had passed through its ranks. In August 1945 the Corps' strength stood at 458,000 officers and men. Between 1941 and 1945 it had met and overcome every challenge thrown at it by a ferociously determined enemy. Many new challenges lay ahead in the postwar world.

# 5: KEEPING THE PEACE:
## The Postwar World 1946-1988

### THE COLD WAR

In the immediate aftermath of the war, Marines of 4th, 2nd and 5th Marine Divisions formed part of the occupation forces in Japan. Other Marine units went to China to repatriate Japanese troops and to maintain the peace between Chiang Kai-shek's Nationalist forces and the Communists led by Mao Tse-tung. Marines also provided the garrisons in a number of Pacific islands.

Meanwhile, demobilization gathered pace. Within five months of the end of the war, 3rd, 4th and 5th Marine Divisions had been disbanded; 18 months later the strength of the Corps had fallen from a wartime peak of 485,000 to 92,000. Marine units were withdrawn from Japan in 1946, and the peacekeeping force in China was steadily reduced. The last Marines were withdrawn from China in May 1949. By the end of the year, the Communists had triumphed in China and Chiang Kai-shek's remaining forces had been driven from the mainland to the island of Formosa.

At home, the Corp's independence once more came under threat. The atom bomb appeared to be the harbinger of a revolution in the nature of warfare far more terrible than anything envisaged by Mitchell and Douhet in the 1920s. An amphibious force seemed an irrelevance in a world where the giant fist of air power cast its shadow. The United States Air Force, which was given independent status in 1947 by the National Security Act, was eager to swallow up Marine aviation. The Army maneuvered to absorb the remainder. But the National Security Act, which created a co-ordinated command of all the US armed forces under the Department of Defense, ensured that the Marine Corps retained its status as a separate military service within the US Department of the Navy. In January 1951, Congress passed the Douglas-Mansfield Bill, which formalized the Marines' separate identity and fixed the Corps' strength at four divisions and four air wings. The Commandant of the Marines was made a member of the US Joint Chiefs of Staff. By then, the Corps was involved in the largest military confrontation of the Cold War.

*Left:* On guard by dawn's early light.

*Right:* Two North Korean T-34 tanks destroyed by Marines in heavy fighting in the Naktong sector in August 1950.

## Korea

Encircled by China, Japan and the Soviet Union, the mountainous and largely inhospitable peninsula of Korea had long been coveted by its powerful neighbours. In 1942 Korea was made an integral part of Japan. At the Cairo conference in December 1943, the Allies promised Korea its independence, a decision confirmed at the Potsdam Conference in July 1945. On 15 August 1945 the Allied Supreme Commander in the Far East, General Douglas MacArthur, directed all Japanese forces north of the 38th parallel in Korea to surrender to the Russians and those in the south to the Americans. Originally conceived as a temporary demarcation line, the 38th parallel quickly became a political frontier. In the South, the US-backed Republic of Korea (ROK) was established in August 1948; in the North, the Soviet Union set up the People's Democratic Republic of Korea (PDRK). By July 1949, all Soviet and US troops had been withdrawn from the peninsula; in their place was the experienced and well-equipped North Korean People's Army (NKPA) and the understrength and poorly-equipped ROK Army, armed with obsolescent weapons left behind by the Americans.

War broke out on 25 June 1950 when seven infantry divisions and a tank division of the NKPA attacked across the 38th parallel. Brushing aside the four ROK divisions in their path, the NKPA forces drove on the South Korean capital, Seoul. On the same day, the United Nations (UN) declared the invasion a "breach of the peace" and requested military aid for the ROK Army. On 27 June President Truman sent orders to MacArthur, now the US Commander Far East, to lend American air and naval assistance. Seoul fell on the 28th and two days later President Truman authorized the use of ground forces in Korea. American troops nearest to the battle zone were 7th, 24th and 25th Infantry Divisions, which made up part of Eighth Army's occupation forces in Japan. The US 24th Division, under General William Dean, began moving into Korea on 30 June. US troops engaged the NKPA for the first time on 5 July, near Osan, when a North Korean infantry division supported by tanks ran into "Task Force Smith", a makeshift American advance unit comprising a 105-mm howitzer battery, two rifle companies, two mortar platoons, six bazooka teams and a 75-mm recoilless rifle unit, under the command of Lieutenant-Colonel Charles B. Smith.

On 7 July, General MacArthur was appointed C-in-C UN Command. (British 27th Infantry Brigade arrived in Korea on 14 September 1950, and by the end of the war UN forces also included contingents from Turkey, Canada, Australia, Thailand, France, Greece, New Zealand, Holland, Colombia, Belgium, Ethiopia, Luxembourg and South Africa.) US 24th Division fought a gallant holding action against the NKPA — during which General Dean fell into the hands of the enemy — buying time until the arrival of two more US divisions, 25th Infantry and 1st Cavalry. By the beginning of August the ROK and US forces — now designated Eighth Army — had been pushed back into a confined area around Pusan on Korea's south-east coast, the so-called "Pusan Perimeter".

*Opposite bottom:* A marine takes up a firing position in a Korean schoolhouse.

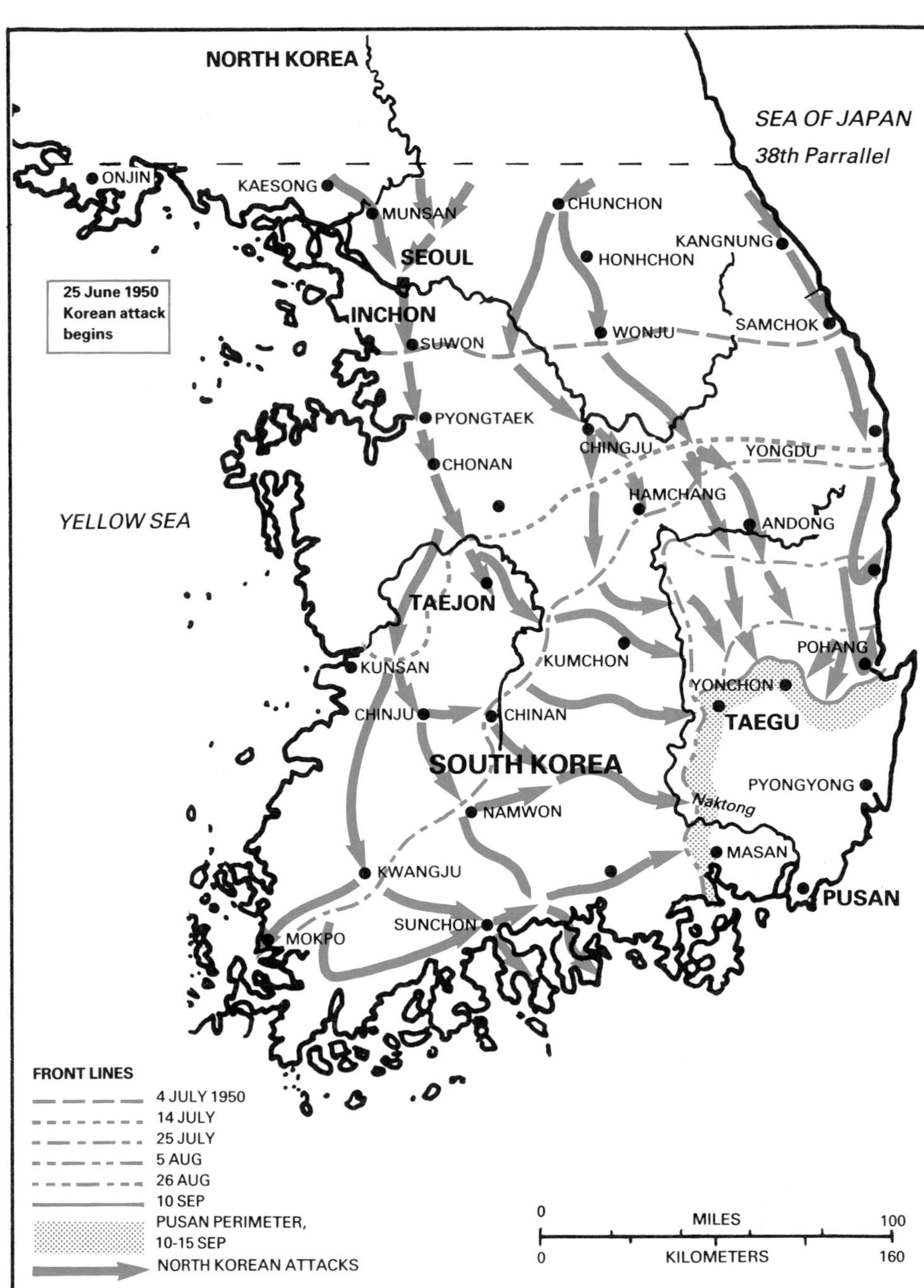
NORTH KOREA
SEA OF JAPAN
38th Parrallel
ONJIN
KAESONG
MUNSAN
CHUNCHON
KANGNUNG
HONHCHON
SEOUL
25 June 1950
Korean attack
begins
INCHON
SUWON
WONJU
SAMCHOK
PYONGTAEK
CHINGJU
YONGDU
CHONAN
HAMCHANG
YELLOW SEA
ANDONG
TAEJON
POHANG
KUNSAN
KUMCHON
YONCHON
CHINJU
CHINAN
TAEGU
SOUTH KOREA
PYONGYONG
Naktong
NAMWON
MASAN
KWANGJU
PUSAN
SUNCHON
MOKPO
FRONT LINES
4 JULY 1950
14 JULY
25 JULY
5 AUG
26 AUG
10 SEP
PUSAN PERIMETER,
10-15 SEP
NORTH KOREAN ATTACKS
0
MILES
100
0
KILOMETERS
160

*Opposite:* Marine tank crewmen prepare ammunition for their M-26 Pershings aboard ship on their way to the Inchon beach-head, 13 September 1950.

*Right:* Marines of 5th regiment, 1st Marine Corps search two captured North Korean soldiers for concealed weapons.

As early as 2 July, General MacArthur had asked the US Joint Chiefs of Staff for a Marine Brigade. Within a week, 1st Provisional Marine Brigade had been activated at Camp Pendleton, taking most of the assets of the half-strength 1st Marine Division and 1st Marine Aircraft Wing. The core of the ground element was 5th Marine Regiment, commanded by Lieutenant-Colonel Raymond L. Murray, a veteran of Guadalcanal and Tarawa. The air elements came from Marine Aircraft Group 33 (MAG-33), including three squadrons of late-model F-4U Corsair fighter-bombers. The Brigade's 6,534 men sailed from San Diego on 12 July, arriving in Pusan on 2 August.

The Marines' immediate task was to plug holes in the buckling perimeter as they

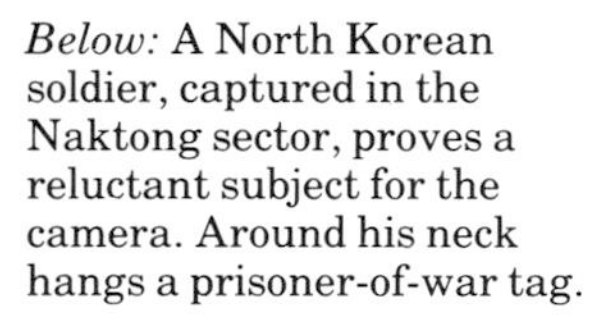

*Below:* A North Korean soldier, captured in the Naktong sector, proves a reluctant subject for the camera. Around his neck hangs a prisoner-of-war tag.

opened. Their Brigade commander, General Edward A. Craig, told them: "It will be costly fighting against a numerically superior enemy . . . Marines have never lost a battle. This Brigade will not be the first to establish such a precedent".

The 1st Marine Brigade entered action on 7 August as part of Task Force Kean (1st Marines, an ROK Army battalion and 5th and 35th Army Regimental Combat teams), named after the commander of 25th Infantry Division, Major-General William Kean. Having blunted a drive on the Pusan Perimeter from the south-west by the NKPA 6th Division, Task Force Kean launched a counter-offensive against Chinju, enemy headquarters for the south-western sector. By nightfall on 11 August, 1st Marine Brigade was dug in above Changchon, 26 miles deep into enemy territory.

Shortly afterwards, the Marines were withdrawn to shore up another hard-pressed stretch of the perimeter along the southern section of the Naktong River, fighting alongside 24th Infantry Division. MAG-33 was also in action: two fighter-bomber squadrons were flying close-support missions from the decks of carriers of US Seventh Fleet; a night-fighter squadron (VMF (N)-513) was flying missions from Japan; and an observation squadron (VMO-6), equipped with helicopters and light aircraft, supported ground elements in the Pusan perimeter.

Fighting in the Naktong sector became critical in mid-August as the NKPA 4th Division drove a salient across the river, threatening the provincial capital of Taegu, at the north-western tip of the UN enclave. From its position on the right of US 24th Division, 1st Marine Brigade drove the North Koreans from their dominating position of "No-Name Ridge" and back across the Naktong River.

With the Pusan perimeter temporarily secured, the Marines were withdrawn to act as the reserve for 25th Infantry Division and to rest and replenish their equipment. On 31 August the NKPA renewed its offensive along the Naktong, breaking the line in many places. The 1st Marine Brigade was rushed into the front line, flanking 2nd Infantry Division in the Yongsan–Changnyong sector. After three days of hard fighting, the Marines mauled the NKPA 9th Division, retrieving many pieces of abandoned American ordnance and leaving the countryside "littered with enough North Korean arms, tanks and vehicles to equip a small army". In the space of six weeks the Marines had destroyed two crack North Korean divisions.

On 5 September the Brigade was ordered back to a staging area in Pusan "for further operations against the enemy". A week later the Brigade was absorbed by the newly-arrived 1st Marine Division.

From the outset, General MacArthur had determined on reversing the desperate situation in Korea with an amphibious assault in the enemy's rear. On 25 July he secured permission from the Joint Chiefs of Staff to bring the "skeletonized" 1st Marine Division up to wartime strength in readiness for an amphibious operation in Korea. This required a supreme effort of organization. The activation of the Provisional Brigade had reduced 1st Marine Division to 3,386 officers and men, less than half the strength of a single regiment.

Within 53 days its strength had been increased to 17,162 men. The understrength 2nd Marine Division had provided 7,812 men; 3,630 Marines had been pulled in from posts and stations throughout the world; and 2,891 combat-ready Reservists, most of them World War Two veterans, had been provided by a mobilization of the entire Organized Reserve. A second infantry regiment, 1st Marines, was assembled in ten days by Colonel Lewis B. "Chesty" Puller, who had commanded the same regiment at Cape Gloucester and Peleliu. The 1st Marine Division would become the spearhead of the newly activated X Corps, which would also include US 7th Infantry Division, reinforced with 8,000 ROK troops.

## Inchon

X Corps, commanded by Major-General Edward M. Almond, was to deliver the first major UN counterstroke at Inchon, on Korea's western coast, 150 miles north of Pusan and about 20 miles west of Seoul.

The amphibious landings at Inchon were MacArthur's last great strategic stroke, both daring in conception and posing formidable problems of execution. In the headlong postwar demobilization, most of the US Navy's amphibious shipping had been given away or allowed to fall into disrepair. Ironically, 30 of the 47 LSTs required for the operation had to be retrieved complete with their crews from the Japanese, who were using them as inter-island ferries.

Intelligence reports indicated that there were about 21,000 enemy troops in the immediate area of Inchon — most of them of poor quality — with about 2,000 stationed in the town itself. These were less problematic than the hydrographic idiosyncracies of the target area. Inchon's harbor — guarded by the shore batteries on Wolmi-do Island — could be reached only through the narrow, winding Flying Fish Channel, which was subject to daily tidal variations of 30ft. On 15 September, the day scheduled for the landings (Operation Chromite), morning tide would be at 0659 hrs and evening tide at 1919 hrs. When the tide fell, the currents ripped out of the channel at up to eight knots, exposing glutinous mud flats on which even the assault force's amphibious tractors would stick fast. Pinpoint navigation would be essential for the success of the operation; it was the typhoon season; and there would be no time for rehearsals.

The assault force for the landing was Amphibious Group One, with 1st Marine Division embarked, under the US Navy's amphibious expert, Rear-Admiral James H. Doyle. The 7th Marines, the Division's third infantry regiment, were still *en route* to Korea and would not be there in time for the operation. A reserve regiment was provided by the newly-formed 1st Korean Marine Corps (KMC) Regiment along with its Marine Corps advisers.

The 3rd Battalion, 5th Marines, was to seize Wolmi-do — which was connected to the Inchon docks by a 600-yd causeway — on the

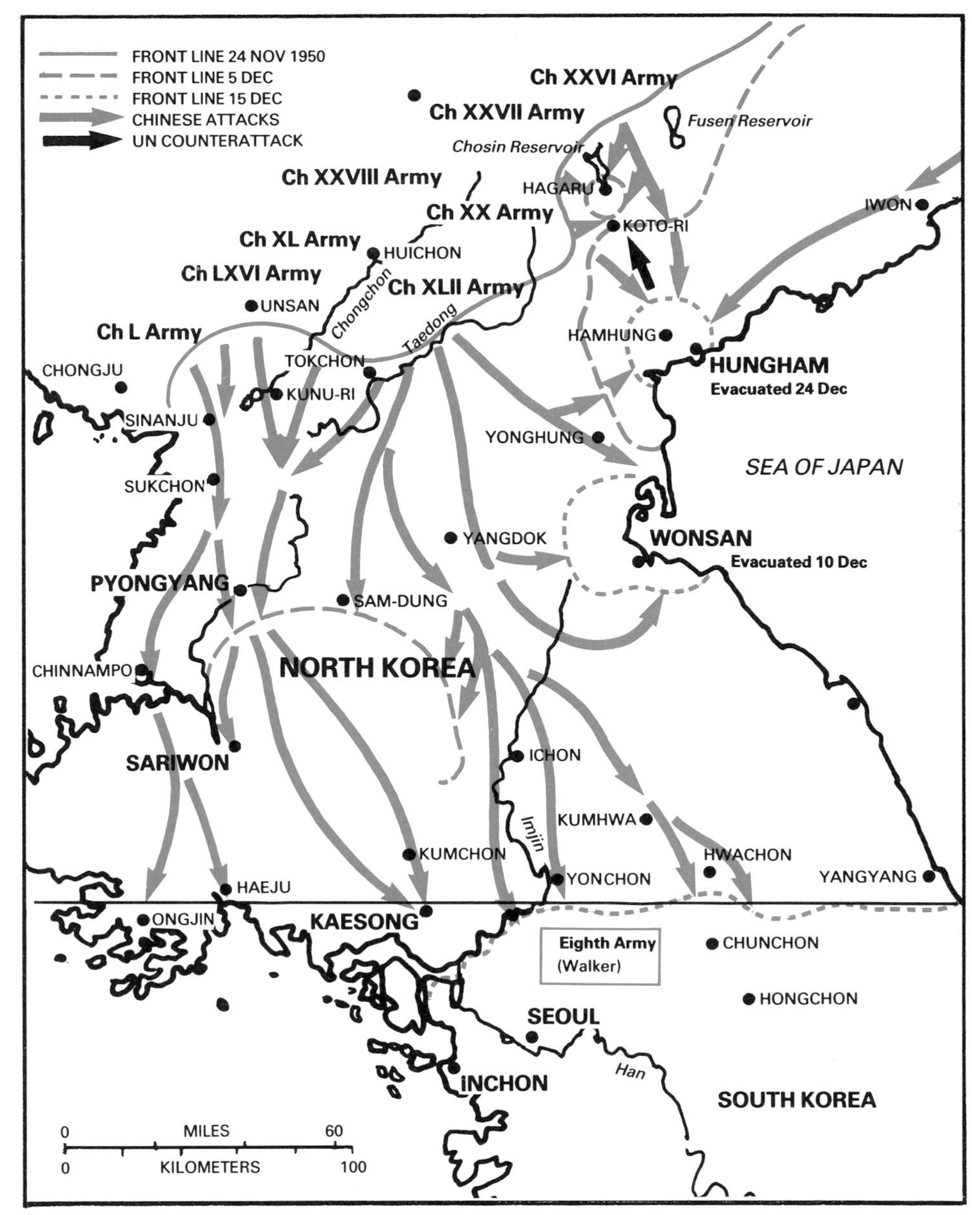

*Left:* Smoke raised by naval gunfire covers the landing areas at Inchon. Geysers of water can be seen near Inchon's docks, in the center of the picture.

*Right:* Marines use scaling ladders during the amphibious assault at Inchon, 15 September 1950. Only on Blue Beach, where 1st Marines landed, were there any problems. Some landing craft ran aground on mud flats 500yds from the shore and part of the reserve battalion, confused by the smoke-shrouded landing area, came ashore in the wrong place.
*Far right:* A tank-infantry team of 1st Marine Division pushes inland after the Inchon landings.
*Below:* Marines and an M-26 Pershing tank move through the bullet-swept outskirts of Seoul on 25 September. In Korea, 1st Marine Division's three infantry regiments and single artillery regiment (11th Marines) were supported by a number of organic and attached battalions, including: 1st Amphibian Tractor, 1st Armored Amphibian, 1st Combat Service, 1st Engineer, 1st Medical, 1st Motor Transport, 7th Motor Transport, 1st Ordnance, 1st Service, 1st Shore Party, 1st Signal, 1st Tank (with M-26 Pershings), the Headquarters Battalion, and 1st Combat Service Group. Attached to the Division were two aviation units — Marine Observation Squadron 6 and Marine Helicopter Transport Squadron 161.

morning tide across Green Beach. There would then be a 12-hour delay until the evening tide, when the remainder of 5th Marines would land on Red Beach, to the north of Wolmi-do, while 1st Marines came ashore at Blue Beach in the inner harbor. These landing areas were not "beaches" in the strict sense of the term. The harbor had granite walls at the sea's edge, which would have to be scaled.

Tasked with close air support was 1st Marine Aircraft Wing, flying from the decks of Seventh Fleet's light carriers USS *Sicily* and *Baodeng Strait* (dubbed the "Bing Ding" by the Marines). The "softening-up" of Wolmi-do began on 10 September with napalm strikes flown by Marine squadrons VMF-214 and VMF-323. For two days before the landing, US and British cruisers and destroyers pounded Wolmi-do and the Inchon waterfront.

Before daylight on 15 September, the Attack Force moved up the channel towards Inchon, with General MacArthur aboard the command ship *McKinley*. The shore bombardment lifted at 0545 hrs and within 15 minutes the men of 3rd Battalion, 5th Marines, were aboard their landing craft. The air attacks lifted at 0615 hrs and were followed by a blanket salvo of 5-in rockets from three rocket boats. The first wave of Marines went ashore on Green Beach at 0633 hrs, meeting only light resistance. By noon the battalion had secured the island and eliminated the enemy positions flanking the approaches to the main landing area at Inchon.

Naval gunfire and air strikes continued to plaster Inchon, and at 1733 hrs leading elements of 1st and 2nd Battalions, 5th Marines, scaled the sea wall at Red Beach and began to push south and south-east. On the right flank, another naval bombardment preceded the first wave of Puller's 1st Marines, aiming a swinging right hook to cut off Inchon from Seoul.

By the afternoon of D+1, the force beach-head line had been secured. The assault phase of the operation, launched under the most difficult hydrographic conditions, had been a stunning success. Marine casualties were 20 killed in action, one dead from wounds, one missing in action and 174 wounded. On the same day, 1st and 5th Marines began to push down the road to Seoul, leaving the Korean Marines to mop up resistance in Inchon. On the 17th, 5th Marines secured Kimpo airfield, north-east of Inchon, and soon US C-54 and C-119 transports were landing every few minutes under the direction of Major-General William H. Tunner, mastermind of the 1948 Berlin Airlift. On the 18th, 7th Infantry Division began to come ashore at Inchon, moving up on the Marines' right flank. Two days later 3rd Battalion, 5th Marines, crossed the Han River in amphibious tractors. Enemy resistance was now stiffening, but by 25 September the Marines had fought their way through to the outskirts of Seoul. On the 26th an armored breakout from the Pusan perimeter joined hands with the Inchon landing force. The battle for Seoul lasted for two days before NKPA resistance collapsed. On the 29th South Korea's President Syngman Rhee, escorted by General MacArthur, entered Seoul, three months and four days after the NKPA had launched its invasion of South Korea.

## Retreat from Chosin

On 27 September General MacArthur was ordered by President Truman to "complete the destruction of the North Korean forces", with authority to cross the 38th parallel into North Korea. At the beginning of October, the UN General Assembly passed a resolution calling for the "establishment of a united, independent and democratic government in the sovereign state of Korea". The roles had been reversed; now the UN was attempting to unite the Korean peninsula by force of arms. The North Korean capital, Pyongyang, fell on 20 October. By the third week in November, UN forces had occupied two-thirds of North Korea, pressing to within a few miles of the Yalu River, which marked the border with China.

On 26 October, 1st Marine Division had been landed at Wonsan, on Korea's east coast, where it formed part of X Corps' three-pronged advance on the Yalu River, which forms the border between North Korea and Manchuria. ROK I Corps was assigned to the right flank; US 7th Infantry Division was in the center; and 1st Marines took up the left flank; corps reserve was provided by US 3rd Infantry Division.

The only route to the Marines' objective was over a narrow road through wild mountain terrain which rose to a height of 4,000ft. Winter was closing in, bringing sub-zero temperatures and marrow-chilling winds. The Marines began their advance to the Yalu at Hamhung, 70 miles north of Wonsan. Their sector of responsibility — approximately 200 miles long and 40 miles wide — would have taxed the abilities of a corps-sized formation. The Marines' commander, Major-General Oliver P. Smith, was not only worried about his division's widely dispersed positions. He was also concerned about the 80-mile gap which separated X Corps' left flank from Eighth Army, advancing in the west but cut off from 1st Marines by Korea's mountainous spine. Another cause for alarm came with intelligence reports that elements of 12 Chinese divisions had been identified in the Chosin reservoir area, 70 miles to the north.

At the beginning of October, the UN high command had been confident that their troops would be "home by Christmas", an unfortunate echo of the mood in August 1914 and as equally ill-founded. As he pushed northwards, the wary General Smith left behind stockpiles of arms, ammunition, fuel and supplies, to minimize 1st Marines' vulnerability if they were obliged to withdraw through the granite gullies and gorges of the road which led to the Chosin reservoir.

On 4 November, 7th Marines' Regimental Combat Team reached Chinhung-ni, where they encountered Chinese Communist forces (CCF) dug-in in strength. In a five-day battle the Marines so severely mauled major

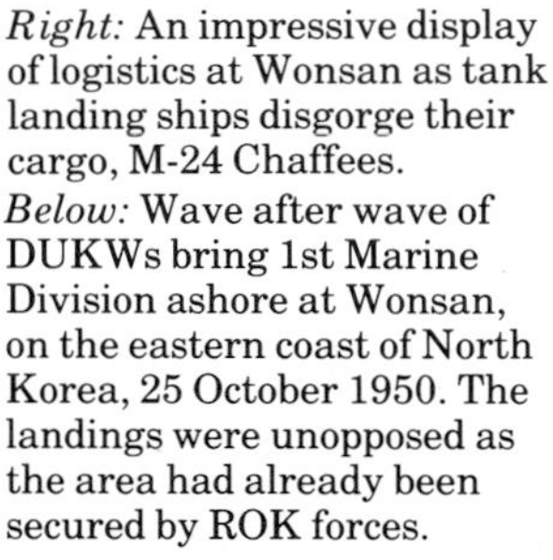

*Right:* An impressive display of logistics at Wonsan as tank landing ships disgorge their cargo, M-24 Chaffees.
*Below:* Wave after wave of DUKWs bring 1st Marine Division ashore at Wonsan, on the eastern coast of North Korea, 25 October 1950. The landings were unopposed as the area had already been secured by ROK forces.

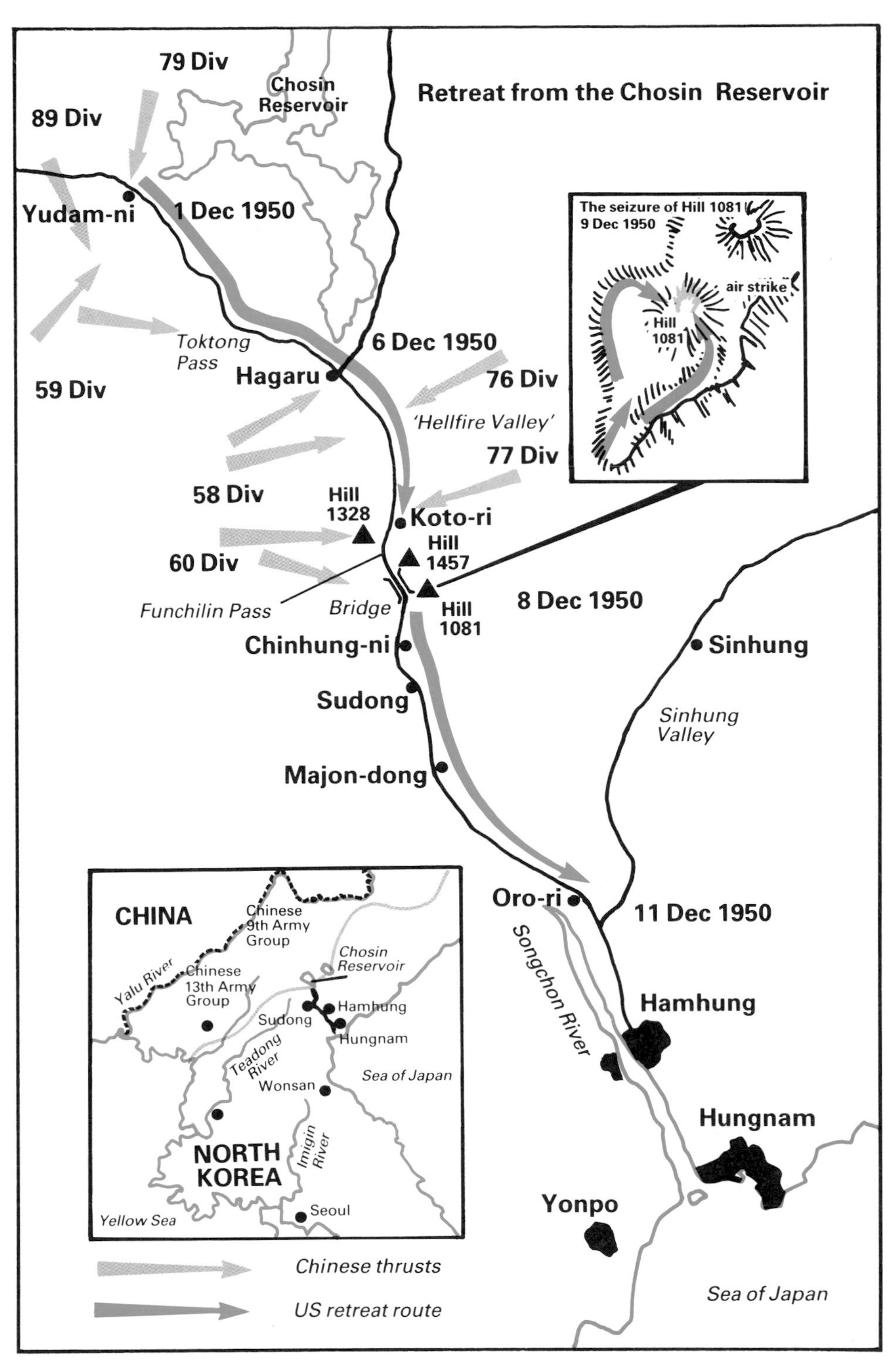


elements of 124th CCF Division that it was never effective again as an organic unit.

By 25 November, 5th and 7th Marines were on the western side of the Chosin reservoir, preparing to launch a westward thrust out of its mountain valley. Fourteen miles to the south-east, across a frozen, windswept plateau, the forward elements of the divisional command post and a battalion of 1st Marines held Hagaru-ri at the southern tip of the reservoir. Further south were the remaining two battalions of 1st Marines, dug in on the icy slopes of Koto-ri. Behind them lay the Funchilin Pass, gateway to the high plateau of the Tobaksan Mountain range which cradles the Chosin reservoir.

On that day the Korean War entered its second phase. The NKPA, reinforced by 200,000 CCF troops acting as "volunteers", launched a massive counter-offensive across the Yalu. The main blow fell on the right flank of Eighth Army, which by the end of the year had been bundled back to the 38th parallel. On 26 November, 1st Marine Division had been ordered to attack westwards to sever the enemy lines of communication at Mupyong-ri. But before this operation could gain any momentum, the Chinese delivered their second blow, this time aimed at X Corps.

On the night of 27 November, the assault battlions of the CCF North Army Group hurled themselves against the 5th and 7th Marines' perimeter at Yudam-ni, 1st Marines at Koto-ri and the three-battalion task force of US 7th Infantry Division east of the Chosin reservoir. While the Chinese 79th and 89th Divisions battered at the Marines' positions at Yudam-ni, 59th Division cut the 14-mile section of the road back to Hagaru. On the next day the Chinese attacked Hagaru, with its vital fuel dumps and nearly-completed airstrip, opening a gap in its four-mile perimeter at East Hill, a position dominating the town.

The 1st Marine Division was now encircled by Communist forces, and General Almond authorized General Smith to abandon his heavy equipment to speed a breakout and withdrawal. Smith declined to leave his heavy equipment behind him, adding that he would withdraw only as rapidly as he could evacuate his wounded.

On the 29th, operations began to open the road to Hagaru. Six days later, 5th and 7th Marines fought their way through, many of them marching in cadence and singing the Marines' hymn as they arrived. With them

they brought 1,500 casualties. Hagaru's airstrip — hacked out of frozen ground in 12 days — had become operational on 1 December. In five days 3,150 Marines and 1,137 soldiers were evacuated by Marine R4Ds and Air Force C-47s. The same aircraft flew in 537 replacements, some of them recently recovered from the wounds they had received in the fighting for Inchon and Seoul.

Once the Marines were in the Hagaru perimeter, General Smith ordered the division to break out to Hamhung, 56 miles to the south-east. When asked by a newsman if this was a retreat, Smith explained that "retreat" was not the correct term: "Retreat, hell! We're just attacking in another direction!"

On 6 December, 7th Marines struck out for Koto-ri while 5th Marines plugged the gap in East Hill. The two-day breakout to Koto-ri was achieved with the loss of 103 dead, 506 wounded and seven missing in action. Close air support was provided by land- and carrier-based aircraft. Smith had now concentrated 14,000 men — including all three of his infantry regiments and some British commandos — but was keenly aware that the Chinese would reserve their main effort for the ten-mile gauntlet down the Funchilin Pass to Chinhung-ni.

At a hairpin bend, where the road clung to the southern side of Hill 1081, the enemy had blown up a narrow concrete bridge. To save his heavy equipment, particularly his tanks, Smith decided to replace the bridge with a 16-ton steel bridge, air-dropped in sections, an operation never attempted before. On 9 December the site on Hill 1081 was secured by 1st Battalion, 1st Marines. The steel sections were flown in from the emergency airstrip at Koto-ri and assembled in three hours under heavy enemy fire. Throughout the operation there had been fierce fighting along the length of the road, from the rearguard action at Koto-ri to the advanced elements pushing into the outskirts of Chinhung-ni. There, they linked with Brigadier-General Armistead Mead's Task Force Dog, which had fought its way up from Hamhung to clear a path for 1st Marine Division on the last leg of its epic journey. By nightfall on 11 December, all of 1st Marine

*Below:* Corsair fighter-bombers of the four squadrons of MAG-12 at Yonpo airfield, December 1950. They provided crucial close support during 1st Marines' epic withdrawal from Chosin. The very heavy AU-1 attack Corsair saw much action in Korea, carrying a 4,000-lb load at speeds which seldom exceeded 240mph.

*Above:* In heavy snow, 1st Marine Division readies itself for the break-out from Koto-ri. Only about 25 percent of the division had been issued with cold-weather gear — mountain sleeping bags, parkas, wind-proof trousers, shoe-pacs and heavy woolen socks. The parkas were Navy-type, heavy and long cut, better suited to watch-standing than long marches through freezing mountain terrain in which the temperatures plummeted to 20 degrees Fahrenheit below zero with a 20-30 knot wind.

Division's units were safely in their assembly areas in the Hamhung–Hungnam sector.

General Almond had been ordered to redeploy to the Pusan area, and the evacuation of the Hungnam perimeter was completed by 24 December. The 1st Marine Division sailed on 15 December. Since landing at Wonsan, the Marines had suffered 4,418 battle casualties — 718 dead, 192 missing and 3,508 wounded. There were also 7,313 non-combat casualties, most of them suffering the effects of the extreme cold. They had fought the 20th, 26th, 27th and 42nd CCF Armies, 14 divisions in all, inflicting an estimated 40,000 casualties on the enemy. *Time* magazine declared that the Marines' fighting retreat was: "A battle unparalleled in US military history. It has some of the aspects of Bataan, some of Anzio, some of Dunkirk, some of Valley Forge." In less florid but no less telling military language, the 1st Marines Division had achieved a signal tactical triumph by "coming through with operable equipment, with wounded properly evacuated, and with tactical integrity".

## A War of Attrition

No sooner had General Walton Walker stabilized Eighth Army's front on the 38th parallel than the Chinese launched a second offensive, occupying Seoul on 4 January. On 23 December, General Walker was killed in a road accident and replaced by Lieutenant-General Matthew B. Ridgway, who assumed control of all land operations under General MacArthur.

The Marines were now drawn into a savage war of attrition. There were to be no more amphibious landings in Korea. Instead, the Marines were assigned missions similar to those undertaken by Army divisions, and its air elements were placed under the control of the USAF.

After the evacuation of Hungnam, 1st Marine Division had been placed in the Eighth Army reserve to re-equip and receive replenishment. The launching of the renewed Communist offensive brought them back to the front line. On 10 January 1951, Chinese forces broke through the UN lines on the right flank of US 2nd Division, infiltrating ROK III Corps. The Marines were immediately rushed northward from Masan to the Andong–Yondok road, where enemy forces were threatening to cut the supply lines of the ROK troops in the eastern sector.

The Marines stabilized this front and were then assigned the task of destroying enemy guerrilla forces — the remnants of NKPA III Corps — who were conducting harassing

*Above:* A sniper and spotter of 1st Marine Division in search of prey.
*Right:* Marines of 1 Battery, 11th Marines, in action with a 105-mm howitzer in support of 7th Marines in the Yanggu region of North Korea, June 1951.

operations between Andong and Usong. By the beginning of February 1951, the Marines' "Rice Paddy Patrols" had eliminated about 60 percent of the enemy and forced the remainder to pull out of the area.

At the end of February, General Ridgway began a series of limited counterstrokes, aimed at inflicting maximum damage on the enemy at minimum cost to the UN forces. The Marines were transferred to central Korea, where they came under the operational control of IX Corps in Operation Killer, which for public relations was subsequently renamed Operation Ripper. Two weeks later the shattered shell of Seoul was retaken by UN forces, the fourth time it had changed hands in less than nine months. In the central zone, the Marines secured Hungchon and destroyed the important Communist supply and communications center at Chunchon. On 4 April they were among the first UN forces to recross the 38th parallel, probing at a major Communist assembly and supply area between Chorwon, Kumhwa and Pyongyang, known as the "Iron Triangle".

As heavy fighting continued on the battlefield, a different kind of battle reached its climax. On 11 April President Truman replaced General MacArthur. The latter had been chafing at the restrictions placed on him by the UN and Truman; he had not, for example, been allowed to bomb bridges over the Yalu or fly reconnaissance missions over south China, for fear of precipitating full-scale Chinese involvement. The UN commander-in-chief was at loggerheads with the President over the conduct of the war. American B-29s and fighter-bombers had flattened North Korea's relatively primitive industrial infrastructure. Now MacArthur urged a naval blockade of China and a strategic bombing campaign against her industrial complexes in Manchuria. He argued that these operations should be combined with the employment of Chinese Nationalist forces from Formosa and the waging of a guerrilla war in south China. Truman was determined to limit the war to the Korean peninsula. Having abandoned any realistic hope of uniting North and South Korea, the United States and its UN allies were now reconciled to ending the war by negotiation. Relations completely broke down

*Above:* Clad in heavy winter uniforms, Corporal Richard J. Grinnic and Pfc Appleton, 1st Marine Division, undertake a scout-sniper mission in December 1951. Appleton is armed with a .30-caliber M1 Garand rifle with a sniper 'scope.

when MacArthur decided to pre-empt Truman with a public statement of his own, in which he declared that "there is no substitute for victory". Truman had no option but to remove his insubordinate commander-in-chief, replacing him with General Ridgway. Lieutenant-General James A. Van Fleet was despatched to Korea to command UN ground forces.

Van Fleet arrived on 14 April, a week before the Chinese launched their expected spring offensive. By the end of the month it had been contained, and the Communists had suffered 70,000 casualties. The second phase of the offensive opened on 15 May, the main blow falling on the eastern side of the Korean peninsula. After heavy fighting, the attacks petered out on 20 May. Eighth Army immediately counter-attacked, clearing South Korea of practically all the Communist forces by the end of the month. Some of the hardest fighting in Operation Piledriver was experienced by 1st Marine Division and 5th and 3rd ROK Divisions as they advanced on the "Punchbowl", a volcanic crater lying about 25 miles north of Inje in east-central Korea and along the edge of the "Kansas Line", Van Fleet's main defensive line.

As the fighting congealed into a slogging match around the 38th parallel, the Soviet representative at the UN, Jacob Malik, proposed a cease-fire. It was clear that the request had come from the People's Republic of China. Truce talks began on 10 July at Kaejing, just inside the Communist lines. The talks gave the Communists a much-needed breathing space, but achieved little else, and they were broken off in August.

Hostilities continued throughout the negotiations. At this point the front extended from the Imjin River to Chorwon, parallel to the base of the "Iron Triangle", swinging south-east along the southern edge of the "Punchbowl", then north again to come to rest on the Sea of Japan above Kansong.

Some of the fiercest fighting took place in the "Punchbowl", and it was here that the 1st Marine Division opened a new chapter in military history. At the beginning of the war, 1st Provisional Brigade had used Sikorsky HO3S-1 light helicopters in combat for the first time in the Pusan perimeter, flying reconnaissance, casualty evacuation and rescue missions. Unit commanders had used

*Above:* Improvizing front skids for wheels, Captain Grady Holmes, 1st Marine Air Wing, flies his Sikorsky HRS-1 helicopter on a shuttle run between forward and rear areas. In Korea helicopters pioneered airborne assault, rapid battlefield resupply and speedy relocation of mortars and light artillery, often within only a few yards of hostile troops.

them at Inchon to direct fighting over a front of several hundred yards. At the end of August 1951, a Marine medium helicopter squadron, HMR-161 commanded by Lieutenant-Colonel George W. Herring, arrived in Korea equipped with 15 Sikorsky HRS-1s. The HRS-1's sea-level payload of 1,420lb enabled it to carry up to six combat-equipped Marines or up to five casualties on litters. In the hand-to-hand combat over the razor-sharp ridges of the "Punchbowl", the helicopters offered an invaluable tactical advantage, with their ability to ferry quantities of supplies and troops in minutes over terrain which would take several hours to cover on foot or by motor transport.

On 13 September, Herring's HRS-1s were used in the first helicopter re-supply mission, delivering over seven tons of supplies (mostly ammunition) to 2nd Battalion, 1st Marines on Hill 673. Soon the helicopters were flying company-sized units to the combat-zone. A squadron of HRS-1s could carry a company 10–15 miles over terrain which would otherwise take a day to cover. In October the Marines began to move whole battalions by helicopter. The era of air mobility had begun.

The winter of 1951–52 passed with action on both sides confined mainly to raids and patrol skirmishes. In March 1952, after seven months hard campaigning in the "Punchbowl", the Marines were moved west to form part of I Corps, on Eighth Army's left flank, occupying a 35-mile front blocking the approach to Seoul.

From the cessation of major offensive action on 12 November 1951, the Main Line of Resistance (MLR) of the UN forces in Korea was a trench line which in theory ran all the way across the peninsula (the British Commonwealth Division broke the line with an "island" defensive system). The Marines' field fortifications were less impressive than those of the Chinese, behind whose deep-dug MLR complexes stretched echeloned belts of fieldworks some 10 miles deep and as impressive as anything on the Hindenburg Line in 1917. Comparisons with World War One were inevitable in these conditions, although this time the Marines were defending rather than attacking.

Just as in the trenches of 1914–18, there were long periods of inactivity — while both sides considered the results of the stop-go truce talks at Panmunjon — interrupted by bursts of savage fighting. Small, vicious battles were fought for the exchange of a few hundred yards of shell-churned earth or a hill-top which offered a few precious metres of elevation. A typical action was the bitter eight-day battle for the Chinese occupied Hill 122, a feature in no-man's-land dubbed "Bunker Hill" by the Marines and providing a vantage point from which the enemy was directing fire on the Marines' MLR. In a series of bloody actions between 11 and 17 August 1952, units of 1st Marine Division seized the hill at a cost of 48 dead and 313 wounded. Chinese casualties were estimated at about 3,000.

In March 1953, Communist pressure against the MLR began to build up to the level of May 1951, before the start of cease-fire talks. Hand-to-hand fighting occurred at Bunker Hill and other Marine outposts as the enemy probed at I Corps' line. Heavy fighting continued until July. The deadlock was broken by Truman's successor, President Eisenhower, who dropped thinly veiled hints that the United States was prepared to use nuclear weapons if peace talks were not resumed. On 20 July the talks got underway again at Panumnjon and an armistice was signed on the 27th.

Thereafter the Marines were relieved of their combat duties but remained in Korea until April 1955, manning defensive positions

*Above:* Medical corpsmen rush a wounded Marine from a Bell H-13 Sioux helicopter on a casualty evacuation (CASEVAC) mission.
*Left:* An uneasy moment for a North Korean farmer as he is interrogated by men of 1st Marine Division in April 1951.

*Above:* A battery of 4.5-in rockets unleashes a salvo at positions occupied by the Chinese Communist Forces (CCF). Rockets were an important supplement to the Marines 105-mm howitzers in the "war of the outposts", which was punctuated by ferocious artillery duels.

*Right:* An HRS-1 helicopter on a resupply mission in Korea.

along the Demilitarized Zone which separated North and South Korea.

Total US casualties in the war numbered approximately 136,000 men killed, missing or wounded. Marine casualties were listed as 28,011: 3,845 killed, 422 missing and 23,744 wounded. One-third of the Marine dead were victims of the static "outpost warfare" which had been such a feature of the war. Marine aircraft had provided vital close support, particularly during the withdrawal from Chosin. Between August 1950 and 27 July 1953, units of the 1st Marine Aircraft Wing flew more than 118,000 sorties, of which over 39,500 were close air support missions. During the same period, Marine helicopters had evacuated nearly 10,000 personnel.

The Korean war had given the Marines a taste of trench warfare which would have been familiar to the veterans of Belleau Wood. The landings at Inchon had drawn on the experience gained in the "island-hopping" campaign in the Pacific, while the "Rice Paddy Patrols" and the development of embryonic air mobile tactics anticipated a future conflict — in Vietnam.

## VIETNAM

During World War Two, Allied support for resistance to the Japanese in South-East Asia ignited the twin forces of nationalism and Communism, the political effects of which are still working themselves out in the world of the 1980s. In Vietnam these forces were harnessed by the leader of the Viet Minh, the Communist Ho Chi Minh, who on 2 September 1945, from the northern city of Hanoi, issued a Declaration of Independence. A memorable photograph taken on the day shows the Vietnamese Communists giving their clenched-fist salute as the new red flag with the yellow star unfurled above the citadel of the former French colony of Indochina. By the side of these new leaders that day, also saluting the flag, were American officers in uniform.

The Americans would return, in less friendly circumstances. But first came the French, attempting to restore their colonial authority over Vietnam. Nine years later they were forced to admit defeat when 15,000 men, under General de Castries, were isolated and then overwhelmed at Dien Bien Phu by General Giap's Vietnamese People's Army.

At the Geneva Conference (26 April–21 June 1954) the French agreed to the division of Vietnam at the 17th parallel. Neighbouring Laos and Cambodia were recognized as independent, neutral states. The United States accepted the provisions of the Geneva Agreement but reserved the right to take action should they be broken. In North Vietnam a Communist government was established under the leadership of Ho Chi Minh. In the South a corrupt, authoritarian regime, under Ngo Dinh Diem, was set up with US backing.

Between 1954 and 1962 the US Marines provided a small advisory group to work with the South Vietnamese Marine Corps. During this period the situation in the South steadily deteriorated. Lacking popular support, Diem was unable to resolve South Vietnam's internal problems or counter the growing threat posed by Communist guerrilla forces, which in December 1960 formed the National Front for the Liberation of South Vietnam (NLF), called the Viet Cong (VC) by its opponents. By 1960 there were about 6,000 Viet Cong guerrillas operating in South Vietnam. However, the South Victnamese Army (ARVN), advised by the Americans,

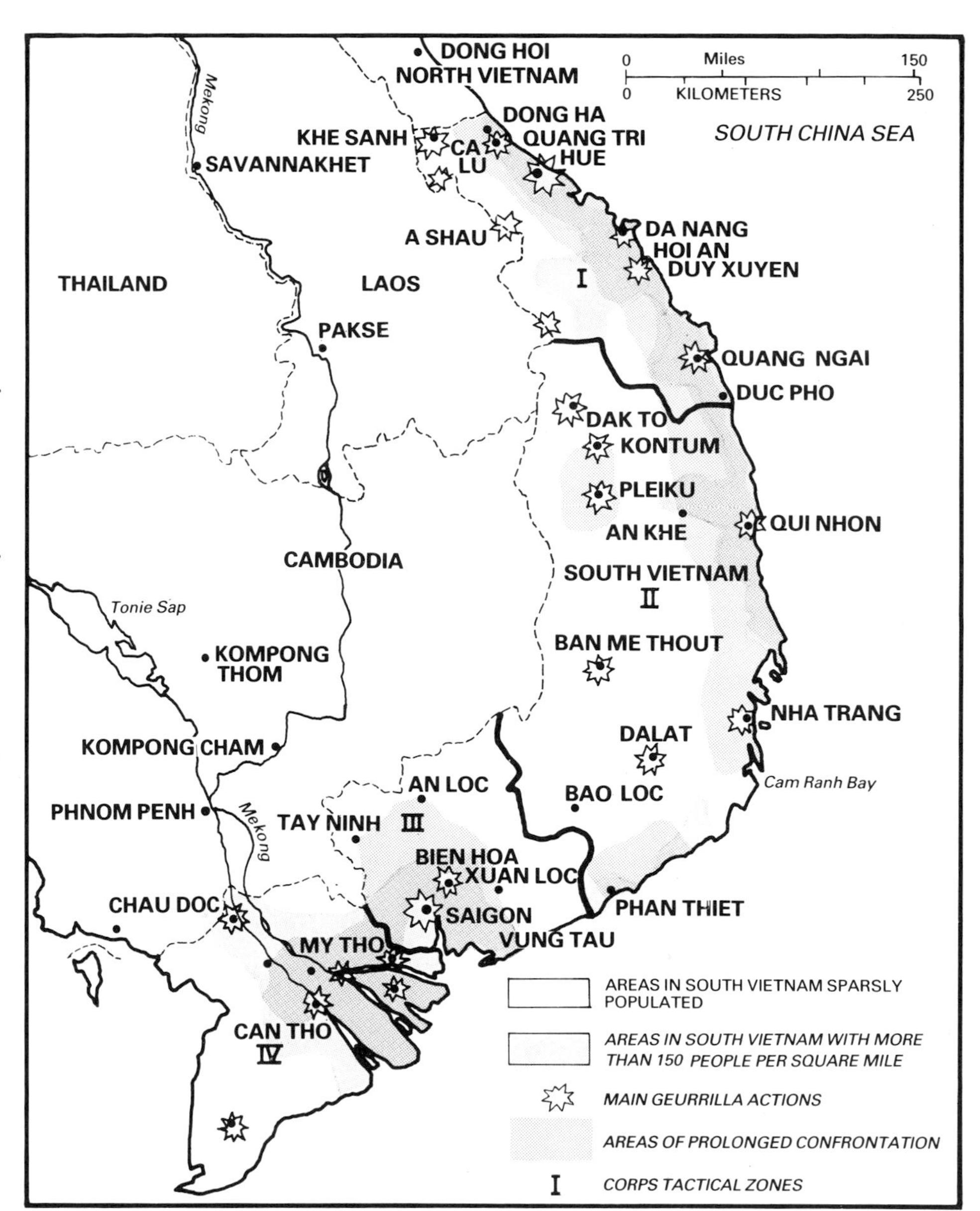


*Above:* The military regions of South Vietnam. Climate and topography had an important influence on the fighting in Vietnam. The Marines operated in I Corps Tactical Zone, where the monsoon occurred in the winter months. During the monsoon, visibility is poor, cross-country movement difficult and flying conditions bad. Health hazards — particularly for non-Asian troops — increased during the monsoon and quartermaster and storage problems multiplied. The North Vietnamese Army and the Viet Cong tended to reduce their levels of activity during the monsoon.

continued to train for conventional rather than counter-insurgency operations.

On 19 October 1961, Diem declared a state of emergency. In November, following a fact-finding mission to South Vietnam by General Maxwell D. Taylor, President Kennedy decided to increase military aid without committing US troops to combat.

Early in 1962, Marine Medium Helicopter Squadron 362 of of 1st Marine Aircraft Wing was ordered to Vietnam to provide support for the AVRN. By now there were 4,000 US military personnel in South Vietnam, of whom 600 were Marines.

The United States had long since lost faith in Diem, and gave tacit support to his assassination on 1 November 1963 by a group of South Vietnamese generals. Three weeks later President Kennedy was also assassinated, in Dallas, Texas, and was succeeded by Lyndon Baines Johnson. In South Vietnam, nine changes of government took place in the next two years as coup followed coup. With the South on the verge of collapse, the decision was taken to initiate active US military intervention. This

*Above:* Getting in. The 9th Marine Expeditionary Brigade comes ashore at Da Nang, South Vietnam, in March 1965. The Vietnam conflict was to be the longest, and in some respects the biggest, war in Marine Corps history. By 1968 III Marine Amphibious Force (III MAF) had a total of 85,755 men in Vietnam, more than were ashore at Okinawa.

resulted in the "Americanization" of the war, which was accomplished in successive stages between August 1964 and June 1965.

On 2 August 1964 the US destroyer *Maddox* was attacked in the Gulf of Tonkin by North Vietnamese torpedo boats. Two days later the destroyer *C. Turner Joy* also came under attack. On 5 August, aircraft from carriers of the US 7th Fleet retaliated by attacking military targets in North Vietnam. On 7 August, the US Congress approved the Gulf of Tonkin resolution, allowing the President to "take all necessary measures to repel any armored attack against the forces of the United States and to prevent further aggression". President Johnson now had a blanket authorization to expand the US military commitment in South-East Asia. By 1 January 1965, US military strength in South Vietnam had risen to 25,000 men.

In February, Viet Cong attacks on US military bases and personnel led to Operation Flaming Dart, in which carrier aircraft from 7th Fleet's Task Force 77 struck at military installations around the Demilitarized Zone (DMZ), the five-mile-wide buffer zone straddling the 17th parallel.

In March the role of US troops in South Vietnam was switched from "advisory" to "combat" and a sustained air offensive — Operation Rolling Thunder — was launched against North Vietnam.

Task Force 77 was not the only active force in the South China Sea. Since January, US Marines of the 9th Marine Expeditionary Brigade (9th MEB), in Task Force 76 shipping, had been steaming off South Vietnam, ready to land. At the end of February, President Johnson ordered the two-battalion brigade ashore to protect the air base at Da Nang, an operation which was already the subject of the Corps Schools' Amphibious Warfare Study No. 16.

At 0918 hrs on 8 March, the first Marines of Battalion Landing Team 3/9 (BLT 3/9) came ashore, to be greeted with garlands of flowers. In the afternoon the Brigade's second battalion, BLT 1/3, was flown in from Okinawa. By 12 March, 9th MEB was in position at Da Nang.

They were followed on 10 April by another Marine battalion, BLT 2/3. Two companies were immediately heli-lifted to defend the airfield at Phu Bai, 42 miles north-west of Da Nang and six miles from the ancient city of Hué. On 11 April, the first Marine fixed-wing

*Left:* McDonnell Douglas A-4E Skyhawk aircraft of Marine Attack Squadron 311 (VMA-311), armed with 750-lb bombs. In spite of its small size, the A-4 packed a considerable punch and, like all classic combat aircraft, was capable of absorbing continual updating and modifications. *Below left:* Troops of 2nd Battalion, 4th Marines, move across a dike during a patrol of the Ly Tin area, north-west of the air base at Chu Lai, in 1966. At the beginning of their involvement in Vietnam, the Marines favored a strategy which gave priority to the establishment of secure coastal positions such as Da Nang from which forces could move out gradually in "clear and hold" operations. In contrast, the Army strategy increasingly favored the aggressive employment of troops in "search and destroy" missions against the enemy.

squadron, Marine Fighter Attack Squadron 531 (VMFA-531), flying McDonnell Douglas F-4B Phantoms, arrived at Da Nang. On 14 April, BLT 3/4 arrived to replace BLT 2/3's companies at Phu Bai. By the end of April, 8,878 Marines were in place in Vietnam.

The two Marine enclaves were situated in the northernmost of South Vietnam's three military regions, designated I Corps Tactical Zone and covering some 10,000 square miles of territory separated from the rest of the South by the rugged peaks of the Annamite Chain. Military control of this predominantly rural region was nominally by ARVN units commanded by General Nguyen Chanh Thi, but in fact their writ ran no further than the cities of Da Nang and Hoi Ann. In the countryside, a number of outpost district headquarters — garrisoned by company-sized ARVN units — floated like small islands in a sea dominated by the Viet Cong.

At the beginning of May, 9th MEB was redesignated III Marine Amphibious Force (III MAF), principally because the US Joint Chiefs of Staff were concerned that the term "Expeditionary" evoked memories of the colonial days of the French Expeditionary Corps. At the same time, it was reinforced by the landing of three more battalions at Chu Lai, 55 miles south-west of Da Nang and the site of a projected airfield.

Within 48 hours, Marine engineers and Seabees were working on the site, which became operational at the beginning of June. The airfield at Chu Lai was a unique Marine development, designated a Short Airfield for Tactical Support (SATS). This was nothing less than an "aircraft carrier on land", consisting of 4,000ft of aluminum matting runway, complete with catapult and arrester wires (the catapult was not installed at Chu Lai until 1967, jet-assisted take-off being used in the interim).

On 6 May, Da Nang-based Marine VMFA-531 Phantoms flew their first mission over North Vietnam and by mid-1965 there were four Marine Aircraft Groups — MAG-11, 12, 16 and 36 — stationed in Vietnam, two of them helicopter and two fixed-wing.

### On to the Offensive

The American military build-up in Vietnam was inexorably gathering pace, and on 28 July President Johnson announced that the US forces in the region were to be increased from 75,000 to 125,000. The increasing demands of the US war machine led directly to an expansion of the Marine Corps, which late in 1965 received authorization for an additional 55,000 men. The Corps set a target of 278,184 men by mid-1967, and in the course of 1966 recruited 80,000 volunteers plus about 19,000 draftees.

In the summer of 1965 the Marines' roles in Vietnam underwent a radical change. Initially they had been required to adopt an "enclave strategy", standing on the defensive and patrolling within a radius of 50 miles around the enclaves to break up the concentration of hostile forces. In June 1965, President Johnson abandoned this strategy, secretly authorizing General William Westmoreland, Commander United States Military Assistance Command, Vietnam (Com USMACV), to engage in "counter-insurgency" combat operations.

At the beginning of August 1965 there were four Marine regiments — 3rd, 4th, 7th and 9th Marines — in Vietnam. Intelligence reports indicated that the 1st Viet Cong Regiment was concentrating on the Van Tuong peninsula, 15 miles south of Chu Lai. On 6 August, III MAF's commander, Lieutenant-General Lewis W. Walt, was authorized to take offensive action in Operation Satellite. However, a clerk's typing error transformed "Satellite" into "Starlite", and that was the way it stayed when the Marines jumped off on 18 August. In the first regimental-sized Marine action of the war, 7th Marines encirled and then severely mauled 1st VC Regiment, killing 614 of the enemy at a cost of 45 Marines dead.

The Viet Cong hit back on the night of 27-28 October when Communist sappers, covered by mortars, blew up 24 helicopters and damaged 23 more at the Marble Mountain Marine helicopter base, south of Da Nang. At Chu Lai, a VC raiding party destroyed two Marine Douglas A-4 Skyhawk fighter-bombers and damaged six more.

January 1966 saw the arrival in Vietnam of the 1st Marine Division. At the same time the Marines' Combined Action Program (CAP), initiated in the Phu Bai area, was extended to the Da Nang sector. The basic tactical unit of the CAP was the Combined Action Company, comprising a squad of Marine volunteers serving in each of the five platoons of local Popular Forces (PF) companies. The Marines were enthusiastic advocates of "winning the hearts and minds"

of the Vietnamese with a vigorous "pacification" program conducted at grass roots level, an approach which the Army treated with some scepticism. In spite of III MAF's considerable efforts in this field, the program was fatally undermined by the inability of the Popular Forces to provide security for an area once it had been cleared of Viet Cong.

The ultimate failure of the "pacification" program can be gauged from the grim fate of the village of My Lai, a hamlet near the provincial capital of Quang Ngai. In 1965 the Marines turned My Lai into a "model protected hamlet". On 16 March 1968 it was the scene of a massacre in which in an inexperienced, ill-disciplined company of 1st Battalion, 20th Infantry, US Americal Division, commanded by Lieutenant William Calley, ran amok, killing 347 Vietnamese civilians.

In January 1966, the four battalions of Marine Task Force Delta combined with the Army's 1st Air Cavalry Division in Operation Double Eagle, launched against the 325A North Vietnamese Army (NVA) Division, which was concentrating on the boundary between I and II Corps Tactical Zones. The operation began with 3rd Battalion, 1st Marines, landing near Thach Tru in the largest amphibious operation of the war up to that time, deploying three attack transports, an attack cargo ship, three LSTs, three LSDs, an LPH, a cruiser, a destroyer and two auxiliaries. On the second day of the operation, 2nd Battalion, 3rd Marines, was heli-lifted to a site five miles west of the beaches. On D+4, 2nd Battalion, 9th Marines, moved out of the Quang Ngai airstrip into the mountains to the north-west of the beaches.

A VC guerrilla is interrogated by men of 3rd Marine Division in 1966. *Above:* Lance Corporal Miller Brown, 3rd Marine Division, fires his flamethrower into a VC position during Operation Cherokee (May 1966), 15 miles north of Hué.

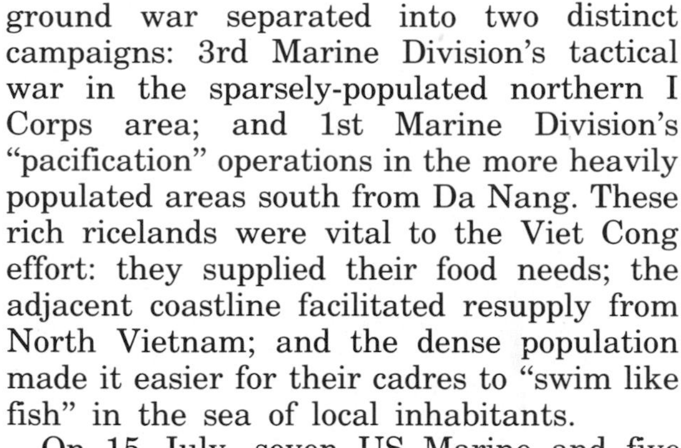

*Opposite, top:* A flame-throwing tank in action, with Corporal Wayne Whiting surveying his handiwork. *Opposite, bottom:* Lance Corporal Jerry Fola, a rifleman in 3 Platoon, E Company, 2nd Battalion, 3rd Marines, at the alert during operation No Name Number 97, December 1967. He is armed with an M16A1 rifle, which can be distinguished from the original M16 by the prominent bolt-closure device above the pistol grip. This was added after combat experience in Vietnam revealed the difficulty of closing the bolt after debris had entered the weapon.

The enemy proved elusive, and in mid-February the Marines moved into the Que San Valley to engage 36th NVA Regiment and the reconstituted 1st VC Regiment in Operation Utah.

In March, the Marines launched two combined operations with the AVRN: Utah/Lien Ket 26, north-west of Quang Ngai; and Texas/Lien Ket 28, to relieve the besieged ARVN outpost at An Hoa. Over 1,000 enemy troops were killed in these operations, but they were overshadowed by the outbreak of large-scale civil unrest in South Vietnam's principal cities as Buddhists mounted a challenge to the military government. On 9 April, Marines at Da Nang had to intervene to prevent rebel ARVN units joining the dissidents. General Walt played a key role in restoring order with the minimum of bloodshed, but a major casualty in the disturbances was the "pacification" program, as Viet Cong infiltrated back into previously "sanitized" hamlets.

In March 1966, two-thirds of 1st Marine Division, commanded by Major-General Lewis J. Fields, was assigned to Quang Tin and Quang Ngai provinces. The 3rd Marine Division, under Major-General Wood B. Kyle, assumed responsibility for the Da Nang-Phu Bai region. By July it was clear that the North Vietnamese 324B Division had crossed the DMZ into northern Quang Tri province. Thus, in the summer of 1966, III MAF's ground war separated into two distinct campaigns: 3rd Marine Division's tactical war in the sparsely-populated northern I Corps area; and 1st Marine Division's "pacification" operations in the more heavily populated areas south from Da Nang. These rich ricelands were vital to the Viet Cong effort: they supplied their food needs; the adjacent coastline facilitated resupply from North Vietnam; and the dense population made it easier for their cadres to "swim like fish" in the sea of local inhabitants.

*Below:* A member of a Marine mine-sweep team carefully probes for hidden VC mines along the strategically vital Route 9 highway to the combat base at Khe Sanh, April 1968. Mines and booby traps accounted for some 11 percent of US combat deaths and 15 percent of wounds in Vietnam. A favorite spot for a mine was around a fallen tree or log lying across a track.

On 15 July, seven US Marine and five ARVN battalions launched Operation Hastings against the 324B NVA Division in Quang Tri province. Bombing support missions were flown by ground-directed Boeing B-52 Stratofortress aircraft of Strategic Air Command. During some of the heaviest large-scale fighting in the war to date, Marines occupied the "Rockpile", a 700ft vantage point from which they could observe west-central Quang Tri province. When the operation ended on 3 August, three Marine battalions remained in the area to seek out and engage NVA regulars in Operation Prairie, which continued until 31 May 1967.

By the autumn of 1966, the Marine presence in Vietnam had increased to 60,000 men. Its zone of responsibility now covered 1,800 square miles containing nearly one million people. It had participated in over 150 operations of battalion or regimental size, killing 7,500 of the enemy; another 4,000 enemy deaths had resulted from 200,000 Marine patrols, ambushes and other small-unit actions. Marine losses in this period were 1,700 killed and 9,000 wounded; over 80 percent of the wounded returned to duty.

Particularly successful had been the Marines' refinement of reconnaissance techniques, formalized under the code-name "Sting Ray", in which seven-man teams were used to observe the enemy and then call in fire missions from artillery, fighter-bombers and helicopter gunships. Two artillery pieces were assigned in direct support of each active Sting Ray team. By the time of the US withdrawal from Vietnam, Marine Reconnaissance teams were operating at will behind enemy lines. An outstanding pioneer of these techniques was Major (later Lieutenant-General) Bernard Trainor, commander of 1st Reconnaissance Squadron of the 1st Marine Division.

Operation Prairie I was brought to an end by the monsoon season at the end of January

1967. In 182 days of hard fighting around Con Thien and Gio Linh, the Marines killed 1,397 of the enemy at a cost of 225 killed and 1,159 wounded. Prairie II began in the same area in February, although on a much-reduced scale. The NVA had withdrawn across the DMZ and were infiltrating South Vietnam through the Ho Chi Minh Trail, a network of paths and trails through the jungle and mountainous terrain of Laos' eastern border, later extended into Cambodia. The Marines' role changed from "search and destroy" to "clear and secure", and the emphasis was placed on supporting the "pacification" efforts of 1st AVRN Division.

Spring 1967 saw the so-called First Battle of Khe Sanh, fought near the US firebase located in the north-west of I Corps Tactical Zone, six miles from the Laotian border and 14 miles south of the DMZ. This encounter battle began when a platoon-sized patrol from 1st Battalion, 9th Marines, made contact with an enemy force occupying the high ground to the north-west of the firebase. The

*Above:* A VC rocket attack lights up the sky over the Da Nang air base on 30 January 1968, at the start of the Tet offensive.

enemy did not return fire, but when the Marine patrol was joined by a second platoon, a furious firefight erupted in which 13 Marines were killed. On the following day it became clear that the enemy was well dug-in, to at least battalion strength, on three peaks, Hills 861, 881 South (881S) and 881 North (881N), apparently as a preliminary to attacking Khe Sanh.

Two Marine battalions were flown in, and the next 18 days saw a fierce battle in which enemy positions were pounded by artillery and air strikes delivered by 1st Marine Aircraft Wing. The Marines fought their way up the slopes and occupied the three peaks, establishing outposts protecting the approaches to Khe Sanh.

Following the First Battle of Khe Sanh, the Marines moved on to the offensive. In the south of I Corps Tactical Zone, 1st Marine Division launched Operations Union I and II, claiming 2,250 dead. There was also heavy fighting around the Marines' forward base at Con Thien, which came under sustained 122-mm and 140-mm rocket fire as the enemy concentrated for an assault.

War correspondents, ever quick to draw an historical parallel, began describing the fighting at Con Thien as the preliminary to a "second Dien Bien Phu". But to Generals Walt (who was succeeded by Lieutenant-General Robert E. Cushman on 1 June) and Westmoreland, the security of Con Thien was underwritten by American firepower. During the fighting at Con Thien, this was co-ordinated by the commander of US 7th Air Force, General William H. Momyer. From his forward headquarters he orchestrated the full range of fire support — tactical aircraft, naval gunfire and ground-directed B-52s, in close co-ordination with artillery and other ground fire — to break up enemy concentrations as they formed. By mid-autumn the "siege" of Con Thien was over.

## The Tet Offensive

In the autumn of 1967, a return to a semblance of constitutional government in South Vietnam was made with the election of General Nguyen Van Thieu as President, with Air Vice Marshal Nguyen Cao Ky as his deputy. US military strength in the South had now risen to 500,000.

In three years of "search and destroy" operations undertaken by US forces, the Viet Cong had taken grievous punishment, frequently in the ratio 10:1. By the beginning of 1968 the Americans were fighting far from the South's main population centres, near the borders of Laos and Cambodia and on the DMZ. General Westmoreland, confident that

*Left:* A Marine Corps M50 "Ontos" — designed as a tank destroyer, mounting six 106-mm recoilless rifles, but widely used for fire support in Vietnam.

*Below:* Marines of A Company, 1st Battalion, 1st Marines, fire from the window of a house during the bitter fighting in Hué.

his victory was in sight, was planning to reduce the number of US troops in South Vietnam.

His optimism was suddenly reduced to ashes. On 22 January, the Marine combat base at Khe Sanh came under a siege which was to last 77 days. At the end of the month the Viet Cong and the NVA launched the "Tet" (Buddhist New Year) Offensive with simultaneous attacks on cities and military installations throughout South Vietnam.

In Saigon, the US embassy came under attack. Savage fighting raged in the beautiful old city of Hué, which was entirely occupied by the enemy with the exception of the ARVN 3rd Division's headquarters inside the citadel and a compound housing US Army advisors.

In some of the most bitter fighting of the war, it took the ARVN division and three battalions of Marines three weeks to clear Hué's Old and New Cities. Most of the Marines at Hué were short-term enlisted men and, although they had been trained to fight in a number of environments, expected to engage the Viet Cong in the countryside, where they could always rely on superior firepower and mobility. In Hué, the fighting was at close quarters, in rubble-strewn, fire-swept streets where blanket shelling was of limited value and heavy overcast skies prevented air strikes. Nevertheless, during the battle Marine artillery fired, 18,091 rounds: high explosive, smoke, white phosphorus, illumination and CS gas. From the Seventh Fleet, three cruisers and five destroyers expended 5,191 rounds; although the weather limited their effectiveness, Marine aircraft flew 113 sorties.

Just as at Iwo Jima and Okinawa, the Marines had to prise a fanatically-

*Above:* An aerial view of Marine Fire Support Base (FSB) Cates. The FSB was a self-contained and self-defending artillery base from which infantry operations could be supported. A typical FSB deployed a battery of six M102 105-mm howitzers; an infantry company for local defense; four 81-mm mortars from an infantry battalion; and communications, medical and administrative personnel.

determined enemy from their positions one by one. The Marines had some support from M48 tanks, which acquitted themselves well in the street fighting, and from the "Ontos", thinly-armored tracked vehicles mounting six recoilless rifles. These directed a great weight of fire against defense positions at close range. The "Ontos" could penetrate areas denied to the tanks, darting in to deliver a salvo before retiring to cover.

By the end of the Tet Offensive, the Viet Cong and the NVA had lost 400,000 men killed. Only at Hué did they hold any objective for an appreciable length of time, and this may explain why the North Vietnamese failed to commit troops held in reserve to exploit successes. The NLF, in particular, had suffered a shattering military defeat and was never the same force again. But they gained a crucial psychological victory. "Pacification" and US control over South Vietnam's cities were shown to be an illusion. The Tet Offensive, although a defeat for the NVA, made the US withdrawal from Vietnam inevitable. General Westmoreland's request for another 200,000 men — half for immediate use and half as a strategic reserve — was refused, and on 10 April President Johnson announced that he would be replaced by his deputy, General Creighton Abrams.

## Khe Sanh

Two days earlier, the siege at Khe Sanh had

come to an end. The Marine combat base at Khe Sanh had been established as one of a series of firebases known as the McNamara line (after the US Secretary of Defense, 1961–68) and stretching from the coast to the Laotian border. Its purpose was to cut troop and supply infiltration into South Vietnam from the North and to block North Vietnamese incursions from Laos along the strategically important Route 9. At the beginning of January 1968, US intelligence sources indicated that a North Vietnamese offensive in the northern provinces was imminent. Two NVA Divisions, 324B and 325C, were identified in the area.

On the base, the Marine commanding officer, Colonel David E. Lownds, had at his disposal 1st, 2nd and 3rd Battalions, 26th Marine Regiment and an artillery unit, 1st Battalion, 13th Marines. As the siege developed, reinforcements were provided by 1st Battalion, 9th Marines, and 37th Rangers, an ARVN unit inserted for purely political reasons. The 6,000 men ultimately deployed at Khe Sanh faced enemy forces estimated at somewhere between 15,000 and 20,000.

The battle opened in earnest on 22 January with a massive rocket, artillery and mortar bombardment by the NVA which blew up 1,340 tons of ammunition in the base's main dump. Throughout February the enemy continued to pound the base and the Marine positions on Hill 881(S),an outpost on the high ground to the north-west of Khe Sanh. Hill 881(S), held by 400 men of 26th Marines, had nearly 50 percent casualties but each morning raised the Stars and Stripes on an improvized flagpole and brought it down at night to the strains of the correct bugle call.

*Previous page, top:* An M60 machine-gun team of 5th Marines in a firefight in 1968. Troops in Vietnam dubbed the M60 "The Pig", as it was trouble-prone and very heavy for a squad-support firearm.
*Previous page, bottom:* Marines train their guns on an enemy bunker, down which they have sent a captured VC to retrieve the bodies of his comrades.
*Right:* Men of 3rd Battalion, 7th Marines, cross a river. They are wearing standard olive-drab combat dress and flak jackets.

Command of the high-ground surrounding the low-lying combat base — Hills 881(S), 861, 558 and 950 (the numbers indicate their height in metres) — was vital to the survival of the garrison at Khe Sanh.

The NVA's siege methods would have won praise from the great 17th-century siege-master, Vauban, as they dug trenches, zig-zag approaches and parallels. Sometimes the NVA would dig 1,000ft of trenches in a night. On the following day A-4 Skyhawks would fly in to saturate them with napalm. NVA infantry attacks were mainly confined to Marine outposts, where the fighting was particularly savage.

The keys to the defense of Khe Sanh were resupply and fire support. The land main supply route — Route 9 — was too open to ambush, with stretches rendered impassable by the north-east monsoon. By the middle of February the landing and take-off of fixed-wing transports from Khe Sanh's airstrip had become too risky an operation. A switch was made to delivering supplies at low-level by the Low Altitude Parachute Extraction System (LAPES) and the Ground Parachute Extraction System (GPES). In the former, the transport made a low-level approach and a parachute dragged the cargo across rollers out of the rear doors. In the latter, the aircraft came in low to snag an arresting line which in turn pulled the cargo out of the rear.

Marine helicopters flying resupply missions were also vulnerable. Marine Helicopter Squadron HMM-262, flying Boeing Vertol CH-46 Sea Knight assault transports, lost half their helicopters in February and had to be replaced by HMM-364. Helicopter deliveries were made three times a day — at 0900, 1300 and 1700 hrs — by "super gaggles" of 12 CH-46s with a standard load of 3,000lb, escorted by two UH-1E gunships, controlled by two UH-1E "slicks" and preceded by up to 12 strike aircraft, usually Marine A-4s from Chu Lai.

At the same time concentrated fire support in Operation Niagara broke the back of the enemy's attacks on Khe Sanh. NVA columns were allowed to advance until their heads approached the US perimeter. Three 105-mm batteries within the base then opened up with fixed concentrations forming three sides of a box around the enemy column with the open end facing the base. A fourth battery fired a walking barrage, moving up and down the box. Simultaneously, two batteries of 175-mm guns from the firebases at the

*Below:* The concept of helicopter-borne air mobility (which originated in Korea) came of age in Vietnam. *Below left:* Pfc John R. Huddeston, "A" gunner on an M-60 tank with 1st Marine Division, sits on the parapet of a fighting hole and watches fellow Marines board a CH-53 Sea King helicopter to return to An Hoa after 90 days in the field.

*Right:* A flame tank sprays napalm.

"Rockpile" and Camp Carroll fired fixed linear concentrations outside the inner box, while fighter-bombers and B-52s, under Combat Skypot radar control, delivered a rolling barrage of ordnance to obliterate the enemy's reserve. NVA troops spilling out of the open end of the box were mopped-up by Marine infantry.

In March, the B-52s began a series of massive close-in strikes, arriving in cells of three over the target area every 90 minutes to hit enemy positions within 1,000yds of Khe Sanh's outer defenses. In all, the B-52s completed 2,548 sorties, dropping 59,542 tons of bombs. Photo-reconnaissance showed that 274 North Vietnamese defensive positions had been completely destroyed and 67 damaged, while 17 weapon positions were annihilated and another eight put out of action. Bomber crews reported 1,382 secondary explosions and 108 secondary fires.

NVA attacks on Khe Sanh began to fall away as the US relief operation, Pegasus, was set in motion, spearheaded by 1st Air Cavalry Division. On 4 April, 1st Battalion, 9th Marines, launched an attack from Khe Sanh to the south-east, capturing the enemy-held Hill 471. Here they linked with 2nd Battalion, 12th Cavalry, on 6 April. The enemy began to withdraw, losing their last strongpoint — Hill 881N — to attack by 3rd Battalion, 26th Marines, on 14 April. Pegasus was declared officially over at 0800 hrs on 15 April.

It has never been clear whether General Giap's intention at Khe Sanh was to force the Marines into a re-run of Dien Bien Phu. If it was, he failed, losing over 10,000 men in the process. Between 19 January and 31 March, the Marines at Khe Sanh lost 199 men killed and 830 wounded. Another 92 Marines died in Operation Pegasus. Two months later, the firebase at Khe Sanh was dismantled and its ammunition and stores moved back to the now secure Route 9. The move seemed to epitomize the American dilemma in Vietnam — the expenditure of colossal resources to no readily-discernible end against an enemy prepared to accept losses which would have been intolerable in a Western army. Pegasus was followed in the Khe Sanh area by Scotland II, which continued until February 1969, by which time the Marines claimed to have killed 3,921 of the enemy.

General Abrams now curtailed "search and destroy" operations, employing mobile helicopter-borne forces to strike at enemy forces where they were located. Two-thirds of US troops in South Vietnam were now tied to the protection of the main population centres. The corrosive effects of the war, watched on television every night by millions of Americans, provoked powerful political reactions at home. The bombing of North Vietnam, in particular, stirred deep controversy, engendered by the image of a superpower belaboring a small country. Ironically, the bombing — which was frequently interrupted in response to North Vietnamese hints that they might negotiate — was seen as a sign of American weakness rather than strength. Moreover, its relatively slow build-up, hampered by close operational control from Washington, enabled the North Vietnamese to put their country on a war footing and establish a formidable defense system, which accounted for 938 US aircraft during Rolling Thunder. As with the strategic air offensives of World War Two, by making the conflict a "total war" for the North Vietnamese people, the bombing strengthened their resolve. In the United States it added fuel to the anti-war movement.

Disillusioned, President Johnson began to cast around for a way out of the war. On 31 March 1968 he announced that he did not intend to seek re-election as President. The bombing of North Vietnam was halted north of the 20th parallel. In May, peace talks began in Paris, chaining the United States to the negotiating table until the North Vietnamese were ready to launch a conventional invasion of the South. On 21 October, bombing of the North ceased completely, bringing an end to Rolling Thunder.

*Below:* A Marine Grumman A-6 Intruder all-weather low-altitude attack aircraft. Marine squadrons at Da Nang and Chu Lai flew the Intruder, whose principal missions were close support, all-weather and night attacks on enemy troop concentrations and night interdiction. A typical load was 30 500lb bombs.

250 CARTRIDGES
CAL .30

Men of the 2nd Marines negotiate a typical piece of Mekong Delta terrain during a sweep for Viet Cong.

Machine gunner Lance Cpl. Kenneth G. Korolyk targets a sniper during Operation NoName No.97, 10 miles south of Da Nang.

A sergeant plots the map coordinates of a Viet Cong unit, while the lance corporal radioes them on to artillery support.

*Right:* A Marine checks in with his command post via field radio in Operation Urgent Fury, Grenada, October 1983. He is armed with an M-16A1, with improvized lanyard, and a small fragmentation grenade hanging from his webbing.

On 5 November Johnson was succeeded as President by Richard Milhous Nixon, who had pledged to seek an end to US involvement in the war. The "Americanization" of the conflict was put in reverse, and its "Vietnamization" began.

As the American commitment to South Vietnam began to wind down, III MAF launched its last major action of the war on 22 January 1969. Operation Dewey Canyon, in the Da Krong valley, Quang Tri province, was ironically perhaps the most successful regimental-sized action of the war, involving 9th Marine Regiment, two battalions of 1st ARVN Division and the entire resources of 1st Marine Aircraft Wing. Over 1,000 enemy were killed in the operation, which ended on 19 March, and great quantities of arms and ammunition captured.

Now the newsreel started running backwards. On 8 June 1969 President Nixon announced the first US troop withdrawal. In July, 9th Marines left Vietnam; the 3rd Marines followed in October and, by the end of October, 3rd Marine Division had also gone. In April 1971 the headquarters of III MAF, 1st Marine Division and 1st Marine Aircraft Wing left Da Nang. All that remained was 3rd Marine Amphibious Brigade. Ground and air operations ceased on 7 May and, by the end of July 1971, 3rd Marine Amphibious Brigade had sailed away. Only a handful of US Marines remained in Vietnam, as artillery observers, advisors and embassy guards. They had grandstand seats when Saigon fell to the NVA on 30 April 1975. Marine losses in Vietnam (1962–72) were 12,936 killed, 88,594 wounded and 26 captured. Aircraft losses (to October 1970) were 252 helicopters and 173 fixed-wing aircraft lost in combat; 172 helicopters and 81 fixed-wing aircraft lost in operations.

## AFTER VIETNAM

The Vietnam war dealt a heavy blow to American prestige and self-confidence from which it took a long time to recover. For the Marine Corps it was doubly galling. They had maintained their proud boast that they had never lost a battle, but the United States had lost the war.

On 10 November 1975, the Marine Corps celebrated its 200th birthday. Amid the junketings, many gave pause for somber reflection about the future. The Corps had come a long way since the days of the "Original Eight", but it was now moving into an era of political and economic uncertainty in which many of its precepts could no longer be taken for granted.

Training of an exceptionally rigorous kind has always been one of the cornerstones of the Marine Corps' effectiveness. But changing attitudes to authority resulted in an accelerating desertion rate which by 1976 was running at 69.2 men per 1,000 enlistees, compared with 31.7 per 1,000 for the US Navy and 11.7 per 1,000 for the US Army. A disproportionately high black intake — 22 percent, compared with 12 percent of the overall population — reflected the economic problems afflicting the United States and the difficulty young blacks were experiencing in finding regular employment. In 1979 the new Commandant of the Corps, General Robert H. Barrow, briefly considered tackling these problems by cutting the authorized strength of the Corps from 195,000 men to 175,000.

Gone were the days when a Marine force posted offshore could restore order to a troublespot threatened by civil unrest or civil war. The United States was now obliged to move more cautiously in a world of political and strategic complexities beyond the scope of gunboat diplomacy.

### The Caribbean

Nevertheless, when it came to securing the

*Above:* Marines gather round a Soviet AN-26 Curl transport aircraft of Cubana airlines seized at Pearls Airport during Operation Urgent Fury.

interests of the United States in a traditional sphere of influence, the Marine Corps could still be called upon to move as decisively as it did in the days before World War One.

In the Dominican Republic, the assassination of the pro-US dictator Rafael Trujillo on 30 May 1961 was followed by a prolonged period of political turmoil. In April 1965, a left-leaning faction in the Army overthrew the conservative Cahral regime. Fearful that the Dominican Republic might follow Cuba into the Soviet camp, President Johnson ordered a six-ship squadron of the US Navy's Caribbean Ready Group, with some 1,700 Marines, to sail from Puerto Rico, ostensibly to protect the lives of US nationals and evacuate them if necessary.

On 27 April, while fierce fighting raged in Santo Domingo between the leftist insurgents and a new military junta, Marines using helicopter and amphibious transports succeeded in evacuating 1,200 US nationals aboard US ships. The next day the Dominican junta requested military aid. The platoons of Marines which were sent ashore quickly came under fire from rebel snipers. In Washington the decision was taken to commit more Marines in order to prevent a Communist coup.

On the 29th, 1,500 Marines were landed, followed by elements of the US 82nd Airborne Division. Heavy fighting followed as they pushed into Santo Domingo. Eventually, the number of US troops in the Dominican Republic reached 32,000, including 14,000 Army personnel, 8,000 Marines, 9,000 Navy personnel and 1,000 airmen. On 6 May a peace force created by the Organisation of American States (OAS) came into being, at the request of the United States. Once the OAS units were in place in the Dominican Republic, the United States began to reduce its military presence. The first to go were the Marine battalions, and by early June over 10,000 troops had been withdrawn. The remainder left in the summer of 1966, following the election of a new President, Dr Joaquin Balaguer.

The Marines went into action again in the Caribbean in October 1983, on the tiny island of Grenada. In-fighting between competing factions in Grenada's Marxist government led to the seizure of power by an extreme left-winger, Bernard Coard, and the summary execution by firing squad of the Prime Minister, Maurice Bishop. Of particular concern to the United States was the 10,000ft runway under construction at Point Salines airfield on the western tip of the island. Funded with Russian money and built by Cuban combat construction workers, it threatened to provide the Soviet Union with a crucial toehold in the region from which it could "service" client states.

The Organisation of Central Caribbean States (OCCS), together with Jamaica and Barbados, called upon President Ronald Reagan to provide military intervention.

Reagan was not slow to comply. The chaotic situation on Grenada was seen as a direct threat to American security. By deploying a military force to eliminate the threat before it fully developed, Reagan hoped simultaneously to restore a pro-American government in a strategic location and also to demonstrate the United States' resolve to maintain the *status quo* in the Caribbean. A viable pretext for intervention was supplied by the presence on Grenada of several hundred US medical students.

The units selected for Operation Urgent Fury were US Army Rangers of the 75th Infantry (Ranger) Regiment; US Army paratroops of 82nd Airborne Division; and Marines of the 22nd Marine Amphibious Unit (MAU), who had been diverted from another troublespot, the Lebanon, to take part in the operation. Additionally, there were small contingents from special operations units: Navy SEALs, US Army Special Forces, USAF Combat Control Teams (CCTs), and the Delta anti-terrorist unit, which was standing by to act if any of the American students were taken hostage. A force of 400 police and military personnel was provided by Grenada's Caribbean neighbours, to act as a garrison after the island had been secured.

The operation began in the small hours of 25 October 1983 when SEAL units came ashore, tasked with the rescue of the island's Governor-General, Sir Paul Scoon, who had been placed under house arrest. At 0536 hrs, the Rangers made an airborne assault on the airfield at Point Salines. Simultaneously, 400 Marines from the assault ship *Guam* made a heli-borne landing at Pearls airport, on the eastern side of the island. Pearls airport was secured with little difficulty, but at Point Salines the Cubans, who were heavily armed, put up a stiff fight. However, the runway was cleared and operable by 1400 hrs, when two battalions of 82nd Airborne were flown in to relieve the Rangers and free them for other operations.

Meanwhile, *Guam* was moving round the island and at 1930 hrs landed 250 Marines, five tanks and 13 LVPT-7 amphibious assault vehicles at Grand Mal Bay, near St George's, the island's capital. Their objective was Fort Frederick and its Richmond Hill prison, on the high ground above St George's, where the SEALs and the Governor-General were now besieged.

At 0700 hrs on the 26th the Marines secured Fort Frederick, which had been abandoned by its defenders. Moving eastward from Point Salines, the Rangers and 82nd Airborne took Frequente and at 1600 hrs secured Grande Anse campus, where the majority of the students had taken refuge. The students were heli-lifted out on the same day. Throughout the rest of the 26th, men of 22nd MAU and 82nd Airborne swept the island for Cubans and troops of the Grenadan People's Revolutionary Army. A curfew was imposed during darkness.

By the third day of the invasion, all resistance had evaporated and the Cuban barracks at Edgmont were taken without a fight. Large quantities of light and heavy weapons were discovered, including AK-47 assault rifles, 120-mm mortars, machine-guns, anti-aircraft weapons and rocket launchers. Total US casualties in the operation were 18 dead and 113 injured. More than 1,100 Cubans and Grenadans had been taken prisoner, and Cuban casualties had been considerable. A week later all the US Rangers and Marines had left Grenada, and within six weeks there were only about 300 US military personnel left on the island.

*Left:* Marine Sea Stallion helicopters on the flight deck of the carrier *Nimitz* at the start of the ill-fated mission to rescue the US hostages in Teheran. The failure of the mission stirred memories of the "*Mayaguez* incident" of May 1975. On 12 May of that year a Cambodian gunboat had seized the American merchantman *Mayaguez*. An operation to recover the ship and rescue its crew (who had been imprisoned on the mainland at Koh Tang) resulted in the loss of four Marine helicopters and 18 men (11 of them Marines). Nevertheless, the crew and the ship were retrieved.

**The Middle East**

The politics of the Caribbean seem relatively uncomplicated when compared with the murderous complexities of the Middle East. On 16 January 1979, the Shah of Iran left the country in the face of relentless mass demonstrations. On 1 February, the Ayatollah Khomeini returned from exile to gather to himself the reins of power of the Islamic revolution.

On 4 November 1979, 400 militant Islamic students occupied the United States embassy in Teheran. Its Marine guards were among the 66 US citizens taken prisoner during the occupation. Three other US citizens were also held hostage in the Iranian Foreign Ministry.

Marine pilots were involved in an ill-fated American rescue bid of 14/15 April 1980 by Colonel Charles Beckwith's 1st Special Forces Operational Detachment (Delta).

The plan was for the Marines to fly eight Sikorsky RH-53 Sea Stallion helicopters from the carrier *Nimitz* to a secret rendezvous in the desert 200 miles south-east of Teheran with three troop-carrying Lockheed MC-130 Hercules transports accompanied by three fuel-carrying EC-130s. Delta's assault force of 118 men and their equipment were to be loaded on to the helicopters and, after refueling, flown on to a hide-site near Teheran, from which they would launch a complicated operation to free the hostages. Covered by the massive firepower of C-130 gunships, the Sea Stallions were to fly in to pick up the assault teams and hostages from the embassy compound or, if requested, from a nearby soccer stadium. The Sea Stallions would then ferry the hostages and assault teams to Manzariyeh airfield, 35 miles to the south, where a contingent of US Rangers would be defending a flight of Lockheed C-114 Starlifter transports waiting to airlift everyone out of Iran.

The plan broke down in chaos at the initial "Desert One" rendezvous south of Teheran. Only six helicopters arrived, an hour late and long after first light, having been delayed by severe dust storms which had forced one pilot back to the *Nimitz* with navigational and flight instrument failure; a second had come

*Opposite:* The USS *Fort Snelling*, a Thomaston class Landing Ship, Dock (LSD). *Fort Snelling* is capable of accommodating 21 LCM(6) landing craft or three LCUs (Landing Craft, Utility) and six LCMs, or 50 LVTP amphibious tractors, with another 30 LVTPs housed in the mezzanine and upper decks; troop capacity is 340.

down with rotorblade trouble only 80 miles inside Iranian airspace.

After refueling and loading, a third helicopter suffered hydraulic failure and the mission was abandoned. The withdrawal plan was for everyone to offload and rejoin the transports. The five Sea Stallions would then fly back to *Nimitz*. As one of the Sea Stallions was changing position it collided with a troop-laden Hercules and burst into flames. In the ensuing conflagration, Redeye missiles exploded in all directions. Miraculously, all the troops inside the Hercules managed to disembark as the C-130 caught fire. Eight men crewing the C-130 and the Sea Stallion were killed. Boarding the remaining aircraft, Delta Force swiftly abandoned "Desert One", leaving five helicopters behind on the ground and the eight charred bodies of the men who had died in the mission.

The hostages were finally released in January 1981 after prolonged negotiations. The "military solution" had not only proved a humiliating failure for the United States — it had in the final analysis proved unnecessary. In the process, it dealt a terminal blow to the Presidency of Jimmy Carter.

The situation in the Persian Gulf was also part of an array of long-term strategic problems facing the United States. The violent anti-Americanism of the Khomeini regime, the prolonged hostage crisis, and the Soviet intervention in Afghanistan in November 1979, seemed to pose a direct

*Below:* The AV-8 Harrier, which equips four Marine squadrons.

*Below:* Marine training has a well-earned reputation for toughness. The cream of the Corps volunteer for the Force Reconnaissance Units, whose task is to gather intelligence prior to a landing. "Recon" units are divided into Force Recon Company groups, which operate covertly in specialist four-man teams somewhat in the style of the British SAS, and Battalion Recon Company Groups. Battalion Recon is larger, each Division having a battalion of around 500 men. Divided into platoons and companies, its members are attached to specific battalions. Utilizing SCUBA diving techniques, helicopters and light vechicles, they obtain general intelligence regarding beaches to be used for landing by the parent battalion.

threat to Western oil supplied from the Gulf and the stability and security of the pro-Western states in the region. In his State of the Union message of 21 January 1981, President Carter made a clear commitment to the security of the Gulf, and indicated an American, readiness to defend its interests there, if necessary by military force. Within a month a Marine Amphibious Task Force, including four vessels led by the amphibious assault ship *Okinawa* and carrying some 1,800 men, left the Pacific for the Indian Ocean for maneuvers with Carrier Task 70 on station in the Arabian Sea. Since then, similar Marine Task Forces have been rotated to the Arabian Sea to maintain a permanent presence there.

The deployment of the Marine Amphibious Task Force in the Arabian Sea was a significant step in the progress towards the creation of the Rapid Deployment Joint Task Force (RDJTF). The idea of a quick-reaction force, capable of worldwide deployment, had first been canvassed in the early 1960s by the US Secretary of Defense, Robert McNamara. Drawing from the lessons of the Cuban missile crisis of 1962, McNamara concluded that the advantage in sub-nuclear superpower confrontations would go to the side which could deploy a decisive local military superiority. Such a capability would also help prevent an escalation of such confrontations to the nuclear level.

The situation in the Middle East in the late 1970s gave the concept a new urgency. The Rapid Deployment Joint Task Force was established on 1 March 1980, with its HQ at McDill Air Base, Tampa, Florida; in October 1981 it became a separate task force with joint command and control of the forces designated to it; and on 1 January 1983 the RDJTF became a separate unified command, US Central Command (CENTCOM). The importance of the amphibious element of the RDJTF was indicated by the appointment as its first commander of Marine Lieutenant-General Paul X. Kelley. The Marine element of the RDJTF includes three Maritime Prepositioning Ship (MPS) task forces, each of which can carry sufficient supplies for a highly mechanized Marine Amphibious Brigade.

*Left:* One of the Marine Corps' 720 M-60A1 tanks, with wading exhaust.

*Below:* Marines armed with M-16s take cover behind sandbags in Beirut. The Corps had first fulfilled a peace-keeping role in the troubled Lebanon in July-September 1958, on that occasion suffering only two deaths, both accidental shootings by other Marines. Their second tour of duty, in 1984, was to prove more traumatic.

## The Lebanon

Nowhere are the intractable problems of the Middle East more dramatically demonstrated than in thc Lcbanon, which since the summer of 1975 has been torn apart by a civil war between rival Christian and Islamic factions. The arrival of the Palestinian Liberation Organisation (PLO) in southern Lebanon injected a factor guaranteed to increase Lebanon's chronic instability. In mid-1976 the President of Lebanon appealed to Syria for help. Syrian intervention secured a temporary cessation of the fighting, but the warring factions failed to reach any agreement among themselves. While the Syrians remained the only guarantors of a semblance of internal security, they quickly became an army of occupation. A United Nations force — UNIFIL, based in southern Lebanon — was little more than a helpless bystander in the conflict.

Reacting to the Syrian presence, and determined to put an end once and for all to the PLO, the Israelis invaded Lebanon in June 1982, driving northward to Beirut. In August 1982, an agreement was negotiated by the US envoy Philip Habib, calling for an Israeli withdrawal from the Lebanese capital. In response to a request from the Lebanese government, an international peacekeeping

The carnage of the US Embassy in Beirut resulting from the action of a single suicide lorry bomber.

force, comprising French and Italian troops and 800 US Marines, arrived in Beirut at the end of August. By the beginning of September, all the Syrian and PLO fighting units had been evacuated from Beirut. On 13 September, the newly-elected President of the Lebanon, the Maronite Christian Bashir Gemayel, was assassinated with Syrian connivance.

On the following day the Israelis marched back into Beirut. They saw themselves as the only force for stability in an increasingly chaotic situation, but they immediately made a major miscalculation. On 16 September their troops stood idly by while Maronite Christian militiamen massacred Palestinian refugees in Beirut's Sabra and Shatila camps.

The US Marines had returned to their ships offshore on 10 September. Now President Reagan ordered them back into

Lebanon, and on 29 September they were detailed to guard Beirut International Airport. On 23 October a Muslim suicide bomber drove a truck packed with explosives into the Marine compound, where it blew up with tremendous force, killing 240 Marines. The Americans, naively perhaps, had seen their role as that of peacekeepers. But to the suicide bomber — a member of the extreme Iranian-backed Shi'ite Hizbollah faction — they were just another militia and representatives of "The Great Satan" — the United States. A fatal incomprehension of the tortuous coils of Lebanese politics, and insuffcent vigilance, had led to one of the blackest days in the Marine Corps' history. The Marines left Beirut in the spring of 1984, having lost 260 men during their tour of duty.

*Left:* Marine sniper scouts survey an infinitely hostile terrain in Beirut.

*Bottom:* A Marine LVTP-7 tracked landing vehicle in the streets of Beirut. This amphibious assault vehicle can carry up to 25 fully-equipped Marines, propelling itself through the water with twin water-jets. The LVTP-7 is equipped with passive night vision equipment, smoke-generating capacity and automatic fire detection and suppression system. Armament is provided by a 12.7-mm M85 machine-gun. It has a 40mph road speed and 8.39mph water speed, with a road range of 300 miles.

The shattered ruins of the compound in which 240 Marines died on 23 October 1983.

*Opposite, top:* The USS *Inchon*, an Iwo Jima class LPH (Landing Platform, Helicopter). The seven LPH ships of the class, commissioned in 1961-79, were the world's first assault ships designed and constructed specifically to operate helicopters. The LPH can accommodate 11 CH-53 Sea Stallions or 20 Boeing-Vertol CH-46 Sea Knights. Each can carry a Marine battalion landing team, its artillery, vehicles and equipment plus a reinforced squadron of assault helicopters. Anti-aircraft defence is provided by Sea Sparrow SAMs and Phalanx CIWS. In the late 1980s each full-strength Marine battalion consists of a headquarters company, three rifle companies divided into 13-man squads, and a weapons company. The standard squad weapon is the improved M16A2 rifle supported by a 5.56-mm Squad Automatic Weapon (SAW) issued one per fire team. The weapons companies are acquiring a new heavy machine-gun platoon with eight firing teams each allotted a vehicle armed with a 0.5-in and a Mk19 40-mm heavy machine-gun.

## MARINE TRAINING

At the Marine Corps Recruit Depots a gruelling training program and iron discipline transform new civilian trainees into closely-welded platoons of combat-ready fighting men. The recruits pass through three clearly-defined phases of training, the first of which can best be described as "shock treatment" — an intensive introduction to the fundamentals of military life. From their arrival in "boot camp", the recruits are put through a highly ritualized psychological assault course by their drill instructors (DIs), aimed at stripping away all vestiges of civilian attitudes and reducing the recruits to the same level. Complete denial of personal privacy, ruthless attention to the minutest details of dress and kit maintenance — all accompanied by the eyeball-to-eyeball verbal pyrotechnics of the DIs — combine to produce an automatic response to orders. "Problem" recruits are assigned to a special "motivation platoon", whose program includes the screening of inspirationl feature films like *The Sands of Iwo Jima*, starring John Wayne. Long hours of drilling on the parade ground (the "grinder") and punishing daily exercises rapidly increase discipline. The second phase concentrates on marksmanship and the maintenance of personal small arms. After three weeks on the range the recruits qualify as riflemen. Out of a possible 250 points (five points for each of the 50 rounds fired) a man needs 190 to qualify as a "marksman", 210 for "sharpshooter", and 220 for "expert". By now, competition between platoons encourages unit loyalty and pride. Non-qualifiers in the marksmanship course are often made to wear their shooting jackets backwards and march away from the range at the rear of their platoons, carrying their rifles upside down. After a week of mess and maintenance duty, the third phase begins. The DIs now foster maximum competition between the platoons for the prize of honor platoon on graduation day. This phase of training includes a day on the Confidence Course — an assault course designed to test the recruits' strength, agility and physical courage — and the issuing of metal identification tags ("dog tags"), which reinforces the recruits' growing sense of experience. The final days of recruit training are spent preparing for a series of written tests, which are followed by a last physical fitness test and the series drill competition, judged by senior NCOs. The last hurdle for every platoon is the "Final Field Inspection", by a team of officers and senior NCOs from the recruit training battalion. The subsequent graduation parade is conducted with great ceremony and watched by the recruits' families and friends. This is a marked change from the days in the 1950s when, on graduation, recruits simply packed their gear in a seabag and joined an operating unit.

*Below:* A Marine Corps Honor Guard. The Guard is wearing the Marines Dress Blue "B" uniforms. The "blood stripes" on the trouser seams of the corporal nearest the camera distinguish NCOs, WOs and officers from other ranks.

*Below:* A vision of the future — a Marine in an NBC (Nuclear-Biological-Chemical) warfare kit.

### Looking to the Future

Throughout its history, the Marine Corps has resisted determined attacks on its independence. Today the Corps' powerful lobby in Congress ensures that it will retain its unique identity into the foreseeable future.

The active strength of the Corps is currently around 199,000, including 9,700 women, divided into three Marine Divisions, two Marine Security Force battalions and three active Air Wings. The Air Wings consist of over 40 squadrons of fixed and 30 squadrons of rotary wing aircraft. The 472 combat aircraft, together with the 84 armored and approximately 450 support helicopters, provide the Marines with a unique versatility. They are capable of undertaking a number of battlefield roles, including close support, transportation and combat air patrols. Mobility is provided by helicopter units capable of lifting men and equipment into and out of action. The Marine Air Wings also deploy early warning and reconnaissance aircraft. The concept of the all-arms force is embedded in the structure of the Marine division. In addition to its three rifle regiments, each division has an artillery regiment, a tank battalion, an amphibious battalion, a light armored assault battalion, reconnaissance battalion, air defence battalion, engineering battalion and other support and ancillary units. Although Marine Corps divisions are some 20 percent larger than their Army equivalents, financial constraints make their battalions smaller.

Despite the recent Soviet build-up of its amphibious forces and the technical innovations in equipping them, they remain small in comparison with the US Marines and the large number of specialized ships which support them, sufficient to lift one and one-third Marine Amphibious Forces (MAFs). A

MAF comprises three reinforced battalions, plus an air wing — a total of 45,000 Marines and 6,000 Navy personnel. Although the MAF is used as a standard measurement criterion for amphibious lift, a more realistic indicator is provided by the number of reinforced battalions which can be maintained in forward areas, primarily the Mediterranean, Western Pacific and Indian Oceans, supported by Maritime Prepositioning Ships. The US Navy is capable of keeping two reinforced battalions continuously afloat in the Western Pacific and one in the Mediterranean. In addition, a reinforced battalion is intermittently deployed in the Atlantic.

Among the 60 active and reserve ships are Amphibious Assault Ships (LHAs), Landing Platform Helicopter (LPHs), Command and Control Ships (LCCs), Amphibious Transport Docks (LPDs), Landing Ships, Dock (LSDs), Landing Ships, Tank (LSTs) and Amphibious Cargo Ships (LKAs).

The five ships of the "Tarawa" LHA class are the largest purpose-built assault ships in service, capable of accommodating a reinforced battalion, 19 Sea Stallion helicopters and a large number of fighting vehicles and palletized stores. Beneath the full-length flight decks are two half-length hangar decks connected by lifts. Under the aft elevator is a floodable dock capable of accommodating four LCU1610 landing craft. In addition there are extensive hospital facilities and storage for 10,000 gallons of vehicle fuel and 400,000 gallons of helicopter fuel.

In spite of this formidable display of military technology, the US Marine Corps remains faithful to the traditions which began in the fighting tops of tiny frigates during the American War of Independence. The future will see them on station, and on alert, throughout the world.

The US Navy operated dock landing strip, *USS Vancouver,* LPD-2.

HISTORY OF THE UNITED STATES
NAVY

206
43

212

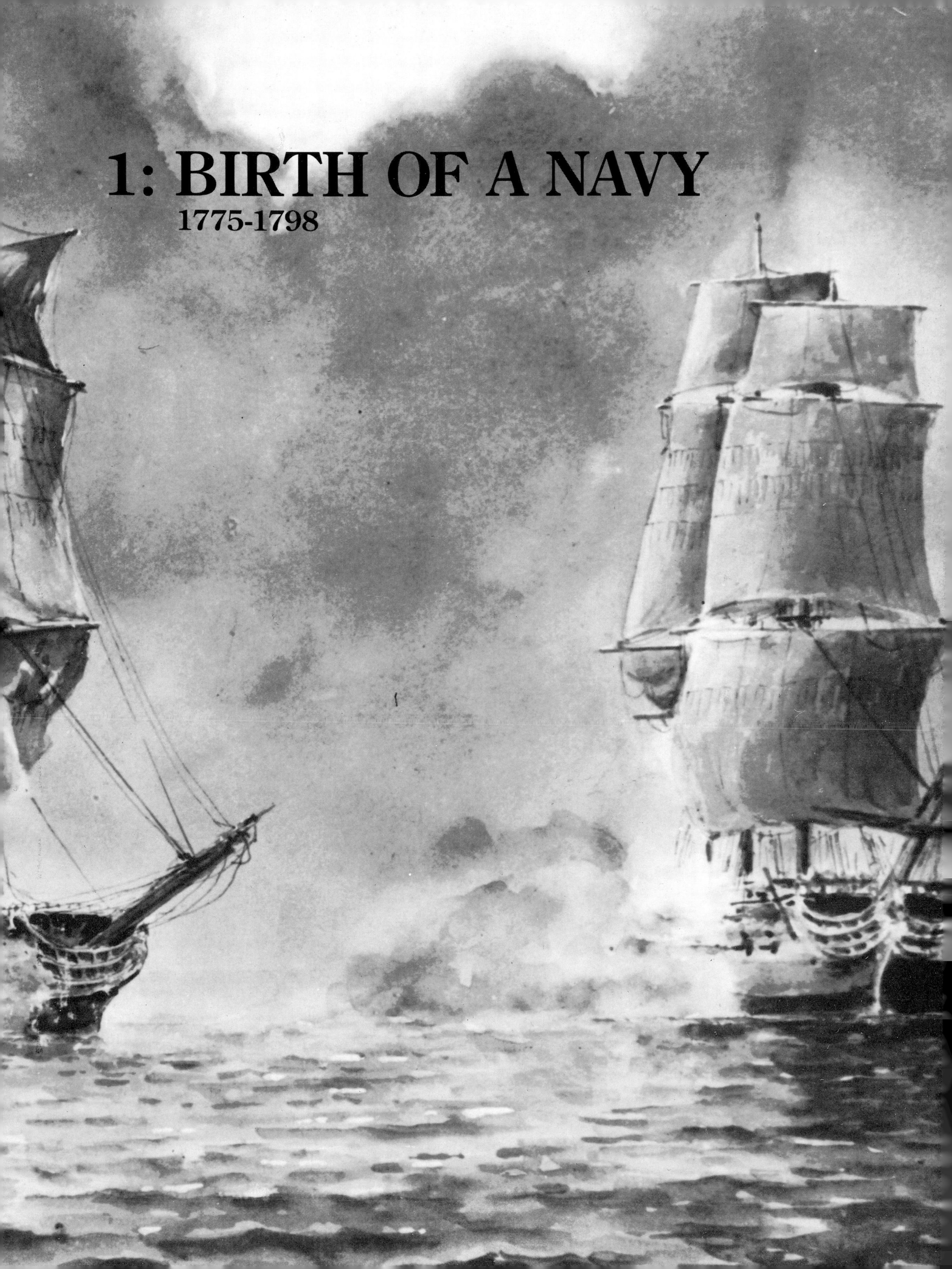

# 1: BIRTH OF A NAVY

## 1775-1798

When a new or reconstituted nation decides that its security and prosperity depends on maintaining an ocean-going navy, the results are liable to be as far-reaching as the oceans themselves. Over the past 120 years, culminating in the two World Wars of the 20th Century, this has certainly been the case with the new navies of Italy, Germany, and Japan. Remembering their influence on the Second World War alone, the creation of an ocean-going Soviet Navy since 1945 has been a most ominous accompaniment to the rapid decline, after centuries of paramountcy, of British sea power, the world's strongest until postwar relinquishment of Empire.

The mantle of global naval supremacy passed from the British to the United States Navy 40 years ago, in the latter years of the Second World War; and fortunately for the Free World the United States Navy remains the world's strongest in the 1980s. But the origins of American sea power present a startling contrast to the 'instant navies' so eagerly created by Italy, Germany, and Japan in their demand for recognition as world powers. Far from being an aggressive or nationalist demand for a 'place in the sun,' the creation of the United States Navy in the last decade of the 18th Century was a grudging, reluctant acceptance of unwelcome necessity. And this is all the more surprising because the United States only emerged as a new nation after successfully defying the most renowned naval supremacy since the Roman Republic defeated Carthage.

When resistance to the force of British arms began in the American 'Thirteen Colonies' in the spring of 1775, only a minority of American activists really believed that total independence from British rule was their true goal. There was little to indicate that 200 years later the colonists' descendants would be citizens of the world's most powerful nation, possessed of the strongest armed forces on the planet. Indeed, in 1775 this was virtually the status of Britain, whose control the American colonists felt driven to challenge. Only 12 years earlier, Britain had emerged as the victor in the first true world war: the Seven Years War (1756–63), which had seen France and her allies confounded in land and sea battles from Canada to Bengal. As British subjects, the American colonists had played their part in that victory, on land against the French and their surrogate Indian 'troops' in Canada, and at sea as privateers preying on French trade. The Colonies had also supplied some 18,000 seamen to the Royal Navy. In its origins, the War of American Independence should be seen as a violent series of strikes by the colonists against what they saw as arbitrary and unfair taxation to pay for a war which they had helped to win, and against the garrisonning of regular troops on American soil (also to be paid for by the colonists) to enforce British authority.

In 1763 the 'Thirteen Colonies' consisted, from south to north, of Georgia, South Carolina, North Carolina, Virginia, Maryland, Delaware, Pennsylvania, New Jersey, New York, Connecticut, Rhode Island, Massachusetts, and New Hampshire, the latter extending up to French Canada and including what later became the State of Maine (in 1820). Together they amounted to a settled land area of around 250,000 square miles (almost three times the size of England and Scotland) inhabited by about 1.25 million colonists of European descent or birth, with about 250,000 negro slaves – already an impressive population compared with the 7 million of Britain. The era of purely English emigration to 'The Americas' was long gone, and by the early 1770s America's population was swelled by many Irish, Scottish, German, Dutch and Scandinavian families. Since 1717, there had also been repeated shiploads of English convicts dumped or 'transported' to the New World colonies – in theory for hard labor until their deaths but more often than not, as in Australia in the following century, to begin new lives on and behind the steadily expanding colonial frontiers.

Convict transportation, incidentally, was another anti-British grievance harbored by Americans. 'What would you say if we were to transport our rattlesnakes to England?' was the famous protest of Benjamin Franklin. But it helped swell a population containing many elements – the Irish and Scots to the fore, not to mention the jailbirds – naturally ill-disposed to put up with high-handed decrees from the King of England's haughty ministers. The growing cities of the Atlantic 'Tidewater' already boasted their own aristocracies and snobberies; the colonies contained thousands of 'Loyalists' who later moved to British Canada rather than endorse American independence. In the main, however, the colonies of America contained a potent human brew which spurted to defiance under the pressure of British governmental obstinacy, misplaced contempt and woeful miscalculation. If pushed, they were ready to fight – and that included an increasingly numerous and confident seafaring population, merchant traders, whalers and deepsea fishermen, operating out of ports along a thousand miles of coast between New England and the Carolinas.

After the defeats which the Royal Navy had inflicted on the navies of France and Spain in the Seven Years War, the prospects for American colonists seriously challenging British sea power were almost ludicrously bad – when measured in terms of heavy warships, custom-built for decisive fleet actions. Of these the colonists had none, nor any experience in building them or casting heavy guns. But commerce warfare, hitting at British merchant shipping, was a very different story. Even the lightest vessel able to cruise the Atlantic, though armed with the most modest array of guns, could achieve success out of all proportion to the number of merchantmen it might capture or sink. Such attacks would force the British Admiralty to sail merchant ships in convoy, dislocating the normal pattern and profits of Britain's merchant trade and sending costs soaring; warships detached to escort convoys would be unable to blockade American ports or attack American shipping.

Commerce warfare of this nature was ideal for the Americans, being cheap and easy to wage. It could be entrusted to privateers. armed vessels manned if necessary by their normal civilian crews motivated by a personal stake in the plunder, licensed by 'letters of marque' authorising them to take prizes from a designated enemy. A commerce war waged by privateers, with the patriotism of their skippers and crews sharpened by the profit motive, could enable the Americans to wage a highly effective naval campaign as far as British home waters. If there seemed little chance of American victory in an all-out land and sea war with Britain, there was still every chance of pressurizing the powerful British merchants interest into joining the sympathetic voices advizing a settlement with the indignant colonies. Every colony from which ocean-going ships put to sea could contribute to such a campaign, which could well be a long one. Though British naval countermoves could be expected to inflict heavy losses, American shipyards had the capacity to replace every privateer captured or sunk. By 1775, Massachusetts alone was turning out 150 ships a year, and American shipbuilding was becoming more economic than in England (£2,600 for a 200-ton ship built in Philadephia; £3,000 for an equivalent vessel built on the Thames).

As the cheapest and easiest method of waging maritime war against such a powerful naval opponent as Britain, privateering could be conducted on a single-ship basis by individual colonies. For anything more ambitious – even the smallest armed squadron capable, say, of tackling an escorted convoy or raiding British island possessions in the Carribbean – inter-colonial collaboration was essential, if only because of the limited supply of guns in the colonies. Because of this, privateering remained the most important American strategy against Britain in the War of Independence and the succeeding War of 1812, 30 years later.

The events leading to the first shots in the War of Independence were complex, but may be briefly summarised here. In their first attempt at concerted action against British taxation, nine of the 13 colonies sent delegates to the 'Stamp Act Congress' which met at New York in October 1765. Unprecedented as it was, this disconcerting display of colonial solidarity achieved the repeal of the hated Stamp Act in March 1766, but only led succeeding British governments to seek other ways of showing the colonies who was master. The fateful catalyst was the British attempt to rescue the failing East India Company by 'dumping' its surplus of teas, taxed at the full rate and sold only by carefully selected agents, on the American colonies. This was in the autumn of 1773, and when the first shipment of tea reached the ports of Charleston, Philadelphia, New York and Boston it was to encounter a mixed campaign of passive and active resistance. The humiliation of being used, financially exploited to bail out a British company, had resulted in outrage in the colonies, carefully orchestrated by 'corresponding committees.' The tea unloaded at Charleston was stored in cellars, with not an ounce sold. At New York and Philadelphia the ships were refused permission to unload and returned to Britain with their cargoes. At Boston the world knows what happened: the ships were boarded by demonstrators of the 'Sons of Liberty,' disguised as Indians, and the tea dumped into the harbour. The 'Boston Tea Party' of 16 December 1773 established Massachusetts, and the port of Boston in Particular, as the center of colonial obduracy, to be chastized by economic pressure and if need be by military force.

The ensuing British 'Coercive Acts' of early 1774 were aimed at forcing Boston to make full restitution for the 'Tea Party,' but also intended effectively to place Massachusetts under much tighter political control. The Acts led to the summoning of the 'First Continental Congress' at Philadelphia in September 1775. Attended by 56 delegates from 12 of the colonies (all but Georgia), this second colonial congress rejected the Coercive Acts as unconstitutional and promised support for Massachusetts in ignoring them. Massachusetts was advized that it should form its own elected government, collect its own taxes and run its own revenue – and arm itself with a citizen militia to resist further attempts at coercion. The Congress finally drew up a 'Declaration of Rights and Grievances' for the edification of King George III, and approved an American boycott of all British goods to help this petition to bite. May 1775 was set as the date for Congress to reassemble, if American grievances had not been redressed in the meantime.

All this dictated the way in which the war broke out in the spring of 1775. Massachusetts stood out as the number-one troublemaker, and the enthusiastic recruiting of the Massachusetts militia was an obvious direct challenge to the 4,000 British troops in Boston. General Gage, Military Governor of Massachusetts, did what he could to lessen the threat by seizing all arsenals and ammunition depots likely to fall into colonial hands. One of these attempts sent 800 British troops from Boston to Concord in April 1775. On 19 April 'the shots heard round the world' were fired against 70 militiamen at Lexington, with the British marching on Concord after a heartening skirmish which had cost them one man hit in the leg, eight militiamen dead and ten wounded. The day ended with the British fighing a miserable and costly retreat back to Boston, sniped at all the way by militiamen, and an aggregate British loss of 73 killed, 174 wounded and 26 missing. American losses were only 49 killed, 41 wounded and five missing. By the end of the month, Gage's men in Boston were hemmed in by 15,000 militiamen from all over New England.

There never was a hope of confining the flare-up of colonial resistance to the Boston region. On 10 May, 170 miles away to the north-west, Colonel Benedict Arnold of the Massachusetts militia and Ethan Allen's 'Green Mountain Boys' rowed across Lake Champlain and caught the British garrison of Fort Ticonderoga completely by surprise. Two days later, 10 miles further north, Fort Crown Point was taken as well. Rough and ready though it was, this was an inspired stroke, severing the British in Boston from any hope of prompt overland relief from Canada. Gage could only hold on at Boston and await reinforcement by sea, with his troops controlling no more than the ground they stood on – and hope that the colonial delegates who convened the 'Second Continental Congress' at Philadelphia on 10 May would fall out.

But the second Philadelphia Congress did no such thing. It was confronted with a war in which the Americans seemed to have a far better chance of victory than had ever been envisaged. The New England militiamen had Gage cooped up in Boston, and the news from the Canadian frontier could not have been more promising. There was plenty of support for reorganizing the militiamen around Boston as an inter-colonial 'Continental Army'. The biggest stumbling-block, however, was the unwillingness of the other colonial delegates to agree to the appointment of a Massachusetts officer as supreme commander. This would effectively have left Massachusetts, widely mistrusted for its cantankerous extremism, running the whole show – but the problem was brilliantly surmounted by the eventual appointment of the respected Virginian, George Washington. All this took time to be hammered out; the Continental Army was not proclaimed until 14 June, with Washington receiving his appointment on the following day. Before he could even take up his duties, the deliberations of Congress were again overtaken by dramatic events at Boston.

Inevitably out of touch with the course of events in America, the British Government sent Gage reinforcements – and orders to disperse the rebels and capture their leaders. By mid-June 1775, with about 6,000 British troops ready for action, Gage prepared to clear the decks by pushing the Americans off the heights round Boston, thus ensuring the security of the only British military foothold in the colonies. But the result was the near-disaster of 17 June 1775: the Battle of Bunker Hill, which the British took at bayonet point only after the American defenders had run out of ammunition. British casualties at Bunker Hill were appalling: 1,054 out of 2,200 with at least 226 killed. It was more than enough to force Gage back on to the defensive, pleading for massive reinforcements which never came. Meanwhile, through the summer of 1775, Washington and his generals began to lick the Continental Army into a semblance of regular order, their sights set on an eventual move to expel the British from Boston.

As the Continental Army embarked on the siege of Boston, Congress – its hand strengthened even further by the object-lesson of Bunker Hill – was still prepared to try for a negotiated settlement with Britain. The 'Olive Branch Petition,' signed by Congress on 8 July 1775, offered no American concessions to King George. It was a protestation of unchanged colonial loyalty, coupled with a request for redress of grievances to bring about an end to hostilities. Determined never to negotiate with rebels, the King refused the Petition point-blank on 1 September: a stubborn, if hardly realistic, statement that Britain was not prepared to consider the faintest likelihood of ultimate defeat. The failure of the 'Olive Branch Petition' left Congress with no option but to prepare for all-out war with Britain by land and sea. With its Continental Army already in the field before Boston, Congress authorized the formation of a Continental Navy on 13 October 1775.

Creating the Continental Navy was an infinitely harder task than shaping the Army, the raw formations of which were already in the field in June 1775. The biggest problem was the artillery shortage, which bedevilled American operations for the first three years of the war. With no gun foundries in the colonies, every popgun six-pounder embarked in a Navy commerce raider was one field gun less for the Army. Then again, it took time to conduct the necessary stock-taking of colonial vessels suitable for commerce raiding – and time was on the side of the British, enabling them to recommission a score of laid-up warships for every American raider sent out to prey on British commerce.

American colors fly over the British as the Continental schooner *Lee*, commanded by Captain John Manley, escorts the captured British brig *Nancy* into captivity on 28 November 1775. *Nancy*, with her cargo of gunpowder, was a prize of immense value at this early stage of the War of Independence.

Commodore Esek Hopkins, first commander-in-chief of the American Continental fleet. His lackluster performance contrasted ill with the more dashing successes of the American single-ship raiders and he was relieved of his command after failing to capture the British frigate HMS *Glasgow* off Block Island on 6 April 1776.

Inevitably the Continental Navy, so-called, at first consisted of a number of 'navies' raised by the different colonies. Apart from the shortage of guns, the Continental Navy suffered from an incurable dilemma. Its best privateer captains were, from the nature of such warfare, individualists, most effective when left virtually to their own devices. Congress, however, was obsessed from the start by the need to show its likeliest European allies that emergent America was far more than a mere nest of licensed pirates, hence the early attempt, late in 1775, to form a Continental 'fleet,' scraped together to make at least a show of conventional naval capacity, whose operations were always far less effective than those of individual raiders.

The fleet's commander, the first American to hold flag rank with the status of commodore, was Esek Hopkins of Rhode Island. Born in 1718 at Scituate, R.I., Hopkins had been a privateer commander in the Seven Years War and in 1775 owned a fleet of merchantmen. He was therefore qualified to command the Continental fleet on the dual grounds of previous war experience and financial self-sufficiency, and being the younger brother of the head of the Naval Committee of Congress was no hindrance. For a flagship Hopkins was given the new merchant ship *Black Prince* of Philadelphia, hastily armed with 20 nine-pounders and 10 six-pounders and renamed *Alfred*. Her complement consisted of about 160 officers and seamen and 60 militiamen embarked as marines. 'Keeping it in the family', Hopkins' eldest son John Burroughs Hopkins commanded the brig *Cabot,* with her single deck of 14 six-pounders and 12 light swivel guns, 90 officers and seamen and 30 marines.

Apart from *Alfred,* the only other ship in the fleet with two decks of guns was *Columbus* (18 nine-pounders and 10 six-pounders). Her commander, Captain Abraham Whipple, was another Rhode Islander, born in 1733 at Providence, R.I. Getting a command in this threadbare squadron was bad luck for Whipple because he was a commerce-raiding lone wolf *par excellence*. Commanding the privateer *Gamecock* in the Seven Years War, he had captured 23 French merchantmen in six months. When hostilities against the British broke out in 1775, the Rhode Island assembly gave Whipple two ships fitted out to protect the colony's seaborne commerce. He had wasted no time in capturing the armed tender of the British frigate HMS *Rose,* the first enemy prize taken by an American warship. Though Whipple was adept at the type of naval warfare on which the Continental Navy would have to rely – hit-and-run, with maximum nuisance value – few such opportunities to shine came his way under Hopkins' command.

Captain Nicholas Biddle commanded the brig *Andrea Doria* of 16 six-pounders and 12 swivel guns, 100 officers and seamen and 30 marines. A most promising young officer, Biddle was a Pennsylvanian, born in 1750 in Philadelphia, and had gone to sea at the age of 13. Biddle was an excellent example of the fine human material suddenly denied to the Royal Navy by the breach with the American colonies, having served as a midshipman in the King's Navy in 1770. In 1773 he had requested an appointment to the Royal Society's forthcoming expedition to the North Pole, but on being refused he resigned his rank and enlisted before the mast in the bomb-ketch *Carcass*. (One of his shipmates on this abortive expedition, which returned after being halted by ice in August 1773, was the young Horatio Nelson, serving as coxswain of the captain's gig in the same spirit of adventure). When the Polar expedition returned to England in October 1773, the 'tea crisis' with the American colonies was already well advanced and Biddle returned to America. *Andrea Doria* was his first command in the service of the Pennsylvanian 'navy.'

The fifth and most junior command in the Continental fleet was Captain Hazard's light sloop *Providence,* with 12 six-pounders, ten swivel guns, 62 seamen and 28 marines. Together, the five ships of the fleet mounted 38 nine-pounders and 62 six-pounders – an extravagant concentration of guns which would have been far better employed with the Army, which in the winter of 1775-76 was preparing to batter the British out of Boston. This must be counted as a serious misapplication of the scanty resources at the disposal of Congress, which had the inevitable result of delaying the build-up of Washington's Army with no compensating gains at sea. In its anxiety to fit out a recognizable colonial fleet, Congress was forgetting that it was bound to be brutally out-gunned in any action. British frigates, the likeliest class of warship which the Colonial fleet could expect to fight, carried far heavier guns: 18-pounders, 12-pounders, on average from two to three times the weight of metal than that of the lightweight American six-pounders with their top-dressing of nine-pounders. Even a single British frigate, well handled and given the right conditions, might be expected to give a good

*Below:* A typically spirited encounter of the early days of the war: the capture of the British armed schooner HMS *Margaretta* off the port of Machias, Maine (11 May 1775) by 35 Patriots embarked in a lumber sloop armed with muskets, pitchforks and axes. The British captain was killed. 19 other British crewmen were killed or wounded, and the spoils included 40 cutlasses, 40 boarding axes and 40 muskets, plus grenades, pistols and two wall guns.

account itself against Hopkins' motley armada. And so it proved.

The first mission ordered by Congress for the Continental Navy was to stop the savaging of the Virginian coast in Chesapeake Bay by the dispossessed British governor, Lord Dunmore. With a handful of light warships and a force composed of Royal Marines and negro slaves enlisted on (empty) promises of freedom, Dunmore earned the nickname of 'bloody butcher' for his raids on Virginian Patriots. Unable to maintain a base ashore, Dunmore was a menance who, if not eliminated, might conceivably tempt the British into sending a reinforcing army for the subjugation of Virginia. Dunmore's flotilla was not, in fact, an objective hopelessly beyond the capacity of the Continental fleet, but Hopkins felt otherwise. He was convinced that his ships would be far better employed in beating up the British sealanes between the American coast and the Bahamas, thus forcing the British to spread their available naval force as thinly as possible.

There was no direct collaboration between the Continental Army and the Navy's only fleet in March 1776, when the siege of Boston came to an unexpectedly early climax. On 4 March Washington occupied the commanding eminence of Dorchester Heights, emplacing heavy guns (captured at Fort Ticonderoga the previous year and painfully dragged south by sledge) to menance the city and harbor. Thus surprised, the British evacuated Boston on 17 March and shipped their garrison to Halifax, Nova Scotia. While this was going on, Hopkins and the American fleet were 1,300 miles to the south, raiding Nassau in the Bahamas. With the British fleet momentarily committed to the safe transfer of the Boston garrison to Nova Scotia, Hopkins would have been able to blockade Dunmore in Chesapeake Bay without undue molestation, but the opportunity was missed.

April 1776 came in with a symbolic pair of engagements for the Continental Navy: a humiliation for the fleet, followed within 24 hours by a brilliantly successful single-ship action.

The first event took place on 6 April: a miserable encounter between Hopkins' fleet and the British frigate HMS *Glasgow,* patrolling the mouth of Long Island Sound and the southern approaches to Rhode Island. Hopkins badly needed a solid victory, to exonerate himself to the Naval Committee for not having gone to the Chesapeake as ordered. He had won little success at Nassau, where he had failed to capture more than a small portion of the invaluable British naval stores. Passing up an action with favorable odds of five-to-one would have crowned his failure. He had little choice but to attack *Glasgow,* but he also knew that his fleet was the only one which Congress was likely to raise, and shrank from the prospect of excessive losses. The result was an inconclusive sparring-match off Block Island from which *Glasgow* escaped with comparative ease. Though his best chance would have been a converging attack by all five American ships, culminating in boarding with overwhelming manpower, Hopkins kept the range open and tried to disable *Glasgow* with long-range sniping – over-cautious tactics ideally suited to *Glasgow,* with her heavier fire-power.

*Glasgow's* dry record of the encounter – the only attack ever made by an American fleet on a British warship – has survived. It is notable for its detail and the surprising extent of information which the British clearly had about the American warships (or 'Rebel Armed Vessels' as they were dismissively called). All five ships names were known, with their captains, though *Andrea Doria* and *Cabot* are spelled as 'Annadona' and 'Cabinet'. The differing armaments and complements of the ships were also noted, with brief notes on the ships' appearances. *Alfred,* the flagship, was described as 'A Figure head and Yellow Sides, her Lower Deck Ports not above eighteen inches from the Water; Mizen Topgallant Sail.' Yellow seems to have been a Hopkins trademark, with *Cabot* described as 'A small white Figure head, and Yellow sides with hanging Ports;' *Columbus, Andrea Doria* and *Providence* were all black-painted, without figureheads.

Observers in *Glasgow* also noted that *Alfred* and *Columbus,* contrary to the normal practice of mounting light guns above heavy guns, carried their nine-pounders on the upper deck and their six-pounders below. This top-heavy arrangement, which can have done little to improve the ships' stability in a seaway, was intended to permit the nine-pounders to fire even in rough weather or during points of sailing which made it impossible to open lower-deck ports.

The humiliation of the Continental fleet off Block Island was increased when the news came through of an American single-ship victory 400 miles to the south, won on 7 April 1776. It was the first of many triumphs for

Captain John Barry, born about 1745 in County Wexford, Ireland, for whom Philadelphia had been home since 1760. He had become a merchant captain by the age of 21 and his last peacetime command had been the *Black Prince,* subsequently requisitioned as *Alfred.* Barry was commissioned as a Captain in the Continental Navy on 14 March 1776. He was appointed to command the armed brigantine *Wild Duck* which had been re-christened *Lexington,* the first of seven American warships destined to bear that illustrious name. Superbly handled by Barry, the handy *Lexington* evaded the British frigate HMS *Roebuck,* patrolling the entrance to Delaware Bay, and escaped to sea. Barry then headed south for the Chesapeake and on 7 April fell in with the British sloop HMS *Edward,* tender to the frigate HMS *Liverpool,* off Cape Charles. A communications vessel rather than a fighting ship, *Edward* had a complement of only 29 and surrendered after a running fight lasting nearly an hour – the first American prize to be brought into Philadelphia.

Though the opposition had been modest, Barry's performance had been sharply competent throughout. It was considered all the more credible that a two-masted brigantine (with square rig on the foremast only, and fore-and-aft rig on the mainmast) had captured a normally more powerful sloop. The lackluster performance of the Continental fleet appeared all the more depressing in the light of this timely demonstration of what could be achieved by American warships, and Esek Hopkins had to endure a vote of censure from Congress. He was given no further chance to redeem himself, being suspended from his command prior to formal dismissal. This unforgiving treatment of naval commanders who failed to fulfil the politician's expectations was to remain a characteristic of the American naval service. Though not without value, *pour encourager les autres,* it was not invariably successful, let alone just. In the case of the Royal Navy the British often preferred to give another chance to a man who had done good service in the past, and if Hopkins had been over-cautious he had at least kept the fleet in being. Whipple of the *Columbus,* incidentally, demanded a court martial to absolve himself of imputations of blame for the Block Island Fiasco, and was cleared.

Such were the uncertain origins of American sea power in the first year of the War of Independence: tentaive, inglorious, and yet by no means disastrous or even lacking in promise. The *Glasgow* fiasco was a sharp reminder that the Continental Navy was pitted against real professionals: the *Edward* success was a solid hint that any successes which American sailors might win would come from lucky or well-chosen encounters with opposition of suitably modest dimensions. If concentrated, vainly trying to imitate conventional fleets, the Continental Navy would be risking disaster. If dispersed in privateer commerce-raiding, it could at least continue to make an intolerable nuisance of itself. But one ugly fact was grimly obvious. Alone and unsupported, the Continental Navy had no chance of stopping the British from shipping troops anywhere they chose.

This was the hardest reality facing the American Congress as its delegates steeled themselves to sign the colonies' Declaration of Independence on 4 July 1776. At the very moment at which the American 'Founding Fathers' were signing that immortal document, British and mercenary German troops were pouring into New York, chosen as the main base from which the reconquest of the American colonies would be launched. The British build-up continued throughout July and August 1776 and by early autumn the Continental Army was confronted by about 45,000 British and German troops, 10,000 of them in Canada and the rest massed in New York. In the face of this massive new development, the only discernible American naval success was the capture of three armed transports on 16–17 June. This was achieved by Captain Seth Harding of Massachusetts in the brig *Defence,* fitted out by the Connecticut State Navy – a pinprick against an elephant.

The summer and early autumn of 1776 saw the British complete their ominous new troop concentration in New York, with the Continental Navy completely unable to stop or even delay it. Extreme measures were called for, and none was more extreme than the attempt to blow up the British naval C-in-C, Admiral Howe, in his flagship. This took place in August 1776 and, though a failure, was an historic event: the first attack by a submersible craft with an explosive warhead. The 'submarine' in question was the brain-child of David Bushnell, who had graduated from Yale in 1775. Bushnell's *Turtle* was a wooden egg enclosing a single crewman and hand-pumped buoyancy tanks by which the craft could be 'trimmed down'

U.S. S/M "TURTLE" 1776.

just below the surface. Feeble power was provided by hand-cranked screws, and *Turtle* was also fitted with a vertical gimlet for screwing into the bottom planking of the target ship. To this gimlet was attached an explosive charge, to be left beneath the target as *Turtle* made its escape.

The *Turtle* attack was not, however, a Navy affair: it was carried out by Sergeant Ezra Lee of the Continental Army, against Howe's flagship HMS *Eagle*, lying in the lower East River. It was a gallant effort deserving of better success. Lee did extraordinarily well to fetch up under *Eagle's* stern after a downstream approach, but he was beaten by a new British 'secret weapon' for which *Turtle's* designer had not bargained: the new technique of protecting ships' hulls with copper sheathing. This defeated all Lee's efforts to force home *Turtle's* gimlet and in the end he was forced to beat a retreat, chased by boats from *Eagle*. Lee managed to escape them by slipping the explosive charge and detonating it in the face of his pursuers.

The *Turtle* incident is usually remembered as an untimely freak of naval history, but it has more significance than that. In its audacity alone, it perfectly demonstrated American desperation in the face of a relentless British amphibious build-up against which available American naval resources were useless. As a might-have-been – Lee came close to success – it is on a par with wondering what would have happened if Hitler had not declared war on the United States when the Japanese attacked Pearl Harbor in December 1941. If Lee *had* succeeded in blowing one of Britain's most respected admirals sky-high it would have

The first 'submarine attack' in naval history: Ezra Lee's gallant but unavailing foray against HMS *Eagle*, flagship of the British Admiral Howe, in the East River on 7 September 1776.

been remembered as an atrocity, a renunciation of the rules of civilized warfare; and one of the biggest paradoxes of the War of Independence was that the British fought it very much according to the rules of civilized warfare. Though the British officially regarded the war, from start to finish, as the suppression of rebellion, captured American captains were not hanged or shot as rebels. They were offered the same niceties expected by any European belligerent of the day: release on parole, or imprisonment pending exchange for a captured British officer of equivalent rank.

Under this polite system, many American officers underwent more than one spell of British captivity before either escaping or being exchanged, returning to sea to fight the British again. They included John Barry, Gustavus Conyngham, Richard Dale, John Manley, and Samuel Tucker. A harder British line towards prisoners of war could easily have resulted from a successful attack by *Turtle,* progressively depriving the struggling Congress of its best seagoing commanders.

American fortunes reached a nadir in the autumn and winter of 1776-77, with Washington's army successively pushed out of Long Island, away from New York and

The Stars and Stripes in the English Channel: USS *Revenge*, commanded by the aggressive commerce raider Captain Gustavus Conyngham (1777-1778).

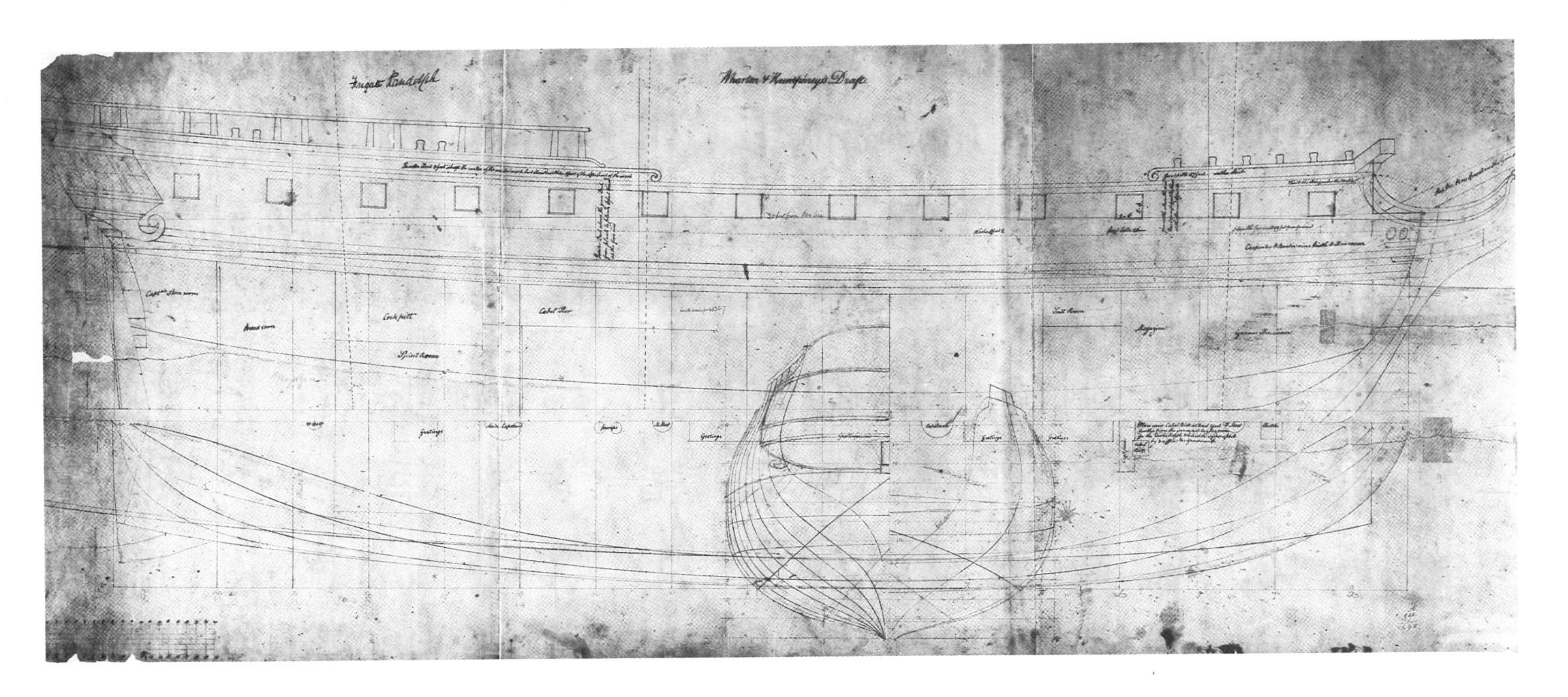


The only surviving plan drawn for one of the new frigates of the Continental Navy: USS *Randolph*, built at Philadelphia in 1776 to the design of Wharton and Humphries. Sadly, *Randolph's* service career was brief: she blew up in action with the British 64-gun *Yarmouth* in March 1778, near Barbados.

across New Jersey into Pennsylvania. Across the Atlantic, however, French sympathy for the American cause burgeoned under the subtle hand of envoy Benjamin Franklin, who arrived in Paris in December 1776. Though the French held back from a formal alliance until February 1778, Franklin did win permission for American raiders to refit and operate from French ports. One of his first achievements was to secure the release of Gustavus Conyngham, jailed by the French for operating out of Dunkirk in the lugger *Surprise* and bringing his prizes into French ports. Conyngham, another Irish-born Philadelphian, had learned navigation in his cousin's merchant ship, and had been stranded in Europe when the war broke out in 1775. The first American raider to carry the naval war into British waters, Conyngham was commissioned Captain in the Continental Navy by Franklin. He made a successful raiding cruise in the North and Irish Seas in the cutter *Revenge* before shifting to Spanish ports when France and Spain entered the war. By the time Conyngham returned to Philadelphia via the West Indies in February 1779 he had taken 60 prizes in 18 months.

The year 1777 was the turning-point of the war, seeing General Sir William Howe fail to destroy Washington's army and switching his objective to capturing Philadelphia. British sea power enabled Howe to shift his army from New York to Chesapeake Bay, but this move left General Burgoyne unsupported as he began what was intended to be a decisive southward march from Canada. The result was not the planned British isolation and reconquest of New England by the united armies of Burgoyne and Howe, but the isolation of Burgoyne's army and its surrender at Saratoga on 17 October 1777. This triumph more than atoned for the loss of Philadelphia to Howe in late September, and the discomfiture of Washington's army at Valley Forge in the winter of 1777-78. The most important direct result of Saratoga was the signing of treaties of commerce and alliance on 6 February 1778 between France and the newly-styled 'United States of America.' Assuming, after Saratoga, that there was no longer any danger of the American colonies falling to converging attack, the alliance guaranteed them the aid of the French battle fleet and the eventual despatch (July 1780) of a French expeditionary force to fight alongside the Continental Army.

Thanks to Franklin's advocacy, however, the first fruits of the alliance were gathered even before the treaties were signed. French co-operation in the naval war saw the stepping-up of American activity in British home waters, and an increased flow of military and naval supplies from France to America. These vital facilities saved the United States from the humiliation of having to entrust the naval war entirely to the French fleet. In 1777-78 it enabled the fitting-out of a new generation of American warships, the light frigates *Randolph, Warren, Hancock, Confederacy* and *Boston,* the first of which were ready for sea in the early summer of 1777.

The new raiders scored an early success, but this was cancelled almost at once. In June 1777, with *Boston* in company, John Manley in *Hancock* captured the British light frigate HMS *Fox*. Manley continued his cruise with *Fox* under an American prize crew, but within a month of this cheering victory he had the bad luck to fall in with two British frigates and a brig detached to hunt him down. With his manpower spread too

American frigates *Boston* and *Hancock* in action against the British *Flora* and *Rainbow* off Cape Sable, Newfoundland (7 July 1777).

thinly between *Hancock* and *Fox,* Manley was forced to strike his colors while *Fox* was speedily recaptured. Manley was exchanged after a year in British captivity and returned to face an American court-martial for losing *Hancock*. He was acquitted, and returned to sea with more successes in store for him.

By this time, however, the Continental Navy had lost not only the second of its new frigates, but one of its most promising captains. Biddle, formerly commanding *Andrea Doria* under Esek Hopkins, was fifth in the captains' list by the New Year of 1778 and promoted to the new *Randolph*. In March

1778, having sailed from Charleston with four light warships of the South Carolina State Navy in company, Biddle in *Randolph* fell in with the British 64-gun HMS *Yarmouth* near Barbados, and boldly engaged this much stronger adversary. It was an obvious bid to wipe out the shame of the Block Island fiasco against *Glasgow,* and at first *Randolph,* excellently handled, stood up well to *Yarmouth's* greatly superior firepower. But it ended disastrously when *Randolph* blew up – a most unusual end to a single-ship duel, indicative of inadequate magazine protection – with Biddle among the many dead.

The tragic loss of Biddle and *Randolph* in March 1778 was rapidly followed by the first exploits of one of the most celebrated of all American naval heroes: John Paul Jones. Born in 1747 at Kirkbean, Galloway, he was the son of an Irish gardener named John Paul, and, bearing the same name, first went to sea in the British merchant service in 1761. At Tobago in 1773, John Paul killed a mutinous seaman. This was in self-defense but he still had to flee to Virginia, where his elder brother was a tailor, taking the name 'Jones' in the process. After service as a lieutenant in the Continental Navy, Jones got his first command, the new sloop *Ranger,* in 1777. His first task was to supervize

Captain John Paul Jones and *(below)* a recruiting poster soliciting recruitment of 'gentlemen volunteers' for his first command, the new sloop *Ranger,* in March 1777.

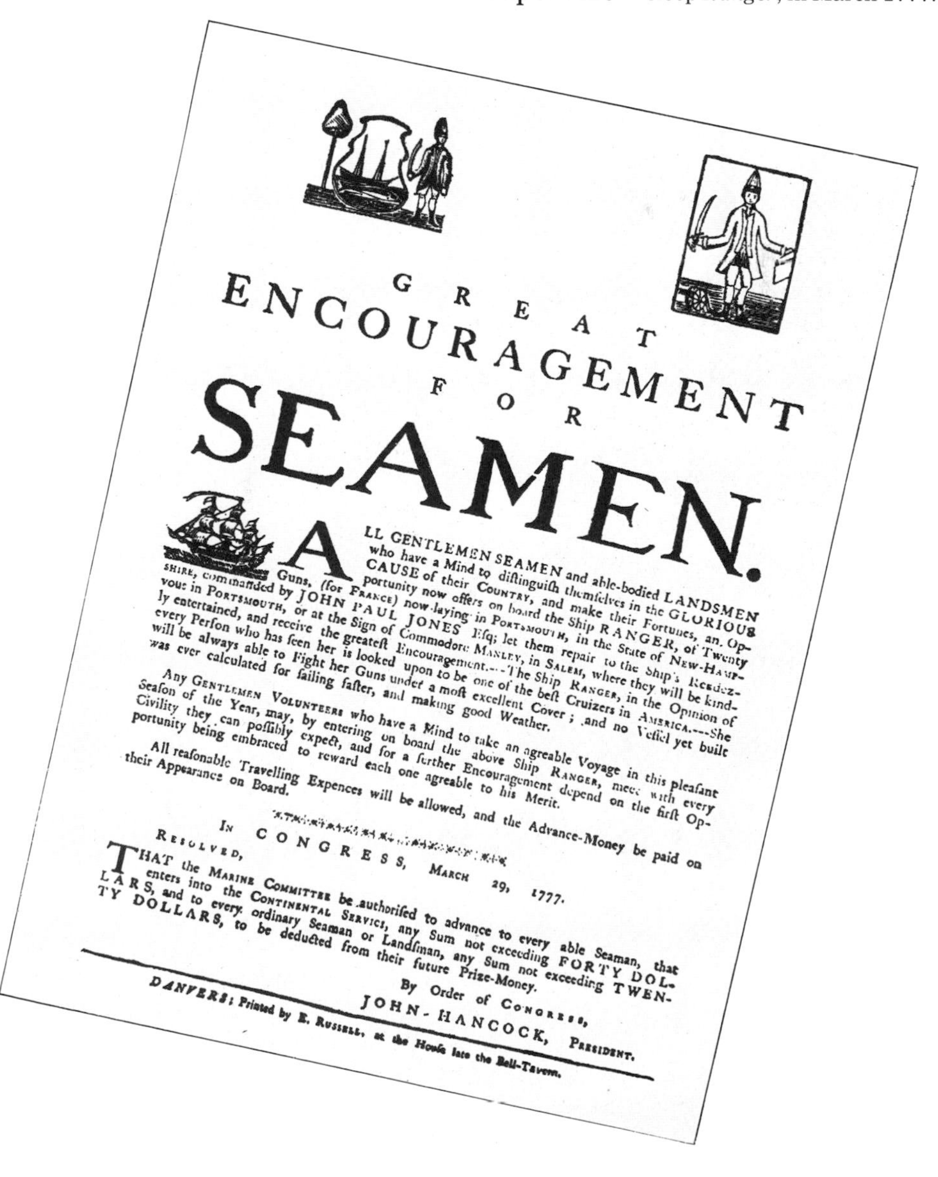

GREAT ENCOURAGEMENT FOR SEAMEN.

ALL GENTLEMEN SEAMEN and able-bodied LANDSMEN who have a Mind to diſtinguiſh themſelves in the GLORIOUS CAUSE of their COUNTRY, and make their Fortunes, an Opportunity now offers on board the Ship RANGER, of Twenty Guns, (for FRANCE) now laying in PORTSMOUTH, in the State of NEW-HAMPSHIRE, commanded by JOHN PAUL JONES Eſq; let them repair to the Ship's Rendezvous in PORTSMOUTH, or at the Sign of Commodore MANLEY, in SALEM, where they will be kindly entertained, and receive the greateſt Encouragement.---The Ship RANGER, in the Opinion of every Perſon who has ſeen her is looked upon to be one of the beſt Cruizers in AMERICA.---She will be always able to Fight her Guns under a moſt excellent Cover; and no Veſſel yet built was ever calculated for ſailing faſter, and making good Weather.

Any GENTLEMEN VOLUNTEERS who have a Mind to take an agreable Voyage in this pleaſant Seaſon of the Year, may, by entering on board the above Ship RANGER, meet with every Civility they can poſſibly expect, and for a further Encouragement depend on the firſt Opportunity being embraced to reward each one agreable to his Merit.

All reaſonable Travelling Expences will be allowed, and the Advance-Money be paid on their Appearance on Board.

IN CONGRESS, MARCH 29, 1777.

RESOLVED,

THAT the MARINE COMMITTEE be authoriſed to advance to every able Seaman, that enters into the CONTINENTAL SERVICE, any Sum not exceeding FORTY DOLLARS, and to every ordinary Seaman or Landſman, any Sum not exceeding TWENTY DOLLARS, to be deducted from their future Prize-Money.

By Order of CONGRESS,
JOHN-HANCOCK, PRESIDENT.

DANVERS: Printed by E. RUSSELL, at the House late the Bell-Tavern.

*Ranger's* completion and fitting-out at Portsmouth, New Hampshire, before sailing for France, arriving at Nantes on 2 December.

When he met Franklin in Paris, Jones learned that *Ranger's* arrival could not have been more timely. It coincided with that of confirmatory news of the British capitulation at Saratoga and the acceleration of Franco-American alliance talks. As the most convincing demonstration of the American will to carry the war to the British enemy, Franklin ordered Jones to raid in British home waters in the spring of 1778. This was preceded on 14 February by the first-ever formal salute of a ship flying the 'Stars and Stripes' by warships of a foreign power, rendered to *Ranger* in Quiberon Bay.

*Ranger's* cruise of March-May 1778 began with an abortive night raid on the Cumbrian port of Whitehaven during 22-23 April. This caused little material damage, but the moral effect of American raiders landing on British soil was naturally immense. On the following day, Jones raided the home of the Earl of Selkirk at St Mary's, planning to take the Earl as a hostage for a mass release of American prisoners of war. Unfortunately the Earl was not at home. The raiders made off with his family silver instead, but Jones subsequently demonstrated his hold over his men by returning the silver with a note of apology.

The highlight of the cruise came on 24 April when *Ranger*, approaching Belfast Lough, encountered the British sloop HMS *Drake*. It was one of the most equally-matched single-ship actions of the war and Jones fought it brilliantly, concentrating on cutting his opponent's rigging to pieces with disabling fire. Finally, when the British commander had been killed, the master of *Drake* surrendered. Jones crowned his vic-

The first 'famous victory' for John Paul Jones, 24 April 1778. At left the British sloop HMS *Drake*, her rigging already showing the effects of American disabling shot, trails her shattered bowsprit overside at the outset of the action off Belfast which ended in her capture.

Woodcut of the 32-gun American frigate *Alliance*, commanded by the unreliable French expatriate Pierre Landais during the epic cruise of John Paul Jones in *Bonhomme Richard*.

tory by fitting *Drake* with a jury rig and bringing her triumphantly into Brest – an additional humiliation for the Royal Navy in home waters, on a par with the successful running of the English Channel by the German warships *Scharnhorst* and *Gneisenau* in February 1942. From France, 200 British prisoners were subsequently exchanged for American prisoners in British hands. Deeply impressed by Jones's achievement, the French agreed to contribute warships to a Franco-American squadron to be commanded by Jones on a second cruise in 1779.

As the French authorities had all they could do to render their battle fleet fit for action in American waters, Jones got the scrapings. His 'flagship' was the old French East Indiaman *Duc de Duras,* renamed *Bonhomme Richard*. She took a year to fit out at Lorient, modified to carry the motley armament of six 18-pounders, 28 12-pounders and eight nine-pounders. Jones was also given the 30-gun *Pallas* and 12-gun *Vengeance* – both armed merchantmen – and the 18-gun cutter *Cerf*. The American contribution to the squadron was the new Continental frigate *Alliance,* of 32 guns. As her name implied, she was a reciprocal compliment to the Franco-American alignment and, to the disappointment of many better-qualified American officers, was commanded by a Frenchman. He was Pierre Landais, a French naval officer who had gone to fight for the American Patriots in 1777 and had been commissioned into the Continental Navy. His undoubted propaganda value could not, as it proved, atone for his erratic and unstable behaviour in command. Landais brought *Alliance* into Brest in February 1779, but it was June before Jones had his squadron fit for sea. When it sailed, on 19 June, *Bonhomme Richard* and *Alliance* collided heavily and the need for repairs meant a further delay until 14 August.

Safely to sea at last, Jones pressed ahead with his planned circumnavigation of the British Isles, despite the weakening of his force by the incompetence and wilfulness of his junior commanders. The cutter *Cerf* lost touch with the squadron off south-west Ireland, and never rejoined; Landais in *Alliance* kept taking off on what appeared to be his private commerce-raiding war. Thanks to Landais's refusal to co-operate, Jones had to abandon his intended entry of the Firth of Forth to raise Cain off the Scottish capital of Edinburgh. But the squadron's fortunes improved on the voyage down the English east coast, with three prizes snapped up off Flamborough Head on 21 September, and Jones remained in what seemed a promising hunting-ground. He was right. On the 23rd, the ideal target hove into view: a 41-ship convoy from the Baltic, scantily escorted by the 20-gun *Countess of Scarborough* and the 44-gun frigate *Serapis,* commanded by Captain Richard Pearson.

There was no choice but to fight, as Pearson stoutly positioned *Serapis* and *Countess of Scarborough* between this unex-

Robert Dodd's painting of the famous duel between John Paul Jones in *Bonhomme Richard (at centre left)* and HMS *Serapis* off Flamborough Head (23 September 1779). *Alliance,* firing indiscriminately into both friend and foe, is shown circling the main action at right, with the secondary duel between the American *Pallas* and HMS *Countess of Scarborough* at left.

pected enemy force and the helpless merchantmen of the convoy. Jones duly headed in to take out *Serapis,* reckoning that this would be straightforward enough with *Alliance* in support; but he was again let down, with near-fatal consequences, by the maddening behaviour of Landais. In the ensuing epic Battle of Flamborough Head, *Pallas* battered the weaker *Countess of Scarborough* while *Bonhomme Richard* and *Serapis* fought it out, with Landais in *Alliance* circling the fray and firing into both friend and foe alike.

In the duel between *Bonhomme Richard* and *Serapis,* British gunnery and seamanship told from the first. Pearson managed to rake *Bonhomme Richard,* two of whose 18-pounders burst at the beginning of the action. *Bonhomme Richard* took a fearful battering for two hours, at the end of which she was leaking like a sieve (kept afloat largely by the efforts of the prisoners of war turned loose by Jones to labor at the pumps) with only three nine-pounders still able to fire. Pearson then called on Jones to surrender – as did several of Jones's own men – only to receive the immortal defiance, 'I have not yet begun to fight!' Jones made good his words by laying *Bonhomme Richard* alongside *Serapis* and boarding: the only option left to him. *Serapis* was carried against stiff resistance, which only wilted when Landais belatedly closed and opened a devastating raking fire. At 10.30pm, knowing that he had saved his convoy and that his men could do no more, Pearson surrendered to Jones – whose first act was to transfer his men from the foundering *Bonhomme Richard* to *Serapis.*

It had been a bloody encounter, with 128 killed and wounded in *Serapis* and 150 in *Bonhomme Richard.* Jones painfully crossed the North Sea to the Texel and the temporary shelter of Dutch neutrality. There, now flying his commodore's broad pendant in *Alliance,* he managed to repair *Serapis* before sailing again on 27 December. On 19 February 1780, after evading the British squadrons hunting for him and making a cruise across the Bay of Biscay to Corunna, Jones reached Lorient. In Holland Jones had been joined by Gustavus Conyngham, who had been captured off New York earlier in the year and imprisoned in England before escaping with the help of friends in London. (Conyngham returned to America from Corunna only to be captured again, this time spending a year in prison before being released under exchange.) Meanwhile, back in Paris, Jones revelled in a well-earned hero's welcome before returning to America in the sloop *Ariel.* Congress appointed him to complete and command the Continental Navy's first battleship, the 74-gun *America,* under construction at Portsmouth, New Hampshire.

Though naturally high in propaganda value and dramatic impact, the exploits of Conyngham and Jones in British home waters had no direct effect on the course of the war in America. The spring of 1778 had seen Washington's army speedily restored from the hardships of the winter, improved by European drill, and able to take the field. The British in Philadelphia, unable to destroy Washington, were now faced with imminent French intervention; Philadelphia was therefore abandoned to permit a concentration at New York. In July 1778 the Comte d'Estaing arrived off the Delaware Capes with a battle fleet 11 strong. When he moved to New York Admiral Howe, momentarily outnumbered, kept his ships close inshore to cover the British garrison, but d'Estaing failed to combine with Washington in a joint attack on the city. The moment of danger passed with d'Estaing's removal, first to support an abortive siege of Newport, Rhode Island, and then in August 1778 to Boston. The British were not slow to profit from d'Estaing's hesitation. At the end of 1778 they took the offensive again, sending forces from New York to occupy French St Lucia in the Caribbean and Savannah in Georgia.

Apart from New York, the British had effectively cut their losses in the north and it was in the Southern States – Georgia (1778-79), the Carolinas (1779-80) and Virginia (1781) – that the war was fought to its conclusion. Apart from fleeting successes in the field, the last solid British success was the capture of Charleston on 12 May 1780, together with a squadron of four American warships (*Providence, Ranger, Queen of France* and *Boston*) trying to emulate Howe's defense of New York in 1778. The senior American naval officer at Charleston was Abraham Whipple, deploring this misuse of the Continental Navy's still-modest resources. Only one year previously, Whipple in *Providence,* with two auxiliaries, had got in among a British homebound convoy and captured ten of its ships before the escorting British warships could react. But Charleston was the last major American naval setback of the war, which was effectively won by the

The decisive fleet action of the War of Independence (5 September 1781) ended with the defeat of the British battle fleet under Admiral Graves (*right*) by the French under the Comte de Grasse.

Comte de Grasse's defeat of Admiral Graves's fleet at the entrance to Chesapeake Bay on 5 September 1781. This crucial defeat left General Cornwallis's army isolated on Virginia's Yorktown peninsula, with the French fleet to seaward and the Franco-American army to landward. Cornwallis bowed to the inevitable and surrendered on 19 October 1781.

It was clear to all that Britain had no hope of regaining her former American colonies by force, being now at war not only with France but with Spain (from June 1779) and the Dutch Republic (from December 1780). During the two years which separated the Yorktown surrender from the signing of the definitive Peace of Paris on 3 September 1783, American privateers and ships of the Continental Navy kept up the attack on

British commerce. The last important prize of the war was the merchant ship *Baille,* captured by John Manley in the Continental frigate *Hague* in January 1783. Two months later came the last clash with the Royal Navy. In March 1783, escorting a bullion ship carrying 72,000 dollars, John Barry in *Alliance* fought the British frigate HMS *Sybil,* brought down her foretopmast with his first broadside, and drove her off after 40 minutes. This action, in its sharp competence, was reminiscent of the skill with which Barry had extricated *Alliance* from attack by HMS *Atlanta* and *Trepassy* two years before.

The Continental Navy's contribution to American victory was always secondary: the commerce-raiding campaign, in which it accounted for about 200 British ships. American privateering, however, had always been far more popular and profitable than service with the Navy of Congress. It has been estimated that at the time of Yorktown in 1781 there were more Americans involved in privateering than there were serving in Washington's army. American privateers took nearly four British ships for every one which fell to the Continental Navy, estimates of the joint tally ranging from 800 to 1,000 vessels. A contemporary English estimate put the financial loss to the British war effort caused by American raiders at some £2 million.

Faced with swarming political, constitutional and financial problems of the utmost urgency, Congress had no intention whatever of maintaining a peacetime fleet of any kind. It took the States until April 1789 to agree on a joint constitution and swear in Washington as first President of the United States, and until this had been done Congress had no authority to levy taxes for such costly peacetime expenditure. Indeed, Congress began selling off ships of the Continental fleet long before the Peace of Paris was signed. The new '74', *America,* went to

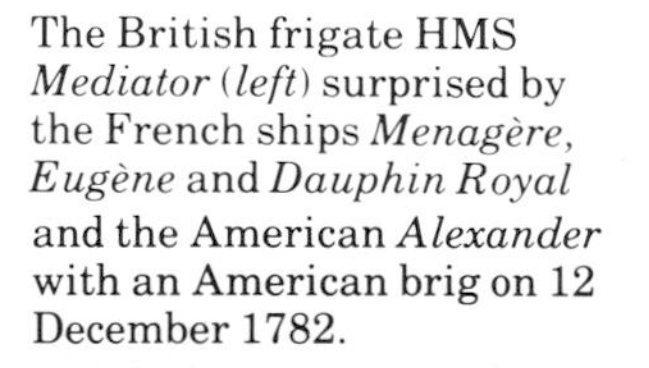

The British frigate HMS *Mediator* (*left*) surprised by the French ships *Menagère, Eugène* and *Dauphin Royal* and the American *Alexander* with an American brig on 12 December 1782.

Captain John Barry, senior captain of the new US Navy (by virtue of his services in the War of Independence) when the new service was formed by Act of Congress in March 1794.

France in 1782, thus abruptly and ungratefully ending the career of John Paul Jones in American service. (He died of pneumonia in Paris ten years later, having briefly served as a rear-admiral in the Russian Navy of Catherine the Great). By the time of the Peace of Paris Barry's *Alliance* was the last warship left flying the American flag, and she was sold in 1785. For the Continental Navy, the price of American victory in the War of Independence was immediate dissolution, in the vague hope that friendly powers would in future give the United States any naval protection that might be needed.

It took little over ten years for the American Republic to accept hard reality: that the United States' essential seaborne trade would remain vulnerable as long as naval protection was lacking. From the middle 1780s, attacks on American merchant shipping by corsairs from Algiers and Tripoli – international pests swarming inside and outside the Mediterranean – left the United States with no choice but to pay the corsairs protection-money, or leave American merchantmen to their fate. Nor, when Europe became involved in war against Revolutionary France in 1792-93, was it feasible for American seaborne trade in the Mediterranean to claim the already-dubious protection of European navies. American refusal to become involved in the European conflict, signified by Washington's proclamation of neutrality in April 1793, only spelled out the fact that the American merchant marine was overdue for at least a token measure of American naval protection.

On 27 March 1794, a special Act of Congress provided for the formation of the United States Navy. Admittedly, 'navy' could be described as a grandiose term for the six frigates provided for in the Act, but there was a vital difference from the hodge-podge nature of the old Continental Navy. The new United States Navy was to be nationally funded, with an initial appropriation of two-thirds of a million dollars, not scraped together from the contributions of the individual states.

Bringing the 'original six frigates' from approval on paper into reality could well be called Washington's last great service to his country. He picked the captains who would oversee completion of the new ships – respected veterans from the War of Independence, men like John Barry, Richard Dale, Thomas Truxton. Most important of all, it was Washington who appointed the remarkable naval designer Joshua Humphreys, a supreme pragmatist who realized that the new frigates must be able to out-sail and out-gun all contemporary ships of their class. As Humphreys put it, 'As our navy for a considerable time will be inferior in numbers, we are to consider what size ships will be most formidable and be an overmatch for those of an enemy.' Humphreys opted for 'qualities of strength, durability, swiftness of sailing and force – superior to any frigate.'

Thanks to Washington and Humphreys, the 'original six frigates' of the United States Navy – *Constellation, Constitution, Congress, Chesapeake, United States,* and *President* – were the pocket-battleships of the age of sail. Their completion was supervised by the specially-formed Department of the Navy, created with the US Marine Corps on 30 April 1798. It was none too soon. By June 1798, the United States was already involved in its first naval war.

# 2: SURVIVAL AND TRIUMPH

1798-1823

It was certainly an irony of history that the first war which the United States had to fight was against France, the erstwhile liberator of the American colonies, but the Revolutionary France of the 1790s was a very different power from the Bourbon France of the 1770s. Luckily, the Franco-American confrontation resulted in the only form of warfare which the United States was able to wage, and no conflict could have done more to justify and expand the new United States Navy. It lasted from 1797 to 1800 and luckily for the United States was a purely naval struggle, sporadic and low key. An outright declaration of war between France and the United States was never in fact made, and hostilities took the form of mutual harrassment at sea.

The root cause of this war was French resentment and distrust not only of American neutrality, but of the successful resolution of Anglo-American frontier and trade disagreements outstanding from the Peace of Paris. These disagreements were momentarily resolved by Jay's Treaty, negotiated in London by John Jay and signed on 19 November 1794. The Revolutionary French Directory which followed Robespierre's Terror in 1795 took Jay's Treaty as a sign that the United States had become a British client in an act of 'hostile neutrality.' The Directory refused to receive Charles Pinckney as American minister in December 1796, and when he was summoned to Paris in October 1797 to smooth over the differences between France and the United States it was to receive unashamed French demands for cash payments to secure peace – nothing less than protection-money if paid. Pinckney indignantly rejected these demands while John Adams, Washington's successor as President, reaped political kudos by publishing details of the affair (the 'XYZ Affair', as it is known, 'X', 'Y' and 'Z' referring to the three French agents involved).

These events determined the diplomatic rupture between France and the United States, but a campaign of intimidation at the expense of American shipping had already begun, with several American merchant ships falling prey to French raiders by the summer of 1797. The United States Navy was in no condition to retaliate until the first of the new frigates were ready for sea in the following year. Naturally the greatest support for the Navy came from the big merchant seaports, whose prosperity was most at risk; one of the most-resented French outrages was the destruction by a French privateer of a British merchantman in Charleston Harbour. Several seaports raised funds to build warships which were then loaned indefinitely to the Navy. The most valuable of these were light frigates with broadsides about 10-15 guns lighter than those of the 'original six'. A typical example was the 36-gun *Essex,* funded by and built at Salem, Massachusetts, between April and September 1799. Pennsylvania's *Philadelphia* was another. Other seaports fitted out lighter warships, sloops, brigs and schooners, as tenders and scouts for the frigates.

As long as the conflict dragged on, the main American defensive measure was the convoying of merchant ships. As soon as *Essex* was completed and handed over to the US Navy in December 1799 she was ordered to make a maiden cruise to Batavia, Java, thence to escort home a rich convoy from the Far East trade. *Congress,* one of the 'original six', was to have gone with *Essex,* but had to turn back for repairs. This left *Essex* to become the first US warship to double the Cape of Good Hope. Her Captain, Edward Preble, had been born at Falmouth (then New Hampshire) in 1761, and had first gone to sea at the age of 16 in a privateer. In 1779 he had transferred to the Massachusetts State Navy as a midshipman. Captured in the *Proctor* in 1781, Preble was subsequently exchanged, ended the war in the Massachusetts frigate *Winthrop,* then returned to civilian life and 15 years in the merchant service. Preble's success in single-handedly bringing home the Batavia convoy in November 1800 made him a man of mark in the US Navy.

Before the undeclared Franco-American war was ended by the Treaty of Mortfontaine in September 1800, France and the United States lost about 100 merchant ships apiece in three years of sporadic raiding and retaliation. The outstanding American achievement during the conflict was the first battle fought by one of the 'original six' frigates, when the Baltimore-built *Constellation* fought and captured the French frigate *l'Insurgente* on 9 February 1799. Born at Jamaica, Long Island in 1755, Captain Thomas Truxton of *Constellation* had gone to sea at the age of 12 and in 1771 had been impressed into the Royal Navy, briefly serving in HMS *Prudent.* Truxton had been a successful privateer commander in the War of Independence, returning to the merchant service and voyaging as far afield as China

The spirited single-ship duel between Captain Thomas Truxton in USS *Constellation (right)* and the French frigate *Vengeance* (1 February 1800). Truxton was robbed of victory by the untimely loss of *Constellation*'s mainmast, but emerged with credit from the encounter.

before being selected for the US Navy in 1794. After his triumph over *l'Insurgente,* Truxton fought a second single-ship action in February 1800: a night encounter with *la Vengeance* of 40 guns, slightly greater than the broadside of *Constellation.* This time, however, Truxton's luck was out: he was robbed of a second victory by *Constellation's* mainmast going over the side, but emerged safely with enhanced credit from this encounter with a ship of superior force.

The foremost younger officer to make his name in the 'quasi-war' with France was Lieutenant Charles Stewart, born at Philadelphia in 1778. After first going to sea as a cabin-boy in the merchant service, Stewart was commissioned lieutenant in the US Navy in 1798, his first ship being John Barry's frigate *United States.* Here Stewart shone to such good effect that in January 1800, aged 22, he was given command of the armed schooner *Experiment.* In her, Stewart not only captured two armed French merchantmen but recaptured several American ships which had fallen victim to the French raiders. It was a brilliant beginning to a unique career in the US Navy.

In contrast to these successes, *Constitution,* destined to become the most famous of all the 'original six' frigates, had a frustrating debut in the 'quasi-war'. Of the two prizes she took, one turned out to be a British ship, while the second proved to be a British ship recently captured by the French. Because of the overriding need to preserve American neutrality in the Anglo-French conflict, *Con-*

Prize crew away: the men of USS *Enterprise* prepare to board the battered Corsair *Tripoli* – only to be forced to release their prey under the complex niceties of international law which bedevilled the US Navy during its struggle with the Barbary Corsairs (1801-1805).

*stitution* was robbed of her prey, her crew suffering the mortification of having to turn a prize loose and watch it sail off under the enemy's colours.

On balance, the US Navy had stood up well to its first trial, against the commerce-raiders of a major European sea power with the bulk of its navy tied down in a major European war. It was perhaps inevitable that the next exercise of sea power by President and Congress falsely sought to apply the experiences of the Franco-American 'quasi-war' to an entirely different set of circumstances.

The problem was the old one of the Barbary Corsairs in the Mediterranean, or more accurately the easternmost nest of them: Tripoli. In May 1801 the Pasha of Tripoli, discontented with the takings of peacetime extortion, decided to boost his profits from American shipping by going to war with the United States, barely three months after the third President, Thomas Jefferson, had taken office. Jefferson's options were strictly limited. The rough-hewn American Constitution prevented him from committing the United States to war. He could send a squadron to the Mediterranean in defence of American shipping, but only with a strictly defensive brief. American warships could defend themselves and any other American vessel from attack, but could not take Tripolitan prizes, destroy Tripolitan shipping or bombard Tripolitan property, let alone Tripoli itself. The most promising bloodless way of putting pressure on Tripoli seemed to be by blockade – but without injuring the trade of Tripoli's Corsair neighbours – Tunis, Algiers and Morocco, which was impossible.

From 4,000 miles away, however, it was easy for politicians to imagine that the softest option of blockade would, after less than a year's application, end with the Pasha suing for peace on American terms. It was only after the first American squadron arrived in the Mediterranean that the men on the spot found out the hard way that any blockade of Tripoli was bound to leak like a sieve, and that more forceful measures were essential.

Command of the expedition was to have gone to Truxton after his prowess in the 'quasi-war' against France, but he turned it down in a fit of pique caused by a disagreement over the appointment of his flag captain. It passed to Captain Richard Dale, onetime first lieutenant to Jones in *Bonhomme Richard,* and justly famed in the US Navy as having been the first man into *Serapis* during the Flamborough Head battle. Dale, a Virginian from Norfolk County, was 45 years old in 1801. His command consisted of the big frigate *President,* light frigates *Essex* and *Philadelphia,* and the schooner *Enterprise.* They sailed for the Mediterranean in June 1801.

The American squadron arrived at Gibraltar in July, and at once it seemed that all the confidence had been justified. Dale's force found two Tripolitan raiders – one-third of the estimated Tripolitan fleet – making ready in Gibraltar for their next foray into the Atlantic. Dale politely informed the Tripolitan commander that he would sail only at his peril, then left *Philadelphia* to stand over the cornered raiders. When the Tripolitan crews ran out of supplies they abandoned their ships, leaving them to swing round their anchors in British custody while the Tripolitans took to the boats and headed for the North African shore across the Straits.

This was exactly the sort of bloodless happy ending for which Jefferson and his advisers had hoped, but it proved to be the last of its kind. Dale headed east towards Tripoli, looking in at Algiers and Tunis to make a polite show of force, but was then obliged to detach *Essex* on convoy escort duty and *Enterprise* to replenish water supplies at Malta.

*President's* arrival off Tripoli certainly made a powerful impression, and Tripolitan seaborne traffic ceased as long as she remained; but this impression swiftly evaporated when Dale, after two and a half weeks' patrolling, also ran short of water and headed for Malta. The American naval presence seemed even flimsier to the Pasha when, before the week was out, the extremely battered *Tripoli* returned to her home port. *Tripoli* had had the bad luck to fall in with *Enterprise* while the latter was still on her way to Malta, and had been captured without the loss of a single American life. But then the American commander, well aware of the constitutional shackles clamped round his country's belligerency, had turned *Tripoli* loose without taking prisoners, hostages or even loot. So far from being the hoped-for show of strength, *Tripoli's* capture and release had precisely the opposite effect. The Tripolitan Corsairs had never met an enemy like this – amateur, weak, and apparently plain stupid as far as the waging of war at sea was concerned. After the *Tripoli* incident,

Another Tripolitan Corsair falls victim to the American armed schooner *Enterprise (left)* during the war with Tripoli.

Dale's hopes of negotiating from a show of strength never stood a chance, and he soon made matters worse. On his way back to Tripoli from Malta, *President* stopped a Greek ship bound for Tripoli, took off 40 Tripolitans found aboard (20 of them soldiers), then landed these prisoners at Tripoli on the verbal assurance that American captives would be released in exchange. Apart from the fact that such false assurances had been a Corsair stock-in-trade for centuries, there were no American prisoners in Tripoli at the time.

Dale stuck to his thankless task for as long as he could, from September 1801 to February 1802, but with two frigates always on convoy escort duty and one ship always in transit to replenish at Malta, this left only one ship to keep an intermittent watch on Tripoli. Moreover, by the New Year of 1802, Dale was being bombarded with unhelpful advice from the American consuls in Tunis, Algiers and Morocco, warning that the other Corsair states were preparing to raise the ante – not only with increased cash demands, but with raiders already being fitted out. Dale finally headed for home in *President* in February 1802 with his crew's commission left with barely two months to run; the fact that the squadron's sailors had only been recruited for one year's service was the most telling proof that the problem of bringing Tripoli to heel had been grossly underestimated.

Much had been learned about the practical side of that problem, however, and Jefferson's Government prepared for a second try – this time with a stronger squadron, recruited for long-term service. With *Essex, Philadelphia* and *Enterprise* as the foundation, remaining in the Mediterranean after Dale's departure, it was hoped that no less than 12 American warships could be concentrated there. But, although Congress had empowered the President to declare war on avowed enemies of the Union, the new commodore, Captain Richard Morris, was still under orders to negotiate from strength rather than fight. He was authorized to offer up to $20,000 in securing a lasting settlement with the Corsairs.

Morris's squadron, based on the big frigates *Chesapeake* and *Constellation,* with the light frigates *New York, Boston* and *John Adams,* arrived in Gibraltar in June 1802. There the first task was to repair *Che-*

*sapeake's* mainmast, which had split on the Atlantic crossing. At once, Morris was plunged into the morass of problems which had bedevilled his predecessor. With Morocco now peremptorily demanding the two Tripolitan ships at Gibraltar and threatening war, Morris lacked the ships with which to watch Morocco, convoy warships and settle accounts with Tripoli.

It was now clear that only a close blockade of Tripoli would bring the Pasha to heel, but this was impossible without the shallow-draught warships (brigs and schooners) which alone could venture close inshore amid the treacherous shoals outside the port. Though *Chesapeake's* mainmast had been repaired, her bowsprit had been found to be rotten, necessitating more lengthy repairs at Malta. *New York* was badly damaged by an accidental powder explosion. The squadron's manpower constantly dropped towards danger level, due to the need to keep sending home men whose enlistments had expired. The independently-minded Captain McNeill of *Boston* remained out of touch for weeks on end. To cap it all, Congress baulked at the cost of the expedition and insisted on the recall of *Constellation* and *Chesapeake*. Morris was a dogged, honest officer of no more than average competence, when it needed a genius to overcome the problems surrounding him at every turn.

The only highlights of the cruise were provided by Captain John Rodgers of *John Adams,* born in 1773 in Harford County, Maryland. Rodgers had been Truxton's executive officer in *Constellation* in 1799 and had been appointed prize commander of the captured *l'Insurgente.* In *John Adams,* Rodgers took the first prize achieved during the cruise: the former Tripolitan raider *Meshuda,* which in the spring of 1803 made a run for Tripoli crammed with Moroccan stores. *Meshuda* was in fact American in origin – the *Betsey* of Boston, taken by the Corsairs back in 1784 – and her recapture naturally boosted American morale. But Morris failed to follow up this success. An abortive attack

by *New York, John Adams* and *Enterprise* failed to prevent a shallow-draught convoy of grain ships from reaching Tripoli protected by gunboats, and a half-hearted attack on the gunboats in Tripoli harbour was also beaten off. Morris then tried negotiation, offering $5,000 for a settlement with Tripoli (he had to keep back the other $15,000 to settle with Morocco, Algiers and Tunis) but this only produced a contemptuous counter-demand for the impossible sum of $200,000 in cash, plus compensation in full for Tripoli's costs in the war.

After this humiliating rebuff Morris sailed for Malta, leaving Rodgers to maintain the blockade of Tripoli with *Enterprise* and *John Adams*. In June 1803, with a brilliant display of ship-handling, Rodgers fought and blew up a Tripolitan blockade-runner in sight of the Tripolitan army, but Morris did not exploit this success by renewing pressure on Tripoli harbour. Instead he raised the blockade and sailed for Gibraltar, only to encounter official notification of his recall. A court of enquiry ruled that Morris be dismissed from the service – a grossly unfair sentence, with Morris denied the right to defend himself in a proper court martial. But though Morris had been cast in the role of scapegoat, Jefferson and Secretary of the Navy Robert Smith were determined to fight on, accepting the futility of the half-measures enjoined upon both Dale and Morris. Congress had also been persuaded to vote $96,000 to fit out the light warships required to close the stranglehold on Tripoli: the schooners *Nautilus* and *Vixen,* and brigs *Argus* and *Siren*. To replace Morris as commodore in the Mediterranean, Jefferson and Smith made what proved to be an inspired appointment: Edward Preble, famous for his command of *Essex* during the 'quasi-war' with France.

With *Constitution* as his flagship, Preble reached Gibraltar in September 1803. He had been preceded by the light frigate *Philadelphia* under Captain William Bainbridge, who was sent on ahead with *Vixen* to

Preble's abortive assault on Tripoli (4 August 1804) with USS *Constitution*, the only ship of force available to support the lightweight US squadron, at right. It was a forlorn hope: even the firepower of *Constitution*'s broadside was not enough to silence the fire of the Tripolitan shore batteries.

waste no time in resuming the blockade of Tripoli. Preble meanwhile concentrated his force and entered Tangier, where he intimidated the Emperor of Morocco into agreeing a separate peace with the United States without American tribute or even the customary presents. Preble lingered to proclaim the blockade of Tripoli and set up a new cycle of convoys, then headed east – to receive the appalling news that *Philadelphia* was in Tripolitan hands. Bainbridge, chasing a blockade-runner too close inshore, had grounded her on the Kaliusa reef and had been taken into captivity with the whole of his crew, while the exultant Tripolitans refloated *Philadelphia*.

Preble's whole mission now hung in the balance, with the diplomatic triumph over Morocco abruptly wiped out by *Philadelphia's* loss. If *Philadelphia* could not be recovered by negotiation (and the Pasha dispelled that hope by demanding another American warship in exchange) she must be recaptured or destroyed. Preble took his time, maintaining the blockade of Tripoli throughout the winter of 1803–4 while he examined the problem for all angles. He negotiated the sending of supplies to the American prisoners in Tripoli, and corresponded secretly with Bainbridge (the latter using invisible ink). A shred of Credit was recovered by the capture of the Tripolitan ketch *Mastico* by *Enterprise,* the latter now commanded by Lieutenant Stephen Decatur, an officer of high ability. It was Decatur (another Marylander, born in 1779) who came up with the plan for destroying *Philadelphia* where she lay. There was no other option. With barely a thousand men under his command, Preble lacked the manpower to send a cutting-out expedition of sufficient strength to recover *Philadelphia,* and another American repulse under the guns of Tripoli would be disastrous.

Decatur's plan was to use the captured *Mastico* (now renamed *Intrepid*) to approach *Philadelphia* without arousing undue suspicion; the Tripolitans would probably decide that the weak-kneed Americans had let her go. In support would be Stewart in the *Siren,* whose rig resembled that of a two-masted ship recently purchased by the Tripolitan agents in Sicily. A storming-party from *Intrepid* would then board *Philadelphia,* set her on fire, take the boats and be brought out by *Siren.* Commanded in person by Decatur, the attack went in on the night of 16 February 1804 and was a complete success. When the fire reached *Philadelphia's* magazine she blew up, and Decatur brought out the attacking party intact. He even saved *Intrepid,* which he had planned to use as a fireship if necessary. This feat earned Decatur immediate promotion to Captain as soon as the news reached home. But a hit-and-run operation of this nature was a far easier proposition than the close bombardment of Tripoli which Preble knew was essential, yet for which his ships lacked the necessary resources.

Preble's foremost need was for a friendly base of operations where American warships could repair and replenish without undue loss of time. With Britain and France at war again (the frail Peace of Amiens had expired in May 1803) the British at Malta had few spare facilities for the American squadron. This was a problem from which Morris, at least, had been mercifully spared. As a substitute, Preble turned to the vacillating Bourbon Kingdom of Naples with his eye on the ports of Sicily, its southernmost province. Before he could assault Tripoli, however, Preble needed the loan of gunboats and bomb vessels armed with mortars for precision bombardment, and when it came to these practical matters the professionalism of the Neapolitan Navy left much to be desired. In the end he secured the loan of eight Neapolitan gunboats, two of them bomb vessels, all manned by Neapolitan crews; but the summer of 1804 was well advanced before he judged his force to be ready to attack.

Preble finally launched his bombardment of Tripoli on 4 August 1804, pushing his gunboats inshore to close with the Tripolitan light craft and keeping *Constitution,* his only ship of force, ready to give fire support. Decatur, commanding a division of three gunboats, boarded and captured one Tripolitan vessel; in boarding a second he was momentarily overpowered, narrowly escaping death in a desperate hand-to-hand fight which became a favourite scene with American naval artists. Preble ventured inshore to sink two or three gunboats but *Constitution's* broadside, devastating though it was in frigate actions out at sea, lacked the power to destroy the all-important Tripolitan shore batteries. When an afternoon sea breeze set in, threatening to pen the attackers in dangerous shoal waters, Preble signalled the withdrawal of his force to the open sea.

Without the vital element of a landing force in sufficient strength to storm the forts, blow up the magazines and destroy the guns, there was little more that Preble's ships could do, and the Tripolitans knew it. With admirable pertinacity, however, Preble ordered his crews to repair battle damage and continue with successive day and night attacks throughout August, hoping against hope that the Pasha would lose heart and start negotiating. But it was not to be. The Tripolitans never dropped their guard enough to allow a really punishing attack to be made, and their gunnery certainly did not deteriorate. For what proved to be his last night attack (on 4 September 1804) Preble planned to send in *Intrepid,* packed with seven tons of powder charges, to explode amid the crowded shipping off the Tripoli waterfront, hopefully causing extensive damage in the city, and so cracking the Corsairs' morale. It may have been a moment's carelessness on the part of *Intrepid's* volunteer skeleton crew or it may have been a lucky shot from the shore, but *Intrepid,* which was certainly under long-range fire at the time, blew up before she was fairly into the harbor. Her brave crew – a dozen men commanded by Master-Commandant Richard Somers – had been sacrificed in vain.

It was the last disappointment for the gallant and capable Edward Preble. Though he had raised the discipline and morale of the Mediterranean Squadron to unheard-of-heights, he already knew that Commodore James Barron was on his way out to relieve him, under the inflexible promotion principle followed by the Department of the Navy in those early years. These constant changes of command were naturally the foe of continuity and tended to deny worthy officers the opportunity to overcome early setbacks. They did, however, have the advantages of exposing a wide range of officers on the Captains' List to the strains and stresses of high command and, though one unfortunate by-product was constant wrangling over seniority, the experience thus gained was a definite asset to the young US Navy. Unfavorable weather prevented Preble from launching a last attack on Tripoli before Barron arrived with no less than four frigates – reinforcements which Preble would have found invaluable the month before. In mid-September 1804 Preble, already suffering from the illness which was to result in his untimely death in 1807, sailed for home.

Barron, whose most powerful ships in late 1804 were *President* and *Essex,* had entered the US Navy in 1798 at the age of 30. High-quality service under John Barry in *United States* had won him early promotion, but his performance in the Mediterranean belied his first impression in naval service. Barron had little of the natural leadership qualities of Preble, let alone the aggressive instinct and dogged endurance which Preble had displayed throughout his command. Ill health led Barron to conduct a distant blockade of Tripoli throughout the winter of 1804–5, and in the spring he handed over command to John Rodgers – the fifth American commodore appointed in as many years. It therefore fell to Rogers to handle the naval end of the amazing combined operation which, after so many previous failures, brought the war with Tripoli to a successful conclusion in the summer of 1805.

The new plan was the brainchild of William Eaton, American consul in the Mediterranean since 1799. Eaton proposed a flanking march against Tripoli from Egypt, using an Arab army raised in the name of Hamet Pasha, brother and rival of Tripoli's ruler, Yusuf Pasha. Eaton eventually raised a motley force of about 400 Arabs, led by himself with a bodyguard of seven United States Marines. Supported at sea by *Argus, Hornet* and *Nautilus,* detached from the close blockade of Tripoli which Rogers simultaneously resumed, Eaton's 'army' made an arduous 500-mile march along the coast to the Tripolitan outpost of Derna, and captured it on 27 April 1805. Two of the seven US Marines were killed leading the attack.

Unexpectedly assailed by land as well as by sea (he had no idea of the real weakness of Eaton's force) Yusuf Pasha immediately sued for peace. In an unprecedented gesture, Yusuf actualy released the captives from *Philadelphia* before receiving the token ransom which the American negotiators agreed to pay. The less attractive side of the treaty with Yusuf, signed on 4 June 1805, was the prompt American abandonment of Hamet Pasha's cause and of Eaton's 'army' in Derna (though Eaton managed to get Hamet out by sea before Yusuf's warriors reoccupied Derna). Apart from this disagreeable flash of *realpolitik,* the United States could claim to have won through to 'peace with honour' in their five-year struggle against the Corsairs of Tripoli.

The US Navy had learned much from the conflict, not only in practice but in theory. Bainbridge and his fellow captives had put their 19-month incarceration to excellent use, studying their trade with debates and lecturers – the 'University of the Prison,' in

which a leading name was that of David Porter. And it is certain that without the considerable expansion of the American fleet during the war with Tripoli, the US Navy would have been in far worse condition to face its next major trial: the 'War of 1812' with Britain.

By no means all of the maritime outrages which led to the Anglo-American War of 1812 were British-inspired. This is the incident of 16 May 1811 in which the USS *President* chased and battered the British sloop HMS *Little Belt* in the belief that she was a marauding frigate.

The War of 1812 was declared by the United States under the slogan 'Free Trade and Sailors' Rights.' Like the 'quasi-war' with France in the late 1790s, it resulted from American determination to pursue neutral trade and profit in a world at war, defying two superpowers each of which was trying to blockade the other into starvation at the cost of excluding neutral trade. Maritime grievances between the United States and Britain dated back even before the outbreak of the Revolutionary War in 1792-93. Though the US Navy also used flogging to enforce discipline, and continued to do so until 1861, the far harsher British naval discipline made American ships natural havens for British deserters, at a rate of about 2,500 per year. The British resented American refusal to give up such deserters on demand; the United States equally resented the peremptory British habit of stopping American ships to search for deserters and, as likely as not, forcibly impress 'volunteers' into the Royal Navy.

An early example of these tensions occurred in June 1807, when *Chesapeake* sailed from Norfolk, Virginia for the Mediterranean under James Barron. Even though this was a peacetime cruise, it soon proved that she was in no condition to cope with unexpected trouble. Off Cape Henry, *Chesapeake* was pounced on by the British frigate HMS *Leopard,* whose captain demanded the right to search for four British deserters. When Barron refused, *Leopard* opened fire, killing three and wounding 18; *Chesapeake,* her decks still cluttered with stores, was unable to defend herself. Barron surrendered, the British boarded her and hauled off four American crewmen identified as deserters. Though the '*Chesapeake* Incident' predictably aroused American public outrage, it was the end of Barron's active career, crowning his lacklustre performance in the Mediterranean. Suspended from duty for five years (though found not guilty of cowardice), Barron spent them with the French Navy, but was refused another command when he returned to the United States after the outbreak of war.

*Chesapeake's* humiliation nevertheless gave timely warning of the likely penalty for unpreparedness by American warships and in the next Anglo-American naval incident of note, four years later, it was a very different story. In May 1811 Rodgers took *President* to sea to warn off the British frigate HMS *Guerrière,* which had been impressing American seamen off New York. Late on 16 May Rodgers sighted and chased a British warship which he believed to be *Guerrière* and came up with her after dark. An exchange of hails was followed by a totally one-sided gun action in favour of *President,* with each side subsequently accusing the other of having fired first. Daylight revealed that the British warship was not a frigate at all, but the puny 20-gun sloop HMS *Little Belt.* With a firepower advantage of nearly three to one, *President* was virtually unscathed but *Little Belt* was badly cut up, with 11 dead and 21 wounded. Rodgers was exonerated by the subsequent Court of Enquiry, but the '*Little Belt* Incident' did nothing to modify Britain's high-handed attitude towards American shipping and neutrality.

These two incidents did not mean that British and American warships were invariably poised to fly at each others' throats; in the last five years of peace, there were occasional courteous exchanges between warships of the rival navies. In one such encounter, Captain Isaac Hull of *Constitution* and Captain James Dacres of *Guerrière,* over a glass of wine, discussed the fighting qualities of each other's ship and good-humoredly wagered a hat on which would win in a single-ship action. That friendly bet on a theoretical encounter was destined to become grim reality only two months after the outbreak of war, reluctantly declared by President James Madison (who had succeeded Jefferson in 1809) on 18 June 1812.

Though American myth naturally prefers to cast the War of 1812 as the American David again gallantly defying the bullying British Goliath, as in the War of Independence, the reality was somewhat different. In 1775 the British Government had not been willing to negotiate reasonably on every American grievance, as it was in 1812. There was a good deal more greed in the American declaration of war in 1812 than Americans like to remember. The 1810 census had shown that the population of the United States, at 7,239,881, was about two and a half times greater than it had been in 1783; conquering British Canada, with its population of half a million protected by no more than 4,000 British regular troops, seemed an easy prospect. It was all very well for the 'War Hawks' in Congress (a term with a disconcertingly modern ring) to claim that Britain was again locked in war with the whole of Europe, and that conditions were ripe for another British humiliation. But this was a false comparison: in the early 1780s American victory had been clinched by the French battle fleet. In June 1812, nearly seven years had passed since British naval superiority had been secured by Nelson's destruction of the French battle fleet at Trafalgar.

Of course there was an equal excess of confidence on the British side in 1812. After Trafalgar, a total victory over 33 Franco-Spanish ships of the line, it was impossible to envisage defeat by a navy consisting only of a handful of frigates, without a single ship of the line. After their roll of naval victories since the outbreak of the French Revolutionary War nearly 20 years before, few Britons remembered the occasions when isolated British warships had been beaten fair and square, in untimely encounters with superior American warships, back in the War of Independence. There was altogether too much over-confidence on both sides in June 1812, and both sides soon paid for it in full measure.

Madison's administration had even less idea of how to fight a naval war with Britain than the Continental Congress had had in 1775. At one stage he toyed with the idea of keeping all American warships in home waters to serve as floating batteries, but happily Captains Bainbridge and Stewart, who happened to be in the new capital of Washington at the time, talked him out of it. Madison's biggest problem was that the mercantile states of New England, cradle of the American Revolution, were firmly opposed to war and virtually opted out of it, trading with Canada and Britain throughout. As a result the main American squadron was at New York, under Rodgers: the frigates *President, United States, Essex* (completing repairs at the outbreak of war), and *Congress,* with the sloop *Hornet* and the brig *Argus.* The nearest British force was at Halifax, under Vice-Admiral Sawyer; it was known to consist of the ship-of-the-line *Africa* (64 guns) and about seven frigates, and Rodger's main concern was to get to sea and start raiding before the British force could come south and blockade him at New York. He sailed at once, leaving Porter in *Essex* to complete his repairs.

It was a sound move, but the first American brush with the British was not propitious. Only 36 hours after leaving New York, Rodgers sighted the British frigate *Belvidera* and gave chase in *President*. The excellently-handled *Belvidera,* though damaged, got clean away to Halifax with news of the American strength, while Rodgers was left to nurse a broken leg caused by the bursting of one of *President's* maindeck guns. He then set off on a 10-week Atlantic cruise, sweeping as far as Madeira, during which no more than seven small prizes were taken.

Meanwhile, the land war had opened disastrously. Without support from New England, the ambitious triple invasion of Canada planned with such confidence by the 'War Hawks' collapsed in ruin. The Great Lakes were commanded by British flotillas. The Indians beaten at the battle of Tippecanoe in November 1811 rallied, under their great leader Tecumseh, to the British. After the briefest foray into Canada, General William Hull retreated to Detroit. There he surrendered to a handful of British regulars on 16 August, appalled by the Indian threat to massacre the 5,000 American civilians in his charge. This disaster was echoed by setbacks at sea in the first two months of the war, with *Nautilus* sailing straight into British hands off New York; the brig *Viper* was captured off Havana after a seven-week cruise with no prizes, as was her sister-ship *Vixen*.

After such a dismal prelude the remarkable run of American naval victories which began in the third week of August 1812 appeared all the more dazzling, the news of the first breaking hard on the heels of the gloom caused by the fall of Detroit.

The first victory was that of Porter in *Essex* over the sloop HMS *Alert* on 13 August. By the time *Essex* was ready for sea after the departure of Rodgers, *Belvidera* had been chased off station and New York was momentarily unwatched. Porter therefore got away unmolested on 3 July and headed for Bermuda, planning to harrass British convoys in the Caribbean. He had the luck to fall in with seven troopships escorted by the light frigate HMS *Minerva,* eluded her in a well-judged night attack, and captured a troopship with 200 soldiers. He took eight further prizes before falling in with *Alert* on the 13th and smashing her with two broadsides; the British captain surrendered to avoid a useless slaughter. The captured *Alert,* once repaired, was used as a cartel to convey prisoners to Halifax under parole while *Essex* headed for home, taking a tenth prize before returning to New York on 7 September.

Captain William Bainbridge, whose timely eloquence dissuaded President Madison from keeping the warships of the US fleet in home waters to serve as floating batteries.

The news of the capture of *Alert* by Porter broke a week after Isaac Hull – nephew of the man who had surrendered Detroit – had brought *Constitution* into Boston with stunning news of his own: a crushing victory over the British frigate *Guerrière* on 19 August. Hull had sailed from Annapolis on the Chesapeake three weeks after the declaration of war and had headed north, hoping to join Rodgers whom he knew to be at sea. But what he actually sighted on 17 July was the British squadron from Halifax, commanded by Captain Philip Broke: the 64-gun *Africa* and frigates *Guerrière, Belvidera, Shannon* and *Aeolus.* A prolonged spell of still weather left *Constitution* becalmed just outside gunshot and an agonising three-day chase ensued under tow, with boats' crews trying to close within range on the British side and escape on the American. Hull, using the superior technique of kedging (winching his ship up to alternating anchors instead of relying solely on the muscle-power of his boats' crews) edged *Constitution* gradually out of reach and, as soon as the wind returned, sailed clean out of sight of his pursuers. It was a convincing demonstration of American seamanship and the impressive sailing qualities of the US Navy's big frigates.

After escaping from Broke, Hull put in at Boston to replenish the 10 tons of water pumped overside during the chase. He then headed for Nova Scotia and the Gulf of St Lawrence, beat up British shipping for just long enough to draw Broke's squadron north from American waters, then set off south to shift his hunting-ground to Bermuda – the natural tactical thinking of a born commerce raider. But on 19 August, a month after they had last been seen vanishing astern of *Constitution,* a familiar set of topsails was sighted. They were those of *Guerrière,* detached by Broke to return to Halifax. Now that prewar bet between Hull and Dacres was put to the test, with much more at stake than a hat.

Dacres' only real hope was that superior British gun drill, yielding a higher rate of fire, would cancel *Constitution's* much heavier broadside (about 684 lbs to *Guerrière's* 556). In going for speed, however, the British frigate's accuracy suffered badly, her all-important first broadside missing completely. As it happened, the decisive factors were superior American ship-handling and strength of construction; it was in this fight that *Constitution* earned the deathless nickname of 'Old Ironsides' from her apparent immunity to British shot. After a 15-minute cannonade, broadside to broadside, *Constitution* had only suffered minor damage aloft and light casualties; *Guerrière's* casualty rate was far higher, due to splinter wounds from her smashed scantlings. Her mizzenmast was the first to go, slowing *Guerrière* and allowing Hull to swing *Constitution* across his enemy's bows, raking *Guerrière* from stem to stern with two devastating broadsides. For a moment the ships hung clipped together, with *Guerrière's* bowsprit caught in *Constitution's* mizzen rigging. The last British guns able to fire and bear started a fire in Hull's cabin, but this was quickly extinguished. Then the ships tore free, leaving *Guerrière* a dismasted, beaten wreck. Having done all that duty demanded, Dacres wisely surrendered. The two captains met again, and Dacres offered his sword to the victor. Hull declined, telling Dacres to keep it after such a gallant fight – 'but I will trouble you for that hat.'

*Guerrière* was so badly damaged that Hull had no choice but to take off the British wounded and survivors (*Guerrière* had lost 78 killed and wounded out of 272) and set her ablaze. Instead of continuing his cruise and hoping to offload his captive passengers on to prizes, Hull humanely headed for Boston where he arrived, to wild acclaim, on 30 August. Viewed coldly, ship for ship and gun for gun, the *Constitution/Guerrière* fight was not that remarkable an achievement – certainly not when compared with the circumstances of the *Bon Homme Richard/Serapis* fight back in 1779. What made the capture of the *Guerrière* an historic event was its timeliness, instantly dispelling the gloom caused by the preceding run of American failures. Arguably the most surprising aftermath of the encounter was the fact that Hull was never given another fighting command, though he lived until 1843 – yet another instance of the Department of the Navy's misuse of its best commanders.

The next encounter was unique, the only occasion when an American warship has captured an enemy warship, only to be captured itself within hours. Fleeting though it proved, the new victory was won by Master Commandant Jacob Jones in the sloop *Wasp,* working the Gulf Stream trade route between Halifax and the West Indies. On 18 October Jones sighted a British convoy escorted by the brig HMS *Frolic,* commanded by Captain Whinyates. Both warships had suffered rigging damage in a storm on the previous day but *Frolic* had come off worst, having her mainyard brought down. This naturally proved a considerable handicap in the ensuing action, competently won by Jones with his superior fire-power. *Wasp* was still standing by *Frolic,* with the American prize crew making repairs in the captured brig, when the British ship-of-the-line *Poictiers* (a '74') hove into view, heading for Bermuda. Because of their storm and battle damage, plus boisterous weather conditions which perfectly suited a ship-of-the-line, *Frolic* was soon recaptured and *Wasp* taken. Jones and his men, however, were returned to New York under cartel and were received as heroes, their surrender forgotten in the light of their earlier victory. At least they

had managed to tie down a vital British '74' to the tedious and distracting job of rounding up *Frolic's* convoy and seeing it safely to Bermuda.

Meanwhile two other sorties had been made by Rodgers with *Congress* and *President,* and Decatur with *United States,* with *Argus* in company. This imposing force sailed from Boston on 8 October, dispersing three days later once it was safely out to sea. Rodgers again had bad luck in not falling-in with any major convoys on a huge Atlantic sweep – south of the Azores to the Cape Verdes, and back by way of Bermuda – which lasted to the end of the year. In all this time he took only two prizes, though one of them turned out to be a bullion ship with nearly $200,000 on board. It was Decatur who had the real luck. After parting company with Rodgers on 11 October he headed towards Madeira in *United States* while *Argus* turned south to work the South American coast. Approaching Madeira on 25 October he sighted the British frigate *Macedonian* (38), heading west to join the British West Indies Command. To Decatur's relish, *Macedonian's* Captain Carden wasted no time to coming in to attack.

Carden was foolish in doing this, for *United States* held all the hitting-power. Her broader beam made her a much steadier gun platform and her heavier guns had a longer range. *Macedonian's* only real advantages were greater speed and the upwind position or 'weather gauge,' possession of which enabled the owner to dictate the opening stage of the battle. Both these advantages were thrown away by Carden's gallant but stupid attempt to close the range at once, enabling *United States* to maul *Macedonian* to a wreck. *Macedonian* lost 100 men killed and wounded (over one-third of her crew); her mizzenmast, maintopmast and foretopmast were shot away, and 12 of her guns were knocked out. *United States* suffered only 12 casualties overall and her most serious dam-

The American sloop *Wasp*, at right of picture, crosses the bows of the British brig HMS *Frolic* (18 October 1812). The artist has missed the important fact that the beaten British ship had gone into action minus her mainyard, as a result of storm damage, but the superior seamanship of the American raking attack is still clear to see.

age was the loss of her mizzen topgallant mast. Decatur did not have to prolong the slaughter. He indicated that he was able and ready to take up a raking position and Carden, now completely unable to defend himself, surrendered.

Unlike *Guerrière, Macedonian* had been refitted shortly before the action. Though holed below the waterline, she still had two lower masts standing and was not in a sinking condition. Decatur therefore transferred a prize crew which succeeded in bringing *Macedonian* into Newport under jury rig, himself returning to New England with *United States*. Repaired and refitted at New York, *Macedonian* became the first command of Jacob Jones, former commander of *Wasp*, who was promoted Captain on his return from British captivity – another notable contrast with the churlish treatment accorded to Isaac Hull.

Decatur's capture of *Macedonian* coincided with the second war cruise of *Constitution*. She was now commanded by Bainbridge, who sailed from Boston on 26 October with the sloop *Hornet*. The latter was commanded by Master Commandant James Lawrence, noted for having been Decatur's second-in-com-

Another view of the duel between USS *United States* and HMS *Macedonian* in October 1812. Apart from her short-torn sails the US frigate appears unscathed as the rigging of her British opponent dissolves in ruin.

mand during the burning of *Philadelphia* at Tripoli. Bainbridge had hoped to sail in collaboration with Porter and *Essex,* but the latter was not ready for sea until a fortnight later. Bainbridge therefore forwarded rendezvous instructions to Porter and sailed without him, planning to work the South American trade route. At Bahia, Bainbridge left Lawrence to blockade the British sloop *Bonne Citoyenne* (which was laden with bullion and therefore sensibly declined Bainbridge's challenge to come out and fight *Hornet*). On 29 December he was cruising offshore, on the lookout for possible prizes, when he sighted the British frigate HMS *Java,* under the command of Captain Lambert.

Lambert was not on the hunt for American raiders as he was on his way out to the East Indies, carrying a reinforcement draft of seamen, naval building materials, the new Governor-General of Bombay and several civilian passengers. He was calling at Bahia to top up with water before picking up the south-west trades for the long haul down to St Helena and the Cape of Good Hope. Like *Guerrière, Java* was French-built (the former *Renommée,* captured off Madagascar in May 1811). Like *Macedonian,* she was newly refitted and faster than her more powerful American opponent. Bainbridge countered this by setting his maincourse and forecourse (the big 'driving' sails, usually kept clewed-up during action). The gamble paid off. With her edge in maneuverability blunted, *Java* was unable to get across *Constitution's* bows or stern for a raking attack; instead she was subjected to another merciless American cannonade.

One of the most devastating encounters of the War of 1812: the attack by USS *Hornet* on the British brig HMS *Peacock* which left the British ship defenceless and sinking in less than 15 minutes.

This was the toughest fight yet, with *Java* shooting away *Constitution's* wheel and forcing Bainbridge to con his ship with a chain of men passing orders to crews on the relieving tackle at the tiller. Then *Java's* headsails were left dangling when her jib-boom and bowsprit were shattered – a crippling loss of maneuverability. Lambert's only chance now was to close and board, but *Java's* faltering lunge at *Constitution* missed, enabling *Constitution* to rake her twice, bow and stern. Lambert fell mortally wounded and *Java's* First Lieutenant, Chads, accepted the inevitable and surrendered. An important American bonus was the capture of *Java's* codebooks and despatches which Chads, who was also wounded, had no time to drop overside. Bainbridge himself had been wounded twice. He decided that the battered *Java* was not worth saving, and burned her on 31 December. After landing his prisoners at San Salvador (where Captain Lambert died of his wounds) Bainbridge left Lawrence to continue the cruise and returned to Boston, arriving on 27 February 1813.

Three weeks later, Lawrence brought *Hornet* into Martha's Vineyard with $20,000 in captured bullion and news of yet another victory, which he had won on 24 February. Lawrence had kept *Hornet* at the mousehole outside Bahia, watching *Bonne Citoyenne,* until the arrival of the British '74' *Montagu* forced him to escape north-east along the Brazilian coast. As he prepared to round the 'corner' of Brazil at Pernambuco, Lawrence encountered and took the bullion brig *Resolution,* then headed for the Guianas. His plan was to seek what he might devour along the Guianan coast, then try out the West Indies on the voyage home. Off the mouth of the Demerara River in British Guiana, *Hornet* had additional luck by falling in with the British brig *Peacock*.

This was an interesting battle in that both ships were armed with carronades: short-range battering guns, known as 'smashers' in the Royal Navy, useless for long-distance sparring and disabling fire. Despite the fact that *Peacock* was a far flimsier vessel than *Hornet,* the British Lieutenant William Peake displayed all the bull-at-a-gate rashness which had undone Carden of *Macedonian* in the fight with *United States*. Peake's rapid approach was suicidal. Much better handled than the British ship, *Hornet* swung in close off *Peacock's* quarter (where hardly a British gun could bear) and hammered her defenseless and sinking in less than 15

The unlucky ship of the US Navy's 'Original Six' frigates: USS *Chesapeake*, captured by HMS *Shannon* on 1 June 1813, under full sail.

minutes. *Peacock* sank so rapidly that she took with her several members of the American prize crew sent across by Lawrence. *Hornet's* triumphant voyage home, with 277 men aboard (127 prisoners above *Hornet's* normal complement) was made in increasing hardship due to water shortage, victors and vanquished suffering alike.

Such was the fifth and last of an unbroken string of American single-ship victories over the Royal Navy, still justly remembered with pride by the US Navy. In these repeated humiliations of the most powerful navy on the planet, it may be said that the US Navy had truly come of age. And yet, lumped together and weighed against the overall war situation, the American naval successes came to very little. They were really only a fivefold fleabite against the massive strength of the Royal Navy – now fully on its guard and hot for revenge – which by February 1813 had hardly begun to deploy its full strength against the United States. The British reinforcements already sent across the Atlantic were formidable enough. Deployed from Halifax to Brazil, it all came to 17 '74s', two 50-gun ships, 27 frigates and 56 sloops, brigs and smaller warships – odds which the US Navy, for all its mood of justified triumph, could never hope to beat.

A British blockade of increasing severity was already withering American coastal trade and communications. The Federal Government was facing bankruptcy, and it was becoming harder and harder to repair and replenish the US Navy's warships between cruises. There was no hope of any early end to the conflict, and no hope of any delivering battle fleet and expeditionary force coming from France, as in 1779-81. The only real comfort was that with Napoleon still unbeaten in Germany (despite the disastrous Russian adventure of June-December 1812) the main British Army was still pinned to Europe. Until this situation changed, the British would be unable to invade from Canada. If the United States could win command of the Lakes, the British would not be able to invade at all.

In 1813 the balance swung back in favour of the British. Rodgers sailed again with *President* and *Congress* on 23 April, but took only 12 mediocre prizes in five months. At New York, *Chesapeake* was painfully refitting after a four-month cruise in which only three prizes had been taken. Stewart in *Constellation* lay blockaded at Norfolk by a powerful British squadron; *United States* and *Macedonian,* under similar blockade in Long Island Sound, were soon abandoned and their

Security won on the Canadian frontier: Commodore Perry's victory in the battle of Lake Erie (10 September 1813).

crews transferred to other ships. Then, on 1 June 1813, came the famous fight outside New York between Captain Philip Broke of HMS *Shannon* and *Chesapeake,* now commanded by Lawrence. *Chesapeake's* men had only stayed with the ship in the hope of getting the pay due to them. Higher American morale might conceivably have checked the fury with which the British boarded *Chesapeake* and captured her, virtually intact, after less than 15 minutes' fight. Lawrence died with another of the US Navy's immortal slogans on his lips – 'Don't give up the ship'! Apart from Rodgers, only Commander William Allen in *Argus* managed to slip the British blockade, in June 1813; after a promising cruise in the Irish Sea, destroying 19 ships in 31 days he was captured off St David's Head in August 1813 by the British brig HMS *Pelican*.

The only notable American naval victory in 1813 was the battle of Lake Erie on 10 September, which took place nearly 500 miles from the open sea and was won by Commodore Oliver Hazard Perry. Both the British and American flotillas consisted of two square-rigged brigs and a motley collection of schooners and gunboats, all built on the Lake from local green timber. Perry's flagship *Lawrence* was disabled at the start of the battle but he shifted his flag to *Niagara,* resumed the attack, and won through by superior weight of shot. Twelve months later, on 11 September 1814, a second American victory on Lake Champlain, won by Commodore Thomas Macdonough in his flagship *Saratoga,* rendered the Canadian frontier virtually secure. The solid gain of the Lake Champlain victory amply compensated for the British 'hate raid' of 24 August 1814, in which Washington had been burned. Three days after Lake Champlain, the gallant defence of Fort McHenry not only foiled the British attempt to give Baltimore the same treatment but also inspired Francis Scott Key to write *The Star-Spangled Banner,* in memory of how:

'... the rockets' red glare, the bombs bursting in air, gave proof through the night that our flag was still there.'

It was symbolic that the US Navy's proudest achievement in 1813-14 was the 17-month cruise of David Porter in *Essex,* although it did nothing whatsoever to relax the tightening economic stranglehold inflicted by the British blockade. After narrowly failing to make rendezvous with Bainbridge in December 1812, Porter decided single-handedly to extend the commerce war to the Pacific. This gave *Essex* a unique 'double': back in 1800 it had been the first American warship to enter the Indian Ocean by passing the Cape of Good Hope, and was now the first to enter the Pacific via Cape Horn. Displaying leadership, ingenuity and professional skills of the very highest, Porter kept *Essex* operational in the Pacific from February 1813 to March 1814, using a captured vessel renamed *Essex Junior* as a

At the crisis of the Lake Erie battle, Perry defiantly shifts his flag from USS *Lawrence* to USS *Niagara* before resuming his attack.

tender; but in all those months he only managed to take 15 prizes. Crippled by weather damage, *Essex* was finally brought to action by the British frigate HMS *Phoebe* off Valparaiso on 28 March 1814. It was the bloodiest single-ship action of the war, with Porter only surrendering after over half his crew had become casualties: 89 American dead, and another 66 wounded. Among the survivors was 13-year-old Midshipman David Glasgow Farragut, destined half a century later to become the foremost admiral of the American Civil War.

By the time *Essex* fought her last battle, Anglo-American peace negotiations had been under way for months. It was obvious that with Napoleon defeated at last (he finally abdicated on 11 April 1814) neither Britain nor the United States had anything to gain from a stand-off war which might drag on for years, with the rest of the world reaping the profits of peace. Though the Treaty of Ghent formally ended hostilities on 24 December 1814, it took time for the news to arrive in American waters. By the time it did, a final British amphibious assault had been repulsed by General Jackson at New Orleans on 8 January. Attempting to break out from Long Island Sound in *President,* Decatur had been captured on 16 January by HMS *Endymion, Pomone* and *Tenedos.* But the last word had gone to Stewart in *Constitution,* who on 20 February 1815 captured both the sloop HMS *Levant* and the corvette HMS *Cyane* off Madeira. To a large extent these final actions perfectly symbolised the futility of the Anglo-American conflict, fortunately destined to be the last of its kind.

One of the lesser-known axioms of naval history is that when peace breaks out, politicians usually overstep the mark when reducing their country's navy to a reasonable peacetime strength. It has been shown above (p.00) how this syndrome had, in the 1780s, resulted in the early liquidation of the first Continental Navy. Between 1815 and 1818 the gigantic British fleet was reduced by two-thirds, and its manpower dropped from 145,000 to 19,000. It is easy to imagine the effects on the diminutive US Navy of peacetime economies on a similar scale; but in 1815 the US Navy was lucky. Encouraged by the disappearance of US warships from the Mediterranean during the War of 1812, the Barbary Corsairs had resumed their attacks on American shipping, this time with Algiers taking the lead.

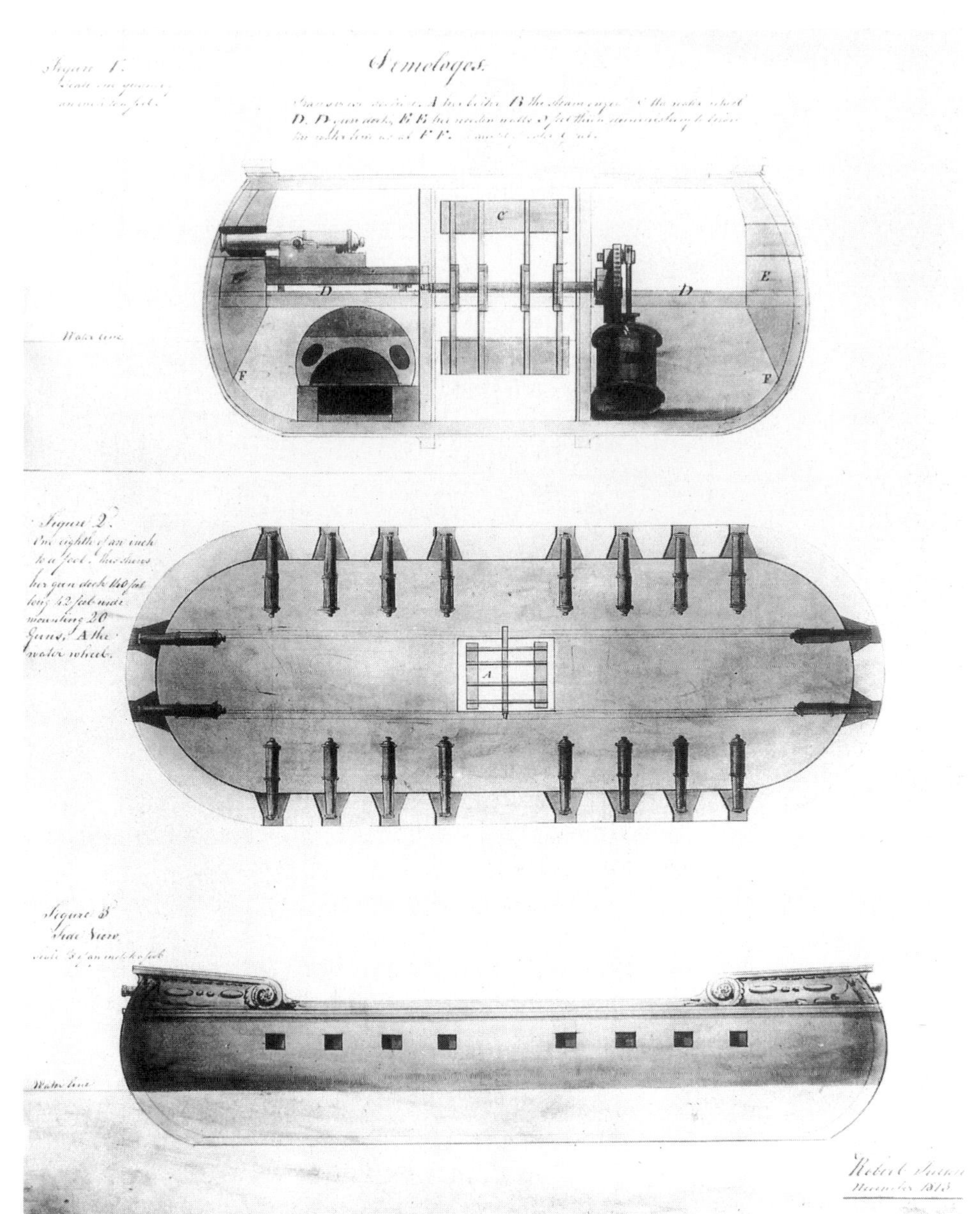

With memories of the Tripolitan War still barely ten years old, the Madison administration reacted with energy and promptitude. The right man was picked for the job, and given all the force and discretion he needed. Decatur sailed in May 1815 with a squadron ten strong (including the refitted British captures, *Guerrière* and *Macedonian*). This time there was no weak-kneed bargaining at the outset: Decatur settled the business

*Above: Demologos* (renamed *Fulton*), the US Navy's first steam 'warship', designed 1813. *Below*: End of an epic war cruise: USS *Essex* is captured by HMS *Phoebe* and *Cherub* off Valparaiso, 28 March 1814.

ENDYMION

*Above:* The US squadron triumphantly cruises past Gibraltar in October 1815 after its resounding defeat of the Barbary Corsairs.

*Left*: 'A View of the Gallant Action between his Majestys ship the ENDYMION and the United States Ship the PRESIDENT' – 15 January 1815. Trying to break out from Long Island Sound, Decatur had damaged his ship in a temporary grounding on the eve of the action.

within ten weeks. On 17 June 1815, Captain Downes of *Epervier* (Porter's former First Lieutenant in *Essex*) captured the Algerine flagship *Mashuda,* the Algerine admiral being killed in the fight. Decatur then entered Algiers harbor and dictated peace terms, including a healthy cash payment of reparations to the United States; this was paid within the week. He then moved on to Tunis and Tripoli, in each case achieving the same result. By the end of June 1815 Decatur was free to return in triumph to the United States. By waging one of the briefest, most economical and effective naval campaigns in American history, he had safeguarded American Mediterranean commerce for the first decade of peace.

Decatur's success in the Mediterranean confirmed every essential point of President Madison's peacetime message to Congress, in which Madison affirmed that 'a certain degree of preparation for war is not only indispensable to avert disaster in the onset, but affords also the best security for the continuance of peace.' He was confident that Congress would in future continue to 'provide for the maintenance of an adequate regular force,' with particular regard to 'the gradual advance of the naval establishment.' Nor were these words spoken in vain. Twenty-one years after its foundation by George Washington, the US Navy had indeed come of age and the need for its continued maintenance was self-evident.

After 1815 there could be no doubting that the future of the United States, with immediate regard to the early break-up of the Spanish and Portuguese empires in Central and South America, would largely depend on the effectiveness of American sea power. The 'Monroe Doctrine' promulgated by Madison's successor in December 1823, warning off any European inclination to intervene in the development of the Americas, was less a statement of defiance than of confidence in this new role.

# 3: THE UNION PRESERVED

1823-1865

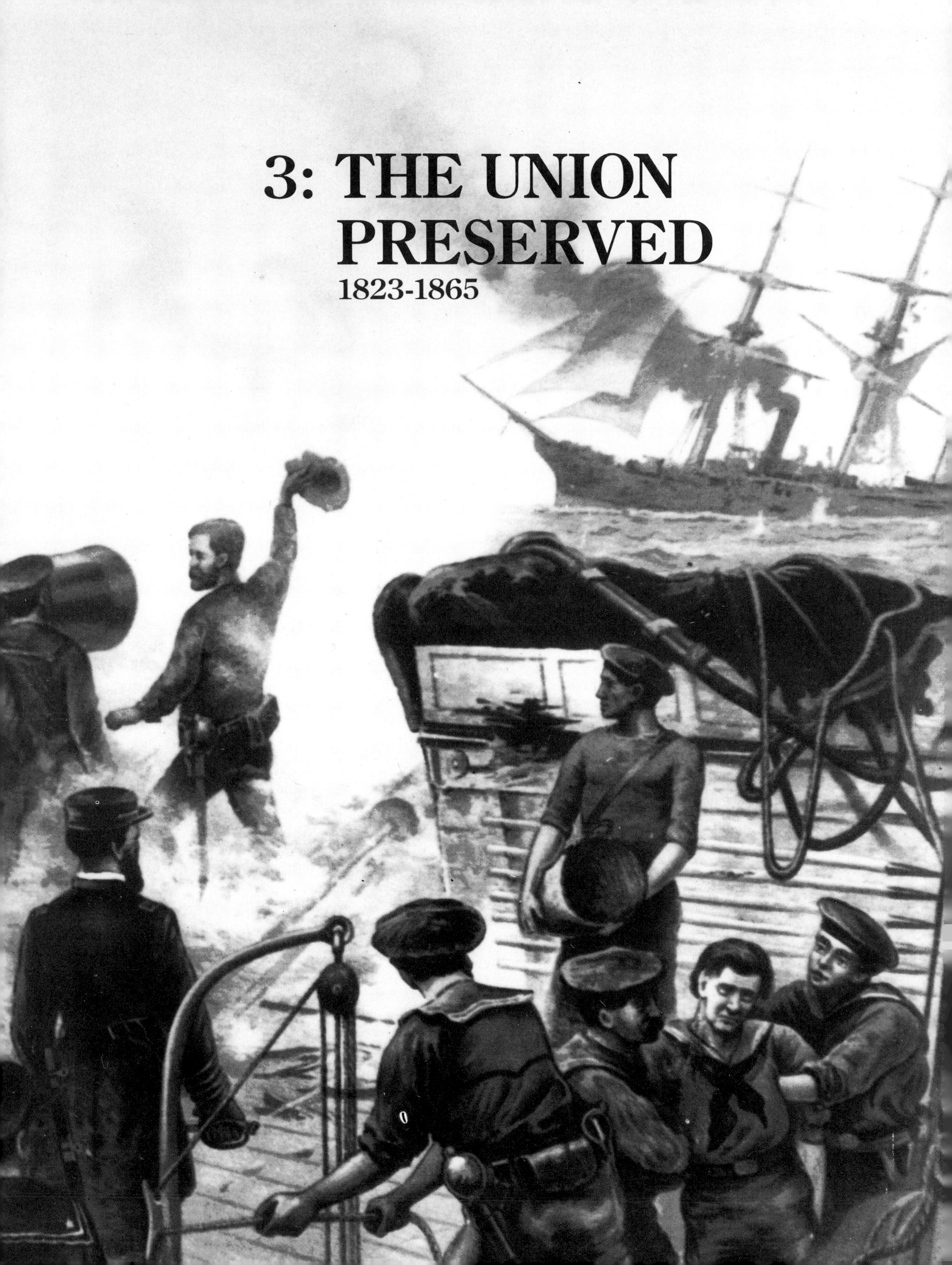

During the half-century which followed the peace of 1815, the US Navy enjoyed several advantages over its enormous British counterpart, and profited by them.

First and foremost, the US Navy was a young service. It was thus largely free of the more unfortunate encrustations of tradition which, throughout the 19th century, opposed change and sapped the fighting efficiency of the Royal Navy. To take just one example, the US Navy had gone into its first trial against France with nothing more inhibiting in the way of tradition than the example set by the sailors of the War of Independence. In 1797, on the other hand, the morale of the British fleet was shaken from top to bottom by widespread mutinies caused by miserable pay and ferocious discipline, very largely unchanged from the days of Cromwell in the 1650s. Not the least practical benefit of American independence was the US Navy's natural tendency, right from the beginning, to regard the Royal Navy as a useful model rather than an object for slavish imitation.

This tendency was, of course, most marked in the field of the technological improvements which completely transformed every class of warship by the end of the century. The US Navy was in the forefront of experiments with steam-powered vessels; then of steam-powered warships driven by screw rather than by paddlewheel; with guns firing explosive shell rather than solid shot; with ships protected by armor plate. The US Navy ended the century pioneering the fighting submarine, having joined with the British and French navies in rejecting submarines 80 years previously. From the 1860s the British repeatedly found themselves in the embarrassing position of building warships for foreign customers which were better vessels than those serving in, or even envisaged for, the Royal Navy. It was an embarrassment from which the US Navy was spared.

Certainly, during the years before trans-oceanic voyages under steam became truly practicable (about 1830-70), the US Navy had a vociferous cross-section of anti-steam diehards. The more vehement advocates – with no little justification in the early years – despised the newfangled steam 'teakettles' as detrimental to seamanship and pledged undying faith in 'ships of wood and men of iron.' But American naval conservatism never had the time to grow the deep roots of its British counterpart. It was not a century, and the United States was not a country – with its phenomenal growth in territory, population and industry – which gladly suffered resistance to change. The American Civil War duly furnished the most devastating proof.

The US Navy enjoyed another important advantage over the British after 1815. Already swollen to massive proportions by the Napoleonic Wars, the Royal Navy's Admirals' and Captains' Lists set like concrete after 1815, due largely to the refusal of veteran officers to die off and make room for younger men. The results were naturally inimical to change and reform as well as being frustrating to new talent. The Royal Navy's performance in its next major test, the Crimean War of 1854-56, was predictably lackluster and, in at least one instance, positively unbalanced. (The British Rear-Admiral in the Far East, who had waited a soul-destroying *39 years* for promotion to the Admirals' List, went mad and shot himself on the eve of his first action in command.)

There was no such stagnation in the US Navy's pool of senior officers after 1815. The American service, until the Civil War, stuck to its original system of selecting 'Flag Officers' from the Captains' List to command the various active squadrons, and the Captains' List was nothing if not fluid. In 1820, for instance, Decatur was killed in a duel with Barron, who had never forgiven Decatur for giving what Barron regarded as malicious evidence during the enquiry into the '*Chesapeake/Leopard* Incident' back in 1807. The duel ended the careers not only of Decatur but of Barron (who otherwise might have hoped for a Flag Officer's command,) and of Bainbridge, censured for his insistence on acting as Decatur's second. Perry, the hero of Lake Erie, had died of Yellow Fever the year before, a victim of Venezuela's fight for independence from Spanish rule. (Perry had been on a mission up the Orinoco to persuade Simon Bolivar to refrain from attacking American ships with Venezuelan privateers.

Porter, of *Essex* fame, had the distinction of commanding the US Navy's first experimental steam 'warship,' the paddle-wheeler *Fulton,* in 1815. He then joined Hull and Rodgers as the first three members of the Board of Navy Commissioners. In 1823 Porter was appointed Flag Officer West Indies, but his excessive zeal in suppressing piracy in those waters (always a task rife with international sensitivities) earned him a court-martial and reprimand. He resigned from the US Navy in 1826 and served for the next three years as commander-in-chief of

*Previous pages:* Gunners of USS *Kearsarge* cheer as the Confederate raider *Alabama*, battered to defeat, sinks off Cherbourg in June 1864.

the Mexican Navy. The last 12 years of Porter's eventful life were spent as US Minister to Turkey; he died at Istanbul in 1843. Of the 'first-generation' heroes of the US Navy still alive in 1815, this left only John Rodgers, Thomas Macdonough (the victor of Lake Champlain) and Charles Stewart. Macdonough died in 1825 after a final seagoing command as Flag Officer Mediterranean and was succeeded in the Mediterranean by Rodgers, subsequently reappointed as a Navy Commissioner and serving until 1837, when he resigned on grounds of ill health; he died the following year. Charles Stewart, born in 1778 – who had first gone to sea as a merchant-service cabin boy before Washington's creation of the US Navy in the 1790s – alone lived on to become the US Navy's immensely respected 'grand old man,' outliving Isaac Hull, who died in 1843. A special Act of Congress created the post of Senior Flag Officer for Stewart in 1859; when the Civil War broke out in 1861 he lamented the fact that he was too old to go back to sea. It was fitting that he was appointed Rear-Admiral (retired) on the new List in 1862. He lived to see the victory of the Union he had served so well and died, full of honours, in 1869.

A healthy early clearance at the top of the Captains' List was matched by the service longevity of the frigates, the US Navy's staple warships. Though Congress had authorized the building of three ships-of-the-line during the War of 1812, these were never completed. Until the outbreak of the Civil War in 1861, frigates remained the heaviest warships in the American fleet – one of the most impressive characteristics of the US Navy, from its earliest years, being its knack of repeatedly renovating heavy warships for long-term service, giving the American taxpayer excellent value for money. (The most remarkable modern instance of this technique has been the appearance of the reactivated Second World War battleship *New Jersey* amid the 6th Fleet support force off Beirut in 1983-84.)

Two of the 'original six' frigates had been taken during the War of 1812: *Chesapeake* and *President.* Of the surviving four, *Congress* was broken up in 1834, the deterioration of her hull too far advanced to permit reconstruction. A second *Congress* was launched in 1841. A similar fate would have overtaken *Constitution,* condemned as unseaworthy in 1828, had there not been an immediate public outcry against the idea of breaking up or selling 'Old Ironsides.' After reconstruction, *Constitution* returned to service in 1835 and remained with the fleet until 1860, when she was relegated to sail-training duties. *Constellation's* record was easily the best: she was still at sea, in the Mediterranean, when the Civil War broke out. Today lovingly preserved as national shrines, *Constitution* and *Constellation* are the only two frigates of the Napoleonic era left in the world.

The US Mediterranean squadron sails from Port Mahon in 1823. *Left to right: North Carolina* (flying the pennant of Commodore John Rodgers), frigates *Constitution* and *Brandywine,* and sloops *Erie* and *Ontario.*

*United States* was less fortunate. Unfit for sea in 1861, she fell into Confederate hands when Virginia seceded and was used as a Confederate 'receiving ship', or floating barracks, for the first year of the war. The Confederates burned her when they evacuated Norfolk in the spring of 1862. Her name has never been used since in the US Navy, though twice chosen for 20th century warships (a battle-cruiser and aircraft-carrier, neither of which was completed).

In any event, the survivors of the 'original six' frigates served the US Navy well for 40 years after the end of the War of 1812. It was not until 1854 that Congress authorized their replacement by six new frigates, named after rivers and powered by auxiliary steam engines. One of these, *Merrimack,* was destined to begin a new chapter in naval history by becoming the world's first fighting ironclad.

Though steam power was widely used in shallow-draught paddlewheelers for inshore work, the US Navy was still predominantly a sailing navy in 1861. So, for that matter, were the leading European fleets, in comparison with which the US Navy was by no means obsolete. It had made the vital transfer from solid shot to explosive shell, pioneered by the French General Paixhans in

the 1820s, and in this respect owed much to the calculations of J.A. Dahlgren, whose massive 'beer-bottle'-shaped guns were adopted in 1859. Once the Dahlgren gun was in service, it was only a matter of time before the US Navy followed the French and British in producing warships protected against explosive shell by armor plate. In the event, the US Navy Department ordered its first two ironclads, *Galena* and *New Ironsides,* in the summer of 1861 – only one year behind the British *Warrior* and two years behind the French *Gloire*. Yet, at the outset of the Civil War, the US Navy consisted of no more than

42 warships of all types.

This modest force had been more than enough for the US Navy's only 'shooting war' since 1815, the Mexican War of 1846-48. In this conflict the Navy's role was secondary to that of the Army: blockade and troop convoy followed by coastal support, one notable action being the forcing of the Tabasco River in 1847. (This was the war in which the US Marine Corps, serving with the Army, earned the second half of the battle honours remembered in the stirring Corps Hymn – 'From the halls of Montezuma to the shores of Tripoli'.) The main objective of the war was the conquest of New Mexico and California, and a squadron rounded Cape Horn to operate off the Californian coast. A leading light in this squadron was Commander Samuel Francis Dupont, born in 1803 at Bergen Point, New Jersey, who had joined the US Navy as a midshipman in 1815. In the Mexican War he distinguished himself as commander of the sloop *Cyane* in operations off San Diego and in the Gulf of California.

Apart from playing an active part in the crushing of piracy in the Caribbean in the 1820s, the US Navy's most enduring 'police duty' down to 1861 was the pursuit and

*Above left:* The steam frigate USS *Merrimack* as completed, before her half-burning and reconstruction as a mastless ironclad by the Confederates. *Below*: Union punch – an 11-inch Dahlgren gun on its slide-pivot mounting in an unidentified Northern warship during the Civil War.

interception of slavers. These operations were not limited to the African coast: they extended to the Caribbean and the Gulf, covering the slavers' home run to the markets of the Southern States. Anti-slavery patrols increased after the Northern crusade for the abolition of slavery got under way in the early 1830s – the powder-trail leading to the explosion of the Civil War. In directing anti-slavery patrols, the Federal Government had to walk on eggshells, wary of alienating either the Southern States or countries under whose flags slavers constantly sailed in camouflage. In 1847 the American Colonization Society finally achieved its aim of setting up a colony of freed African slaves on the west coast of Africa, the foundation of the Republic of Liberia. The commander of the American naval squadron entrusted with the job was Commodore Matthew Galbraith Perry, younger brother of the victor of Lake Erie.

Matthew G. Perry's greatest achievement, however, was his pair of missions to Japan (1852-53) in command of the East India Squadron, operating from Hong Kong. Perry's goal, the opening of diplomatic and commercial intercourse between the United States and Japan after centuries of self-imposed Japanese isolation, was brilliantly attained by the Treaty of Kanagawa on 31 March 1854. Much of Perry's success, which no career diplomat could have bettered, was due to the imposing appearance of his famous 'Black Ships': the steam frigates *Susquehanna* and *Mississippi,* aboard which the Japanese representatives were introduced to the delights of whisky and champagne. In his patient and sensitive negotiations, however, Perry took pains to give no impression of intimidation and succeeded by demanding nothing which the Japanese might regard as a national humiliation.

Apart from scoring one of the most important diplomatic breakthroughs of the century, the US Navy made a vital contribution to the drawing science of polar exploration. This was the first sighting and naming of the mainland of the Antartic continent on 30 January 1840 by Commander Charles Wilkes (1798–1877). He was given command of an expedition of six sailing ships, headed by the sloop *Vincennes* and lamentably prepared for the rigors of Antarctic cruising, which sailed south in August 1838. In two Antarctic forays, separated by seven months of laborious repairs at Sydney, Wilkes followed 1,500 miles of the Antarctic coastline. But Antarctic exploration was only one task in an immensely ambitious surveying cruise which extended to the South Pacific Islands and the length of the American western seaboard. It could hardly have been completed without the ferocious discipline upon which Wilkes insisted – and for which he was repaid, on his return to New York in June 1842, by court-martial charges of having exceeded his authority. Though acquitted, his troubles were not over: he was starved of funds with which to publish the full official account of the expedition. For all that – as Mark Twain bears witness in his autobiography, referring to his boyhood on the Mississippi – Wilkes became a national hero. Fame of a very different kind awaited him in the opening year of the Civil War.

Wilkes was not unique in his contribution to the enlargement of maritime knowledge and exploration. An equally famous name was that of Lieutenant Matthew Fontaine Maury (1806–73), who succeeded Wilkes as superintendent of the Navy Department's new Depot of Charts and Instruments. Maury's genius lay in charting and oceanography. In 1847 he produced his classic 'Wind and Current Chart of the North Atlantic', and in the following year produced its practical supplement: *Abstract Log for the Use of American Navigators*. Maury's sailing directions, based on the scientific exploitation of the predictable vagaries of wind and weather, yielded impressive savings in travel time and expense. Up-dated from observations sent him by the masters of ships, Maury's *Abstract Log* was republished in 1850 and 1851, and in 1853 Maury represented the United States at the great international conference on oceanography held in Brussels.

Maury's works earned him international fame and placed the United States in the front rank of maritime science. His system did for oceanography what the Swede Linaeus had done for the classification of animals and plants in the previous century: it provided a comprehensive international framework for the advancement of science. Maury's crowning work, *The Physical Geography of the Sea,* appeared in 1855. Its practical yield was a profile chart of the Atlantic ocean floor between America and Europe, showing the feasibility of linking the continents with a submarine telegraph cable (achieved by the British in 1866). But for all his worldwide fame as a man of science, Maury considered himself first and foremost a Virginian. When, after months of hesitation, Virginia quit the Federal Union and joined the new 'Confederacy' of slave-owning states in April 1861, Maury resigned his commission in the Navy and went with her.

It was a decision taken with varying degrees of sadness and exultation by scores of other American naval officers, of both low and high rank. Some, indeed, jumped the gun, like Captain Franklin Buchanan of Maryland. Born in 1800 and joining the US Navy in 1815, he had risen to become flag captain and chief of staff to Perry during the 'Black Ships' mission to Japan, and had played a key role in the tricky negotiations with the Japanese. For this his reward was his appointment in 1854 as first Superintendent of the new US Naval Academy at Annapolis. When Abraham Lincoln was inaugurated in March 1861, as 16th President of a Union which no longer existed, Buchanan was in command at the Washington Navy Yard; his last duty there consisted of drawing up plans for the Yard's defense. Buchanan resigned his commission in the belief that his home state, Maryland, would follow Virginia into Confederacy, and was not allowed to withdraw his resignation when she failed to do so. This error of judgement went almost unnoticed in the stream of miscalculations made by the Federal Government in 1861. Another seceding Marylander destined for high renown in Confederate naval service was 52-year-old Commander Raphael Semmes, who had distinguished himself at the bombardment of Vera Cruz in the Mexican War. Under the flag of the 'Stars and Bars,' Semmes was destined to become the most effective commerce raider before the German 'raider aces' of the two World Wars.

At its fullest, fleeting strength in the summer of 1861, the Southern Confederacy consisted of 11 states: South Carolina (the first to secede from the Union), Georgia, Florida, Alabama, Louisiana, Mississippi, Texas, Arkansas, Tennessee, North Carolina and Virginia. Apart from Marland the three 'border states' of Kentucky, Missouri and Kansas, despite strong southern sympathies, were kept in the Union, so were the mountain territories which formed the new State of West Virginia. The Confederacy was formed as the ultimate protest against what Southerners considered to be a tyrannical new Republican Administration, pledged to the abolition of slavery and the consequent destruction of the Southern way of life. The hopes of the South rested on the false belief that industrial Europe could not do without Southern cotton, and that the European powers would speedily recognise and support the Confederacy in its bid for independence.

Such foreign aid was vital, for in manpower and industrial resources the Confederacy never stood a chance against the North. The South's population was some 9 millions (of which 3.5 millions were negro slaves) against the 22 millions of the North. As for industrial establishments, the entire South could muster a grand total of no more than 16,896 against 99,564 in the North (with another 6,532 lost to the South in Kentucky and Missouri). In 1860, only one in ten of the total of manufactured articles turned out in the United States had been produced in the South. The same applied to the ships which carried the South's exports to the markets of Europe. Unless supplied from overseas the Confederacy would never be able, from its own resources, to replace the weapons and stores seized from Federal arsenals and shipyards after secession, once these had been expended.

On the other hand, the North could not mobilize all its undoubted resources overnight. The prewar US Army had barely topped 16,000 men in 1860 and 92 percent of them – 183 out of 198 companies of regular troops – were garrissoned in the West along the vast inland frontier. As for the naval front, the Confederacy's coastline stretched some 2,700 miles from the Rio Grande to the Potomac: a blockade-runner's paradise, against an enemy fleet no more than 40 strong at the outset of hostilities. The self-evident fact that the tiny US Navy could not support the Northern garrisons stranded, by secession, in Southern forts led to the firing of the first shots of the war. This was the notorious bombardment of Fort Sumter at Charleston (12–13 April 1861).

Virginia's secession followed hard on the Northern surrender of Fort Sumter, and was the first real Northern defeat of the war. Virginia was not only historically the most prestigious of the Southern States, but the most advanced in population and industry. Richmond became the new Confederate capital. The Navy Yard at Norfolk, on southern shore of the James River estuary, was hastily evacuated by the Federals but they held on to powerful Fort Monroe, north across Hampton Roads at the tip of the Yorktown peninsula. The big frigate *Merrimack* was still refitting at Norfolk and was unable

In the Civil War the North held nearly every card when it came to technological know-how. This imposing group shows Benjamin F. Isherwood (*seated at center*) with personnel of the US Navy's Bureau of Steam Engineering.

to escape to sea; the flustered Yard commander therefore ordered her to be burned and scuttled. This seemed infinitely preferable to allowing *Merrimack* to be captured intact, but it was, in fact, a fateful error of judgement. Though the flames destroyed her as a sailing ship above the waterline, *Merrimack* sank with her main hull and engines intact. Once the Confederates had raised her and pumped her out, they had the makings of a steam-driven ironclad warship – once they had found enough iron.

President Jefferson Davis's Confederate Government, taking up its duties in February 1861, was realistic enough to foresee the deadliness of a prolonged Union blockade, even if only applied at obvious pressure points like Hampton Roads. As Secretary of the virtually non-existent Confederate States Navy, Stephen Mallory of Florida was empowered to build and man ships able to challenge the Union blockade. He knew that any new warships built in the North were bound to follow the current European adoption of ironclad warships, and insisted on 'the wisdom and expediency of fighting with iron against wood.' In this, Mallory was at least one jump ahead of his Northern counterpart, Gideon Welles, whose priority was commandeering enough suitable vessels to be armed as warships and sent out on blockade duties. By the time the US Navy asked shipbuilders to consider ideas for ironclads on the latest European model, it was August 1861 and the Confederate transformation of *Merrimack* was already under way.

With Norfolk separated from the Federal capital by less than 150 miles, it was not long before details of the new Southern ironclad began to filter north to Washington. Even when the wildest rumours were discounted, it was still clear that she was obviously being built for strength, and apparently more strength than that envisaged for the first Northern ironclads, *Galena* and *New Ironsides*. The Confederate Army had already shattered the first clumsy Northern invasion of Virginia, in the first Battle of Bull Run on

21 July 1861. In the shaken aftermath of Bull Run, the prospect of a Confederate ironclad able to break out from Norfolk and maybe even attack Washington was too awful to consider. The result was a panic search for an 'instant' Northern ironclad to set against *Merrimack;* and in October 1861 the US Navy decided that there was no choice but to gamble on the outlandish design for an ironclad 'monitor' (supervisor) put forward by the Swedish-born engineer John Ericsson.

Ericsson was, like Britain's Isambard Kingdom Brunel, one of the most versatile inventive geniuses of the new Industrial Age. By 1841, when he settled in the United States, he had designed railway locomotives and powered fire engines before turning his hand to screw-driven warships, naval shell-firing guns and their antidote: armor plate. In the 1840s he had built the first screw-driven warship for the US Navy (USS *Princeton*) only to fall out of favor when a gun designed (but not built)by him burst on her trials, killing two Cabinet ministers.

Still under a cloud in 1861, Ericsson was nevertheless consulted by Cornelius Bushnell, the Connecticut shipbuilder who had won the contract for *Galena*. It was Bushnell who acted as go-between for Ericsson, urging the Navy Department to consider a cardboard model which looked like nothing on earth. It had no masts; it had no apparent freeboard; it had no conventional broadside of guns, but only two guns in a rotating pillbox turret. All the experts laughed Ericsson's model to scorn. But none of them could produce so much as a sketch for an ironclad which could be built in as little as 100 days (as Ericsson insisted was possible for his 'monitor'), and so wipe out the Confederate lead with *Merrimack*. It was to give the US Navy *something* with which to fight *Merrimack* that Ericsson was contracted, in October 1861, to build USS *Monitor*.

By this time the Confederate Navy had already given embarrassing proof of what it could do with conventional craft. CSS *Sumter* was the former mail packet *Havannah,* armed as a commerce raider with four 24-pounders and an 8-inch swivel gun. Under Commander Raphael Semmes, she slipped out of New Orleans in June 1861, easily dodging the lone USS *Brooklyn* patrolling

Forging the new steam-and-iron Navy – factory chimneys and gaunt new hulls at Washington Navy Yard, DC, about 1862.

the Mississippi approaches, and set off on a six-and-a-half-month commerce-raiding cruise through the Caribbean and Atlantic in which 17 Northern merchantmen were destroyed. By January 1862 the Confederacy had produced a commerce-raiding 'ace' fit to rank with the American naval heroes of the War of Independence and the War of 1812.

Moreover, by the fifth month of *Sumter's* cruise the Confederacy's wildest dream seemed on the verge of realization. The Northern blockade had laid heavy hands on a British ship, bringing the United States and Britain to the brink of war. The culprit was Captain Charles Wilkes, the former Antarctic hero. He had been at Norfolk when Virginia seceded, waiting to take command of *Merrimack;* instead he had had the job of burning her, before being appointed to *San Jacinto* and sent down to the Caribbean to hunt for Confederate blockade-runners. On 8 November 1861 Wilkes had stopped the British mail steamer and arrested two Confederate envoys (Senators James Mason and John Slidell) on their way to plead the Confederate cause in France and Britain.

It has been said that the absence of an Atlantic telegraph cable, providing a natural 'cooling-off period,' kept the peace; this was precisely the sort of act for which the two nations had gone to war in 1812. On both sides of the Atlantic the popular press yelped war-talk, hailing Wilkes as a hero in the United States and calling for direct action to avenge the insult in Britain. The two Governments showed far more sense, Whitehall accepting that Wilkes had not been carrying out deliberate orders and Washington releasing Mason and Slidell without a formal apology to Britain (the arrest having been disavowed). As for Wilkes, he was promoted Acting Rear-Admiral in 1862 and kept in the Caribbean to keep up the pressure on Confederate blockade-runners. (Undoubted success in this role did not, however, save him from court-martial two years later and conviction for 'disobedience, disrespect, insubordination, and conduct unbecoming an officer'. After one year's suspension from duty he was finally retired with the rank of rear-admiral in 1866.)

The New Year of 1862 therefore came in with Confederates beginning to accept that they were on their own, forced to save themselves by their own exertions without foreign aid; and the building race between *Merrimack* and *Monitor* continued apace. Inventing and correcting as he went along, Ericsson proved as good as his word: *Monitor* was launched at New York on 30 January 1862. She was the first wartime naval achievement of the Industrial Revolution, her construction having been farmed out to different firms for the separate manufacture of hull, engines, turret, and armor plate – a facility denied the Confederacy, with its lack of industrial plant. Not surprisingly, *Monitor* was riddled with teething troubles (mostly concerned with the steering gear) and she was not ready to be towed down to Hampton Roads until 6 March. This enabled *Merrimack* (now re-christened CSS *Virginia*) to beat *Monitor* into action by less than a day.

The ungainly Southern ironclad had been rebuilt with a massive angled penthouse running fore and aft, of heavy timbers sheathed in armor plate (the latter mostly contrived from railway iron). She carried eight guns in broadside (four per side) plus a bow and stern gun, each of the latter swiveled for a choice of fire through three ports. Unlike *Monitor, Virginia* had been given an armored spur with which to ram enemy ships below the waterline: an attack technique wholly unsuited to sailing warships. *Virginia* was so unweatherly that she could only operate safely in a calm; a storm on 7 March (which all but sank *Monitor* on her way down from New York) delayed her first sortie by a day. But on 8 March 1862 *Virginia* became the world's first ironclad to go into action. Under Captain Franklin Buchanan, commanding the Confederate James River Flotilla, *Virginia* lumbered across Hampton Roads to sink the becalmed sailing sloop USS *Cumberland* with a ramming attack, then turned on the nearby frigate *Congress* and set her ablaze with shellfire and red-hot shot.

All this was accomplished in the teeth of point-blank fire from the Union ships and their covering shore batteries. *Virginia's* armor survived the lot, though Buchanan (venturing outside for a better view) was wounded by a rifle bullet; he was replaced in command by Lieutenant Jones. With evening approaching and the tide on the ebb, restricting *Virginia's* already limited maneuverability, Jones prudently decided to withdraw for the night and finish off *Minnesota, St Lawrence* and *Roanoke* on the morrow. As night fell, however, the insignificant shape of *Monitor* came steaming in past Fort Monroe, and daybreak on 9 March found her poised to defend *Virginia's* intended victims.

The extraordinary fight between *Virginia*

and *Monitor* on the forenoon of 9 March 1862, the first-ever battle between ironclad warships, ended with neither ship having inflicted vital damage on the other. *Monitor's* heavier guns were frustrated by *Virginia's* sloping armor. Though the two ships battered each other for three hours, there was only one serious casualty: Lieutenant John Worden, commander of *Monitor*, Momentarily blinded by a direct hit on the observation-slit through which he was peering. Until Lieutenant Greene took over command and brought *Monitor* back into the fight, *Virginia* seemed on the point of adding *Minnesota* to her tally of victims, but prudently retired again with the ebb of the tide, rather than risk being stranded. On balance *Virginia* had taken the heavier damage, with the muzzles of two guns shattered, her tall stack shot away and a leak in the bows from the loss of her ram during the earlier attack on *Cumberland*, aggravated by an abortive attempt to ram *Monitor*. Though *Monitor* had undoubtedly frustrated *Virginia's* attempt to break the Union blockade of the James River, the Battle of Hampton Roads ended in a stalemate which seemed destined to last as long as the two ironclads confronted each other.

The stalemate was abruptly broken in just over two months by the movement of the land armies, beginning on 4 April with a Northern advance on Richmond up the Yorktown peninsula. This forced the Confederates to evacuate first Yorktown and then Norfolk (4-10 May 1862). When it proved impossible to move *Virginia* up the James to defend Richmond, she was set on fire and blown up by her crew on 11 May. Four days later her gunners helped repel an attempt by the US Navy to force open a direct route to Richmond up the James by bombarding and passing Fort Darling. The Northern flotilla consisted of *Monitor*, the new ironclad *Galena* and three gunboats, and its defeat revealed the limitations of ironclads when opposed by well-emplaced shore batteries. Hit 43 times, *Galena* was reduced to a wreck, her frail 4-inch armor shattered. She never saw service as an ironclad again. *Monitor* again came through unscathed, but her guns could not be elevated enough to silence the Confederate fire.

Richmond was saved by Robert E. Lee's victory in the Battle of the Seven Days (25

*Above:* Union gunboat USS *Choctaw* off the battered city of Vicksburg in 1863. *Below:* The distinctive pill-box turret of a Northern monitor: USS *Lehigh* in the James River, spring 1863.

Distinctive features of the river gunboats during the Civil War were the sloping, armored sides of the casemate and broadside guns protected by armored ports. *Right:* The crew of USS *Cincinnati* take advantage of a quiet spell and good laundry-drying weather. *Below:* USS *Cairo* in more martial guise, 'showing her teeth' for the camera.

June-1 July 1862), after which the Union field army was withdrawn from the Yorktown Peninsula. Apart from a two-month withdrawal to New York for repairs, *Monitor* remained on the lower James River until December 1862. On the last day of the year, while attempting another sea voyage to join the naval blockade of Wilmington, North Carolina, *Monitor* foundered and sank off Cape Hatteras – a sad end to an astonishing operational career which had changed warship design for good.

Whilst 1862 was a year of repeated Union frustration and defeat in the East, it was a very different story in the West. There the US Navy, though operating hundreds of miles from salt water, played a vital role in helping slice the Confederacy in two down the line of the Mississippi. The armored river gunboats of the North were essential in overwhelming or by-passing the Confederate strongpoints barring the southward Union advance.

Building the Union gunboat fleet was, like the breakneck construction of *Monitor,* another remarkable demonstration of the North's industrial muscle. It was achieved largely by the organising genius of millionaire industrialist James B. Eads, who masterminded the construction of seven new ironclad gunboats well within the promised 65 days. These were *St Louis, Carondelet, Cincinatti, Louisville, Mound City, Cairo* and *Pittsburgh,* built piecemeal in timber yards, foundries and workshops scattered across eight of the Northern states. Eads then added two more gunboats, one converted from a river salvage boat (*Benton*) and one

*Above:* Mass production of Mississippi gunboats at the Eads works, Carondelet, Missouri, in October 1861. *Right:* The screw, unarmored under-hull and waterline armor belt of USS *Dictator*, probably photographed shortly before her launch on 26 December 1863 – Delameter Iron Works, New York.

from a ferry (*Essex*). All were broad in the beam, flat-bottomed stern-wheelers, known generically as 'Pook's Turtles' after Samuel M. Pook, the naval architect working in harness with Eads. Commanded by Flag Officer Andrew Foote, the Northern gunboat fleet mustered at Cairo, Illinois, to support the first drives against the Confederate river strongholds in the New Year of 1862.

The gunboats got off to a resounding start with the shattering bombardment which assisted General Ulysses S. Grant to capture Fort Henry on the Tennessee River on 6 February 1862. They moved to the Cumberland River to spearhead Grant's follow-up capture of Fort Donelson on 16 February, then returned to Cairo to make repairs before tackling the first major barrier on the Mississippi: 'Island Number 10', north-western bastion of the Tennessee frontier. Here, frustrated by the well-sited Confederate batteries, the Union advance stuck until *Carondelet* ran the gauntlet on the night of 4-5 April and silenced the guns preventing Union troops from crossing to surround the fortress. This early winning of Northern supremacy on the central Mississippi was followed at once by one of the US Navy's finest feats of the Civil War: nothing less than the capture of New Orleans, the Confederacy's second city.

The victor of New Orleans was 61-year-old Flag Officer David Glasgow Farragut, a veteran of the War of 1812 who had sailed the Pacific under Porter in *Essex,* and had been captured in her. The plan to take New Orleans was formed after the first Northern footholds on the Confederate Atlantic coast had been won with comparative ease: Hatteras Inlet (29 August 1861) and Port Royal (7 November 1861), followed by Roanoke Island on 7 February 1862. To tackle New Orleans, Farragut was given 10,000 troops and a fleet consisting of eight steam-powered warships,

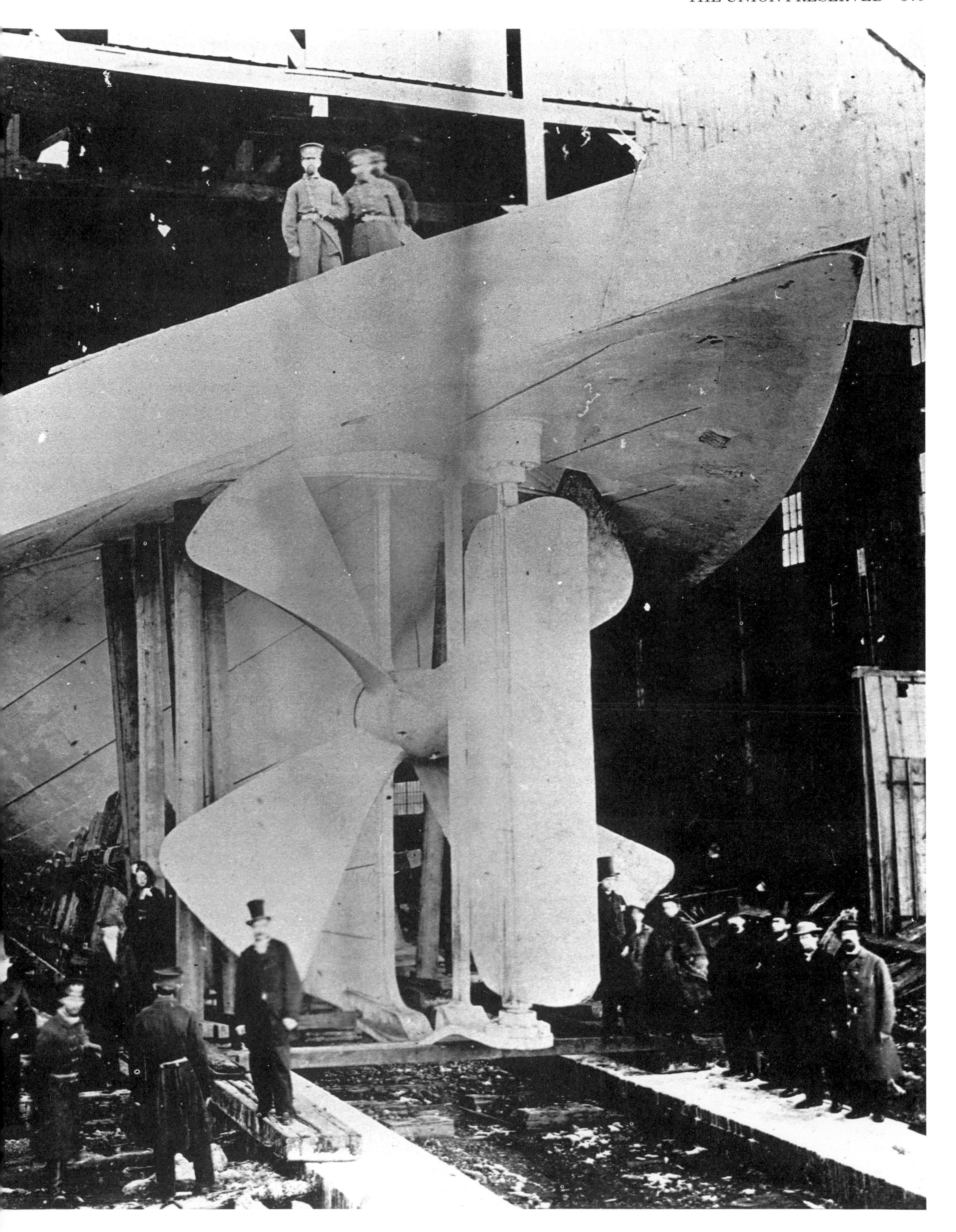

Victor of New Orleans and Mobile Bay: Admiral David G. Farragut strikes a suitably heroic pose beside the wheel of his flagship, USS *Hartford*, at Mobile in 1864. With Farragut is the bearded Captain Percival Drayton, USN.

*Opposite, below:* Northern and Southern gunboats clash at Memphis, 6 June 1862. At center, the USS *Monarch* rams the Confederate *General Beauregard*; the Confederate *General Price* can be seen at left, with the Confederate flagship *Little Rebel* in the background.

nine gunboats and a flotilla of mortar schooners. None of these were ironclads, and when Farragut heard that the Confederates were building two large ironclads (*Louisiana* and *Mississippi*) for the defense of New Orleans, he decided to attack before they were ready. Farragut was not deterred by the pair of forts, Jackson and St Philip, commanding the channel leading north to New Orleans; he intended to pass them, not match them in fire-power, and he did just that. Within 24 hours after fighting his way past the forts, Farragut's ships anchored off the New Orleans waterfront to receive the surrender of the defenseless city on 25 April 1862.

By the end of June 1862 Fort Pillow and Memphis had followed New Orleans, Island No. 10 and Forts Henry and Donelson, and Confederate control of the Mississippi had shrunk to the three-mile waterfront of Vicksburg, Mississippi. Farragut had cruised up from New Orleans to join hands with the Northern gunboats, now commanded by Flag Officer Charles H. Davis – but, even when the two forces joined above Vicksburg, they proved unable to capture the town without a powerful land army attacking from the east. Silencing the guns of Vicksburg on their commanding bluffs above the town was a task beyond Farragut's warships and gunboats. As *Monitor* had discovered at Fort Darling on the James River, two months before, not even the most powerful ironclad could neutralize positions sited on high ground beyond the limited elevation of its guns. In October 1862 Farragut, now a rear-admiral, withdrew his seagoing ships to New Orleans. His replacement as the new Flag Officer on the Mississippi was the commander of his mortar boats during the assault on New Orleans: David Dixon Porter, son of Farragut's old commander in the War of 1812.

The fate of the war hung in the balance from the high summer of 1862 to that of 1863. The string of famous Confederate land victories won in the East by Robert E. Lee and 'Stonewall' Jackson, went hand in hand with a succession of failures for the US Navy. On the high seas, Raphael Semmes was on the loose in a new Confederate raider, CSS *Alabama,* secretly built in Britain, which began a remarkable two-year cruise in August 1862 and destroyed 20 US ships in her

The Confederate ironclad Arkansas, at center, running through the Union fleet off Vicksburg, 15 July 1862.

first two months of operations alone. In January 1863 she sank the Union gunboat *Hatteras* off Galveston before extending her hunting grounds to the South Atlantic, Indian Ocean and China Sea – a range remarkable by the standards of the day, and destined not to be surpassed until the disguised German merchant-raiders of the two World Wars. In March 1863 Porter's gunboats, frankly attempting the impossible, failed to break through to the upper Yazoo River in Vicksburg's rear by forcing a channel from bayou to vegetation-clogged bayou. In the following month Rear-Admiral Samuel Du Pont, victor at Hatteras Inlet in November 1861, tried to take Charleston with a bold frontal assault by nine ironclads, seven of them turretted monitors. Though their armor stood up well to a formidable hammering by the guns of Fort Sumter and the other Charleston forts – they fired an astonishing 2,209 rounds to only 139 from Du Pont's ships – Du Pont was forced to order a humiliating withdrawal after two hours. Like Vicksburg, Charleston was a target beyond the US Navy's capacity and held out until invested from the landward by the Army.

After the tide turned for good with the twin Confederate defeats at Vicksburg and Gettysburg in July 1863, the biggest threat to units of the US Navy was posed by weapons born of desperation: the mine and the torpedo (both referred to as 'torpedo'). Torpedoes of the Civil War were of the spar variety: extended from the bow of a fast boat, manned by what amounted to a suicide crew. The first Confederate torpedo attack was against *New Ironsides* off Charleston in October 1863, but though the ironclad's plates were started by the explosion the ship survived. It was a very different story with the wooden-hulled *Housatonic,* ripped open and sunk by a spar torpedo on 7 February 1864. A new factor had entered naval warfare. It was one which the Confederate Admiral Buchanan hoped would keep Farragut's fleet out of Mobile Bay, the last Confederate naval base on the Gulf by the summer of 1864.

Well aware of the 'torpedo' menace, Farragut was more concerned with running his

*Opposite, top:* Confederate commerce-raider supreme – Captain Raphael Semmes of CSS *Alabama*, standing by the 110-pounder gun while his ship replenishes at Cape Town in August 1863. *Below:* CSS *Hunley*, one of the justly-famed Confederate submersibles which achieved the first sinking of an enemy warship by submarine attack: USS *Housatonic*, ripped open and sunk on 7 February 1864.

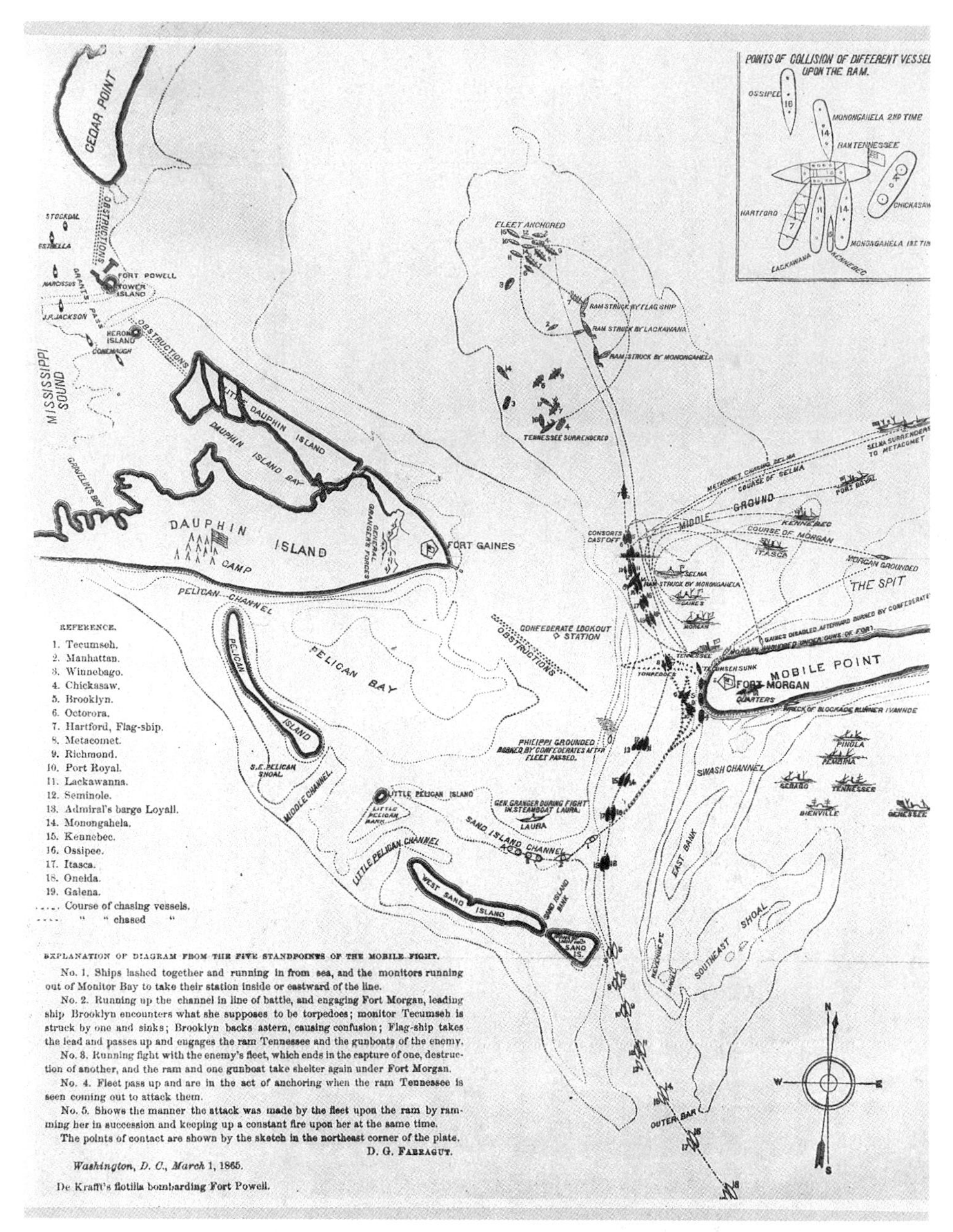


Map of the Battle of Mobile Bay (5 August 1864) showing Farragut's line of approach and *(inset)* the massive concentration of fire-power brought to bear on the Confederate ironclad *Tennessee*.

fleet in past Fort Morgan, guarding the entrance to the Bay. He used his four monitors as a line-ahead screen for his wooden ships, which he had lashed together in pairs for safety. This level-headed deployment had the desired result, with the monitors drawing the bulk of Fort Morgan's fire during the critical entry to Mobile Bay – but the Union fleet was thrown into momentary disarray when the leading monitor *Tecumseh* hit a 'torpedo' and sank with 93 of her crew of 114. Farragut rose splendidly to the crisis, giving the US Navy a watchword fit to rank beside 'Don't give up the ship!' and 'I have not yet begun to fight!' 'Damn the torpedoes!' he barked. 'Full speed ahead!'

Having failed to keep Farragut's fleet out of the Bay, Buchanan's last hope was the prowess of his flagship *Tennessee*, the South's last heavy ironclad – but she stood no chance against the terrible combined pounding, at point-blank range, by the Union monitors *Winnebago* and *Chickasaw*. After a heroic fight, with her steering gone and her armor

being blown off in great chunks, *Tennessee* surrendered and the battle was over.

The Battle of Mobile Bay on 5 August 1864 was the last fleet action of the American Civil War. It was fought two months after *Alabama* was finally caught off Cherbourg by Captain John A. Winslow of USS *Kearsarge,* and sunk after a no less dramatic single-ship action. Extraordinary honors

Position of the ships at the moment of *Tennessee*'s surrender, hemmed in on all sides.

were paid to Winslow by a grateful government, as had been paid to Britain's Captain Broke after his capture of USS *Chesapeake* in 1813. Apart from an immediate promotion to Flag Officer and unusually early postwar advancement to Rear-Admiral, Winslow was ordered to be kept on the active list for the rest of his life.

When Lee's Army surrendered to Grant at Appomattox on 9 April 1865, the US Navy could claim to have played a full and varied part in the victory of the Union. Indeed, no other Navy had ever been forced to undergo a greater transformation in a mere four years of war. It now remained to be seen how much of this impetus would be lost, and how much retained, as the battle-scarred American nation prepared to heal its wounds in peace.

# 4: IRONCLADS AND DREADNOUGHTS
## 1865-1918

In the summer of 1865 the US Navy was taking stock after one of the most remarkable transformations ever experienced by any navy in so short a time. Only four years before, on the brink of the Civil War, the US Navy had been no more than a numerically modest fleet of sailing wooden warships with auxiliary steam power. After the war, thanks to the first total harnessing of the Industrial Revolution to meet the demands of modern sea power, the US Navy found itself leading the world in the development of armored steam warships with turretted gun armament – and these new warships were only part of the story. The American Civil War had proved that mine warfare, first used with any effect in the Crimean War of 1854-56, was much more than a worrying novelty: it now had to be considered an integral part of naval warfare. So had the torpedo-boat, though admittedly to a lesser degree (until the British perfected the self-propelled torpedo in the 1870s). After its loss of the wooden *Housatonic* to a Confederate torpedo-boat in February 1864, the US Navy had used a torpedo-boat to sink the Confederate river ironclad *Albemarle* on the Roanoke in October of the same year, proving that ironclads were no more proof against torpedo attack than wooden warships.

Though nearly all these lessons had been learned in coastal and riverine waters, the Civil War had also proved that steam power, armor plate and heavy-caliber gunnery were perfectly suited to the ancient ploy of commerce-raiding. In a way, the depredations inflicted by the Confederate commerce-raiders *Sumter, Alabama, Florida* and *Shenandoah* (the last-named of which was still at sea when the war ended) were a more valuable experience to the US Navy than that gained with the new ironclad types. They were a reminder that the US Navy must retain an oceanic cruiser force for the defense of the sealanes against enemy raiders – and that these cruisers (like mine warfare, the name 'Cruiser' in its modern sense dated from the Crimean War) had to be of the most modern and best-armed type. *Alabama* and *Keasarge* had fought their famous duel off Cherbourg under steam; *Alabama's* fate had been sealed by a heavy shell bursting in the engine room, whereas the Union captain had cannily contrived a measure of armored protection by draping his anchor-chains over the side.

As a final example of what the US Navy had learned from the Civil War, mention should be made of the *Dunderberg,* the enormous Union ironclad nearing completion at New York when the war ended. *Dunderberg* ('thunder mountain') was 373 feet (114 meters) long – 50 feet (15.2 meters) more than Brunel's famous iron liner *Great Britain* – and was designed to carry two revolving gun casemates as well as broadside batteries under an angled penthouse. From her bow there jutted an awe-inspiring ram shaped like a plowshare. With her low silhouette, sloped armor and ferocious ram, *Dunderberg* would probably have proved a match for the heaviest battleship anywhere in the world.

However, for the postwar US Navy, inevitably shrunk by a cost-conscious administration struggling with a wealth of domestic crises, there was no place for a monster like *Dunderberg*. She was eventually sold to the French Navy, whose warship design over the ensuing 30 years bore the unmistakable stamp of *Dunderberg's* influence.

Despite all these undoubted improvements brought about by the Civil War, the postwar US Navy nevertheless fell victim to an unfailing natural law. Any fighting service raised to an unprecedented state of development by the pressures of war inevitably suffers from the ensuing peace, with its automatic tendency towards demobilisation, retrenchment, domestic reconstruction and economy. In the case of a navy, these peacetime influences wither the size of the fleet, its trained manpower and consequently its combat experience (the most rapidly waning asset of them all). No less is true of the will to improvise and innovate, which had applied to the naval war of 1861-65 far more than to land warfare. An automatic extension of this natural law is that the longer the peace endures, the more damaging its effects will

*Previous pages:* The shape of things to come – one of the Confederate submersibles or 'Davids' driven by steam or an eight-man hand-cranked shaft, with the spar for its torpedo at right, beached at Charleston at the end of the American Civil War.
*Below:* First warship lost to submarine attack was the unarmored USS *Housatonic*, sunk by a hand-driven 'David' on 7 February 1864.

Replete with battle honors: Farragut's flagship USS *Hartford*, completed in 1859, showing her starboard battery of 9-inch Dahlgren guns.

be on the fighting services.

The US Navy was saved from the worst results of this syndrome by the increasing awareness of its strength and potential as a world power with imperial interests. The purchase of Alaska and the Aleutian Islands from Russia in 1867 could be said to have an obvious precedent in American history: the purchase of the Louisiana territory from Napoleon's France in 1803. But the Louisiana Purchase had only facilitated the exploration and settlement of the continent west of the Mississippi. The Alaska Purchase gave the United States a vital stake in the North Pacific, and this was reflected in the same year, 1867, by the securing of American rights over the Midway Islands, 1,200 miles west of the kingdom of Hawaii. Eight years later, in January 1875, the United States negotiated a 'reciprocity treaty' with Hawaii, admitting Hawaiian sugar into the United States free of duty – but in exchange rapidly reducing the islands to economic dependence on the United States. In 1887 the treaty was extended, giving the US Navy the use of Pearl Harbor, where the building of a naval station with coaling facilities rapidly followed. The next step, in January 1893, was the landing of US Marines to defend American residents in Hawaii against the results of growing constitutional unrest; this was followed by the American establishment of a Hawaiian Republic (July 1894) and the final ratification of a treaty of annexation with the United States by the Hawaiian Senate in June 1897. The Hawaiian Islands were formally transferred to the United States in the following August – a classic pattern of imperial expansion which Americans, naturally prone to sneers at *British* imperialism, would do well to remember.

This new role for the United States as a North Pacific power, no more than a debating-point before the Civil War, effectively cancelled domestic pressure for really damaging service economies. It led to the rapid development of San Francisco as the permanent 'rear base' of the US Pacific

*Below:* Paving the way to an American 'Two-Ocean' battle fleet – the coastal battleship USS *Iowa* (BB.4) as completed, before a towering 'cage' mainmast was installed aft of the stacks. Launched in 1896, *Iowa* served through the First World War in the training role, being expended as a gunnery target in 1923.

Squadron, with other naval bases subsequently added at Bremerton, Puget Sound, to the north and finally at San Diego to the south. By the middle 1890s, the transformation of the US Navy into a permanently 'two-ocean' navy was an accomplished fact.

Though the enduring years of peace saw the lead in warship and gunnery design recross the Atlantic to Europe, this also had direct advantages for the US Navy. With money kept tight by Congress, American designers were denied the costly interim experiments made by their European counterparts. British and French designers came up with many a weird and wonderful hybrid design between 1865 and 1885, as the full sailing-ship rig of masts and yards passed into final obsolescence. The US Navy Department could afford to lie back and opt for the best of the European designs for application to American needs – and this by no means implied excessive reliance on European experience.

One of the greatest American naval assets in these years was the remarkable shipbuilder Charles H. Cramp (1828-1912), who gave the US Navy an invaluable continuity in ship design from the ironclads of the Civil War to the battleships and cruisers of the

Dreadnought era. Cramp had given the US Navy its first seagoing ironclad, *New Ironsides,* in 1862; 30 years later, with *Indiana, Massachusetts,* and *Iowa* (BBs. 1-3, laid down 1891-93) he produced the first modern American battleships. These were only the precursors of four more battleships built at Cramp's Philadelphia yard before his death: *Alabama* (BB.8), *Maine* (BB.10), *South Carolina* (BB.26), and *Wyoming* (BB.32) – the latter a full-blown Dreadnought with twelve 12-inch guns.

No less important, though overshadowed in the prevailing anxiety not to be outstripped in the development of conventional sur-

*Above:* A typical cruiser of the post-Civil War years – USS *Richmond* as she looked after receiving an 8-inch rifled pivot gun in her refit of 1877-78, and before her bridge was rebuilt forward of the stack in her refit of 1884-87.

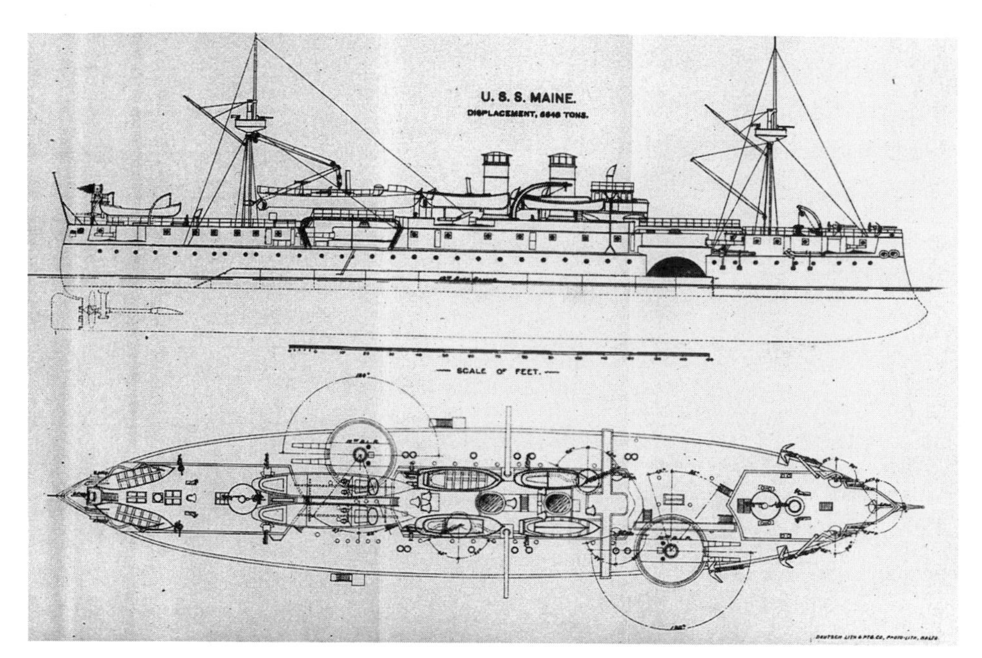


*Above:* Melting-pot years in battleship design, midway between broadside and center-line turret armament. This plan for the ill-fated USS *Maine* (1839) placed the turrets in wing mountings instead of on the centerline.

face warships, was the American inventor John P. Holland. He provided another direct link with the lessons of the Civil War by building on the experience gained by the Confederate 'Davids': the semi-submersible torpedo-boats which had attacked *New Ironsides* and *Housatonic* in the latter years of the war. Thanks to his persistent experiments, Holland emerged head and shoulders above his contemporary submarine pioneers: Garrett (Britain), Nordenfeldt (Sweden), Goubet and Dupuy de Lôme (France), and Peral (Spain). After a long succession of prototypes throughout the 1880s there emerged the *Holland VII* of 1895 and the *Holland VIII* of 1900. The latter was the forerunner of every non-nuclear submarine still in service in the 1980s: a pressure hull surrounded by flooding ballast tanks for submerging and surfacing; an air-breathing engine for running on the surface and electric motors for running submerged; and a bow torpedo tube.

These vital developments in *materiel* did not come about in isolation, prompted solely by the need to copy European models. They were matched by an ever-deepening professionalism in the US Navy's infrastructure, in which the leading lights were Stephen Bleecker Luce and his far more famous *protégé,* Alfred Thayer Mahan. Luce (1827-1917) had published a textbook on seamanship before commanding *Pontiac* while supporting Sherman's capture of Charleston in February 1865. After serving as commandant of midshipmen at the US Naval Academy, Annapolis, Luce became the foremost champion of a college for advanced naval studies, and was appointed first president of the US Naval War College when this was founded at Newport, Rhode Island, in October 1884. This splendid institution became a model of its kind for other navies; and it was also Luce who appointed Captain Mahan as lecturer in naval history.

Mahan (1840-1914) succeeded Luce as president of the Naval War College in 1886. He had also served during the Civil War, on blockade duty, but will always be remembered for his classic studies of sea power – *The Influence of Sea Power upon History, 1660-1783* (1890); *The Influence of Sea Power upon the French Revolution and Empire* (1892); biographies of Farragut (1892) and Nelson (1897); *Sea Power in its Relation to the War of 1812* (1905); and *The Major Operations of the Navies in the War of American Independence* (1913).

*Below:* Blueprint for the future. Only five years later, the lines of the *Holland VIII* already anticipated the streamlined 'teardrop' hull familiar in US submarines of the 1980s.

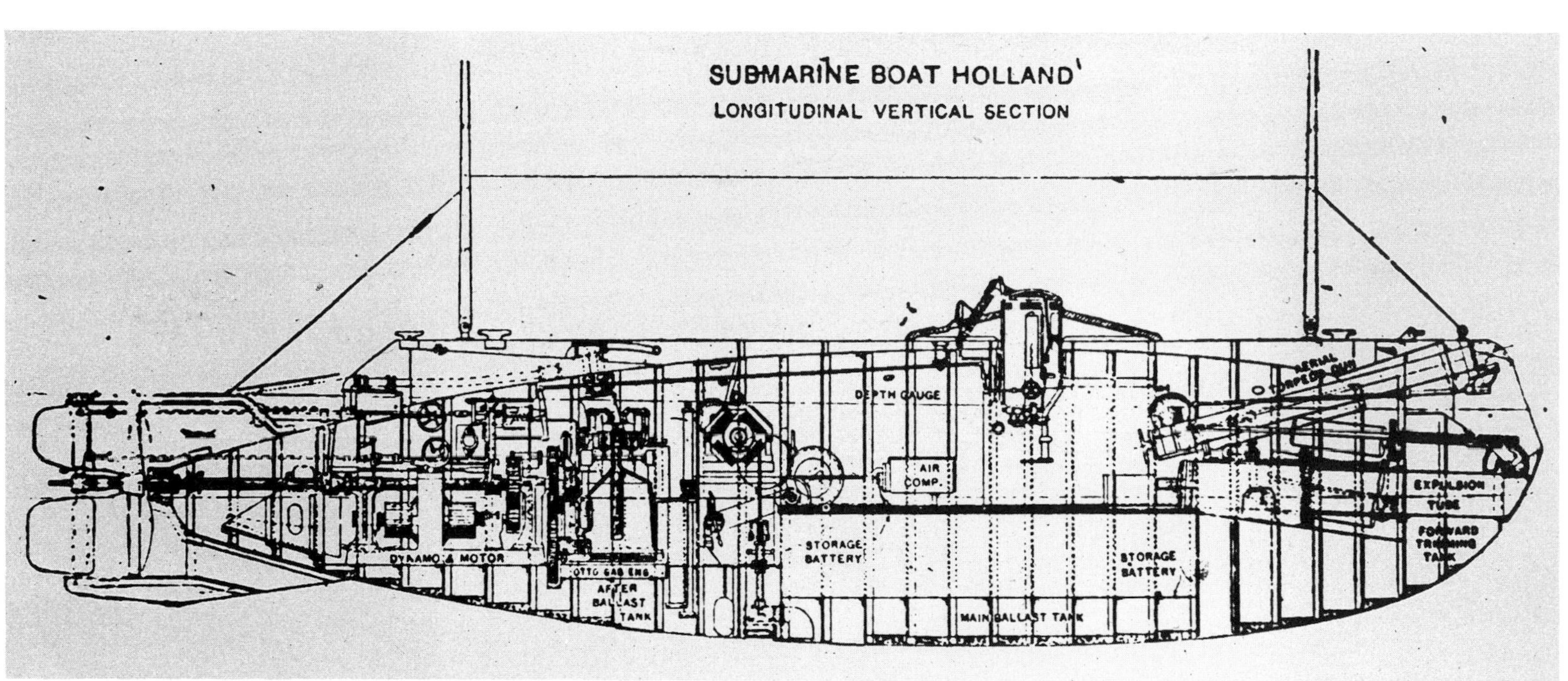

These masterpieces earned Mahan worldwide fame in his lifetime and entitle him to be remembered as the Clausewitz of naval theory (though Mahan's scholarship and clarity of style are infinitely superior to the unfinished works of the Prussian). Mahan's most famous doctrine, traced through every era in naval history, was that of the *fleet in being:* the outnumbered, perhaps even insignificant naval force which, by merely existing as a potential threat, prevents a more powerful enemy from deploying his full naval strength as he would. The exploits of the Confederate Navy between 1861 and 1865 had alone offered convincing proof of this.

The US Navy's continued advances both in *materiel* and in professional studies took place in a period of extended *détente* with the old enemy, Britain. Though postwar US governments accepted that the Confederate raiders of the Civil War had not been built or sustained with British governmental approval, American claims for postwar compensation by Britain were politely but firmly maintained. The result was an extension of the common sense which had resolved the '*Trent* Incident' of November 1861. Both cases, American and British, were submitted to international arbitration at Geneva in 1872, British liabilities being assessed at £3,100,000 – and both fully and promptly paid. The same solution was chosen for the next falling-out between the United States and Britain. This occurred in 1895, when President Grover Cleveland's administration cited the Monroe Doctrine during a boundary dispute between Venezuela and British Guiana. On this occasion the arbitrators decided in Britain's favor.

The inevitable result of continued equal and amicable relations with Britain was the sharpening of American imperial ambitions in the Pacific, which received their most disagreeable outlet in the Spanish-American War of 1898. The cause of the war was a Cuban revolt against Spanish rule, and American outrage against Spanish atrocities committed on the rebels – the said outrage being deliberately fanned for the sake of increased circulation by William Randolph Hearst, king of the popular press. Then, on 15 February, the US battleship *Maine* blew up and sank in Havana harbor. The disaster could quite easily have been spontaneous

A US Navy hallmark has always been the extraction of maximum utility from every class of ship by virtue of long-term service. This is the USS *Pensacola*, already obsolete less than 20 years after completion but serving as flagship of the Mediterranean squadron, at Alexandria in 1886.

*Right:* Heavy metal for the Pacific theater – 'Indiana' class battleship USS *Oregon* (BB.3) sets out from New York on the long haul round Cape Horn, bound for Manila in the Philippines, on 12 October 1898. Like her sister-ships *Indiana* and *Massachusetts*, she carried a main armament of four 13-inch guns in centerline turrets, with a secondary armament of eight 8-inch guns.

ammunition explosion (a tragedy known to all battleship navies down to and including the Second World War), but Hearst's newspapers shrieked accusations of Spanish sabotage. The fact that Spain apologized unreservedly and offered all sympathy, plus practical suggestions for resolving the crisis, went for nothing: the real American goal was not Cuba but the Spanish Philippines, on China's doorstep. On 21 April 1898, President William McKinley approved the Congressional resolution for armed intervention.

Meanwhile, bellicose Assistant Navy Secretary 'Teddy' Roosevelt had, without any authorization, briefed the commander of the US Pacific Squadron to move from Hawaii to Hong Kong. Thence, as soon as he heard that war with Spain had been declared, he was to descend on Manila and attack the Spanish fleet. Commodore George Dewey (1827-1917) had served under Farragut during the capture of New Orleans in 1862 and had a distinguished Civil War career. After running the gauntlet of Forts Jackson and St Philip he was not deterred by the prospect of the Spanish batteries commanding Manila Bay, and sailed from Hong Kong with his six cruisers on 25 April. Shortly after midnight on 1 May, Dewey sailed past the outermost forts, ignored the shore batteries and headed straight for the ramshackle fleet.

Rarely, if ever, can American warships have had softer opponents. Admiral Montojo had seven ships in all, only three of them armored, and one a hulk which could only move under tow. So far from being drawn up in line of battle, Montojo had anchored close inshore to save as many of his crewmen as possible when the moment came to abandon ship. Dewey's chosen tactics were redolent of Civil War ironclad experience. Instead of anchoring to slug it out ship to ship, he made five slow runs past his victims, retiring to send the American crews to breakfast to give the smoke a chance to clear. It was typical of this war that Dewey went into US naval legend for his perfectly natural order to his gunnery officer on the eve of the first attack-

ing pass: 'You may fire when you are ready, Gridley.' By noon, what was left of Montojo's fleet surrendered, Spanish casualties totaling 381 in exchange for eight Americans lightly wounded and an overweight American chief engineer dead from heatstroke after collapsing below decks.

The Battle of Manila Bay established Dewey as the greatest American naval hero since Farragut, but ironically it was not for the battle but for its aftermath that Dewey deserved the fullest praise. He had no troops. He could not land to capture Manila. All he could do was stay on station, waging a magnificent game of bluff, until General Merritt arrived with an American expeditionary force. It took *14 weeks* before the troops arrived; landed; fought a brisk skirmish (six Americans and 49 Spaniards dead); and accepted the surrender of Manila on 13 August. The hardest fighting in this 'splendid little war' (as Secretary of State John Hay expressed it to Roosevelt) was in the Cuban theater, where 509 American troops

were killed in battle and 1,800 died of disease. The big naval victory of the Cuban theater was the Battle of Santiago on 3 July 1898, won by Commodore William T. Sampson (1840-1902). Santiago was Manila Bay reversed, with Sampson's squadron destroying that of Admiral Cervera as it tried to break out; the victory made possible the American invasion of Puerto Rico on 25 July, which clinched the American victory.

However squalid the circumstances which had precipitated the conflict, the Spanish-American War of 1898 had one unanswerable result. Thanks mainly to the prowess of her Navy, the United States was now a global power, having gained not only Spanish withdrawal from Cuba but from the Philippines (in return for an inducement of $20 million paid to Spain). The United States also gained Guam in the Marianas and

*Below:* Victory review in New York Harbor (21 August 1898) after the defeat of Spain. *Left to right:* cruiser *New York*, battleships *Iowa* and *Oregon*.

*Above:* Rare photograph of American gunners during the Battle of Santiago (3 July 1898).

Puerto Rico in the Caribbean. The newly-acquired Philippines immediately proved their worth by serving as the advance base for the American forces which joined in the international force sent to crush the Boxer Rising in China (July-August 1900).

Even before the American successes in the Spanish War of 1898 had been fairly won, it had always been clear that the United States would never be able to enjoy a free hand in the exploitation of China, whether politically or economically. Apart from the British with

*Above*: View from the USS *Oregon* of the victors of Santiago during the victory review.

A trio of US pre-Dreadnoughts. *Top:* USS *Maine* (BB.10) as completed in 1902.
*Above:* USS *Kearsarge* (BB.5), with her imaginative but unworkable superimposition of co-axial 8-inch turrets atop the main 13-inch turrets.

their base at Hong Kong, there were the Russians at Port Arthur and Vladivostok, the Germans at Tsingtau – and, newest entrants of all, the newly-reconstituted Japanese Empire, making use of the latest European models to be ready to take on all rivals for the domination of China by land and sea. The decks were cleared by the Russo-Japanese War of 1904-5, in which the shattering defeat of Russian ambitions in the Far East left Japan – an ally of Britain since 1902 – as the most potent rival of the US Pacific Fleet. But Japan was not the only naval rival to the United States. On the Atlantic front, the Anglo-German naval building race, measured primarily in numbers of new battleships, was already fast accelerating by 1905. For the US Navy, faced with potential naval rivals from both East and West, there could be no withdrawal now from its costly 'two-ocean' status.

*Right:* Superb shot of USS *Connecticut* (BB.18) at full speed in 1907.

*Above:* Airborne watch over a First World War convoy by a US Naval Airship or 'blimp'.

*Below:* The filthy job of coaling ship – one of the 'Florida' class Dreadnoughts (*Florida* or *Utah*) in May 1917.

Thanks largely to the excellent groundwork of shipbuilders like Charles H. Cramp, the US Navy adapted with comparative ease to the radically improved battleship concept brought in by the British with HMS *Dreadnought* (1906). American naval designers – like their new Japanese rivals – also declined to ape the British and Germans and start building costly squadrons of the new 'battle-cruiser' type. These lightly-armored super-cruisers, armed with battleship-sized guns, were designed to annihilate enemy raiders and cruiser squadrons scouting ahead of the battle fleet, and 'take their place in the line' to augment, when required, the fire-power of the battle fleet. Both American and Japanese sensed the fallacy (as propounded by the British Admiral Fisher) that 'speed is armor.' There could be no substitute for adequate armored protection, which made the *fast battleship* the ideal choice.

When Britain, France and Japan went to war with Germany in August 1914, the US Navy had eight Dreadnought battleships completed and two more building. This gave a clear lead over the Japanese battle fleet, with its six Dreadnoughts and two hybrid 'semi-Dreadnoughts' completed and two building. With the might of the British Grand Fleet holding the German High Seas Fleet in check (29 British Dreadnoughts and battle-cruisers against 20 German) the Pacific and Atlantic wings of the US Navy seemed safe enough. Though Japan clearly had her eyes on Germany's Pacific Island territories, Japan would never be given unrestricted play by her British ally. Even if, by some unimaginable chance, the German High Seas Fleet managed to defeat the Grand Fleet, this could hardly be achieved with the High Seas Fleet left intact. By any reckoning, American neutrality seemed to be the ideal course for the US Navy in 1914.

In fact this was not the case, and there were three reasons why not.

In 1914 the one factor under-estimated by all naval powers, belligerent and neutral alike, was an unknown one: the extent of the change about to be made in naval warfare by the ocean-going submarine, as demonstrated by Germany's U-boat fleet. On the high seas

Eugene B. Ely shortly after landing on the cruiser USS *Pennsylvania* on 18 January 1911, before he took off again and landed safely ashore. Despite this historic 'first', the US Navy lagged behind the British and Japanese in naval aviation development until the 1920s.

the raiding submarine – unable to disembark prize crews or give full warning to its victim without exposing itself to mortal danger – was about to bring total war into being in the naval dimension. American failure to recognize this, and how it must result in loss of American life at sea, meant that once Germany resorted to fully unrestricted submarine warfare American entry into the war could only be a matter of time.

The second reason why American neutrality worked against the US Navy's best interests was even harder to see in August 1914. This lay in the pioneer field of naval aviation, in which the United States had made a promising start in 1910-12. It was an American pilot (Eugene Ely) who had made the first successful take-off from, and subsequently the first landing on, a warship fitted with a flight-deck. This had been achieved during an anxious prewar interlude when there were rumors that Germany was experimenting with spying aircraft, which would fly off Atlantic liners and reconnoiter the American coast – a prospect not to be borne. American experiments with naval aviation were suspended with the proclamation of American neutrality; and when the US Navy did enter the war it found itself at least five years behind its allies in aircraft-carrier development.

The third reason was, perhaps, the most obvious in 1914: the fact that a neutral US Navy would not be accumulating the vital combat experience being amassed by its allies and likeliest enemies. Nor, on a peacetime footing, could the pace of American naval construction hope to match that of the combatant powers. As a result, the immediate contribution of the US Navy, after the United States joined the Allies on 6 April 1917, was painfully limited. The US Navy had never had to undergo the humiliating experience of being a poor relation in its entire existence, and it was not an easy experience to live with.

The fact that Anglo-American naval collaboration worked out superbly in 1917-18 was due to the high tact and ready diplomacy displayed by the American naval commanders in European waters. Rear-Admiral William S. Sims (1858-1936) was 'Commander of the US Naval Forces Operating in European Waters.' His task, coming under the British Admiral Sir Lewis Bayly, based on Queenstown, Ireland, was to collaborate in the provision of Atlantic convoy escorts against the U-boats. Admiral Hugh Rodman (1959-1940) commanded the American Dreadnought battle squadron which joined the ranks of the British Grand Fleet, under the overall British command of Admiral Sir David Beatty. As an element of the Grand Fleet the American force was designated '6th Battle Squadron,' adopting British methods of signalling and fire control. The original battleships of 6th Battle Squadron (BatDiv 6, in US naval parlance) were *New York* (flag), *Florida*, *Wyoming* and *Delaware*.

It was with the fully-justified pride in faith kept and a job well done that Rodman's squadron deployed with its Grand Fleet comrades, on 21 November 1918, to receive the German High Seas Fleet as it came steaming duly west to surrender off the Firth of Forth. The German naval threat to American sea power had been destroyed – to all appearances, for ever. The Japanese naval threat continued to grow. How the peacetime naval powers could achieve a mutually satisfactory balance of strength – assuming such a feat were possible – remained to be seen.

*Opposite, top:* The amazing capacity of American warship production. In the summer of 1918, less than three weeks from laying-down to launch, the destroyer DD.139 (USS *Ward*) prepares to take the water.
*Above:* Scene of bleak discomfort on the exposed bridge of a US destroyer in the First World War.
*Below:* Over there – the destroyer USS *Stockton* (DD.73) in British waters.

# 5: INSTRUMENT OF VICTORY
## 1918-1945

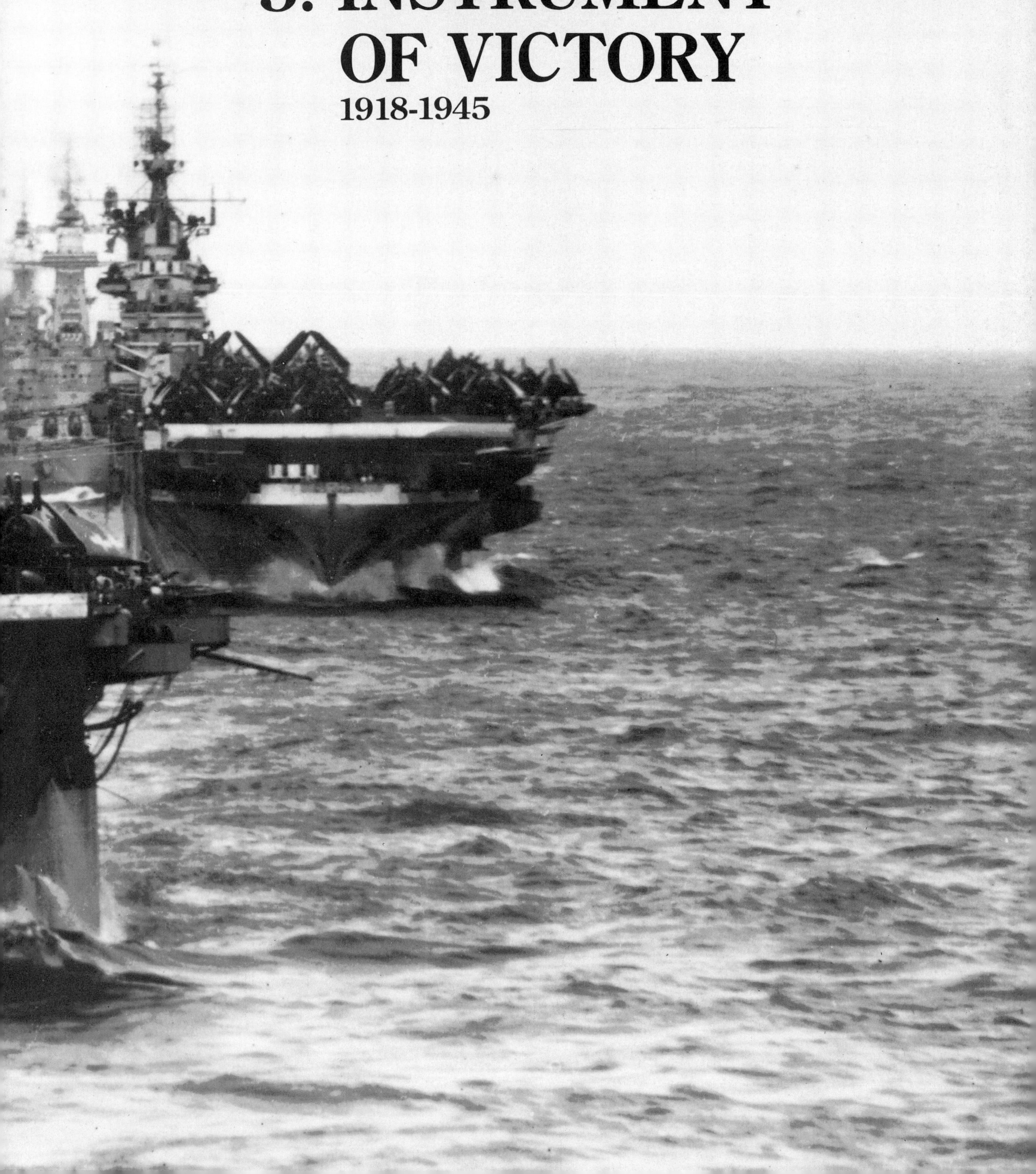

*Previous pages:* Ships of Admiral Halsey's 3rd Fleet during the battle for the Philippines in December 1944. Task Group 38.3 returns to its advance base at Ulithi Atoll, in line-ahead led by the light carrier USS *Langley* (CVL. 27) and 'Essex' class fleet carrier USS *Ticonderoga* (CV.14).

After the defeat of Germany and her allies in November 1918, the future of the US Navy was more uncertain than at any other time in its history. The US Navy's two previous trials – in the Spanish-American War of 1898 and the American Civil War of 1861-65 – had ended with the enemy prostrate and all objectives for the conceivable future secured. This was not the case in 1918, and even the scuttling of the surrendered German fleet in Scapa Flow in the following April failed to dispel the clouds. It was true that one of the US Navy's potential rivals, that of Germany, had been liquidated. But that of Japan had not only emerged from the First World War in a much stronger strategic position, but had already embarked on a new spate of naval construction which could only be aimed at eclipsing American sea power in the Pacific.

Under the terms of the Treaty of Versailles, Germany was to be stripped of all her global colonies. These were to be shared out among the victorious powers and organised as mandates under supervision of the newly-formed League of Nations. In the case of Germany's colonies in the western and southern Pacific, these were divided north and south of the line of the Equator between the Japanese and British Empires, Japan took the Marianas (with the exception of American-held Guam), the Palaus, Carolines and Marshalls. The Bismarck Archipelago – New Britain and New Ireland – passed into Australian control, Samoa into that of New Zealand.

The former German presence in the western Pacific had been tolerable to the United States because it was not sustained by a powerful German Pacific Fleet. But the transfer of these possessions to Japan was a very different story, creating as it did an enormous bastion of Japanese-controlled ocean stretching from the Japanese home islands south to the Equator. Viewed in the light of possible future hostilities between the United States and Japan, the situation could not have been less promising for the United States. The Philippines now lay isolated to the west of Japan's new island empire; Guam lay, completely surrounded by Japanese possessions, plumb in the middle; and the widely-separated American-held islands of Marcus, Wake, Midway, and the Hawaiian group lay to the east. The strategic possibilities in the western Pacific, after the postwar settlement came into effect, amounted to all weakness for the Americans and all strength for the Japanese.

Times had also changed since Japan had won the reputation as the plucky underdog which had made good against the might of Tsarist Russia in the war of 1904-5. But this approving reputation had begun to wane with the unabated growth of the Japanese Navy in the decade before the First World War. The British had begun to have second thoughts about their former client (most of the Japanese fleet which had shattered the Russians at Tsushima in 1905 was of British manufacture or design) when Japan ordered a new battle-cruiser, *Kongo,* in 1911. No navy in the world had yet moved up from the 12-inch gun to the 14-inch; *Kongo* had eight 14-inch guns, 10 inches of armor and a speed of 27 knots. She was, in effect, a fast battleship, superior to any comparable ship in British service, and she was a profound embarrassment to the British who built her. But *Kongo* was also the last capital ship built for Japan by a foreign power. Using *Kongo* as a model, the Japanese went on to complete three sister-ships – *Hiei, Haruna* and *Kirishima* – in their own yards.

When war broke out in 1914, Japan loyally collaborated with her British ally in hunting for German surface raiders in the Pacific, but there could be no mistaking the single-mindedness with which Japan attacked the German colonies north of the Equator. After seizing Tsingtau and the Shantung peninsula, Japan had then served China with her notorious '21 Demands' (January 1915). China's acceptance gave Japan a virtual monopoly of future foreign intervention in China and, after news of the '21 Demands' broke, the pre-1914 image of 'plucky little Japan' was gone for ever. At the same time the Japanese battle fleet continued to grow, four more 14-inch gun battleships being followed by *Nagato* and *Mutsu,* the world's first 16-inch gun battleships. Their completion ensured that the US Navy, which had moved up to the 14-inch gun with *New York* and *Texas* (BBs. 34 and 35, laid down in 1911) would go on to produce its own classes of 16-inch gun battleships in emulation.

The United States had one obvious disadvantage compared with Japan. American naval construction had to be planned with one eye on the Atlantic and the leading European navies and one eye on the Pacific and Japan, and in effect build two battleships for every one built in Japan. To offset this, however, the Panama Canal had finally been opened in August 1914, making it easier to

The US Navy's first carrier was the USS *Langley* (CV.1), a flush-decked conversion from the fleet collier *Jupiter*. Here she is shown under way with her radio masts lowered, recovering aircraft in the 1920s. *Langley's* affectionate Fleet nickname (as with Britain's *Furious* of similar vintage) was 'The Covered Wagon'.

adjust the balance between the Atlantic and Pacific fleets as required. In 1916, the last year of American neutrality, Congress authorized the construction of a huge new fleet of 16-inch gun battleships intended to ensure a 'two-ocean' comparability for the US Navy. The new program fell into two parts: four 'Colorados' authorized in 1916, and six 'South Dakotas' authorized in 1917. Only one of these, *Maryland* (BB.46) had been laid down by the end of the war, and none of the 'South Dakotas' was laid down before 1920. But by then it was already clear that a new naval building race was under way between the United States and Japan, no less financially crippling and dangerous to world peace than the pre-1914 contest between Britain and Germany had been.

Japan's reply to the American 1916 program had been the '8-8' Program of 1918: a total of eight battleships (four 14-inch and four 16-inch) and eight battle-cruisers of similar armament. News of the '8-8' Program confirmed the American decision to add a third element to the 1916 expansion program: six 16-inch gun battle-cruisers ('Lexingtons'), a type which the US Navy had hitherto avoided. Britain, which had planned extensive fleet reductions for the 1920s, was distractedly obliged to order a new class of super-battle-cruiser to keep pace. By the spring of 1921 another global warship-building racc was under way.

This renewed outburst of battleship mania had serious results for the planned composition of the American fleet. One of the most valuable fruits of the close Anglo-American naval relationship in the last 18 months of the war had been access to the unrivaled British expertise in building aircraft-carriers: 'custom-built' for the job with workshops and hangars below a long flight-deck left unimpeded by a compact 'island' superstructure offset to one side. The addition of four 38,000-ton aircraft-carriers to the March 1919 Estimates was intended to give the US Navy carrier parity at a stroke – and outright carrier superiority over the Japanese, who had one small carrier (*Hosho*) building. The new American carriers were intended to operate with the 'Lexington' class battle-cruisers – but it was only with the greatest reluctance that Congress voted funds for the 'South Dakotas' and 'Lexingtons' in the 1920-21 Estimates. The proposed four carriers were rejected outright on grounds of cost, the only concession being permission to convert the fleet collier *Jupiter* as an experimental carrier.

*Jupiter* was taken in hand for conversion in March 1920 at the Norfolk Navy Yard – most appropriately, for it was here that the burned-out hulk of *Merrimack* had been converted into the ironclad *Virginia* in 1861-62. She recommissioned as USS *Langley*, Carrier Number One (CV.1) in March 1922 – by which time the naval construction story had been completely changed. Thanks to a remarkable international exercise in arms limitations, the battleship building race was over – at least for the foreseeable future.

This was the work of the Washington Naval Conference and Treaty (November 1921-February 1922), convened on the invitation of American President Warren Harding. The main items of agenda, from which there was no dissent, were that the situation in the Pacific and China needed definition by treaty and that the prospect of another international building race was intolerable. Separate treaties (with Japan agreeing to restore the Shantung peninsula to China) settled the political scene before the details of the naval agreement were hammered out. These proscribed the super-battleship as the world's most dangerous military status symbol, imposed restrictive limitations on future battleship tonnage and armament, and agreed on a ten-year 'holiday' from new battleship construction. The tonnage and armament restrictions were an attempt to scotch battleship development by imposing what were then believed to be irreconcilable specifications: 35,000 tons maximum displacement and 16-inch maximum caliber for main armament.

The Washington Treaty also sought to make future building races among the signatory powers impossible, by assigning maximum permitted tonnage totals on a ratio basis: Britain 5, United States 5, Japan 3, France and Italy 1.67. Here was a special landmark in the history of the US Navy: the official grant of battleship parity between the British and American fleets. But the Treaty's most celebrated ploy was to tolerate new aircraft-carrier construction as a way of 'recycling' the battleship and battle-cruiser hulls already being built when the Washington Conference met. The carrier's maximum tonnage was set at 27,000 tons and its gun armament limited to a battery of no more than 10 guns with a maximum caliber of eight inches. But the naval powers at present locked into the battleship building race – the United States, Japan and latterly Britain – were given the option of converting two of their uncompleted hulls into heavy carriers of no more than 33,000 tons. For the rest, future carrier-building tonnage was allocated by ratio: Britain 5, United States 5, Japan 3, France and Italy 2.2. This worked out at 135,000 tons of carriers for Britain and the United States, 81,000 tons to Japan and

With the US Battle Fleet in March 1926, probably in Cuban waters. Identifiable are two battleships of the 'New Mexico' class and four destroyers – *Lavalette* (DD.315), *Wood* (DD.317), *Kidder* (DD.319) and *Chase* (DD.323) – all from the Battle Fleet; and one destroyer from the Scouting Fleet. Also present are an 'Omaha' class cruiser, an oiler, and other destroyers.

The battleship USS *New York* (BB.34) leads USS *Nevada* (BB.36) and USS *Oklahoma* (BB.37) during Fleet exercises in 1932. On the horizon can be seen the unmistakable silhouette of the carrier USS *Langley*.

60,000 tons to France and Italy.

The trouble was that few in early 1922 had any clear idea what the carrier's true role should be. In general it was vaguely assumed to be an extension of the cruiser's traditional scouting role, with the carrier's gun armament envisaged for defense as much against surface as against air attack. There was virtually no notion of using carriers as a separate striking task force, with the battleships of the fleet offering heavy-gun support against enemy surface attack. Such thinking on tactics as existed saw the carrier's fleet role as primary reconnaissance, making the battleships' job easier – with the useful facility of being able to launch air attacks on enemy ships sheltering behind minefields or in anchorages too remote to be bombarded by an offshore battle fleet.

The first-fruit of the Washington Naval Treaty was the birth of the heavy fleet carrier: the US Navy's *Lexington* and *Saratoga,* Japan's *Kaga* and *Akagi,* all four converted from Treaty-banned capital ship hulls. All four, entering service in the later 1920s, demonstrated the Washington Treaty's gravest flaw: that there was no way of enforcing the Treaty's restrictions short of war, the avoidance of which was the Treaty's ultimate objective. All four of the heavy carriers were way over the specially-expanded limit of 33,000 tons permitted for these conversions, but both the US Navy and Japan 'bent the rules' in concocting acceptable figures. This process needed very little extension to become an easy way in which to flout the Treaty restrictions without calling down international censure. By the time of the London Naval Conference of 1930, which sought with considerably less success to extend the naval 'holiday,' there were already signs (most notably the increasing truculence of Japan) that the Washington Treaty's most solid achievements were short-term and impossible to repeat.

Meanwhile, the heavy-carrier conversions were put to work in fleet exercises which showed considerable promise for carrier task

At the time of Pearl Harbor in December 1941 the US Navy had 112 submarines in commission with another 65 completed. These are all of the 'New "S"' class, launched in 1937-38: USS *Stingray* (SS.186), *Sturgeon* (SS.187), *Salmon* (SS.182) and *Seal* (SS.183), exercising with the Battle Force in 1939. All four survived the Second World War.

groups operating independently of the main battle fleet. The big question for the US Navy was whether its remaining allocated carrier tonnage should be taken up with a few more large carriers, or several smaller ones. The disappointing performance of the lightweight *Ranger* (launched in 1933) tipped the scale in favor of larger carriers (*Yorktown* and *Enterprise,* launched in 1936). After one last experiment with the light-carrier format with *Wasp* (launched in 1939) the carrier type chosen for the US Navy was the 'medium-heavy', 27,000-ton 'Essex' class, the first of which were ordered in the 1940 Construction Program. But none of the 'Essex' class carriers was ready for service before Japan attacked the United States in December 1941. Nor were the first of the fast 16-inch gun battleships ('North Carolina' and 'South Dakota' classes) ordered in the 1937 and 1938 Programs. Ironically, these new battleships solved the problem of getting a full battery of 16-inch guns into 35,000 tons displacement (by using triple instead of twin turret mountings) long after the Washington Treaty was dead in spirit as well as in letter.

In its two years and three months of wartime neutrality before Pearl Harbor, the US Navy benefited enormously from British wartime experience in the Narrow Seas, Atlantic, Arctic and Mediterranean. The two most obvious of these British-inspired benefits were sonar, for detecting submerged submarines, and radar for surface and air surveillance, invented by the British and perfected by American technology. The British also served as guinea-pigs in the hitherto unknown field of how modern warships would stand up to expert air attack, showing that no anti-aircraft battery of rapid-firing guns could really be considered sufficient. The loss of the British carrier *Courageous* in September 1939 and of *Glorious* in June 1940, respectively to U-boat and surface attack, showed the supreme vulnerability of carriers when exposed without adequate anti-submarine screening or heavy ship support. Finally, the British search for auxiliary air cover which could be extended to cover convoys produced the new concept of the escort carrier, converted from merchant ships. When mass-produced by American shipyards with their world-beating capacity, escort carriers became the means by which the fleet carriers were completely freed for purely offensive instead of supportive opera-

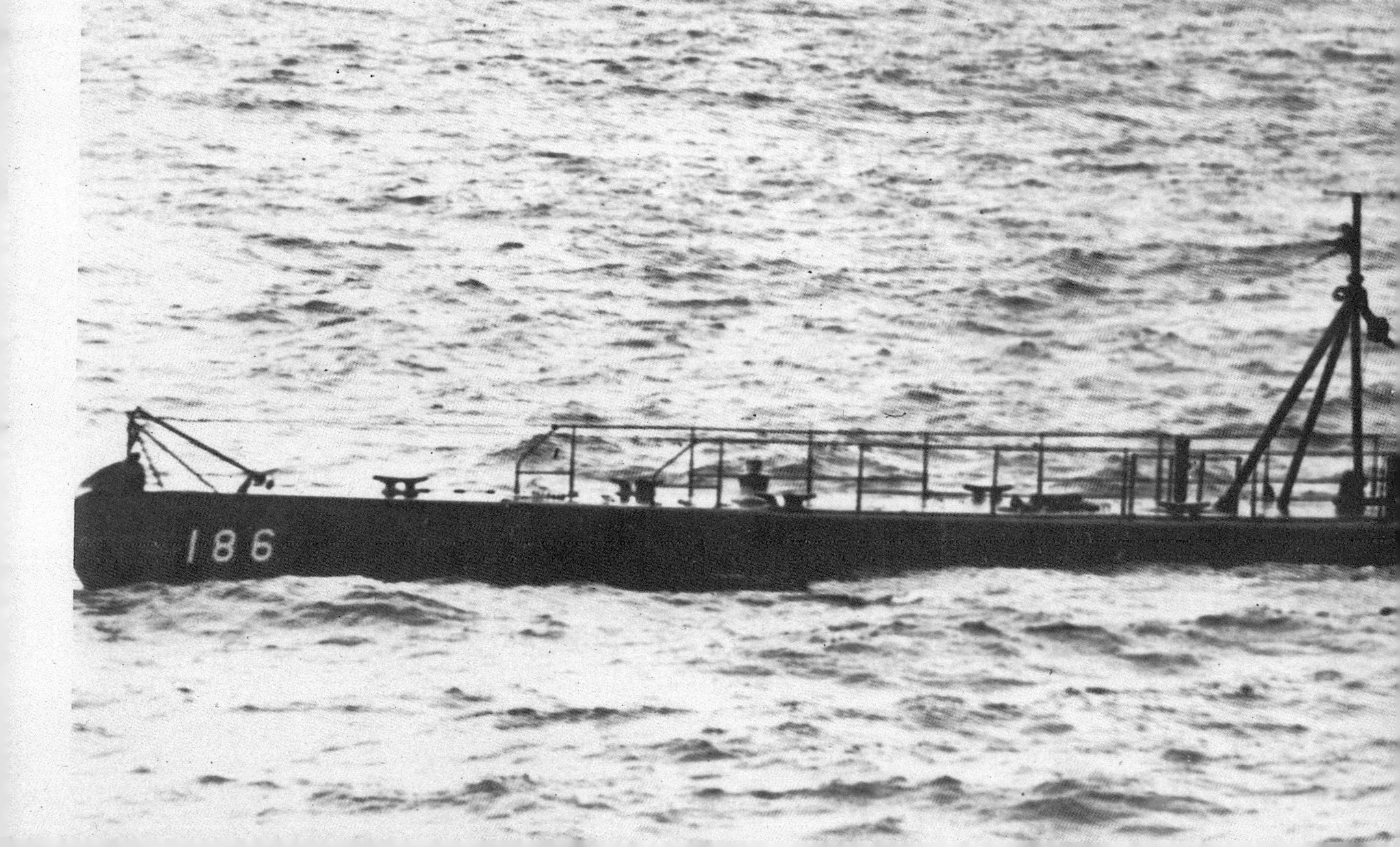

tions. *Long Island,* the US Navy's first escort carrier (CVE), was completed over six months before Pearl Harbor, at the beginning of June 1941.

Setting aside these crucial debts to British technology and combat experience, in the renewal of basic warship types the US Navy had been far better served than the Royal Navy during the 1930s. (Having a 'Navy-minded' President in Franklin D. Roosevelt, who as a rising young politician had served as Assistant Navy Secretary, was an invaluable boon.) In the seven years between Roosevelt's first inauguration as President in 1933 and the outbreak of the European war in September 1939, successive Construction Programs ordered a total of four aircraft-carriers, six battleships, three heavy cruisers, 13 light cruisers, 83 destroyers and 38 submarines. But the emergency 1940 Program – cast in the light of the German bid for mastery in Europe – alone ordered nine battleships, 17 carriers, eight heavy cruisers, 38 light cruisers, 196 destroyers and 73 submarines. This was virtually *double* the *combined total* of the Programs *for the previous seven years,* most of whose ships were completed in time to help bear the brunt of the Japanese offensive in 1941-42. The new ships coming forward in the last five years of peace before Pearl Harbor were ample to replace those lost in the US Navy's first year of war: two battleships, four carriers, five heavy cruisers, two light cruisers, 27 destroyers and eight submarines.

The assurance of ample warship replacements, however, only spelled comfort for the future; they could do nothing to halt the

*Above:* Fine shot of the Battle Force at sea in 1939. It was not until the Pacific Fleet's battle line was liquidated at Pearl Harbor that the new carrier arm became the US Navy's dominant arm.

WAR EXTRA

WAR DECLARED!

U. S. FLEET SAILS!

BATTLESHIP BOMBED

2ND RAID ON HONOLULU!

3RD SUNDAY EXTRA!

America's Best Evening Newspaper

The Seattle Daily Times

PRICE FIVE CENTS

SEATTLE, WASHINGTON, MONDAY, DECEMBER 8, 1941.

Published Daily and Sunday and Entered as Second Class Matter at Seattle, Washington. Vol. LXIV. No. 342.

The hecatomb of battleships at Pearl Harbor, with smoke belching from USS *Tennessee* (BB.43) at left. A small boat heads in to pluck a survivor from the upperworks of USS *West Virginia* (BB.48) at right foreground. Excellent counter-flooding work saved the 'Weavie' from capsizing, allowing her to settle on the bottom on an even keel. Both battleships were repaired and returned to service in 1943-44.

initial run of Japanese victories in 1941-42. Nothing remotely approaching the breadth of the Japanese offensive – from Wake Island and the Gilberts in the Central Pacific, south to the Dutch East Indies, New Guinea and the Solomons, and west to Malaya and Burma – had ever been dreamed of by American strategists. Still very much battleship-orientated, American prewar naval strategy had envisaged a 'one-front' Japanese offensive, with the Philippines high on the list of likely targets. Once committed to such an offensive, the Japanese could then be taken in flank by the advance of the US Pacific Fleet from Hawaii into the Central Pacific, to fight a predominantly battleship action somewhere in the Philippine Sea. But this scenario was liquidated on 7 December 1941, when the six carriers of the Japanese task force sank or crippled every one of the US Pacific Fleet's eight battleships at Pearl Harbor. The often-cited British carrier attack on the Italian battle fleet at Taranto on 11 November 1940 pales into insignificance by comparison with Pearl Harbor. For the only time in all naval history, one of the world's most powerful navies had been forced onto the defensive by a major disaster, suffered on the first day of hostilities, with not one of the enemy warships responsible having been sighted. This was a humiliating fate for America's much-vaunted 'Two-Ocean Navy.'

Because of the simultaneous German declaration of war on the United States, there could be no question of rushing instant reinforcements from the Atlantic to the Pacific Fleet. Only driblet reinforcements could

The cruiser USS *Phoenix* (CVL.46) passes the funeral pyre of the battle line at Pearl Harbor.
*Inset:* USS *Nevada*, beached and burning after failing to escape to the open sea during the Japanese attack.

be spared from the Atlantic, where the battle against Germany's U-boats was necessarily left to the hard-pressed Royal Navy in 1942. In the Pacific, therefore, the traditional concept of an American battle fleet supported by carriers was shattered for ever by the Pearl Harbor disaster. Only a handful of American carriers and cruisers remained, apparently the flimsiest of weapons with which to oppose the Japanese Combined Fleet at the peak of its strength.

Yet they were just enough. Within six months of Pearl Harbor, two major Japanese offensives had been frustrated by carrier battles in which, for the first time, neither fleet ever sighted the other. And in these battles – the Coral Sea (May 1942) and Midway (June 1942) – the Japanese superiority in carriers was wiped out. For this reversal, Japanese over-confidence and unrealistic planning played a major part. But there can be no detracting from the US Navy's achievement against all odds, for which five American admirals claim an enduring share of fame.

Ernest J. King (1878-1956) was the man at the top, directly under Roosevelt as Commander-in-Chief of the US Armed Forces. In the inevitable command changes after Pearl Harbor, King was advanced from C-in-C

Atlantic Fleet (CINCLANT) to Commander-in-Chief, US Fleet (COMUNCH). A hard-core professional who never lost faith that the US Navy would come through to win the war, King's greatest achievement was in picking the man who would start the job by restoring faith and fighting efficiency to the US Pacific Fleet: Admiral Chester W. Nimitz (1885-1966).

Patient, shrewd, with all the warmer human qualities lacking in the more forbidding character of King, Nimitz had the gift of extracting the maximum results from the minimum resources – human and *materiel*. He was the ideal commander to take up King's brief in December 1941: 'Hold what you've got and hit them where you can.' Few commanders ever showed more skill in exploiting that most unpredictable of factors in war: the enemy's mistakes.

The gutsy and ebullient William F. Halsey (1882-1959) embodied the fighting spirit of the US carrier arm, with his slogans, 'Before we've finished with 'em, the Japanese language will be spoken only in hell!' and 'Kill Japs, kill Japs, kill more Japs!' He commanded the carrier raid which on 18 April 1942 launched Army B-25s to bomb Tokyo – the most convincing proof possible that the US Pacific Fleet was still a force to be reckoned with. The Tokyo Raid deprived Halsey of the chance of joining the fray in the Coral Sea battle (4-8 May 1942), which foiled the Japanese conquest of Port Moresby and saved a vital foothold in New Guinea for the

*Right:* USS *Enterprise* (CV.6) recovering Dauntless strike aircraft off Guadalcanal in December 1942, with USS *Saratoga* (CV.3) in background. Three other aircraft can be seen above the tailfin of the Dauntless in foreground.

*Below:* A Hellcat of VF-1 'Top Hat' Squadron, poised for take-off from the second *Yorktown* (CV.10) during the 'Great Marianas Turkey Shoot' in June 1944.

S-13

Allies. When sickness forced Halsey ashore on the eve of the supreme trial at Midway, his choice of successor proved to be one of the greatest naval tacticians of the new carrier era.

Frank Jack Fletcher (1885-1973) was, with Halsey, the foremost carrier task force commander in the hit-and-run raids on the Japanese perimeter, ordered by Nimitz in the spring of 1942. Fletcher won the Battle of the Coral Sea and, until his flagship *Yorktown* was mortally damaged, commanded the US carrier ambush on the Japanese at Midway on 4 June 1942. Thus deprived of effective command with the Midway battle still hanging in the balance, Fletcher wisely decided to conform to the movements of Halsey's chosen successor, Raymond A. Spruance (1886-1969), who until Halsey's illness had commanded the cruiser element in Halsey's task Force. Thanks to the combined judgment of Fletcher and Spruance and the supreme gallantry of the aircrews of *Yorktown, Enterprise* and *Hornet*, four of the six Japanese carriers which had struck at Pearl Harbor were sunk and carrier parity between the American and Japanese navies precariously restored.

After Midway came the long agony of Guadalcanal (August 1942-February 1943): a merciless battle of attrition in the central Solomon Islands, with both navies at full stretch to supply their troops locked in combat on Guadalcanal. The campaign was fought to the limit of endurance, with two more daytime carrier battles (Eastern Solomons on 24 August and Santa Cruz on 26 October), and a string of vicious night actions between the rival cruiser/destroyer forces. By November 1942 the US Pacific Fleet was down to its last operational carrier, *Enterprise*. *Wasp* and *Hornet* had followed *Yorktown* (lost at Midway) and *Lexington* (lost at the Coral Sea). Both sides finally committed battleships to the Guadalcanal night fighting, with the new American *Washington* and *South Dakota* finally tipping the balance on the night of 14-15 November 1942. From then on the Japanese were reduced to supplying their army on Guadalcanal with clandestine night runs, having lost the equivalent of an entire peacetime fleet since the

*Previous pages:* Hellcat fighters (foreground) and Avenger strike aircraft ranged for take-off on a US carrier.
*Left:* The first two US fleet carriers lost in the Pacific War were USS *Lexington* (CV.2) at Coral Sea in May 1942, and *(below)* the first *Yorktown* (CV.5) at Midway in June 1942. By the end of the year *Wasp* and *Hornet* had followed, both sunk off Guadalcanal; with *Saratoga* damaged, this briefly left *Enterprise* as the only operational US fleet carrier in the Pacific.

The battleship *New Mexico* (BB.40) added fire power to every major US Pacific amphibious operation, from the recapture of the western Aleutians in 1943 to Okinawa in 1945.

*Right:* The two forward turrets of the main battery: 14-inch guns in triple mountings. *Opposite:* The heavy guns of the vital anti-aircraft umbrella – 5-inch AA guns at exercise.

A B C

*Above:* Devastator torpedo-bombers prepare for launch from *Enterprise* during the Battle of Midway (June 1942). Bereft of close fighter cover, slow and vulnerable, only four of the aircraft in this picture came back.

start of the campaign: two battleships, one carrier, five cruisers, 12 destroyers and eight submarines. When this last desperate venture failed, the Japanese High Command accepted the inevitable and ordered the evacuation of Guadalcanal.

The Guadalcanal victory was an extraordinary achievement by the US Navy. The campaign was fought and won on two levels: the Navy's determination not to leave the Marine garrison to its fate, and the attempt to maintain naval air cover until the troops on the ground had conquered enough real estate for land-based air cover to take over. The inevitable result was to deprive the US carriers of their most valuable asset – operating from 'no fixed address' – thus exposing them to heavy losses from Japanese submarine and carrier attack. The victory was another triumph for Nimitz, who refused to despair when American prospects seemed darkest; and for Halsey, appointed by Nimitz as Commander-in-Chief, South Pacific (ComSoPac).

After Guadalcanal, Halsey remained as ComSoPac to direct the dogged advance up the Solomons chain which culminated in the invasion of Bougainville on 31 October 1943. Spruance was meanwhile appointed by Nimitz to command the 5th Fleet: the ever-increasing concentration of new carriers ('Essex' and 'Independence' classes) which arrived in the Pacific from the autumn of 1943. Backed by an armada of storeships and tankers to remain at sea for weeks on end, withdrawing between attacks to advance bases created from empty coral atolls, the 5th Fleet launched the long-awaited break-in to the Central Pacific with its attack on the Gilberts in November 1943. The Marshalls followed in February 1944 and then on 16 June 1944 the 5th Fleet covered the invasion of Saipan in the Marianas, which brought on the last great carrier battle of the Pacific War: the Battle of the Philippine Sea (19-20

June 1944).

The Philippine Sea was Spruance's greatest tactical triumph, in which he refused to expose the Saipan invasion fleet and waited for the Japanese to come to him – to be shot down in scores by the 5th Fleet's carrier fighters. It was the swansong of the Japanese carrier arm, which went into battle with 430 aircraft against 891 and came out with only 35 – the 'Great Marianas Turkey Shoot,' as the Americans exultingly dubbed the engagement. After the Philippine Sea, the last operational Japanese carriers were toothless tigers, useful only as decoys in the extraordinary plan concocted for the defense of the Philippines: 'Sho-Go'.

*Above:* Top brass on Saipan – the leading UD admirals of the Second World War, with Fleet Admiral 'Ernie' King (COMINCH) at center.

*Below: Enterprise* at speed during the Battle of Midway, with a cruiser of the screen at right of picture.

3A

*Above:* Destroyer ordeal off Samar in the Battle of Leyte Gulf. USS *Meermann* (DD.532) lays a smoke screen, viewed from the fleeing escort carrier *Kalinin Bay* (CVE.68). Three of the destroyers escorting the escort carriers surprised on 25 October 1944 were lost.

This involved using empty Japanese carriers as decoys to lure away the massed American fleet carriers, exposing the American invasion fleet, as it lay off the invasion beaches, to a devastating attack by the Japanese battleships and cruisers. The result was the Battle of Leyte Gulf (23-25 October 1944), the greatest sea battle of all time, in which 244 ships on both sides were engaged.

Halsey had returned to sea for the assault on the Philippines, replacing Spruance in command of what was redesignated the '3rd Fleet.' That the Japanese decoy plan came perilously close to success was due to Halsey's aggressive desire to pursue and engage the enemy, giving the Japanese battle fleet a clear run through San Bernadino Strait. The morning of 25 October found the escort carriers of Admiral Kinkaid's 7th Fleet, screening the invasion fleet's northern flank, forced to run for dear life from the battleships until the latter, fearing renewed carrier air attack, turned and withdrew. Halsey's conduct earned a sharp rebuke from Nimitz, who intervened with a direct order to Halsey to cease his pursuit of the Japanese carriers and support 7th Fleet. Though Halsey's carriers duly caught and massacred the Japanese decoy carriers off Cape Engano, the 3rd Fleet's 'Battle Line' failed to intercept the retreating Japanese battleships. For all that, Leyte Gulf was a decisive American victory. It secured the vital beach-head for the reconquest of the Philippines and broke the back of what was left of the Japanese Fleet. At Leyte Gulf the Japanese lost three battleships, four carriers, ten cruisers and nine destroyers; American losses were one carrier, two escort carriers and three destroyers.

Though Leyte Gulf was the last battle fought by the Japanese Fleet, the 3rd/5th Fleet had one prolonged ordeal in store. This was the attempt to decimate the American warships with attacks by *kamikazes:* suicide aircraft, the pledged watchword of whose pilots was 'one plane, one warship.' The *kamikaze* attacks reached their zenith in

*Left:* The 'Great Marianas Turkey Shoot' in the Philippine Sea – 18 June 1944. A blazing Japanese bomber hurtles towards the sea, shot down while trying to attack the escort carrier *Kitkun Bay* (CVE.71).

*Right: Kamikaze* ordeal off Okinawa, 28 April 1945. Too close for the AA guns to bear, a bomb-laden Zero aims for the side of USS *Missouri* (BB.63). This attack was unsuccessful, the Zero crashing into the sea only a few feet short of its target.

April-May 1945 as Spruance's 5th Fleet covered the invasion of Okinawa. All in all, 5th Fleet beat off 1,809 *kamikaze* sorties, shooting down 930 aircraft in the process. Though no American carriers were sunk, 5th Fleet suffered 17 ships sunk and 198 damaged, including 12 fleet carriers and three battleships. In this ordeal the support of the newly-formed British Pacific Fleet, operating with 5th Fleet as 'Task Force 57,' was welcomed in most generous terms by both Spruance and Nimitz. No more than a standard American task force in strength, the British Pacific Fleet readily adjusted to American command and signalling techniques. The wheel had indeed come full circle since the American battle fleet had formed a lone squadron in Beatty's Grand Fleet in the last year of the First World War.

After Okinawa, Halsey returned to begin the softening-up of the Japanese home islands for 'Olympic,' the invasion of Kyushu scheduled for November 1945. The strength of 3rd Fleet, as it sortied from Leyte on its last campaign in July 1945, was ten fleet and six light carriers, eight battleships, 19 cruisers, and over 60 destroyers – a far cry from the threadbare force which had sailed into immortality at Midway barely three years before. What proved to be the last month of the Pacific War was abruptly cut short by the atomic bombs which fell on Hiroshima on 6 August and Nagasaki on 9 August. When the Japanese made their surrender on the deck of the battleship USS *Missouri* in Tokyo Bay on 2 September, the triumph of the US Navy was complete.

Below: 'Independence' class light fleet carrier *Langley* (CVL.27), with fleet carrier *Ticonderoga* (CV.14) in background.

# 6: SHIELD OF THE FREE WORLD

## 1945-1984

With the defeat of Japan in the late summer of 1945 – 170 years since the Continental Congress had first set about organising a Patriot navy with which to fight the British at sea – the US Navy stood revealed as the mightiest instrument of sea power in world history. Perhaps the most amazing aspect of this growth to world supremacy is the fact that it was largely crammed into the last two of those 170 years. The US Navy and the Royal Navy reached their most exact point of balance in the spring of 1943, before the flood of new American carriers entered service. It was in 1943 that US warships, for the last time, served in European waters under British supreme command – when units of the US Atlantic Fleet reinforced the British Home Fleet against the threat of the German battleship *Tirpitz*.

The pace of the US Navy's wartime expansion was staggering. In June 1942, the month of Midway, the US Navy had numbered 5,612 ships of all types and a manpower strength (including Marines and Coast Guards) of 843,096. In June 1945, it numbered 67,952 ships and a manpower strength of 4,031,097 – and it was still expanding in preparation for the invasion of Japan, which, judged by the time it had taken to reconquer the Philippines, was not expected to be completed until the summer of 1946.

The unexpectedly early end of the Pacific War in 1945 was not followed by the classic peacetime levelling-off and downturn in American naval development. No sooner had Japan surrendered than American sea power was given new impetus by three completely novel phenomena. The first of these, born of the war, was technological: the urgent need to adjust naval equipment and strategy to the advent of the atom bomb, jet aircraft and helicopter. The second was political. The hostile attitude of the Soviet Union, the imposition of Communist regimes under Soviet control on the whole of eastern Europe, and the Communist victory in China were to American eyes, the manifestation of a new global threat as great as that so recently posed by Germany, Italy and Japan. The third was the vacuum caused by the impending dissolution of the British Empire, starting with Indian independence in 1948, and the accelerated postwar shrinkage of the hitherto supreme Royal Navy.

Britain was bankrupt and economically ravaged after six years of war; the British economy in 1945-46 was only saved by a massive American dollar loan. One of Britain's most urgent postwar needs was to get as many men as possible out of the Services and into the factories. Between 1945 and 1948 the Royal Navy's manpower fell from 863,000 to 147,000 and there was a massive shake-out in warships of prewar vintage: 10 old battleships and a battle-cruiser, 20 cruisers, 61 destroyers and 77 corvettes. Britain's entire fleet of 37 escort carriers, built in the United States, was handed back under the terms of Lend-Lease. On VJ-Day in 1945, the overall strength of the British Pacific Fleet had consisted of four battleships, 10 fleet carriers, nine escort carriers, 11 cruisers, 40 destroyers and 29 submarines. Three years later, the strength *of the entire British Fleet,* in all waters, had dwindled to four battleships, eight carriers, 17 cruisers, 52 destroyers and 34 submarines (excluding the Reserve). By 1950 the British strength in the Pacific was a ghost of what it had been only five years before. The heaviest Royal Naval contribution to the United Nations fleet in the Korean War was one light fleet carrier.

This tremendous postwar run-down of the British Fleet confirmed that the mantle of global sea power *in strength* had passed to the US Navy, which in 1945 had over 3,600 named ships of all types, and thousands more bearing numbers only. The excellent prewar groundwork in modernising the American fleet meant that immediate postwar disposals (1945-48) weeded out fewer heavy ships than in the Royal Navy: seven old battleships to the British ten, 11 escort carriers to the British 37, 11 cruisers to the British 20. Even after 132 old American destroyers had been sold or scrapped between 1945 and 1948, this still left over 500 available for service.

Inevitably, therefore, the US Navy played a dominant role in the crucial operations in Korea of 1950-51. When Communist North Korea invaded South Korea at 11 points in June 1950, the force best placed to rush support to the faltering South Koreans was the US 7th Fleet of Vice-Admiral Arthur Struble, based on Japan. Struble was unusually well qualified for the job. He had been chief of staff during the US naval planning for the invasion of Normandy in 1944, commanded an attack group at Leyte Gulf, and had been promoted commander of US amphibious forces in the Pacific in September 1945. He now became the first American admiral required to fight a naval war exclusively tailored to the demands of the land forces, with no enemy naval chal-

The awesome streamlined bulk of USS *Ohio* (SSBN.726), the first of the Trident-firing giant ballistic missile submarines, commissioned in 1981. Each of these giants carries firing tubes for 24 Trident missiles with over ten warheads per missile. Trident's range (at over 4,000 miles (6,437 km) nearly double that of the earlier Poseidon) enables the 'Ohio' class ships to menace targets in the Soviet Union from waters where the Soviet anti-submarine fleet dare not venture. An 'Ohio' has a displacement greater than most light aircraft-carriers at 18,700 tons (18,999 tonnes) submerged.

The old and the new in Korean waters (February 1952). In the center, USS *Rainier* (AE.5) pulls away after simultaneously replenishing the carrier USS *Antietam* (CV.36) and the 'Iowa' class battleship USS *Wisconsin* (BB.64).

lenge to meet – a far cry from the days of Guadalcanal, the Marianas and the Philippines in 1942-45. Korea was also the only war in which an American fleet has formed the core of a United Nations force called into being to resist aggression. The 7th Fleet off Korea was ably seconded by contingents from the British, Canadian, Australian, New Zealand, French and Dutch navies.

The naval war off Korea started promisingly enough for the UN naval forces, with the virtual elimination of North Korea's scanty coastal navy in the first weeks of the war (July-September 1950) by carrier air attacks and gun actions by surface warships. Over the following year, however, the dramatic swings of fortune on land finally took the form of a strategic stalemate. The further south the North Koreans advanced the heavier they were hammered by UN air attacks, with carriers playing an increasing role. Conversely, the further north the UN forces advanced, the harder it proved to give them adequate support. UN sea power (with the US 7th Fleet covering the Korean east coast and the other UN naval forces the west) enabled the UN counter-offensive of autumn 1950 to be speeded by two impressive amphibious 'hooks' behind the Communist lines, at Inchon (September) and Wonsan (October). UN advances north beyond the Yalu River, however, proved impossible to sustain, and after another Communist assault was repelled in May 1951 armistice talks got warily under way at Kaesong. They were to drag on for another two years before the armistice ending the war was finally signed at Panmunjom, in July 1953.

For the US Navy, the legacy of Korea was a mixed one. The war confirmed the versatility of the big carrier as an 'all-arms' air support and strike force, able to provide fighter cover as well as tactical air/ground support. As in 1941-45, this applied both to amphibious landings and to subsequent operations ashore. The wisdom of 'mothballing' older ships (particularly carriers) was also proven. But Korea also showed that land targets within reach of naval gunfire can be far more economically destroyed by cruisers and battleships than by carrier aircraft. Expressed as 'cost effectiveness', shells are cheaper to make, store, and unleash on the enemy than piloted aircraft; the expenditure of radar-directed heavy shells is far less costly than that of shot-down sophisticated aircraft and trained aircrew.

One of the greatest paradoxes of the international naval scene since 1945 is that the United States, home of the world's most wasteful 'throw-away' consumer culture, has practised unequalled thrift with regard to its warships. Many years have to pass before an American warship is declared unfit for furth-

Mothballed American destroyers, all capable of speedy return to front-line service, on the Pacific coast in July 1966. Preserving obsolescent ships instead of scrapping them has always been a prudent hallmark of the US Navy.

The guided missile frigate USS *Oliver Hazard Perry* (FFG.7), commissioned in December 1977. She carries 40 Harpoon/Standard surface/AA missiles, two helicopters in the after hangar, a 76mm gun, and two triple torpedo tubes for anti-submarine work – all-round potential in a hull displacing 3,605 tons (3,663 tonnes) at full load.

Scene on the flight deck of the amphibious warfare ship USS *Guam* (LPH.9) during the American intervention in Grenada (October 1983), with troop-carrying Chinook helicopter in background.

Pacific War veteran USS *Ticonderoga* in service in 1961, extensively rebuilt with a portside angled flight deck and fully-enclosed or 'hurricane' bow.

er service, and consigned for sale or scrap. The essence of the US Navy's postwar policy on warship strengths has always been to go, wherever possible, for the longest feasible service life through repeated modernisation. This again has presented a total contrast to British practice, and has remained unchanged for nearly four decades. When HMS *Victorious,* Britain's last wartime heavy fleet carrier, was phased out in 1968, the US Navy still had 13 wartime 'Essex' class carriers in service. Two of these were offered to the Royal Navy in 1981 by President Reagan's Government, alarmed at the apparent British determination to do away with carriers completely. (This was the year before the total insanity of Britain's carrier policy was exposed by the Falklands War.) The last British fleet carrier, HMS *Ark Royal,* was axed in 1978 – though she was ten years 'younger' than the first class of American postwar heavy carriers, the 'Midways'. At the time of going to press, in the spring of 1984, the 'Midway' class *Coral Sea* is undergoing a refit which will extend her operational career to no less than 50 years: 1945-1995.

On a far more modest but inevitably more controversial scale, the same has applied to the US Navy's battleships. Fifteen years on, the lessons of Korea were re-taught in the Vietnam War. In this conflict the US 7th Fleet provided offshore support for the South Vietnamese and American forces with six carriers (450 aircraft). By 1968, however, aircraft and aircrew losses to North Vietnamese anti-aircraft fire had become so costly that the US Army and Marine Corps – not the Navy – were urging the reactivation of the veteran battleship *New Jersey*. Over 1,000 targets hitherto accessible only to strike aircraft lay within the range of her 16-inch guns, which fired 5,688 rounds (com-

*Above:* A US Navy F-4B Phantom in a high-level bombing attack over Vietnam.

*Right:* The battleship USS *New Jersey* (BB.62) firing her full 16-inch broadside during her 1968-69 recommission for service in the Vietnam War.

USS *Long Beach* (CGN.9) was the first American cruiser designed since 1941; the world's first nuclear-powered surface warship; and the first surface warship armed with a guided-missile main battery. She was brought into service in September 1961.

June 1982: USS *Ticonderoga*, first ship of the newest American class of guided-missile cruisers, armed with the Aegis missile system, underway in the Gulf of Mexico.

pared with only 771 between 1943 and 1945) during her experimental recommission in 1968-69. It was calculated that the $21 million cost of her refit and recommission was equal to the value of six shot-down F4 Phantom aircraft. Within another ten years the heartfelt advocacy of former pilots was pressing for yet another return of *New Jersey* to active service, this time as a combined missile and big-gun platform. In this new guise her awesome silhouette appeared off the strife-torn coast of Beirut in the New Year of 1984, supporting the 6th Fleet's abortive 'peace-keeping' mission, hurling 16-inch shells across the Shouf Moutains onto rebel PLO gun positions.

Extending the operational careers of veteran warships past all known limits has gone hand in hand with a formidable inventiveness in new technologies and new ship types. This has been most obvious in the two mainstays of American sea power since 1945: the giant carrier and the submarine.

The big carrier was the natural legacy of the Pacific War in which, after 1942, the only American carriers lost were the lightweight 'Independence' class *Princeton* and five escort carriers. From this experience, American carrier doctrine argues that a big carrier stands a better chance of surviving submarine or air attack, and can also mount more anti-aircraft guns (or, latterly, missiles). More obviously, the bigger the carrier, the bigger (and better balanced) the air group can be. This means more fighters both for defense from air attacks, and for escorting attack missions flown by the carrier's strike aircraft. Big carriers also proved perfectly suited to operating the new jet aircraft of the postwar era, with their increased deadweights and flying speeds. The first jet-powered carrier launch (of a McDonnell FH-1 Phantom) was made from *Coral Sea* in July 1946.

After a false start with *United States* (aborted in 1949) American heavy-carrier development was resumed in the light of

The Combat Information Center (CIC) in USS *Ticonderoga*. Here are displayed the data gathered by the ship's four fixed-array AN/SPY 1A radars, revealing situations which might threaten the ship and the battle group she is designed to protect. The ship's weapons – AA and surface missiles, rapid-firing deck guns, anti submarine torpedoes and rockets – are all directed and fired from the CIC.

Sonar Technicians man their underwater watch stations at the console aboard the 'Los Angeles' class nuclear-powered attack submarine USS *La Jolla*.

Korean War experience. The result was the four-ship 'Forrestal' class (*Forrestal, Saratoga, Ranger,* and *Independence*), the first of which was ordered in 1952. These mighty ships, with their full-displacement of 78,000 tons, were the first post-1945 heavy carriers, designed and built specifically for operating jet aircraft. They gave the US Navy an entirely new strategic function: as a global vehicle for the American nuclear deterrent. Though the simultaneous development of the ballistic missile-firing submarine (SSBN) soon robbed the American carrier arm of a monopoly in nuclear 'clout', the Forrestals served as prototypes for the mightiest floating structures ever built by man: the nuclear-powered *Enterprise* which was commissioned in 1961 and ultimately the 91,500-ton *Nimitz* (commissioned 1975) and her successors.

Not content with transforming the role of the heavy fleet carrier, the US Navy was simultaneously achieving the same for its submarine arm. The end of the Pacific War had carried the American submarine arm to an unprecedented eminence. In the submarine 'Battle of the Pacific' against Japanese shipping, the US Navy's submarines – though only amounting to two percent of the total American naval strength in the Pacific, destroyed 61 percent of the Japanese merchant fleet. The ravages caused by the American submarines made it impossible for the Japanese to ship troops and supplies to the island garrisons menaced by the US carrier task forces, completely distrupted the internal sealanes of the Japanese Empire, and were a major factor in bringing about the early end of the war. They succeeded, in short, where Germany's U-boats had failed in the Atlantic, and the significance of this was not forgotten after the Japanese defeat.

American submarine development after 1945 was aimed at pushing the conventional diesel/electric submarine to the limit and to developing a practicable nuclear power plant. The first stage was perfecting a streamlined hull which would yield high submerged speeds. The now-familiar 'teardrop' or 'whale' shape was proven by the experimental *Albacore* (1953), the first submarine to break 30 knots when submerged. The first nuclear-powered submarines,

Stunning head-on shot of the 'super-carrier' USS *Carl Vinson* (CVN.70), third ship of the nuclear-powered 'Nimitz' class. With a deep-load displacement of 91,487 tons (92,951 tonnes), these carriers are the biggest warships of all time.

Poised for launch from the steam catapult: a Grumman F-14 Tomcat. This advanced 'swing-wing' all-weather fighter (the wings retract aft for high-speed flight) has a maximum speed of Mach 2.4.

USS *Enterprise*, the US Navy's first nuclear-powered 'super-carrier'. When completed in 1961 she was the largest floating structure ever built by man, but still took only 31 months from laying-down to launch.

*Above:* The first nuclear-powered aircraft carrier USS *Enterprise* (CVN-65) and USS *Truxton* (CGN-35), the nuclear-powered 'Belknap' class cruiser.

*Nautilus* (1955) and *Seawolf* (1956) retained a conventional submarine hull design, the full 'teardrop' hull being used in *Skipjack* (laid down in May 1956).

Long before the 'Skipjacks' had even been launched, however, it was clear that even more fundamental changes must be made. The shift of nuclear weapons delivery from conventional bombing aircraft to ballistic rocket missile threw a new burden on the US Navy: providing submarine launching-platforms for ballistic missiles which cannot – unlike land-based missile sites – be 'taken out' with the first enemy strike. This was achieved with the 'George Washingtons', first of the US Navy's SSBN fleet within a fleet, designed to lurk unseen in the ocean wastes with their batteries of Polaris missiles.

This development, modified and expanded to keep pace with the parallel advances in missile development, has produced warships which stagger the imagination. *George Washington,* commissioned in the same year as *Skipjack* (1959), displaced 6,888 tons to *Skipjack's* 3,513 tons. Their successors were the 'Ethan Allens' (7,880 tons), and the 'Benjamin Franklins' and 'Lafayettes' (8,250 tons), yielding a total of 41 SSBNs in service with the US Navy by the end of 1967. After less than a decade in service for the earlier SSBNs, they were being converted to carry the more powerful Poseidon missile with its multiple-warhead punch. But all were dwarfed by the 'Ohio' class giants, built to carry the Trident missile in 24 launching tubes: 18,700 tons submerged displacement and 560 feet in length, larger than most light aircraft-carriers of the Second World War.

The US Navy of the 1980s therefore has a greater range of major capacities than at any other time of technical peace. Its SSBNs and carriers have a crucial nuclear strike potential; in the conventional carrier task force role, its surface forces have retained all the versatility in support and strike potential, which their predecessors perfected in the Pacific War. Its 'hunter-killer' submarines, both nuclear and conventionally powered, maintain the triple task of enemy commerce destruction and enemy warship-hunting, both surface and submarine. Its amphibious capacity, with helicopter carriers and support ships, is one of the greatest assets of the North Atlantic Treaty Organisation in which the US Navy has played the dominant role since the formation of the Alliance in 1949.

The formation of NATO set the seal on the recasting of global sea power which had emerged from the Second World War. A NATO Supreme Command for the Atlantic (SACLANT) was established at Norfork, Virginia, with the US 2nd Fleet and the Royal Navy undertaking joint responsibility for Europe's Atlantic lifeline. The former British paramountcy in the Mediterranean passed to the US 6th Fleet, with the US 7th Fleet continuing to watch the western Pacific and the US 3rd Fleet the eastern Pacific. This 'all-ocean' capability extends to the maintenance of powerful US forces in the Indian Ocean and approaches to the Persian Gulf.

Yet fellow-members of NATO have no grounds for complacency. The rise of a powerful Soviet fleet, with all essential capabilities matching those of the US Navy save in numbers and technological excellence, has proceeded unabated over the past 25 years. Soviet naval growth has not, however, been matched by similar efforts on the part of the US Navy's NATO allies, predominantly Britain. Even when all the capacities of the US Navy are listed, the combined NATO naval deployment has shrunk from 35 carriers and 440 destroyers and frigates in 1960 to 13 carriers and 333 destroyers and frigates in 1980. The day may yet come when the US Navy, increasingly the seaborne shield of the Free World, is called upon to shoulder a burden beyond even its mighty strength.

*Left:* The nuclear-powered fleet ballistic missile submarine USS *Ohio*, SSBN–726, at the electric boat division of General Dynamics. The *Ohio* was the first of the Navy's nuclear-powered Trident missile submarines.

2

# 7: THE U.S. NAVY TODAY

The US Navy is the largest and most powerful navy the world has yet seen, possessing truly global capability for the protection for the USA and its interests, and for the projection of American power. The three principal components of the US Navy are its submarine arm, heavily biased in favour of nuclear-powered boats; its maritime air arm, centred on multi-role aircraft-carriers carrying a diversity of offensive/ defensive aircraft and protected by missile-armed cruisers and destroyers; and its amphibious arm, dedicated to the carriage and shoreward delivery of the US Marine Corps, and usually protected by frigates. The submarine arm is being rationalised at the moment, with heavy emphasis on the rapid construction of the 'Ohio' class SSBN and 'Los Angeles' class SSN to allow the retirement of older classes. The SSBN's are being equipped with the Trident I C4 strategic missiles as a replacement for the older Poseidon C3, and will soon begin to receive the definitive Trident II D5; combined with improved communications capability for submerged submarines (thanks to the development of ELF and new TACAMO systems), greater reliance can be placed on the rapid and accurate response capabilities of the SSBN force, helping to promote it towards the primary position amongst the elements of the US offensive strategic triad (land-based missiles, air-released bombs and missiles and submarine-launched missiles). The SSN force is designed for two offensive/ defensive functions, namely the defence of the USA by attacks on Soviet missile-carrying submarines, and the defence of carrier task groups by attacks on Soviet submarines equipped with torpedoes (of which about half are nuclear-tipped). But while in theory the concentration on the 'Ohio' and 'Los Angeles' classes is excellent, offering the possibility of large standardized forces, the programme has run into immense problems of cost escalation and production slippages, requiring the retention of older vessels as a stop-gap. Moreover, while the capability of the new classes is unquestionable, so too is their vulnerability, for both classes are extremely large and relatively noisy. And the very size of the 'Los Angeles' class raises another problem, for it makes it difficult for the boats of the class to operate in the shallow waters of the large continental shelf areas, where Soviet boats could well lurk for some time. It would seem sensible, therefore, for the US Navy to develop a new class of diesel-electric hunter-killer submarine for this specific purpose, but so entrenched is the position of the nuclear-boat lobby that this seems impossibly difficult to achieve.

Naval aviation in the US Navy rests with the aircraft-carrier force, planned at 15 carrier air wings (one per carrier) but currently operational as only 12 carrier air wings. This is still a formidable capability, given that each carrier air wing can muster up to 80 or more aircraft (usually two fighter squadrons, one medium attack squadron, one light attack squadron and two anti-submarine squadrons, plus support aircraft) of the US Navy and US Marine Corps, but leaves the US Navy with little reserve capacity. Four more of the massive nuclear-powered 'Nimitz' class carriers are planned or building, which will improve matters considerably, but in the short term the deficiency is being made good in an alternative fashion by the reactivation and modernization (with missiles and modern sensors) of two (possibly four) 'Iowa' class battleships. Though these cannot carry the aircraft of a carrier air wing (though a complement of V/STOL strike aircraft is planned when the ships are modernised yet further), they do have formidable gun and missile firepower.

Escort of each carrier task group is theoretically entrusted to two missile-armed cruisers (nuclear-powered in groups which are centred on a nuclear carrier) plus a number of missile-armed destroyers. A shortfall in numbers has often meant, however, that frigates have to be included in the escort force as part of the outer screen. The situation should be improved greatly with the delivery of additional 'Ticonderoga' class cruisers, with their highly capable AEGIS analysis and control functions, and with the first arrivals of the 'Arleigh Burke' class destroyers at the end of the decade. Hand-in-hand with this ship and sensor modification programme goes a constant upgrading of the vital Standard missile, designed principally as an air-defence weapon but possessing a limited anti-ship capability and being developed into a longer-range and more accurate weapon system. Other missile developments centre on the widespread deployment of the medium-range Harpoon anti-ship missile, and the installation on larger ships of the Tomahawk cruise missile for long-range anti-ship defence. Close-range air-defence remains a problem, the Sea Sparrow system being too slow in launch, and the Phalanx 20-mm CIWS mounting lacking sufficient punch for last-ditch defence against sea-skimming anti-ship missiles. It is anticipated that the capability and versatility of ship-board missile systems will be much enhanced later in the decade by the adoption of vertical-launch systems capable of handling anti-ship, anti-aircraft and anti-submarine missiles of several types.

Amphibious forces are in something of a quandary at the moment, for the precise role of the US Marine Corps remains uncertain. Amphibious operations are clearly important, but their precise nature (and perhaps their vulnerability) remains open to question. Nevertheless their ships are being developed and built as a matter of urgency as the need to replace older units becomes more apparent. One of the problems is that these large and lightly defended targets require extensive escort protection from frigates armed with anti-ship and anti-aircraft missiles, and that the frigates are in short supply because of the need for their deployment in carrier task group escort forces.

The US Navy has an all-volunteer personnel strength, this amounting at the moment to some 569,000 including 42,700 women. Naval air-power, which has about 1,450 combat aircraft and 160 combat helicopters, is included in this total, and operates 24 fighter squadrons, 12 medium attack squadrons, 24 light attack squadrons, 11 shipboard anti-submarine squadrons, 11 fixed- and 17 rotary-wing anti-submarine squadrons, 12 airborne early warning squadrons, 24 land-based maritime reconnaissance and anti-submarine squadrons, two mine countermeasures helicopter squadrons, 22 operational conversion units, 18 training squadrons and 17 miscellaneous squadrons.

Operationally, the US Navy is divided into four fleets controlled by two command organizations: headquartered at Norfolk, Virginia, the Atlantic Fleet contols the 2nd Fleet (headquarters in Norfolk) and the 6th Fleet (headquarters at Gaeta in Italy) for operations in the Mediterranean; and headquartered at Pearl Harbour, Hawaii, the Pacific Fleet controls the 3rd Fleet (headquarters at Pearl Harbour) and the 7th Fleet (headquarters at Yokohama in Japan for operations in the western Pacific with detachments into the Indian Ocean and Persian Gulf areas). With other continental bases at Bangor, Boston, Brunswick, Charleston, Jacksonville, Kings Bay, New London, New Orleans and Newport, the 2nd Fleet has overseas bases at Guantanamo Bay (Cuba), Holy Loch (UK), Keflavik (Iceland) and Roosevelt Roads (Puerto Rico), and generally deploys 31 SSBNs, 41 SSNs, 76 surface combatants and 27 amphibious warfare vessels. Apart from its base at Gaeta, the 6th Fleet has a base at La Rota in Spain and at La Maddalena, Naples and Sigonella in Italy, and usually musters some two SSNs, one or two aircraft-carriers and about 38 other surface combatants and amphibious warfare vessels. The 3rd Fleet has additional bases at Adak, Long Beach, San Diego, San Francisco and Whidbey Island, and has a typical strength of two SSBNs, 30 SSNs, three carriers, one battleship and about 44 other surface combatants plus 31 amphibious warfare vessels. And the 7th Fleet, with additional bases at Agena and Apra Harbor on Guam, Midway Island, Subic Bay in the Philippines and forward facilities in the Indian Ocean at Diego Suarez, operates a few SSNs on temporary assignment, plus some 45 surface combatants including three or four carriers; the detachments in the Indian Ocean and Persian Gulf, often supported by vessels from the 6th Fleet, generally comprise a carrier task group with five escorts in the former, and two destroyers plus a command ship in the latter.

US Navy Reserves amount to an extra 87,900 men, and these man a varying number of ships, normally about three destroyers and six frigates, and also provide the manpower strength for two additional carrier air wings, two maritime reconnaissance wings and one tactical support wing (all with fixed-wing aircraft), plus one helicopter wing.

The US Coast Guard service is administered by the Department of Transportation, but in war comes under the operational control of the US Navy as part of the armed forces. Regular strength is 38,800 including 1,800 women, and there are 11,800 reservists. Ship assets comprise 17 high-endurance cutters (small destroyers), 28 medium-endurance cutters (lightweight frigates), six icebreakers, 76 patrol craft, and 118 other craft. The US Coast Guard also possesses a small air arm with 41 fixed- and rotary-wing aircraft, most of them dedicated to patrol and search-and-rescue.

**USN ship strength**

| *type* | *class* | *number* |
|---|---|---|
| SUBMARINES | | |
| strategic, | 'Ohio' | 8 (+6 ordered) |
| ballistic-missile, | 'Benjamin Franklin' | 12 |
| nuclear-powered | 'James Madison' | 8 |
| | 'Lafayette' | 8 |
| fleet attack | 'Los Angeles' | 36 |
| nuclear-powered | 'Sturgeon' | 35 |
| (SSN) | 'Permit' (ex 'Thresher') | 13 |
| | 'Glenard P. Lipscomb' | 1 |
| | 'Narwhal' | 1 |
| | 'Skipjack' | 4 (3 in 87/88) |
| | 'Skate' | 2 (1 in 87/88) |
| attack, diesel-powered | 'Barbel' | 2 |
| (SS) | 'Darter' | 1 |
| SSNs, other roles | | |
| Deep SAR | 'Sturgeon' | 2 |
| SF transport | 'Ethan Allen' | 2 |
| transport | 'Tullibee' | 1 |
| AIRCRAFT CARRIERS | | |
| nuclear (CVN) | 'Nimitz' | 4 |
| | 'Enterprise' | 1 |
| conventional (CV) | 'Kitty Hawk' | 3 |
| | 'John F. Kennedy' | 1 |
| | 'Forrestal' | 4 |
| | 'Midway' | 2 |
| BATTLESHIP (BBG) | 'Iowa' | 3 (+1 refit) |
| CRUISERS | | |
| nuclear-powered | 'Virginia' | 4 |
| (CGN) | 'California' | 2 |
| | 'Truxton' | 1 |
| | 'Long Beach' | 1 |
| | 'Bainbridge' | 1 |
| conventionally- | 'Ticonderoga' | 9 |
| powered (CG) | 'Belknap' | 9 |
| | 'Leahy' | 9 |
| DESTROYERS | | |
| guided missile | 'Kidd' | 4 |
| (DDG) | 'Coontz' | 10 |
| | 'Charles F. Adams' | 23 |
| anti-submarine (DD) | 'Spruance' | 31 |
| FRIGATES | | |
| guided missile | 'Oliver Hazard Perry' | 50 |
| (FFG) | 'Brook' | 6 |
| gun/ASW | 'Knox' | 46 |
| | Garcia' | 10 |
| | 'Glover' | 1 |
| | 'Bronstein' | 2 |
| AMPHIBIOUS OPERATIONS | | |
| command (LCC) | 'Blue Ridge' | 2 |
| assault (LHA) | 'Tarawa' | 5 |
| assault (LPH) | 'Iwo Jima' | 7 |
| assault (LPD) | 'Austin' | 11 |
| | 'Raleigh' | 2 |
| assault (LSD) | 'Whidbey' | 2 |
| | 'Anchorage' | 5 |
| | 'Thomaston' | 3 |
| (LST) | 'Newport' | 18 |
| cargo (LKA) | 'Charleston' | 5 |
| landing craft | Air cushion (LCAC) | 9 (+27 ordered) |
| | Utility: Type 1610 | 53 |
| | Type 1466 | 4 |
| patrol craft | | |
| hydrofoil (PHM) | 'Pegasus' | 6 |
| inshore & river (PB, PCF, PBR) | | 85 |
| MINESWEEPERS | | |
| ocean | 'Aggressive' | 3 |
| inshore boats (MSB) | | 7 |

Figures do not include Active Auxiliary Ships: 84; Military Sealift Command: 123; Ready Reserve Force: 85; National Defense Reserve Fleet: 176; Ships on Inactive Reserve/Storage: 46.

HISTORY OF THE UNITED STATES

# AIR FORCE

*Right:* P-47N Thunderbolts, produced from late 1944 for service in the Pacific.

488577
488589
488576

PA
92

# 1: SIGNAL CORPS TO AIR CORPS

*Overleaf:* P-36As, seen here in the markings of the 1st Pursuit Group, were supplied to the Army Air Corps from April 1938.

American military aviation had its formal beginning with the establishment of the Aeronautical Division, US Army Signal Corps, on August 1, 1909. Its staff of three was given the task of studying flying machines and their possible military applications. By the end of the year they had defined their first requirement, and advertised for an aircraft able to carry two men, for an hour, with a range of 125 miles (200 km) and a minimum average speed of 40 mph (64 km/h).

The successful aircraft – the world's first military airplane – was, predictably, built by the Wright brothers, though the original was destroyed in a crash during trials at Fort Myer, Virginia, in September 1908, and it was not until August 2, 1909, that a rebuilt example was accepted by the Signal Corps. No more aircraft could be afforded until 1911, and only 56 altogether had been procured by the end of 1915. A handful of these were sent to the Philippines, while others were used for experiments involving firing machine guns and dropping bombs, though the inventors of the machine gun and the bomb sight were soon promoting their inventions in Europe instead: official policy in the US was to discontinue such practices. Wireless telegraphy for communicating with artillery batteries on the ground was more readily accepted.

It was America's involvement in World War I that inspired real development of both the aircraft industry and military aviation. When the German submarine offensive in the Atlantic in 1915 prompted an assessment of military preparedness, the Signal Corps Aviation Section, as the Aeronautical Division had become in 1914, comprised 46 officers, 243 enlisted men, and 23 aircraft. Soon after, experience on the Mexican border, where a squadron of eight R-2s had been sent in support of General Pershing's campaign against Pancho Villa in the spring of 1916, showed the aircraft to be virtually useless because they were underpowered and prone to disintegrate. Thus nearly $14 million was allocated to the Aviation Section. At the same time, the National Defense Act of 1916 removed the restriction of flying training to bachelor officers under 30 that had been imposed in 1914.

The American declaration of war in April 1917 stimulated further action. In July Congress voted the astonishing sum of $640 million to support a military aviation program that envisaged production of 22,625 aircraft, along with twice that number of engines, to equip 345 combat and 118 supporting squadrons, of which 263 were to be in action in France within a year. This target was clearly impossible, and by the end of the year the

*Below:* The standard Army Air Service trainer in World War I, the JN-4 'Jenny', provided inadequate preparation for the high-performance fighters in service on the Western Front by 1917.

numbers were being revised to meet a target of 202 squadrons by July 1919.

Compared with the 532 aircraft ordered, and 272 delivered, by April 1917, the following 19 months brought deliveries of 11,754 American and Canadian airplanes, along with nearly 31,000 engines. The appointment of the first Chief of the Air Service, American Expeditionary Force in France, was confirmed in September 1917, and the following May brought the establishment of the Army Air Service, along with the Bureaus of Military Aeronautics and of Aircraft Production. The Expeditionary Force accepted more than 5,000 aircraft from European – predominantly French – manufacturers, and the scale of production that had been initiated is indicated by the acceptance of another 2,317 American aircraft after the Armistice of November 1918, as well as the cancellation of more than 61,000.

The majority of the US-built aircraft were JN-4, JN-6 and SJ-1 trainers, and license-built versions of the British D.H.4, a light bomber already obsolescent when deliveries began in 1918. Nevertheless, from August 1918 13 squadrons were equipped with the type. Fighter squadrons, meanwhile, generally categorized as pursuit squadrons, had to rely on French and British aircraft. Various models of Nieuport scouts were used for training American pilots, whose experience of the JN-4 had hardly equipped them for the high-performance machines in use on the Western Front by 1918; four squadrons were equipped with the Nieuport 28 for a time, but by the Armistice the Spad XIII was used by 16 of the 18 pursuit squadrons, another had the British S.E.5a and the last used the F.1 Camel, generally for night operations.

With the exception of the small number of Americans who had served with the French and British forces, and who ultimately transferred to the AAS as the 17th, 48th, and 103d Pursuit Squadrons, it was March 1918 before the first American unit – 1st Aero Squadron – was ready for active service, and late summer before the Air Service had reached a substantial level. However, under the control of Colonel Billy Mitchell, Chief of Air Service with Pershing's First Army, AEF, all American squadrons were combined with French and British units to produce a force of 49 squadrons mustering nearly 1,500 aircraft to support the First Army's Saint-Mihiel offensive in September 1918. These were used with great success, carrying out the classic missions of air superiority, interdiction, and close air support, albeit against greatly inferior opposition.

*Below:* Large numbers of D.H.4 light bombers were produced before the end of the war, and many were modified for other roles after the Armistice.

9241
F4B-4

Of course, these missions were still to be defined in such terms: in the context of the Western Front they amounted to bombing and strafing German airfields, troop concentrations, and lines of communication, but their use of aircraft in superior strength as part of a coordinated air and ground offensive held important lessons for the future. Like so many advocates of air power, Mitchell, promoted to brigadier-general in command of the Air Service Army Group, as a result of the Saint-Mihiel success, was convinced that aircraft alone, carrying out strategic raids against the enemy rear, could turn the tide of war.

In the event, there was no time to test the theory. From September 26 the AEF was busy with the Meuse-Argonne offensive, and supporting the ground forces took priority, though there was one mass raid against a rear-echelon German formation on October 9, involving 253 bombers escorted by 110 fighters. Barely a month later the war was over, and the force began the process of demobilization.

The size of the force in November 1918 is a measure of the progress made in less than two years of war. Its total strength of 20,000 officers and 170,000 men included nearly 800 pilots with 45 front-line squadrons, equipped with 740 aircraft. In combat 781 enemy aircraft and 73 observation balloons had been shot down, for the loss of 289 American airplanes. During 215 bombing raids nearly 114 tons (115,831 kg) of bombs had been dropped.

The end of the war put an end to the expansion it had engendered. Mitchell was appointed Director of Military Aeronautics, only to discover on his return to Washington, DC, in March 1919 that the post had been abolished: instead, he was appointed Third Assistant Executive and Chief of the Training and Operations Group. He advocated universal military training to produce a reserve force 7,000,000 strong, the construction of transatlantic bombers, and the means of defense against them, but without the capacity for the kind of decisive independent action he envisaged, the Air Service stood no chance of forming the basis of the independent air arm controlling both military and naval aviation that he recommended.

With the limited funds made available in 1920 and 1921 some improved versions of wartime aircraft were ordered, including 200 MB-3A pursuits, updated from the useful but unreliable MB-3, and 20 MB-2 bombers. At the same time, Mitchell instigated a series of experimental flights aimed at extending the capabilities of men and machines and demonstrating the possibilities of organized aviation.

In 1919 a transcontinental reliability test saw a number of war-surplus aircraft complete the coast-to-coast journey; the following year brought a return flight by four Air Service DH-4s between New York and Nome, Alaska, and the laying out of the first of a proposed national network of airways, involving landing fields and navigational aids on a route between Washington, DC, and Dayton, Ohio: and 1924 was marked by the first nonstop and the first dawn-to-dusk transcontinental flights, and a successful "world cruise," when two of the original four Douglas seaplanes built for the purpose took 175 days to accomplish a journey of 27,553 miles.

While such flights provided vital experience in the engineering and organizational fields, Mitchell's most famous and most spectacular demonstrations were of an entirely different kind. In trying to block development of the airplane as an instrument of war, the Navy attempted to show its ineffectiveness. This backfired, when pictures of the battleship *Indiana* were published, revealing the damage caused by bombs placed on her deck in an intended display of the vessel's invulnerability. In 1921 Mitchell offered to prove his point by sinking some of the obsolete German ships awaiting disposal.

The Navy accepted, though limiting the number of bombs allowed, and Mitchell ordered the construction of 2,000 lb (907 kg) bombs for the purpose. The trials began in June, with the sinking of a German U-Boat and the location of the battleship *Iowa* in a

*Opposite, top:* A grotesquely decorated Nieuport 17, one of the 75 procured by the American Expeditionary in France from September 1917.

*Opposite, bottom:* A total of 143 Sopwith Camels were bought by the AEF, and used primarily as night fighters, though the two squadrons equipped with the type did not transfer from the RAF until November 1918.

*Below:* Line-up of Nieuport 17s at the American Aviation School, Isseudon, in March 1918, when this was the standard pursuit trainer.

25,600 square mile (66,360 km$^2$) search zone, and were resumed in July with the destroyer *G-102*, the cruiser *Frankfurt*, and the battleship *Ostfriesland* as targets. The destroyer was despatched within 19 minutes by 300 lb (136 kg) bombs dropped from 1,500 ft (460 m) on July 13; *Frankfurt* resisted similar bombs, but succumbed to the 600 lb (272 kg) weapons that followed; and in the climax on July 21, the *Ostfriesland*, which had withstood 600 lb (272 kg) bombs in the previous day, was attacked with Mitchell's secret 2,000-pounders (907 kg).

The rules allowed two direct hits with the largest bombs available, but after three direct hits with 1,000 lb (454 kg) bombs the hull of the battleship was still intact. However, the plan was to drop the bigger bombs alongside the *Ostfriesland*, and six of these in 12 minutes caused the battleship to capsize and sink. Though the violations of the rules gave the Navy an excuse to ignore the results, a naval air arm was formed soon afterward, and subsequent tests, when the battleships *Alabama*, *Virginia*, and *New Jersey* were sunk in September 1921 and September 1923, proved Mitchell's point. Mitchell himself continued his campaign, becoming a popular hero, but his outspokenness could not be tolerated indefinitely, and after his court-martial at the end of 1925, Mitchell resigned from the army.

In July 1926 the Air Service was redesignated the Army Air Corps, and the legislation effecting this change included provisions for an expansion program intended to achieve a strength of 1,518 officers, 16,000 enlisted men,

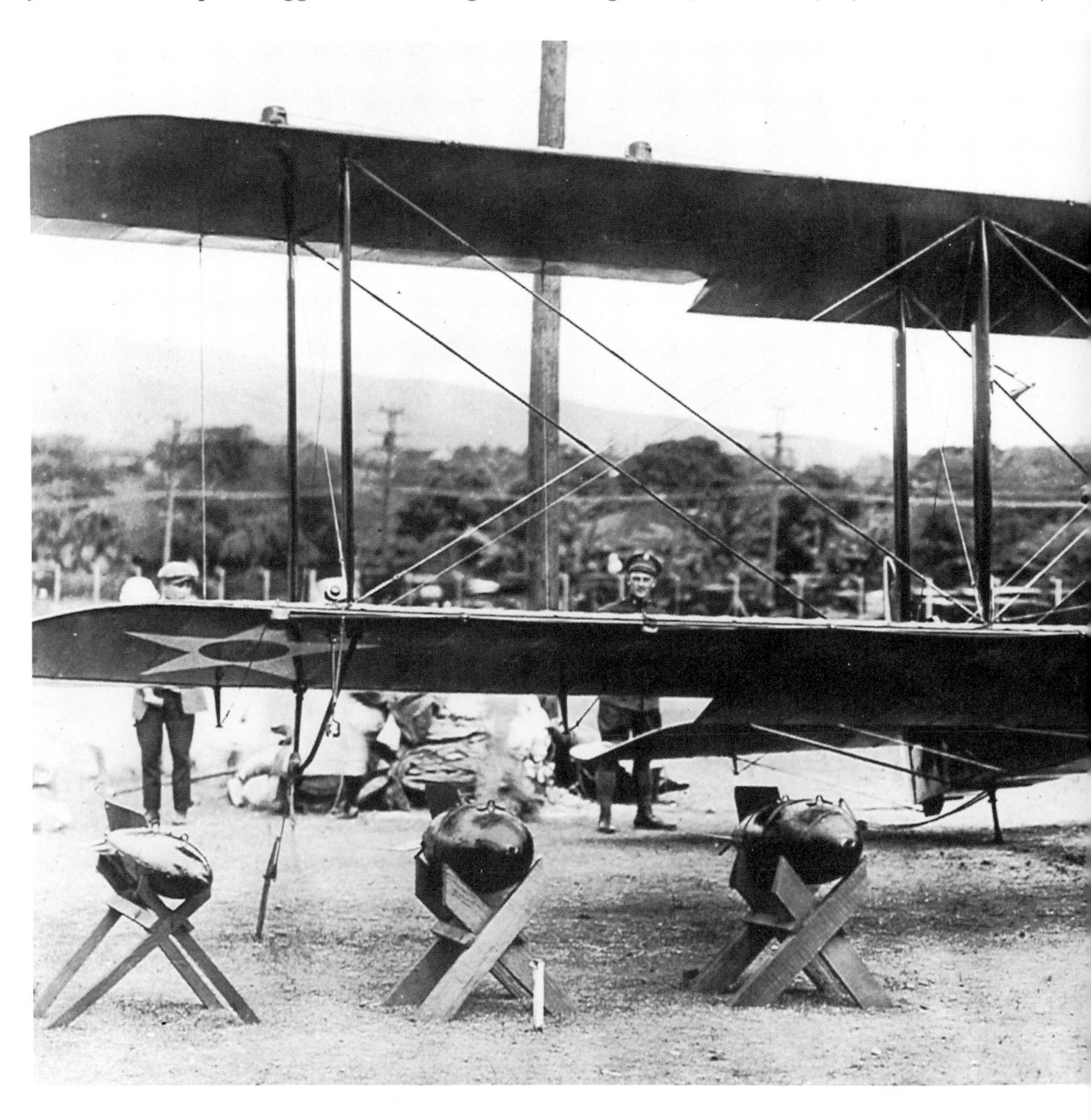

2,500 flying cadets, and 1,800 aircraft within five years. The necessary funds were not provided however, and by March 1935, when the GHQ Air Force came into existence, the various units attached to the nine army corps were still not enough to form the recommended 1,800-aircraft force. The units available were organized into three wings, at Langley Field, Virginia, also the headquarters of GHQ Air Force, and at Barksdale, Louisiana and March, California; the new organization's commander was responsible to the Chief of Staff for its organization, training, and operation.

Meanwhile, despite the relatively small sums made available for research, development, and procurement, and the limited number of airplanes acquired, there had been

*Above:* The B-10B of the mid-1930s represented a marked advance on the biplane bombers that had preceded it in Army Air Corps Service.

*Left:* The B-4, one of a series of Keystone bombers used by the Air Corps in the early 1930s, had a top speed of only 120 mph (193 km/h) and suffered from severe limitations in payload/range performance.

considerable progress in the matter of equipment. Bombing, and particularly strategic bombing, was at the heart of Mitchell's doctrine, and was widely accepted within the service as being the most useful activity for an air force. The success of the bombing trials had resulted in the production of 110 improved MB-2s with the designation NBS-1, indicating their role as short-range night bombers.

Their successors later in the 1920s were designated light bombers until 1930, when the single B for bomber designation was introduced; by that stage a total of 158 prototype and production aircraft had been ordered. Main types were the Keystone LB-5, LB-6, LB-7, and LB-10A, these last becoming the B-3A under the new system. With two engines of up to 575 hp, weighing around 13,000 lb (5,900 kg) and with top speeds of around 115

mph (185 km/h) with their five-man crews these were hardly the instruments of an overwhelming strategic offensive, and even the B-6A of 1932, the last of the Keystone series, was capable of only a 180-mile (290-km) radius of action with its maximum 2,200 lb (998 kg) bombload. The more promising B-2 of 1928 was also more expensive, and only one squadron was equipped with the end bough, compared with 12 squadrons using the Keystone machines.

*Left:* By mid-1937 the first Y1B-17s, service test examples of the new Flying Fortress bomber, were being evaluated by the 2d Bombardment Group, which was assigned the task of working out operational techniques.

By 1934, however, the first B-10Bs were in service. These all-metal monoplanes featured a number of technical advances, including a glazed nose-gunner's position, an internal bomb bay, and variable-pitch propellers. More than 100 were procured, along with 25 B-12s, and their 675 hp radial engines and aerodynamic refinement produced a maximum speed of over 200 mph (322 km/h) at 6,000 ft (1,830 m). The contemporary B-9 had been bought in small numbers for evaluation, and by 1937 two much bigger bombers, the B-17 and B-18, were being evaluated.

Both B-17 and B-18 were four-engined metal monoplanes, the former able to carry 2,200 lb (998 kg) of bombs 1,000 miles (1,600 km), twice the range of the latter, and having a cruising speed of over 200 mph (322 km/h), compared with 170 mph (274 km/h) for the B-18. The price of the B-17 reflected this superiority, however, and only 13 YB-17s, the Y prefix indicating their status as service test examples, were ordered, compared with 133 B-18s ordered initially and another 217 in 1937–38. The promise of the B-17 could not be ignored, and small numbers of improved models continued to be ordered, paving the way for the thousands of Flying Fortresses that would follow during World War II.

One of the consequences of the improved performance offered by the first monoplane bombers was their ability to outpace the Air Corps' contemporary pursuit aircraft, as fighters continued to be called. The MB-3As of the early 1920s had been followed by a series of Curtiss designs, starting with the Orenco D, developed by the Air Service Engineering Division and originally built by the Ordnance Engineering Company. During the early 1920s Curtiss produced a series of high-performance racing aircraft for the Army and Navy, as well as the PW-8 for the Air Service, and these won numerous prizes and established a series of speed records. By 1925 the first P-1 Hawks, derived from the racers, had been produced, and during the remainder of the decade small quantities of improved variants, principally the P-1B, P-1C, and P-6, followed. The Hawks were used by the 1st Pursuit Group, and annually contested the Mitchell Trophy race at the National Air Races that were a feature of the 1920s.

Boeing, who by the 1930s were making a name with their heavy bombers, had produced another series of fighters during the 1920s, starting with the PW-9 ordered in 1924, and again small numbers of developed versions,

*Right:* P-1 Hawks, the principal fighters produced for the Army Air Corps during the late 1920s, in formation over the Sacramento Valley, California.

*Below:* Air racing provided the stimulus for technical development in the early 1920s: this D-12-engined R-6 was one of an impressive series of racers produced by Curtiss, and finished second to its twin in the 1922 Pulitzer Trophy.

*Opposite, top:* By the late 1930s monoplane fighters were the norm: these P-36As entered service with the 20th Pursuit Group, the first to be equipped with the type, from April 1938.

*Opposite, bottom:* Bridging the gap between the 1920s biplanes and the modern monoplanes of the late 1930s, the P-26A was the first all-metal monoplane fighter in Army Air Corps service, and the last to have a fixed undercarriage.

*Below:* An advanced design when it was introduced in 1934, the P-26A was thoroughly obsolete by March 1939, when this 18th Pursuit Group example was photographed over Oahu, Hawaii.

followed. By 1930 the company had produced the P-12, derived from the Navy F4B, and during the next three years the Air Corps bought 350 of various models. At the same time, development of an all-metal monoplane fighter was proceeding, and in 1933 the first production P-26s were ordered, a total of 136 being delivered in 1934, of which 25 were P-26Bs. The P-26 equipped seven pursuit groups during the late 1930s.

The P-26 was joined in service by the two-seat P-30 and single-seat P-35 and P-36A, all of which had retractable undercarriages, but none of which was equipped for the conditions of a few years later. In the meantime, the Air Corps was trying to find the best method of employment for its comparatively advanced aircraft. The influence of Mitchell was still strong, and the new monoplane bombers seemed to offer the possibility of real strategic offensives, concentrating on early strikes against the industrial base on which an enemy's war effort would depend. An exercise at March Field in May 1933, when the dry bed of Muroc Lake was used as a bombing range, seemed to vindicate this theory, when the opposing pursuits experienced great difficulty in intercepting the new bombers.

By the late 1930s the B-17, equipped with the Norden bombsight, was demonstrating impressive accuracy in runs over Muroc at altitudes of up to 15,000 ft (4,570 m), though the perfect visibility of the Mojave desert did not represent conditions typical of those that would be encountered a few years later over Europe. The improving performance of fighters, especially the new P-38 Lightning of 1939, was rapidly outstripping that of the bombers: the Lightning's armament of four machine guns and a cannon was also a severe threat to the bombers, whose typical armament of four or five machine guns was generally considered to constitute an impregnable defense, especially when deployed in formation.

The validity of these theories would soon be put to the test. In September 1939 war was declared in Europe, and the rearmament that had started at the beginning of the year was accelerated. In early 1939 the Air Corps com-

U.S.
ARMY

00
102

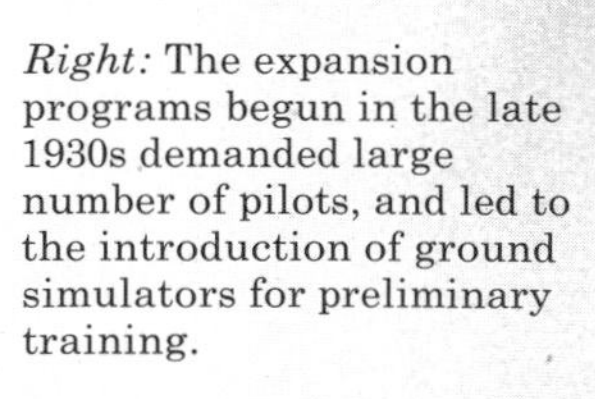

*Right:* The expansion programs begun in the late 1930s demanded large number of pilots, and led to the introduction of ground simulators for preliminary training.

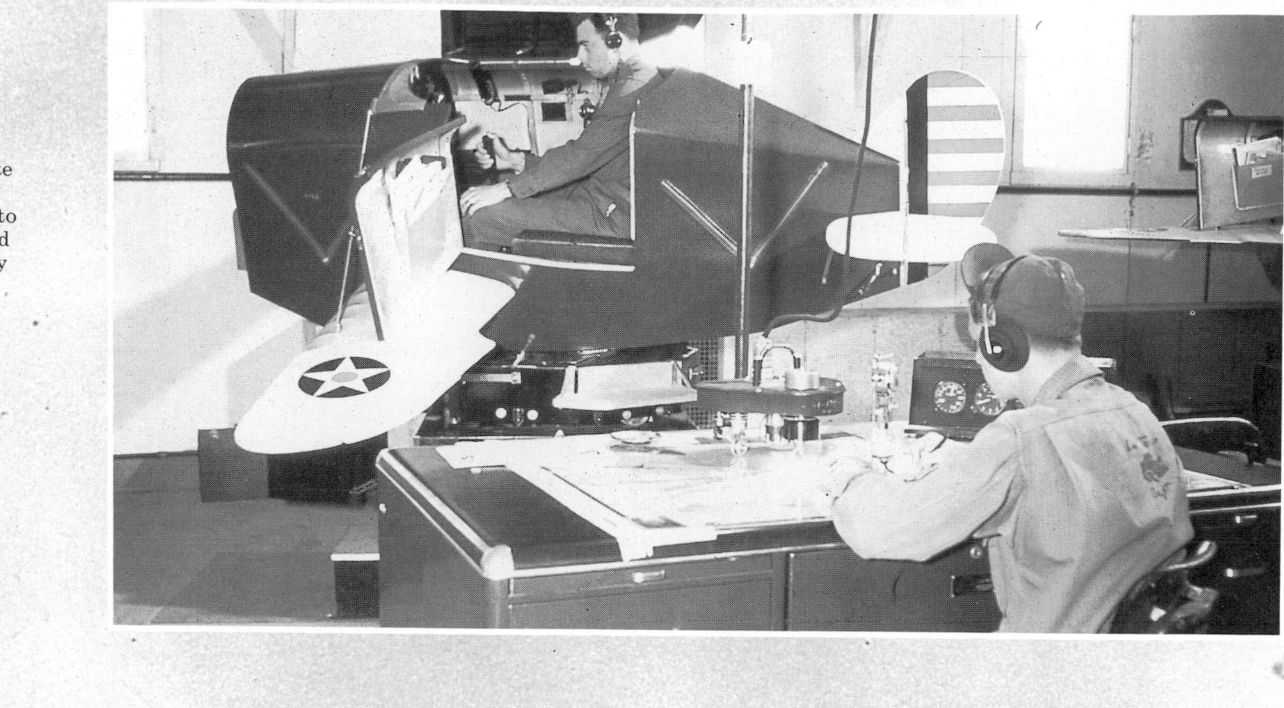

prised 1,600 officers and 18,000 men, with some 1,700 airplanes, of which many were trainers or observation types used for cooperation with ground forces. Within three months the target for the expanded force had been set at 5,500 aircraft and nearly 50,000 personnel: operationally, the Air Corps envisaged a strength of 24 tactical groups by mid-1941.

These targets were frequently revised. By July 1940 the required strength had been raised to 54 groups, involving 4,000 combat aircraft, and more than 200,000 personnel. Among the new equipment ordered were large quantities of the B-17 and a new bomber, the B-24, while many new types were under development, but the demands on the aircraft industry for vastly increased production would not be met for some time.

In the meantime there was an urgent requirement for a new organization to replace the peacetime Army Air Corps and GHQ Air Force. The two parallel organizations were combined in March 1939, only to be separated again in November 1940, when GHQ Air Force was placed under the command of Army field forces. The final step was taken on June 21, 1941, with the creation of Army Air Forces, responsible to the Army Chief of Staff for the formulation of Army aviation policy and plans.

*Below:* 1st Pursuit Group P-1B Hawks line up at the start of the Mitchell Trophy race, one of the events of the 1929 National Air Races at Cleveland.

# 2: THE ARMY AIR FORCES AND WORLD WAR II

*Overleaf:* One of the main instruments of Army Air Force power, the B-24 Liberator was only just entering service at the time of the attack on Pearl Harbor.

At the time of its formation on June 20, 1941, the Army Air Force was only starting to show the effects of the expansion program begun more than two years earlier. Manpower strength had risen to 9,078 officers and 143,563 men, and the inventory of aircraft to 6,102. While these totals were impressive compared with those of early 1939, they were still some way short of the planned figures, and the conduct of the war in Europe had highlighted the inadequacy of US air defenses.

The first priority, therefore, was to assure the defense of North America, especially after the mutual assistance agreement between Japan and the Axis powers had been reached the previous year, and Britain faced the possibility of falling like the rest of western Europe under the German war machine. Accordingly, Air Defense Command was created early in 1940, and the 1st, 2nd, 3d, and 4th Air Forces were allocated to the Northeastern, Southern, Central, and Western Defense Commands. In accordance with the concept of hemisphere defense, the 1st AF supported the buildup of bases in Newfoundland, Greenland, and Iceland, as links in both the chain of defense and the air route to Britain.

At the same time, the Panama Canal zone's existing air defense force was expanded to form the basis of the Caribbean Air Force, using new bases in the Caribbean islands obtained under the Lend-Lease agreement. Alaska was something of a weak link, and as part of the strengthening of the presence there the Air Field Forces became the Air Force, Alaska Defense Command in October 1941, though only a few obsolescent aircraft could be spared to equip it. In the Pacific, the Hawaiian Air Force had been activated in November 1940, but the fear of Japanese intentions led to the formation in the Philippines of US Army Forces in the Far East in July 1941 and an Air Force component in the following month. Because of the distances involved, new aircraft were shipped to the Philippines, but the heavy bombers, which were too big to be ferried, had to be flown on a week-long excursion from Hawaii via Midway, Wake, and Australia.

Despite the urgency of these preparations, the Japanese attacks on Pearl Harbor, Oahu, and on Clark Field in the Philippines on December 7/8 (the international date line lay between the two) met with little resistance. While the entire battleship force of the Pacific Fleet was being put out of action in Pearl Harbor, the Air Force installations at Hickam, Wheeler, and Bellows Fields also came under attack: a handful of P-36s and P-40s managed to get airborne and shot down a few of the attacking aircraft, but by the end of the raid only 79 of the Hawaiian Air Force's 231 aircraft were still fit for use. The story was repeated in the Philippines, where the initial destruction of half the Far East Air Force's aircraft was followed by a Japanese invasion.

For six months the series of Japanese victories continued, as the Americans found their aircraft outnumbered and outclassed by a superior fighter – the Zero – in the hands of pilots with long combat experience over China. While the British were defeated in Hong Kong, Malaya, and Burma, the Americans withdrew to the Netherlands East Indies. Small numbers of FEAF B-17s withdrawn from Luzon, and a few more which arrived to supplement them, carried out sporadic raids against Japanese shipping during January and February 1942, and P-40s made the difficult journey from Darwin, Australia. The Japanese occupation of New Britain, the Celebes, and Borneo, followed by invasions of Sumatra and Bali, left the forces on Java isolated, and by March 3 they had withdrawn again, to Australia.

Even Australia was not immune to attack. The first air raid against Darwin came on February 19, and not until mid-March, with the arrival of three squadrons of P-40s, did these begin to diminish. The invasion of New Guinea, and the advance toward Port Moresby, posed an immediate threat to Australia. Port Moresby became the staging post for B-17 attacks on the new Japanese base at Rabaul, while the surviving Dutch and American air units, along with Australian air elements, were consolidated into the Allied Air Force. The immediate priority was the maintenance of the South Pacific route along the chain of islands between Hawaii and Australia, and fighter reinforcements were dispatched to Samoa, Fiji, New Caledonia, and the other links in the chain.

At the same time, the defeats in the Pacific were provoking anxiety about the defense of the mainland United States. In March 1942 the air forces were reorganized, with the 1st and 4th Air Forces assigned to the Eastern and Western Defense Commands, while the 2d and 3d AFs became training elements of the USAAF. The Army Air Force itself became one of three autonomous departments of the War Department, along with the ground and supply forces. The emphasis in early 1942 was on defense of the west coast,

Panama, and Alaska: the focus of the Caribbean Air Force shifted to the west of the Panama Canal zone, the Alaskan Air Force became 11th Air Force in February 1942, with a rapid expansion of facilities and equipment, and the available fighter reinforcements were based along the west coast.

Previously, the Allied leaders had agreed that Germany, as the stronger potential enemy, would have priority as a target for air operations, and early efforts had been devoted to developing the North Atlantic staging posts in Newfoundland, Iceland, and Greenland. In January 1942 it was decided to establish the 5th Air Force to support a projected invasion of northwest Africa, but by January 28, when its headquarters were established at Savannah, Georgia, the designation had been changed to the 8th AF. During February VIII Bomber and Interceptor Commands were located at Savannah and Charleston (pursuit and interceptor units were redesignated fighter in May 1942) under the aegis of the 3d AF.

As soon as it was formed, the 8th AF's mission began to change. The invasion of northwest Africa was postponed as impractical for the time being, and in February 20 B-25s were diverted to the Pacific, where they were used for the Doolittle raid on Japan. This was the first attack on the Japanese homeland, and though its primary importance was symbolic, it represented a remarkable achievement. The twin-engined B-25 Mitchell had been flown for the first time in August 1940 and was originally armed with nose, tail, and beam machine guns, though the B-25Bs used for the Doolittle raid had dummy guns fitted in the normally unarmed tail, and the lower of the two turrets that had replaced the beam guns was removed to make way for extra fuel.

On April 1, 16 of the B-25s were loaded aboard the carrier USS *Hornet*, after intensive training in takeoffs from very short runways designed to approximate the size of the carrier deck. The plan was to launch the bombers no more than 550 miles (886 km) from Tokyo, and after the attack to continue to airfields in China, but the risk to the carrier was such that the raid was launched at a range of more than 800 miles (1,290 km). The bomber force reached the Japanese mainland safely, attacking Tokyo, Kobe, Yokohama, and Nagoya and causing damage much greater than expected, but the distance already covered left them no chance of reaching their intended destinations. However, all but one of 50 crew members survived subsequent bale-outs over China, though one crew was interned in Russia after landing near Vladivostock; others were injured in crash-landings and two crews were captured.

*Above:* Still at peace on October 30, 1941, Pearl Harbor and Hickam Field, Hawaii, were soon to be the subjects of a devastating Japanese attack.

Meanwhile, the 8th AF had been reassigned as a strategic bomber force for service with Army Air Force in Britain, resulting in a change in its planned equipment. The basic tactical unit of the AAF was the squadron, differentiated by type of aircraft – heavy bomber, fighter, and so on – with up to 300 officers and men and an establishment of 25 fighters, eight heavy bombers or 13 medium or light bombers. For administrative purposes squadrons were organized into groups, normally three fighter or four bomber squadrons, and for tactical and operational purposes two groups would normally constitute a wing. Two or more wings formed a command, usually of a single type of combat aircraft and incorporating supporting elements. Commands could be organized in separate air divisions if the number of wings required an additional administrative level, and the combat commands would be combined with a service command and other commands, such as troop carrier or air support, as its role demanded, to form an air force. The air force was the largest single unit, and was designed to meet the demands of a theater of operations, where it would be under operational control of the theater command.

The 8th AF was originally a tactical force, but its reassignment to England called for an emphasis on heavy bomber elements. However, despite the rise in B-17 and B-24 produc-

*Below:* The Army Air Force's first air raid on Japan was carried out by 16 B-25 Mitchells launched from the deck of the aircraft carrier *Hornet* on April 18, 1942.

tion – from three a day at the beginning of the year to four times that number by the end of 1942, and an ultimate peak of 50 a day by the spring of 1944 – the demands of other theaters left the 8th in a state of constant flux as groups were assigned only to be diverted elsewhere. Nevertheless, the advance elements arrived in Britain in May, and eventually selected the level expanses of East Anglia as the location for the new bases that would be needed. It was the end of August before the first three bomber groups were stationed at their new homes, though on the 17th of that month the first raid, by 12 B-17s on a marshaling yard near Rouen, had been mounted.

Despite the diversion of some groups to northwest Africa in late 1942 and early 1943, strength continued to increase, and daylight raids were mounted with increasing frequency against coastal targets in occupied France. American bombers were dedicated to high-altitude raids in good visibility, even after the RAF had switched entirely to night raids by heavy bombers, and the early successes over France, where RAF and later USAAF P-47 Thunderbolts were available for escorts, encouraged the continuance of this policy. However, the Casablanca conference of January 1943 resulted in the 8th AF being directed to join the RAF in attacking Germany itself.

Early attempts at such raids were often frustrated by the weather, and in the three that were mounted during February 1943 losses of aircraft amounted to 13 percent. This was a pointer to the future: as the daylight raids increased in frequency and strength, so losses mounted ominously. By May VIII Bomber Command had more than 200 bombers available, allowing attacks on multiple targets, and the use of diversionary tactics to confuse the defenses, though the unpredictable weather frequently degraded bombing accuracy, or prevented the attackers from even finding their targets.

Among the targets selected for attack, the submarine pens along the coast receded in importance as their threat to the Atlantic convoys was brought under control, and oil installations, ball bearing factories, and aircraft plants became the primary objectives. Even with the new auxiliary fuel tanks the

P-47 escorts were limited to a range of about 300 miles (480 km), while increasingly distant targets were attacked; losses of the bomber force were running above the level of replacements, and exaggerated claims of enemy aircraft destroyed by the gunners aboard the B-17s and B-24s resulted in misleading estimates of the likely fighter opposition.

Following losses of 6 percent in June and 5.5 percent in August, September brought some relief with less costly attacks on airfields in occupied countries, though a raid on Stuttgart saw the loss of 45 of the 300 bombers involved. The climax of the daylight raids came in October, when 88 bombers were lost in the space of three days before the notorious Schweinfurt raid on the 14th. Only 291 B-17s were available after the earlier losses, of which 60 were shot down, and another 133 damaged. Despite the heavy damage inflicted on the ball bearing factories that were the subject of the attack, a 30 percent loss rate was clearly unacceptable, and this would be the last unescorted raid: by the time the weather allowed the offensive to be resumed, new long-range P-51 Mustangs would be available, and all missions would be provided with fighter escorts.

At the same time, there was extensive reorganization of the heavy bomber forces. In November 1943 the 15th Air Force was established in Italy, absorbing the heavy bomber elements of the 12th Air Force in the Mediterranean along with the B-17 groups diverted from the 8th AF to the Northwest African Strategic Air Force formed earlier in the year.

*Opposite, top:* 8th Air Force B-17 Flying Fortresses in one of the daylight formations employed in the early stages of the strategic bombing offensive against Germany.

*Opposite, center:* Early losses on daylight bombing raids led to increasingly heavy armament being carried by the B-17.

*Opposite, bottom:* Number 5,000 of a total of over 12,700 B-17s built.

*Below:* The B-24 Liberator proved more versatile than the B-17, and a total of over 18,000 were built.

With the invasion of Sicily and Italy the Northwest African Air Forces had been replaced by Mediterranean Allied Air Forces, of which the 15th AF was the strategic bombing component.

In fact, the Mediterranean had seen little use of strategic bombing, apart from the Ploesti raid in August, when 177 B-24s, drawn from the 9th Air Force in Libya and the groups detached from the 8th AF, were dispatched on a 1,900-mile (3,060-km) round trip from North Africa to the oilfields around Ploesti, in Rumania. The low-level attack resulted in the loss of 54 of the Liberators, and oil production was disrupted for only a month. However, the availability of bases in Italy brought more targets within range, and B-24s had already carried out attacks on the Messerschmitt factories at Wiener Neustadt in Austria before the formation of the 15th AF.

While the 15th AF was forming in Italy, the B-17G model of the Flying Fortress was appearing with new 8th AF units in England. The B-17G had an additional chin turret to improve the inadequate nose defense of the earlier models, and in conjunction with the P-51s, whose range with auxiliary fuel tanks was increased to 500 miles (805 km), promised to halt the fearful attrition rate experienced during 1943. By April the two strategic air forces had a combined strength of more than 1,500 heavy bombers. By this stage the earlier attacks on strategic industries had resulted in the widespread dispersal of aircraft and other plants, while the needs of the ground forces in Italy and Normandy commanded the majority of the bombers' attention.

Before the strategic bombing offensive officially ended on April 16, 1945, there were many new techniques to be learned, including the use of airborne radar for navigation and countermeasures to the German interceptor radar systems. New adversaries appeared in the form of Me 262 jet fighters, though these were handicapped by their high speed when attacking the relatively slow-moving bombers. The 15th Air Force, while continuing to mount regular attacks on the Rumanian oilfields, began to use bases in Russia to enable more distant targets to be attacked. This

method was also adopted by the 8th Air Force, with the bombers carrying on to land in Russia after making their attacks, and occasionally carrying out further raids from the Russian bases before returning to their regular homes in England and Italy. Air superiority had been won by the Allies by mid-1944, but improving antiaircraft defenses continued to take their toll on the bomber forces.

The 8th Air Force reached its peak strength in June 1944, when 21 groups of B-17s and 19 of B-24s, plus a mixed Pathfinder group, were operational. In total, the 8th flew just over a million sorties, losing 11,687 aircraft in the process, including 5,548 heavy bombers, and dropping a total of 624,141 tons (1,368,528,800 kg) of bombs. Comparable figures for the 15th AF were 242,377 sorties, losses of 3,410 aircraft, of which 2,519 heavy bombers, and the dropping of 341,378 tons (714,042,696 kg) of bombs. Of the 20,419 enemy aircraft claimed destroyed by the 8th, and 6,258 by the 15th AF, 6,098 and 2,110 respectively were credited to the bombers' own guns.

While the 8th Air Force was learning a hard lesson in the skies over Germany, the tactical units supporting the Allied troops in North Africa were also having to revise their operating methods. The importance of air superiority had been demonstrated in the Pacific from the beginning of the war, and the RAF in Egypt had made command of the air its first objective. In August 1942 the 12th Air Force was formed to support the joint Torch landings in Morocco and Algeria; it included two B-17 groups from the 8th AF, four fighter groups, two with British Spitfires and two with P-38 Lightnings, and a light bombardment group with DB-7s, the British equivalent of the A-20 Havoc. All of these were already in England, having been assigned initially to the 8th AF, but the additional units from the US, including two groups of B-25s, three of B-26s, two and a half of P-39 Airacobras, and one of A-20s, took some time to complete the crossing of the Atlantic.

As a result, only part of the planned force was available when the landings at Casablanca, Oran, and Algiers began on November 8. Operations were governed by the existing air support doctrines, which stipulated that, while local air superiority might be desirable, the air elements must be subordinate to the ground commander, and that the most important target at a given time was that posing the most immediate threat to the ground force. In any event, the decision as to the priority of targets was to rest with the

*Right:* The heavy fighting that followed the Japanese invasion of New Guinea is reflected in the missions recorded on the nose of this B-25 Mitchell.

*Below:* The P-39 Airacrobra was something of a disappointment as a fighter, but proved useful as a ground-attack aircraft.

ground commander, who was also to be responsible for deciding on the necessity for any air superiority mission.

Accordingly, during the advance into Tunisia in January and February 1943, the support element of the 12th AF found itself called on to provide air cover for Allied ground troops, a far less effective measure than direct counter-air missions. On the occasions when the latter were carried out, substantial numbers of enemy aircraft were destroyed on the ground; when the fighters were obliged to wait for attackers to show up, they were too thinly spread to cope with the concentrated attack formations, and it was the defenders

who suffered the heavier losses.

The formation of Northwest African Air Forces in February 1943, brought together the 12th AF and its counterpart in the Western Desert, the 9th Air Force, formed in November 1942, along with British and Commonwealth units in a joint organization under Mediterranean Air Command. The air support and heavy bomber elements of the 12th AF became part of Northwest African Air Forces, which included tactical and strategic air forces and a troop carrier command, while the fighter command became part of the Northwest African Coastal Air Force, responsible for air defense and for air-sea reconnaissance and anti-shipping operations over the Mediterranean.

The integration of British and American units at operational level was accompanied by a wholesale adoption of the methods developed by the RAF, and already followed by the 9th AF in the Western Desert. First priority was given to the continual offensive against the enemy in the air, accompanied by concerted attacks on enemy airfields; ground support missions could then be carried out free of interference. The availability of Spitfires for air superiority, in combination with P-38s, left P-40s and the recently arrived P-39 Airacobras free to concentrate on bomb and machine-gun attacks in support of ground forces. By early 1943 the latter types were being supplemented by A-36 dive-bomber variants of the P-51, armed with eight machine guns and able to carry a 500 lb (227 kg) bomb under each wing.

By July 1943 the tactical bomber element of NAAF Tactical Air Force included two groups of B-25s and one of A-20s, while the Air Support Command had two fighter groups of P-40s and one of Spitfires, plus two fighter-bomber groups using the new A-36 and a tactical reconnaissance squadron of camera-equipped Mustangs. Another two fighter groups of P-40s were attached to the Western Desert Air Force, the third element of the Tactical Air Force. The Coastal Air Force was charged with covering the convoy en route to the landings on Sicily on July 10.

As a prelude to the operation, the Strategic Air Force had bombarded the Italian stronghold on Pantelleria, and with support from the light and medium bombers, and from naval gunfire, succeeded in reducing the defenses to the point where the garrison surrendered before the assault force had even reached the beaches. The significance of this achievement lay not so much in the surrender itself, since the island proved to be unusually vulnerable to air attack and the defenders low in morale, but in the opportunity it provided for study of the precise effects of the air action. In particular, analysis of the damage indicated the poor accuracy of the bombing, and underlined the need for more precise target analysis.

By this stage the bombing offensive was turning on Sicily, and repeated attacks were carried out on airfields, harbors, and other installations, with the air bases the principal targets. During the landings, as a result, the covering fighters were able to keep the air opposition to a minimum, and within a week several NAAF squadrons were established at a series of captured bases on the island, of which nearly a third was already occupied. For the next month the tactical elements continued to support the land battle, while the strategic bombers were able to turn to the mainland, where massive attacks on Rome and Naples severely disrupted the Italian rail system.

With Sicily occupied, the next task was the invasion of Italy, and after continuing air strikes against the mainland the British Eighth Army landed across the Strait of Messina on the lightly defended "toe" of Italy, preceded by air attacks to neutralize airfields and isolate the landing areas. Following the initial landings, there were further assaults on the beaches at Salerno, south of Naples, and at Taranto.

In contrast to the virtually unopposed landings in the south, there was fierce resistance at Salerno. Airborne troops were dropped inland near Avellino, and airstrips constructed in the area of the beachhead, so that P-40s and A-36s were soon available for support. However following the capture of Naples the Ger-

*Right:* A P-51B Mustang of the 354th Fighter Squadron, 355th Fighter Group, carrying the distinctive markings adopted for the June, 1944, invasion of Europe and carrying the long-range fuel tanks that helped to make the Mustang such a valuable escort for the 8th Air Force's heavy bombers.

mans – the Italians had reached an Armistice at the same time as the invasion – withdrew to well-defended positions, and the winter brought a halt to the advance. Consolidation of the command structure in Italy involved the formation of Mediterranean Allied Air Forces in December, with the 15th Air Force forming the strategic element and the former Tactical Air Force of Northwest African Air Forces occupying a similar place in the new command structure.

At the same time, the procedure for ground support became more formalized, with the adoption of a system of forward controllers on the ground. Communicating by radio with "cab ranks" of fighter bombers, the controllers would call for strikes on targets designated by grid references of a standard map, either in response to specific requests from ground commanders or as a result of reports from reconnaissance aircraft. By the end of 1944, too, the P-47D had been adapted for the fighter-bomber role, carrying guns, rockets, or bombs as required, and proving much more resistant to battle damage, with its air-cooled radial engine, than the P-40 and A-36 with their more complicated liquid-cooled powerplants.

During 1944 the P-47 became the standard ground attack aircraft, and while the long struggle in Italy continued into 1945 the focus of attention had shifted to England, where preparations had been under way since mid-1943 for the invasion of occupied France. By October 1943 the headquarters elements of the 9th Air Force had moved to England, leaving the combat units with Northwest African Air Forces, and taking over the 8th Air Force's four B-26 groups. To this nucleus many more groups were added, so that by June 1944 the 9th AF had a troop carrier command with 15 groups, a bomber command with eight B-26 and three A-20 groups, and two tactical air commands, IX TAC and XIX TAC, disposing of 13 groups of P-47s, three of P-38s and two of P-51s. Supporting units included engineer regiments for the preparation and maintenance of airfields, an air defense command to control antiaircraft batteries assigned by the ground forces, and a photo-reconnaissance group.

During the buildup to D-Day, the 9th AF's fighter groups supported the 8th AF operations in Europe, as well as escorting IX Bomber Command's light and medium bombers in raids on France. At the same time, the support services trained and stockpiled supplies and equipment for the enormous task of keeping the combat units active after the move to France. Mobility was the keynote, and the lessons of North Africa and Italy were reflected in the assignment of priorities to IX and XIX TACs, which were dedicated to the support of the US 1st and 3d Armies respectively. Air defense of the armies and their lines of communication was the principal task, followed by direct and indirect support of battlefield operations, tactical medium bombing and tactical reconnaissance.

In the initial stages of the D-Day landings on June 6 the 9th AF was busy providing air cover for the invasion force, but airstrips were soon established within the beachheads, and following the breakout and the advance through northern France new bases were occupied, consolidated, and abandoned. The arrival of the US Ninth Army in September led to the creation of a third tactical air command, and following the success of the landings in southern France, other P-47 groups were detached to the joint US-French 1st Tactical Air Force. Weapons used in support of the advance toward the Rhine included 500 lb (227 kg) and 1,000 lb (454 kg) high explosive bombs, clusters of 20 lb (9 kg) fragmentation bombs and napalm, while new aircraft appeared in the form of the P-61 Black Widow night fighter and the A-26 Invader, the latter designed for a 4,000 lb (1,814 kg) bombload as well as a nose armament of either two or eight .50 in machine guns, plus remote-controlled twin-gun upper and lower turrets and more guns or rockets under the wings.

Some of the fiercest fighting of the campaign in northwest Europe came in December, with the last German offensive in the Ardennes, known as the Battle of the Bulge. Weather restricted air operations for the first week, but when a change came on December 23 there was frantic activity. The medium bombers flew hundreds of interdiction sorties

*Right:* P-47D Thunderbolts of the 78th Fighter Group, 8th Air Force, equipped with long-range tanks and wearing D-Day markings, at their base at Boxted, England, in the summer of 1944.

against road and rail bridges and other supply routes, while the fighter-bombers attacked airfields and supported the armored divisions on the ground, as well as carrying out armed reconnaissance missions.

By the beginning of the following month the German armies were in retreat, though continuing to mount determined rearguard actions, and despite the virtually absolute air superiority now enjoyed by the Allies, the excellent light AA guns deployed by the Germans continued to make low-level missions hazardous. The pattern of interdiction and close support was well established however, and continued up to the crossings of the Rhine in March and the eventual end of resistance on May 8, ironically echoing the manner of the German advance across western Europe five years before, though more slowly and on a much more massive scale.

Similarly, in the Pacific, the long process of pushing the Japanese back through the territory they had occupied in such alarming fashion during the early part of 1942 was still under way. The first of many amphibious operations was mounted against Guadalcanal in the southern Solomons on August 7, 1942, in order to forestall the construction of an airfield there by the Japanese and the resulting threat to the air route between Hawaii and Australia. Because of the distances involved in the Central Pacific, initial air support during the landings was generally provided by carrier-based Navy and Marine Corps aircraft, but in the southwest Pacific the islands' relative proximity to each other enabled land-based aircraft to be used, and in September the 7th Air Force was formed from the air units in Australia and New Guinea.

In February 1943 the Hawaiian Air Force had become the 7th Air Force, and in January a new air force, the 13th, was formed in the New Hebrides for the South Pacific area. The position on Guadalcanal was being consolidated by the end of 1943, and Henderson Field became the principal base for the air war in the Solomons, where the struggle focussed on Rabaul. At the same time, the 5th Air Force was severely stretched in the struggle to repel the Japanese in New Guinea, and the shortage of aircraft caused serious problems. The P-39s and P-40s were coping well with the ground-support requirements, but the limited number of heavy bombers available, the long distances over which they had to operate, and the long escort missions that only the P-38s could manage, coupled with the shortages of spares and the arduous operating conditions, all compounded the difficulties.

During 1943, however, as aircraft production steadily increased, the problems began to ease. The longer-range B-24 had replaced the B-17 by the end of the year, and B-25s took over from the B-26s. In the Solomons AAF, Navy, Marine Corps, and Royal New Zealand Air Force units were all under the control of Air Command, Solomons, a naval command, and all the various types of aircraft were employed in roles that suited them best. Particularly useful were the radar-equipped SB-24s, used for night attacks on Japanese shipping, though the P-70 night fighters were something of a failure in their intended role.

*Inset:* The A-20 Havoc light bomber served as the basis for the P-70, the USAAF's first radar-equipped night fighter.

The 7th Air Force, meanwhile, was occupied with reconnaissance from Hawaii and occasional bombing raids against Wake, Tarawa, and Nauru, the B-17s and later B-24s staging through intermediate islands. It was the obvious need for a series of bases as the advance against the Japanese-held islands progressed that led to the decision to occupy first the Gilbert and then the Marshall Islands, starting in November 1943.

New bases were constructed on Tarawa and other islands in the Gilbert chain, and occupied by 7th Air Force squadrons ready for the assault on Kwajalein which came at the beginning of February 1943. By this stage American air power was growing steadily, while the Japanese resources were becoming hopelessly over-stretched. The Aleutians were secured in the northern Pacific, by August the central Pacific drive had reached the Marianas, where bases on Guam, Saipan, and Tinian brought the heavy bombers within reach of the Japanese mainland, and in October the return to the Philippines was under way, bases such as Rabaul having been isolated and neutralized. Subsequently the 13th Air Force was absorbed by the 5th on Luzon, as the strategic bombing offensive began to gather momentum.

The other main front against the Japanese was in China and Burma. As early as February 1942 the 10th Air Force had been formed in India, but the handful of heavy bomber P-40s available were not in a position to offer more than token resistance to the Japanese occupation of Burma. For its mission to support operations in China, where the American Volunteer Group had been fighting alongside Chiang Kai-shek's forces since the attack on Pearl Harbor, the 10th was hardly better equipped: a dozen or so DC-3 and C-47 transports were based in India, but the loss of Burma meant supplies had to be flown across the Himalayas from Assam in northeastern India. In August the China Air Task Force, with new Army Air Force squadrons, took over from the Flying Tigers, as the AVG had become known, and in January 1943 this became the 14th Air Force.

*Below:* Massive production was the basis for the overwhelming superiority enjoyed by the Allied air forces in the later stages of the war: the P-39 was ordered just before the start of World War II, and half the 8,500 built were supplied to the Soviet Union.

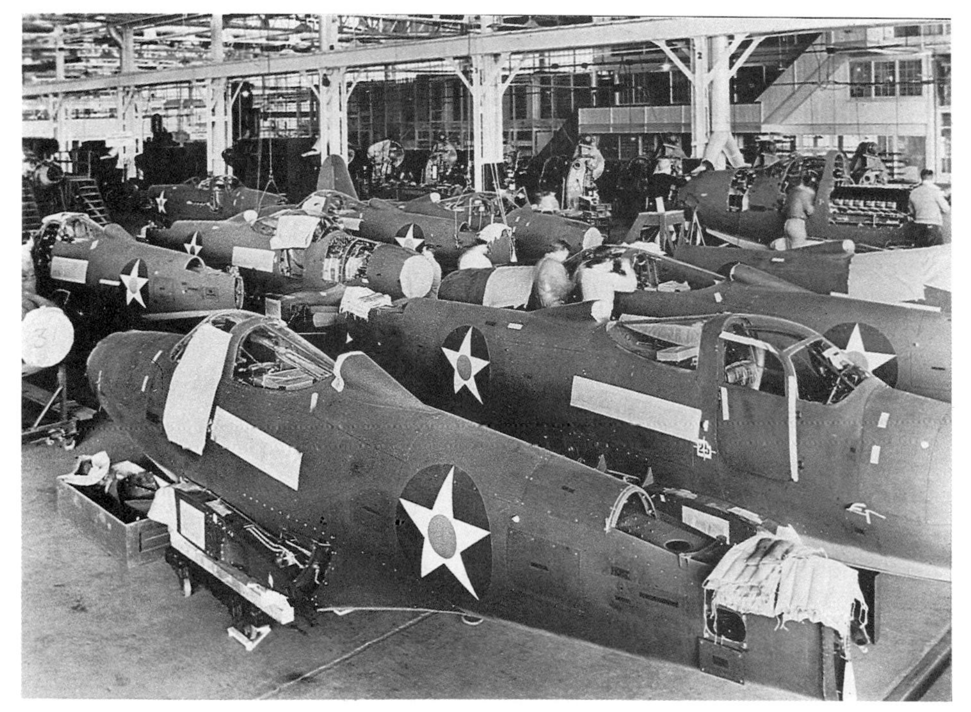

After a year of consolidation, the end of 1943 brought the formation of the joint RAF-AAF Eastern Air Command, and in the first half of 1944 Allied air power was able to establish complete air superiority during the Arakan campaign in Burma. Among the notable achievements of the supply aircraft were the maintenance of the isolated garrison at Imphal, and in the subsequent drive into Burma close air support from P-47s and P-51s followed the pattern established in Italy, with the fighter-bombers flying cab-rank cover, ready to respond to requests from the ground commanders with guns, bombs, rockets, and napalm.

Another development in the early part of 1944 was the arrival of the first B-29 Superfortress group in eastern India. With twice the radius of action of the B-17 and B-24, the B-29 was earmarked for use against Japan at an early stage, and in April, with the first wing of 150 aircraft leaving for India, the 20th Air Force was formed to operate the new bomber. Its mission was defined as the progressive reduction of the Japanese military, industrial, and economic systems and the undermining of national morale, and forward bases were constructed in China to launch the offensive.

The first raids were mounted in June against railroad yards in Bangkok and then against the steel works in the southern Japanese island of Kyushu, though in these and subsequent raids on steel works in Manchuria and oil centers in Sumatra substantial numbers of aircraft were lost through engine failures and other malfunctions. Not until

March 1945 would the failure rate fall below 17 percent.

Meanwhile, the first B-29s had arrived in the Marianas during the previous October, and in November 1944 the first raid was mounted against the Nakajima aircraft engine factory near Tokyo. The effectiveness of these raids was still low as a result of mechanical failure and poor bombing accuracy over the targets, and in December it was decided to investigate the potential of fire raids, using incendiary bombs to destroy the thousands of small workshops on which the major industries depended. The first such raid was carried out on January 3, 1945, against Nagoya, but poor accuracy limited the extent of the damage.

As a result, there was a change of tactics to low-altitude attacks by massed formations flying at 5,000–6,000 ft (1,525–1,830 m), and the first such raid against Tokyo on March 9–10, when 325 B-29s dropped 1,665 tons (1,691,746 kg) of incendiaries. The results were spectacular: nearly 16 square miles (41 $km^2$) of the city were destroyed, and more than a million people left homeless, and the next few days brought similar attacks on Nagoya, Osaka, and Kobe. From mid-June, with fighter opposition almost negligible, the campaign switched to the secondary urban areas, and during the next two months, while occasional precision attacks and the mining of Japanese ports were also carried out, the total area destroyed by the fire raids was increased to more than 200 square miles (518 $km^2$).

The climax to the strategic bombing campaign came early in August with the introduction of a completely new type of weapon. On August 6 a single B-29 from the specialist 509th Composite Wing, formed for the purpose the previous September, dropped an atomic bomb over the city of Hiroshima. With estimates of casualties ranging from 78,000 dead to four times that number, the Hiroshima attack would have a fundamental effect on postwar military policy; in the meantime, three days later a second atomic bomb was dropped over Nagasaki, and five days after that, on August 14, the biggest B-29 attack of all was mounted, with 809 bombers taking part. The same day brought Japanese acceptance of the American demand for unconditional surrender.

*Left:* The B-29 Superfortress represented the peak of wartime heavy bomber design. Operationally, the heaviest bomber of the war was used only against Japan.

USAF

# 3: STRATEGIC AIR COMMAND

*Overleaf:* Strategic air power in the 1950s: a B-47 Stratojet refuels from a KC-97, a facility that transformed the B-47 into an intercontinental bomber.

The rapid postwar demobilization that saw Army Air Force manpower reduced to around 300,000 within two years was accompanied by a reorganization of its resources. In March 1946 the Continental Air Forces were divided between three new commands, Air Defense, Tactical Air, and Strategic Air, the last having as its mission the conduct of long-range offensive and reconnaissance operations in any part of the world using "the latest and most advanced weapons." Concepts such as deterrence and mutually assured destruction were yet to be formulated, but there could be no mistaking the nature of the most advanced weapons. Atomic bombs had introduced an entirely new factor into the military equation, and while conventional forces were drastically reduced, the means of delivering the "ultimate weapon" provided the justification for the creation of the independent Air Force in the following year.

By the end of 1948 Headquarters Strategic Air Command was established in the redundant Martin bomber plant, where B-26 Marauders and B-29 Superfortresses had been built a few years earlier, at Offutt AFB, near Omaha, Nebraska. The testing of further atomic bombs at Bikini Atoll in July 1946 had underlined the urgency of the nuclear weapon program, and as well as producing the weapons, there was a clear need for new aircraft. Only about 30 of the 279 B-29s equipping six Very Heavy Bomb Groups that formed the command's initial combat strength were capable of delivering nuclear weapons, and while the number of B-29s reached a peak of over 500 in 1948, many would soon be converted to other roles.

*Opposite:* B-47s over Washington, DC, in 1957. The unusual sight of a massed formation of six-jet swept-wing bombers emphasizes the changes that had occurred since World War II.

*Below:* The reason for Strategic Air Command's existence: the awesome power of an atomic device detonated for experimental purposes at Bikini Atoll.

By 1950 SAC's organization had been rationalized. The 8th Air Force, headquartered at Carswell AFB, near Fort Worth, Texas, had both medium and heavy bombers; the 15th AF, with headquarters at March AFB, California, operated medium bombers; and the 2d AF, at Barksdale AFB, Louisiana, was devoted almost exclusively to reconnaissance. The disappearance of the Very Heavy bomber category was explained by the appearance in SAC service of the gigantic B-36, which prompted a redesignation of the B-29 as a medium bomber, while the new type was known as a heavy bomber.

Conceived in 1941 as a transatlantic bomber able to carry a 10,000 lb (4,536 kg) bombload against a target 5,000 miles (8,050 km) away in case Britain should be invaded by Germany, the B-36 was not ordered into production until 1943, and the prototype did not fly until 1946. The majority of the 446 built had four turbojets in underwing pods to supplement the original six pusher propellers, allowing them to carry a maximum load of two 42,000 lb (19,050 kg) high-explosive bombs, though the normal maximum load was 72,000 lb (32,660 kg) in four separate weapons bays. The first B-36A was delivered to the 7th Bomb Group at Carswell in June 1948, and by 1954 six Heavy Bomb Wings and four Heavy Strategic Reconnaissance Wings were equipped with B-36 and RB-36 variants. The following year all B-36 units were classified as Heavy Bombs Wings, the number reducing steadily until the last B-36 was retired in February 1959.

The end of the B-36 was also the end of the propeller-driven bomber in SAC. The B-29 had been followed by the B-50 derivative, delivered from February 1948 and equipping five Medium Bomb Wings by 1952 before the last of 370 built was retired in October 1955. The RB-45C reconnaissance counterpart of the B-45 Tornado equipped one medium reconnaissance wing briefly in the early 1950s, but the first all-jet bomber to serve with the command was the B-47 Stratojet.

The first B-47 was delivered to SAC in October 1951, and it represented a startling advance over any previous type. Its thin, swept wings and six J47 turbojets gave it a maximum speed of over 600 mph (965 km/h), and by 1957 over 1,200 were in service with 28 Medium Bomb Wings. Another five Medium Strategic Reconnaissance Wings used the RB-47, with 11 cameras in the bomb bay, and a total of over 2,000 were built.

By that stage the Heavy Bomb Wings were

*Above:* An F-84F engages the trapeze under a B-36 during trials that led to brief operational service for GRF-84F reconnaissance fighters carried in a similar fashion. High-altitude reconnaissance aircraft and satellites soon made such complication unnecessary.

starting to convert from the B-36 to the eight-jet B-52 Stratofortress, still the command's principal bomber, the first production B-52B having been delivered in June 1955 to the 93d HBW at Castle AFB, California. In 1958 the one-third alert system, under which a third of SAC's bombers would be on ground alert at any time, was introduced, and at the same time new Strategic Wings were created by dispersing individual B-52 squadrons along with supporting squadrons of tankers, to other bases. By this time the old KB-29 had been phased out, and 34 of the 41 air refueling squadrons were flying KC-97 Stratofreighters. The other seven were equipped with the new KC-135 Stratotanker, whose jet propulsion enabled it to match the operational speeds and altitudes of the bombers, rather than forcing them to slow down at low levels to refuel.

The performance of the jet bombers was enough to minimize the threat of intercep-

tion, and in 1957 the four surviving Strategic Fighter Wings were transferred to other commands or inactivated. SAC had included a fighter component for bomber escort from its inception, and from two groups of P-51 Mustangs in 1946 its fighter strength had grown to a peak of six fighter and one fighter-reconnaissance wings flying F-84F Thunderstreaks capable of delivering nuclear weapons and RF-84F Thunderflashes by 1955.

In one scheme to provide B-36s with long-range escorts the XF-85 Goblin was designed to fit into the bomber's weapon bay, to be launched when required and retrieved by means of a trapeze arrangement. Two Goblins were built in the late 1940s but the project was abandoned. In 1955, however, the 91st SRS was equipped with 25 GRF-84Fs (later redesignated RF-84K), the G (for parasite) prefix indicating their modification under the Ficon (Fighter conveyor) program with nose hooks to engage trapezes carried by a dozen

*Above:* The U-2 of the late 1950s was SAC's first specialized high-altitude strategic reconnaissance aircraft. Many of those built were lost on clandestine missions.

GRB-36Ds.

New aircraft soon made such arrangements unnecessary. SAC's original reconnaissance force comprised camera-equipped variants of the B-29, B-17, and C-45 Expeditor, initially with the old designations F-13, F-9, and F-2, and supplemented by small numbers of C-82 Packets and RC-45s. Heavy and medium reconnaissance wings flew RB-36s and reconnaissance versions of the smaller bombers until the former were redesignated as bomb wings in 1955, leaving five medium wings with RB-47s. In May 1956 the 4080th SRW received the first RB-57D, a high-altitude photographic and radar reconnaissance development of the B-57 Night Intruder, itself a derivative of the British Canberra light bomber. The greatly enlarged 106 ft (32 m) span wings of the 20 RB-57Ds built suffered a number of failures, and a number of RB-57Fs were rebuilt from early models with entirely new wings of 2,000 sq ft (186 $m^2$) area.

All SAC's RB-57s had been passed to other commands by April 1960, and in the meantime the 4080th SRW, based at Laughlin AFB, Texas, had received its first U-2A in April 1957. Specially designed for high-altitude photographic and electronic reconnaissance missions over the Soviet Union, the U-2 was built in limited numbers but in a variety of configurations, including a new series of much bigger U-2Rs produced in the late 1960s, and the current production version, the TR-1, which will be used to support tactical operations in Europe. The type was used by the CIA as well as SAC, and a few were ostensibly

*Below:* Designed for high-altitude cruising flight, both the U-2 and its current derivative, the TR-1, are extremely difficult to land.

transferred to the Nationalist Chinese Air Force in Taiwan, and several were lost on missions over China and Cuba as well as the one in which CIA pilot Gary Powers was shot down near Sverdlovsk on May 1, 1960.

Operationally, during its first decade and a half, SAC's preoccupations included extending its mission capabilities through regular overseas deployments and a series of long-distance exercises and demonstration flights. The first overseas deployment was in November 1946, when six B-29s flew to Rhein-Main AB, Germany, and spent two weeks touring Europe, surveying airfields in a symbolic show of strength after two US Army C-47s had been shot down over Yugoslavia. In 1947 B-29 squadrons began rotational assignments to Yokota AB, Japan, and after the imposition of the Berlin blockade in the summer of 1948 the whole of SAC was placed on 24-hour alert, and three B-29 groups deployed to England and Germany. The same year brought a round-the-world flight, three B-29s taking 15 days to cover some 20,000 miles (32,200 km): less than a year later a B-50 went round the world non-stop, flying more than 23,000 miles (37,030 km) in 94 hours with the aid of four refuelings, while a B-36 made an unrefueled flight of 9,600 miles (15,460 km) in 43 hours 37 minutes.

War in Korea brought four groups of B-29s and a reconnaissance squadron of RB-29s to Japanese air bases in July, and after all strategic targets in North Korea had been attacked two of the bomb groups returned to the US in September, while the other units continued to serve with Far East Air Forces until after the fighting ended in July 1953. By that time overseas Air Division headquarters had been established in England and Morocco, and another was activated at Andersen AFB, Guam, in 1954, to oversee SAC operations in the respective areas. Later in the decade the 16th AF was established in Spain and assigned to SAC, taking over control of Moroccan operations from 2d AF. In 1953 B-47 wings started rotational training missions to England, and until 1958 there was always at least one wing based in the UK.

The geographical disposition of the three US Air Forces in the US was revised in 1955, with 8th AF HQ moving from Texas to West-

*Above:* Crew member at the control panel in a Minuteman II silo. ICBMs can only be launched on the instruction of the National Command Authority – the president, the secretary of defense or their deputies.

*Top:* The single warhead of a Minuteman I missile, which became operational in 1963 but has now been superseded by the Mks II and III.

over AFB, Massachussetts, to be responsible for the northeastern and central areas, while the 2d and 15th controlled activities in the southeast and the southwest and west respectively. The Suez crisis of 1956 saw air refueling squadrons based in the northern US, Greenland, Newfoundland, and Labrador ready to support a mass exercise involving 1,000 B-47s and KC-97s in simulated missions extending over the Arctic. Two years later, with extended ranges and reduced flight times made possible by the KC-135, the 90-day wing rotations to bases in England and Morocco were replaced by more frequent deployments of smaller detachments, maintaining the one-third alert system.

Perhaps the most significant development of the late 1950s was the activations of SAC's first missile units. The weapons were developed by the Ballistic Systems Division of Air Research and Development Command (Air Force Systems Command from April 1961), as described in the chapter on Space Command. The first Atlas ICBMs were declared operational in 1958, later models remaining in service with up to 13 squadrons until 1965. The Snark intercontinental cruise missile became operational for only a few months in 1960, while the intermediate-range Thor ballistic missile was based in England, operated in conjunction with 20 RAF squadrons, from 1959 to 1963.

The Thors were made redundant by the new Titan and Minuteman ICBMs, early models of which became operational in 1962. The later Titan II, Minuteman II, and III, operational from 1963, 1966, and 1970 respectively, continue in service, although the remaining Titans, their number down to 52 from a peak of 63 in 1967, started to be phased out in a five-year program begun in October 1982.

The introduction of the land-based ICBMs, along with the manned bombers and the Navy's submarine-launched Polaris ballistic missiles, completed the triad of strategic weapon systems, each with its own characteristics. In conjunction, these weapons were the concrete expression of the concept of assured destruction and its derivative, mutually assured destruction, on which American strategic defense was based from the early 1960s. The level of ICBMs was established at 1,000 Minuteman missiles, the original Minuteman I and II carrying single reentry vehicles with one- or two-megaton warheads, while the Mk III has triple independently targettable RVs, each with a 200-kiloton warhead. The last Minuteman I was retired in 1974, and production of Minuteman III ended in 1977, but 300 of the latter were scheduled to have new reentry vehicles carrying 330-kiloton warheads in a program started in 1979, while 50 Mk IIs were due to be replaced by Mk IIIs, producing a balance of 400 and 600 of the older and newer models.

The bigger, heavier Titan carries a 10-megaton warhead and has a range of 9,600 miles (15,460 km) compared with the 7,000 and 8,000 miles (11,270 and 12,880 km) of the Minuteman II and III. Titan's long-delayed replacement, the MX Peacekeeper, with a range of over 8,000 miles (12,880 km) and 10 of the new Advanced Ballistic Reentry Vehicles, has been a controversial subject for some years. Most of the arguments have concerned the proposed basing modes: by the time the first of 20 test flights had been made in the summer of 1983 it had been decided that

*Left:* Test launch of two Minuteman missiles as seen from a safe distance through the side door of a UH-1 helicopter.

*Below left:* The small number of B-58 Hustlers that served with SAC throughout the 1960s were the command's only supersonic bomber before the B-1B of the 1980s.

the dense pack system would be adopted. The dense pack involves 100 missiles in superhardened capsules 1,800 ft (550 m) apart in a rectangular pattern 14 miles (23 km) long and a mile (1.6 km) wide.

The theory behind dense pack is that a first strike on the site – the first is expected to be operational in the vicinity of Francis E. Warren AFB, near Cheyenne, Wyoming, current base of the 90th Strategic Missile Wing with its four squadrons of 50 Minuteman III missiles, by the end of the decade – would destroy no more than 20 missiles before the effects of the first rounds began to destroy succeeding incoming missiles. The DoD budget request for Fiscal Year 1985 included five billion dollars for the MX program, roughly three-fifths of which would be for the production of 40 missiles to follow the 21 authorized in FY 1984.

The initial deployment of ICBMs in the late 1950s and the new missiles under development were responsible for a rapid run-down of the B-47 force, the last bombers being retired in 1966 and the last RB-47s in the following year, and the cancelation in 1959 of the enormous B-70 Valkyrie Mach 3 bomber, intended to replace the B-52. One new supersonic bomber was produced, however, in the form of the B-58 Hustler, which equipped two

*Right:* The controversial MX ICBM, the subject of continuing debate both about the safest basing method and the cost of deploying a new generation of land-based ICBMs.

Medium Bomb Wings between 1961 and 1969. Designed for high-altitude penetration with a dash range of 1,500 miles (2,415 km) at Mach 2, the Hustler was faster but more limited in range and payload than the B-52. It carried a nuclear weapon along with extra fuel in an external 62 ft (19 m) pod to be released over the target, with reconnaissance or electronic warfare equipment as alternative payloads.

In terms of performance the B-58 was unique, but high-speed, high-altitude bombing attacks were impractical in the face of

*Left:* Among the B-58's many unusual features was the mission pod carried under the fuselage and used to carry both supplementary fuel and weapons, the whole assembly being jetisonned over the target.

new surface-to-air missile systems. As a result, the B-47, B-52, and B-58 were all required to switch from their original mission profiles to low-altitude approaches at high subsonic speeds, using the Low-Altitude Bombing System (LABS) to deliver their weapons. LABS was developed to give the low-flying bombers a chance to escape the effects of the nuclear detonation, and involved the bomber pulling up in the start of a loop from its approach altitude of around 500 ft (152 m). The weapon was released during the upward zoom, flying several thousand feet (well over 500 m) up in the air before falling back to earth while the launch aircraft rolled out of the top of the loop and dived back to low altitude and a hasty exit.

Another means of distancing the bomber from the detonation was to launch stand-off missiles from a safe distance, and the first such weapon to become operational was the Hound Dog. Two Hound Dogs could be car-

*Left:* A Hound Dog standoff attack missile is test-launched from a B-52. The weapon was intended to assist in penetration by destroying air defenses in the bomber's path.

*Opposite:* Successor to the Hustler, the FB-111 was an even more radical design and the subject of massive controversy over escalating costs, with the result that only a few dozen were built.

ried by G and H models of the B-52, and their turbojet engines could be used to provide extra thrust for takeoff, the missiles then being refueled before launch. Carrying a one-megaton warhead 500 miles (800 km) or more at just over Mach 2, and using inertial navigation, supplemented by terrain-following radar in some versions, to locate its target, the Hound Dog was operational with SAC from 1961 to 1976.

One result of the increasingly sophisticated air defense systems faced by SAC's bombers was the need to deceive hostile radars. This can be done electronically by transmitting jamming signals, or mechanically by releasing decoys or clouds of reflective material to clutter the hostile radar screens with false signals. The Quail decoy missile, built of fiberglass and powered by a J85 turbojet, was introduced in 1961 and remained in service until 1978: two could be carried in a B-52 bomb bay, and on release they would follow a similar flight path to that of the bomber, and despite their overall length of only 13 ft (4 m) they would produce a radar return similar to that of a B-52.

Standard equipment on current B-52s include chaff to confuse radar signal returns, flares to decoy heat-seeking missiles, radar detection sensors, and jamming equipment which has been repeatedly updated. The B-52G and H also feature improved inertial navigation systems and Tercom (terrain contour matching), the latter a system of measuring the contours of the terrain below the flight path and comparing them with stored map information. Large nose blisters on the updated aircraft house ECM antennae, as well as low-light-level television and FLIR sensors whose images are displayed on a

*Below:* SAC's newest bomber, the B-1B, is designed for low-level penetration at high subsonic speeds: like the FB-111, it has swing wings, and despite its small size it will carry a heavier weapon load than the B-52.

cockpit cathode ray tube (TV screen) as part of the million-dollar (per aircraft) electro-optical viewing system installed in the mid-1970s.

Complementing the B-52s are a small number – less than 60 of the 76 built were still operational in 1984 – of the FB-111A, strategic counterpart of the F-111 tactical attack aircraft developed amid endless controversy in the 1960s. With variable geometry swing wings for optimum low-level performance, automatic terrain-following radar navigation that can maintain a programed flight path as little as 300 ft (91 m) above ground level, and a bomb/nav system that can deliver its weapons within 50 ft (15 m) of a pre-selected target in darkness and all weathers, the FB-111 is extremely well suited to the low-level penetration mission.

Among the weapons available to the FB-111

is the SRAM (Short Range Attack Missile), which has both inertial and terrain-following navigation systems to permit a variety of delivery techniques to be used. Carrying a 200-kiloton warhead over a range of 100 miles (160 km), the SRAM is designed to destroy air defense radar installations and missile sites. It became operational in 1972, and a maximum of six can be carried by the FB-111, two internally and four under the wings: the B-52G and H can carry up to 20, with eight on a rotary launcher in the bomb bay and another six on a single pylon under each wing.

Although designed for intercontinental nuclear strikes, the B-52 saw extensive service during the war in Vietnam, delivering heavy weights of conventional ordnance against a variety of targets. The B-52Fs of the 2d and 320th Bomb Wings were modified to carry 12 bombs on each of the Hound Dog pylons, in addition to the internal load of 27, and were based on Guam in February 1965. The first operations over southeast Asia were carried out by 30 aircraft in June, and although their attempts to destroy suspected Viet Cong bases in Bin Duong province were unsuccessful, General Westmoreland, Commander of the US Military Assistance Command, Vietnam, was so keen on their use that he personally allocated the Stratofortresses their targets.

At the end of 1965 the Big Belly modification program to enable 82 B-52Ds of the 28th and 484th Bomb Wings to carry 42 750 lb or 500 lb (340 or 230 kg) bombs internally, in addition to the 24 similar weapons on the wing pylons. The two wings arrived in Guam

*Below:* The bulges around the nose of this B-52G house ECM antennae and low-light television and infra-red sensors; the weapons under its wings are Air Launched Cruise Missiles.

in April 1966. The number of sorties flown was steadily increased, reaching a peak of 1,800 per month by 1968, when the bases at Kadena, Okinawa, and U-Tapao, Thailand began to be used to launch strikes in the theater. Just over half the total of 126,615 B-52 sorties launched between June 1965 and August 1973 were in support of ground forces in South Vietnam, including 2,700 during the siege of Khe Sanh in early 1968, when 110,000 tons (246,400,000 kg) of ordnance was dropped. Just over a quarter of the total were aimed at cutting the Ho Chi Minh Trail in Laos, with another 12 percent against suspected North Vietnamese lines of communication in Cambodia.

Only six percent of the total were flown against North Vietnam, where the antiaircraft defenses were responsible for all 17 B-52s shot down during the conflict. The north was on the receiving end of the most concentrated B-52 offensive of the war in December 1972, when 740 sorties were flown against Hanoi and Haiphong in an 11-day period which saw nearly 49,000 bombs dropped on 34 targets. Nearly a thousand missiles were launched against the attackers, and 15 of the bombers were shot down, but under the combined effects of the bombing, a naval blockade and the failure of that year's offensive in the south peace negotiations were resumed and a truce was concluded in January 1973.

The B-52Ds are now being phased out, and after nearly 30 years a replacement for the Stratofortress is on the way. The B-1B, derived from the B-1A that was canceled in 1977, is optimized for the low-level penetration

mission, equipped with extensive electronic warfare equipment and using radar-absorbent materials to reduce its radar cross-section to less than one percent of that of the B-52. Current plans call for 100 production B-1Bs, with the first becoming operational in late 1986 and deliveries completed by 1988.

The B-1B will have almost double the weapons payload of the B-52 being able to carry three 8-round SRAM launchers internally and an external load of 14 of the new Air-Launched Cruise Missile (ALCM). The ALCM is powered by a low-thrust turbofan engine and uses Tercom to follow a low-altitude, subsonic flight path to its target. With a range of around 2,000 miles (3,220 km) and a 200-kiloton warhead, the ALCM became operational on the B-52Gs of the 416th BW in 1982, and a total of 96 B-52Gs were scheduled to be equipped for the weapon. Originally intended to use the same rotary launchers as the SRAM, the ALCM ended up too long, and until a new launcher becomes available a maximum of 12 will be carried externally. A similar launcher will be available for the B-1B, and a total of 1,500 ALCMs are being produced.

In fact, the B-1Bs will supplement rather than replace the B-52. SAC's bomber force will continue to include eight Bomb Wings with B-52Gs and five using the turbofan-powered H model. Two of the latter are designated as part of the Strategic Protection Force, the SAC element of the Rapid Deployment Joint Task Force, supported by SR-71A, U-2R, and RC-135 reconnaissance aircraft and KC-135 tankers.

Several variants of the RC-135 are used for electronic intelligence work, while the SR-71A is a high-speed, high-altitude reconnaissance aircraft developed in unusual secrecy from 1959 and first flown in 1964. Operated by the 1st Strategic Reconnaissance Squadron, 9th SRW, based at Beale AFB, California, the SR-71 is regularly operated by detachments based at Kadena AFB, Okinawa, Eielson AFB, Alaska and RAF Mildenhall in England on clandestine missions.

Because of the specialized JP-7 fuel burned by its J58 turbojets for continuous operation at speeds of Mach 3 at altitudes of over 60,000 ft (18,300 m), the SR-71 is supported by special KC-135Q tankers. Standard tanker is the KC-135A, of which some 500 are operated by 33 regular SAC squadrons, with another 128 in service with 16 Air Force Reserve and Air National Guard squadrons stationed at SAC bases. SAC is responsible for all USAF flight

*Overleaf*: Since the first KC-135A tanker was delivered to SAC in 1957 numerous specialized variants have been produced including RC-135 radar and electronic intelligence aircraft.

*Opposite*: A Strategic Air Command tanker refuels a modified version of this prolific family.

*Below*: One of the SR-71A Blackbirds operated by the 9th Strategic Reconnaissance Wing deploys its brake parachute as it lands on a wet runway while on detachment to England.

refueling, and 300 of its KC-135As are scheduled to have quieter and more efficient CFM56 turbofan engines. In 1981 the first KC-10A Extender was delivered: based on the DC-10 airliner, the new tanker/transport has considerably greater range than the KC-135, and can carry support equipment and personnel as well as fuel when supporting overseas deployments.

It is fundamental to SAC's task that it should be able to maintain control of its forces in any circumstance. One aspect of this control is the need to guard against the accidental or unauthorized launch of a nuclear attack. SAC's bombers and missiles can only be committed on the orders of the National Command Authority – the President, the Secretary of Defense, or their deputies – and once the bombers have taken off to ensure their survival they initially proceed to their allotted turnaround points. Only on receipt of the "go code," authenticated voice commands originating from the NCA verified by at least two crew members, are they allowed to carry out an attack, and only after the go code has been received can the arming process, which itself requires several crew members to carry out coordinated procedures, be initiated. Similarly authenticated commands are required before a missile launch, and the launch can only be effected by two men, since simultaneous key turns are required in control panels too far apart for one person to manipulate both.

The other side of the coin is the need to ensure that the commands can be given. In 1957 SAC headquarters was relocated in a new complex at Offutt, incorporating a three-storey underground command post, and in 1962 the Post Attack Command Control System was expanded to include a number of EC-135 airborne control centers, one of which was to be airborne at any given time with an SAC general aboard. The "Looking Glass" EC-135s continue in service, principal operator being the 2d Airborne Command and

U.S. AIR FORCE

Control Squadron at Offutt, though the 4th ACCS at Ellsworth AFB, South Dakota, operates an auxiliary command post and three Airborne Launch Control Center EC-135s equipped to launch Minuteman missiles by remote control.

The 1st ACCS, also based at Offutt, is responsible for the four E-4 National Emergency Command Posts, variants of the Boeing 747 airliner equipped to accommodate the NCA, the joint Chiefs of Staff, and essential personnel and to remain airborne for up to 72 hours. One of the E-4s is always on alert at Andrews AFB, Maryland, just outside Washington, DC, and all the airborne command post aircraft are linked by worldwide communications networks maintained by the Strategic Communications Division of Communications Command. Targets for the strategic forces are defined by the Joint Strategic Target Planning Staff, a joint service agency established in 1960 within the Joint Chiefs of Staff organization which prepares both the National Strategic Target List and the Single Integrated Operational Plan under which they would be attacked.

*Above right:* Some of the massive quantity of data produced by SAC's worldwide reconnaissance systems is displayed at the command's underground headquarters at Offutt AFB, Nebraska.

*Above:* One of the E-4B Sentry airborne national command post aircraft that maintain a constant alert at Andrews AFB, Maryland, ready to take to the air for up to 72 hours with the President, the Joint Chiefs of Staff and communications equipment to enable them to exercise control over strategic forces.

*Left:* The unique outline of the SR-71A, designed to cruise at Mach 3 at stratospheric heights on clandestine reconnaissance missions.

U.S. AIR FORCE

# 4: WAR IN KOREA

*Overleaf:* The B-57 was developed as a night intruder in the 1950s: this B-57B has been rebuilt as an EB-57E for service with an Air National Guard Defense Systems Evaluation Squadron, simulating enemy air raids to test air defenses.

*Opposite:* C-54 transports at Wiesbaden continue to operate supply flights to West Berlin during the blockade of the city, despite the heaviest snowfall of the year in March 1949.

The end of World War II, and the new era of warfare inaugurated by the destruction of Hiroshima and Nagasaki, resulted in a rapid rundown of conventional forces, but not the period of peace that had followed the Armistice of 1918. On September 18, 1947, the United States Air Force officially came into being as an independent service, though it was some months before complete autonomy was established. Already, in March 1946, the formation of Strategic Air Command had been accompanied by the establishment of Air Defense and Tactical Air Commands, with Air Training and Alaska Air Commands joining them later that year. Among the consequences of the 1947 reorganization were the merger of Air Transport Command and the Naval Air Transport Service to form Military Air Transport Service, and the elimination of the strategic from US Strategic Air Forces in Europe.

The formation of MATS coincided with the first major confrontation between the recent allies, when the Soviet armies in eastern Germany imposed a blockade on surface access to the western sector of Berlin. In response, an airborne supply operation was mounted by the Western Allies, with the first USAF C-47 landing at Tempelhof airport in the city on June 26. Between then and the end of the airlift on October 1, 1949, as many as 300 C-54s, along with five C-82s, were assembled in Germany, and until the lifting of the blockade in May 1949 aircraft were arriving at Tempelhof at three-minute intervals, with more than three-quarters of a million flights being completed.

There was to be little relaxation following the end of the airlift. On June 25, 1950 North Korean troops launched an invasion of the southern part of the country, and the United Nations, under the leadership of the United States, sent in troops to meet this threat. While SAC B-29s moved to Japan for a campaign against the relatively limited number of strategic targets available, the Far East Air Forces, formed in December 1945, were committed to the support of South Korea.

By this stage the FEAF was but a shadow of the force built up in the Pacific a few years earlier. The 20th Air Force in Guam and Okinawa had one group of B-29s and a SAC squadron of RB-29s, plus a fighter interceptor group and an all-weather fighter squadron; 13th AF at Clark, in the Philippines, had a single fighter-bomber group and a few RB-29s. Main air power was concentrated in Japan with the 5th Air Force, but even this

400
3
437

amounted to only six squadrons of fighter-bombers, three of interceptors and four of all-weather fighters, plus single groups of B-26 bombers and C-54 troop carriers, along with supporting rescue and reconnaissance units and a weather reconnaissance squadron.

Perhaps the most significant difference between the FEAF in 1950 and the force of five years earlier was the aircraft used by the fighter squadrons. The interceptors and fighter-bombers were F-80C Shooting Stars, the all-weather fighters F-82 Twin Mustangs, and while the latter, with their twin P-51 fuselages married to a new wing center section, were rather extraordinary in appearance, the F-80 was the more significant. The Twin Mustang was the last propeller-driven fighter produced in substantial numbers for the Air Force, having originated in 1944 as a long-range escort but subsequently being adapted to carry a radar pod as a night fighter. The F-80, on the other hand, was the USAF's first front-line fighter to use jet propulsion, the F-80C fighter-bomber variant being equipped to carry a 1,000 lb (454 kg) bomb, four rockets, or three napalm bombs under each wing.

The first task after the start of the invasion was the evacuation of American personnel, covered by the 5th Air Force fighters, the second was to move troops and air support to South Korea, and before the end of June the process was under way. Unfortunately, the expertise in air-ground cooperation built up during World War II had apparently been dissipated, and the lack of effective communications was highlighted early in July, when a Royal Australian Air Force squadron received a delayed report of a North Korean advance and attacked a retreating South Korean column instead.

Another handicap was the limited range of the aircraft available. The B-26s, with longer endurance and a heavy gun armament, enjoyed great success against the advancing North Koreans, but the F-80Cs were limited to a range of 225 miles (362 km) with 16 rockets, or only 165 miles (266 km) with a pair

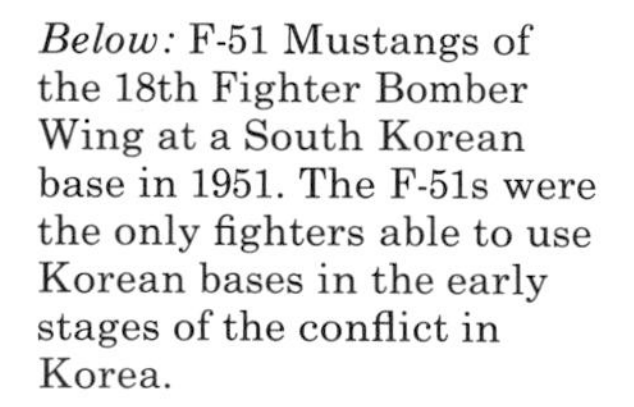

*Below:* F-51 Mustangs of the 18th Fighter Bomber Wing at a South Korean base in 1951. The F-51s were the only fighters able to use Korean bases in the early stages of the conflict in Korea.

of 1,000 lb (454 kg) bombs, with only 15 minutes in the target area. Bigger wingtip fuel tanks allowed the loiter time to be increased to 45 minutes, and the Shooting Star proved an adept ground-attack type. By the middle of August air strikes on North Korean airfields had all but eliminated opposition, and bases adequate for piston-engined operations had been opened at Taegu and Pohang. As a result, FEAF squadrons began to exchange their F-80s for F-51 Mustangs (the old P designations having been superseded) and by mid-August there were six 5th AF Mustang squadrons in Korea ready to take part in the crucial battle for Pusan along with carrier-based Navy and Marine Corps units.

Air power was vital in stemming the North Korean advance, and by September 12 the offensive against the Pusan perimeter had failed and a counteroffensive was under way. By the end of the month the North Korean army was virtually destroyed, and the American and South Korean armies pushed on into North Korea in October. By the end of the month, however, there was a new factor involved: as the advance neared the Yalu River that formed the border with China it met sudden strong opposition from Chinese ground troops, and on November 1 the first Chinese MiG-15s were encountered by a flight of Mustangs.

The appearance of the MiG-15 had serious implications. With performance far superior to that of the F-80 it represented a deadly threat to the United Nations air power, and only the relative inexperience of the Chinese pilots allowed the Mustang and Shooting Star pilots to escape undamaged from their early encounters. Clearly, new aircraft would be needed to combat the MiGs, and by December the first wings of F-86A Sabres and F-84E Thunderjets were established at Kimpo and Taegu respectively. The Sabre was a close match for the MiG-15 in terms of performance, and the first engagements in December resulted in the claimed destruction of eight MiGs for the loss of one F-86. The F-84 was designed as a jet-propelled successor to

*Below:* The F-86 Sabre came to symbolize the air war over Korea. These F-86Fs served with the 51st Fighter Interceptor Wing in Korea during 1953.

*Opposite, top:* B-29Ds over Korea in 1951.

*Opposite, below:* B-29Ds at a Far East Air Forces base. Virtually every strategic target in North Korea had been destroyed within a few weeks, but the bombers continued to be used until the end of the conflict.

the P-47 Thunderbolt, and the first wing to serve in Korea was assigned to escort B-29s.

The Chinese intervention brought the UN advance to a halt during December, and the aircraft of FEAF were stretched to the limit dropping supplies to isolated ground units as well as carrying out close support and interdiction missions in an attempt to stem the Chinese advance. By the end of January 1951 the offensive had been halted, and the F-84s and F-86s were withdrawn to Japan. This also halted the B-29 attacks for the time being, until forward air bases could be made serviceable in March. The F-86s were then able to reassert a measure of air superiority, despite growing confidence and improved accuracy at hitting targets on the part of the MiG pilots, while the F-80s and F-84s tended to keep to lower altitudes where the MiG-15's superiority was less marked.

Meanwhile, the B-29s were beginning to use radio-guided bombs, initially the Razon type developed during the closing stages of World War II, and then with a much bigger version, the 12,000 lb (5,440 kg) Tarzon. Both used a radio receiver attached to the bomb to allow steerable tail fins to modify the weapon's trajectory in response to commands transmitted from the bomber, and both were used to attack the bridges that were the main targets of the bombing effort and required direct hits if they were to be destroyed. The Tarzon was abandoned as unsafe in August, though the 30 dropped had succeeded in destroying six bridges and damaging a seventh.

By this stage the emphasis of the bombing had switched to other targets. The B-29s were redirected to more accessible targets such as railroad yards, while the 5th Air Force fighter-bombers and B-26s concentrated on a sustained campaign of road and rail interdiction aimed at isolating the Chinese forces south of the old border at the 38th parallel. The latter was a failure, however, since it proved impossible to halt the transport of supplies by air action alone, damage being repaired quickly and movements being effected under cover of darkness, while the main supply bases remained well protected against air attacks.

The difficulty of attacking surface transport at night was underlined by the occasional droppings of loads of tacks intended to puncture tyres and thus immobilize vehicles until they could be attacked by daylight. The more normal method was to use B-26s against

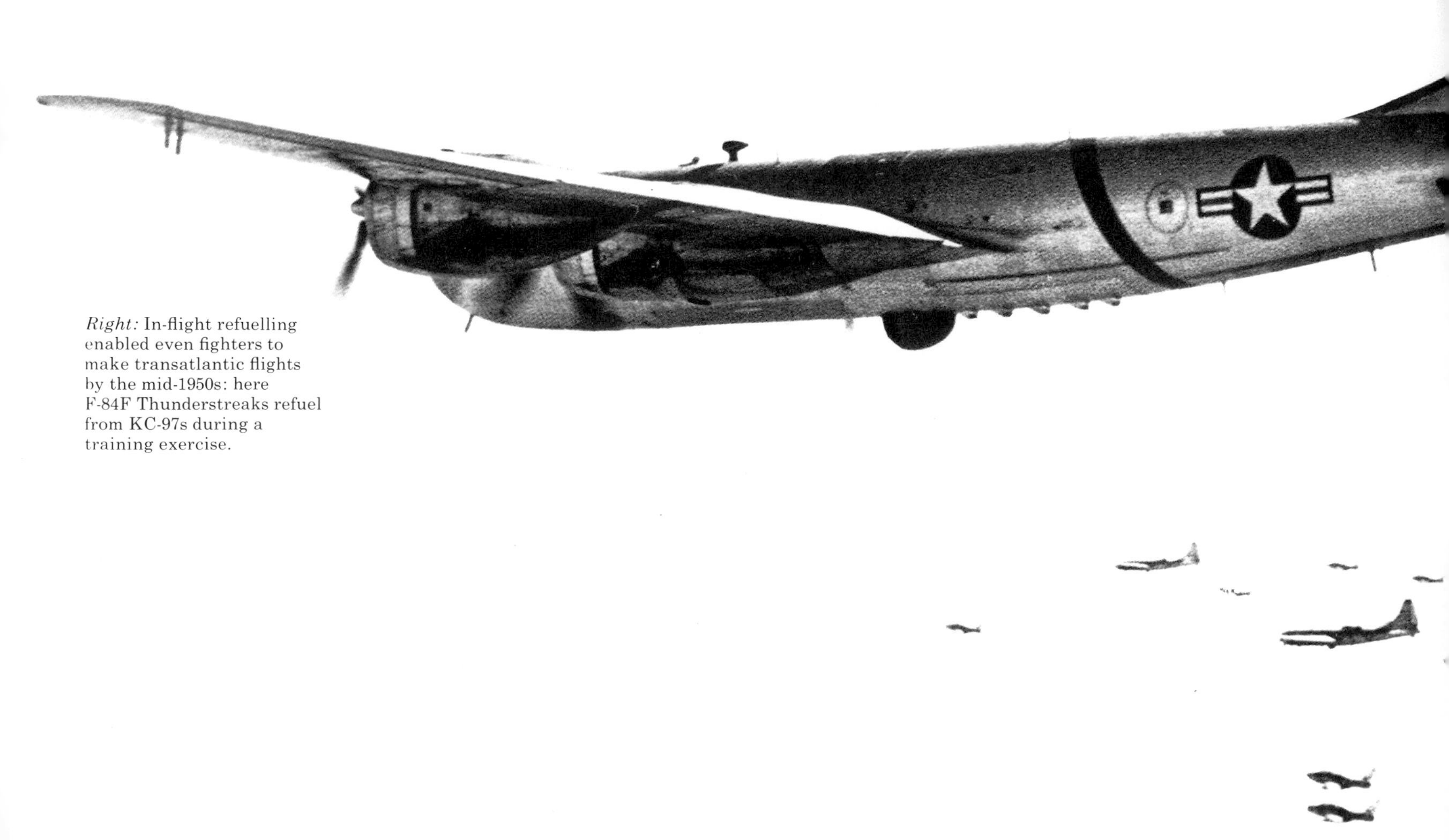

*Right:* In-flight refuelling enabled even fighters to make transatlantic flights by the mid-1950s: here F-84F Thunderstreaks refuel from KC-97s during a training exercise.

targets illuminated by flares dropped from C-47s. By day, too, the old Mustangs proved more successful in attacks on road convoys than the faster jets, whose endurance was much more limited, but improving antiaircraft defenses made low-level operations increasingly costly.

By August 1951 a new Chinese tactic imposed severe limitations on air operations over northwestern Korea. Massive formations of MiGs crossing the Yalu at high altitudes detached individual flights and attacked any UN aircraft encountered withdrawing in strength. However the arrival of the first wing of F-86Es in December enabled some opposition to be mounted to the high-altitude MiG

USAF
819
UNITED STATES AIR FORCE

formations. The return of the MiGs to low-altitude combat in March brought more successes for the Sabre pilots.

Losses among the fighter-bomber squadrons were particularly heavy during the second half of 1951 as the campaign against the railroad system continued, and severe shortages of aircraft resulted. The situation did not improve in the early months of 1952, as antiaircraft weapons grew more numerous, and in the absence of a new ground offensive losing aircraft in attacks on railroad lines that were soon repaired made little sense. Consequently, in June a new series of attacks began against hydro-electric installations in the north. These were accompanied by the arrival of new aircraft in substantial numbers, including F-84Gs whose in-flight refueling equipment allowed them to be flown rather than shipped across the Pacific.

At this point the air offensive switched to enemy morale, and in July the biggest attack of the war, involving all the United Nations elements – US Air Force, Navy, and Marine Corps, Republic of Korea Air Force, and Royal Navy Fleet Air Arm – in a concerted series of strikes against the North Korean capital of Pyongyang. Neither these nor the simultaneous bombing of North Korean industrial centers had any effect on the continuing negotiations between United Nations and North Korean representatives, and with virtually every fixed target already destroyed the UN planners resorted to a simulated amphibious landing at a village north of Wosan in an attempt to lure the North Korean forces into a position where they could be attacked.

During the ensuing winter the F-86s established firm superiority in the air, though interceptors guided by radar-directed searchlights took a heavy toll of the B-29s on night raids. By 1953 the specialized F-94B Starfire night fighters, previously restricted to the south to avoid their radar equipment falling into enemy hands, were allowed to escort the bombers over the north, providing their crews with some relief from the attentions of the North Korean interceptors.

In May 1953, with the cease-fire negotiations under way again, but with little progress being made, one last air offensive was mounted. This time the targets were provided by the irrigation dams on which much of North Korea's rice supply depended. Then, with an armistice imminent, airfields were attacked in order to prevent any buildup of reinforcements before the cease-fire came into effect. A final Chinese offensive in mid-July

*Opposite:* The C-119 Flying Boxcar was a standard freight and troop transport aircraft of the 1950s.

was halted after a week of fighting which cost the northern forces 72,000 casualties, and on July 27 the armistice came into effect.

In terms of aircraft, the USAF losses amounted to 139, of which 78 were Sabres, a relatively modest total compared with the total of nearly 721,000 sorties flown. In terms of strategy, the outcome of the war in Korea was determined in the end by the threat of nuclear attack on China: the nominal participants were apparently prepared to go on fighting for ever, and it was only under pressure from the Americans on the one side and the Chinese and Soviets on the other, with the atom bomb hanging over all of them, that the final agreement was reached. As a battlefield weapon, the atomic bomb might have been employed decisively, according to US Army studies, in late 1950, and one consequence of the war was the development of tactical nuclear weapons, designed to be fired by guns, carried by short-range missiles or dropped by fighter-bombers.

The remainder of the 1950s saw some dramatic improvements in USAF capability, as technology was applied systematically to the development of advanced aircraft and weapon systems for a variety of purposes. The penetration of the "sound barrier" by the rocket-powered X-1 in October 1947 had naturally induced aircraft designers to start thinking in terms of supersonic fighters, and the development of aircraft radar and guided missiles offered the obvious complements to such weapons. By February 1950 the need for systematic investigation of new technological advances had inspired the formation of Air Research and Development Command to evaluate new weapon systems.

The first of the supersonic fighters, and of the appropriately designated "Century series" fighters, was the F-100 Super Sabre, which began to replace the F-86 in 1954. A temporarily unexplained midair breakup of one of the flight-test Super Sabres in 1954 led to the type being grounded for a time, and most F-100s were of the C and D fighter-bomber version, equipped for low-altitude delivery of tactical nuclear weapons but destined to spend much of their careers dropping

*Below:* B-26 Invaders serving with the 452d Bomb Wing, 5th Air Force. Formerly designated A-26, the Invader was used extensively against North Korean communications.

conventional weapons on Vietnam.

At the same time, the F-86F had replaced the F-51 and F-80 fighter-bombers, and another version of the Sabre, the F-86D, was produced as an all-weather interceptor with a radar and fire-control system and an armament of 24 Mighty Mouse unguided rockets in a retractable tray. A similar system was used in the F-94C Starfire two-seat, all-weather fighter, while the later F-89D Scorpion had improved radar and fire control and an armament of 104 Mighty Mouse rockets carried in the front part of two large wing-tip pods whose rear sections contained fuel tanks. The purpose of the fire-control systems was to compute a collision course with the target and automatically guide the fighter into position and launch the rockets.

Meanwhile, a radical new development of the Thunderjet had been produced in the form of the swept-wing F-84F Thunderstreak and a further derivative, the RF-84F Thunderflash, carried cameras in the nose for photo-reconnaissance work. Like the F-84G, the Thunderstreak was equipped with the Low Altitude Bombing System, but later in the decade far more sophisticated equipment was provided for the F-105 Thunderchief, early versions of which were first ordered in 1952, but which did not reach service until 1958. The principal variant, the F-105D, carried a doppler all-weather navigation system, air-data computer, toss-bombing computer and an air-to-ground search and ranging radar; standard armament was an M61 Vulcan six-barrel cannon, firing 20 mm rounds at a rate of 6,000 per minute.

Experience in Vietnam would underline the need for a gun to be carried by fighter aircraft, but during the 1950s it appeared that aircraft speeds were reaching the point where only missiles would be capable of hitting a hostile aircraft, and the new supersonic interceptors of the late 1950s dispensed with guns in favor of new guided missiles of the Falcon series, and unguided Genie missiles, which carried a 1.5-kiloton nuclear warhead. Both were first used by variants of the Scorpion, the Falcon entering service with the F-89H in January 1956 and the Genie on the modified

*Below:* Long-range fuel tanks as carried by these 51st Fighter Interceptor Wing F-86Fs were needed to give the early jet fighters a useful endurance.

32430
U.S. AIR FORCE
USAF
USAF
USAF
U.S. AIR FORCE
37786
FG-786
USAF
U.S. AIR FORCE

F-89J a year later. The F-89J carried two Genies and four Falcons under the wings, while the F-89H retained 42 of the Mighty Mouse rockets along with six Falcons in the wingtip pods.

In order to make the best use of the new interceptors, the SAGE (Semi-automatic Ground Environment) system was built up during the 1950s. This system is based on centralized data processing, using information from a network of ground radars supplemented by additional inputs from airborne and naval early warning systems, meteorological data, weapon status information, and logs of civil and military flight plans, so that air defenses can be controlled over the whole of North America. Alongside SAGE is the Back-up Interceptor Control system, or BUIC, whose local control centers are designed to take over in the event of the centralized SAGE system ceasing to function during an attack.

Air Defense Command's first supersonic interceptor was the F-102 Delta Dagger, of which 875 were delivered in 1955-57. Armed with six Falcon missiles, normally three each of the semi-active radar guided AIM-4A or -4E and the AIM-4C or -4F infrared homing versions, carried in an internal bay whose doors incorporated launch tubes for 24 Mighty Mouse rockets, the F-102 was provided with SAGE data link equipment in the early 1960s. Using this in conjunction with the MG-3 or later MG-10 fire-control system, the normal system of voice commands from the ground controller and manual operation by the pilot could be replaced by direct data inputs to the autopilot. To use the radar scope the pilot needed to position his head directly over a viewing hood, and with the autopilot providing attitude hold or heading or height lock he adjusted the scan pattern and range gate, and with infrared or radar missiles selected the MG-10 system would take over to launch the weapon when lock-on had been achieved and the target was within range. An infrared seeker was added to help the IR Falcon to lock on, and the Mighty Mouse rockets were later dispensed with.

The successor to the F-102 was the F-106 Delta Dart, still in service in the early 1980s. The F-106 has an improved weapon system, including the data link but with an added onboard computer to provide rapid solutions to interception requirements. Armament was six Falcons plus two Genies, and in the 1970s an internal Vulcan cannon was added, as it was considered that visual identification and

*Opposite:* Century-series fighters at Edwards AFB: (clockwise from foreground) F-104 Starfighter, F-100 Super Sabre, F-102 Delta Dagger, F-101 Voodoo and F-105 Thunderchief.

*Below:* Fly-past of F-100As. The first version of the Super Sabre suffered a high casualty rate, but later versions saw extensive action in Vietnam, and continued in service through the 1970s.

*Opposite, top:* An F-106A Delta Dart of the 5th Fighter Interceptor Squadron, formerly part of Aerospace Defense Command but still in service with Air Defense, TAC.

*Opposite, center:* F-101B Voodoo all-weather interceptors in service with the Air National Guard in the 1980s.

*Opposite, bottom:* An F-104G Starfighter of the 69th TFTS, 58th TTW, which for several years trained Luftwaffe F-104 pilots.

*Right:* Two examples of the USAF's first delta-winged interceptor, the F-102A Delta Dagger, in Air National Guard service in the early 1970s.

*Right:* Fighter armament of the 1950s: an F-89D Scorpion fires a salvo of Mighty Mouse rockets from its starboard wingtip pod.

consequent short-range attacks might be required.

A contemporary of the F-106 in Air Defense Command, and one which survived in ANG units into the early 1980s, was the F-101 Voodoo, originally ordered as a long-range escort fighter for SAC. The F-101A and C versions produced to meet this requirement were diverted to TAC when SAC decided to dispense with fighter escorts, but the principal version was the F-101B interceptor, of which more than 400 were supplied to ADC. Unlike the original single-seat version, the F-101C was a two-seat all-weather interceptor, carrying armament similar to that of the F-106, while around 200 RF-101A and C unarmed tactical reconnaissance Voodoos were also produced for TAC.

One of the most radical new fighters of the 1950s was the F-104 Starfighter, which served in comparatively small numbers with the USAF but which was built in considerable numbers for other air forces. Intended as a lightweight high-performance interceptor, the original F-104A had only a brief career with ADC in 1958–59, though two squadrons reequipped with the type in 1963, and only one TAC wing used the F-104C fighter-bomber, from 1958 until 1965. Its mission was the delivery of tactical nuclear weapons.

While the fighters were the most spectacular of the Air Force's new aircraft during the 1950s, there were other important new types to fill other roles. B-45A and RB-45C Tornados, tactical bomber and reconnaissance versions of the USAF's first jet bomber, remained in service until late in the decade, the bomber variant being stationed in Britain with USAFE from 1952. Following the Korean experience another tactical bomber was produced in the form of the B-57 Night Intruder, built in a number of variants and serving in a wide variety of roles. Also the B-66 and RB-66 Destroyers, based on the Navy's A-3 Skywarrior, were in service from 1955, their primary role being tactical reconnaissance. RC-121 and EC-121 reconnaissance and airborne early warning versions of the C-121 Constellation transport made their appearance in 1953 and 1954 respectively.

With this new equipment, and with new transports such as the C-130 Hercules, the USAF was able to respond rapidly to international crises, such as the erection of the Berlin Wall in 1961, when several squadrons were deployed to Europe. Before long, however, the USAF would find itself preoccupied with a new conflict in Asia.

# 5: WAR IN SE ASIA

*Overleaf:* An AC-130, one of several gunship conversions of transport aircraft modified to provide heavy supporting fire in Vietnam.

*Opposite, top:* Supersonic jets were not ideal close-support aircraft, but they were pressed into service as such in Vietnam: an F-100 Super Sabre fires a salvo of air-to-surface rockets in May 1967.

*Opposite, bottom:* Thunderchiefs carried out more strikes against North Vietnam, and suffered more losses, than any other US combat aircraft. F-105Ds are bombed up ready for a mission in 1965.

The massive research and development programs of the 1950s had produced missile-armed Mach 2 interceptors, supersonic fighter-bombers able to carry tactical nuclear weapons and hundreds of heavy transport aircraft, and the early 1960s brought some impressive demonstrations of tactical air power mobility during the series of confrontations with the Soviet Union known as the cold war. The formation of the 4400th Combat Crew Training Squadron at Eglin AFB, Florida, in April 1961, was insignificant in comparison, but its role in training South Vietnamese personnel to resist the infiltration from north of South Vietnam's demilitarized zone would soon become the Air Force's major preoccupation.

The first confrontation with the Soviet Union came in 1961 with the erection of the Berlin Wall and the accompanying build-up of Warsaw Pact forces in eastern Europe in 1961. In response, 10 squadrons of ANG F-84F and F-86H fighter-bombers and RF-84F photo-reconnaissance fighters, along with one of the 479th TFW's three squadrons of F-104C Starfighters, were flown to France in November. Most of the aircraft returned to the US the following year, but a new wing, the 366th TFW, was formed to operate the F-84Fs in Europe.

October 1962 brought the most serious confrontation of all, when the revelation of Soviet bombers and missiles based in Cuba resulted in a worldwide alert of US forces. During the six days for which the island was blockaded, TAC's Composite Air Strike Force was assembled at Florida AFBs and MATS was busy supporting the build-up and ferrying Marines to Guantanamo Bay base on the island.

A year later Exercise Big Lift was staged to demonstrate the Air Force's ability to transport a complete armored division to Europe within two and a half days. More than 300 transport aircraft were involved in ferrying the 15,000 men and 450 tons (457 tonnes) of equipment that formed the 2d Armored Division from Texas to Rhein-Main, Sembach, and Ramstein ABs in Germany, and while the C-135s flew back and forth nonstop the shorter-range C-124, C-133, C-118, and C-130 transports made single crossings via intermediate stops in Bermuda, the Azores, Greenland, and the UK. At the same time the Air Strike Force was deployed to French bases.

By this stage Air Force units were already directly involved in the Vietnam conflict. In 1961 a detachment of the 4400th CCTS deployed to Bien Hoa AB under the codename Farm Gate with a small force of T-28s, EC-47s, and RB-26s in South Vietnamese Air Force (SVnAF) markings. At the same time, detachments of PACAF RF-101Cs and C-123s were located at Tan Son Nhut AB, where they were joined the following year by four F-102s from the 509th FIS, Clark AFB in the Philippines. Initial duties included reconnaissance, light attack, transport, and electronic surveillance of the border and coastal areas, while the C-123s, converted for aerial spraying with the designation UC-123B Ranch Hand, carried out defoliation missions along major highways and in areas under Viet Cong control.

Although the early incursions were contained, and the Air Force units were present in a nominal advisory capacity, American political involvement in Vietnam was growing. In February 1962 the Military Assistance Advisory Group, set up in 1956 when the French started to withdraw from the country, was replaced by the Military Assistance Command, Vietnam (MACV). By this stage there were 4,000 advisers in the country, but in the following year the number grew to 15,000. Among the new arrivals was a squadron of F-100D Super Sabres from Clark AFB stationed at Da Nang.

South Vietnam's political instability, combined with the determination of Presidents Kennedy and Johnson to maintain a bulwark against Communism, was drawing America inexorably into full-scale military involvement since the South Vietnamese forces proved unable to resist growing North Vietnamese and Viet Cong pressure. Johnson resisted the calls for direct action against the north, apart from limited air strikes by US Navy aircraft after the Gulf of Tonkin incident in August 1964. The incident, which involved one actual and one alleged attack on US destroyers monitoring South Vietnamese commando raids on naval bases in the north, allowed him to win Congressional approval for such military action as he might consider appropriate either to protect US forces or to assist any member state of the Southeast Asia Treaty Organization.

There was no immediate escalation of the air offensive, despite the destruction by the Viet Cong of six RB-57s at Bien Hoa on November 1, 1964 and the Christmas Eve bombing of a Saigon hotel used by American personnel. Limited strikes by US Navy aircraft were carried out in February 1965 after Viet Cong attacks on US Special Forces

U.S. AIR FORCE
FH-195
FH-279

bases, and on March 2, with South Vietnam's military situation deteriorating rapidly, the instigation of Operation Rolling Thunder marked a new stage in the air war.

The theory behind Rolling Thunder was that an escalating series of air strikes against selected targets would persuade the North Vietnamese to stop their attacks on the south. Accordingly, squadrons of F-105Ds from PACAF and US-based TAC units were based in Thailand to form the 388th (originally 6234th) and 355th (originally 6235th) TFWs at Korat and Tahkli RTAFBs (Royal Thai Air Force Bases) respectively, supported by RB-66C (later (EB-66C) squadrons, while the 3d TFW brought three squadrons of F-100Ds from the US to Bien Hoa AB, near Saigon, where it was joined by a squadron of B-57Bs. In April the 552d AW&CW arrived at Korat with its EC-121 Warning Stars to monitor enemy interceptor activity.

From an early stage the pattern of attacks on targets on North Vietnam was established, and while new aircraft would appear and techniques would be refined the basic roles would remain. A typical attack formation would include F-105D strike aircraft, F-100Ds for combat air patrol (CAP) duties, guarding against interception and covering downed aircrew while rescuc helicopters were dis-

*Opposite:* B-52s were converted to carry heavy weights of conventional bombs and used in support of ground operations, notably during the siege of Khe Sanh.

*Below:* Among the earliest US aircraft deployed to Vietnam were these B-57s, which arrived in strength at Bien Hoa in 1964. In November, five were destroyed and 15 damaged by a Viet Cong rocket attack.

patched, and RF-101s for photographic assessment of the damage caused. For difficult targets EB-66s would provide a navigational lead, while the EC-121s monitored aerial activity and SAC's tankers would top up the strike force's fuel tanks.

During 1965 the first F-4 Phantoms, originally designed as interceptors for the US Navy but subsequently adopted in various models by Air Force and Marine Corps, would take over almost all these roles, though the F-105D carried out more strikes over the north than any other type. By the end of the year two Phantom wings, the 12th TFW at Cam Ranh Bay AB and the 8th TFW at Ubon RTAFB, were operational in Southeast Asia, and the 388th TFW had received the first examples of the F-100F Wild Weasel, specially equipped to detect and attack surface-to-air missile sites. The EB-66 Destroyers were also given jamming equipment in addition to their electronic reconnaissance outfits for added protection.

During 1966 the strike force continued to build up. By the end of the year new units had arrived from the US to form the 366th TFW with F-4Cs at Da Nang and the 31st and 35th TFWs, both with F-100Ds, at Tuy Hoa and Phan Rang. In addition, the 460th TRW had been organized, with two squadrons of the

RF-4C photographic and electronic reconnaissance variant of the Phantom, at Tan Son Nhut AB, while the 432d TRW at Udorn RTAFB had two squadrons each of the RF-101C, RF-4C, and F-4D. The F-4D had new equipment specified by the Air Force, only minimal changes having been allowed in production of the F-4C, and included improved avionics, a central air data computer for navigation and bombing, a lead-computing optical sight, and equipment for launching electro-optical and laser-guided weapons.

The new precision weapons used either a television camera in the nose allowing the operator to guide the bomb to its target, or in later versions to designate the target before launch and leave the missile to find its own way; or a laser seeker, which enables the weapon to steer itself toward the target using reflections of laser energy transmitted by either the launch aircraft or another aircraft. The earlier Bullpup, which required the operator to observe the weapon's flight and transmit guidance commands to steer it onto the target, had the drawback of requiring the launch aircraft to remain in the vicinity until impact, but the electro-optical Walleye and laser-guided Paveway systems, which could be fitted to standard bombs of various sizes, enabled the bombs to do the work while the aircraft took evasive action.

Meanwhile, the emphasis of Rolling Thunder gradually changed. At first only a small number of targets were cleared for attack, the North Vietnamese capital of Hanoi and the main port of Haiphong being off limits, and even missile sites were excluded until the first F-4C was shot down by a SAM in July 1965. By the end of the year armed reconnaissance missions were being flown against rail, road, and river traffic in the north, and in 1966 principal targets were oil storage depots and the limited number of industrial plants. The difficulty of finding worthwhile targets for the huge formations of expensive jets was highlighted by the strikes against oil storage facilities at Haiphong, when their destruction accounted for an estimated 90 percent of the country's oil reserves, but which in the longer term resulted in the dispersal of oil

*Below:* An early formation of F-4C Phantoms over Vietnam, before green and brown camouflage became standard.

reserves to less accessible sites.

In 1967 the list of targets was extended to include the NVnAF interceptor bases, targets closer to Hanoi and rail links with China and Haiphong. The latter included the Paul Doumer and Thanh Hoa rail and road bridges, which were the subject of repeated attacks, though such damage as was caused was rapidly repaired, and the switch to classical interdiction tactics from the initial straightforward intimidation was no more successful. Finally, on March 31, 1968, the bombing of North Vietnam north of the 20th parallel was suspended by President Johnson, and in November the offensive against the north was halted altogether.

By this stage the emphasis had switched to the interdiction of supplies carried along the Ho Chi Minh Trail through Laos, and a grandiose strategy was evolved to use remote sensors to monitor movements. Under the Igloo White program thousands of acoustic and seismic sensors were dropped along the trail: vibrations, noise from truck engines or exploding antipersonnel mines would activate the sensors, causing them to transmit a signal which was picked up by patrolling EC-121s and relayed to the infiltration surveillance center at Nakhon Phanom RTAFB. Computers analyzed the resulting data, and air strikes were directed against areas where movement was detected.

Many techniques were used to attack the traffic on the trails. By day conventional air strikes could be mounted, but since most movement took place at night more sophisticated methods had to be developed. F-4s could use their inertial navigation to bomb on predetermined coordinates, and later the Pave Phantom technique linked the INS to Loran radio navigation. Three B-57Bs were fitted with infrared detection equipment in 1967, and subsequently 16 B-57Gs were given additional radar, infrared, and laser designators, along with appropriate weapons, and based at Ubon in 1970.

More concentrated firepower was provided by the series of gunship conversions of transport aircraft starting with the AC-74D Spooky. This conversion of the C-47D in-

*Below:* RF-4C tactical reconnaissance Phantoms in protective pens at their base in 1966. RF-4Cs supplemented and later replaced RF-101 Voodoos in the tactical reconnaissance role.

*Below:* By the later stages of the war new weapons were available: an F-4C Phantom of the 479th TFS, 8th TFW, based at Ubon RTAFB, releases a laser-guided bomb in November 1971.

volved the installation of three multi-barrel miniguns, with a combined rate of fire of 18,000 7.62 mm rounds per minute, which were aimed at targets illuminated by flares while the aircraft circled overhead. Later gunships included the AC-130A Spectre, in service from 1967, with four miniguns and four 20 mm cannon plus light-intensification, infrared and radar sensors linked to a computer which dictated the pilot's course while aiming the weapons automatically. Both this and the later AC-130E, which carried one 105 mm, one 40 mm, two 20 mm and two 7.62 mm guns plus low-light level television, were operated by the 8th TFW at Ubon RTAFB; E models were subsequently given new engines and the designation AC-130H.

Meanwhile, the 14th SOW at Nha Trang AB, which had operated AC-47s from several bases in Vietnam and Thailand, received the new AC-119G Shadow gunship in 1969, when its headquarters moved to Phan Rang. This conversion of the C-119 Flying Boxcar had four miniguns and a computerized fire-control system, the crew using flares, searchlight and night vision equipment for target identification. The AC-119G had inadequate performance for use along the increasingly heavily defended Ho Chi Minh Trail, and the AC-119K Stinger, with two 20 mm cannon and auxiliary jet engines in wing pods, was produced for use in Laos.

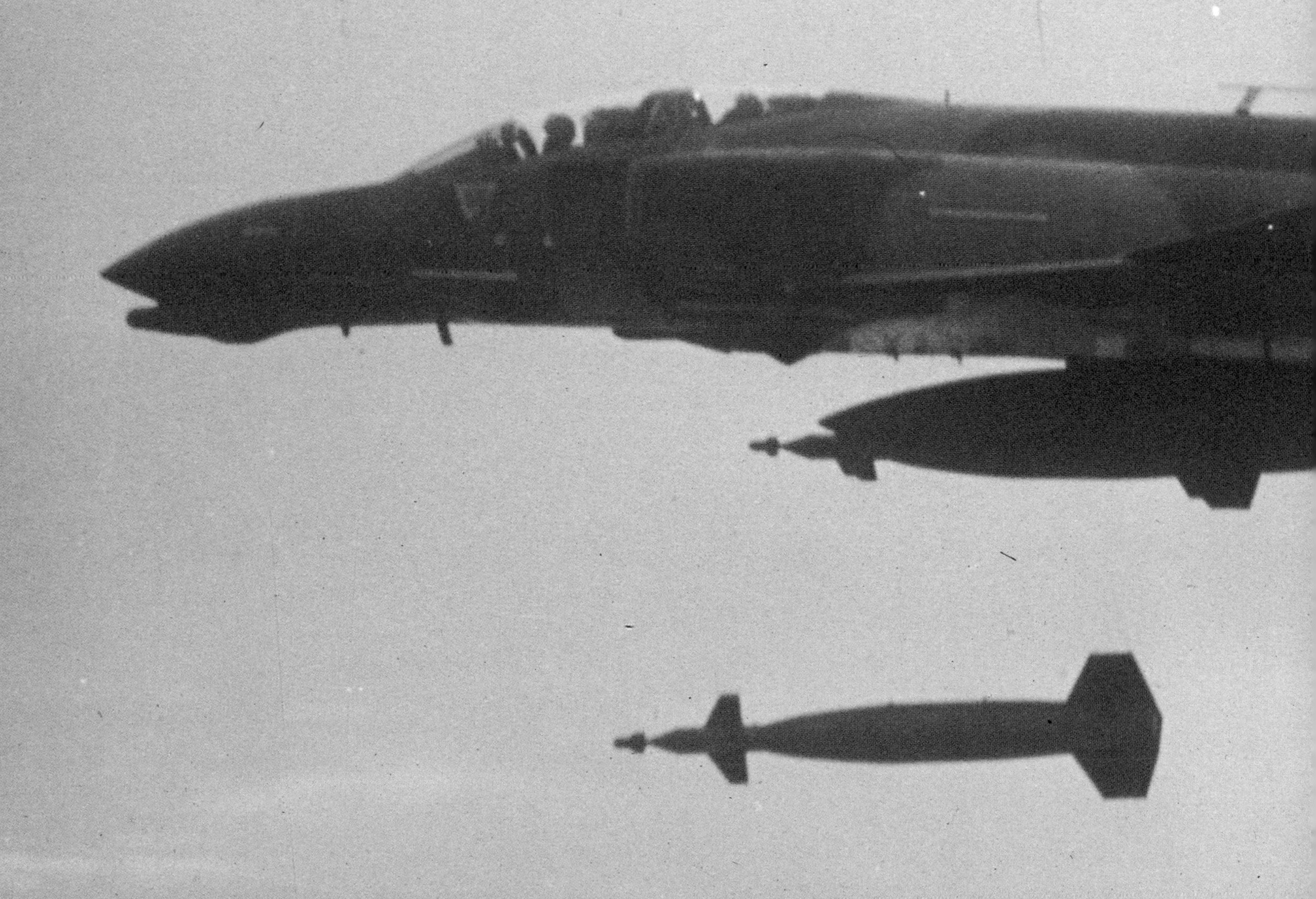

The North Vietnamese Tet offensive early in 1968 drew sensors and firepower away from the Ho Chi Minh Trail as they were pressed into the defense of the strongpoints, notably the Marine Corps base at Khe Sanh, which were intended to form a defensive line across the country south of the demilitarized zone, and which constituted the second half of the plan to halt North Vietnamese infiltration. However, with the ultimate failure of the Tet offensive, the end of Rolling Thunder and the provision of the specialized attack aircraft described, the campaign of interdiction in Laos was resumed.

By May 1971, at the end of the annual five-month dry season when traffic began to be

*Below:* Conventional ordnance was dispensed in vast quantities in support of ground troops: an F-100 lets go a bomb in a diving attack in December 1965.

*Opposite:* The OV-10A Bronco was developed as a counter-insurgency aircraft. In the mid-1960s, it was used in Vietnam for FAC and armed reconnaissance, and now serves with various specialized units.

*Below:* A rocket pod is attached to the wing of an O-2A FAC aircraft at Phu Cat AB in March 1970. The O-2 was too lightly armed, and was replaced by the OV-10.

slowed by the monsoons, the Air Force was claiming a total of 25,000 trucks destroyed since the previous November. This was only an estimate, based on sensor data and intelligence analysis, and subsequent events would cast doubt on its validity.

The difficulty of obtaining reliable evidence of the effects of the air action, and the problems involved in keeping track of an enemy that moved mainly by night and under the cover of dense jungle, resulted in a number of innovatory reconnaissance techniques being evolved during the course of the war. SAC's SR-71s and U-2s carried out photo-reconnaissance missions at high altitudes, while the RF-101C and later RF-4C routinely preceded and followed air strikes to provide target information and damage assessment. By the end of 1967 new MiG-21 interceptors had made the skies over North Vietnam unsafe for the Voodoos, and by 1971 the RF-101C had been replaced completely by the RF-4C, faster and with a wider range of sensors which enabled it to provide radar and infrared linescan images as well as photographs of the area under surveillance.

In connection with Igloo White novel techniques were employed. The QU-22, a modifi-

cation of the Beech Bonanza, was designed as a remotely-piloted, long-endurance relay aircraft to supplement the EC-121Rs in relaying signals from the air-dropped sensors. Both types were operated by the 553d Strategic Reconnaissance Wing at Korat RTAFB, though the QU-22 normally carried a pilot on operations.

A true RPV was the AQM-34 drone, powered by a J69 tuborjet and operating under radio command or automatic Loran navigation. Various sensors could be carried, and the drones were launched from specially modified aircraft, originally A-26 or P-2 types,

*Above:* One of the three miniguns mounted in an AC-47 is silhouetted against the muzzle flash from another.

*Top:* Red tracer rounds against the night sky mark the cones of fire from an AC-47 operating from Saigon.

but eventually the standard launcher was the C-130. DC-130A and later DC-130E aircraft were operated by detachments of the 100th SRW at U-Tapao RTAFB and Bien Hoa AB; recovery was carried out by CH-3 helicopters based at Da Nang using a net to catch the drone after its engines cut out on command and a parachute was deployed.

Throughout the campaign in Vietnam, despite the enormous effort put into strategic bombing, interdiction, and reconnaissance, the bulk of the air operations were in support of ground forces. The vital function of coordinating air support was the responsibility of the Forward Air Controllers (FACs), who used a variety of aircraft for the job. First was the O-1 Bird Dog, derived from the Army's L-19, and using marking rockets to designate targets for tactical air strikes summoned by radio. The O-2 which followed had double the range and twice the rocket capacity of its predecessor, though it still lacked armor protection. By 1968 the earlier types were being replaced by the OV-10 Bronco, purpose-built for the task and able to carry a variety of bombs, rockets, and machine gun pods.

Principal operator of the FAC aircraft was the 14th SOW, based at Nha Trang and, from 1969, at Phan Rang, though the aircraft operated from many forward bases. The F-4 was widely used to deliver heavy weights of ordnance as required by FACs, but its high speed was something of a drawback when trying to locate and attack small, well-camouflaged positions, and many other types were used for close air support. Another Navy aircraft, the A-1E Skyraider, was operated by the 56th Air Commando Wing (later 56th SOW) at Nakhon Phanom RTAFB and from the 14th SOW's forward operating base at Pleiku AB. Along with A-1H and J models acquired subsequently, the A-1Es could carry substantial loads of weapons on 15 wing and fuselage hardpoints, and its low speed and long endurance made it particularly suitable for the close air support mission.

By 1969 the specialized A-37 Dragonfly was available, entering service with the 3d TFW at Bien Hoa AB and in the following year joining the 14th SOW. Equipped with an internal minigun and eight wing pylons for bombs or rocket pods, the A-37 was a useful replacement for the A-1 and B-57.

Meanwhile, the A-1s had come to be used increasingly to escort rescue helicopters, combat rescue being a vital part of the air war with so many operations conducted over hostile territory. The original rescue helicopter was the rather inadequate H-43 Huskie, and at the beginning of 1966 the 3d Aerospace Rescue and Recovery Group was activated at Tan Son Nhut to coordinate all rescue operations, with helicopters based at Nakhon Phanom and Bien Hoa, plus a small number of Hu-16 Albatross amphibians for use over the Gulf of Tonkin.

The small H-43 was not really suitable, however, and by November 1965 the 3d ARRG had received the first HH-3E Jolly Green Giants. With additional fuel tanks to give them a range of 625 miles (1,006 km), the CH-3Es were based at Da Nang, Tan Son Nhut, Tuy Hoa, and Udorn, enabling them to cover the whole of Vietnam. Many rescue operations demanded long periods over the rescue site while the crew was located, and to extend the endurance of the helicopters HC-130H variants of the Hercules, equipped to control and coordinate the rescue were fitted with additional fuel tanks and equipment for refueling the helicopters. The HC-130P, as the converted Hercules was designated, extended the Jolly Green Giant's endurance to eight hours, and as escorts, to suppress enemy fire and hold off hostile ground forces while the downed airmen were retrieved, up to eight A-1s would normally join the formation.

In 1967 the bigger, faster and more powerful HH-53 'Super Jolly Green' appeared in Vietnam and Thailand, and efforts began to be directed toward providing a night rescue capability. This was achieved by 1971, when five HH-53Es were fitted with searchlights and infrared sensors for night navigation and crew location, but the noise of the machines in the jungle night tended to alert the enemy of their whereabouts and the experiment was abandoned for the time being.

Airlift support for all these operations was provided by the C-123 Provider and C-130 Hercules, the former serving from 1961 and the latter from 1965. The 315th Air Commando Wing was formed at Tan Son Nhut in March 1966 to control C-123 operations, but no C-130 wings were based in Vietnam, detachments from PACAF wings operating the type from principal bases at Cam Ranh Bay and Tan Son Nhut, the latter being the headquarters of the Airlift Control Center.

In October 1966 the 483d Troop Carrier Wing was formed at Cam Ranh Bay to operate 134 C-7 Caribou STOL transports taken over from the Army. Main bases for the Caribou were at Phu Cat and Vang Tau ABs, with a forward operating location at Da Nang, and their principal duties included supplying assault forces in the field and the Special Forces camps established in remote locations along the western border of South Vietnam. Their short takeoff and landing performance made them particularly useful in the latter role.

There was also a continuing need for long-range transport across the Pacific, much of which was provided by chartered airliners. However, Military Air Transport Service, which became Military Airlift Command in January 1966, operated its own fleet of long-range transports. In the early stages of the conflict the aging C-124 Globemaster, with its 10,000 cu ft (280 m$^3$) hold, was the most widely used transport for cargo, though wrinkling skins and old engines were becom-

*Below:* One of the first AC-47 conversions. The early gunships proved so useful that more modern transports were later equipped with substantially heavier armament.

*Right:* C-141 transports at Cam Ranh Bay in 1967. The StarLifter started regular flights carrying freight, troop and casualties between the US and Vietnam in 1965.

ing a problem and a round trip between Travis AFB, California, and Tan Son Nhut AB, Saigon, took as much as four days. By the time of the big American buildup in 1965 the first C-141A StarLifters were entering service, and the new type soon became the principal strategic transport, carrying wounded personnel back to the US as well as freight to Vietnam. In the interim, until the StarLifter became available in greater numbers, the C-133 Cargomaster, despite its frequent engine troubles, did the bulk of the work.

The bulk of the passenger transport capacity was provided by the C-135 Stratolifter, which entered service in 1962 and could carry 126 personnel on the outward journey to Vietnam, returning with up to 98 wounded. By 1963 design was under way of the C-5 Galaxy, with capacity for 345 troops, though its primary role was as a cargo transport, and it was 1971 before the first examples entered regular service.

By this stage the American forces in Vietnam had seen a dramatic reduction from their peak strength of over half a million in 1968. The 'Vietnamization' policy was adopted in 1969 in the face of growing anti-war sentiment in the US and with the start of peace negotiations in Paris in May 1968. Many USAF aircraft were turned over to the SVnAF, and many of the remaining Air Force units were withdrawn to bases in Thailand. Missions continued to be flown in support of the incursions into Cambodia in 1970 and Laos in 1971. The renewed North Vietnamese offensive early in 1972, whose strength called into question the claims for trucks destroyed on the Ho Chi Minh Trail, found US strength reduced to 95,000 including 20,000 USAF personnel, although another 27,000 were in Thailand, and during February 1972 American air strikes in the south had fallen to only 700.

Following the opening of the North Vietnamese offensive at the end of March the third of a series of US deployments under the codename Constant Guard was mounted. Already two PACAF squadrons of F-4Ds had been moved from Clark AB in the Philippines and Kunsan AB in Korea to Udorn, Da Nang, and Ubon, but the new series of deployments

*Below:* The A-7D Corsairs of the 354th TFW were deployed from Myrtle Beach AFB, South Carolina, to Korat RTAFB, Thailand, in October 1972. They participated in the Linebacker II bombing offensive against North Vietnam and subsequently attacked the Khmer Rouge in Kampuchea.

*Below:* C-130Ds at Bien Hoa AB prepare to take a battalion of the 173d Airborne Brigade into action during Operation Junction City early in 1967.

involved the transfer of squadrons from the US directly to bases in Thailand. Altogether four squadrons of F-4Ds from the 49th TFW at Holloman AFB, New Mexico and four of F-4Es from Seymour Johnson AFB, Texas, and Holloman and Eglin AFBs, Florida, were dispatched to Thailand, flying via Hickam AFB, Hawaii and arriving at Ubon, Udorn, and Tahkli to be ready for action within a week of departure.

As well as supporting the South Vietnamese forces, which succeeded in containing the invasion, bombing attacks on the north were resumed. This time the tactical units were much better equipped for the task: although North Vietnamese air defenses, combining surface-to-air missiles, radar-directed antiaircraft artillery, and ground-controlled interceptors, had reached formidable proportions, specialized counters to these had been developed. The new F-105G Wild Weasels, replacing the earlier F-100s used for defense suppression, were equipped with improved electronics and radar-homing missiles; the F-4E variant of the Phantom had been produced with an internal gun, remedying a

*Left*: A-1E Skyraider escorts an HH-3C Jolly Green Giant helicopter on a combat rescue mission in 1966. Auxiliary fuel tanks gave the HH-3C a 625-mile (1,000-km) range, enabling it to cover the whole of North Vietnam from bases at Udorn and Da Nang; the Skyraider's job was to deliver suppressive fire during the rescue.

severe deficiency in the original missile-only models, which had often been forced to carry gun pods in order to deal with the close-range encounters demanded by the rules of visual identification; and the new laser-guided bombs were now in service, along with electronic pods which gave individual aircraft the capacity to jam radar-guided missiles.

There were new aircraft, too. In October 1972 the 354th TFW arrived at Korat RTAFB with three squadrons of A-7D Corsairs, derived from the Navy A-7A attack bomber and equipped with a radar navigation and bombing system. Even more capable was the F-

111A, two squadrons of which arrived at Tahkli in September. The F-111A had been briefly deployed to Tahkli in 1968, when a series of unexplained losses, later attributed to failure of the wing pivot fitting, caused its operations to be curtailed. With terrain-following radar for low-level operations at night or in bad weather, and extremely sophisticated navigation and attack system, the F-111s carried out their missions alone and without radio contact, and on November 8 they were able to carry out strikes over North Vietnam in weather so bad that all other aircraft in the theater were grounded.

*Opposite:* The C-5A Galaxy began transport flights between the US and South Vietnam in 1970, and was soon participating in, first, the reinforcement of the country following the North Vietnamese invasion of March 1972, and subsequently the 1975 evacuation.

The climax of the bombing campaign against the north came with Operation Linebacker II in December 1972 and January 1973, which was followed by the signing of the peace accords on January 23. By March the last ground troops had been withdrawn from Vietnam, and although operations continued against the Khmer Rouge in Cambodia, these too were halted by Congress in August. The last strike of the war was flown by an A-7D against a target in Cambodia on August 15.

A number of Air Force units remained in Thailand until 1975, including the F-111As of the 347th TFW at Tahkli, and the Phantoms of the 388th TFW at Tahkli and the 8th TFW at Ubon. The last unit transferred to Kunsan AB, Korea, while the others returned to the US. By this time South Vietnam had fallen, and by the end of the year both Laos and Cambodia had new communist governments.

An epilogue to the American involvement in southeast Asia came in May 1975 with the combined assault on the island of Koh Tang, off the coast of Cambodia, where the US merchant vessel *Mayaguez* and its crew were being held after their seizure by Khmer gunboats. The ship was located by two F-111s diverted to the area, and an AC-130 maintained surveillance, attacking a number of gunboats while a Navy carrier made for the Gulf of Thailand. The assault force of Marines was transported to the island by CH-53s from the 56th SOW at Nakhon Phanom and HH-53Cs from the 56th ARRS at Korat, but the island was more heavily defended than had been realized, and five helicopters were lost. The crew of the *Mayaguez* was rescued, but at the cost of 18 lives and in circumstances that might easily have resulted in more serious losses.

The end of American involvement in southeast Asia marked another step in the evolution of US foreign policy that has seen the Air Force's role and equipment extensively revised, as described in the following chapter. Much of that equipment, particularly in the emphasis on electronic warfare and close air support, has been developed in the light of experience in Vietnam, where the tactics and technology of air warfare underwent some fundamental revisions.

SOUTH CAROLINA
SC
AF 79 289

# 6: MODERN TACTICAL AIR POWER

*Overleaf:* An F-111D lands at a Middle Eastern airfield in front of a stationary B-52 during a Bright Star exercise.

Since the withdrawal from Vietnam the Air Force has undergone significant changes in both role and equipment. Although the fundamental missions of the tactical units – air superiority, interdiction, and close air support – remain, the relative emphasis on each, the means of achieving them and the circumstances in which their use can be envisaged have all been modified by political and technological considerations.

Politically, the relationship between the United States and the rest of the world has seen substantial changes under successive presidents, most notably following the abandonment of the detente with the Soviet Union pursued by Nixon. As the area of immediate confrontation with the Warsaw Pact, Europe continues to be the most important area of deployment for American forces, though the divergence of interests between the US and its European allies has led to strains in the NATO alliance. Moreover, NATO's insistence on allowing the deployment of American ground-launched cruise missiles (GLCMs) and Pershing II ballistic missiles has resulted in many USAF bases in Europe being besieged by semi-permanent camps of antinuclear protesters.

Across the Pacific, meanwhile, China has come to be perceived as a potential ally against the Soviet Union rather than a sinister menace, resulting in an end to active support of Taiwan; the withdrawal of American ground forces from South Korea begun by President Carter was halted temporarily in 1979 and stopped altogether by President Reagan; the commitment to Japan has come under severe strain as a result of the imbalance of trade and a Japanese defense budget seen in Washington as inadequate.

In the early 1970s American policy was to maintain forces adequate to fight one war in Europe (against the Warsaw Pact) and one in Asia (against China), plus a "half-war" wherever else a secondary threat might arise. The obvious setting for the half-war remains the Middle East, where the US has a continuing commitment to the independence of Israel, as well as a keen interest in oil supplies from the Persian Gulf, and where the Iranian revolution and ensuing war with Iraq put an end to the policy of promoting Iran as a stabilizing influence in the region, as well as a bulwark against Soviet expansion. At the same time, Central America has attracted renewed attention.

Against this background, the "two-and-a-half war" policy has been replaced by an emphasis on strategic weapons, with SAC about to become the recipient of new B-1B bombers and MX ICBMs, and the Navy deploying the new Trident-armed *Ohio* class submarines, along with plans for more rapid deployment of conventional forces. Europe is still the front line as far as the Air Force is concerned, while air defense of the continental United States (Conus) has been downgraded almost out of existence.

Meanwhile, the results of the Vietnam experience can be seen most clearly in the emphasis on technology and its application to new and improved electronic warfare equipment, guided weapons and better targetting systems, command, control and communications ($C^3$) and, particularly, all-weather operations. The air defenses encountered over North Vietnam underlined the need for such systems, and the possibility of a NATO-Warsaw Pact conflict in Europe, where the weather is just as bad, the AA environment still more lethal and the opposing air and ground forces vastly superior, has made their development essential.

Ramstein AB in Germany is the headquarters of United States Air Forces in Europe: 3d in England (HQ RAF Mildenhall), 17th in Germany (HQ Sembach AB) and 16th in Spain (HQ Torrejon AB). Until 1977 its six Tactical Fighter and two Tactical Reconnaissance Wings were equipped primarily with F-4 and RF-4 Phantoms, though the 20th TFW's F-111Es had been at RAF Upper Heyford since 1970. In 1977, however, the 48th TFW at RAF Lakenheath traded in its F-4s for F-111Fs and the 36th TFW at Bitburg AB, Germany, transferred from the Phantom to the F-15. The following year saw A-10s replace the 81st TFW's F-4s at RAF Woodbridge/Bentwaters and more F-15s taking over from F-4s with the 32d TFS at Soesterberg AB in the Netherlands.

Five years later both the 50th TFW at Hahn AB, Germany, and the 401st TFW at Torrejon had converted from F-4 to F-16, with the 86th TFW at Ramstein scheduled to follow suit in 1986. The 52d TFW at Spandgahlen AB, Germany, has a squadron of F-4G Wild Weasel defense suppression aircraft alongside its two of F-4Es, and the Eagle units received the improved F-15C/D in 1980–81. The 10th TRW at RAF Alconbury and the 26th TRW at Zweibrucken AB, Germany, continue to operate single squadrons of RF-4Cs, but the former also has a squadron of Aggressor F-5Es for dissimilar air combat training, and the TR-1 tactical reconnaissance type was based at Alconbury in early 1983. With EC-130H Com-

*Left:* A BGM-105G Tomahawk cruise missile launcher of the type currently deployed by TAC in Europe is erected during a demonstration of the dispersal tactics to be employed in the event of their use.

*Left:* F-16As of the 50th Tactical Fighter Wing, United States Air Forces in Europe, based at Torrejon AB, Spain, airborne over Madrid.

*Right:* LTV (Vought) A-10 Corsair II land-based attack bomber from 354th TFW, Myrtle Beach AFB, South Carolina.
*Below:* F-15s flying out of Bitburg AFB, Germany.

BT
AF
79 058
BT
AF
78 549

pass Call and EF-111 electronic warfare aircraft due to be deployed in the near future, the latter with the 42d Electronic Combat Squadron at RAF Upper Heyford from early 1984, USAFE will have a potent combination of modern aircraft for the conventional tactical roles, backed up by a sophisticated reconnaissance and electronic warfare capability.

The F-15 air-superiority fighter, big, heavy, and expensive, is also extremely powerful, with impressive performance and comprehensive equipment, including a versatile long-range radar. The latter has been further improved in the C/D model (the A and C are single-seat, the B and D two-seat versions) by the addition of a programmable signal processor, and the standard armament is a 20 mm M61 gun plus four Sparrow and four Sidewinder missiles. The newer F-16 Fighting Falcon, smaller, lighter, armed with gun and Sidewinders, and with only one F100 engine to the Eagle's two, has a dual role as an outstandingly agile air combat fighter and a surprisingly accurate attack aircraft, though it lacks the F-15's all-weather capability.

For close air support the A-10 Thunderbolt II, based in England but regularly deployed to six forward operating bases in Germany, mounts the highly lethal 30 mm GAU-8 Avenger cannon. Big and slow, but well protected against AA weapons, the A-10 is very maneuverable for enhanced survivability and to enable its antitank gun to be brought to bear quickly. It can also carry a wide range of external stores on its 11 wing and fuselage pylons. Interdiction is the job of the two F-111 wings, whose first pass blind attack capability is being enhanced by the Pave Tack pods fitted to F-111Fs. Pave Tack provides both optical and FLIR (forward-looking infrared) tracking systems and a laser designator for manual or automatic delivery of precision weapons.

Pave Tack is also intended to be fitted to F-4s, but the latest version of the Phantom, the F-4G Wild Weasel, has been developed for the defense suppression role, replacing the F-105F and G. The F-4G's APR-38 radar detection and homing system uses 52 aerials to detect, identify, and locate the source of hostile radar emissions, so that Shrike, Standard ARM, or HARM radar-homing missiles, Maverick electro-optically guided missiles or standard cluster bombs can be launched to destroy them. Backing up the Wild Weasels will be the EF-111A Raven,

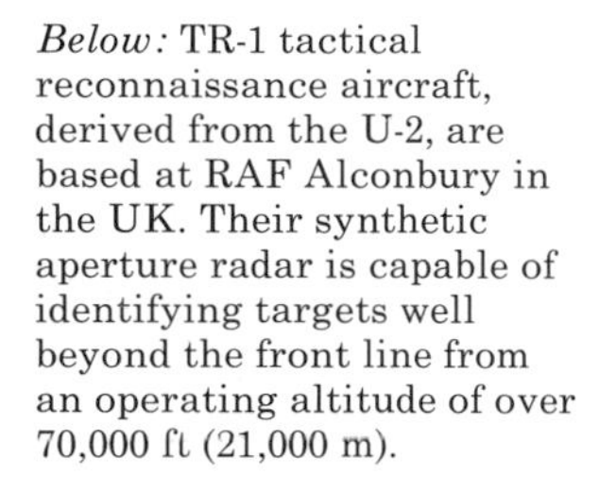

*Below:* TR-1 tactical reconnaissance aircraft, derived from the U-2, are based at RAF Alconbury in the UK. Their synthetic aperture radar is capable of identifying targets well beyond the front line from an operating altitude of over 70,000 ft (21,000 m).

whose powerful ALQ-99E tactical jamming system is designed to respond almost instantaneously to radar signals, analyzing their characteristics, identifying their source and transmitting an appropriate jamming signal.

In addition, the EC-130H Compass Call variant of the Hercules will provide further protection by working in conjunction with mobile ground-based $C^3$CM (command, control, and communications counter measures) systems to jam or otherwise interfere with enemy $C^3$ systems. The EC-130H will presumably carry out its mission from within friendly airspace, but the EF-111 can operate either from a standoff position, guarding supporting aircraft such as tankers, reconnaissance, and AWAC (airborne warning and control) platforms from both ground-launched missiles and enemy fighters while covering penetrating attack formations, or accompany the attack aircraft on deep penetration missions.

Alongside this upgrading of electronic warfare capability, the USAF is pursuing improvements to target location systems. The Pave Tack pods, and the LANTIRN system under consideration for both A-10 and F-16, the latter combining terrain-following radar and FLIR for night or all-weather navigation with a separate FLIR and laser designator for automatic or visual target acquisition and weapon delivery, are one aspect of this effort; another is the new dedicated aircraft being introduced. The Alconbury TR-1s carry side-looking radar to look up to 35 miles (56 km) inside enemy territory, and are intended to form part of the PLSS (Precision Location Strike System), involving data links between the TR-1, ground processing stations and strike aircraft to enable the last to attack enemy radars identified by the reconnaissance aircraft.

USAFE's remaining flying units include the 601st Tactical Airborne Control Wing at Sembach, with two Tactical Air Support Squadrons of OV-10A Broncos for FAC duties and another of CH-53C helicopters for combat rescue, as well as supporting elements of MAC. Tanker support is provided by SAC.

Operationally, the emphasis in USAFE is on realistic training and combat-readiness. The Aggressor squadron, trained in Warsaw Pact tactics, provides realistic air combat training; weapon ranges at Zaragoza in Spain, Aviano in Italy, and elsewhere provide practice facilities; and extensive $C^3$ and other support installations are available. Most

*Below:* Prototype of another new type deployed in Europe, the EF-111A Raven, whose powerful jamming system is designed to suppress Warsaw Pact air defense and surveillance radars.

*Right:* An F-5E of an Aggressor Squadron, whose pilots and ground controllers simulate Warsaw Pact fighter tactics for air combat training.

controversial of the command's activities is the operation of Tomahawk GLCM batteries, already installed at RAF Greenham Common and scheduled for other bases in Germany, Belgium, and Italy, from which they will be driven to dispersed locations at times of heightened international tension.

Pacific Air Forces, with headquarters at Hickam AFB, Hawaii, comprise the 5th Air Force (HQ Yokota AB, Japan) and 13th Air Force (HQ Clark AB, Philippines). The latter has only the 3d TFW at Clark, comprising one TFS with F-4Es, another with F-4Gs, a Tactical Fighter Training Squadron with Aggressor F-5Es and T-38As, and a Special Operations Squadron whose MC-130Es have special avionics for low-level clandestine missions in darkness or bad weather.

The 5th AF has undergone a transformation similar to that of USAFE, with F-15C/D Eagles replacing Phantoms with three of the

18th TFW's squadrons at Kadena AB, Okinawa, while a fourth continues to use the RF-4C. A new two-squadron F-16 wing will be based at Misawa, Japan in 1985. The 8th TFW in South Korea has three squadrons of F-16s at Kunsan and Taegu ABs, and a fourth of A-10s at Suwon, while the 51st Composite Wing at Osan AB, Korea, has replaced its FAC squadron of OV-10s with OA-37Bs; the 51st CW's other squadron is equipped with F-4Es. A squadron of TAC E-3A Sentry AWACS aircraft is also based at Kadena, and these impressive aircraft with their distinctive radomes can track both friendly and hostile aircraft right down to ground level to a range of some 250 miles (400 km), as well as assimilating and processing much additional information, providing an invaluable aid to control and coordination. Later production models of the E-3A include a maritime surveillance capacity, beneficial in the Pacific.

Because of the vast distances involved in PACAF's operational area long-range deployments are a standard feature of the regular exercises carried out. Another requirement is the ability to operate in conjunction with friendly air forces in the region, and such exercises as Team Spirit, involving the Republic of Korea Air Force and units deployed from CONUS, Cope North, carried out jointly with the Japan Air Self-Defense Force, and Cope Thunder, which brings together elements of all the US armed forces with aircraft from the Philippines, New Zealand, and Thailand, are regular training features.

Both USAFE and PACAF regularly play host to CONUS-based TAC units, and Tactical Air Command generally forms a ready reserve force to reinforce the overseas commands as required. TAC has its headquarters at Langley AFB, Virginia, and includes the 9th Air Force (HQ Shaw AFB, South Caro-

*Below:* Another Aggressor F-5E. Warsaw Pact camouflage and markings add another touch of realism to the simulated combat exercises.

lina) and 12th Air Force (HQ Bergstrom AFB, Texas) as well as a variety of other components.

The 9th AF's 10 wings include the 1st TFW at Langley and the 33d TFW at Eglin AFB, Florida, with F-15s; the 56th Tactical Training Wing at MacDill AFB, Florida, and 363d TFW at Shaw with F-16s; the 31st TTW with F-4Ds at Homestead AFB, Florida and the 4th TFW at Seymour Johnson AFB, North Carolina and 347th TFW at Moody AFB, Georgia, both with F-4Es; two TFWs of A-10s, the 23d at England AFB, Louisiana and the 354th at Myrtle Beach AFB, South Carolina; and a Tactical Air Control Wing, the 507th, with a squadron each of O-2s and CH-3Es at Shaw.

The 12th AF comprises four Tactical Fighter and one Tactical Reconnaissance Wings, the latter (the 67th) with RF-4Cs at Bergstrom. The 27th TFW at Cannon AFB, New Mexico, and the 366th at Mountain Home AFB, Idaho, operate the F-111D and A respectively, the latter including the first operational EF-111As, while the 388th and 474th TFWs, at Hill AFB, Utah and Nellis AFB, Nevada, are equipped with F-16s. There are also four Air Divisions in 12th AF: the 831st AD at George AFB, California, includes the 35th TFW (F-4E) and 37th TFW (F-4G); the 832d AD at Luke AFB, Arizona, has two TTWs, the 58th with F-16s and the 405th with F-15s and F-5s; Holloman AFB, New Mexico, is the home of 833d AD, composed of the 49th TFW (F-15) and 479th TTW (T-38); and the 836th AD at Davis-Monthan AFB, Arizona, includes the A-10s of the 355th TTW and the OA-37s of the 602d TACW.

The reduction of Aerospace Defense Command, whose strength shrank from 28 squadrons in 1968 to only seven in 1974, culminated in its disappearance as a separate command on December 1, 1979. It was replaced by the Aerospace Defense Center at Peterson AFB, Colorado, which in turn became part of the newly formed Space Command on September 1, 1982. Space Command retains responsibility for the worldwide communications, early warning and Spacetrack systems previously operated by ADCOM, while the flying units became Air Defense, Tactical Air Com-

*Below:* The special equipment on the nose of this ARRS HC-130H is a fold-out assembly designed to retrieve personnel or payloads from the ground.

*Above:* The MC-130E special operations variant of the Hercules is equipped with special avionics for low-level clandestine missions.

mand (ADTAC).

The four Air Divisions within ADTAC control a network of air defense radars, including the Distant Early Warning (DEW) Line across North America from Alaska to Greenland, and each is responsible for one of the four NORAD (North American Air Defense, a joint US-Canadian command) districts in the US. The Joint Surveillance System, with a total of 84 radars – 46 in CONUS, 24 in Canada, and 14 in Alaska – and seven Regional Operational Control Centers – four in the US, two in Canada and one in Alaska – has been developed to replace the old SAGE (Semi-Automatic Ground Environment) system for control of the Fighter Interceptor Squadrons, though in the event of war control would pass to AWACS E-3As.

Two of the six FIS, the 48th at Langley and the 318th at McChord AFB, Washington, have converted from the veteran F-106 to the F-15, with which they will also provide anti-satellite capability as described in the next chapter, and the remainder – the 5th at Minot AFB, North Dakota, the 49th at Griffiss AFB, New York, the 84th at Castle AFB, California, and the 87th at Sawyer AFB, Michigan – will soon transfer to the newer fighter. Air Forces Iceland, with a squadron of F-4Es at Keflavik AB, where it is supported by a squadron of E-3As, is also part of ADTAC, as is the 325th Fighter Weapons Wing, with two FI Training Squadrons and a Test Squadron of target drones, at the USAF Air Defense Weapons Center, Tyndall AFB, Florida, scene of regular Copper Flag exercises. Another FITS has been formed at Peterson AFB.

Alaskan Air Command, whose 21st TFW at Elmendorf AFB, near Anchorage, has a squadron each of F-15s and T-33s, while the 343d Composite Wing at Eielson has a squadron of A-10s and another of O-2s, has an air defense function as a region of NORAD, as well as manning a network of radar installations and supporting ground forces in the region. TAC's Southern Air Division at Howard AFB, Panama, has the 24th Composite Wing, with a squadron of O-2s.

Back in the US, the three-million-acre Nellis AFB in Nevada, houses the USAF Fighter

Weapons School and the 57th Fighter Weapons Wing, which operates examples of all current tactical fighters and is responsible for the test and evaluation of air tactics and new equipment, and for advanced tactical fighter training and realistic combat training. One of its principal activities is the Red Flag series of exercises, which involves as many as 250 aircraft at a time flying sorties against simulated enemy interceptors and AA defenses. Nellis is also home to the USAF's Thunderbirds Air Demonstration Squadron, which swapped its T-38s for F-16s in 1982.

Finally, Tinker AFB, Oklahoma, is the headquarters of TAC's 552d Airborne Warning and Control Wing, responsible for the three squadrons of E-3A Sentrys based at Tinker and one each at Keflavik, Iceland, and Kadena AB, Okinawa. Another squadron at Tinker operates the older EC-135K, used for control of tactical fighters on overseas deployments, while EC-130E battlefield command and control posts and the 41st Electronic Combat Squadron, with EC-130H Compass Call $C^3CM$ aircraft are stationed at Keesler AFB, Mississippi, and Davis-Monthan AFB, Arizona, respectively.

TAC's own training programs concentrate on operational aspects, while the Air Training Command claims to be the West's biggest training-educational complex. Responsible for recruiting, flying, and other training, ATC has six installations devoted to technical training, five for undergraduate flying training and one for navigators, and operates T-41, T-37B, T-38, and T-43 aircraft. Maxwell

*Opposite:* One of the Distant Early Warning Line radars located across northern North America, this one at Greenland Icecap.

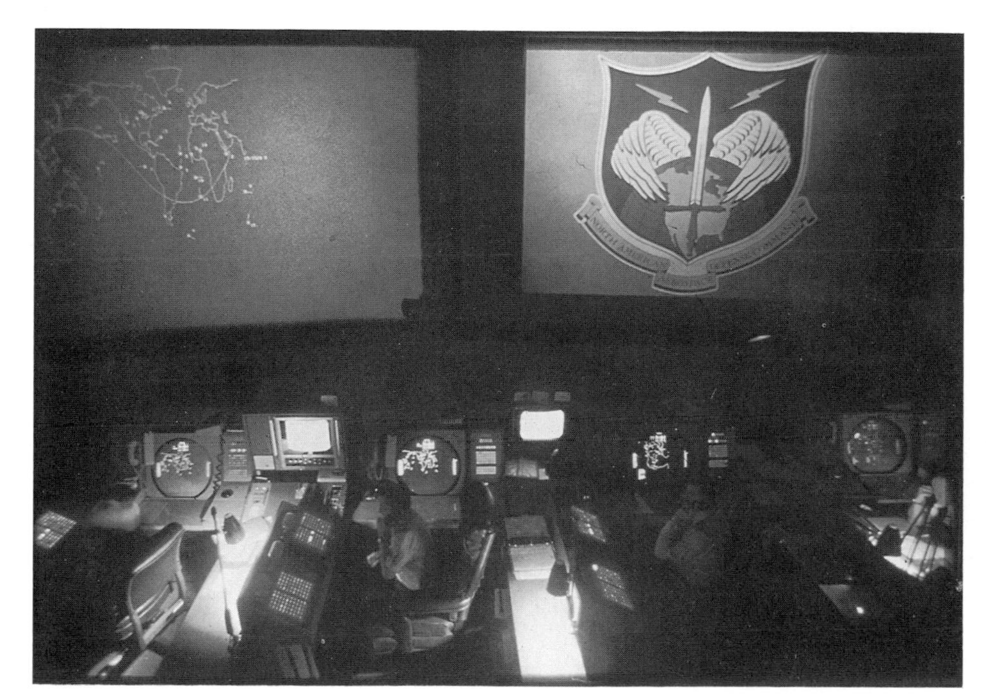

*Below:* Headquarters of NORAD, the joint US/ Canadian North American Aerospace Defense Command. NORAD's Commander-in-Chief is also Commander of Space Command.

One of the fleet of E-3A AWACS (Airborne Warning and Control System) aircraft operated by the 552d AW&CW from its base at Tinker AFB, Oklahoma.

AFB, Alabama, houses the Air University – which became a Major Command in its own right in July 1983 – and several other educational facilities, and the command's annual output includes some 2,000 pilots and 1,000 navigators.

In the event of mobilization, the Air Force strength would be boosted by the Air Force Reserve (AFRES), whose 4th AF (HQ McClellan AFB, California) and 14th AF (HQ Dobbins AFB, Georgia) support Military Airlift Command, while the 10th AF (HQ Berstrom AFB, Texas) trains to reinforce TAC and SAC. Between them, the 4th and 14th AFs control six Military Airlift Wings, with four squadrons of C-5As and 13 of C-141Bs, and five Tactical Airlift Wings, with 14 squadrons of C-130s and one of C-7s. In addition, a Weather Reconnaissance Squadron flies the WC-130H and an Aeromedical Airlift Squadron is equipped with the C-9A, and four Aerospace Rescue and Recovery Squadrons operate HC-130H/N search and rescue aircraft and rescue helicopters.

The 10th AF's four Tactical Fighter Wings comprise five squadrons of F-4s, four of A-10s and one of F-16s. Two Special Operations Squadrons fly CH-3E helicopters and AC-130A gunships, and there are five Heavy Air Refueling Squadrons, three using the KC-135 and two with the new KC-10A Extender. The latter, like the Military Airlift Wings of the 4th and 14th AFs, are Associate squadrons, providing half the crews for regular squadrons at the bases where they are located.

Further augmentation for the active Air Force comes from the Air National Guard, which can be called to active status by Congress or summoned to Federal service by the President, but which is normally under the authority of state governors. ANG wings and groups, usually with one squadron each, are assigned to major commands and trained and equipped appropriately. There are 13 Air Refueling Squadrons with KC-135s for SAC support, 19 C-130 Tactical Airlift Squadrons and two ARRS units with HC-130s and helicopters are assigned to MAC, and eleven FIS, six with F-4s and five with F-106s support ADTAC and PACAF.

The remaining ANG squadrons, just over half the total of 91, are assigned to TAC, with equipment that would be the envy of many regular air forces. There are 14 squadrons each of A-7Ds and F-4Cs and Ds, plus another seven of RF-4Cs, along with five squadrons of A-10s, three of OA-37Bs, and one each with the F-16, O-2 and EC-13OE. Providing a sub-

13244
RESCUE
U.S. AIR FORCE

*Overleaf:* More than 50,000 pilots have qualified on the T-38A Talon, ATC's supersonic trainer which undergraduate pilots only fly after mastering the piston-engined T-41A and T-37A jet trainers.

stantial part of TAC's operational strength, these squadrons, like those assigned to the other commands, regularly participate in exercises along with regular units and carry out operational duties such as air defense alert and air refueling and airlift.

Main responsibility for strategic and tactical airlift in support of all US armed forces lies with Military Airlift Command, which, like SAC, is a US Specified Command reporting direct to the Joint Chiefs of Staff. From its headquarters at Scott AFB, Illinois, MAC controls three Air Forces, two of which, the 21st and 22d, provide strategic and tactical airlift.

The 21st AF, with HQ at McGuire AFB, New Jersey, includes two Airlift Divisions with three Military Airlift Wings, two Tactical Airlift Wings and the 89th Military Airlift Group, based at Andrews AFB, Maryland, which operates a variety of VIP aircraft for transport of government personnel. The 436th

*Right:* Gaudily painted F-16s of the Air Force's Thunderbirds display team in formation over Nevada.

*Left:* Two of the dozen or more AWAC specialists carried by the E-3A at one of the nine multi-purpose consoles with which the aircraft is equipped.

*Left:* Seen through the head-up display of an A-7D, another Corsair replenishes its fuel tanks via the boom of a KC-137.

*Right*: A C-130-H demonstrates its remarkable handling qualities, one of the attributes that have made it the Hercules Military Airlift Command's most versatile aircraft.

*Opposite*: A whole series of specialized aircraft have been developed to take over some of the F-4's many roles, but the Phantom is still in widespread service.

*Below*: One of Air Force Systems Command's most urgent tasks is the development of a new generation Advanced Tactical Fighter. Some of the advances the ATF might incorporate are already being evaluated by the AFTI F-16.

MAW at Dover AFB, Delaware, has two squadrons of C-5A Galaxy strategic transports, while the 437th and 438th MAWs, at Charleston AFB, South Carolina, and McGuire, have three squadrons each of C-141 StarLifters; along with the 317th TAW's three squadrons of C-130Es at Pope AFB, North Carolina, these constitute the 76th Airlift Division. The 322d AD is headquartered at Ramstein AB, Germany, and administers the air bases at RAF Mildenhall in England and Lajes Field in the Azores. Stationed at Rhein-Main AB, Germany, is the 435th TAW, with two squadrons of C-130s, two of C-9s and another with various types at Ramstein, headquarters of USAFE.

Just as the 21st AF covers the eastern US

AFTI/F-16
AF
75
750

RESCUE

and Europe, the 22d AF covers the western US and Pacific. The 60th MAW at Travis AFB, California, the 62d at McChord AFB, Washington and the 63d at Norton AFB, California, between them dispose of four squadrons of C-141s, three of C-5s and one of C-130s, while the 443d MAW at Little Rock AFB, Arkansas, has training squadrons using the C-5 and C-141. The 314th TAW at Little Rock has four squadrons, one of them for training, with the C-130, and another three squadrons of C-130s form the 463d TAW at Dyess AFB, Texas. In Alaska, the 616th MAG at Elmendorf AFB has one TAS of C-130s, while the 834th Airlift Division has bases for an Aeromedical Airlift Squadron of C-9s and a TAS of C-130s at Clark AFB, in the Philippines and a squadron of C-130s at Yokota AB in Japan, respective formations being the 374th TAW and 316th TAG.

Until March 1982 the Aerospace Rescue and Recovery Service was a separate component of MAC, but in that month it was united with the newly activated 2d Air Division to form the 23d AF, with headquarters at Scott. The ARRS element of 23d AF includes the 39th ARRW, based at Eglin AFB, Florida, which deploys helicopters at a total of 26 bases in the US, England, Germany, and Iceland; the 41st Rescue and Weather Reconnaissance Wing, with ARRS helicopters at Kadena, Clark, and Osan PACAF bases and at McClellan AFB, California, as well as three Weather Reconnaissance Squadrons with WC-130s or WC-135s at McClellan, Keesler and Andersen AFB, Guam; and the 37th ARRS, which deploys HH-1H and UH-1F helicopters at SAC missile bases.

The 2d AD, at Hurlburt Field, Florida, is responsible for all USAF's special operations, defined as including unconventional warfare, collective security, psychological operations, and civil affairs measures. It includes the 1st Special Operations Squadron at PACAF's Clark AFB in the Philippines and the 7th SOS at USAFE's Rhein-Main AB, as well as the 1st SOW at Hurlburt Field, with a squadron each of the Combat Talon MC-130E, the AC-130H Spectre gunship and the HH-53H Pave Low III night/all-weather combat rescue helicopter. The USAF Special Operations School and various supporting units share the base, which is actually located in AF Systems Command's 465,000-acre Eglin AFB, home of TAC's Tactical Air Warfare Center, and a detachment of UH-1N Twin Huey helicopters is stationed at Howard AFB in Panama.

Other elements of MAC include the 375th Aeromedical Airlift Wing, based at Scott, with C-9As, the Air Weather Service, both at Scott; the Aerospace Audiovisual Service, at Norton AFB, California; and the three Military Airlift Squadrons with CT-39 Sabreliner transports based at 15 AFBs throughout the US for government transport.

During the 1970s the Air Force held a competition for a new tactical transport aircraft designated AMST (Advanced Medium STOL Transport) to find a successor to the C-130, but in the event the AMST program was canceled and the C-130 has remained in production. However, the establishment of the Rapid Deployment Joint Task Force, with its requirement for 100 heavy cargo aircraft, highlighted a shortage of capacity should the new force be called on simultaneously with a requirement for reinforcement of NATO in Europe. The RDJTF has been replaced by a new unified Central Command, responsible for any deployment in southeast Asia or the Indian Ocean, and the expansion of MAC's capacity is continuing.

SAC's new KC-10 will be an important factor, increasing the refueled range of MAC's existing transports, and many of the latter have had their capacity increased by modification. The entire fleet of 268 C-141s have had their fuselages lengthened by 23 ft 4 in (7 m), providing the equivalent of 90 new aircraft in increased capacity, and in 1982 another program was begun to fit new wings to the 77 C-5As. This work is due for completion by 1987, and in 1986 the first of 50 C-5Bs, similar to the modified C-5As, should be delivered. The immediate requirement for the new wing stemmed from the unforeseen fatigue damage to the original wings, but the modified aircraft will also have substantially better payload/range performance.

Meanwhile, the C-X competition of the late 1970s resulted in the selection of the McDonnell Douglas C-17 though only R&D funding has been approved so far. The four-turbofan C-17 has been designed to fly loads such as M1 tanks, which only the C-5 can accommodate at the moment, into 3,000 ft (910 m) airstrips too small for the C-5. Should procurement go ahead, a total of up to 125 is planned, with the first examples in service by 1990.

On a smaller scale the first of 80 new Learjet 35As was delivered in March 1984; designated C-21, they will replace some of the CT-39s currently used for operational support. In 1983 nine UH-60A Blackhawk helicopters were delivered for aircrew training and familiarization in preparation for trials

*Above:* C-130s on an Egyptian airfield during one of the Bright Star exercises that are a recent addition to the list of Tactical Air Command's regular overseas deployments.

of the HH-60D Nighthawk variant. Two of the latter have been modified with terrain-following/terrain-avoidance radar, FLIR and other equipment for low-level rescue at night and in all weathers, and if they prove capable of meeting the requirement up to 243 could be ordered to replace the current HH-3 and HH-53 search and rescue types.

Further capacity is available to MAC under the CRAF (Civil Reserve Air Fleet) Enhancement scheme. A total of 65 wide-bodied airliners will be fitted with additional cargo doors and floors under this program. CRAF already provides for more than 300 passenger and cargo aircraft operated by 21 airlines to be made available in time of emergency.

There are four other major commands. Communications, Logistics, Systems, and Electronic Security Commands all have vital parts to play, but the big spender is Systems Command, which is responsible for the design, construction, testing, and purchase of Air Force weapons and equipment. Among AFSC's major recent projects have been development of the B-1 and KC-10 for SAC, the Titan 34D and IUS for Space Command and the C-17 for MAC. Its major installations include the Flight Test Center at Edwards AFB, California, Armament Division at Eglin AFB, Florida, and Aeronautical Systems Division at Wright-Patterson AFB, Ohio.

Among AFSC's most significant projects for the future are the production of an Advanced Tactical Fighter for the 1990s and an interim derivative of either F-15 or F-16 for delivery in the late 1980s. In November 1983 seven companies were invited to submit conceptual studies for the ATF by the spring of 1984, principal requirements including the best possible use of new materials, advanced electronics, possibly vectored thrust for short-strip operation, and so-called 'stealth' technology, which involves various techniques for minimizing visibility to hostile radar and other sensors. The aim will be a balance between maximum performance against antiaircraft weapons and electronic warfare, and minimum cost, risk, and support requirement. The last is an important consideration in view of the contrast between the elaborate organization and large areas of concrete on which the current Air Force depends, and the unlikelihood of these being available in any European war scenario.

For the time being, Systems Command has tested dual-role derivatives of both Eagle and Fighting Falcon, as well as advanced technology demonstrators based on examples of each. The dual-role fighter is required to have a more useful attack capability than the standard models, including longer range and night/all-weather operation. Both single-seat and two-seat versions of the arrow-wing F-

*Below:* A UH-60A, the type on which the HH-60D Night Hawk is based. Night Hawks will equip both ARR and Special Operations Squadrons.

A C-141 StarLifter of Military Airlift Command on Grenada after the US occupation of the Caribbean island in October 1983.

*Right:* High-altitude formation of F-16s of the 8th TFW – the Wolf Pack – which is based in Korea as part of Pacific Air Forces.

16XL have been tested, the new wing shape reportedly giving improved performance even with heavy weapon loads, while systems such as Lantirn could theoretically enable a pilot alone to negotiate hostile airspace at night, locate a target using FLIR and carry out a successful attack with the aid of laser designation. The makers of Strike Eagle consider all this a two-man job, and have added extensive avionics and refined radar signal-processing techniques to produce the Strike Eagle, which is intended to be as capable as an F-111.

The Advanced Fighter Technology Integration F-16, on the other hand, is a research aircraft designed to examine the possibilities of unconventional maneuvers made possible by digital flight control, and the potential for using voice controls, helmet-mounted sights for target acquisition, and an Automated Maneuvering Attack System to enable weapons to be launched accurately at ground targets without interrupting low-level evasive maneuvers for a conventional pop-up attack. AMAS is derived from the Integrated Flight and Fire Control system tested on the Firefly III F-15, which automatically combines inputs from the pilot and the aircraft's inertial navigation, radar or electro-optical sensors to calculate unconventional pre-launch flight paths, or to adjust the aircraft's attitude for more accurate air-to-air gunnery.

The decision on the dual-role fighter was reached in February 1984, when it was announced that $1.5 billion would be spent to modify 392 F-15s for the all-weather attack role, in addition to the planned force of 969 air-superiority Eagles, highlighting Tactical Air Command's stated goal of achieving night and bad-weather capabilities as its top priority. In this context, the command lists the Lantirn pod, with its combination of infrared navigation and targetting, laser designator and terrain-following radar, as its prime requirement. Lantirn is earmarked for installation on all F-15Es, plus 200 F-16s and 100 A-10s.

At the same time, TAC is planning to increase the tactical fighter force from 36 to 40 72-aircraft wings, and it has a long list of additional requirements, headed by the JTIDS (Joint tactical information distribution system) secure voice communications system, followed by the AMRAAM missile. AMRAAM (Advanced medium-range air-to-air missile) is a launch-and-leave weapon with an active radar seeker which will provide the F-16, otherwise restricted to visual-range Sidewinders and gun for air combat, with a weapon for use at radar ranges. The F-16 itself is the next priority, the target being an inventory of 2,651 Fighting Falcons, many of which are expected to incorporate features of the F-16XL dual-role demonstrator, and 100 of which will have PLSS equipment, as later aircraft are dedicated increasingly to the air-to-ground role.

The Advanced Tactical Fighter to succeed the F-16 and F-15E is next on TAC's list, followed by the TR-1's PLSS for all-weather

*Left:* Fuselage-mounted data-link pod and GBU-15 guided glide bomb under the wing of a Pave Strike F-4E Phantom.

location of targets on the battlefield; the AGM-130 boosted version of the GBU-15 electro-optical and infrared guided bombs to hit them in the dark in conjunction with Pave Tack or Lantirn pods; the EC-130H Compass Call to suppress enemy $C^3$ while they do so; the secret Tactical Improvement Program for the application of advanced technology; and new IFF systems, possibly identifying hostile aircraft by their engine harmonics, to make sure the new weapons can be used without danger to friendly aircraft.

Other requirements include a replacement for the RF-4C tactical reconnaissance aircraft, possibly in the form of two-seat F-16Ds with podded sensors; improved ECM; enhancements to the Aggressor squadrons' F-5Es to enable them to simulate MiG-23s in air combat training; fitting Sidewinders for self-protection to A-10s, F-4s and F-111s; and improvements to the E-3A AWACS aircraft, as well as procurement of an additional 12 E-3As for defense of the US against cruise missiles.

Along with the improved aircraft, weapons and systems, revised operating procedures are aimed at increasing combat readiness. Accordingly, the accent is on realism, both in training exercises – such as routine low flying and dissimilar air combat practice – and in day-to-day operations: active duty combat squadrons are ready for overseas deployment at any time, all within 24 hours and some within 12 hours, and units on rotational deployments to Europe land to refuel en route, rather than using the aerial tankers that might not be available in wartime.

Readiness is also a function of maintenance, and under the new combat-oriented maintenance organization (COMO) the aircraft parts supply system has been streamlined and ground crews operate as parts of specified squadrons, rather than being assigned to base maintenance squadrons as in the past, with each aircraft assigned to a specified crew chief. The result is a marked improvement in aircraft availability since the late 1970s, and still further improvement is part of the Advanced Tactical Fighter requirement whose target is a turnaround time between sorties of only 15 minutes.

Finally, alongside the emphasis on overseas deployment, there are the improvements scheduled for US air defences. As well as the additional AWACS aircraft new ground-based radar installations will be provided to detect cruise missiles launched from ships or submarines in the Atlantic or the Pacific. A total of eight over-the-horizon backscatter (OTH-B) radar stations are to be built, three each on the east and west coasts with another two looking south, and each providing coverage of a 60-degree segment. The OTH-B radars bounce their signals off the ionosphere to provide surveillance from sea level to an altitude of 100,000 ft and at ranges of up to 2,000 miles, though other radars will be needed for surveillance of the area inside the OTH-B system's 575-mile minimum range.

Nor do TAC's preoccupations end at the ionosphere: as the continuing efforts to develop the F-15's antisatellite missile to the operational stage indicate, space is an area of growing importance to an air force whose operations are no longer confined to the atmosphere.

# 7: THE AIR FORCE IN SPACE

The formation of Air Force Space Command on September 1, 1982, with the motto "Guardians of the High Frontier," marked the importance of space operations in modern military strategy. The new command structure is designed to provide overall management of space operations and to coordinate research and development efforts with military objectives. Those objectives are defined as the maintenance of freedom in space, ensuring that it is not used as a sanctuary for aggressive systems and guarding against threats in, through, and from space; and to increase the effectiveness, readiness, and survivability of military forces. In terms of hardware, that means satellites and ground-based sensors for surveillance, early warning, communications, and navigational data, and an effective means of neutralizing threats, all of which have been in use or under development for some time.

Space Command traces its ancestry back almost 30 years to the establishment in July 1954 of the Western Development Division of Air Research and Development Command, the forerunner of Systems Command. With headquarters at Inglewood, Calif., the Division was initially responsible for development of the Convair Atlas ICBM, and by July 1957, when its name was changed to the Ballistic Missile Division, it had added the intercontinental Martin Titan and intermediate-range Douglas Thor.

Flight testing of Atlas began in 1957, and although two early launches from Cape Canaveral using only the booster motors ended in unscheduled explosions, a successful booster-only launch in December was followed by a satisfactory test with all engines live in August 1958. By the end of 1959 the first Atlas D missiles were operational with Strategic Air Command. The more advanced Titan, built of light alloy and with two stages rather than the stage-and-a-half configuration of the steel Atlas, was test flown for the first time in February 1959, and after a series of 47 firings the first Titans became operational in March 1962.

The same month saw the first flight of the inertially guided Titan II, and by June 1963 the improved version was operational. As well as the new guidance system, replacing the original radio-inertial system, Titan II used a new propellant which could be stored in the missile fuel tanks, allowing it to be launched directly from its silo. The original Titan I had to be raised to the surface for fueling with liquid oxygen before it could be launched.

Meanwhile, the first Thor had been delivered in October 1957, but during the first test launch three months later the missile only managed to raise itself six inches off the pad before exploding, and it was not until the fifth launch in September 1958 that a successful flight was completed. By the end of 1959 Thor was operational with five Royal Air Force squadrons in the United Kingdom, but with the rapid deployment of intercontinental and submarine-launched ballistic missiles it soon became redundant, and its operational career ended in August 1963. The same year saw the delivery to SAC of another second-generation missile, the Boeing Minuteman, which along with Titan II had replaced Atlas and Titan I by 1965. In succeeding models Minuteman has continued to form the major part of the US ICBM fleet, and it was not until the current MX Peacekeeper program that an entirely new missile arrived to supplement it.

Deployment of missiles was SAC's business, however, and the operational career of the missiles has been dealt with in the relevant chapter. Even before the first generation of missiles had completed their deployment, on April 1, 1961, the Ballistic Missile Division was split into separate functions. Ballistic Systems Division, with new headquarters at Norton AFB, California, was to be responsible for rocket and missile technology, while Space Systems Division, initially at Inglewood but later at El Segundo, California, tackled the even newer area of orbiting spacecraft and their associated equipment.

There had already been numerous suggestions for earth-orbiting satellites, space stations and interplanetary exploration, and as early as 1946 a Rand Corporation report commissioned by the USAAF had recommended a scheme for an Experimental World-Circling Spaceship. A growing conviction in some quarters that surveillance from space was an essential complement to the development of nuclear weapons failed to win much political support until the launch of the Soviet satellite Sputnik I on October 4, 1957, concentrated attention on space. Within three months Explorer I had been placed in orbit by an Army Jupiter C rocket, and by the end of 1958 the National Aeronautics and Space Administration (NASA) had been formed to pursue the scientific – as distinct from military – exploration of space. The Army's Ballistic Missile Agency, responsible for the Redstone and Jupiter rockets, became part of NASA, which took over the manned spaceflight program, while the Air Force retained control of military space systems.

There was continuing apathy toward the military role in space until May 1960, when a CIA U-2 was shot down during a reconnaissance mission over the Soviet Union. It became clear that such missions could no longer be carried out safely within the earth's atmosphere, and following the shock of the Sputnik the U-2 incident emphasized the necessity for space-based monitoring and reconnaissance systems.

In fact, the Air Force had already made considerable progress with its reconnaissance satellite program. The redundant Thor, Titan I, and Jupiter rockets were obvious candidates as launch vehicles, and the development of the Agena second-stage rocket had been under way since 1954. By 1958 a concrete program for the development of reconnaissance satellites had been outlined, starting with Discoverer capsules for basic research and followed by operational Sentry photographic and Midas early warning satellites. Vandenberg AFB, Calif., was to be the launch site, allowing satellites to be placed in polar orbit without the overland launch trajectories that would have to be followed from Cape Canaveral. In addition, tracking stations to monitor the flights and maintain communications were set up in Alaska, New Hampshire, and Hawaii, and Hickham AFB, Hawaii, was made the center for capsule re-

*Left:* An early Atlas rocket is prepared for a launch from Vandenberg AFB, California, in 1960. Originally developed as an ICBM, Atlas has become more familiar as a booster for space vehicles.

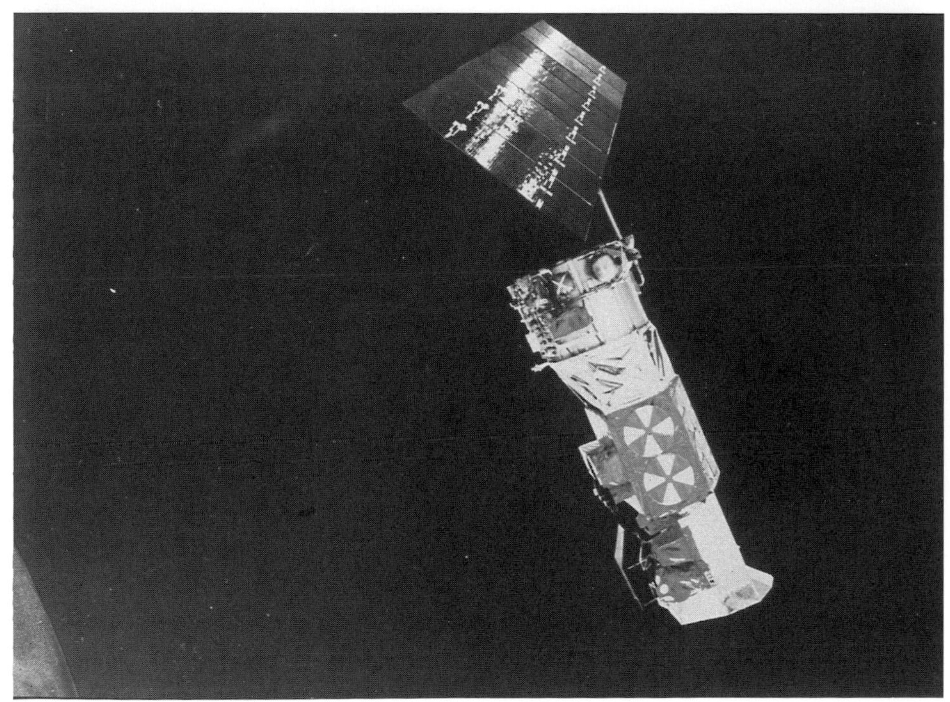

covery operations.

Discoverer 13 was the first of the research series to enjoy a successful launch, on August 10, 1960, and although it splashed down in the Pacific and had to be recovered by helicopter, the aerial recovery system, involving C-119s and later C-130s equipped with trapezes to catch the capsule's parachute lines, was used to retrieve Discoverer 14 the following week. By the time Discoverer 38 completed the initial series in 1962 the first operational satellites had already been launched. Sentry had become Samos, or satellite and missile observation system, and was launched successfully at the second attempt on January 31, 1961, and after two more failures another success was achieved with the fifth and last Samos in December.

The year 1962 saw the introduction of new types of photographic satellite, using line-scan techniques to transmit photographs of large areas, or recoverable capsules for higher-resolution images taken from lower altitudes, as well as electronic intelligence satellites to monitor radio and radar emissions. During the rest of the decade progressively more powerful and more versatile combinations of rocket stages were used to put steadily more refined reconnaissance systems into orbit, using multi-spectral and infrared photography, higher resolution films, and digital data transmission.

The final generation of rocket-launched reconnaissance satellites appeared in the 1970s in the form of the Big Bird, first launched in June 1971, and the improved KH-11, which followed in December 1976. With flight times of around five months and 12 months respectively, these were launched in much smaller numbers than the earlier models, but carried far more sophisticated sensors, including subsidiary electronic satellites which could be carried by Big Bird and detached to follow their own orbits as required.

Reconnaissance was the most immediate requirement of the military satellite program, and the equipment involved has been subject to the most stringent security, but there are a number of other uses for orbiting systems. One is early warning of ICBM launches, and the first Midas (missile defense alarm system) satellite carried its infrared sensors into orbit in 1960, but several more launches yielded only disappointing results. More successful were the pairs of Vela satellites, for the related task of detecting nuclear explosions in support of the 1963 Partial Test Ban Treaty, launched for the first time in October of that year, and their successors built under Program 647 in the 1970s to combine the early warning and nuclear detection roles.

Another area of intense concern to military planners is the weather, and under the Defense Meteorological Satellite Program pairs of satellites have been orbited since 1965. The current model, known as Block 5D, can provide pictures in the visible or infrared bands directly to field units on land or ships at sea, as well as to the Air Weather Service's Global Weather Central at Offutt AFB, Nebraska. In addition to the cameras, several other sensors are carried by the Block 5D satellites, and the data transmitted to Offutt has many applications, such as analyzing atmospheric conditions for optimum reconnaissance photography, as well as more obvious uses such as planning air strikes.

An essential part of the intelligence-gathering activities is the dissemination of the resulting information, and communications is another area where satellites have provided new capabilities. The Initial Defense Satellite Communications System (IDSCS) consisted of 26 small satellites with simple transponders for relaying radio signals. These were placed in orbit between 1966 and 1968, and were followed by a series of experimental satellites as predecessors to the four-satellite DSCS-2. This involves the satellites placed in longitudinally stationary orbit above the equator, where they receive and transmit both wide and narrow beam signals using steerable antennas.

Because of problems with DSCS-2, the first follow-up DSCS-3, bigger, more powerful, and using steerable multiple beams was launched on a prototype basis along with the penultimate DSCS-2 in October 1982. Like its predecessors, the DSCS-3 satellite can relay voice, teletype, facsimile image, or digital transmissions, but with much greater frequency versatility.

The DSCS systems are administered by the Defense Communications Agency, which reports direct to the Joint Chiefs of Staff, though support is provided by various Air Force units. The Air Force's own command, control, and communications ($C^3$) system is known as Afsatcom (Air Force satellite communications), and uses transponders on the Navy's Fleetsatcom satellites to provide secure communications between the National Command Authority (the President or his deputy) and the various elements of the strategic forces.

The remaining satellite system, Navstar or GPS (Global Positioning System), is designed to provide users in all armed forces with positional information accurate in three dimensions to within 30 feet (9 m), velocities to within 0.3 ft/sec (0.09 m/sec), and timing accurate to within one millionth of a second anywhere around the globe. The satellites form part of a planned network of 18, the first of which was launched in February 1978 and they carry atomic clocks and transmit continuous binary pulses. Receivers which can be mounted in aircraft, ships, or vehicles, or carried in back-packs, select signals from four satellites on which to base their computations of position and velocity.

*Above:* A Titan 34D lifts off from Cape Canaveral with a payload of Defense Satellite Communications System satellites in October 1982.

*Opposite, top:* A Thor rocket, originally a medium-range ballistic missile, soon found a new career as a launcher for satellites.

*Opposite, bottom:* One of the Block 5D meteorological satellites which carry optical and infra-red cameras and other sensors to monitor global weather patterns.

*Overleaf:* The Space Shuttle Orbiter *Columbia* touches down at the end of the first orbital test flight in April 1981. *Inset:* Solid-fuel rocket boosters lift a Shuttle Orbiter and its fuel tank off the launch pad at Kennedy Space Center, Florida. Although the Shuttle is a NASA project, the Air Force is heavily involved in its development and operations, and will be a major customer for its services.

*Opposite:* A US Navy FLTSATCOM satellite, which also carries transponders for USAF communications, waits for lift-off atop its Atlas-Centaur launcher.

*Below:* Artist's impression of a Navstar satellite, part of a system designed to provide extremely accurate, almost instantaneous position and time information on a world-wide basis.

Later Navstar satellites, and other space systems, will in future be carried into orbit aboard the NASA Space Shuttle, which will also have the ability to retrieve satellites in orbit and return them to earth. Space Shuttle represents the culmination of a long train of development that began at Muroc Lake, in southern California's Mojave Desert, in the 1940s. It was at Muroc on October 14, 1947, that Capt Charles E. Yeager, in a rocket-powered Bell XS-1, became the first man to exceed the speed of sound; renamed Edwards AFB in 1949, housing the Air Force Flight Test Center, Systems Command, along with a host of associated research establishments, Muroc was the scene of numerous tests of advanced aircraft and systems.

In 1952 the National Advisory Committee on Aeronautics (NACA) produced a specification for a rocket-powered hypersonic research aircraft. The resulting North American X-15 was air-launched from a B-52, and ultimately reached a speed of Mach 6.72 (4,534 mph/7,300 km/h) in 1967, in the course of its career reaching an altitude of 354,200 feet (107,960 m) and providing invaluable data in such areas as hypersonic aerodynamics, life-support systems, and winged reentry from space. A proposed X-20 Dyna-Soar, intended to be launched by a Titan and to return from orbit by gliding down to a skid landing, was canceled in December 1963, and another ambitious project for a Manned Orbiting Laboratory was canceled in favor of the NASA Skylab in June 1969. However, research had continued at Edwards with a series of lifting-body aircraft, designed to investigate the problems of returning from orbit, and it was these that proved the basic concept of the Space Shuttle's unpowered glide back to land after reentry.

Of course, Space Shuttle is a NASA project, but the Air Force has made several major contributions to its success, and will be a principal customer for its services. For example, Military Airlift Command provides detachments from its Aerospace Rescue and Recovery wings trained in techniques for rescuing Shuttle crew members during landings, as well as ensuring that the launch area

UNITED STATES
49

NASA
United States

Columbia

*Opposite, top:* Aerodynamic research at Edwards AFB using these low-speed "lifting body" aircraft paved the way for the Shuttle Orbiter's unpowered precision landings.

*Opposite, bottom:* The NKC-135 airborne laser laboratory knocked out five Sidewinder air-to-air missiles in 1983 as research continued into laser weapons.

is clear of other aircraft or surface ships; Space Command tracking stations monitor the flights; and the 6555th Aerospace Test Group, part of Systems Command's Space Division, works directly with NASA in the development and operation of the hardware.

Space Division, headquartered at Los Angeles AFS, California, is responsible for the development and launch of most of the military space programs. It includes the Space and Missile Test Organization (SAMTO), the Western Space and Missile Test Center (WSMC), and the Shuttle Activation Task Force, all at Vandenberg AFB, California; and the Air Force Space Technology Center at Kirtland AFB, New Mexico, which develops the hardware, along with subordinate research establishments. SAMTO is responsible for management and field test of all DoD space programs, and, via the WSMC and its equivalent Eastern SMC at Patrick AFB, Florida, for the western (Vandenberg) and eastern (Cape Canaveral) test ranges. The Air Force Satellite Control Facility, based at Sunnyvale AFS, California, runs the worldwide network of tracking stations, while the Manned Spaceflight Support Group at Johnson Space Center, Houston, Texas, is responsible for Air Force participation in Space Shuttle Missions.

Space Division was formerly part of Systems Command's Space and Missile Systems Organization, formed in 1967 by reuniting the Space Systems and Ballistic Systems Divisions, and its commander is also the deputy commander of Space Command. The latter, with headquarters at Peterson AFB, Colorado, is responsible for control, management, and protection of space systems, and its first commander, General James V. Hartinger, continued to serve as Commander in Chief of NORAD, based at the nearby Cheyenne Mountain underground complex. The Consolidated Space Operations Center at Peterson will act as the control center for operational spacecraft and DoD Space Shuttle flights, while the Space Defense Operations Center (SPADOC) has been formed alongside NORAD's Aerospace Defense Operations Center at Cheyenne Mountain.

*Below:* A rocket-powered X-15, the first manned aircraft to venture beyond the atmosphere, is launched from the wing of a B-52.

USAF
U.S. AIR FORCE X-24A
NASA
803
804

U.S. AIR FORCE
USAF
ASD
0-53123

086

*Left:* The antisatellite missile is designed to be carried to a height of around 60,000 ft (18,000 m) by an F-15 before launch.

Via the 1st Space Wing at Peterson, Space Command is also responsible for the missile warning and space surveillance network, originally established by SAC, with 24 radar and optical sensor sites. The early warning systems include the Ballistic Missile Early Warning System (BMEWS) radars at Clear AFS, Alaska, Thule AB in Greenland and Fylingdales in England; the Cobra Dane phased-array radar at Shemya AFB in the Aleutians; and the Pave Paws radars at Beale AFB, California, and Otis AFB, Massachusetts, which operate with the FPS-85 radar at Eglin AFB, Florida, to warn of SLBM attacks.

SPADOC's SPADATS (Space Detection and Tracking System) includes the Spacetrack system, with a radar site in Turkey plus optical tracking stations in New Mexico, California, New Brunswick in Canada, South Korea, Italy, Hawaii, and New Zealand, and the Pacific Radar Barrier, two of whose scheduled three sites are in the Philippines and at Kwajalein Atoll. The PARCS (Perimeter Acquisition Radar Attack Characterization System) radar at Grand Forks, North Dakota, looks north toward the Arctic, while the newest space surveillance system, known as GEODSS (Ground-based Electro-Optical Deep Space Surveillance), will include five sites, the first four located at the White Sands Missile Range in New Mexico, Taegu in South Korea, Maui in Hawaii, and Diego Garcia in the Indian Ocean. The GEODSS system uses video sensors to convert images from powerful telescopes into digital data.

Of course, the importance of the current and planned systems is such that they need to be defended, and in January 1984 the USAF's new antisatellite system was tested for the first time. As well as designing new satellites to be difficult to see, or to track by radar or infrared sensors mounted on hostile killer satellites, and providing spare capacity, such as the extra Navstar satellites planned as orbiting reserves for the 18 in the operational network, the Air Force has developed the new three-stage missile specifically to knock out satellites at ranges of up to 620 miles (998 km). The missiles will be launched at around 60,000 feet (18,288 m) by F-15s stationed at

*Below:* Monitoring one of the data terminals at NORAD's Space Surveillance Center, where Space Command personnel keep track of thousands of man-made objects in space.

Langley AFB, Virginia, and McChord AFB, Washington, and use an infrared seeker to home on their target.

For the future, the Air Force is investigating a number of projects. The DoD has shown little interest in NASA's projected Space Station, though NASA believes military uses will certainly be found for such a platform once it is in service. Instead, the Air Force has been active in developing alternative means of launching and retrieving satellites, and in October 1982 the first Titan III(34)D was launched. This new version of Titan III is designed as a backup to the Space Shuttle, and is intended for use with the Inertial Upper Stage (IUS), a two-stage rocket vehicle able to boost payloads to geostationary orbits some 22,300 miles (35,900 km) above the earth's surface. IUS can be used with either the new Titan or the Space Shuttle, which is designed only to reach much lower orbits.

The Air Force would also like a more versatile version of the Shuttle itself, able to be launched on demand and with enough maneuverability after reentry to be recalled at any time and land close to its launch site. A first step toward this goal is the Maneuverable Reentry Research Vehicle, proposed as a flying testbed to examine the aerodynamics of reentry maneuvers.

A number of satellite applications involve the use of lasers, both for communications, in which role pulses of light could carry enormous quantities of information and, equally important, be almost impervious to jamming or interception, and as weapons of destruction. The latter, denounced by some experts as totally impractical and advocated by others as ideal antisatellite or antiballistic missile devices when carried by orbiting satellites, are the subject of intense security. The Air Force would like to use aircraft-mounted lasers as air-to-air, air-to-surface, or antisatellite weapons, and it has produced the NKC-135 Airborne Laser Laboratory for research purposes. During 1983 a carbon dioxide laser carried aboard this aircraft was used to destroy five Sidewinder air-to-air missiles, and to bring down one BQM-34A drone and inflict damage on two others.

*Below:* Global Weather Central at Offutt AFB, Nebraska, receives and processes data from satellites and other sensors worldwide.

291

# 8: TODAY'S AIR FORCE

*Above:* The B-52s of Strategic Air Command can carry 12 Boeing AGM-86B ALCMs (Air Launched Cruise Missiles) on underwing pylons. A further eight are carried internally on a rotary launcher.

*Right:* The McDonnell Douglas KC-10A 'Extender' is operated by SAC in the dual tanker/cargo role. It can deliver 200,000lb (91,000kg) of fuel, using either rigid boom or hose and drogue systems, up to 2,200 statute miles from base.

*Below:* Initially designated TF-15, the F-15D two-seat version of the Eagle was the basis for the Strike Eagle.

*Above:* Ships and low-flying aircraft can be detected at ranges up to 250 miles by the Boeing E-3A Sentry AWACS. Its distinctive 30ft radome sweeps through 360° every 10 seconds.

*Left:* In service with the USAF and Air National Guard, the A-7D Corsair II can deliver 15,000lb (6,800kg) of assorted weapons with pinpoint accuracy using the Pave Penny laser target designator.

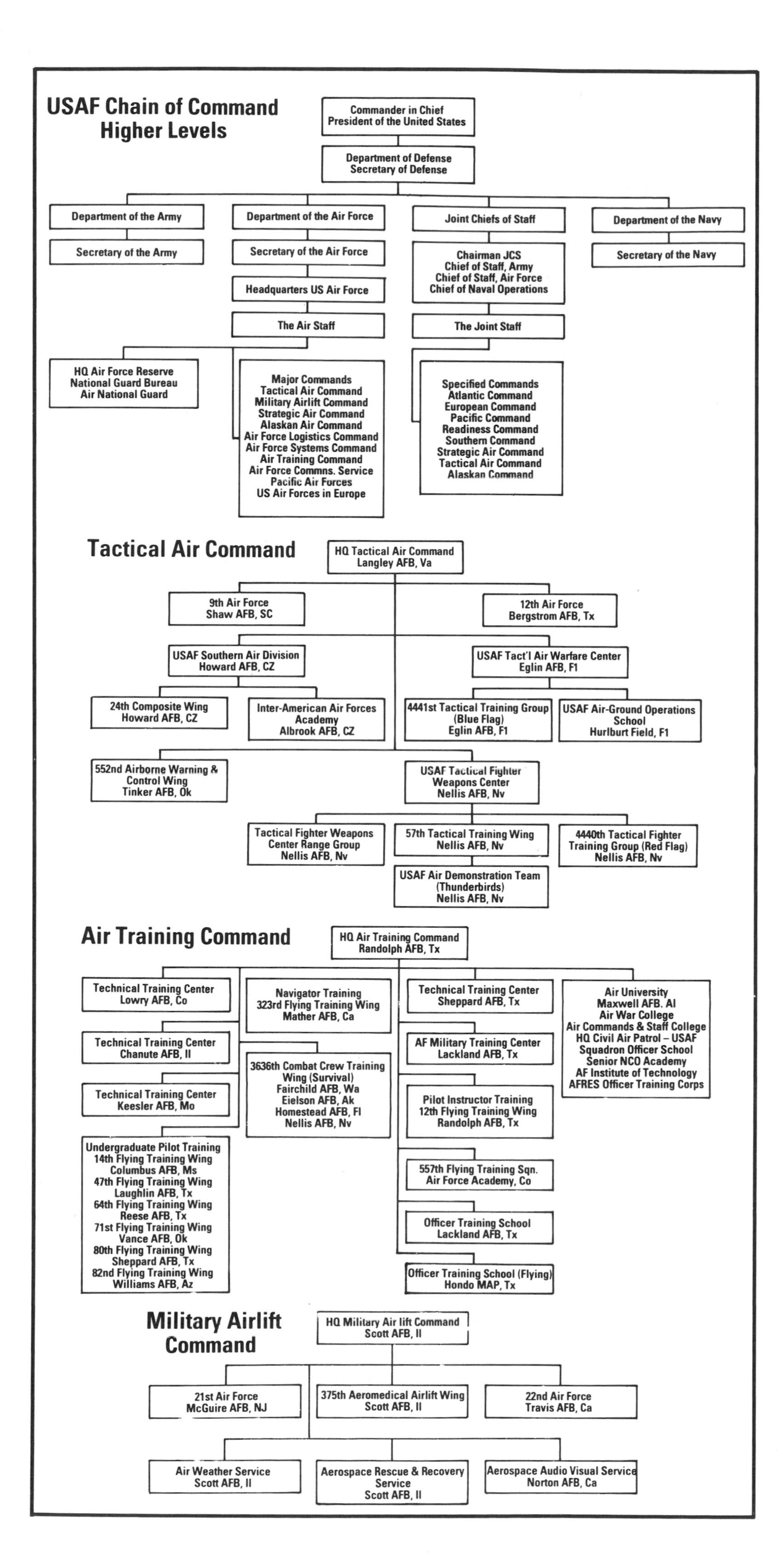


**USAF aircraft strength**
(including Air Force Reserve and Air National Guard)

| *type* | *number* |
|---|---|
| Beech C-12 | 80 |
| Bell H-1 | 76 |
| Boeing | |
| 737A | 15 |
| B-52H/G | 96/167 |
| C-22 | 5 |
| C-137 | 7 |
| E-3 | 34 |
| E-4 | 4 |
| EC-135 | 41 |
| KC-135 | 639 |
| RC-135 | 20 |
| T-43 | 22 |
| WC-135 | 7 |
| Cessna | |
| OA-37 | 139 |
| T-37 | 608 |
| T-41 | 100 |
| de Havilland Canada UV-18 | 2 |
| Fairchild A-10 | 723 (+98) |
| Gates C-21 | 79 |
| General Dynamics | |
| F-16 | 1,285 |
| FB-111/F-111/EF-111 | 61/256/36 |
| T-39 | 8 |
| Gulfstream C-20 | 8 |
| Lockheed | |
| AC-130 | 19 |

The T-37 trainer provided the basis for the A-37/OA-37 Dragonfly. 139 examples are still flying with the USAF and ANG.

| | |
|---|---|
| C-5 | 89 |
| C-130 | 494 |
| C-141 | 250 |
| EC-130 | 15 |
| HC-130 | 53 |
| MC-130 | 11 |
| SR-71A/B | 11 |
| T-33 | 40 |
| TR-1A/B | 13/2 |
| U-2CT/R | 2/11 |
| WC-130 | 12 |
| McDonnell Douglas | |
| C-9 | 17 |
| F-4/F-4G/RF-4C | 1,300/84/430 |
| F-15 | 786 |
| KC-10 | 57 |
| Mikoyan-Gurevich | |
| MiG-21 | 24 |
| MiG-23 | 4 |
| Northrop | |
| F-5 | 101 |
| T-38 | 812 |
| Rockwell | |
| B-1B | 54+ |
| CT-39 | 14 |
| Rockwell OV-10/Cessna 0-2 | 145 |
| Short C-23 | 18 |
| Sikorsky | |
| H-3/CH-3 | 65/34 |
| H-53 | 31 |
| UH-60 | 9 |
| Vought A-7 | 638 |

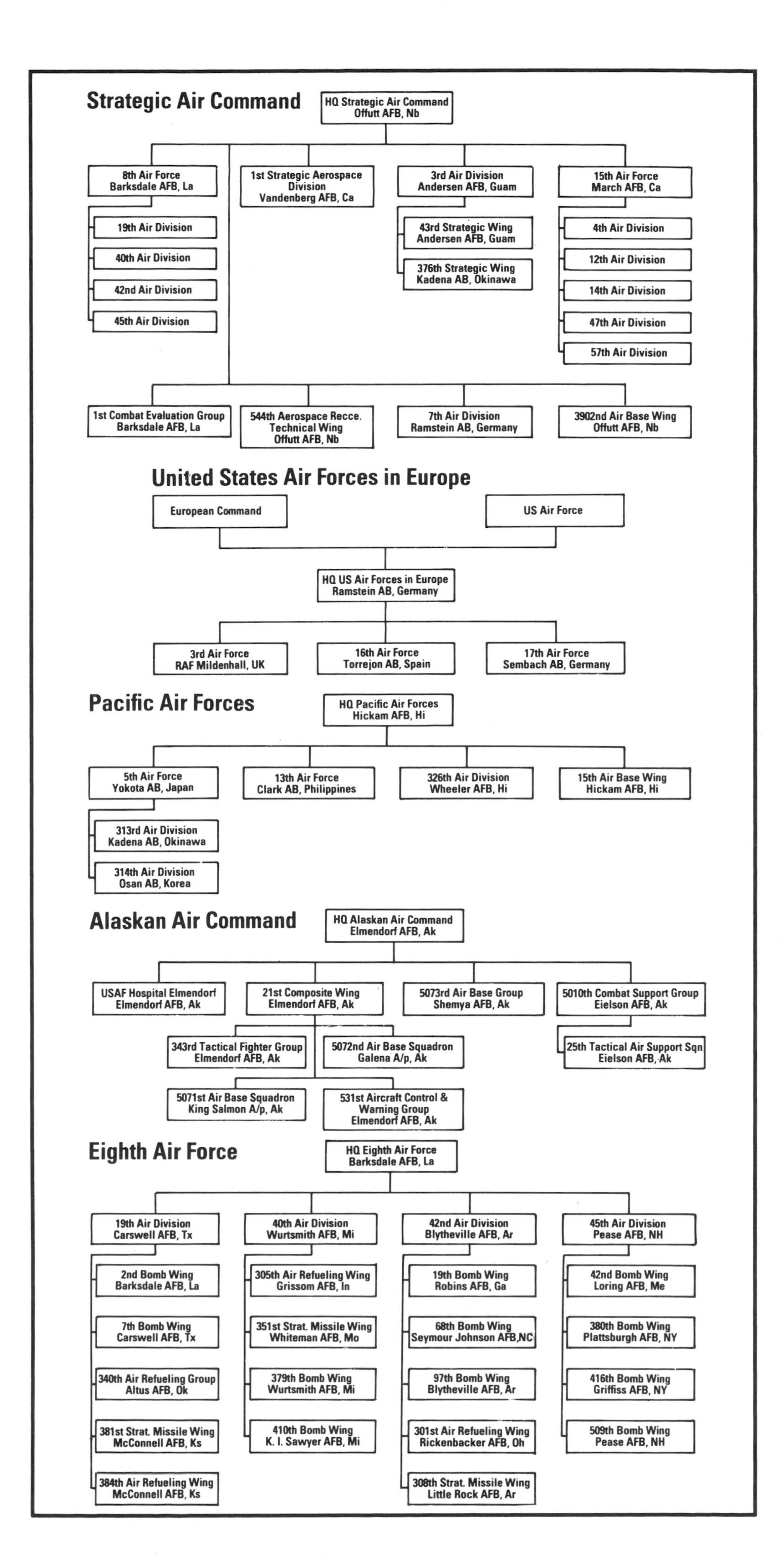

*Right:* The built-in survivability features of the A-10 Thunderbolt, augmented by the pylon-mounted AN-ALQ 119 ECM jammer system, help this battlefield support aircraft to survive in a hostile environment.

**Below:** Increased power and modified wing design make the F-5E Tiger II a potent adversary, ideal for "aggressor" training.

*Above:* The 80ft wingspan of the TR-1 makes landing a very delicate operation, especially after an eight-hour mission.

*Left:* After the B-1B programme was revived in 1981, three wings have become operational. More B-1Bs will replace the ageing B-52G.

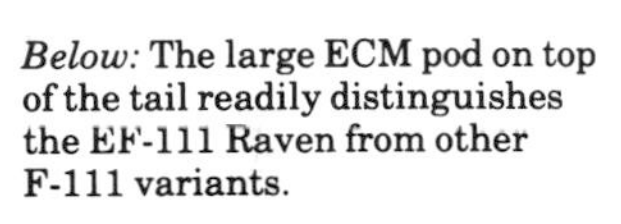

*Below:* The large ECM pod on top of the tail readily distinguishes the EF-111 Raven from other F-111 variants.

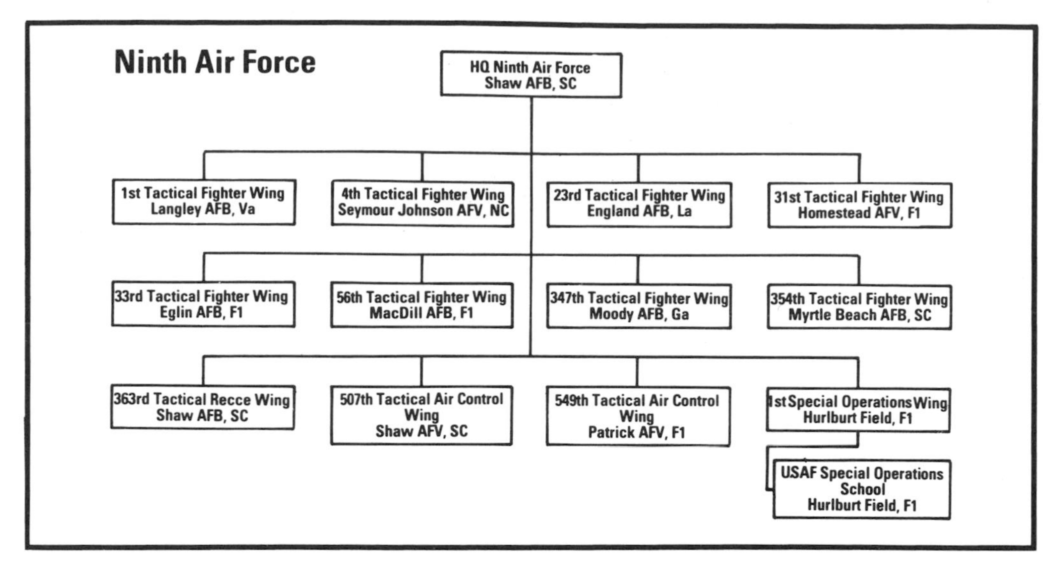

*Above, right:* Optical and electronic reconnaissance can be carried out at Mach 3 from over 80,000 feet by the SR-71 Blackbirds operated by the 9th Strategic Reconnaissance Wing from Beale AFB.

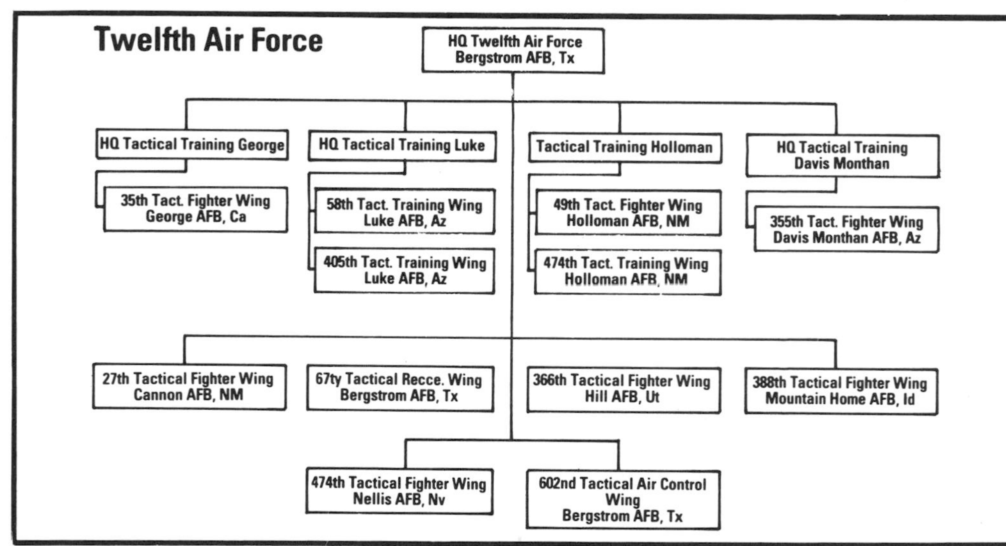


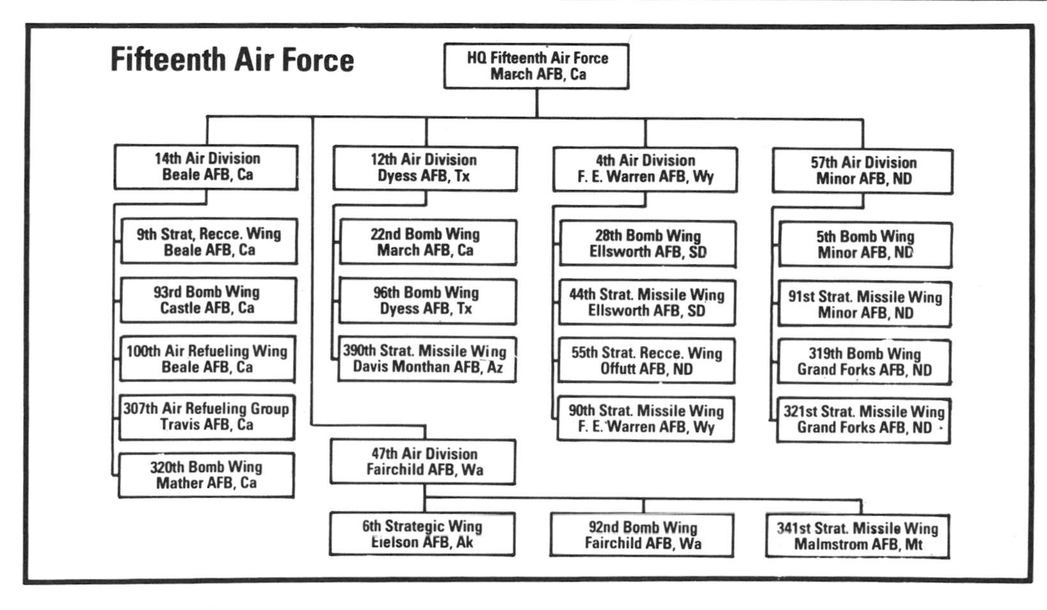

*Right:* An F-16A Fighting Falcon displays part of its armoury: two AIM-7 Sidewinder missiles on its wingtips and a 20mm Vulcan cannon in the port (left) wing root.

*Above, left:* In service for over 20 years, the T-37 basic trainer is familiar to most USAF pilots.

*Above, right:* The DHC-4 Caribou STOL transport entered USAF service as the C-7A/B in 1967, when 134 aircraft were transferred from the Army.

*Left:* Developed from the Boeing 737-200 commercial transport, the T-43A can accomodate up to 16 trainee navigators.

*Left:* A giant C-5A Galaxy effortlessly disgorges part of its 265,000lb (120,200kg) cargo. The 83 C-5s of Military Airlift Command represent a phenomenal load-carrying capacity.

The F-4 Phantom is still in service with the US Air Force after more than 20 years.

# U.S. Army Index

Page numbers in *italics* refer to illustrations.

# U.S. Marine Corps Index

Page numbers in *italics* refer to illustrations.

# U.S. Navy Index

Page numbers in *italics* refer to illustrations.

# U.S. Airforce Index

Page numbers in *italics* refer to illustrations.